The flag shown above is the original "Star Spangled Banner" that flew victoriously over Fort McHenry in Baltimore Harbor after a battle in the War of 1812, inspiring our national anthem. The earliest photo of the flag, taken in 1874, showed that one end of it had been cut away, a star was missing, and a mysterious V had been affixed to a white stripe. In 1914, two years after the flag was donated to the Smithsonian Institution, a team of seven needlewomen began work to slow further deterioration. They removed the canvas backing and replaced it with hand-stitched Irish linen. The missing star was replaced by sketching and stitches and has since faded. The flag hangs today inside the Mall entrance to the National Museum of American History in Washington, D.C.

The Politics of American Government

Second Edition

Basic Version

STEPHEN J. WAYNE
Georgetown University

G. CALVIN MACKENZIE
Colby College

DAVID M. O'BRIEN
University of Virginia

RICHARD L. COLE
University of Texas at Arlington

St. Martin's Press
New York

Sponsoring editor: Beth A. Gillett
Development editor: John Elliott
Managing editor: Patricia Mansfield Phelan
Project editor: Diana M. Puglisi
Production supervisor: Dennis J. Para
Art director and cover designer: Lucy Krikorian
Text design: Jill Little, Lucy Krikorian
Graphics: Burmar
Photo research: Rose Corbett Gordon
Cover art: The Smithsonian Institution
Library of Congress Catalog Card Number: 96-69852

Manufactured in the United States of America.

1 0 9 8 7
f e d c b a

For information, write:
St. Martin's Press, Inc.
175 Fifth Avenue
New York, NY 10010

ISBN: 0-312-13915-2

DEDICATION

These pages bear the fruits of our country's proud
political tradition. Enjoy them. Improve them. Live them.
And give them to your children.

To
Jonathan C. Cole
Mary Ashley Cole
Andrew C. Mackenzie
Peter W. Mackenzie
Rebecca M. Knight
Benjamin M. O'Brien
Sara A. O'Brien
Talia M. O'Brien
Jared B. Wayne
Jeremy B. Wayne

BRIEF CONTENTS

FEATURES

CONTENTS

PREFACE

S ince the first edition of *The Politics of American Government* was
published, dramatic change has shaken the American political landscape. The 1994 elections ended forty years of Democratic dominance
of Congress and ushered in a period of sharp partisan debate over the
nation's policy agenda. Throughout 1995 and 1996 the new Republican
congressional majority battled President Clinton and his fellow Democrats in an
effort to reverse longstanding federal policies and shift the terms of political debate
in a much more conservative direction. So fierce did the conflict become that twice
much of the government had to shut down for several weeks because the two sides
could not agree on a federal budget.

For many Americans, partisan wrangling in Washington served only to heighten
their cynicism about government. Mistrust of public officials spurred interest in candidates who were not career politicians, such as General Colin Powell, and in alternatives to the two major parties, such as the Reform party begun by Ross Perot.
Meanwhile, outright anger toward government led to the growth of private militias
in several states, to a long armed standoff between a group known as the Freemen
and the FBI in Montana, and apparently to the bombing of the federal office building
in Oklahoma City.

Despite these undercurrents of public malaise, however, the economy grew, crime
declined, and the United States continued to exercise superpower influence throughout the world. Moreover, the politics of American government continued in much
the same vein as it has for decades, with conflicts between House and Senate, president and Congress, and Democrats and Republicans characterizing much of the
newsworthy political activity. In short, the political struggle has persisted, adapting
itself to the changing domestic and foreign policy environment in which the United
States finds itself at the end of the twentieth century. This is a book about that struggle. It is about *politics*, pure and simple.

We stress politics because we believe it is the lifeblood of government—its
dynamic, living quality. We view politics as the process through which people struggle to better themselves, to pursue their own interests within society. There is nothing inherently wrong with that pursuit, although sometimes it can lead to consequences that are not beneficial to some individuals and groups. That is why political
activities must be both protected *and* constrained. It is the job of our government
to achieve these two sometimes contradictory goals within the framework established by the Constitution and laws of this country.

Therefore politics and government are closely and inevitably interrelated. One
cannot be considered without the other. Politics influences government; government makes public policy; public policy generates political activity—this is the life
cycle of the politics of American government.

The Interrelationship of Politics and Government

In placing the focus of **The Politics of American Government** on the drama of American political life, we do not argue that politics is good or bad but rather that it is a necessary means of expression for citizens of a democracy, both individually and in groups. To help students more easily understand the intricacies of the connections between the struggle of politics and the structure of government, we examine government in terms of both its inputs and its outputs. Central to this discussion is the role of equity in a democratic political system. We take a careful look at the outputs of government—its authoritative decisions and actions and their consequences for society. Do the same people benefit or the same ones suffer most of the time? The answer to this question suggests the capacity or incapacity of the system to be fair and just to everyone. At the same time, we also examine the inputs of government—the effects that different political actors achieve through elections and their access to policy makers. Do some groups exercise more influence than others? Identifying influential political groups, understanding their sources of power, and evaluating their motivations and strategies for affecting public policy enable us to determine how fairly and effectively the democratic process is working.

A Critical, Not Cynical, View of Politics

In emphasizing the struggle between politics and government, we have tried to maintain a perspective that is critical but not cynical. One of the greatest challenges facing American government instructors is engaging students to think politically both in and out of the classroom—in other words, to show them that politics matters to them both as individuals and as members of a community. To this end, we have taken great care in this edition to integrate more opportunities for student participation into the text, through boxes labeled *Practicing Democracy* and *Where on the Web?* In addition, ample opportunity to promote participation is available through an enhanced ancillary package, including the second edition of the Ralph Nader Institute's *Practicing Democracy*, and The St. Martin's Student Survey of Political Attitudes.

An Eye Toward the Future

As the world becomes more interdependent through trade and political and military alliances and as countries become more closely linked by instantaneous communications, students no longer view American government in a vacuum. Their desire to put current events in a broader perspective has led us to include more focused comparative information where appropriate. We have also created a new feature called *Hot-Button Issues*—boxes that give students a forum for exploring and discussing contemporary political issues. The results of the 1996 elections are woven into the narrative and provide a basis for understanding how the most recent changes in American politics and government will shape institutions and policy making into the twenty-first century.

THE SECOND EDITION

In addition to the thorough, balanced analysis of politics and government offered in the first edition, the second edition reflects the following changes and additions

Thorough Updating

The text, tables, figures, photographs, and reference sources have been thoroughly updated; you will find coverage of current political figures and significant recent events in the United States, including the results of both the 1994 and 1996 elections.

Focus on Student Involvement: Practicing Democracy

The focus on student involvement in politics has been enhanced through the addition of *Practicing Democracy* boxes. Topics include contacting legislators, using the Freedom of Information Act and the Privacy Act, doing jury duty, and getting involved in a political party. Many of these boxes feature new means of participation via the Internet and e-mail.

Where on the Web?

The Internet and the World Wide Web offer instant access to a wealth of primary resources that can be used to create an interactive course in American government, and new *Where on the Web?* boxes provide students with the information they need to use these technologies. Students can find information on interest groups they want to get involved in, check the status of items in this year's budget, contact their congressional representative, or research Supreme Court decisions or White House press releases. Not only are these sources helpful to students doing academic research, but they also encourage them to get involved in politics on their own.

Hot-Button Issue Boxes

These boxes explore some of the social issues that arouse the most passionate political feelings in the United States today, from immigration to affirmative action, from same-sex marriage to censorship of the Internet. They frame the issue at stake, explore the differing nuances of positions, and tell students how to get more information about the issue and become involved in groups on either side.

Extensive Comparative Material

New material throughout the text helps students view the American political system in a comparative perspective. With a globally linked economy, agreements like GATT and NAFTA, and many international commitments borne by the United States as the only remaining superpower, it is important that American students fully understand their country's place in the context of its North American neighbors, its European allies, and the world as a whole.

CHAPTER HIGHLIGHTS

Every chapter opens with an engaging story about politics. Throughout the text, a series of boxed features, many of which fall into the following categories in addition to those already described, appeal to student interests and provide insight into the ways in which politics is at work in so many aspects of American life.

People in Politics

These informative profiles provide brief biographies of people who have made a difference in American political life. Spanning the political spectrum from Ruth Bader Ginsburg to Christine Todd Whitman and from Thurgood Marshall to Newt Gingrich, they also focus on younger and lesser-known figures involved in party organizing and political journalism.

Constitutional Conflict

These essays examine core constitutional issues that are involved in contemporary debates in American government. They include the line-item veto, the right of defendants to confront their accusers in child abuse cases, and the struggle between Congress and the president over the War Powers Act.

Case Studies

Highlighting our focus on the drama of politics, these case studies analyze issues and pose questions for discussions. Among the topics covered are the controversies over the flat tax, the exclusionary rule of evidence in criminal trials, and the admission of women to the Virginia Military Institute.

INSTRUCTIONAL PACKAGE

As authors, publishers, and instructors, we continue to seek to create and assemble the most diverse range of materials to support the teaching of American government and contribute to the most complete and purposeful instructional package available today. Each component of *The Politics of American Government* is designed to make teaching more effective and to heighten students' interest in American government and, particularly, their American government course.

Instructor's Manual   For each chapter of our book, the guide includes an outline and overview, learning objectives, key terms and concepts, recommended assignments, and discussion questions.

Lecture Outlines and Lectures   The outlines list topics that follow the major headings of each chapter of the textbook; they also suggest a range of supplementary topics and issues that relate to, but do not repeat, material in the text. The lectures provide topical narratives of two to three pages that can be expanded into 50-minute lectures. These outlines and lectures are also available on-line to allow you to access, customize, and print at will.

Documents   These primary sources include Supreme Court cases, political speeches, and excerpts from *The Federalist* papers. The documents can be copied and given to students either for homework assignments or for advance preparation for class.

The Politics of American Government **Interactive Web Page** When you log on to this page, you will find a bulletin board where instructors can exchange ideas, activities, and syllabi with the authors and other instructors. The page is updated weekly by the authors to offer suggestions for incorporating current debates into your classroom. An Internet activities and exercise section offers a series of Internet activities that give your students practice in finding the electronic information they need to do further research. Exercises correspond to the chapters of the book so that they can easily be worked into any lecture. *The St. Martin's Political Science Links* page gives professors and students over 1,000 linked references to topics in every chapter. Students can also access current results from *The St. Martin's Student Survey of Political Attitudes.* The Web Page can be found at **http://www.smpcol lege.com/smp_govt/**.

Untangling the Web: A Beginner's Guide to Politics on the World Wide Web
For instructors and students who might not be comfortable "surfing the Net," this guide by Brian Werner of St. John's University offers hands-on advice for learning how to get onto the Internet and access information. It also provides novice instructors with ways to incorporate the Internet in the classroom. By using the guide in conjunction with *The Politics of American Government*'s Web page, instructors can offer a whole new dimension for classroom activities and exercise.

The St. Martin's Student Survey of Political Attitudes Developed by Clyde Wilcox of Georgetown University, this survey is designed for use in American government classes. When the survey is given at the beginning of the course and sent to St. Martin's Press for tabulation, the results will be returned to the professor for use during the semester. The results allow students to explore the relationship between their political opinions and those of students across the country.

The St. Martin's Resource Library in Political Science In recognition of the rising cost of books, shrinking budgets, and continued requests from instructors and students for briefer reading materials, St. Martin's Press publishes a series of brief, inexpensive supplementary books on a range of topics to complement your teaching and customize your focus. Each book in the series is fewer than 120 pages so that students can easily and quickly read and understand the material. Upon adoption of *The Politics of American Government* an instructor can select one of these texts to receive free of charge with the main text. The series includes:

- *Ralph Nader's Practicing Democracy, 1997: A Guide to Student Action.* This book introduces students to the many ways that they can become politically active on the local, state, and federal levels and provides a wealth of information on numerous political organizations.
- *Big Ideas: An Introduction to Ideologies in American Politics,* by Mark Tiller of Houston Community College. For instructors who wish to give their students more grounding in political theory, this book offers an introduction to the predominant political ideas that shape American politics.
- *The Real Thing: Contemporary Documents in American Government,* by Fengyan Shi of Georgetown University. This collection of actual memos, bills, ballots, briefs, grants, and other materials allows students to see for themselves the types of documents that are produced and used in government on a day-to-day basis. The chapters of this book parallel those of *The Politics of American Government* so that instructors can easily work these materials into their lectures.

The St. Martin's Guide to the Movies   This guide to popular films dealing with issues in American government provides summaries, teaching suggestions, discussion questions, and activities for such movies as *Mr. Smith Goes to Washington, Bob Roberts, All the President's Men,* and more. With each adoption, professors are entitled to receive a videocassette of one of these films to use in conjunction with the guide.

***The Politics of American Government* Presentation CD-ROM**   In response to instructors' requests for multimedia, we have developed an easy-to-use CD-ROM that allows professors to enhance their lectures with graphics from the text. By simply "pointing and clicking," an instructor can create his or her own customized disk of the art, including figures and tables.

Software   St. Martin's offers the following software:

- Computerized Test Item File.
- *Micrograde*, a program for recordkeeping and tracking student grades.
- *Presidential Campaign!*—This software program allows a student to run a simulated presidential campaign from April to November, as a challenger or an incumbent, and as a Republican, a Democrat, or an independent.
- Documents Collection: available on disk.

"In Action: Students Making It Happen in Government"   In keeping with the theme of student involvement, St. Martin's Press has produced a new 25-minute video that follows students as they work on the Republican and Democratic campaigns for the 1996 elections. This documentary allows students to see, hear, and understand firsthand the excitement and energy found inside the political system from the point of view of their peers, increasing their ability to look at government critically but not cynically.

St. Martin's Video Resource Library   In addition to "In Action," St. Martin's has developed a series of other 25-minute videos for use in class. Each video is accompanied by a guide that includes a summary of the video, a copy of the narrator's script, test and discussion questions, and a list of supplemental classroom activities. Titles in this series include:
"Women and Politics"
"Interest Groups in America"
"Presidential Leadership"
"The Selection and Confirmation of Supreme Court Justices"
"The Politics of Midterm Elections: The Case of the 104th Congress."

State and Local Supplement   For instructors who like to emphasize state and local politics in their American government classes, this chapter-length supplement, written by Richard Cole of the University of Texas at Arlington, provides additional material, including tables, graphs, and case studies, that is easily incorporated into any syllabus.

Study Guide   Available for sale to students is the Study Guide, which includes introductory essays about how to study and how to do a research paper on American government. Each chapter includes an interactive review section, practice tests, and an in-depth assignment.

Test Item File This comprehensive test item file contains almost 4,000 questions to choose from, including multiple choice, fill-in, true/false, and essay questions with multiple levels of difficulty. It is available to professors in a hard copy or on disk with full authoring capability.

For information about these ancillaries or about special packages and discounts for those who want to use *The Politics of American Government* with other readers and topical books published by St. Martin's Press, please contact your local representative or call or write St. Martin's Press, College Desk, 345 Park Avenue South, New York, NY 10010 (phone 1-800-446-8923).

ACKNOWLEDGMENTS

We wish to acknowledge and thank some of the many people who contributed to this book. Bert Lummus conceived of the text, initially contracted for it, and encouraged us with good humor, patience, support, and many meals. Don Reisman orchestrated the first edition at St. Martin's with skill and imagination, never losing sight of our principal objective—to excite and educate our readers. Beth Gillett, current political science editor, presided over the second edition, making numerous suggestions on how to improve and enliven the book. She is responsible for the more practical, "hands-on" orientation of this edition, as is Rob Mejia, who also contributed many good ideas that we incorporated into the design and text.

Caroline Smith, Cheryl Kupper, and Doug Bell converted our original manuscript into book form. John Elliott, the developmental editor for the second edition, greatly improved its style, organization, and presentation. He made this edition into a much more engaging text. Anne Dempsey, associate developmental editor, helped as well, particularly with the artwork. Diana Puglisi served as a skillful project editor, moving the manuscript through the publication process and keeping it on schedule. Thanks also to others at St. Martin's who helped us with this edition: photo researcher Rose Corbett Gordon, art director Lucy Krikorian, production supervisor Dennis Para, project editorial assistant Christopher Steighner, copyeditor Alice Vigliani, political science marketing manager Chris Helms, and senior editorial assistant Kimberly Wurtzel.

The authors owe a considerable debt to our research assistants, who have helped us immensely and saved us time and effort. Many thanks to Lisa Prenaveau Andrzejewski, Geertruida C. Degoede, Mark Drozdowski, Colin Harrington, Peter Mackenzie, Kathy Naff, Janet Newcity, Eric Pages, Fengyan Shi, and Molly Sonner.

We cannot close without saying how much we have appreciated the sacrifices and support we have received from our families as we worked on this book. Our children, especially, have patiently endured our weekend writing. We have dedicated this book to them, not only because of their patience but also because they and their peers, who will read this book, embody the hopes and hold the keys to the future of our political system.

Finally, we wish to thank our many colleagues in the political science profession who have answered questionnaires, reviewed chapters, found mistakes, and conveyed extremely useful suggestions to us—all of which have helped us improve this book:

Phillip J. Ardoin, Louisiana State University; David G. Adler, Idaho State University; Claude W. Barnes, North Carolina Agricultural and Technical State University; William T. Bianco, Duke University; Stephen A. Borrelli, University of Alabama; John Burke, University of Vermont; William E. Carroll, Sam Houston State University; Roger H.

Davidson, University of Maryland at College Park; David E. England, Arkansas State University; Brian L. Fife, Ball State University; Janet E. Frantz, University of Southwest Louisiana; Nirmal Goswami, Texas A & M University–Kingsville; David R. Harding, Arkansas State University; Michael W. Hirlinger, Oklahoma State University; Herbert Hirsch, Virginia Commonwealth University; Michael J. Horan, University of Wyoming; Leon H. Hurwitz, Cleveland State University; Matthew R. Kerbel, Villanova University; James P. Lester, Colorado State University; Brad Lockerbie, University of Georgia; Burdett A. Loomis, University of Kansas; Bonnie G. Mani, East Carolina University; Cecilia G. Manrique, University of Wisconsin–La Crosse; Janet M. Martin, Bowdoin College; Valerie Martinez-Ebers, University of North Texas; James L. McDowell, Indiana State University; Lauri McNown, University of Colorado at Boulder; Donald Melton, Arapahoe Community College; J. Keith Nicholls, University of South Alabama; Arthur Paulson, Southern Connecticut State University; George Pippin, Jones County Junior College; Edward E. Platt, Indiana University of Pennsylvania; Ronald G. Shaiko, The American University; Steven S. Smith, University of Minnesota; John W. Soule, San Diego State University; Bartholomew Sparrow, University of Texas at Austin; C. Michael Swinford, Kennesaw State College; Andrew J. Taylor, North Carolina State University; Roy Thoman, West Texas State University; Roberto J. Vichot, Florida International University; David J. Webber, University of Missouri; Herbert F. Weisberg, The Ohio State University; Gary D. Wekkin, University of Central Arkansas.

Stephen J. Wayne
G. Calvin Mackenzie
David M. O'Brien
Richard L. Cole

ABOUT THE AUTHORS

 STEPHEN J. WAYNE (Ph.D., Columbia University) is a professor and the head of the American government section at Georgetown University. Besides being a veteran instructor of American government, he has been a Washington insider specializing in presidential politics for over twenty-five years. He has authored numerous articles and published several books about the presidency, including *The Road to the White House, The Legislative Presidency,* and *Presidential Leadership* (with George C. Edwards III). Invited frequently to testify before Congress and to lecture to senior federal executives, distinguished international visitors, and college students in the United States and abroad, Wayne also has shaped public opinion about the presidency and electoral politics as a commentator for radio, television, and newspapers.

 G. CALVIN MACKENZIE (Ph.D., Harvard University) is the Distinguished Presidential Professor of American Government at Colby College. With expertise in presidential appointments, Congress, and public policy, Mackenzie is among the foremost American scholars and commentators on the staffing of national administrations. He is a former congressional staff member and has worked in or advised executive-branch agencies, including the departments of Defense and the Treasury. *The Politics of Presidential Appointments* and *The Irony of Reform* are among his many books; he also has contributed to a wide range of academic and popular journals and is interviewed often on television and radio.

 DAVID M. O'BRIEN (Ph.D., University of California, Santa Barbara) is the Leone Reaves and George W. Spicer Professor in the Department of Government and Foreign Affairs at the University of Virginia. A former Judicial Fellow at the Supreme Court and Fulbright Scholar in Great Britain and Japan, O'Brien is one of the most prominent political scientists studying the Supreme Court. His several books about the judiciary include *Storm Center: The Supreme Court in American Politics,* which in 1987 received the American Bar Association's Silver Gavel Award. His most recent publication is *To Dream of Dreams: Religious Freedom in Postwar Japan.*

 RICHARD L. COLE (Ph.D., Purdue University) is dean of the School of Urban and Public Affairs at the University of Texas, Arlington, where he is also a professor specializing in political science methodology, urban politics, and public policy. He is a former president of the Southwest Political Science Association and former president of the North Texas chapter of the American Society for Public Administration. In addition to dozens of monographs, journal articles, and book reviews, Cole's publications include *Texas Politics and Public Policy* and *An Introduction to Political Inquiry.* His latest book is *Introduction to Political Science and Policy Research,* also with St. Martin's Press.

The Politics of American Government

Second Edition

Basic Version

The American Political Environment

I t was a bitter, no-holds-barred battle, a fight to the finish, pitting political parties, governing institutions, and strong and ambitious people against one another. Ostensibly it was about money: could a balanced federal budget be achieved after decades of deficit spending? The Republicans believed that it could and should; their candidates for the House of Representatives campaigned on this proposition in 1994 and won a majority of seats for the first time in forty years. The Democrats were more wary. Where would spending cuts be made? Who would be affected? Would the public approve?

In the House Republicans' 1994 campaign platform, which they called the Contract with America, they had listed a constitutional amendment requiring a balanced budget as their number one priority. That amendment was to provide the framework and justification for other changes the Republicans wished to make: shrinking the size of the federal government, overhauling and reducing its programs and regulations, and transferring responsibilities for many of these programs to the states.

Within the first 100 days of the 104th Congress, the House of Representatives enacted a balanced budget amendment; but it fell one vote short of the required two-thirds majority in the Senate. With their amendment defeated, the Republicans then turned to ordinary legislation that required only a majority vote, proposing a budget that would eliminate the deficit in seven years. President Clinton's support was crucial since the Republicans did not have the two-thirds majority in both houses required to override a presidential veto. Although Clinton had said that he favored a balanced budget, he had not submitted one in his first three years in office, nor did he agree with the Republicans on their timetable for such a budget or their methods for achieving it.

Preventing a presidential veto was only part of the problem. Garnering public support for specific cuts in government programs, particularly popular programs, was another. Although most Americans agreed with the goal of a balanced budget, they did not agree on how to achieve it.

The Republicans' task was also complicated by the promise contained in the Contract with America to reduce taxes as well as spending. The only way to meet these dual objectives was to shrink expenditures on so-called entitlements, ongoing programs that account for more than half of federal spending and that automatically give benefits to all individuals who meet certain qualifications. With both the Republicans and Clinton unwilling to risk the political dangers of cutting back the largest entitlement program, Social Security, the main targets for cuts included Medicare, which provides health-care coverage for those age 65 and older; Medicaid, a health-care program for the poor; and various welfare programs such as food stamps and Aid to Families with Dependent Children.

The Republicans wanted to raise the premiums paid by Medicare recipients and reduce future benefits paid to them and to health-care providers, as well as to end federal entitlements for Medicaid and most welfare programs by turning the responsibility for them over to the states. Each of these proposals provoked controversy, but none was more contentious and politically explosive than the Medicare issue.

Ever since Medicare began in 1965, it has enjoyed broad and strong public support. Realizing this, the Democrats began to link Republican proposals to save billions by changing Medicare to their proposal to cut income taxes for those earning up to $200,000 a year—a proposal that would cost the government approximately what it would save from the proposed changes in Medicare. The implication was hardly subtle: the elderly were being asked to sacrifice to benefit the wealthy.

Interest groups entered the fray. The American Association of Retired Persons, with a membership of 33 million, announced its opposition to the Medicare premium increases and benefit cuts. The American Medical Association objected to any plan that might benefit group health organizations at the expense of private physicians; naturally, the Health Insurance Association of America and the Group Health Association of America took the opposite stand. Meanwhile, groups especially concerned about budget deficit reduction, such as the Concord Coalition, or about lower taxes, such as the National Taxpayers Union, weighed in with their own public statements and lobbying efforts.

With the political debate heating up, the Republicans needed a strategy to force the president's hand, and they turned to the "power of the purse to do so." The Constitution states that no money can be drawn from the treasury unless it is appropriated by Congress. That is why Congress must enact annual appropriations bills; without them or a resolution to continue spending at a certain level, the government cannot operate.

The political struggle came to its first crisis on November 14, 1995, the expiration date of the continuing resolution that had kept most of the government funded since October 1, the beginning of the 1996 fiscal year.[1] In the absence of a new resolution, agencies that had not received their annual appropriation were forced to shut down and furlough 800,000 workers classified as nonessential. The president used his legal authority to order essential workers to remain on the job, but their paychecks could not be issued if their department or agency had no money.

The shutdown lasted six days. Only after the Clinton administration agreed in principle to achieve a balanced budget within seven years did the Republicans relent and Congress enact an interim spending bill to fund the government until mid-December. However, the agreement between the Republicans and the administration had a caveat: "the balanced budget must protect future generations, ensure Medicare solvency, reform welfare and provide adequate funding for Medicaid, education, agriculture, national defense, veterans and the environment." Republicans interpreted this language as a face-saving effort by the president; the president, however, took it literally. The morning after Congress passed the interim bill, senior White House staff indicated that the caveat made it impossible for Clinton to accept the specific components in the Republican budget. The Republicans were shocked, dismayed, and furious.

The battle continued with much harsh rhetoric but little real compromise. In early December Clinton vetoed the Republican budget plan and the Republicans rejected his counterproposal, claiming that it fell far short of balancing the budget. On December 15, the interim spending bill expired and another shutdown began, this time involving 280,000 government workers and lasting for three weeks.[2]

Unable to visit national parks and museums, obtain passports, or get federally guaranteed mortgages, the public was becoming weary of and angry about the stalemate, blaming the Republicans for it more than the president. Polls conducted in December and January also found many more people sympathetic to the president's position on the issues than to the Republicans'.[3] With the polls evidencing a deterioration in their support, with only two of ten proposals in the Contract with America enacted into law, with the conservative freshman Republicans in Congress increasingly at odds with their own leadership and Democrats increasingly united behind Clinton, a change in Republican strategy seemed inevitable.

Throughout the spring negotiations between the White House and Congress continued, with the Republicans proposing temporary spending bills and the president reluctantly approving them. By the end of April, six months into the fiscal year, a compromise was finally reached on a budget for that year alone—one that allowed both sides to claim victory but neither to achieve its ultimate objective, a balanced budget on its own terms. The president had protected his priorities in education, the environment, health care, and national service. The Republicans had achieved a $23 billion cut in discretionary domestic spending, the largest cut since the first year of the Reagan administration in 1981–1982.[4] The battle was over, but the war was not.

The battle of the budget demonstrates the political character of the American electoral and governing systems: the volatility of public opinion, and the responsiveness of most elected officials to that opinion, but also the resistance of the constitutional framework to major policy changes. It indicates how the public can alter the political climate; how its voting decisions affect what policies government pursues; how newly elected officials can run into trouble by acting on their campaign promises; and how the self-interest of political parties and government institutions influences policy making. It also points to the impact of policy itself on the political process: how the public responds to the costs and benefits of differing policy solutions and how their responses can transform policy debate among governing officials, shape the policy outcomes, and ultimately affect the electoral fortunes of those involved. In this way the battle of the budget reveals the *life cycle of American politics:* how politics affects government, how government tries to resolve contentious political issues, and how that resolution or lack of it generates new political pressures and policy solutions.

Disagreement is normal. In a nation of a quarter of a billion people, representing dozens of different ethnic, religious, and racial identities, spread across thousands of miles of varied terrain, involved in tens of thousands of competing economic enterprises, disagreement is bound to occur on all types of political, social, and economic issues. For example, some Americans believe that government should keep its hands off the economy; others believe it should actively shape and regulate economic life. Some Americans think that government's first priority should be a strong national defense; others think a decent standard of living for everyone should come first. Some argue that abortion is a private matter beyond the proper reach of government; others argue that government should prohibit abortion on the same grounds that it prohibits people from killing one another.

In every dimension and on every plane of American life, disagreement abounds. It is a way of life. If we had no place to resolve our differences, they would tear the country apart. But we do have such a place. In *government* we have a set of institutions and procedures through which we may express and seek to work out our problems.

Although we disagree about many things, government is possible because almost all of us agree about some things—about the need for government, for example. On other fundamental principles and values, and even on some important matters of policy, there is also broad consensus. That consensus has allowed us to create institutions, laws, and procedures that most Americans regard as proper and legitimate. None of us agrees with all the decisions Congress makes, but most of us believe that a representative legislature such as Congress is the proper place for those decisions to be made. Consensus on how to resolve issues, then, allows us to do so; it provides the basis for governing.

Yet in spite of this consensus, differences of opinion persist over what government should do, how it should do it, and for whose benefit and at whose expense. These differences of opinion constitute the sources of and motivation for political activity; they are the basis of politics. If **politics** consists of struggles by individuals and groups in pursuit of their own interests and goals, then practically everything government does, every action it takes, is the result of political activity of one kind or another.

That is why we have titled our book *The Politics of American Government.* We believe that government can be best understood when it is viewed through the lens of politics. *Politics* provides the framework for understanding how *government* works and what it does.

ONE BASIC CONCEPT: POLITICS

Today the word *politics,* like *politician,* is often used disparagingly. Political candidates who accuse their opponents of "playing politics" imply that they are doing things primarily to enhance themselves in the eyes of those whose support they need. In the 1996 presidential campaign, the stands Robert Dole and Bill Clinton took in favor of lowering taxes after they had supported sizable tax increases in 1993 made them look like "typical politicians."

Originally, however, *politics* had a positive meaning. The modern term derives from the Greek word *polis,* roughly translated as "city-state." In ancient Greece, the polis, an independent city and the land that surrounded it, formed the basic unit of political organization. Early Greek philosophers such as Plato and Aristotle believed that loyalty to a polis was part and parcel of being human; in fact, Aristotle referred to the citizens of a city-state as "political animals." In these small communities, "government" meant face-to-face discussions of community issues among all citizens.

In the ancient world, politics was the process by which the community determined how its will would be implemented. Politics involves that same process today. Contemporary society has become much more diverse and complex, of course, and so has politics. But it is still the means through which who gets what, when, and how is determined, and it is still fundamental to the operation of government. In a world where values and beliefs conflict, where resources are limited and desires and ambitions seem virtually limitless, the quest for political gain is inevitable.

Although politics sometimes leads to excesses and abuses, in itself it is neither bad nor dangerous. Insofar as it facilitates the expression of disagreement and the

People get politically involved in various ways. (Top left) *Rock the Vote aimed to register voters between the ages of 18 and 25 at rock concerts across the country.* (Bottom left) *Women chained themselves to concrete blocks inside a truck in front of the White House to protest a toxic waste incinerator in Liverpool, Ohio, in 1993.* (Top right) *African-American men showed their solidarity and potential political power by joining together in a "Million Man March" on Washington in 1995.*

building of consensus, politics is critical to the health of a democratic society. Without it, there would be no mechanism other than force to resolve disagreements.

Politics is an end as well as a means. It is an *end* because it is an activity that has value in and of itself. It links citizens to their government and guides that government as it goes about its principal tasks. It is a *means* to other ends because it gives people the opportunity and the tools to advance their own interests by influencing who gets into office and what actions those officeholders take while they are there.

TWO OTHER CONCEPTS: GOVERNMENT AND PUBLIC POLICY

The term **government** refers to the *formal institutions* within which decisions about public policy are made and to the *processes and procedures* of decision making. For example, the California State Assembly, the Federal Trade Commission, and the local motor vehicles bureau and school board are all governing institutions. So is your school's student council. They and other governing institutions exercise their authority by means of various processes and procedures that permit policies to be made and carried out and disputes to be judged and settled. The ratification of treaties by the United States Senate, the vetoing of legislation by the president, the inspection of meat-processing plants by the Department of Agriculture, and the conduct of criminal trials all exemplify the exercise of formal government power.

Public policy is what governments decide. Codified in the form of laws, of executive agreements, orders, and actions, and of Supreme Court decisions, public policy consists of established rules, procedures, and practices that are determined by and protected by the authority of government.

The federal government and some state governments impose and collect taxes on personal incomes. They also spend money on public services such as education,

Government's job is to make and enforce public policy, sometimes with unhappy consequences for those who violate it. Fortunately for some, however, the actual enforcers may be more lenient than the law. This speeder got away with a warning.

police, and health-related programs. The personal income tax and public services, therefore, are public policy. The federal government does not ban the ownership of handguns or the drinking of liquor by those over a certain age. The freedom to own handguns or consume alcoholic beverages, therefore, is public policy in the United States. Since some states and many cities ban the possession of handguns and some counties are "dry," however, public policy may differ at the state or local level.

Policies are not necessarily the same as laws, and how laws are implemented has a lot to do with what public policies really are. If the law says that the speed limit is 55 miles per hour on a particular highway but the state police never stop any drivers unless their speed exceeds 65 miles per hour, then public policy is really 65 miles per hour because no penalty is imposed as long as drivers stay under that speed. Those who implement a policy — the state police, in this instance — often have considerable discretion in defining what that policy really is.

POLITICS AND POWER: A CRITICAL RELATIONSHIP

For political activity to succeed, it must be accompanied by the exercise of power. **Power,** in this sense, is the ability to get someone to do something that he or she might not otherwise do. Power may be wielded through persuasive skills, rewards, legal authority, threats, even force.

Power is exerted by and within all institutions of government. Presidents exercise power when they persuade reluctant legislators to support their policy positions, as President Clinton did in 1993 when he convinced a majority of the members of Congress to support his deficit reduction proposal despite their many misgivings. Congress exercises power when it exerts its constitutional authority over government spending, as the Republican majority did in 1995 and 1996 when it got President Clinton to accept reductions in domestic spending that were larger than he wanted. At the state and local levels, power is exercised by governors when they commute a death sentence or allow it to be carried out, as well as by police officers when they make an arrest or even merely cruise the streets in patrol cars. Those outside the government also attempt to get their way by promising support or threatening opposition to legislators before they vote on particular issues.

Does the public exercise power when those in government act in accordance with its opinion? Probably, because in a democracy public officials need to be sensitive to public opinion. Failure to do so could result in their defeat in a subsequent election or, less commonly, their recall by the voters or impeachment by Congress.

Power is a normal, everyday component of politics. There can be no politics without power.

Personal Freedom and Social Welfare

The exercise of power often affects individuals and the community in very different ways. One person's liberty, after all, may be another's constraint. For example, many Americans cherish the right to possess and use firearms. Yet we all know that firearms are dangerous and that their use can cause harm. Legislators have struggled with the dilemma of how to design public policy that satisfies both those who want to own guns and use them legally and those who believe that the very availability of guns contributes significantly to violence in our society and thus restricts their freedom in less obvious ways (by preventing them from walking around their neighborhoods in safety, for example).

To take another example, free speech is a basic individual right without which a democracy could not exist. But speech also can be harmful. Words themselves are not as lethal as bullets, but they can cause psychological injury or lead directly to violence. Should speech, then, be as restricted as the possession of firearms? Should it be limited at all, and if so, under what conditions? Should a society be able to outlaw obscene language on the telephone, obscene pictures on the Internet, or public appeals to break the law?

These questions pit the rights of individuals to say and do what they like, and to protest policies and laws that they believe to be unjust, against the obligation of society to protect the health and well-being of its members, which includes maintaining laws that the majority in the community supports. How can the freedom of an individual be protected while the rights of others are simultaneously preserved? Should people be allowed to protest abortion by blocking entrances to clinics? Should they be allowed to defend animal rights by destroying medical laboratories, sabotaging hunters' traps, or spraying paint on fur coats? Should those who preach hatred and advocate violence be allowed to do so on the public airwaves, on radio talk shows? Would your answer be the same if they did so at a much publicized rally at which violent reactions were likely to occur?

Drawing the line between personal liberty and the needs of the community is a difficult task, but one that government must perform. In accomplishing this function, government makes policy judgments that are shaped and conditioned by the political climate in which they occur. In short, *politics influences government, which in turn influences politics.*

Concentrated Power and Distributed Power

How power is distributed within the government affects not only which public policies are made but also who makes them and who benefits the most from them. When power is concentrated in the hands of a few individuals or groups, decision making is more efficient and government can act more quickly and decisively. But those with the power are likely to make decisions that advance their own goals and interests, often at the expense of others.

When power is widely distributed, there is less opportunity for a few people or groups to dominate decision making and determine policy outcomes. But arriving at a consensus, much less agreeing on the details of public policy, is a much harder undertaking. This is the problem usually faced by the U.S. Congress and other American legislative bodies when they try to draft public policy into law. Both the membership of Congress and the distribution of power within Congress are designed to reflect the diversity of American society; but this diversity makes it difficult, and sometimes impossible, for the party in control of Congress to agree among itself on legislation. In more homogeneous countries such as the United Kingdom and Germany, the legislative majority tends to be more cohesive.

How to overcome the lack of concentrated power evident in large, broad-based parties is the challenge legislatures encounter in the United States. One technique is for the winners of an election to claim a public mandate and use that claim to help them achieve a consensus. Newt Gingrich, the newly elected Republican Speaker of the House of Representatives, used this tactic with considerable success in the first 100 days of 1995. Pointing to the Contract with America, the platform on which Republican candidates for the House had campaigned in 1994, he introduced legislation to fulfill its promises. Republican House members felt obliged to support the legislation even though some of them had philosophical or practical objections to it. A partisan platform, however, is less compelling for those who did not campaign on it. Thus Gingrich had difficulty extending the consensus on the contract to the Senate, most of whose Republican members were holdovers from the previous Congress.

Crises are another coalition-building device. During periods of national peril, support for public officials tends to be maximized, opposition to them muted, and partisanship suspended. Deliberation gives way to action. But reason may also be supplemented by emotion, and the rights of individuals, particularly those in the minority may be jeopardized by government responses to the needs and fears of the majority. After the bombing of the federal office building in Oklahoma City on April 19, 1995, the Senate quickly enacted antiterrorist legislation proposed by President Clinton. The bill gave broad investigative powers to the FBI and other law enforcement agencies, powers that some claimed infringe on individual rights protected by the First Amendment to the Constitution. Partly because of this concern, the House did not rush to support this legislation; it enacted a modified bill almost a year later.

Obviously, then, there are tradeoffs between concentrated and distributed power, tradeoffs that can have a profound effect on politics and policy making. Generally speaking, widely distributed power impedes the functioning of government and perpetuates the status quo, even when change is clearly necessary or would benefit a majority of citizens. On the other hand, the more power is distributed, the better able minorities are to protect their legitimate rights and interests, even against the majority.

Majority Rule and Minority Rights

The tension between minorities and majorities, especially when it involves the exercise of personal freedom and the establishment of community standards that restrict that freedom, is one of the principal ongoing problems in the American political sys-

Sometimes the imposition of "community standards," the norms of the majority, violates the rights of a minority. So-called Jim Crow laws in the South discriminated against African Americans by segregating them in many basic daily activities, from attending school or the movies to sleeping, eating, drinking, and using rest rooms. The "Colored Only" drinking fountain was only one of these many separate facilities.

tem. It is inherent in any democracy, although different societies try to resolve this tension in different ways. What is a democracy, and why does it inevitably produce this clash between the majority and various minorities?

A **democracy** is a form of government in which citizens have a right to control their own destiny. Democracy works on the principle of popular consent. The term itself comes from the Greek words *demos,* meaning "people," and *kratos,* meaning "authority." In a democracy the people have the final authority; they have the right to make or at least influence decisions that affect their everyday lives.

Thus in a democracy every citizen should have an equal opportunity to influence public policy through equal representation in government. Rule by the people, or "popular rule," is accomplished by having a majority of citizens or their representatives decide the policies that affect the whole society. If the wishes of the majority are *not* reflected in such decisions, the system itself is not democratic, even though public officials may have been selected in a democratic manner.

Majority rule is vital for a democracy, but it has its dangers. Those in the majority can—and sometimes do—disregard the needs of those in the minority, threaten their interests, and deny them their basic rights. Consider the issue of smoking in public places, for example. When government bans that activity, the ability of smokers to satisfy their needs and desires is adversely affected, yet the health of the majority is enhanced. Is that an acceptable tradeoff? Most people believe it is, or antismoking laws would not have been enacted and would not remain public policy today.

However, the majority cannot always have its way. The principle of majority rule sometimes must be modified in practice. As limits are placed on individual behavior, so too must they be placed on group behavior, *even if the group constitutes a majority.*

The United States Constitution was designed to do just that—to create a government that people of all opinions could influence but that no single group, including the majority, could easily control. James Madison, one of the architects of the Constitution, argued that this was a major strength of the new system. But it has also

The interests of the community often conflict with the rights of individuals. (Left) *Ordinances that prohibit smoking in office buildings constrain the rights of smokers, and* (right) *rules prohibiting prayers as part of school events like graduations and football games may clash with religious freedom, community norms, and longstanding tradition.*

been perceived by some as a major weakness. The very difficulty that people have in manipulating the system to their own advantage makes that system resistant to change. This resistance is a source of constant frustration to those who want quick, efficient, and popular solutions to problems.

Individual Liberty and the Common Good

Government exists to protect the lives and liberties of the people who live within its jurisdiction, and to provide for their well-being and happiness. However, these lofty ideals sometimes clash with one another. Which is more important — protecting the liberty of individuals, or providing for the well-being of society? The competing priorities of government are well illustrated by comparing the goals articulated in the Declaration of Independence with those in the Constitution.

The authors of the Declaration talked about "life, liberty, and the pursuit of happiness." If securing these rights is the purpose of government, and if the British government failed to secure them, then these American revolutionaries believed that the colonies had good reason to declare independence and establish a government that would protect their rights.

The Declaration of Independence is important not only for its statement of the purpose of government but also for its identification of the foundation on which government rests. The second paragraph of the Declaration sets forth the assumptions and logic of a government based on popular consent:

> We hold these truths to be self-evident, that all men are created equal, that they are endowed by their Creator with certain unalienable Rights, that among these are Life, Liberty, and the pursuit of Happiness. That to secure these rights, Governments are instituted among Men, deriving their just powers from the consent of the governed, That whenever any Form of Government becomes destructive of these ends, it is the Right of the People to alter or to abolish it, and to institute new Government, laying its foundation on such principles and organizing its powers in such form, as to them shall seem most likely to effect their Safety and Happiness.

In 1776 the signers of the Declaration needed to justify the American Revolution in terms of a fundamental goal of government — to protect and preserve rights such as liberty and equality and to do so in a system based on popular consent. By 1787, however, the delegates to the Constitutional Convention that met in Philadelphia to restructure the new government defined their needs differently. After nearly a decade of living in a loose confederation of states with little effective central authority, they perceived the need for greater economic, social, and political stability. Their objective was thus to improve the national government's capacity to make and implement public policy for the country as a whole.

In the preamble to their new constitution, the framers enunciated a set of values different from those articulated by the signers of the Declaration. Their goal was "to form a more perfect Union, establish Justice, insure domestic Tranquility, provide for the common defence, promote the general Welfare, and secure the Blessings of Liberty."

Do these two eloquent statements of the purpose of American government conflict? Perhaps not, but their emphasis is certainly different. The Declaration of Independence stresses *individual* liberties, whereas the Constitution emphasizes *social* values. And as we have noted earlier, the unavoidable tension between individual liberties and broad social goals has been evident throughout American history.

The duty of government is to defuse situations in which that tension occurs and try to resolve them by establishing public policy.

Authority and the Rule of Law

When a government makes public policy, it does so on the basis of its **authority,** that is, its lawful power. In a democratic society that authority is derived, directly or indirectly, from the people. In most cases, people do not make policy decisions themselves; but by voting, they have a voice in selecting those who do. Voters choose policy makers to represent them, and then they may try to influence the decisions their representatives make. Thus we frequently hear the terms "representative democracy" or "representative government" used to describe the American political system and to distinguish it from "direct democracy," in which every citizen has an opportunity to participate in making policy decisions (such as in town meetings).

The authority of the government is embodied in *law.* The Constitution is the supreme law of the United States, but it is not the only law. Treaties, statutes, executive orders, and judicial opinions are also part of the body of rules that must be observed by all members of the society, including those in government.

Like decisions themselves, the rules by which decisions are made benefit some people and hurt others. Thus they can impinge both on the principle of majority rule and on the rights of individuals and groups in the minority. For example, the power of the Supreme Court to determine the constitutionality of both local and national laws restricts the ability of those in the majority to determine public policy, because

Besieged by angry constitutents after being accused of sexual harassment and other misconduct, Senator Robert Packwood (wearing necktie), *an Oregon Republican, was forced to resign in 1995. In a democratic society, not even lawmakers are above the law.*

no legislature can take any action that violates the Constitution. In 1995, for instance, the Supreme Court's decision in *U.S. Term Limits v. Thornton* overturned the laws of twenty-two states that had imposed limits on the number of terms members of Congress from those states could serve.

Because procedural rules shape policy outcomes, political struggles often focus on the rules themselves. During the Constitutional Convention, for example, delegates from large and small states clashed over how the states would be represented in Congress. An even more contentious issue was suffrage, specifically the question of who should be able to vote. Here the framers decided not to decide, giving the states the authority and responsibility of determining this issue in general, but also retaining for Congress the power to legislate about suffrage in federal elections. And Congress has used this power, initiating constitutional amendments that have extended the right to vote to all citizens 18 years of age and older and enacting laws to make it easier for citizens to register to vote. It is no coincidence that as the electorate has expanded, public policy has become more sensitive to the needs and interests of a more diverse group of voters.

Another, more recent example of the interrelationship among politics, procedures, and policy occurred following the 1994 congressional elections. In an effort to make House committee chairs more responsive to his leadership, Speaker Gingrich insisted upon approving their appointment and limiting their terms of office. By appointing those who were sympathetic to his policy goals and willing to follow his lead, he was able to move legislation to implement the Republicans' Contract with America through the House. The committee chairs remained loyal to the Speaker even after House freshmen opposed some of Gingrich's compromises with the Senate and the president on the budget and other policy issues.

The divisions of authority mandated by the Constitution have also contributed to the politics of the governing process. By separating the institutions of government and assigning each one a primary sphere of authority, then imposing elaborate internal checks and balances on the exercise of that authority, the Constitution builds competition into the system. The president cannot appoint officials to the executive departments and agencies without Senate approval. Congress cannot appropriate money unless the president approves; however, Congress can override presidential disapproval of its legislation by a two-thirds vote in each house. The Supreme Court cannot enforce its own rulings; only the president has that power. Congress cannot determine the constitutionality of its own legislation; the Supreme Court has assumed that prerogative. The federal system, too, with its divisions of authority between the national government and the states, often plays off competing interests, needs, and policy goals against each other. In short, politics—the competition among conflicting interests—is built into the design and operation of the system.

Beneficiaries of Government Action

Over the years, the dispersion of authority among the branches and levels of government has given well-organized and well-funded groups more opportunities to exert influence on public officials than those with fewer resources at their disposal have had. This influence is often used to prevent policies that adversely affect the interests of powerful groups from becoming law. For years, for example, the American Medical Association effectively prevented Congress from enacting legislation creating a government-run health-care system for the general population. Similarly, domestic automobile manufacturers delayed and subsequently weakened the automobile emissions standards that environmentalists sought to impose on them. But powerful groups do not always get their way. The tobacco industry has not been able to prevent the passage of laws that restrict smoking in public places, and the gambling industry has not been able to overcome local opposition in several states to legalized casinos.

The dispersion of authority also leads to the dilution of policy decisions. To make policies acceptable to as many people as possible and to gain sufficient support to get them enacted, policy makers find they must add, alter, or remove items that particular groups desire or oppose. This practice builds consensus, but it often weakens a policy's scope or impact and may even change its character. Consider an issue that arose when Congress was debating welfare reform: Should additional payments be given to unmarried women on welfare who have more children? House Republicans proposed to end such payments, but a combination of pro-life legislators (who feared that more abortions would result from such a policy) and liberals (who believed that innocent children would suffer) led the Republican-controlled Senate to modify the proposal, giving individual states the discretion to make that decision.

In normal times, then, politics usually produces only small, incremental changes in public policy. In determining what those changes will be, the advantage clearly goes to those with the resources to influence who is selected to hold political power and what decisions they make. Those with greater resources are also likely to be benefiting from government policy already, and thus they are reluctant to support changes that might undercut their advantage. For this reason, government officials tend more often to tinker with the distribution of resources rather than to redistribute them on a larger scale.

Occasionally, however, a sense of national crisis propels the public to demand more sweeping changes. In the Great Depression of the 1930s, for example, President Franklin Roosevelt proposed and Congress promptly enacted legislation to provide federal aid to small farmers, unemployed laborers, and older Americans, all of whom had been hit especially hard by the economic downturn. Though modest by

In times of crisis, the power of government expands, but the rights of individuals shrink. At the outset of World War II, Congress authorized the detention of over 100,000 Americans of Japanese ancestry for "security reasons." Their property was confiscated, and most were forced to spend the war years in government-run camps. The 237 residents of Bainbridge Island in Washington State, for example, were evacuated under armed guard and sent to camps in California. In 1988 Congress apologized to the Japanese-American community and offered each detained family $20,000.

the standards of later social welfare programs, these measures were unprecedented in the United States and seemed almost revolutionary at the time — especially to Roosevelt's Republican critics. In the early 1980s, reacting to a public perception of a weakened United States (a perception fueled by the holding of American diplomats as hostages in Iran and the invasion of Afghanistan by the Soviet Union), President Ronald Reagan got Congress to agree to a large increase in defense spending to bolster the country's national security and image as a superpower. During 1995–1996, the Republican-controlled Congress responded to public displeasure with the size, cost, and implementation of the national government's welfare programs by devolving financial and administrative responsibility for one of these programs, Aid to Families with Dependent Children, to the states.

THE AMERICAN POLITICAL CULTURE

Even during the worst crises, however, most Americans would not allow their leaders to do certain things, such as assume dictatorial powers in violation of the Constitution and laws of the land. Underlying the political system of any nation are the dominant values, beliefs, and attitudes held by citizens about their governance, their nation's unique history, and their rights and responsibilities in society. Together these values, beliefs, and attitudes constitute the unique **political culture** of a people. That culture largely determines the structure and rules of a political system and the bounds of acceptable behavior within it.

The political culture of the United States has been unusually hospitable to a republican form of government, one that is based on popular consent, as opposed to one in which a central authority imposes its will on the people. That culture also favors democratic rules of participation in which citizens can influence who gets elected, what decisions they make, and when and how they make them. Indeed, over time, principles of both republicanism and democracy have become enshrined in America's public institutions. Whether they be a student council, local school board, state legislature, or even the presidency, these institutions are expected to be sensitive to public opinion and responsive to public needs and interests.

Strongly held beliefs about individual initiative and opportunity lie at the core of American democracy. In the last century, the westward expansion of the United States was justified by the doctrine of "manifest destiny," which held it the right and duty of white Americans to settle and subdue the entire continent, displacing the native peoples and wildlife. Thousands of prints of the 1872 painting America's Progress, *by John Gast, hung on living-room walls during the 1890s.*

However, American political life is not guided by a single, cohesive theory like monarchism or communism. Even the American Revolution lacked the kind of guiding idea that has inspired other national revolutions. Most of the American revolutionaries seemed to mean it when they said that they simply wanted protection of their rights as Englishmen, even as that desire led them to the conclusion that they could no longer endure British rule. It was not the charm of a new or more appealing philosophy that lured them away from their British loyalties; it was a practical need to run their own affairs in a way they thought would best suit their interests.

Throughout subsequent American history, practical needs, not theoretical concerns, have given rise to the major political issues that the country has had to address: how to broaden political participation; how to meet the challenges of industrialization and immigration; how to adjust to new realities wrought by technological sophistication, including nuclear weapons. In recent years public officials have been debating how and at which level of government to address the problems of the poor, not whether those problems are a legitimate concern of government. It is politics, not philosophy, that shapes the issue and conditions the solution.

The "American Ethos"

Although the American political culture is a composite of pragmatic attitudes, values, and traditions, two beliefs lie at its core: (1) the commitment to democracy, a political system that stresses personal liberty and political equality, and (2) the commitment to capitalism, an economic system based on individual initiative and private property. These ideas are the basis of the **American ethos.**

Democracy In democratic America, many people believe that a primary responsibility of government is to protect individual liberty. This belief, articulated in the Declaration of Independence, was reaffirmed in the Bill of Rights, the first ten amend-

FIGURE 1-1
Changes in public attitudes toward government efforts to improve equality of opportunity.

SOURCE: General Social Surveys, University of Chicago, National Opinion Research Center.

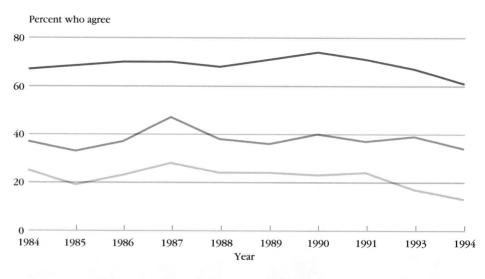

Government should do something to reduce the income differences between rich and poor.

We are spending too little money on improving the conditions of African Americans.

We are spending too little money on welfare.

No data available for 1992.

ments to the Constitution, which guarantee freedom of speech, freedom of religion, and other basic forms of liberty.

To preserve liberty, Americans believe that political processes must be open and responsive to the needs and opinions of individual citizens. As the late senator J. William Fulbright put it, "The values of democracy are in large part the processes of democracy — the way in which we pass laws, the way in which we administer justice, the way in which government deals with individuals."[5] The best way to protect one's liberty, the thinking goes, is to be able to speak on one's own behalf in the councils of power, to be present — or at least represented — in the places where public policy decisions are made.

But people must have more than mere *access* to government. They must also be *equal* in its eyes. In general, the American ethos enshrines equality in two different forms: political equality and equality of opportunity.

In application, *political equality* means that every citizen's vote counts the same, that all citizens have the same rights and obligations, that they are all subject to the same laws and entitled by government to the same treatment. Americans have consistently supported this kind of equality.

They have differed, however, over how to achieve *equality of opportunity*. Although Americans widely endorse the principle, they disagree over its applications. Should government take steps to improve opportunities for those who start out or become "less equal," even if they do so by reason of their own shortcomings? Americans disagree, often violently, on their answers to this question (see Figure 1-1 and Tables 1-1 and 1-2).

Why the disagreements? Intrinsic tensions between equality and liberty are to blame, as they have been for much of the conflict in American political history. The contemporary debate over affirmative action is a good example. Some people believe that the achievement of genuine equality of opportunity requires policies designed to make up for previous practices of discrimination. They feel that extraordinary measures are necessary to offset previously limited opportunities for disad-

TABLE 1-1   **CHANGES IN PUBLIC ATTITUDES TOWARD POLITICAL EQUALITY**

STATEMENT	THOSE WHO AGREE (PERCENT)	
	1984	1994
1. Our society should do whatever is necessary to make sure that everyone has an equal opportunity to succeed.	90	88
2. We have gone too far in pushing equal rights in this country.	45	53
3. One of the big problems in this country is that we don't give everyone an equal chance.	49	53
4. It is not really that big a problem if some people have more of a chance in life than others.	36	32
5. The country would be better off if we worried less about how equal people are.	53	54
6. If people were treated more equally in this country, we would have many fewer problems.	64	64

Source: Based on data from the American National Election Studies, conducted by the University of Michigan, Center for Political Studies, and provided by the Inter-University Consortium for Political and Social Research, Ann Arbor, Michigan.

TABLE 1-2	CHANGES IN PUBLIC ATTITUDES TOWARD THE ROLE OF GOVERNMENT (PERCENT)		
STATEMENT	1972	1984	1994
1. There is much concern about the rapid rise in medical and hospital costs. Some feel there should be a government insurance plan that would cover all medical and hospital expenses. Others feel that medical expenses should be paid by individuals and through private insurance. What is your position? **There should be a government insurance plan**	46	38	38
2. Some people feel that the government should see to it that every person has a job and a good standard of living. Others think the government should just let each person get ahead on his or her own. What is your position? **Government should see to a job and good standard of living**	32	34	29
3. Some people feel that the government should make every possible effort to improve the social and economic positions of African Americans. Others feel that the government should not make any special effort to help them because they should help themselves. What is your position? **Government should help African Americans**	34	32	21
4. Some people think the government should provide fewer services, even in areas such as health and education, in order to reduce spending. Others feel that it is important for the government to provide many more services, even if it means an increase in spending. What is your position? **Government should decrease services and spending**	—	34	42

Source: Based on data from the 1972, 1984, and 1994 American National Election Studies, conducted by the University of Michigan, Center for Political Studies, Ann Arbor, Michigan. Data provided by the Inter-University Consortium for Political and Social Research, Ann Arbor, Michigan.

vantaged groups. Employers, for example, may be forced by affirmative action guidelines to undertake vigorous recruitment programs for female or minority-group job applicants. Failure to do so would leave them open to loss of government contracts or benefits or to lawsuits by those who claim discrimination.

But is such "increased equality" true "equality"? Critics argue that most if not all affirmative action policies put members of historically advantaged groups—generally whites, males, and members of the middle and upper classes—at a competitive disadvantage, depriving them of a fair shake when they compete with members of the groups targeted by affirmative action programs for jobs, college admissions, loans, and scholarships. Further, it is argued that these programs curtail individual liberties because they limit the freedom of employers or others, such as college administrations and banks, to choose whomever they wish. The political debate on this issue, waged with great intensity and emotion in the mid 1990s between liberals and conservatives, Democrats and Republicans, and minority and majority racial groups, forced policy makers at the national and state levels to modify and curtail many affirmative action programs.

Affirmative action is not the only kind of policy that helps some at the expense of others and exacerbates the natural tensions between liberty and equality. In fact, it is difficult to think of any policy decision that does not benefit some people and hurt others. As noted previously in this chapter, the challenge for any democratic government, then, is to respond appropriately to the interests of the majority without impinging on the rights of any minorities.

Capitalism   Americans believe not only in political liberty but also in economic liberty. The American economy operates as a **free-enterprise system.** The "free" in "free enterprise" means that individuals are encouraged to pursue their own financial interests, creating products and services that they can sell for a profit.

The American free-enterprise system is an example of **capitalism,** a system of economic organization that is based on private ownership and private control of the means of production and distribution. Its roots lie in a commitment to individualism, which helps explain the lack of interest that collectivist theories like communism and socialism have usually inspired in the United States.[6] Americans have never believed that government, or any designated planning agency, could generate as much productivity or as high a standard of living as a free market in which economic freedom encourages individual initiative and stimulates the creativity that leads to success. Freedom thus fuels the engine of economic progress. This belief in the social benefit of individual initiative is another component of the American ethos.

Subcultures and Diversity

Although certain common values and beliefs shape American culture, there is still considerable diversity within that culture. Many subcultures coexist, such as the Cajuns of Louisiana, the Amish of Pennsylvania, the Cubanos of Miami, the Mexicans

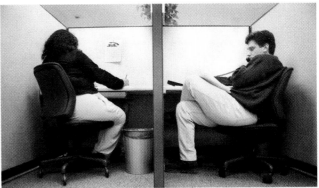

In a capitalist system, one person's gain may be another's loss. Stock prices soared in the mid 1990s as many businesses tried to become more competitive by "downsizing" their work forces. The frenzied floor of the New York Stock Exchange contrasts with the painful task of two soon-to-be-former employees of AT&T, who are using the company's "resource centers" to look for new jobs.

of San Antonio, the Hasidic Jews of Brooklyn. These and many other groups have distinctive traditions, perceptions, interests, and values.

Such diversity has shaped the character of American politics. The indigenous population of the United States was largely supplanted by immigrants, primarily from Europe, who came to America in search of greater economic opportunity, social equality, and religious and political freedom. Others, largely from Africa, came unwillingly — in chains — to plant and harvest crops and work in homes, primarily in the South. The United States continues to attract refugees and other immigrants from all over the world. In recent years much of the immigration has come from south of the border, predominantly from the Spanish-speaking countries of Central and South America.

Although the presence of so many diverse ethnic, racial, and religious groups (see Table 1-3) has often been celebrated as a strength of American society, it has given rise to much of the tension within it. One of the more controversial issues in recent years has been the proposal to establish English as the official language of the United States, a measure already adopted by several states. Proponents argue that a common tongue has helped to unify our diverse society into a single nation, in contrast to other countries in which ethnic and tribal groups who continue to speak different languages and dialects have often come into serious conflict. Opponents, however, contend that the proposal is unnecessary and undesirable: unnecessary because speaking English is essential to advancement in the United States, and undesirable because it may impede learning if it prohibits or discourages bilingual education.

Racial and ethnic groups   For many years the United States was often described as a huge melting pot, a place where Old World cultures were gradually dissolved and blended into the culture of the newer American nation. Today, however, the melting-pot image does not capture America as accurately or stir Americans as powerfully as it once did. Recent immigrants and the descendants of earlier ones have become increasingly conscious of and interested in preserving or rediscovering their ances-

Some groups seek to create traditions that set them apart, while others never give up old ones. (Left) A Chicago family celebrates Kwanza, a new holiday that coincides with Christmas and focuses on the African heritage of African Americans. (Right) Hasidic Jews stop to pray on the way to New York's Catskill Mountains. So many people parked beside the New York State Thruway and flagged down others that they jeopardized highway safety. Finally, officials created a special "Mincha area" for the afternoon prayer.

tral heritages, as have African Americans and indigenous peoples. In general, recent immigrants and racial minorities have felt less of a desire to blend in and adopt the values and mores of the dominant group, whites of European descent.

With this heightened pride in historical roots has come a proliferation of organizations to promote, preserve, and in some cases exalt various ethnic identities. Many of these groups, such as the American Jewish Congress, the Arab American Institute,

TABLE 1-3				IMMIGRANTS TO THE UNITED STATES BY COUNTRY OF BIRTH, 1971 TO 1993 (IN THOUSANDS)			
COUNTRY OF BIRTH	**1971– 1980**	**1981– 1990**	**1991– 1993**	**COUNTRY OF BIRTH**	**1971– 1980**	**1981– 1990**	**1991– 1993**
All countries	**4,493.3**	**7,338.1**	**3,705.4**	**North America[a]**	**1,645.0**	**3,125.0**	**1,896.4**
Europe[a]	**801.3**	**705.6**	**438.9**	Canada	114.8	119.2	45.9
France	17.8	23.1	8.6	Mexico	637.2	1,653.3	1,286.6
Germany	66.0	70.1	23.7	Caribbean[a]	759.8	892.7	337.0
Greece	93.7	29.1	5.8	Barbados	20.9	17.4	3.8
Ireland	14.1	32.8	30.6	Cuba	276.8	159.2	35.8
Italy	130.1	32.9	7.7	Dominican			
Poland	43.6	97.4	72.5	Republic	148.0	251.8	128.8
Portugal	104.5	40.0	9.4	Haiti	58.7	140.2	68.6
Romania	17.5	38.9	20.2	Jamaica	142.0	213.8	59.9
Soviet Union				Trinidad and			
former	43.2	84.0	159.2	Tobago	61.8	39.5	22.0
Spain	30.0	15.8	4.9	Central America	132.4	458.7	226.9
United Kingdom	123.5	142.1	52.7	El Salvador	34.4	214.6	100.3
Yugoslavia	42.1	19.2	8.1	Guatemala	25.6	87.9	47.9
Asia[a]	**1,633.8**	**2,817.4**	**1,073.5**	Honduras	17.2	49.5	25.3
Bangladesh	—	15.2	17.7	Nicaragua	13.0	44.1	33.9
Cambodia	8.4	116.6	7.4	Panama	22.7	29.0	9.7
China	202.5[b]	388.8[b]	137.5	**South America[a]**	**284.4**	**455.9**	**189.1**
Taiwan			43.9	Argentina	25.1	25.7	10.6
Hong Kong	47.5	63.0	30.1	Brazil	13.7	23.7	17.5
India	176.8	261.9	121.9	Chile	17.6	23.4	6.6
Iran	46.2	154.8	47.6	Colombia	77.6	124.4	45.7
Iraq	23.4	19.6	9.7	Ecuador	50.2	56.0	24.5
Israel	26.6	36.3	13.8	Guyana	47.5	95.4	29.1
Japan	47.9	43.2	23.0	Peru	29.1	64.4	36.5
Jordan	29.6	32.6	13.0	**Africa[a]**	**91.5**	**192.3**	**91.1**
Korea	272.0	338.8	63.9	Egypt	25.5	31.4	12.8
Laos	22.6	145.6	25.9	Ethiopia	—	27.2	15.0
Lebanon	33.8	41.6	17.3	Ghana	—	14.9	6.8
Pakistan	31.2	61.3	39.5	Nigeria	8.8	35.3	16.9
Philippines	360.2	495.3	188.1	**Other countries[c]**	**37.3**	**41.9**	**16.4**
Syria	13.3	20.6	8.7				
Thailand	44.1	64.4	21.2				
Turkey	18.6	20.9	7.2				
Vietnam	179.7	401.4	192.6				

[a]Includes countries not shown separately.
[b]Includes Taiwan.
[c]Includes Australia, New Zealand, and unknown countries.

Source: U.S. Immigration and Naturalization Service, Statistical Yearbook, *annual and releases; as appears in U.S. Bureau of the Census,* Statistical Abstract of the United States: 1995 *(115th ed.), Washington, D.C.: 1995, p. 11, Table No. 7. Data are for fiscal years ending in year shown.*

and the Japanese American Foundation, have gotten involved in the political process. In general, their concerns focus on aid to and trade with the members' homelands, foreign policy toward these countries, immigration from them, and certain domestic issues, such as bilingual education.

The increasing self-awareness of racial and ethnic groups has generated conflict among them, as well as between them and groups that are part of or closer to the majority culture. Much of the conflict stems from inequality in wealth and income, education and employment opportunities, and political influence. At the outset of the 1990s, the wealthiest 1 percent of American households controlled approximately 30.4 percent of the country's wealth; the rest of the top 10 percent held almost 37 percent of the wealth.[7] And incomes and wealth differ significantly among

| **TABLE 1-4** | **MONEY INCOME OF HOUSEHOLDS IN CONSTANT (1993) DOLLARS, 1970 TO 1993** |

YEAR	NUMBER OF HOUSE-HOLDS (1,000)	PERCENT DISTRIBUTION							MEDIAN INCOME (DOLLARS)
		UNDER $10,000	$10,000–$14,999	$15,000–$24,999	$25,000–$34,999	$35,000–$49,999	$50,000–$74,999	$75,000 AND OVER	
ALL[a]									
1970	64,778	15.0	8.5	16.9	18.0	20.4	14.8	6.4	30,558
1975	72,867	14.4	9.6	17.2	16.6	19.7	15.5	6.9	30,340
1980	82,368	14.2	9.0	17.4	15.0	19.4	16.3	8.8	31,095
1985	88,458	14.4	8.7	16.7	15.1	17.9	16.5	10.6	31,717
1990	94,312	13.4	8.6	16.4	14.7	17.7	16.6	12.6	33,105
1993	97,107	14.2	9.2	16.9	14.7	16.3	16.1	12.5	31,241
WHITE									
1970	57,575	13.8	8.0	16.3	18.3	21.2	15.5	6.8	31,828
1975	64,392	12.9	9.2	16.9	16.8	20.4	16.4	7.5	31,728
1980	71,872	12.4	8.5	17.0	15.2	20.1	17.2	9.5	32,805
1985	76,576	12.7	8.2	16.5	15.3	18.5	17.2	11.5	33,450
1990	80,968	11.5	8.3	16.2	15.0	18.2	17.5	13.3	34,529
1993	82,387	12.2	8.9	16.6	14.9	17.0	17.0	13.4	32,960
BLACK									
1970	6,180	27.2	13.0	22.2	15.4	13.1	7.4	1.7	19,373
1975	7,489	27.6	14.0	19.7	15.2	13.9	7.7	1.9	19,047
1980	8,847	28.1	13.4	20.7	12.9	13.2	9.0	2.7	18,899
1985	9,797	28.1	12.6	19.4	13.4	13.3	9.7	3.5	19,901
1990	10,671	28.2	11.3	18.3	13.2	13.8	9.6	5.5	20,648
1993	11,281	28.9	11.8	19.2	13.8	12.0	9.3	5.2	19,533
HISPANIC[b]									
1975	2,948	18.5	13.2	22.9	17.8	16.9	8.2	2.4	22,793
1980	3,906	18.2	12.3	22.2	15.9	16.3	11.2	4.1	23,968
1985	5,213	20.4	12.7	19.8	15.8	15.1	11.2	4.8	23,454
1990	6,220	18.6	12.9	19.1	16.3	16.3	10.8	5.9	24,688
1993	7,362	20.0	12.4	21.5	16.5	13.4	10.8	5.4	22,886

[a]Includes other races not shown separately.
[b]Persons of Hispanic origin may be of any race. Income data for Hispanic origin households are not available prior to 1972.

Source: Adapted from U.S. Bureau of the Census, Statistical Abstract of the United States: 1995 *(115th ed.), Washington, D.C.: 1995, p. 469, Table 723.*

racial groups. For example, as Table 1-4 indicates, a much larger proportion of African-American and Hispanic families than white families have incomes at the lower end of the scale.

In the past three decades, much political debate has focused on what, if anything, government should do about this inequality. The debate in 1995 and 1996 over tax and spending cuts is a good example. Republicans, who supported such cuts, contended that they would benefit society as a whole by returning money and political control to individuals and the state governments. Democrats, however, saw the spending cuts, particularly those that would affect health and welfare, as hurting the most vulnerable: minorities, the poor, the young, and the old. They also believed the tax cuts would disproportionately benefit the rich.

In addition to the politics of economic inequality, other issues of social justice have generated considerable political controversy since the 1960s. Congress has debated civil rights legislation, Native American treaty rights, and the eligibility of legal and illegal aliens for government aid. The Supreme Court has considered cases involving school desegregation, financial inequalities in public education, affirmative action, and legislative districts designed to ensure minority representation in Congress. Presidents have been pressured to appoint members of minority groups to public office; to develop and promote programs that prohibit discrimination on the basis of race, gender, and sexual orientation in both the public and private sectors; and to encourage minority businesses.

Interest group activity has fueled the politics of inequality. The Urban League, the Congress of Racial Equality (CORE), the Southern Christian Leadership Conference (SCLC), and many other predominantly African-American groups have championed the cause of the poor within the political arena, as has the "rainbow coalition," a grassroots organization that supported Jesse Jackson's candidacy for the Democratic presidential nomination in 1984 and 1988. More recently, Louis Farrakhan and the organization he heads, the Nation of Islam, have also gotten involved in political activity, sponsoring a "Million Man March" on Washington in October 1995 and a drive to register millions of new African-American voters.

Hispanic-American groups such as the National Council of La Raza and the Mexican American Legal Defense and Education Fund have also become more politically active, particularly in states with large Hispanic populations, such as Florida, Texas, and California. Asian Americans are well organized in California and other Pacific Coast states. These and other, smaller ethnic groups have commanded recognition within the political parties and Congress, and special presidential aides now provide liaison to them.

In sum, the increased self-awareness and unhappiness of racial and ethnic groups about their economic and social conditions has prompted them to organize and enter the political arena. They are not alone.

The women's movement   American women, too, have experienced inequality in various forms; and in the last few decades the women's movement has profoundly changed politics and public policy. During the first half of this century, men took a more active part in politics than did women. Men voted more regularly, and they determined the issues that went on the public policy agenda. American women were not universally guaranteed the right to vote until 1920. Even after they obtained suffrage, their political attitudes and voting behavior did not differ significantly from men's for many years — a fact that some attributed to the stratification of social roles, which encouraged women to be more concerned about family issues and men more concerned about national and world affairs. As a result, most married women—and almost all women were married—tended to follow their husbands' lead on political matters.

Times have changed. In the late 1960s and the 1970s, women surged into the work force and entered the political arena. In both areas they found many traditional patterns and procedures not to their liking, and they became intensely concerned with issues that affected them directly: abortion and other women's health concerns, maternity leave and child-care policies, equal pay and equal job opportunities, legal rights within marriage, and the equity of divorce laws. At the same time, the proportion of women who were divorced or separated or who had never been married increased sharply.

Consistent with the growing awareness of their economic needs, women began to develop distinctive political attitudes. As a group, women became more sympathetic than men to a larger government role within the economic and social spheres and less supportive of a foreign policy based on military force. In response to the differing positions taken by the political parties on these issues, a gender gap emerged, with women more likely than men to vote for Democratic candidates and men more likely than women to support Republicans. This gap in turn has reinforced the ideological differences between the parties, making the Republicans more conservative and the Democrats more liberal.

In addition, women began to form their own interest groups, such as the National Organization for Women (NOW) and the Women's Political Caucus; through them, they began to join causes and support women's issues more successfully than in the past. More women also began to seek and win elective office, at both the state and

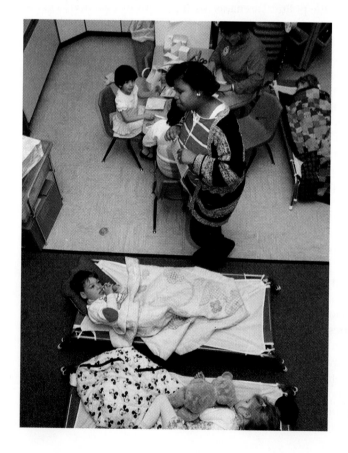

The women's movement has brought a variety of family issues into the public arena, from child care to child custody.

the national levels. These developments have introduced a new gender-based dimension into American politics.

Other sources of diversity   Other differences within the American population have also produced conflicting policy goals and have generated political strife. Geographic differences among and within states, as well as emerging regional identities, have created competition for tax dollars, government grants and services, and special programs. The movement of more of the population to the South and West has turned states in these regions (the so-called Sunbelt) against those in the Northeast and upper Midwest (the Frostbelt); it has pitted the high-technology industries of silicon chips, computer software, robotics, pharmaceuticals, and genetic engineering — industries that promote free trade and seek new markets abroad — against older "smokestack" industries such as steel, automobiles, rubber, and aluminum, which want protection against foreign competition.

Population movements from rural to metropolitan areas and from central-city to suburban areas have set the stage for increasing public concern about street crime, drug abuse, and mass transit as well as environmental and energy policies. The aging of the population has prompted a concern about age discrimination and has intensified demands for policies that benefit older citizens, such as Social Security and Medicare; but it may also eventually lead to age-based cleavages within the political

Among all the sources of diversity in American society, few are more politically divisive than homosexuality. Here opponents of a Colorado constitutional amendment to prohibit gay rights legislation rally in Denver in 1992. Although voters narrowly approved the amendment, in 1996 the United States Supreme Court ruled that it violated the national Constitution.

arena as younger voters are asked to shoulder increasing tax burdens to finance these programs.

Religious diversity has also enlivened American politics, especially in recent years with the growth and activism of the Christian fundamentalist movement. Today approximately 25 percent of all white Protestants consider themselves fundamentalists and another 14 percent evangelicals,[8] and these religious believers have become more politically active in recent years through organizations such as the Christian Coalition. Well-organized, well-funded, with politically skilled leadership, the Christian Coalition regularly speaks out and mobilizes its 1.7 million members on a variety of social issues that have public policy implications—issues such as abortion, homosexuality, school prayer, taxpayer support for religious education, and penalties for criminal behavior. The "religious right" has become an extremely powerful force within the Republican party; it has taken control of a number of state Republican organizations and is courted solicitously by Republican presidential candidates. However, its success within the political arena has also provoked a backlash of activism by groups that oppose its policies, such as the National Abortion and Reproductive Rights Action League, the Human Rights Campaign Fund (a group that supports gay rights), and Americans United for Separation of Church and State.

The list goes on and on. Occupational associations, economic groups, and even leisure-time organizations have become better organized and more involved in the political process. Across the board, interest groups from the Pharmaceutical Manufacturers Association to the National Education Association, from the National Rifle Association to the American Association of Retired Persons, have become more adept at influencing not only the selection of public officials but also the decisions of lawmakers already in office.

Consensus, Conflict, and Apathy in American Democracy

Both consensus and conflict grow from the soil of the American culture, and both help to shape American politics and government. The consensus, which emerges from shared fundamental beliefs and values, embraces the need for government, the rules of the political process, and the general nature of public policy. The conflict, which springs from the diversity of the population and from the different needs, interests, and goals that flow from that pluralism, usually swirls around the content of specific policies and generates much of the activity within the political and governing arenas.

Consensus provides a broad base of support for the government and whatever policies the government produces. The wide diversity of interests, on the other hand, produces political battles over specific issues. Most of this activity occurs among those groups, whether large or small, that are directly interested in or affected by a particular issue. The general public is likely to get involved only when the policy goes into effect or its cost must be paid. Most of the time, only a small portion of the population knows or cares much about public policies, and an even smaller portion gets involved and tries to influence the content of those policies.

Is it unhealthy for a democracy that relatively few people get involved on most issues? Those who answer "yes" point out that apathy increases the likelihood that a well-organized, well-financed group can get its way. The plight of consumers in the United States before the government set safety standards, required warning labels and truth in advertising, and prosecuted violators is a good example of how even a majority of the people can suffer if they are unorganized or underinvolved. A silent or inattentive majority does pose a threat to the democratic process.

However, if most issues aroused most people most of the time, society would be in constant turmoil. Compromise would be even more difficult to achieve than it already is, and decision makers would be pushed and pulled in every direction and, perhaps, unable to act or able to make only minor changes in existing policy. In all likelihood, overall public support for government and law would be weakened because so many people who felt strongly about issues and did not get their way would be discontented.

A vibrant and stable democracy needs both consensus and conflict. *Some* of the people must be well informed and actively involved — preferably not the same ones on every issue — and *most* of the people must generally support the system and the decisions of its policy makers, even though they may not perceive the effects of those decisions on their daily lives.

The strength of the American system is that it permits those who are interested to participate in politics and affect policy outcomes. It also gives the general citizenry regular opportunities to get involved. Thus periodic elections, a free and critical press, and abundant opportunities for citizens to petition and protest keep public officials responsive to society, even though many people choose not to involve themselves in day-to-day political activities.

SUMMARY

In a culture where disagreement and self-interest are the norm, where individual liberty and the common good may be mutually exclusive, and where rewards are limited whereas desires are virtually insatiable, the quest for political gain is never-ending. If *politics* is the ongoing struggle among people to influence the values, beliefs, and policy of the society, then *government* is the institutional mechanism for determining the rules of that contest and, within those rules, who wins and who loses. Government determines who gets what and when by formulating policy decisions that distribute resources, allocate funds, and make and enforce rules.

When government makes decisions, it exercises *authority*. In a democracy, it must do so in a way that reflects the desires of the majority but does not violate the rights of the minority. This is a difficult task. The Constitution provides general guidelines, but each generation must decide for itself how to interpret those guidelines, that is, where to draw the line between the majority's interests, desires, and rights, and the minority's rights.

How government makes decisions may be controversial as well. The rules by which any political system operates are not neutral: they benefit some at the expense of others. Those who understand the rules are best able to benefit from them. And those who understand the rules and can most effectively manipulate them to their advantage have tended to be the best-organized, best-funded, and best-led groups. This is why the political system in the United States seems to advantage the advantaged. This is also why government tends to maintain the status quo, and why policy changes are more often incremental than innovative.

That Americans accept the political system and the rules by which it functions, even though they do not always agree with or benefit from the policy it establishes, is testimony to the consensus underlying the basic values and beliefs of American culture. Most Americans believe that *democracy* is the best type of government and that *capitalism* is the best type of economic system. Both are predicated on the concept of individual liberty — the idea that people should be free to pursue their own interests as long as that pursuit does not impinge on the general welfare of the society. When it does, law may impose restraints. Americans also believe in political equality, the idea that all citizens have equal rights and responsibilities under law. These shared beliefs in individual liberty and political equality provide the foundation on which the political system rests, and the political system in turn provides the mechanisms for the debate and resolution of disagreements.

Society in the United States consists of many different ethnic, racial, and religious groups. This diversity has contributed to the strength and vitality of American society and its political system. But it has also led to continuous struggles over *public policy,* struggles that pit individuals and groups against one another as they pursue their own interests, values, and beliefs. These battles are the essence of contemporary politics, the fuel that fires the engines of government and keeps them running.

This chapter thus ends where it began. Politics motivates and drives the institutions of government. In turn, government makes policy that affects society and influences subsequent political activity. This is the life cycle of the politics of American government.

KEY TERMS

politics
government
public policy
power

democracy
authority
political culture

American ethos
free-enterprise system
capitalism

RESOURCES

SCHOLARLY STUDIES

Dahl, Robert A. *A Preface to Democratic Theory.* Chicago: University of Chicago Press, 1963. An extended discussion of the concept of democracy and its many meanings.

Dionne, E. J. *Why Americans Hate Politics.* New York: Simon and Schuster, 1992. A leading journalist's account of why so many Americans have been turned off by contemporary politics and politicians and what can be done about it.

Ellis, Richard J. *American Political Cultures.* New York: Oxford University Press, 1993. This book postulates the thesis that there are a variety of political cultures in America and that the debate over policy is really a conflict among these cultures.

Greider, William. *Who Will Tell the People: The Betrayal of American Democracy.* New York: Simon and Schuster, 1993. A thoughtful critique of what is wrong with our democratic system and how it can be fixed.

Lasswell, Harold. *Politics: Who Gets What, When, How.* New York: Meridian Books, 1958. A classic study of the politics of influence by a scholar who helped shape the discipline of political science.

Lipset, Seymour Martin. *The First New Nation: The United States in Historical and Comparative Perspective.* New York: Norton, 1979. An inquiry into the economic, historical, and sociological factors that shaped the American character.

Tocqueville, Alexis de. *Democracy in America.* Edited by J. P. Mayer. New York: HarperCollins, 1988. A study of American democracy as seen through the eyes of a French traveler in the United States in the 1830s.

LEISURE READING

Orwell, George. *Animal Farm.* New York: Knopf, 1993 [1946]. A satire about a revolution that went bad. It should be read in conjunction with study of the American struggle for independence.

Orwell, George. *1984.* New York: Knopf, 1992. A powerful fictional description of a totalitarian society.

Smith, Hedrick. *The Power Game: How Washington Works.* New York: Random House, 1989. An insider's account of Washington politics by a journalist who covered the scene for many years.

PRIMARY SOURCES

Safire, William. *Safire's New Political Dictionary.* New York: Random House, 1993. A former presidential speechwriter, now a journalist, explores the language of politics.

Stanley, Harold W., and Richard G. Niemi. *Vital Statistics on American Politics.* Washington, D.C.: Congressional Quarterly, annual. Contains a wealth of statistical data on various aspects of American politics.

Statistical Abstract of the United States. Washington, D.C.: Bureau of the Census, annual. A basic source of information on United States politics, economics, and society collected and updated by the Census Bureau and the Department of Commerce.

ORGANIZATIONS

Center for Democracy, 1101 15th Street, N.W., Suite 505, Washington, DC 20005; phone (202) 429-9141, fax (202) 293-1768, e-mail cfd@netcom.com Promotes democratic values and practices abroad.

Common Cause, 2030 M Street, N.W., Suite 300, Washington, DC 20036; phone (202) 833-1200, fax (202) 659-3716, e-mail 75300.3120@compuserve.com A citizens' lobby. Interested in the operation of government and its responsiveness to the people.

Congress Watch, 215 Pennsylvania Avenue, S.E., Washington, DC 20003; phone (202) 546-4996, fax (202) 547-7392, Internet http://www.citizen.org /public_citizen/congress/cwhome.html A part of activist Ralph Nader's organization. This group examines Congress and the behavior of its members.

National Academy of Public Administration, 1120 G Street, N.W., Suite 850, Washington, DC 20005; phone (202) 347-3190, fax (202) 393-0993, Internet http://relm.lmi.org/napa/ Devoted to the study and improvement of the administration of government. Members are former or current public officials or distinguished students of government.

Public Citizen, 1600 20th Street, N.W., Washington, DC 20009; phone (202) 588-1000, fax (202) 296-1717, Internet http://www.citizen.org/ Another group in Ralph Nader's organization. It promotes democratic practices and tries to coordinate citizen action campaigns.

The Constitutional Basis
of American Politics

H ave you registered to vote? If not, did you know that you will be offered a chance to do so the next time you go to renew your driver's license? The story of how the federal government came to use state motor vehicle offices to register voters—and how state governments unsuccessfully challenged its authority to do so—reveals many facets of the complex relationship between politics and government within the American constitutional system.

Determining who may vote has generated recurring political controversy throughout American history. During the Constitutional Convention the framers struggled with the issue, agreeing on the need for a representative government but disagreeing over who would choose the representatives. In the end they gave the states the right and obligation to conduct elections for federal officials, with such exceptions and regulations as Congress might determine.

The framers' decision not to decide on the voting question did not end the controversy, however. In fact, it ensured that it would be extended to later generations. Over the years Congress has instituted constitutional amendments to extend suffrage to all citizens 18 years of age and older, including racial minorities and women, and has enacted laws limiting the states' discretion in conducting elections for federal officials. The most recent example of this limitation is the so-called "motor-voter" law, officially known as the National Voter Registration Act of 1993. The law requires states to permit registration by mail or in a variety of state offices, including departments of motor vehicles, social services, vocational training, and military recruitment. Moreover, it prohibits states from purging from their registration lists those who have not voted in the past.

Enacted by a Democratic Congress, the motor-voter law aimed to increase the proportion of citizens who actually vote. That proportion had been declining for three decades, leaving voter turnout in the United States lower than in many other democratic countries. But the Democrats had a political motive as well. People who are older, better educated and of higher income levels are more likely to vote than those at the lower end of the age, education, and income scales. Because the

Republicans have tended to receive a larger proportion of their vote than have the Democrats from people in the upper education and income brackets, the Democrats hoped and the Republicans feared that the impact of the law would be to increase the potential Democratic vote. That is one reason why an earlier version of legislation, passed by Congress during the Bush administration, was vetoed by the president. Reenacted during the first year of the Clinton presidency, it was signed into law with considerable fanfare and took effect in 1995, one year before the president was to run for reelection.

After the bill became law, however, a number of states challenged its constitutionality and refused to comply with its requirements. These states — California, Illinois, Kansas, Michigan, Pennsylvania, South Carolina, and Virginia — had one thing in common: they all had Republican governors. The results of the 1994 congressional elections, in which the Republicans gained control of both houses of Congress, reinforced the resolve of these governors and Republican legislators in these states to oppose the law. In response to the states' opposition, the U.S. Justice Department countersued in an attempt to force compliance.

The states could not argue in a court of law that registering more people was bad because the new voters were more likely to register and vote Democratic (a charge that in fact was not borne out by the response to the law in its first year). Instead, their claim had to be couched in constitutional terms. The Tenth Amendment states, "The powers not delegated to the United States by the Constitution, nor prohibited by it to the States, are reserved to the States respectively, or to the people." California's Governor Pete Wilson thus charged that " 'Motor Voter' is the Clinton Administration's latest assault on states' sovereign rights to run their own agencies and to determine the jobs of their own employees." Likewise, Virginia's Governor George F. Allen claimed that the law was "an unfunded mandate" from the federal government that required state employees, in the departments of motor vehicles and social services, to perform work other than that for which they were hired. The governors also claimed that the law would open the door to voter fraud and cost their states "excessive amounts of money."

The federal courts that ruled on the constitutionality of the law unanimously disagreed, however. In rejecting the Republican governors' arguments, the courts cited Article I, Section 4, of the Constitution, which states, "The Time, Places and Manner of holding Elections for Senators and Representatives, shall be prescribed in each State by the Legislature thereof; but the Congress may at any time by Law make or alter such Regulations," except as to the places of choosing senators. Under this provision, Congress had the power to pass the motor-voter law because the Constitution gives it, not the states, the power to alter state voter regulations governing congressional elections. Moreover, the courts noted that although Article I, Section 2, of the Constitution gives the states the power to set the qualifications of voters for senators and representatives, the motor-voter law did not intrude on that power since it did not alter the qualifications themselves. In the words of the Court of Appeals for the Ninth Circuit, "Congress may conscript state agencies to carry out voter registration for the election of representatives and senators." In January 1996 the Supreme Court decided not to review California's appeal of this ruling, thus settling definitively the question of the law's constitutionality.

T he controversy over the motor-voter law illustrates how the Constitution can be both a prescription for political struggle and a framework for resolving political conflict. Politics involves contests over competing interests and powers. The dispute over the motor-voter law was a partisan disagreement between Republicans and Democrats. But when the dispute was taken to the courts, it became a conflict over federalism and the powers of the national government versus the states. The Constitution also provides that the Supreme Court and the lower federal courts may review and decide such cases and controversies. Through constitutional amendments and legislation like the motor-voter law, American government has become more and more democratic. The Constitution thus is as much a framework for government as a blueprint for a dynamic political process in which individuals and interest groups compete for influence and power.

Politics in America differs from politics in other countries because of the nature of the Constitution. The United States Constitution, the oldest written constitution in the world, is unique because it combines the idea of the rule of law with the idea that government is based on the consent of the governed. This chapter examines the basic principles and structure of the Constitution. We discuss the historical context in which the document was drafted and ratified, the original Constitution of 1787, and how the Constitution has changed over the years, as well as the ways in which constitutional change may occur.

THE FOUNDERS' CONSTITUTION

The founders' Constitution, as the historian Max Farrand observed, was a "bundle of compromises."[1] It was forged by a group of pragmatic statesmen who had to overlook, if not reconcile, their conflicting views about the politics of government. How did the Constitution come about? (Key events relating to the creation of the Constitution are listed in the box on page 34.)

The Revolutionary Background

In 1774 twelve of the original thirteen British colonies sent delegates to the First Continental Congress. This gathering had no official status; rather, it was convened to pass resolutions denouncing the British Parliament and Crown. The colonies had unsuccessfully demanded their own representatives in Parliament, arguing that only by this means could they defend their economic interests. When Britain imposed taxes on goods imported into the colonies, the demand for political representation intensified and the slogan "No taxation without representation" became a popular rallying cry. In addition, the colonists opposed the use of judges appointed by King George III to enforce laws they deemed unconstitutional.

In response to growing opposition to the Crown, the First Continental Congress recommended economic sanctions against Britain and boycotts of its goods. It also declared some acts of Parliament unconstitutional and urged colonists to arm themselves and form their own militias. In April 1775 fighting broke out between colonial and British troops, and in May a Second Continental Congress passed a resolution putting the colonies in a state of defense. Hostilities spread, and pressure grew for complete separation from Britain.

In the spring of 1776 a committee of the Continental Congress began work on a resolution proclaiming the colonies free and independent. Committee members decided that Thomas Jefferson would draft the resolution—the Declaration of Inde-

Key Events in the Creation of the Constitution

April 1775
American Revolution begins in Massachusetts, at Lexington and Concord.

July 1776
Declaration of Independence is proclaimed.

November 1777
Articles of Confederation are adopted by the Continental Congress.

March 1781
Articles of Confederation are ratified by the states.

September 1783
Treaty ending the Revolutionary War is signed in Paris.

April 1784
Congress ratifies the Treaty of Paris.

August 1786–February 1787
Shays's Rebellion takes place.

May–September 1787
Constitutional Convention drafts and adopts the Constitution of the United States.

June 1788
Constitution of the United States is ratified.

March 1789
Congress meets for the first time, in New York.

April 1789
George Washington is inaugurated as president, in New York.

September 1789
John Jay becomes the first chief justice of the Supreme Court.

September 1789
Congress proposes the Bill of Rights.

December 1791
The Bill of Rights is ratified.

pendence. Drawing on the Enlightenment philosophy of rationality and a science of human affairs that included the idea of individuals having unalienable rights to "life, liberty and the pursuit of happiness," Jefferson compiled a long list of despotic "abuses and usurpations" of power by King George. On July 1, 1776, the Continental Congress began debating Jefferson's draft and making changes in the wording. Three days later, on July 4, it approved the Declaration of Independence.

Later in 1776 the Continental Congress also considered a proposed set of "Articles of Confederation and Perpetual Union." The **Articles of Confederation,** the United States' first constitution, was approved in 1777 but was not ratified by all thirteen of the former colonies until 1781.

The Articles of Confederation

The Articles of Confederation provided for a unicameral, or one-house, legislature known as the Continental Congress, composed of delegates from the states. But this Congress had no effective power to regulate commerce or collect taxes; and tariffs, weights and measures, and currency varied from state to state. There was no separate executive or national judiciary; neither was there a national army. Instead, each of the original thirteen colonies was an independent and sovereign state that could conduct its own foreign policy without reference to the policies of other states.

This lack of a national political authority presented grave problems. For example, when several states refused to repay debts they had incurred during the Revolutionary War, the Continental Congress had no power to compel them to do so.

Despite artistic renderings like this one by Alonzo Chappel, the Battle of Lexington was no battle at all. In fact, British troops marching through Lexington, Massachusetts, encountered a group of colonial militiamen and ordered them to lay down their arms. The "embattled farmers" obeyed, but a musket accidentally went off. The British then fired into the crowd, killing eight. Although the survivors went quietly, the event became enshrined in American folklore as "the shot heard 'round the world."

In fact, it had no enforcement powers in any area. It could only ask each state to comply with and enforce its laws and policies voluntarily.

Also of growing concern were the economic problems facing the country and the tensions between creditors and debtors. In the aftermath of the Revolutionary War imports and exports declined sharply, wages fell by as much as 20 percent, and money was in short supply. In 1786 and 1787 tensions came to a head in economically depressed western Massachusetts when the state legislature refused to respond to petitions from debt-ridden farmers demanding the issuance of paper money and legislation to stop banks from foreclosing on their homes and farms. The angry farmers, led by Daniel Shays, formerly a captain in the Revolutionary army, rebelled against the state government and eventually marched on the federal arsenal at Springfield. It took the Massachusetts militia a year to put down Shays's Rebellion. (The box on page 36 describes this uprising in more detail.)

Shays's Rebellion dramatically underscored the weakness of the national government under the Articles of Confederation. It also coincided with the states' selection of delegates to the Constitutional Convention, which opened in Philadelphia in May 1787. And it was fresh in the minds of convention delegates, who planned to revise the Articles of Confederation but ended up drafting an entirely new constitution, one that greatly strengthened the powers of the national government.[2]

SHAYS'S REBELLION

On July 8, 1786, the Massachusetts state legislature adjourned without responding to petitions from debt-ridden farmers angered by high taxes and the scarcity of money. The farmers demanded the issuance of paper money and legislation to stop banks from fore-closing on their homes and farms because of nonpay-ment of taxes. Later that summer, at town meetings and at a convention of representatives of some fifty Massachusetts towns, protesters condemned the state legislature for its inaction and for levying high taxes and denounced state judges for enforcing the foreclosures.

By August 31, discontent had turned to violence, as mobs in Northampton, Concord, Worcester, and elsewhere disrupted courts and prevented the judges from hearing cases. In response, the governor of Massachusetts sent 600 of the state militia to protect the state supreme court in Springfield. On September 26 a destitute farmer named Daniel Shays, a former Revolutionary War captain, launched a rebellion against the Massachusetts government. Along with some five hundred insurgents, he confronted the mili-tia in Springfield and forced the supreme court to adjourn.

Shays's uprising in Springfield, the site of a federal arsenal, prompted Congress to authorize General Henry Knox to raise an army of 1,340 to put down the insurrection. But Knox's federal forces never saw any fighting because state troops put down the insur-gents in eastern Massachusetts. In the meantime, though, Shays's insurgents moved to Worcester, where they gathered a force of close to 1,200. On December 26 Shays's new forces began marching west toward Springfield. Now the governor called for 4,400 of the militia to be enlisted for one month, and he ordered them to assemble in both Boston and Springfield.

On January 25, 1787, the insurgents reached Springfield. As they approached the arsenal, the mili-

Debt-ridden farmers and townspeople in western Massachusetts attack a local official who has come to foreclose on a property. Such uprisings grew increasingly common after the Revolution and eventually led to the "rebellion" of Captain Daniel Shays in 1787.

tia greeted them with artillery fire; four insurgents were killed, and the rest broke ranks and fled. Two days later the militia pursued Shays's forces eastward through the state. Then, in a surprise attack on the morning of February 4, the militia captured 150 insur-gents and sent Shays fleeing into Vermont. By the end of the month Shays's Rebellion had been crushed, and the weakness of the Articles of Confederation and the need for a stronger national government had become dramatically clear — at least to some.

BACKGROUNDS OF THE DELEGATES TO THE CONSTITUTIONAL CONVENTION

State legislatures and governors appointed 74 men to go to the Constitutional Convention, but 19 of the appointees declined to attend. Rhode Island was not represented at all. Of the 55 who attended, 14 left before the convention closed, 39 signed the final draft of the Constitution (that number includes the signature of one absentee that was added later), and 3 refused to sign the document. Of these 55 men,

46 had been members of colonial or state legislatures
7 had been governors
42 had been delegates to the Continental Congress

8 had signed the Declaration of Independence
47 had been born in America
31 had attended college—some in Britain; some in America: Princeton (10), William and Mary (4), Yale (3), Harvard (2), Columbia (2)
21 had seen military service—18 as officers in the Continental Army
34 had studied law
13 were in business
10 were planters
21 were younger than 40 years old (the youngest was 26)
14 were over 50 years old (Benjamin Franklin, the oldest, was 81; the average age was 43)

The Constitutional Convention

Despite their diverse interests and conflicting views of government, delegates to the Constitutional Convention agreed that the Articles of Confederation were defective. The Continental Congress lacked three important powers: to regulate commerce, to raise funds to support a national army, and to compel compliance by the states. Within five days after the convention convened, on May 25, 1787, delegates had decided that "a *national* Government ought to be established consisting of a supreme legislative, executive and judiciary."[3]

Although they agreed that government must rest on the consent of the governed, the delegates shared a distrust of direct democracy. They feared a tyranny of the majority as much as they feared the tyranny of a minority—the concentration of power in too few hands. From the outset, therefore, the convention was inclined toward creating a **republic,** or representative form of government. Such a government would have considerable power to make and enforce laws but would derive its authority directly or indirectly from the citizens through popular elections. The objective, in the words of James Madison, a delegate from Virginia, was a "mixed" form of government, one that combined democratic and representative elements so as to minimize the possibility of tyranny by either the majority or a minority.[4]

For information about the makeup of the Constitutional Convention, see the box above.

The Great Compromise   Although in agreement on the broad outlines of the new republic, the delegates were sharply divided over the precise form it should take. Conflicts between large states and small states over their representation in Congress and between states in the North and those in the South over taxation and representation proved to be the major problems.

During the first few weeks debate focused on the **Virginia Plan,** which was drafted by James Madison and presented by Edmund Randolph, the governor of

JAMES MADISON: CONSTRUCTING THE CONSTITUTION

The American Constitution is what it is primarily through the efforts of James Madison. Born into the Virginia planter aristocracy in 1751, Madison entered Princeton University at the age of 15. After taking a four-year course in two years, he returned to Montpelier, the family plantation, and prepared for public life. From then on, Madison advocated religious freedom and independence from Britain.

Madison went to the Virginia Constitutional Convention at age 25, and later served in the Virginia House of Burgesses. At the Continental Congress in 1781, he voted to ratify the Articles of Confederation. His chance to shape the future country came at the Constitutional Convention of 1787. When the Convention delegates threw out the Articles of Confederation, they took as their working document the Virginia Plan, a series of resolutions drafted largely by Madison. The Virginia Plan proposed a federal government divided into legislative, executive, and judicial branches; and that framework was eventually adopted for the Constitution.

Madison then collaborated with two other proponents of the new Constitution, Alexander Hamilton and John Jay, on a series of eighty-five articles urging ratification of the document by the states. These so-called *Federalist* essays were published serially in the New York newspapers under the name "Publius" from October 1787 to August 1788. Madison has been identified as the author of twenty-nine of the essays.

Neither the Virginia Plan nor the Constitution had a bill of rights; and Madison, along with others, believed that the separation of powers within the federal government made guarantees of specific liberties unnecessary. However, opponents of ratification claimed that the absence of such guarantees made federal power dangerous, and the Federalists pledged their support of a formal bill of rights once ratification was achieved. On this basis, Virginia became the tenth state to ratify the Constitution in 1788.

Nearing the end of his presidency at the age of 65, James Madison sat for this portrait by John Vanderlyn.

Seated in the new House of Representatives, Madison began work on the additions to the Constitution. He studied similar bills passed by state governments, particularly Virginia's Declaration of Rights composed by George Mason in 1776. The new amendments were presented for approval in September 1789; and in late 1791, ratification by Virginia made Madison's Bill of Rights part of the Constitution.

Virginia. It called for a strong central government with a *bicameral legislature*—a legislature with two houses. Members of the lower house would be elected by voters in the states, and members of the upper house would be chosen by those in the lower house from nominees submitted by the state legislatures. Representation of states in the national legislature would be based on wealth and population; thus the large states—Virginia, Massachusetts, and Pennsylvania—would dominate. In addition, the Virginia Plan called for an executive chosen by the legislature, for a judiciary with considerable power, and for a council of revision (composed of members of the executive and the judiciary) with the power to veto legislation.

Delegates from small states opposed this plan and supported the **New Jersey Plan,** proposed by William Paterson of New Jersey. It called for a *unicameral legislature* with considerable regulatory and taxing power, in which all states would be represented equally. Executive powers would be exercised by a group that would not have the power to veto legislation.

By the end of June the convention had reached an impasse, and a committee known as the Committee of Eleven was given the task of hammering out a compromise. On July 5 it presented the solution that became known as the **Great Compromise**: a bicameral legislature in which representation in the lower house (the House of Representatives) would be based on population, and representation in the upper house (the Senate) would be equal for every state. House members were to be chosen by popular election, whereas senators were to be chosen by state legislatures.

The three-fifths compromise   Slavery was another divisive issue. Delegates from southern states wanted slaves to be counted as part of a state's population, which would increase the South's representation in the House of Representatives (because most slaves lived in the South). Delegates from northern states insisted on the prin-

The Signing of the Constitution, *painted in 1987 by Louis S. Glanzman, was based on authenticated portraits of those who were at the convention and on architectural records of the time. The Delaware, Pennsylvania, and New Jersey societies of the Daughters of the American Revolution commissioned the painting to celebrate the bicentennial of the Constitution.*

ciple of equal representation of all citizens, which discounted slaves because they were not considered citizens. The delegates finally agreed to the **three-fifths compromise,** which stated that "three-fifths of all other Persons [that is, slaves]" would be counted for purposes of representation but that the same standard would apply for any taxes assessed on the basis of a State's population. As a concession to the southern states, the larger issue of slavery and trading in slaves was put off for two decades by Article I, Section 9, which prohibited Congress from outlawing the slave trade before 1808.

After negotiating the three-fifths compromise, the convention spent more than a month debating issues involving the powers of Congress and those of the president. But the major conflicts over state representation and the structure of government had been resolved. On September 17, 1787, thirty-nine of the remaining delegates signed the document; only three refused to do so.[5]

Ratification

Although the delegates had approved the Constitution, they still had to secure its ratification by the states. To outmaneuver the opposition, they recommended (in Article VII) a novel method of ratification. Amendments to the Articles of Confederation were supposed to be ratified by *all* state legislatures; but instead of submitting the Constitution to the legislatures, the Constitutional Convention recommended that the Congress of the Confederation send the document to the states for ratification by special conventions of the people. Article VII provided that the Constitution would be ratified if at least *nine* of the thirteen states gave their approval. Congress and the thirteen states agreed to this plan.

Ratification by special state conventions was politically significant because, in James Madison's words, it meant that the Constitution was not a mere treaty "among the Governments and Independent States" but the expression of "the supreme authority of the people themselves."[6] Requiring only nine states for ratification was also a defensive strategy, because it was far from certain that all thirteen states would give their approval. The erosion of the states' power and the repudiation of their sovereignty did not escape the attention of those who were opposed to the new

Peter F. Rothermel painted this romantic view of Patrick Henry Before the House of Burgesses *in 1851. Despite his oratorical prowess — his "Give me liberty or give me death!" speech had helped to rouse the colonists to revolution — Henry could not prevent the Virginia legislature from ratifying the Constitution.*

THE BILL OF RIGHTS

First Amendment Freedom of religion, speech, the press, and assembly.

Second Amendment The right to bear arms.

Third Amendment Protection against the quartering of soldiers in one's home.

Fourth Amendment The right to be secure against unreasonable searches and seizures.

Fifth Amendment The right to "due process of law," protection against double jeopardy, and the privilege against self-incrimination.

Sixth Amendment The right to counsel for one's defense

and to a speedy and public trial by an impartial jury.

Seventh Amendment The right to a jury trial in civil law cases.

Eighth Amendment Prohibition of excessive bail and fines and of "cruel and unusual punishment."

Ninth Amendment The retention by the people of rights that are not enumerated in the Constitution.

Tenth Amendment The retention by the states or by the people of powers not delegated to the national government.

Constitution. Known as the Anti-Federalists, they saw the document as concentrating too much power in a national government and retaining too little authority for the states, both individually and collectively. In the words of Patrick Henry of Virginia, "what right had they [the delegates] to say, *We, the People*? . . . Who authorized them to speak the language of, *We, the People,* instead of *We, the States*? States are the characteristics, and the soul of the confederation. If the States are not the agents of this compact, it must be one great consolidated National Government of the people of all the States."[7] But Henry lost, not only in Virginia but in all the other states.

Delaware ratified the Constitution on December 7, 1787. Within weeks Pennsylvania, New Jersey, Georgia, and Connecticut gave their approval. Massachusetts followed in February 1788, but with a close vote of 187 to 168. In the spring of 1788, Maryland and South Carolina gave their overwhelming endorsements. Then, in June, close votes in New Hampshire and Virginia secured the nine states needed for ratification. But the battle was not over. New York's ratification convention was bitterly divided, and New York's approval, however, was crucial for the success of the union because this large commercial state separated New England from the states in the South. Opponents feared that the national government was being granted too much power and that representatives from small states might conspire in Congress against New York's commercial interests. It was largely owing to the leadership of Alexander Hamilton that New York finally voted in favor of ratification.[8] (North Carolina did not ratify until November 1789, and Rhode Island held out until May 1790.)

In New York and several other states—notably Massachusetts and Virginia—the price of ratification was agreement that the First Congress would adopt a bill of rights that specifically guaranteed individuals' civil rights and liberties. In 1789 the First Congress adopted twelve amendments to the Constitution and promptly submitted them to the states. Ten of the amendments, known as the **Bill of Rights,** were ratified by the states on December 15, 1791. The protections contained in the Bill of Rights are listed in the box above.

With the ratification of the Constitution and the Bill of Rights, the framework for a dynamic political process was in place. It remained for succeeding generations to work out the details of government. In fact, Maryland delegate John Mercer observed toward the end of the Constitutional Convention, "It is a great mistake to suppose that the paper we are to propose will govern the United States. It is the men whom it will bring into the government and interest in maintaining it that is to govern them. The paper will only mark out the mode and the form. Men are the substance and must do the business."[9]

The Constitution: Revolutionary or Reactionary?

During much of the nineteenth century, the founders and the constitution they created were revered. But early in the twentieth century Charles A. Beard, along with historians of what is called the progressive school, advanced an economic interpretation of the Constitution as reactionary and antidemocratic. They contended that the founders had thwarted majority rule and created a strong national government in order to protect the proprietary interests of an economic elite.[10] Recently, however, the progressives' evidence and interpretation of the founding period have been disputed by historians such as Bernard Bailyn, Forrest McDonald, and Gordon S. Wood, who claim that the real struggle was not over economic interests but over differing political views of government power.[11] They point out that in late-eighteenth-century America there was no great mass of people without property and that all the founders had an interest in promoting economic prosperity. The deeper political conflict was over republicanism and how to promote civic order while preserving individual liberty.

Indeed, political scientist Martin Diamond argues that the Constitution, far from being reactionary, was revolutionary.[12] It carried forth the revolutionary principles of the Declaration of Independence, respecting individuals' equal freedoms and popular sovereignty as the basis of government. Thus by creating a system of ordered liberty and limited government based on the consent of the governed, the Constitution brought to completion the revolution begun with the Declaration of Independence.

In certain respects the Constitution was both reactionary and revolutionary: reactionary in addressing the defects of the Articles of Confederation; revolutionary in creating a strong central and representative government. The Constitution and the Bill of Rights reflected the political struggles of the founding period and laid the basis for a dynamic political process.

ENDURING IDEAS AND ESSENTIAL TENSIONS

In just forty-three hundred words the Constitution provides a blueprint for self-government. It is a model for free-government-in-the-making, as James Wilson, one of its drafters, observed:

> A free government has often been compared to a pyramid. This allusion is made with peculiar propriety in the system before you; it is laid on the broad basis of the people; its powers gradually rise, while they are confined, in proportion as they ascend, until they end in the most permanent of all forms. When you examine all its parts, they will invariably be found to preserve that essential mark of free governments—a chain of connection with the people.[13]

The Constitution provides for both continuity and change because of the interplay of certain enduring ideas: the principles of popular sovereignty, limited government, and individual unalienable natural rights. These ideas led the founders to establish a system of checks and balances by distributing power among the branches of the national government, dividing power between the national and state governments, and creating the basis for judicial review.

Popular Sovereignty

"A government of our own is our natural right," exclaimed Thomas Paine, the well-known pamphleteer of the American Revolution.[14] As the Declaration of Independence stated, the Revolutionary War was fought because of a "long train of abuses" by the British Crown. The colonists charged that King George III, among other things, taxed them but denied them representation and made judges dependent on his will.

In rejecting the British monarchical model of government, in which sovereignty rested with the Crown, the colonists proposed the revolutionary idea of **popular sovereignty,** the idea that government is based on the consent of the people and is accountable to the people for its actions.[15] Although the framers of the Constitution were not inclined to support direct popular involvement in government, they did subscribe to the principle that government authority is based on the consent of the governed. This principle is expressed in the opening lines of the Preamble to the Constitution: "We, the People of the United States, . . . do ordain and establish this Constitution for the United States of America."

Limited Government

The idea of **limited government** follows from the notion of popular sovereignty. Fearful that the only alternative to constitutionally limited government was political tyranny, the founders sought to ensure that the authority of government—its ability to make and enforce laws that limit individual freedom—would be restricted to **express powers,** that is, powers specified and delegated to the national government by the Constitution.[16] These express powers are listed in the first three articles of the document: Article I details the legislative powers of Congress, Article II describes the executive powers of the president, and Article III indicates the powers of the federal judiciary.

In addition to express powers, the Constitution confers on Congress certain **implied powers,** that is, powers that might be inferred from those that are expressly delegated. The basis for implied powers is the "necessary and proper" clause (Article I, Section 8), which gives Congress the power "to make all laws which shall be necessary and proper for carrying into execution the foregoing powers, and all other powers vested by this Constitution in the government of the United States." Because this clause gives Congress such wide-ranging authority, it is often referred to as the "elastic clause."

How far Congress may go in exercising its implied powers has often been a matter of controversy. Indeed, the scope of Congress's legislative powers became the focus of an enduring struggle almost immediately after ratification of the Constitution. In December 1790, Secretary of the Treasury Alexander Hamilton proposed that Congress charter a national bank. The ensuing debate about the constitutionality of Congress's creating a national bank pitted Hamilton and the Federalists (who favored a strong national government) against Madison and Jefferson over fundamental principles of constitutional interpretation and politics.

Hamilton contended that a national bank would strengthen the national government by aiding in collecting taxes, administering public finances, and securing loans to the government. The Senate, half of whose members had been delegates to the Constitutional Convention, unanimously endorsed Hamilton's proposal. But in the House of Representatives, Madison maintained that creation of the bank was beyond the scope of Congress's delegated powers. Despite Madison's opposition, the House adopted a bill chartering the bank. On February 25, 1791, President George Washington signed the act incorporating the first Bank of the United States and granting it a twenty-year charter.

When the bank's charter expired in 1811, its renewal was defeated in Congress by just one vote; and four years later Congress established the second Bank of the

United States with another twenty-year charter. Economic hardship brought by the War of 1812 and the national government's reliance on state banks for loans were the overriding considerations in Congress. Opposition to a national bank remained strong in the states, however, and eventually it led to the Supreme Court's landmark decision in *McCulloch v. Maryland* (1819). In his decision, Chief Justice John Marshall upheld the constitutionality of the national bank with a broad reading of congressional powers: "Let the end be legitimate, let it be within the scope of the constitution, and all means which are appropriate, which are plainly adapted to that end, which are not prohibited, but consistent with the letter and spirit of the constitution, are constitutional."[17]

Although Madison agreed with the *McCulloch* decision, he continued to bristle at the expansive interpretation of the power of Congress advanced by the Supreme Court. Opposition persisted, and support for the bank gradually diminished. In 1832, Congress passed another bill extending the bank's charter, but President Andrew Jackson vetoed the bill and again challenged the Court's interpretation of and authority over the Constitution. Nevertheless, the Court had successfully established the basis for a broad interpretation of Congress's implied powers.

In addition to express and implied powers, in the conduct of foreign affairs the national government has **inherent powers,** that is, powers that are not specifically enumerated in the Constitution. The states may make no claims in this area. But political contests between Congress and the president occasionally arise over claims of inherent powers, particularly in times of international crisis. These disputes force presidents to defend their actions in terms of the Constitution and to be accountable to Congress and the American people.

Unalienable Rights

One of the founders' main objectives in constraining the powers of government was to ensure the **unalienable rights** of individuals. According to the social theory of the English philosopher John Locke, people are born with certain rights granted to

Alexander Hamilton, portrayed here by John Trumbull, had been George Washington's private secretary during the Revolutionary War. An ardent advocate of a strong central government, he worked hard for ratification of the Constitution; then, as the first secretary of the treasury, he pursued policies that were sharply opposed by Jeffersonian Republicans. Yet in the 1800 presidential election, when Jefferson and Aaron Burr were tied in electoral votes and the president was chosen by the House, Hamilton supported Jefferson. Burr later challenged him to a duel and shot to kill. Hamilton died the next day, July 11, 1804.

them in advance by "nature." Among these, as the Declaration of Independence proclaims, are "Life, Liberty and the Pursuit of Happiness." Because these rights precede the creation of government, they are not granted by government and therefore cannot be taken away by government. Instead, so this thinking goes, it is the duty of government to protect its citizens against any encroachment on those rights.[18]

By limiting government power to that which is specifically granted in the Constitution, the founders hoped to safeguard individuals' unalienable rights. That was one of the arguments used by Madison, Hamilton, and other defenders of the Constitution to win its ratification by the states. In *The Federalist, No. 84*, one of a series of newspaper essays defending the new Constitution, Hamilton wrote: "The Constitution itself, in every rational sense, and to every useful purpose, is a bill of rights." By this he meant that a government with limited and delegated powers would not expand to usurp individuals' rights, and that those rights would be secure.

Those who opposed the Constitution were unpersuaded, however. Fearful that the national government's power would be too great and would expand at the expense of the states and the people, they urged the adoption of a separate bill of rights, which was ratified in December 1791.

Separation of Powers

Because the founders were wary of the concentration of government power, they distributed power among the three branches of the national government (see Figure 2-1). This **separation of powers** was designed to create a delicate structure in which the legislative, executive, and judicial branches would check and balance each other in various ways. "Ambition must be made to counteract ambition," Madison argued in *The Federalist, No. 51*.

The principle of separation of powers is embodied in the Constitution's grant of legislative power to Congress, executive and other powers to the president, and judicial power to the Supreme Court and other federal courts. This system stands in contrast to unitary systems such as that of Britain, in which the majority party in Parliament (the legislative branch) appoints the prime minister and cabinet (the executive branch). Nevertheless, the powers given to the three branches are not entirely or completely separate; the branches are actually separate institutions that share political power. For instance, Congress passes legislation that the president must approve or veto; a two-thirds vote by both the House of Representatives and the Senate may override a presidential veto. The president makes treaties with foreign governments and appoints members of the federal judiciary, but presidential treaty making and judicial appointments are subject to ratification or confirmation by the Senate. (The Constitutional Conflict box on page 47 describes an area where the separation of powers is not clear.)

Congress, the president, and the judiciary share various other powers as well, so that they check and balance each other both directly and indirectly. This division and sharing of powers makes political change difficult and slow. In the words of Justice Louis D. Brandeis,

> The doctrine of the separation of powers was adopted by the Convention of 1787, not to promote efficiency but to preclude the exercise of arbitrary power. The purpose was not to avoid friction, but, by means of the inevitable friction incident to the distribution of the governmental powers among three departments, to save the people from having one institution dominate the government."[19]

The effects of power sharing by separate institutions are evident in the operation of constitutional checks and balances through the years. The president has vetoed

POWERS

President:
- Commander-in-chief of the military
- Makes treaties with other countries
- Appoints ambassadors, federal judges, Supreme Court justices, other federal officials
- Administers U.S. laws
- Acts as head of state

Congress:
- Passes federal laws
- Raises taxes
- Regulates foreign and interstate commerce
- Declares war
- Raises and funds the military
- May borrow money by issuing bonds for sale

Supreme Court:
- Reviews lower federal court rulings and appeals from state courts that involve federal law or constitutional issues
- Hears cases involving foreign ambassadors as first and final court
- Rules on disputes between states

CHECKING POWERS

President:
- Vetoes laws
- Orders special sessions
- Exerts political pressures
- Appeals directly to citizens

Supreme Court:
- Rules on constitutionality and legality of laws passed by Congress and signed by the president

Congress:
- Overrides veto
- Approves or rejects president's budget
- Ratifies treaties (Senate)
- Approves or rejects president's cabinet nominees, ambassadors, and others
- Investigates and reorganizes executive departments
- May impeach the president

Congress:
- Proposes constitutional amendments to override rulings
- Changes size of Supreme Court and numbers of lower federal courts
- Approves or rejects Supreme Court nominees
- May impeach federal judges

President:
- Nominates Supreme Court justices and federal judges
- Pardons those convicted under federal laws
- May refuse to enforce federal court orders

Supreme Court:
- May rule the actions of the president or others in the executive branch unconstitutional or illegal
- Interprets treaties signed by president

FIGURE 2-1

Separate institutions sharing power.

SOURCE: Adapted from *Scholastic Update*, vol. 119, no. 1 (September 8, 1986).

congressional acts more than 2,400 times, and Congress has overridden about 100 of those vetoes. The Supreme Court has ruled more than 180 congressional acts or parts of acts unconstitutional. The Senate has refused to confirm 29 nominees to the Supreme Court (out of 143 nominations) and has rejected at least 9 cabinet nominations as well as many subcabinet appointees. Congress has impeached 14 federal judges and convicted 7. Congress has passed, and the states have ratified, 5 amendments to the Constitution overturning decisions of the Supreme Court. In short, sep-

TERMINATING TREATIES

Who has the power to *terminate* treaties: The president? The Senate? The president with the agreement of the Senate? In Article II, Section 2, the Constitution states: "The President ! . . shall have power, by and with the advice and consent of the Senate, to make treaties." But the Constitution is silent about the power to terminate treaties; and that silence, on at least one occasion, has given rise to a conflict between the president and the Senate.

In 1979 Republican senator Barry Goldwater and several other senators sued Democratic president Jimmy Carter because he had unilaterally terminated a mutual defense treaty with Taiwan without the Senate's approval. Carter claimed that as president he had the inherent power to terminate treaties. But Goldwater and other senators countered that because treaties are made with the Senate's consent, the president must secure the Senate's consent to terminate them.

The Supreme Court was unable to resolve the dispute. In *Goldwater v. Carter* (1979), in a brief unsigned opinion, the Court dismissed the suit and suggested that the case presented a "political question" for the president and the Senate to decide. In a separate opinion, Justice Lewis F. Powell Jr. contended that the case was not ripe for judicial resolution because the full Senate had not passed a resolution barring Carter from terminating the treaty. In another opinion, Justice William H. Rehnquist argued that regardless of whether the conflict involved a few senators or the full Senate, the Court should not decide it but should leave it to be resolved by the president and the Senate. In a dissenting opinion, Justice William J. Brennan Jr. claimed that the president does have the constitutional authority to unilaterally terminate a treaty.

aration of powers is often a prescription for political struggle. The conflict is reflected in President Andrew Jackson's irate response to a Supreme Court decision with which he disagreed: "John Marshall has made his decision, now let him enforce it." Each branch of government at different times and in various ways checks and thwarts the actions of another.

On the other hand, power sharing also encourages cooperation and compromise. For example, Congress and the president must work together to enact legislation and appropriate funds for the operation of government, and the Supreme Court sometimes depends on the other two branches to enforce its rulings. In fact, when the Court handed down its landmark rulings mandating school desegregation, in *Brown v. Board of Education* (1954 and 1955), both presidential action and congressional action were required to overcome opposition in the South.

Federalism

By dividing power not only among the branches of the national government but also between the national and state governments, the Constitution created a system known as **federalism**.[20] The framers of the Constitution had no real alternative to establishing a federal system. They could not abolish the thirteen original states or deny them most of their governing powers, but they *could* establish a national government with its own independent powers and leave intact the powers of the states that were not exclusively delegated to the national government. Thus each state retained its own executive branch, legislature, and judicial system. Individuals were to be subject to both state and national laws. This division has made the politics of government decentralized, as well as flexible and responsive to the heterogeneous population of the United States.

Among countries with federalist systems of government, the United States system is one of three principal models. Another is the Swiss system, in which the subnational units of government are based on ethnic and linguistic differences. The other model, the Canadian system, combines federalism with a parliamentary form of government and a deliberate effort to foster a multicultural society. In addition, the fifteen countries belonging to the European Union have been evolving a federal system to promote free trade and common protection for individual rights.

The Constitution reserves to the states all powers that are not granted to the national government and not expressly denied to the states; these are known as **reserved powers.** In addition to reserved powers, states may exercise other powers that are not given exclusively to the national government. These powers, known as **concurrent powers** because they are exercised by both the national government and the states, include the power to tax, to regulate commerce, and to make and enforce criminal laws. The distribution of power between the national government and the states is shown in Table 2-1.

Because the national and state governments share certain powers, conflicts may arise between them. The Constitution requires that federal law prevail in such conflicts. The **supremacy clause** in Article VI stipulates, "This Constitution, and the Laws of the United States which shall be made in Pursuance thereof; and all Treaties made . . . under the Authority of the United States, shall be the supreme law of the land; and the Judges in every State shall be bound thereby; anything in the Constitution or laws of any State to the contrary notwithstanding." Every government official, state and national, is bound to support the Constitution.

Rarely do state laws directly contradict federal law. More frequent—and more troubling—are cases involving the concurrent powers of the national and state governments, such as the powers to tax and regulate commerce. Conflicts between the national and state governments are ultimately decided by the Supreme Court. For instance, when state and federal laws governing highway safety or telecommunications come into conflict, the Court must decide whether Congress has preempted state regulation or whether the existence of a variety of different state laws interferes with the need for national and uniform regulations.

Throughout the nation's history the Court has generally supported the authority of the national government to regulate interstate commerce and has interpreted that authority more and more broadly. But the Court has also upheld state regulations when they do not "unduly burden" interstate commerce.

Judicial Review

Article III, Section 1, of the Constitution states, "The judicial power of the United States shall be vested in one Supreme Court, and in such inferior courts as the Congress may from time to time ordain and establish." Nowhere does the Constitution give the federal courts the power to strike down any congressional or state legislation or any other government action because it violates a provision of the Constitution. Yet the courts have assumed this power of **judicial review,** a power that makes them the final arbitrator of major political conflicts and places them in the role of guardian of the Constitution.[21]

The power of judicial review was a distinctive American contribution to the practice of government and remains so today. For example, there is no such power in Britain, which does not have a written constitution. In other European democracies, only in the last fifty years have special courts been created to decide constitutional questions.

TABLE 2-1 · DISTRIBUTION OF POWER BETWEEN THE NATIONAL GOVERNMENT AND THE STATES

POWERS RESERVED TO THE NATIONAL GOVERNMENT	POWERS RESERVED TO THE STATES	CONCURRENT POWERS
Coining money and currency	Establishing local governments	Taxing
Conducting foreign relations	Regulating trade within the state	Borrowing money
Making treaties	Conducting elections	Establishing courts
Regulating foreign and interstate commerce	Ratifying amendments to the Constitution	Chartering banks
Providing an army and navy	Exercising powers not granted to the national government or denied to the states	Spending for the general welfare
Declaring war		
Establishing post offices		
Protecting patents and copyrights		
Regulating weights and measures		
Admitting new states		
Making laws necessary and proper to carrying out specifically delegated powers		

Both Alexander Hamilton and James Madison argued that judges should exercise some checking power over state legislatures, but they did not agree on whether the Supreme Court should have the power to strike down acts of Congress and the president. Hamilton contended in *The Federalist, No. 78*, that "independent judges" would prove "an essential safeguard against the effects of occasional ill humors in society," while at the same time deeming the judiciary "the least dangerous branch" of government. In *The Federalist, No. 51*, Madison called the judicial power an "auxiliary precaution" against the possible dominance of one branch over another. Yet during a debate in the First Congress, he observed: "Nothing has been offered to invalidate the [view] that the meaning of the Constitution may as well be ascertained by the legislative as by the judicial authority."[22]

Despite the absence of a specific constitutional provision, the Supreme Court's power to interpret the Constitution is a logical implication of the Constitution. After all, the Constitution is the supreme law of the land, and judges take an oath to uphold it—that was the argument made by Chief Justice John Marshall in *Marbury v. Madison* (1803). The case of *Marbury v. Madison* grew out of one of the great episodes of early American politics. Shortly after the ratification of the Constitution, two rival political parties emerged with widely different views of the Constitution and government power. The Federalists supported a strong national government in which the federal courts would have the power to interpret the Constitution. Their opponents, the Anti-Federalists and later the Jeffersonian Republicans, favored the states and state courts.

The struggle came to a head with the election of Thomas Jefferson as president in 1800. In that election the Jeffersonian Republicans defeated the Federalists, who had held office since the creation of the republic. Fearful of what the Jeffersonian Republicans might do once they assumed office in March 1801, President John Adams and the Federalist-dominated Congress created a number of new judgeships in January and appointed Federalists to fill them all. Appointed as chief justice was Adams's secretary of state, John Marshall. Marshall, continuing to work as secretary of state, delivered commissions for the new judgeships in the final days of Adams's term but failed to deliver them all before Adams's term expired.

The Federalists' attempt to "pack" the courts with Federalist judges infuriated the Jeffersonian Republicans, and President Jefferson instructed his secretary of state, James Madison, not to deliver the rest of the commissions. William Marbury, one of the newly appointed judges whose commission was not delivered, decided to sue to force Madison to give it to him. In his suit he sought a *writ of mandamus,* a court order directing a government official (Madison) to perform a certain act (hand over the commission). Marbury argued that Section 13 of the Judiciary Act of 1789 authorized the Supreme Court to issue such writs. He saw this strategy not only as a way of getting his commission but also as a means by which the Court could take a stand against the Jeffersonians.

The Supreme Court faced a major dilemma. On the one hand, if it ordered Madison to deliver Marbury's commission, President Jefferson would likely refuse to let Madison comply. The Court would then be revealed as powerless, perhaps permanently. On the other hand, if it refused to issue the writ, it could appear to be confirming the Jeffersonian argument that the courts had no power to intrude on the executive branch.

Chief Justice Marshall handed down the Court's decision on February 24, 1803. Marbury had a right to his commission, Marshall observed. But, he went on to say, the Court had no power to issue the writ of mandamus; the Judiciary Act's authorization of the Court to issue such a writ was unconstitutional because it expanded the Court's original jurisdiction beyond that provided in the Constitution. According to Marshall, Article III of the Constitution granted the Court original jurisdiction *only* in cases involving ambassadors, foreign ministers, and states. William Marbury, however, was none of these. Thus the Court declared Section 13 of the Judiciary Act unconstitutional and simultaneously established the Court's power to declare acts of Congress unconstitutional. Marshall's brilliant opinion not only asserted the power of judicial review but defused the political controversy surrounding the case. Because the Court's decision went against Marbury on the immediate point at issue, it gave President Jefferson no opportunity to retaliate. The Jeffersonians fervently disagreed with the reasoning behind the decision, but there was little they could do about it.

John Marshall's opinion in Marbury v. Madison *gave particular pain to President Thomas Jefferson, who distrusted federal power. Author of the Declaration of Independence, Jefferson died on July 4, 1826, its fiftieth anniversary. This portrait is by Rembrandt Peale.*

During the first half of the nineteenth century the Court struck down a number of state laws, thereby reaffirming the power of the national government over the states. But it was not until 1857, in *Dred Scott v. Sanford,* that the Court declared another act of Congress unconstitutional. In that case the Court struck down the Missouri Compromise, which had excluded slavery from the nation's territories. The decision badly damaged the Court's reputation and helped to precipitate the Civil War. However, it confirmed the precedent and practice of judicial review established in *Marbury v. Madison* and reaffirmed the Supreme Court's position as a coequal branch of government having considerable influence on the politics of government and the direction of public policy.

THE LIVING CONSTITUTION

The Constitution is a flexible document. Indeed, the major conflicts of American politics—between the national government and the states, and between majority rule and individual and minority rights—are fueled by conflicting interpretations of the meaning of the Constitution. During the past two hundred years, constitutional change has been in the direction of making the Constitution a more democratic document than it was in 1787 and expanding its protection of the civil liberties and rights of individuals. Change has occurred through applications of the Constitution to the day-to-day operation of government, through formal amendments, and by means of judicial review.

Day-to-Day Operation of Government

The Constitution sets out only a broad framework for the governing process. Within that framework, politics determines the day-to-day workings of government and the outcome of public policies. Through elections and interest group activities the people influence the direction of government and the formulation of public policies, which in turn influence future elections and interest groups as they compete for influence over what the government does.

As the nation's population has increased from barely 4 million in 1787 to over 250 million today, government institutions have changed profoundly. The size of Congress, for instance, has expanded from the 22 senators and 54 representatives elected in 1789 to the 100 senators and 435 representatives (assisted by a staff of more than 25,000) serving today. The power vested in the president now resides in a large executive branch with more than 3 million employees. The federal judiciary has likewise grown, from 19 to more than 1,000 judges, plus more than 15,000 supporting personnel—law clerks, magistrates, and secretaries, among others. In addition, new kinds of government agencies, corporations, and regulatory agencies have powers that cut across and combine the authority of Congress, the executive branch, and the judiciary.

As America's governing institutions have changed, so have government practices; all those changes have established precedents for the future. Not only is the presidency a larger, more central part of government than it was in the century following ratification of the Constitution, but its powers are greater because past presidents vigorously asserted their constitutional authority.

Advances in science and technology—in nuclear energy, telecommunications, biomedicine, and other areas—have created new political conflicts and required numerous adjustments in the workings of government. For example, in the age of sailing ships, when the ocean protected the United States against hostile nations,

THE LIBRARY OF CONGRESS AND THE NATIONAL ARCHIVES

The Library of Congress was established in 1800 as a legislative library, a facility intended for use by members of Congress. The moving spirit behind its creation was Thomas Jefferson, who believed that legislators needed free access to the ideas of the world in order to do their job. After the original collection of the Library was destroyed when British troops burned Washington in 1814, Jefferson sold the nation his treasured personal library of six thousand volumes. Growth has been steady ever since. Today the Library of Congress numbers over 97 million items and occupies three buildings near the Capitol—the Thomas Jefferson Building of 1897, the John Adams Building of 1938, and the James Madison Memorial Building of 1980.

The Library of Congress is a reference and research library, whose twenty-one general reading rooms are open at no charge to all members of the public for research and study. In addition, individuals across the nation are aided by the National Library Service for the Blind and Physically Handicapped. Another important function of the Library of Congress is registering copyrights (for a nominal fee) for American authors. One copy of any formally copyrighted work published in the United States must be deposited with the Library.

The National Archives of the United States is the central depository for the nation's permanently valuable records. Housed in a massive neoclassic building completed in 1937, it is the home of the most cherished documents in America—the Declaration of Independence, the Constitution, and the Bill of Rights. Sealed in special helium-filled cases and guarded around the clock, the documents are displayed to the public daily at the Archives building. At night and in times of emergency, the cases containing the documents sink into a sealed undergound vault.

The records of the Archives span two centuries and total billions of pages of textual material, 6 million photographs, 5 million maps and charts, 100,000 films, and 80,000 sound recordings. Although researchers from across the nation and around the world routinely use the collection to research virtually every aspect of American history, government, and policy, the most popular subject by far is genealogical research. The Archives holds the records of all the agencies ever involved with immigration, as well as pension and cen-

Enshrined in marble and sealed in helium-filled cases to prevent deterioration, original copies of the Declaration of Independence (center) and the Constitution (bottom) are displayed at the National Archives. At night and in emergencies, the cases sink into an underground vault.

sus records dating back many decades. Any member of the public age 16 or over may conduct research at the National Archives at no charge.

In addition to the main archives in Washington, D.C., the National Archives operates presidential libraries containing the papers of all presidents from Herbert Hoover to George Bush except Richard Nixon. Records of primarily regional interest are deposited in the Archives Branches of the fifteen Federal Archives and Record Centers found across the country.

there was ample time for Congress to establish war policy. Now, the existence of nuclear weapons and missiles calls for rapid decision making and action. The result has been a shift of power from Congress to the president in the area of foreign affairs—in effect, a modification of the Constitution.

Social forces, rising expectations, and decreasing resources have resulted in other modifications. For example, interest groups and broad political coalitions forged in the 1960s to promote equal civil rights and liberties succeeded in pressuring the government to enact new laws and to amend the Constitution. As a result, the Constitution became more democratic than it was originally. By the late 1980s and 1990s, however, there was a reaction against the growth of federal bureaucracy and regulation that these changes had produced, and appeals for reducing the size of government become more popular.

Formal Amendment

Although tens of thousands of proposed amendments have been introduced in Congress, the Constitution has been amended only twenty-seven times in two hundred years. These figures give some indication of how difficult the amendment process (spelled out in Article V) was designed to be. Two-thirds of the members of Congress (or a national constitutional convention called for by two-thirds of the states) must pass an amendment, and then three-fourths of the states must ratify it (see Figure 2-2). To date, only Congress has initiated amendments. The idea of a national constitutional convention worries many political observers, who fear that such a gathering might seek to revise the Constitution much as the Constitutional Convention of 1787 "revised" the Articles of Confederation. Among recent proposals that have failed to win approval were the Equal Rights Amendment, which would have outlawed discrimination on the basis of gender, and a proposal to grant home rule (self-government) and Senate representation to residents of the District of Columbia.

As noted earlier, the first ten amendments—the Bill of Rights—were ratified just four years after the adoption of the Constitution. They were necessary to quell fears about the coercive power of the national government and to secure the rights of

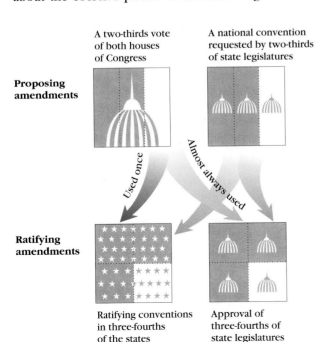

FIGURE 2-2
The amendment process.

A two-thirds vote of both houses of Congress

A national convention requested by two-thirds of state legislatures

Proposing amendments

Used once

Almost always used

Ratifying amendments

Ratifying conventions in three-fourths of the states

Approval of three-fourths of state legislatures

THE WATERGATE CRISIS AND CONSTITUTIONAL POLITICS

On the night of June 17, 1972, five men broke into the headquarters of the Democratic National Committee, housed in the Watergate complex in Washington, D.C. Intending to plant bugging devices so they could monitor the Democratic party's campaign plans for the fall presidential election, the "plumbers," as they came to be called, were caught by off-duty police officers. The next day it was learned that one of them, E. Howard Hunt, a former agent for the Central Intelligence Agency, worked for President Richard Nixon's reelection committee. The stage was set for what would become over the next two years one of the most monumental constitutional crises in American history.

In the immediate aftermath of the break-in, Nixon and his associates managed to cover up their involvement, and the president easily won reelection in November 1972. But reporters and congressional committees continued to search for links between the break-in and the White House. Judge John Sirica, who presided over the trial of the five "plumbers," pressed for a full disclosure of White House involvement. These investigations led to further cover-ups.

In the spring of 1973 the Senate Select Committee on Presidential Activities of 1972, chaired by Senator Sam Ervin of North Carolina, began its investigation before a national television audience. Nixon's former counsel, John Dean, became the star witness, revealing much of the president's involvement in the cover-up. After another aide disclosed that Nixon had installed devices to tape-record conversations in the Oval Office, the possibility that the tapes contained evidence of Nixon's involvement in the cover-up escalated the crisis. The Senate Select Committee and a special prosecutor appointed to investigate illegal activities of the White House, Archibald Cox, immedi-

Attorney General Elliot Richardson resigned (and so did the assistant attorney general) rather than follow President Nixon's order to fire Archibald Cox (left), the special prosecutor investigating illegal activities of the Nixon White House. The third-ranking Justice Department official, Robert H. Bork, did it.

ately sought a small number of the tapes. But Nixon refused to relinquish them, claiming an executive privilege to withhold information that might damage national security interests.

The special prosecutor then subpoenaed Nixon's attorneys to turn over the tapes. When Nixon again refused, Judge Sirica ordered the release of the tapes. But Nixon still did not comply. Cox appealed to the U.S. Court of Appeals for the District of Columbia, which urged that an attempt be made to reach a compromise. When that failed, the court ruled that Nixon had to hand over the tapes.

After the Court of Appeals ruling, Nixon announced his own compromise. On October 19, 1973, he offered to provide summaries of relevant conversations. When Cox declared the offer unacceptable, Nixon ordered him dismissed, thereby unleashing a wave of public anger. Within four days Nixon was forced to tell Sirica that nine tapes would be forthcoming.

The public outcry against Nixon did not subside, nor did the release of the nine tapes end the controversy. Although they did not provide ironclad proof of Nixon's involvement in the cover-up, it was soon discovered that an 18-minute segment of the first conversation between Nixon and his chief of staff after the break-in had been erased. That gap and other revelations about abuses of authority by the Nixon White House prodded the House of Representatives to establish a committee to investigate the possibility of impeachment of the president. Three months later, in February 1974, the House directed its Judiciary Committee to begin hearings on impeachment. Nixon continued to refuse to give additional tapes to the Judiciary Committee or to Leon Jaworski, who had replaced Cox as special prosecutor.

After a federal grand jury investigating Watergate indicted top White House aides and secretly named Nixon as an unindicted co-conspirator, the House Judiciary Committee subpoenaed the release of all documents and tapes related to the Watergate break-in. Nixon remained adamant about his right to decide what to release. This confrontation between the special prosecutor and the president set the stage for the case of *United States v. Nixon.*

The Supreme Court heard oral arguments for the case on July 8, 1974. The fundamental issue, Jaworski contended, was "Who is to be the arbiter of what the Constitution says?" Nixon's claim of executive privilege in withholding the tapes, the prosecutor insisted, was an attempt to place the president above the law. In contrast, Nixon's attorney, James St. Clair, asserted that the case should be dismissed because there was a "fusion" between the criminal prosecution of Nixon's aides and the impeachment proceedings against the president. He argued that this fusion violated the principle of separation of powers and that the president should decide what would be made available to the House Judiciary Committee. The dispute, he insisted, was essentially a political one, one that the Supreme Court should avoid.

The Court disagreed. Just sixteen days after hearing oral arguments, it unanimously rejected Nixon's claim of executive privilege as inconsistent with "the fundamental demands of due process of law in the fair administration of justice."

The new tapes that the ruling forced the president to release contained even stronger evidence of his guilt, and within a week the House Judiciary Committee had voted three articles of impeachment against him. On August 9, facing almost certain impeachment by the full House and conviction by the Senate, Nixon became the first president to resign his office.

Discussion questions

1. How does *United States v. Nixon* illustrate the political struggles that arise over the meaning of the Constitution?
2. What role does the Supreme Court play in resolving political conflicts?
3. Why did President Nixon comply with the ruling in *United States v. Nixon* even though he disagreed with the Court's interpretation of the Constitution, and what is the significance of his doing so?

individuals. Five later amendments overturned rulings by the Supreme Court—a remarkably small number, given the thousands of decisions handed down by the Court. The Eleventh Amendment (1798) granted the states sovereign immunity from suits by citizens of other states. The Thirteenth (1865) and Fourteenth (1868) Amendments (known as the Civil War Amendments) abolished slavery and made African Americans citizens of the United States. The Sixteenth Amendment (1913) gave Congress the power to enact a federal income tax, and the Twenty-Sixth Amendment (1971) extended the right to vote in all federal and state elections to citizens who are age 18 and older.

The majority of the remaining amendments to the Constitution have made government processes more democratic. The Seventeenth Amendment (1913) provided for the popular election of senators. Voting rights were extended to African Americans by the Fifteenth Amendment (1870), to women by the Nineteenth Amendment (1920), to residents of the District of Columbia by the Twenty-Third Amendment (1961), and to indigents (through the ban on poll taxes) by the Twenty-Fourth Amendment (1964). Together with the Supreme Court's rulings promoting the principle of *one person, one vote* (that is, all electoral districts within the same state must be approximately equal in population), these amendments have made the Constitution a more democratic document and the political process more open, accessible, and responsive to the people.

Judicial Review

Chief Justice Charles Evans Hughes once declared, "We are under a Constitution, but the Constitution is what the judges say it is."[23] Through judicial review, the Court gives authoritative meaning to the Constitution in light of new claims and changing conditions. And it does so by bringing new claims, such as a right to privacy, within the language, structure, and spirit of the Constitution.

Through its interpretation of the Constitution, therefore, the Court legitimates and occasionally initiates constitutional change. In the nineteenth century, for example, it expanded the power of Congress to regulate a broad range of social and economic activity. Moreover, it has sanctioned presidents' claims of inherent power in foreign affairs and of *executive privilege*—the power to withhold some White House communications in the interest of national security. In this century the Court has enforced the Bill of Rights against the states. Previously it had interpreted those amendments as applying only to the national government.

Given the enormous power wielded by the Court in interpreting and applying the Constitution, *how* it should interpret that document remains highly controversial. The controversy has embroiled both liberals and conservatives at different times. In the late nineteenth and early twentieth centuries, liberals attacked the Court for becoming a "superlegislature" because it overturned progressive economic legislation. On the other hand, in the last few decades conservatives have cried "judicial imperialism" when criticizing the Court's decisions in the areas of civil liberties and civil rights.

The Watergate controversy (see the Case Study on page 54) illustrates the power of the Court to restrain the other branches of government through its interpretation of the Constitution.[24] In its unanimous ruling in *United States v. Nixon* (1974), the Court held that President Richard Nixon had to release tapes of conversations between the president and his aides that had been recorded in the White House and that contained evidence that the participants had engaged in criminal activities.

Even the justices themselves disagree on how to interpret the Constitution. Some argue for what is known as **strict construction,** that is, interpretation that is confined to a literal reading of the constitutional text, supplemented by historical precedent and whatever can be learned about the historical context of specific provisions. Others urge a **broad reading** of the text, structure, and spirit of the Constitution, an approach that may require judges to formulate a broad principle that is applicable to different cases in light of changing circumstances. The debate over how to interpret the Constitution is almost as old as the document itself and is likely to continue as long as the American system of constitutional politics survives. As Justice Felix Frankfurter wisely observed, "Constitutional law is not at all a science, but applied politics."[25]

Constitutional interpretation evolves with the Court and the country, and constitutional law is best viewed as a constantly evolving dialogue between the Supreme Court and the American people. By deciding particular cases, the Court infuses constitutional meaning into the resolution of the surrounding political controversies that those cases represent. Yet the Court by itself cannot lay political controversies to rest. In *Marbury v. Madison,* for example, Chief Justice Marshall resolved the dispute at hand but by no means laid to rest the larger controversy over judicial review and the Court's power to strike down congressional legislation.

The Court's power turns on the cooperation of other political institutions and, in the end, on the public's acceptance of its rulings. In the words of Chief Justice Edward White, the Court's power to interpret the Constitution "rests solely on the approval of a free people."[26] In sum, the major confrontations that the Court attempts to resolve—such as controversies over school desegregation, school prayer, and abortion—are determined as much by the possibility of developing consensus in a pluralistic society as by what the Court says about the meaning of the Constitution.

SUMMARY

The Constitution is a political document. In laying out a blueprint for government, it provides a basis for political struggles. Based on the ideas of popular sovereignty and limited government as the means for securing individuals' unalienable rights, the Constitution provides for a separation of powers among the three branches of the national government, for a federal system dividing power between the national government and the states, and for judicial review. These divisions of power give rise to ongoing conflicts that animate the politics of American government.

The First Continental Congress met in 1774 to pass resolutions denouncing the English Parliament and Crown. In 1776 the Second Continental Congress drafted a resolution—the Declaration of Independence—that proclaimed the American colonies to be free and independent states. In 1777 it approved the *Articles of Confederation,* the nation's first constitution. Under the Articles, Congress lacked the power to regulate commerce, collect taxes, or enforce its legislation. After the Revolutionary War the nation's economic problems worsened, coming to a head with Shays's Rebellion, a revolt by debt-ridden farmers against the government of Massachusetts.

In 1787 delegates from the states met in Philadelphia to revise the Articles of Confederation but quickly decided to establish a national government with legislative, executive, and judiciary branches. The new government would be a *republic*; it would have the power to make and enforce laws but would derive its authority from the citizens through popular elections.

Two plans for the new government were proposed to the convention. The *Virginia Plan* called for a bicameral legislature in which the representation of states would be based on wealth and population. The *New Jersey Plan*, in contrast, called for a single-house legislature in which all states would have equal representation. A committee was formed to arrive at a compromise between the two plans. Its solution, the *Great Compromise,* was to create a bicameral legislature in which representation in the lower house (the House of Representatives) would be based on population; but in the upper house (the Senate), all states would be represented equally.

Slavery was another divisive issue. Delegates from the southern states wanted slaves to be counted as part of the population for purposes of representation. Delegates from the northern states insisted on equal representation of all citizens, thereby excluding slaves. The delegates finally agreed to the *three-fifths compromise*: three-fifths of a state's slave population would be counted for purposes of taxation and representation.

The Constitutional Convention recommended that the new constitution be sent to the states for ratification by special conventions. The Constitution would be ratified if nine of the thirteen states gave their approval. In some states—especially New York, Virginia, and Massachusetts—the Constitution met with opposition from those who were concerned that it gave the national government too much power. Their approval was finally obtained when it was agreed that the First Congress would adopt a group of amendments that guaranteed the civil rights and liberties of individuals. These first ten amendments constitute the *Bill of Rights.*

Central to the Constitution is the idea of *popular sovereignty,* which holds that government is based on the consent of the people and is accountable to the people for its actions. From this notion follows the idea of *limited government,* the restriction of government authority to *express powers,* which are powers specified and delegated to the national government by the Constitution. The national government also has certain *implied powers,* which can be inferred from its express powers, as well as *inherent powers* in the area of foreign affairs.

One of the main reasons for limiting the powers of government is to safeguard the *unalienable rights* of individuals. These natural rights were ensured not only through the passage of the Bill of Rights but also through the distribution of power among the three branches of the national government. The *separation of powers* creates a delicate structure in which the three branches check and balance each other in various ways. In reality, the powers of the government are not truly separate but are shared.

The Constitution also distributes power between the national and state governments, in a system known as *federalism.* All powers that are not granted to the national government and are not expressly denied the states are known as *reserved powers.* In addition, the national government and the states share some powers, which are known as *concurrent powers.* When conflicts arise between the national government and the states, the *supremacy clause* in Article VI of the Constitution requires that federal law prevail.

Although the Constitution does not give the judiciary the power of *judicial review*—the power to strike down any legislation or other government action that violates constitutional provisions—the federal courts have assumed this power because the Constitution is the supreme law of the land and judges take an oath to uphold it. The Supreme Court first claimed this power in *Marbury v. Madison* (1803).

During the last two hundred years, constitutional change has occurred in three ways: through applications of the Constitution to the day-to-day operation of government, through formal amendments, and through judicial review. Changes in government institutions, scientific and technological advances, and social forces have brought about modifications of the constitutional structure of government. In addition, the Constitution has been amended twenty-seven times, and the Supreme Court has occasionally initiated change through its interpretation of the Constitution. The Court's role in constitutional change has been controversial. Some justices and scholars have argued for a *strict construction,* or literal reading of constitutional text. Others have urged a *broad reading* of the text, structure, and spirit of the Constitution.

KEY TERMS

Articles of Confederation	popular sovereignty	federalism
republic	limited government	reserved powers
Virginia Plan	express powers	concurrent powers
New Jersey Plan	implied powers	supremacy clause
Great Compromise	inherent powers	judicial review
three-fifths compromise	unalienable rights	strict construction
Bill of Rights	separation of powers	broad reading

SCHOLARLY STUDIES

Farrand, Max. *The Framing of the Constitution.* New Haven, Conn.: Yale University Press, 1913 (paperback ed., 1962). A classic introduction to the creation of the Constitution by the editor of the definitive collection of papers and proceedings of the Constitutional Convention.

McDonald, Forrest. *Novus Ordo Seclorum: The Intellectual Origins of the Constitution.* Lawrence: University of Kansas Press, 1985. One of the best contemporary studies of the intellectual background and forces that contributed to the drafting and ratification of the Constitution.

Wood, Gordon S. *The Creation of the American Republic, 1776–1787.* New York: Norton, 1993. A widely acclaimed and pathbreaking study of the intellectual trends and political conflicts that led to the creation of the Constitution.

LEISURE READING

Kammen, Michael. *A Machine That Would Go of Itself: The Constitution in American Culture.* New York: St. Martin's Press, 1994. One of numerous books that appeared during the Constitution's bicentennial year (1987), but one that stands out in showing how the Constitution has survived amid the myriad changes that have taken place in the country over the past two hundred years.

PRIMARY SOURCES

Farrand, Max, ed. *The Records of the Federal Convention of 1787.* 4 vols. New Haven, Conn.: Yale University Press, 1913 (paperback ed., 1986). The definitive collection of the debates at the Constitutional Convention. In 1987 a fifth volume based on additional documents was added to the set.

Hamilton, Alexander, John Jay, and James Madison. *The Federalist Papers.* This collection of eighty-five essays, written to help win support of the Constitution by the New York ratifying convention, contains some of the most illuminating arguments about the nature of the Constitution. It has gone through many editions and many editors; the edition by Clinton Rossiter contains a fine introduction (New American Library, 1961).

Kurland, Philip, and Ralph Lerner. *The Founders' Constitution.* 5 vols. Chicago: University of Chicago Press, 1987. An easy-to-use guide to what the framers said about each part of the Constitution. It contains most of their statements, arranged according to each provision in the Constitution.

Storing, Herbert J. *The Complete Anti-Federalist.* 7 vols. Chicago: University of Chicago Press, 1981. A collection of the arguments made against the Constitution and for the addition of a bill of rights by the opponents of ratification.

Federalism in Theory and Practice

O n March 10, 1992, Alfonso Lopez Jr., a senior at Edison High School in San Antonio, Texas, was caught carrying a .38-caliber handgun, along with five bullets, to school. He was arrested and charged under Texas law with possession of a firearm. The following day, the state charges were dismissed after federal law enforcement agents charged Lopez with violating the 1990 Gun-Free School Zones Act, a federal law banning possession of guns in or near schools. Lopez was convicted in U.S. district court and sentenced to six months in prison.

Lopez and his attorney appealed, claiming the federal law to be "unconstitutional as it is beyond the power of Congress to legislate control over our public schools" [131 L Ed 2d, 632, 1995]. In a stunning 5-to-4 decision announced in April 1995, the U.S. Supreme Court agreed, striking down the Gun-Free School Zones Act.

The decision in *United States v. Lopez*, which directly pitted the constitutional authority of the states against that of the national government, was remarkable because it was the first time in sixty years that the Court had *limited* the reach of national authority under the clause of the Constitution that gives Congress the power to regulate interstate commerce. In its defense, the federal government argued that gun violence represents a drain on national commerce because guns affect learning and learning affects the nation's economic strength. But in this case the Court ruled that Congress had gone too far and that the possession of guns at or near schools was not sufficiently related to interstate commerce to justify federal involvement.

Control of guns in and around public schools, the Court reasoned, was an area legitimate for *state*, but not federal, regulation. (In fact, many state and local governments, including Texas, had already prohibited guns in schools.) Writing for the majority of the Court, Chief Justice William H. Rehnquist stated, "If we were to accept the [federal] Government's arguments, we are hard pressed to posit any activity by an individual that Congress is without power to regulate." In dissent, Justice John Paul Stevens stated, "The welfare of our future . . . is vitally dependent on the character of the education of our children. [Therefore] Congress has ample power to prohibit the possession of firearms in or near schools."

hether *United States v. Lopez* represents a basic shift in Court thinking on federal-state relations and what its ultimate impacts may be for related issues (such as federal laws against drive-by shootings and drug dealing) remain unanswered questions. But the case does illustrate some fundamental principles of politics and decision making in the American federal system. In nonfederal countries such as Great Britain, political debate ordinarily is limited to whether government *should* get involved in some activity. In the United States, the debate is about not only *whether* government should be involved but *which level* of government should be responsible for a particular activity.

Which level of government—national, state, or local—do *you* think should be responsible for firearm regulation? Which level should be responsible for setting education standards, for establishing abortion laws, for setting environmental rules and regulations, for regulating businesses and professions, for establishing welfare policies? Which level should set minimum wage rates for public and private sector employees, determine the appropriate age for alcohol consumption, set speed limits on roads and highways?

FEDERALISM AS A POLITICAL ISSUE

Early in his administration President Clinton expressed the view that "the real genius of the federal system" is the flexibility it gives to states in carrying out policy initiatives. The national government should establish "general principles," the president said, but we should "honor the Founding Fathers by encouraging experimentation in the states."[1] Throughout the nation's history the debate over what the Founding Fathers actually intended when they created a federal form of government has been fueled by the ambiguous language of the Constitution. They provided no clear definition of the precise relationships between the various levels of government. But the debate continues for other reasons as well. For one thing, national legislators are elected from local districts and are responsible to local constituents. In addition, many Americans view government activities at the state and local levels more favorably than those at the national level. Over the past several years, when Americans have been asked which level of government—federal, state, or local—they believe provides the *least* for their tax dollars, their responses indicate that the trend for the federal government has generally worsened, the trend for state governments has improved, and the trend for local governments has improved even more. For those reasons, even more than constitutional vagueness, federalism is likely to remain an intensely political issue.

Debates over the "true" meaning of federalism have been at the heart of some of the most important political battles in United States history, including those over slavery, the regulation of business and industry, the civil rights movement, and environmental protection. The legalistic and scholarly terms in which debates over the proper roles of different levels of government are couched often disguise other, more political concerns. When interest groups, political parties, and individuals advocate more or less control by Washington or by the states, they frequently do so to achieve specific policy goals. People who believe that state and local governments are likely to support their views on an issue—be it welfare, gun control, abortion, or prayer in public schools—will argue that the Constitution "clearly" reserves authority for such decisions to the states and communities. The federal system will suffer, they say, if such decisions are "nationalized." People who believe the national government is likely to be supportive of their views will make the opposite argument. The

FEDERALISM NORTH AND SOUTH OF THE BORDER

Among the countries that have opted for a federal form of government are our closest neighbors to the north and south, Canada and Mexico. Although all federal governments share some characteristics, there are many dissimilarities as well. The governments of Canada and Mexico illustrate this diversity.

The Canadian federal union was created in 1867 and today consists of ten provinces and two territories. Working just after the American Civil War and reflecting on what they saw as defects in the American Constitution that had helped to bring about that conflict, the framers of the Canadian government wanted to make sure that supreme power would not reside at the provincial level. By its act of creation, the Canadian parliament was given explicit control over defense, trade, transportation, and foreign affairs. If only constitutional provisions are considered, Canada appears to be a more centralized federal system than the United States. But because of the country's vast extent, its strong support of local cultural and linguistic heritages (including the legal right of French Canadians to retain their language), and the tendency of the provinces to have developed around a few key metropolitan centers, provincial governments actually exercise considerable power and authority. In fact, the degree of influence exercised by the Canadian provincial governments exceeds that of state and provincial governments in many other federal nations.

Furthermore, the Canadian combination of federalism with a parliamentary form of government has meant that cabinets and cabinet officials, as well as civil service professionals, play a significant role in both levels of government. This characteristic has led some to apply the term "executive federalism" to the Canadian system.

The Mexican constitutional convention of 1917 created a federal system of government that today consists of 31 states and the federal district of Mexico City. From the outset the Mexican system was designed to produce a strong central government, and the persistent strength of the ruling party, Partido Revolucionario Institucional (PRI), has contributed to Mexico's centralizing tendencies. Mexico's president operates with relatively few restraints. Not only are both houses of the federal legislature typically dominated by representatives of the PRI, but those elected to public office at all levels are usually appointed as candidates by higher-ups in the party apparatus.

The Mexican system is sometimes labeled one of "political centralism," meaning that each level of government exercises more political authority than the one below it. The federal government controls most public revenues, so that state and local governments are heavily dependent on it for resources. While creating inequalities in the distribution of public investments and access to services, the resulting system of centralized control has contributed to Mexico's long-term political stability.

SOURCES: Wayne A. Cornelius and Ann L. Craig, *Politics in Mexico: An Introduction and Overview* (Glenview, Ill: Scott, Foresman, 1988); R. MacGregor Dawson and W. F. Dawson, *Democratic Government in Canada,* 4th ed. (Toronto: University of Toronto Press, 1989); and Ronald L. Watts, "Canadian Federalism in the 1990s," *Publius: The Journal of Federalism* (Summer 1991), 169–190.

Constitution, they say, "obviously" delegates responsibility in these areas to the national government.

In this chapter we examine the political aspects of federalism. We trace the evolution of the American federal experience and look at power and influence in the federal system, focusing especially on the ways in which the national government and the states and localities attempt to regulate and influence each other's behavior.

THE CHANGING NATURE OF AMERICAN FEDERALISM

Since the nation's founding, advocates for the national, state, and local governments have sparred over the meaning of federalism and over the proper division of power and responsibility in the American political system. In the 1860s, these debates erupted in the Civil War. In the 1950s and 1960s, the civil rights movement raised the question of whether states had the right to maintain a system of racial segregation in defiance of the federal government. In the 1980s, issues of federalism were again at the forefront of public debate as President Ronald Reagan attempted to get the national government "off the back of the American people." In the 1990s, welfare, health care, abortion, and the environment continue to raise questions about the balance of national, state, and local responsibility.

Not surprisingly, the founders did not foresee all the issues of federalism that would confront subsequent generations. A certain vagueness, however, has contributed to the adaptability of the Constitution and has ultimately strengthened the federal system. It has permitted states to experiment with differing policies and government arrangements, but it has kept those experiments within acceptable bounds. It has permitted—even encouraged—political struggles, and these struggles, in turn, have redefined federalism and made it relevant to contemporary needs.

The concept of federalism has been evolving since 1787, and it will go on evolving as the nation faces new issues and continues to debate how best to deal with old ones. In short, federalism is, as some people say, "unfinished business."

National Supremacy Versus States' Rights, 1787–1865

During the period from the ratification of the Constitution to the end of the Civil War, the constitutional debate continued over the proper role of governments in the American system. Those seeking more power and responsibility for the national government vied for power with those seeking to protect and enhance the rights of the individual states.

Those who maintained a *nation-centered* view—the Federalists—believed that the Constitution emanated from and was applicable to the American people as a whole, that it was not simply a pact among the states. From the Federalist perspective, the national government had a legitimate interest in protecting and promoting the health, safety, and welfare of the people themselves; its interests and obligations did not end with its dealings with state governments. As Chief Justice John Marshall stated in 1819 in the case of *McCulloch v. Maryland*, the national government "is the government of all; its powers are delegated by all; it represents all, and acts for all."[2]

Marshall and other Federalists saw the Constitution as a document of and for national unity. They believed that the national government could draw on a rich array of delegated *and* implied powers to promote the general welfare of the country. As Secretary of the Treasury Alexander Hamilton put it, the test for determining whether an act of Congress is constitutional is the end, or goal, that it addresses:

> If the *end* be clearly comprehended within any of the specified powers, and if the measure have an obvious relation to that *end*, and is not forbidden by any particular provision of the Constitution, it may safely be deemed to come within the compass of the national authority.[3]

In contrast, those who held a *state-centered* view—the Anti-Federalists—believed that the Constitution was a compact among the states and that the states themselves were the legitimate center of power and authority in the federal system. This posi-

JOHN MARSHALL: DEFINING FEDERAL POWER

A successful lawyer and close friend of George Washington, John Marshall served the new federal government as minister to France, was a member for Virginia in the House of Representatives, and as secretary of state in the administration of President John Adams. When Chief Justice Oliver Ellsworth resigned unexpectedly from the Supreme Court in 1800, Adams offered the post to Marshall. He accepted, becoming the fourth Chief Justice. From this exalted position Marshall set forth interpretations of the Constitution that have become the foundations for American constitutional law.

Marshall believed that the Constitution was essentially a flexible document open to judicial interpretation in the light of individual cases and changing times. He also believed strongly in federal supremacy over the states. His opinions helped establish not only the basic principles of constitutional law but also the prestige and independence of the Supreme Court.

Marshall's most famous opinion is undoubtedly the 1803 case of *Marbury v. Madison*, in which he established the Court's power to declare a law unconstitutional and therefore void. Marshall's enunciation of the principle of judicial review firmly established the Supreme Court, not Congress, as the final arbiter of the Constitution.

In *Dartmouth College v. Woodward* (1819), Marshall's opinion established the sanctity of the contracts clause of the Constitution, which prohibits states from passing laws "impairing the obligation of contracts." This ruling, which involved an attempt by New Hampshire to change the college's charter, became the basis for more than a century of judicial defense of private property rights against state action.

In the complicated case of *McCulloch v. Maryland*, the issue was whether the state of Maryland had the right to tax the Baltimore branch of the Bank of the United States. In his opinion, Marshall held that the "necessary and proper" clause of the Constitution gave the federal government the right to

The decisions of John Marshall, the fourth Chief Justice of the Supreme Court, greatly enhanced the powers of the national government and of the Court itself. This portrait is by Rembrandt Peale.

grant corporate charters. He further held that Maryland's attempt to tax the bank clashed with the sovereignty of the federal government established by the Constitution and was thus unconstitutional. Marshall's opinion established the primacy of the federal government over state governments, and his words gave authority to "loose construction" of the Constitution. He wrote, "Let the end be legitimate, let it be within the scope of the Constitution, and all means which are appropriate, which are plainly adapted to that end, which are not prohibited, but consist with the letter and spirit of the Constitution, are constitutional."

In *Gibbins v. Ogden* (1824), Marshall ruled that states cannot interfere with interstate commerce, which is solely in the domain of the federal government under the commerce clause of the Constitution. Today's vast body of regulation of interstate commerce owes its origin to this crucial decision.

South Carolina senator John C. Calhoun championed states' rights and the idea that states could nullify federal rulings if, in their judgment, the national government had exceeded its authority. When slavery became the dominant national political issue, Calhoun's positions became the central planks in the platform of its advocates.

tion was eloquently advanced in 1798 in the Virginia and Kentucky Resolutions, which were drawn up by James Madison and Thomas Jefferson in opposition to the Alien and Sedition Acts of 1798 and were passed by the legislatures in both Virginia and Kentucky.[4] The resolutions implied that the national government did not have *all* government power, that its powers were limited by the language of the Constitution, that some rights were reserved for the states, and that states could protect their rights.[5]

This position was taken to its extreme in the 1820s and 1830s by many advocates of states' rights, especially by Senator John C. Calhoun of South Carolina, whose **doctrine of nullification** argued that *sovereignty*—ultimate government power—could not be divided among levels of government but instead resided with the states. The Constitution, Calhoun thought, was an agreement made by sovereign states that had established a central government to perform certain tasks for them. Viewing the central government as an agent of the states, he argued that whenever a state found an act of Congress to be in violation of the Constitution, that state could declare the congressional act null and void within its own borders. This position was clearly at odds with the views of those advocating a nation-centered form of government.

By the 1840s, slavery had become the dominant issue dividing advocates of the nation-centered and the state-centered notions of federalism. As always, both groups pointed to the Constitution for support. Opponents of slavery cited the due process clause of the Fifth Amendment, which states that "No person . . . shall be . . . deprived of life, liberty, or property, without due process of law." They further argued that since Congress had full sovereignty over the territories by virtue of its treaty and war powers, Congress could limit or abolish slavery in the territories as it wished.

Relying on positions similar to those advanced by Calhoun, proponents of slavery argued that since the national government was merely an agent of the states, it could not administer the territories against the interest of any of the states. Therefore, they said, slaveholders had a constitutional right to bring slaves into any territory without legal hindrance. They also relied on the Fifth Amendment, arguing that since slaves were property, legislation abolishing slavery would be a destruction of property without compensation and therefore a violation of the amendment's due process protections. This argument was accepted by Chief Justice Roger Taney in the *Dred Scott* case.

Scott, a slave, had been taken by his owner from Missouri to Illinois, where slavery was illegal, and later to the Minnesota Territory, where slavery was prohibited under the Missouri Compromise. When his owner died, Scott sued for his freedom, claiming that the years he had spent in Illinois and the free territory had ended his bondage. The case made its way through the state courts in Missouri, moved into federal court, and in 1857 was decided by the Supreme Court.

The Court ruled against Scott, stating that he could not sue because as a Negro and as a slave he was not a citizen of the United States. As for the issue of slavery in the territories, Chief Justice Taney's opinion stated that the federal government had no general sovereignty over the territories at all. Congress had only the powers associated with the right to acquire territories and prepare them for statehood; it could not exercise internal police powers. This meant that Congress could not prevent slavery in the territories and that the Missouri Compromise, which had excluded slavery from the northern territories, was unconstitutional.

The *Dred Scott* decision greatly intensified the crisis that ultimately led to the Civil War. It is often said that even though *Dred Scott* did not "cause" the war, it was the straw that broke the nation's back.

Redefining State and National Roles, 1865–1933

The Civil War permanently altered federal-state relations. Nullification theory was discredited by the outcome of the strife, and the Union was preserved. Since that time, few Americans have seriously proposed that a state can declare an act of Congress null and void or can secede from the Union. But from the perspective of defining federalism, little else was settled.

Between 1865 and 1933 a new relationship known as **dual federalism** emerged, which recognized separate and distinct spheres of authority for the national and state governments. The staunchest advocates of dual federalism viewed the distribution of power between the levels of government as fixed and unchangeable. The states were judged to be on an equal plane with the national government, and the Tenth Amendment was cited as the constitutional evidence of an area of authority reserved for the states.[6]

This philosophy can be seen in the Supreme Court's ruling in the case of *Texas v. White* (1869), which tested whether Texas was responsible for bonds issued by its Confederate government during the Civil War. Chief Justice Salmon P. Chase stated:

> Under the Constitution, though the powers of the States were much restricted, still all the powers not delegated to the United States, nor prohibited to the States, are reserved to the States, respectively, or to the people. . . . Not only . . . can there be no loss of separate and independent autonomy to the States, through their union under the Constitution, but it may be not unreasonably said that the preservation of the States, and the maintenance of their governments, are as much within the design and care of the Constitution as the preservation of the Union and the maintenance of the National Government. The Constitution, in all its provisions, looks to an indestructible Union, composed of indestructible States.[7]

During this period the United States was rapidly industrializing, and the public began looking to government at all levels for greater social and economic regulation. However, because state attempts to curb business excesses and monopolies proved largely ineffective, it fell to Congress to regulate economic practices and the social effects of big railroads and other industrial giants. Much of the debate over proper federal-state relations centered on the interpretation of the interstate commerce clause of the Constitution (Article I, Section 8) and on the proper role of Congress in regulating the nation's commerce.

Attempting to distinguish between *inter*state commerce, which Congress could regulate, and *intra*state commerce, which was under the authority of the states, the Supreme Court invalidated a number of regulatory actions by Congress on the grounds that they usurped state authority. In 1895, for example, the Court significantly weakened the effects of the Sherman Anti-Trust Act of 1890 (a federal act attempting to prevent monopolies) by declaring that monopolistic manufacturing activities were not within the scope of national regulatory influence because manufacturing is not commerce.[8] During the 1890s the Court also severely curtailed the powers of the Interstate Commerce Commission, which had been created in 1887 to regulate commerce, particularly the railroads.

The case of *Hammer v. Dagenhart* (1918) presents most forcefully the doctrine of dual federalism. In that case the Supreme Court invalidated the federal Child Labor Act of 1916—which barred from interstate commerce any commodities produced

Dred Scott was a slave in Missouri but argued that he had become a free man when his owner took him to Illinois and the Minnesota Territory. The controversy over his status led to the 1856 Supreme Court decision that the federal government "had no right to interfere [with slavery] for any purpose but that of protecting the rights of the owner"—a ruling that outraged public opinion in the North and made civil war inevitable.

by manufacturers employing children—on the grounds that the act invaded an area reserved for state activity. Justice William R. Day wrote the following:

> In interpreting the Constitution it must never be forgotten that the nation is made up of states to which are entrusted the powers of local government. And to them and to the people the powers not expressly delegated to the national government are reserved. . . . The power of the states to regulate their purely internal affairs by such laws as seem wise to the local authority is inherent and has never been surrendered to the general government.[9]

Justice Day's use of "expressly" in the *Dagenhart* decision altered the meaning of the Tenth Amendment, since almost 130 years earlier the framers had deliberately rejected the term there.

The Court's affirmation of dual federalism lasted until the Great Depression of the 1930s. After President Franklin Roosevelt took office in 1933, he proposed a number of actions to speed the nation's economic recovery. One of these, the National Industrial Recovery Act of 1933 (NIRA), created a massive public works program and also attempted to establish uniform codes and regulations for much of the nation's business and industry. Reflecting the philosophy of dual federalism, the Court struck down the NIRA in 1935 in the case of *Schechter Poultry Corporation v. United States*. The Court said that "the authority of the federal government may not be pushed to such an extreme as to destroy the distinction . . . between 'commerce among the several states' and the internal commerce of a state."[10] But nullification of the NIRA proved to be the last significant Court decision supporting the concept of dual federalism.

Expansion of the Federal Government, 1933–1968

The Great Depression ended an era and ushered in **cooperative federalism**, which stressed a partnership and a sharing of functions, responsibilities, and programs between the states and the national government. Since the late 1930s, the courts have generally interpreted the Constitution so as to extend the national government's control and regulation of business and commerce. In the case of *United States v. Darby Lumber Company* (1941), for example, the Supreme Court upheld the Fair Labor Standards Act of 1938, which, among other provisions, prohibited the shipment in interstate commerce of goods produced by child labor and thus effectively overturned the *Hammer v. Dagenhart* decision. Subsequent actions by Congress and the courts have greatly enlarged the role of the national government in such areas as education, housing, transportation, civil rights, environmental protection, and social services.

The period from 1933 to 1968 was marked by the increased use of **grants-in-aid**, that is, programs through which the national government shares its fiscal resources with state and local governments (grants-in-aid are described in detail later in this chapter). By 1930, fifteen grant programs were allocating about $120 million to the states annually. Between 1930 and 1960, the number of grants-in-aid programs increased dramatically. During the period sometimes called the "First New Deal"—about 1933 to 1935—new grant programs were enacted for the distribution of surplus farm products to the needy and for free school lunches, emergency highway expenditures, emergency relief work, general relief, administration of unemployment insurance, and assistance in meeting local government costs. During the "Second New Deal"—about 1935 to 1939—additional grant programs were created for child welfare, mothers' and children's health, services for crippled children, old-age assis-

During the Great Depression of the 1930s and the War on Poverty of the 1960s, federal grants to states and localities for social welfare programs rose dramatically. (Left) During the Depression, Works Progress Administration workers in Lawrence County, Tennessee, built a road to link farmers with markets in Memphis. (Right) The Head Start program, a survivor from the 1960s, still provides food, medical care, and early education to prepare disadvantaged children for school.

tance, aid to dependent children, aid to the blind, general health services, fire control, wildlife conservation, public housing, emergency road and bridge construction, and control of venereal disease and tuberculosis.

By 1960, some 132 grant programs existed, allocating almost $7 billion annually. Most of the grants made available during this period went to state governments; a few went directly to cities. Because most of the grants were for specific purposes or programs defined by Congress, the regulatory role of the national government (in the form of rules that had to be followed and conditions that had to be met in order for grants to be awarded) increased significantly. So did national reliance on the grants-in-aid system for achieving a range of objectives, especially in social welfare, housing, and transportation.[11]

During the 1960s the number of federal grants available to state and local governments exploded. Under President Lyndon B. Johnson's Great Society program, grants were used to expand the range of federal activity; in 1965 and 1966 alone, Congress enacted 130 new grant programs. By 1968, almost $19 billion was allocated through the grant programs, many of which provided money directly to cities, bypassing the state governments.

From Grants-in-Aid to Mandates and Regulations, 1968–1994

When the Republicans gained control of the White House in 1968, a new chapter in the history of federalism was written. Calling his approach the **new federalism**, President Richard M. Nixon deemphasized the use of grants for specific purposes and focused instead on large grants to local governments in general policy areas. In theory, such grants, known as block grants, gave the recipient governments greater discretion in the expenditure of funds, and they also removed from the national government a degree of control over how the funds were spent. Throughout the 1970s the amount of money allocated through grants-in-aid programs continued to grow. By 1980, the national government was annually allocating $91.5 billion to states and localities.

In 1980 President Reagan announced a program known as New Federalism, but his approach differed from Nixon's. Reagan called for a significant slowdown in the rate of increase in the funding of grant programs, and in both 1982 and 1987 the amount of money made available actually declined. In addition, the number of programs declined significantly, as did the proportion of state and local budgets funded by grants. In 1980 grants-in-aid accounted for 25.8 percent of total state and local spending, but by the end of the decade the amount had dropped to about 17 percent. This trend turned around somewhat in the early 1990s, and more than sixty new grant programs were enacted from 1993 to 1995. In 1995 grants represented about 22 percent of state and local spending and almost 15 percent of the federal budget. But most of these increases occurred in grants targeted for individuals, not in grants going to local governments for general purposes.

The Reagan administration deemphasized grants-in-aid as a tool for national policy making. But a higher proportion of grants went to state governments than to local governments, and states had greater authority over the funds. This policy continued during the Bush administration, contributing to what some observers believed to be a revitalization of state governments. However, it also left local governments with considerably less revenue to deal with the myriad problems facing America's cities. Bill Clinton, during his presidency, proposed a few modest assistance programs for distressed cities and neighborhoods, but his focus on deficit reduction precluded any major new spending on grants-in-aid.

Throughout this period, whether grants were expanding or shrinking, the federal government—through various mechanisms discussed later in this chapter—greatly increased its *monitoring and regulation* of state and local activities. From 1970 to 1990, for example, it issued over two hundred "preemptive statutes" that displaced or replaced state and local laws. This was twice as many such statutes as had been passed in the *entire history* of the United States until then.

Throughout this period, too, the Supreme Court adopted an increasingly nationalistic perspective on issues of federalism. In an important case in 1976, *National League of Cities v. Usery*, the Court had held that some areas of state activity—in this instance, the setting of minimum wages for municipal employees—are exempt from national-level encroachment. The Tenth Amendment, the Court had ruled, provides absolute protection for at least some areas of state (and municipal) government functions. It said, "There are attributes of sovereignty attaching to every state government which may not be impaired by Congress . . . because the Constitution prohibits [Congress] from exercising [its] authority in that manner."[12]

Soon, however, the Court began issuing decisions that served to erode severely the principle of state sovereignty established in the case.[13] In *Garcia v. San Antonio Metropolitan Transit Authority* (1985), the Court ruled that local governments must adhere to minimum-wage standards set by Congress (at a cost to local governments of about $1.75 billion annually).[14] In this 5-to-4 decision the Court ruled that except in rare situations the Constitution *does not* limit the national government's power to interfere in state affairs. The notion of state functions beyond the control of Congress, the Court said, is "both impracticable and doctrinally barren."[15]

To some, these and other related court decisions seemed virtually to have eliminated any vestige of protected state or local sovereignty. As Justice Sandra Day O'Connor lamented in her dissenting opinion in the *Garcia* case, "The States as States retain no status apart from that which Congress chooses to let them retain." Together, the cases seemed to imply that officials of the national government would be the sole judges of the limits of national power and that, in fact, there would be almost no arena of state activity beyond the regulatory authority of the national government.

Devolution Federalism, 1994–?

Many believe that the stunning Republican party victories in the 1994 elections—in which Republicans won control of both houses of Congress as well as thirty governorships—have ushered in a new era of intergovernmental relations. Called by some **devolution federalism**, this era would be marked by a return to state and local governments of many responsibilities that in recent decades had been assumed by the federal government.

The 1995 *Lopez* decision, in which the Supreme Court curtailed expansion of national power in regulating firearm possession, has already been discussed. In another important case, the Court ruled in *Seminole Tribe v. Florida* in 1996 that the Eleventh Amendment protects states from being sued in federal courts by groups who believe they are victims of wrongdoing. But the center of action for the new emphasis on devolution has been the U.S. Congress. Republicans in 1994 ran on a platform they called the Contract with America, much of which dealt with federal-state relations. Among other provisions, the contract promised a reduction of unfunded mandates—federal requirements imposed on state and local governments without any federal funding to cover the costs of implementation. The contract also promised reductions in grants-in-aid and a greater emphasis on block grants.

After winning majorities in the House and Senate, Republicans were quick to introduce many of their ideas into proposed legislation. Among the first significant pieces of legislation passed by the new Congress—in March 1995—was one limiting congressional use of unfunded mandates; it requires Congress to study the costs of a mandate before imposing it and to find ways to pay those costs—or to vote specifically to waive the funding requirement in that case. A few months later, Congress repealed the national 55-mile-an-hour speed limit it had established twenty-one years earlier, saying states should be permitted to decide speed limits. As Senator Don Nickles (R-Oklahoma) explained, "I just happen to think that the State of Oklahoma and the State of Virginia are just as concerned about safety as the Federal Government."

By far the strongest indication of the shift to devolution federalism, however, was congressional action in 1996 that converted the Aid to Families with Dependent Children program, a central component of the nation's welfare policy, to block grants—an action that virtually ceded control of national welfare policy to the states. Although similar proposals to convert the Medicaid program, along with various employment and job-training programs, to block grants were not enacted, the abolition of AFDC alone represented a significant change of direction in federal responsibilities. "It is finally beginning to dawn on people," noted scholar Richard Nathan, "that this is a big deal. This could produce a series of changes in domestic policy bigger than the Great Society."[16]

THE LIMITS OF FEDERAL AUTHORITY OVER STATE AND LOCAL GOVERNMENTS

The Tenth Amendment says that state and local governments retain powers that are "not delegated to the [national government] by the Constitution." But what exactly are these powers? Throughout American history the answer to that question has been debated.

As recently as 1992, in the case of *New York v. United States*, the Supreme Court ruled that the national government could not force a state to take legal responsibility for disposing of all the low-level radioactive waste produced within its borders, as required by a 1980 federal law. In 1985, the law had been amended both to require states that were unable to dispose of such waste by 1996 to take possession of the waste, and to make them liable in court for any damages caused by their failure to dispose of it previ-

ously. The state of New York and two of its counties sued the federal government, arguing that the law violated the Tenth Amendment. Even though it upheld some parts of the law, the Supreme Court did find the provision that required states to take possession of the waste material by 1996 to be in violation of the states' political autonomy provided by the Tenth Amendment. Writing for the majority in the 6-to-3 decision, Justice Sandra Day O'Connor stated, "In this provision, Congress has crossed the line distinguishing encouragement from coercion."

A continuing source of constitutional controversy in the area of federalism will be the determination of what areas of state activity — if any — are permanently beyond the regulatory control of the national government.

Proponents of greater state and local responsibility argue that governments closest to the people will be able to make better decisions for their citizens. Opponents fear, however, that these governments will not be able to adequately carry out this responsibility. Some even argue that welfare block grants will pit the states against each other in a competition to cut benefits to the poor. It is too early to tell which of these forecasts will be correct. It is too early to tell even if these recent developments really do mark a fundamental shift in American federal-state relations or if they are only temporary aberrations in long-term trends. But they certainly do show that the principle of federalism, created more than 200 years ago by the founders of the Constitution, remains a central feature of American politics today. Federalism, we noted earlier, is "unfinished business." It continues to adapt in response to changing situations and changing public attitudes.

FEDERAL-STATE-LOCAL RELATIONS: POWER AND POLITICS

The federal system of the United States poses particular challenges for the national government, as it attempts to influence and regulate local governments, and for local governments, as they in turn attempt to affect activities at the national level. The national government, in its attempts to regulate states and localities, may issue direct orders and may preempt state and local activities. (The Constitutional Conflict box above describes one such attempt.) Also, through grants-in-aid and the *conditions* attached to these grants, the national government may encourage certain state and local activities and discourage others.

Direct orders   Occasionally the national government issues direct orders that local governments must comply with or else face civil or criminal penalties. The Equal Employment Opportunity Act of 1972, for example, bars job discrimination by state and local governments on the basis of race, color, religion, sex, or national origin. As a result of this law, some localities have been required to reinstate, promote, or pay individuals who have been discriminated against in violation of the act. The 1977 Marine Protection Research and Sanctuaries Act Amendments prohibit cities from dumping sewage sludge in the ocean. The Americans with Disabilities Act of 1990 requires local governments to see to it that all fixed-rate public transportation systems be made accessible to the disabled, that all new buses and transit facilities be equipped with wheelchair lifts, and that transit services be provided to people who cannot use public transit facilities. In 1991 the Environmental Protection Agency issued a ruling requiring all municipal landfills to meet certain conditions designed to prevent contamination of soil and underground water supplies—at a cost to local governments of about $330 million per year—thereby establishing the first comprehensive federal standards for city dumps. The box on page 74 lists major federal statutes that regulate local governments.

Preemption   Early in the nation's history, Congress assumed the authority to *preempt*, or remove from state activity, policy areas having broad national implications. The Copyright Act of 1790 and the Bankruptcy Act of 1898, for example, stipulated

In the crowded Northeast, federal regulations make getting rid of garbage one of government's greatest challenges. (Left) New York City's infamous landfill at Fresh Kills, Staten Island, belches odors and leaches the soil. Worse, it is almost full. (Right) After weeks of wandering at sea, unable to get permission to dump its 3,000 tons of medical and other waste off anyone's coast, this barge from Long Island finally came home still full. Trucks carted the cargo away.

UNBURDENING LOCAL GOVERNMENTS: THE "UNFUNDED MANDATES" ISSUE

In recent decades Congress has increasingly imposed obligations, without accompanying funds, on local governments. Known collectively as "unfunded mandates," these requirements are estimated to cost cities and counties over $10 billion annually. In October 1993, representatives of state and local governments sponsored what was called "National Unfunded Mandates Day," an attempt to bring broad public and congressional attention to the problem faced by local governments. As a result, and with newly elected Republican majorities in the House and Senate, Congress in 1995 passed the Unfunded Mandates Reform Act, which will make it harder for Congress to enact such mandates and conditions in the future.

Some examples of these mandates are the following:

Voter Accessibility for the Elderly and Handicapped Act of 1984. Requires states and political subdivisions to ensure accessible polling places for federal elections and a reasonable number of accessible registration sites.

Asbestos Hazard Emergency Response Act of 1986. Requires local school systems to inspect for asbestos hazards, develop response plans, and take protective actions necessary; requires state review and approval.

Safe Drinking Water Act Amendments of 1986. Sets standards and timetables for removing contaminants from tap water; requires states to monitor their groundwater supplies.

Lead Contamination Control Act of 1988. Requires states to assist schools with testing and remedying lead problems in drinking coolers.

Americans with Disabilities Act of 1990. Requires local governments to ensure that all public transportation systems and other public facilities are made accessible to people with disabilities.

Clean Air Act Amendments of 1990. Imposes strict deadlines and requirements dealing with urban smog, municipal incinerators, and toxic emissions.

Family and Medical Leave Act of 1991. Requires employers to provide family and medical leave to their employees. State and local governments are responsible for all costs associated with providing the leave to their own employees.

National Voter Registration Act of 1993. Requires states to establish procedures for voters to register at local welfare and unemployment compensation offices or when applying for a driver's license by mail.

SOURCES: Timothy J. Conlan, James D. Riggle, and Donna E. Schwartz, "Deregulating Federalism? The Politics of Mandate Reform in the 104th Congress," *Publius: The Journal of Federalism* (Summer 1995), 23–40; U.S. Advisory Commission on Intergovernmental Relations, *Intergovernmental Perspective*, Fall 1992, vol. 18, pp. 5–32.

that all regulatory activity in these fields would be exercised exclusively by the national government. More recently, in 1984, Congress preempted the power of local governments to regulate cable television rates. In such situations national-level authority expands to occupy a field previously administered by state and local governments.

A process known as **partial preemption** occurs when the national government establishes minimum standards in certain areas and authorizes state and local governments to exercise primary responsibility for the function *as long as* they maintain standards at least as high as those set by the national government. States may impose stricter standards, but if a state or locality fails to enforce the base-level standard set by Congress, the national government assumes responsibility for doing so.

Partial preemption occurred, for example, when Congress passed the Water

Quality Act of 1965. The law gave states one year in which to set acceptable standards of quality for interstate waters within their boundaries. After that year passed, the secretary of health, education, and welfare (and, more recently, the head of the Environmental Protection Agency) was authorized to enforce federal standards in any state that failed to do so. Similarly, the Clean Air Act of 1970 set air quality standards throughout the nation and required the states to develop effective plans for their implementation. In 1990 amendments to this act established strict regulations that cities will have to meet in reducing urban smog and required state agencies to prepare new studies of pollution in cities.

Since the ratification of the Constitution, more than 350 preemption statutes have been passed by Congress. However, only a handful were passed prior to 1900, and more than half have been adopted in the past two decades. This concentration reflects the growing complexity of contemporary policy issues and the real need for uniform national standards in many areas. But the increased use of preemptive legislation reflects political considerations as well. In the 1930s, liberals championed the use of preemptive tactics as a means of overcoming the reluctance of many states to pass progressive economic and labor legislation. In the 1960s, liberals again relied on preemptive legislation as a key weapon in implementing policies in the areas of civil rights, fair housing, age discrimination, and voting rights.

In the 1980s and early 1990s, on the other hand, business and industry groups (especially in banking, communications, and transportation) repeatedly sought federal preemption as protection from more aggressive state regulations. For example, the Bus Regulatory Reform Act, signed by President Reagan in 1982, nullified the authority of states to engage in economic regulation of the busing industry. Today virtually all authority to engage in economic regulation of airline, bus, and trucking activities has been removed from the states. Another example is the 1990 Nutritional Labeling and Education Act, signed into law by President Bush, which preempted state nutritional-labeling requirements.

Grants-in-aid The use of grants-in-aid is an even more common, and in many instances more effective, way for the national government to see that its objectives are carried out at the state and local levels. The Sixteenth Amendment to the Constitution, ratified in 1913, gave Congress the power to impose an income tax, and the greatly increased revenues obtained by this means enabled the national government to share extensive resources with the states. This sharing took the form of grants-in-aid.

Today over $225 billion is allocated annually through grants-in-aid, which have enabled the national government to motivate state and local governments to pursue objectives that otherwise might have been politically difficult or impossible. Grants-in-aid have been used to fund projects in mass transportation, urban renewal, housing, drug rehabilitation, crime reduction, health care, low-income home energy assistance, pollution control, nuclear-waste disposal, solid-waste disposal, highway beautification, and aid to homeless youth, as well as in many other areas. In any given year, Congress enacts new grant programs to provide support in areas such as drug abuse and education relating to youth gangs, education for homeless children, living arrangements for runaway youths, prevention of abuse of the aging, lead poisoning prevention, and care services for homebound people with AIDS.

State and local governments have benefited from federal monies in all these areas. Because of the grants they are able to engage in many activities that would not be possible—or at least would be much more costly and difficult—in the absence of federal aid.

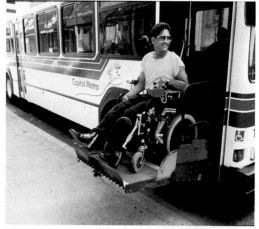

For state and local governments, a federal grant rarely gives a free ride (in any sense of the term). The threat of crossover sanctions pushed states to adopt mandatory motorcycle helmet laws by 1994, but the following year the new Republican Congress repealed the requirement. Under crosscutting requirements like those in the Americans with Disabilities Act of 1990, localities must spend up to $45 million a year to buy and maintain buses with wheelchair lifts.

Conditions of Aid

The many conditions that recipients must satisfy to receive federal grants can influence state and local policies. These conditions are of two types: crosscutting requirements and crossover sanctions.

Crosscutting requirements, which are attached to almost all federal grants, pertain to nondiscrimination, environmental protection, planning and coordination, labor standards, and public access to government information and decision making. As an example, the 1964 Civil Rights Act guarantees nondiscrimination in all federally assisted programs. Today there are approximately sixty such requirements.

Crossover sanctions impose national sanctions or penalties in one area to influence state or local policy in another area. The Intermodal Surface Transportation Act of 1991, for example, contained over a dozen crossover sanctions, including one requiring states to adopt mandatory motorcycle helmet and seat belt laws by 1994. (The motorcycle helmet provisions of this act were repealed in 1995.) States that failed to adopt these laws had to spend up to 3 percent of the federal funds they received for highway projects on highway safety activities. The same strategy had been used in 1984, when Congress passed a law that withheld a portion of federal highway funds from any state that did not set its minimum drinking age at 21 or higher. In 1996, the Health and Human Services Administration issued a ruling threatening states with the loss of federal grants to fight drug and alcohol abuse unless they reduced the easy access of teenagers to cigarettes and other tobacco products. The same year, when Congress renewed the Ryan White Act—a measure funneling millions of dollars to state and local governments to help with the care of people with AIDS—it included a provision to cut off funds to states that do not establish mandatory procedures to test newborns for the virus that causes the disease.

Such requirements almost always reflect worthy objectives. Nevertheless, local officials frequently claim that the requirements fail to take local conditions into account, are unnecessary and duplicative, and are too costly. For example, it was estimated that compliance with the Americans with Disabilities Act of 1990 would cost local governments between $35 and $45 million annually for the purchase and maintenance of lift-equipped buses and several hundred million dollars to modify subways and other transit facilities. By the mid-1990s, it was estimated that the cost of compliance with federal mandates amounted to over $6 billion annually for cities and almost $5 billion annually for counties.[17]

Although conservatives often criticize federal regulations as a liberal tool, they too have used them to achieve broader policy objectives. For example, Ronald Reagan came to office in 1981 promising to eliminate or reduce grant-related regulations. As it turned out, however, Reagan's presidency was associated with a net increase in federal regulations in several policy areas. Political considerations won out over the president's stated philosophy. At the urging of the trucking industry, for example, the administration supported a transportation bill that denied federal highway funds to states that did not approve the use of larger trucks carrying more weight than many states permitted at the time.

Figure 3-1 shows the growth of the major forms of federal regulation of state and local governments between 1931 and 1990.

Grants-in-Aid: A Typology

Historically, there have been three types of grants: categorical grants, block grants, and general revenue sharing. **Categorical grants** are made for specific purposes defined by Congress, such as library construction, child welfare, adoption assistance, and bridge and road construction. Categorical grants can be used only for the purposes stated in the legislation that creates and funds the program, and state and local decision makers thus have little discretion in how the grant money is spent. As of 1995 there were 618 categorical grants, the largest number of categorical grant programs in history. Among the more recently approved are the Drug Abuse Prevention and Education Relating to Youth Gangs program (approximately $12 mil-

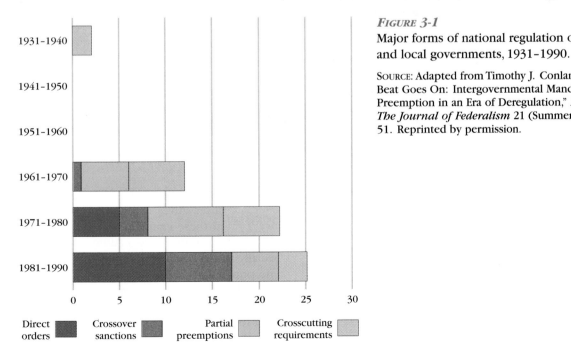

FIGURE 3-1
Major forms of national regulation of state and local governments, 1931–1990.

SOURCE: Adapted from Timothy J. Conlan, "And the Beat Goes On: Intergovernmental Mandates and Preemption in an Era of Deregulation," *Publius: The Journal of Federalism* 21 (Summer 1991): 51. Reprinted by permission.

lion per year), the Emergency Community Services for the Homeless program (about $19 million per year), and the AIDS Education program (about $14 million per year).

Block grants allow appropriated funds to be used in broad policy areas such as job training, health, and public housing. Congress establishes the areas in which the funds are to be used, and state and local officials determine how the money is actually spent. Today there are sixteen block grants in the areas of education, health and human services, housing, criminal justice, job training, and transportation. Mainly because of the consolidation of smaller categorical grants, more block grants were approved during the Reagan administration than during any previous administration. President Bush continued the trend with his proposal to create a $20 billion block grant by consolidating a number of existing grant programs, and President Clinton in his 1996 budget proposal called for combining 271 categorical grant programs into a few block grants. However, the only additional block grant approved in 1996 was the one that replaced the AFDC program.

General revenue sharing (GRS), created by the State and Local Fiscal Assistance Act of 1972, distributed approximately $6 billion annually to state and local governments until 1980 and about $4 billion annually to local governments thereafter until the program was terminated in 1986. These monies were allocated with almost no "strings" attached to nearly 39,000 local governments: the recipient governments could use GRS money for any purpose as long as they did not spend it in a discriminatory manner.

General revenue sharing was the centerpiece of the domestic program of President Nixon, who saw in it opportunities for managerial as well as political reform. From a management perspective, GRS countered the complex and largely unregulated growth of federal grants. Politically, by giving state and local governments maximum flexibility in spending the funds, GRS shifted power away from Congress, the national bureaucracy, and Washington-centered interest groups, all of which Nixon viewed as loyal principally to the Democrats and Democratic constituents. The successful passage of GRS also demonstrated the growing political influence of a new interest group: the intergovernmental lobby, which consists of organizations representing state and local governments. As one observer noted at the time:

> The passage of general revenue sharing is the most successful grassroots lobbying effort undertaken thus far. In spring 1971, delegations of mayors, governors, and county officials swarmed over Capitol Hill demanding congressional passage of this program. . . . The Democratic leadership and Chairman [Wilbur] Mills eventually capitulated to this outpouring of favorable support.[18]

General revenue sharing expired in 1986 as a result of President Reagan's budget reduction efforts and congressional and presidential concern about large federal deficits.

Politics of Grants-in-Aid

In general, block grants are popular among conservatives and advocates of states' rights. Presidents Nixon and Reagan supported these grants in part because they knew full well that most local electorates and local officials would not want to use them for liberal social programs, especially those designed to sharply redistribute resources from upper- to lower-income populations. Block grants also tend to be popular among state and local officials, because they allow them greater discretion in spending the funds.

Categorical grants are more appealing to liberals, particularly those who believe the national government should be actively involved in addressing highly pressing social and urban problems. Congress, too, generally prefers categorical grants, because they allow greater congressional influence in determining and monitoring how the money is spent.

Categorical grants frequently are supported by private interest groups who pressure Congress to approve programs to address their particular needs. Thus each grant tends to build a constituency of people whose programs or projects are funded largely by it. These people naturally become very protective of "their" grant and feel threatened when the grant is considered for termination or conversion to another type.

Consider the 1995 testimony of the Reverend Fred Kammer, president of Catholic Charities USA, presented to Congress during its consideration of the proposal to convert many categorical welfare grants to one, or just a few, large block grants administered by the states. Kammer stated:

> . . . we [Catholic Charities USA] administer model WIC [Special Supplemental Nutrition Program for Women, Infants, and Children] programs, we operate the Commodity Supplemental Food Programs, the Child and Adult Care Food Programs, and the Summer Food Programs, and Catholic schools use the school breakfast and lunch programs to help students from poor and poor working families. Catholic Charities USA opposes block-granting Federal nutrition programs because of the impact on the nation's poorest families. . . . Serious questions exist about the will or ability of the states to protect our poorest families from the worst ravages of hunger and poverty. Despite recent political promises of some governors, state AFDC [Aid to Families with Dependent Children] reforms are as yet untested and unproved.
>
> States have allowed welfare benefits to decline steadily for over 20 years . . . and many states have been very punitive towards poor families. The proposed . . . block grant would deny food to millions of low-income people, a profoundly wrong social, political, and moral outcome.[19]

Table 3-1 compares the outlays of various types of grants-in-aid between 1972 and 1995.

Distribution Criteria

Grants may be categorized as formula grants or as project grants, depending on the criteria used for distribution of the money. **Formula grants** follow a formula that is applied proportionally to all eligible recipients. For example, a grant program to aid education might allocate money to all school districts, with the amount for each district determined by the number of pupils in the district whose families' incomes are

TABLE 3-1	**BILLIONS OF DOLLARS DISTRIBUTED THROUGH GRANTS-IN-AID, 1972–1995 (IN CURRENT DOLLARS)**		
TYPE OF GRANT	1972	1980	1995
Categorical grants	$31.0	$72.5	$202.9
Block grants	2.9	10.3	22.8
General revenue sharing	—	6.8	—
Total	$83.9	$89.6	$225.7

Sources: Congressional Budget Office, The Federal Government in a Federal System: Current Intergovernmental Programs and Options for Change *(Washington, D.C.: U.S. Government Printing Office, 1983), 25; and Advisory Commission on Intergovernmental Relations,* Characteristics of Federal Grants-in-Aid Programs to State and Local Governments *(Washington, D.C.: ACIR, 1995), 3.*

below a certain level. By simply calculating the number of pupils who fall into this category, all school districts across the country will immediately know how much they are entitled to receive.

The political controversies surrounding formula grants concern the elements to be included in the formula and the weighting of those elements. For example, a bitter fight broke out in 1988 when Congress considered changing the formula for distributing money through the Alcohol, Drug Abuse, and Mental Health (ADAMH) block grant. The original formula included a factor that benefited states receiving funds under the older categorical grants that had been eliminated when the ADAMH block grant was approved. Critics argued that this element of the formula gave too much of the ADAMH money to northern states and too little to southern and western states. As an aide to Representative Henry Waxman of California said, "You won't find anyone with a dispassionate interest who would not say the existing formula is an outrage." On the other hand, the deputy director for government and community relations at the New York State Division of Substance Abuse Services commented about the proposed change, "I don't see anything equitable in a proposal which would entail closing down drug treatment programs in high-risk areas like New York."[20]

Project grants are ones for which potential recipients must apply directly to the agency responsible for administering the grant. That agency reviews the proposals and determines which ones are to be funded and at what level. Because there is not enough money to fund every potential project, competition for the funds may be keen.

Federal agencies and departments maintain greater control and authority over project grants than over formula grants. Project grants, which proliferated in the 1960s, have been used for policy areas that might not receive sufficient attention from state and local decision makers in the absence of national funding—areas such as education for disabled youth, programs for the aging, AIDS research, drug rehabilitation, and bilingual education. Like formula grants, however, project grants are often a focus of much political controversy. Those whose applications are not approved may attribute their failure to obtain funds to federal bureaucrats who make poor decisions or are out of touch with local problems. They argue that project grants place too much control at the national level, ignore the specialized needs of local areas, and give an advantage to jurisdictions that are large and wealthy enough to hire staffs with the skills required for drafting federal grant proposals.

The Regional Controversy over Grant Distribution

As the controversy over the ADAMH formula suggests, conflicts sometimes arise over the regional distribution of grants-in-aid funds. Some states and regions receive considerably higher per-person allocations than do others. Table 3–2 shows the per-person distribution of federal grants-in-aid to the top and bottom five states as of 1994.

State and local officials in the Frostbelt (the Midwest and Northeast) often express the opinion that their social and economic problems, such as decaying cities and aging industrial infrastructures, justify higher proportions of federal grant assistance. On the other side, officials in the Sunbelt (the South and Southwest) argue that rapid population growth in their sections of the country brings unique problems calling for increased federal aid. The dispute has led to clashes between coalitions of legislators, mayors, and governors over distribution formulas, a rivalry that has been described as a "regional war."[21]

In 1995, for example, when Congress was debating welfare reform, representatives from the Frostbelt states generally wanted each state's share of the proposed welfare

TABLE 3-2	**PER-PERSON FEDERAL AID RECEIVED BY SELECTED STATES IN FISCAL YEAR 1994**

TOP 5 RECIPIENTS	**PER-PERSON GRANTS TO STATE AND LOCAL GOVERNMENTS**
Wyoming	$1,456
Alaska	1,444
New York	1,058
Rhode Island	1,012
North Dakota	953

BOTTOM 5 RECIPIENTS	**PER-PERSON GRANTS TO STATE AND LOCAL GOVERNMENTS**
Virginia	462
Florida	471
Texas	530
Nevada	535
Kansas	564

Source: Advisory Commission on Intergovernmental Relations, Significant Features of Fiscal Federalism, 1994 Edition, *vol. 2 (Washington, D.C.: ACIR, 1994), 186.*

block grant to be based on what it had previously received from the federal government in categorical grants for welfare programs. Representatives from the Sunbelt states, though, argued that funding should favor those regions with high population growth rates. Criticizing the Frostbelt proposal, Senator Bob Graham (D-Florida) complained, "We start under the banner of 'we're going to end welfare as we've known it,' and yet distribute the money based on a formula which is predicated on welfare as we knew it." [22]

In fact, research centers have sprung up in Washington, D.C., whose sole purpose is to identify and promote public policies that would benefit particular regions. These so-called think tanks often engage in small skirmishes among themselves. In the late 1980s, for example, the Sunbelt Institute (representing the eleven states of the old Confederacy and five border states) issued reports asserting that southern states, on average, send to the national government more than $1.50 in taxes for every dollar returned in federal aid, whereas some northern states receive far more in federal aid than they contribute to the federal treasury. The Northeast-Midwest Institute (representing eighteen northeastern and midwestern states) immediately issued its own report criticizing the Sunbelt Institute's figures. Congressional representatives from each region were drawn into the debate. To the Sunbelt Institute's charges, New York senator Daniel Patrick Moynihan curtly replied that "everybody is entitled to their own opinions, but not their own facts." [23]

Competition for federal funds has been growing as the proportion of dollars distributed by the federal government through grants-in-aid programs has been declining. So regional clashes over federal aid are likely to continue and to increase in intensity.

State and Local Influences on National Policy Making

Officials of state and local governments, and local constituencies in general, use certain tools of their own in an attempt to influence national policy making, including the allocation and distribution of grants. All national legislators are elected from states or local districts and ultimately are responsible to voters at the local level. Thus members of Congress are sure to give some attention to the concerns of their constituents. Also, state and local governments can go to court to challenge the actions of the national government and thus may, at least temporarily, halt or delay national initiatives. Sometimes just the threat of court action will influence an agency or department to modify policy. In 1995, for example, such a threat by several states persuaded the Environmental Protection Agency to significantly relax its proposed timetable and other requirements for states to set up testing programs for automobile exhaust systems. Two additional tools that local officials may use to influence national policies are grantsmanship and the intergovernmental lobby.

Grantsmanship   The efforts of local officials to maximize the amount of federal grants they receive and to have grant rules interpreted so as to achieve the best funding distribution for their areas are termed **grantsmanship**. Cities and states that are most capable of exploiting the various options and opportunities provided by the grant program are able to garner far more than their "fair" share of federal grants. Consider the comments of John Chafee, governor of Rhode Island:

> Let us take the case of a 1-year-old boy on aid to dependent children who has a hearing problem that can be corrected. There is the temptation—and I must say this is a very real one—to refer such a patient, not to the program which is best organized to meet his particular need, but to the program in which the State obtains the best financial advantage. The Federal government will pay 50 percent of the cost when the care is provided by the Crippled Children's Division; it will pay 56 percent under Title XIX since he is on aid to dependent children; and, if he is cared for by vocational rehabilitation, the Federal government will soon pay 75 percent of the bill. Each of these programs has some variation in standards for eligibility, but nonetheless the differences in Federal reimbursement seem extremely puzzling.[24]

Grantsmanship is frequently criticized by those who believe that federal grants should go to local areas because of demonstrated problems or needs, not because of officials' skills in obtaining grants. Moreover, officials at the national level seek to prevent what they consider the "manipulation" of grant programs. In 1991 the Bush administration issued rules preventing states from using money collected from donations or from special taxes paid by hospitals as matching money to qualify for federal Medicaid payments. That ruling, it is estimated, will cost state governments between $3 billion and $5 billion per year.

The intergovernmental lobby   One of the most effective strategies used by state and local governments in recent years has been to organize the **intergovernmental lobby**. Following the explosion of grants-in-aid in the 1960s, representatives of state and local governments began organizing themselves into lobby groups and organizations to press for more federal aid for states and communities, to see that grants are designed to meet state and local needs, and to keep abreast of new rules and regulations affecting grants. Unlike other Washington lobbies, the intergovernmental lobby is funded almost exclusively with public money—state and local funds and even federal grants.

The most important organizations in the intergovernmental lobby are listed in Table 3–3. But these organizations are just a few of the dozens of groups that represent state and local interests. Other members of the growing intergovernmental lobby include the American Association of State Highway and Transportation

TABLE 3-3 THE INTERGOVERNMENTAL LOBBY

ORGANIZATION	EMPLOYEES	BUDGET (APPROX.)	PORTION OF BUDGET FROM FEDERAL GOVERNMENT (PERCENT)	MAJOR ISSUES
National Conference of State Legislatures 40,000 (approx.) legislators and staff of 50 U.S. states, commonwealths, and territories	140	$14 million	20	1. Unfunded federal mandates 2. Medicaid 3. Welfare reform
National League of Cities 20,000 (approx.)	85	$11 million	3	1. Unfunded federal mandates 2. Public safety 3. Tax reform
United States Conference of Mayors Cities with over 30,000 population (approx. 1,000)	57	$10 million	31	1. Unfunded federal mandates 2. Toxic waste 3. Sports franchise relocations
National Association of Counties 2,000 counties	75	$11 million	24	1. Community development 2. Transportation 3. Welfare reform, job training
National Governors' Association 55 state and territorial governors	89	$14 million	35	1. Medicaid 2. Welfare reform 3. Safe drinking water
National Association of Towns and Townships Local governments in small and rural areas mostly with populations of 25,000 or less (13,000 approx.)	4	$700,000	4	1. Rural transportation 2. Indian issues 3. Environment

Source: Authors' interviews with officials of each organization, 1996.

Officials, the Association of State and Interstate Water Pollution Control Officers, the National Association of Attorneys General, the American Association of School Administrators, the National Association of State Budget Officers, the National Association of State Mental Health Program Directors, the Council of State Community Development Agencies, the National Association of State Units on Aging, and the National Association of State Alcohol- and Drug-Abuse Directors.

In addition, many states and cities, believing that these national organizations cannot adequately represent their particular interests, have opened their own offices in Washington. By the mid-1990s about thirty states, one hundred cities, and a dozen counties maintained offices there. California had the largest presence in Washington of all the states: separate offices represented the state, twenty-three cities, and seven counties. Sometimes all this lobbying activity can lead to awkward situations and even conflicting efforts. The state of New York, for example, has separate lobbyists serving the interests of the governor, the state assembly, and the state senate. In the debate over President Reagan's block grant proposals, lobbyists for the Democratic-

STATE GOVERNMENTS

Are you interested in finding information about a particular department or agency of your state government, or in identifying the departments and agencies involved with a specific policy issue? Are you looking for a job with a particular state government? Do you need a list of the hundreds of documents and manuals published by state governments, sorted by subject area—a perfect resource for a research paper?

In the past few years, the amount of information available on-line about state governments has mushroomed. Virtually every state has at least one website where basic facts and figures and general policy information may be accessed; many states have more than one. For example, the site **http://www.ca.gov/** provides basic information about California and links to more than two dozen other websites maintained by California state agencies, such as the education department, the energy commission, and the fish and game department.

To find the website for your state, try asking your instructor or calling your state legislator for the address.

controlled New York state assembly opposed the block grants, and lobbyists for the Republican-controlled state senate supported them.

The 1960s and 1970s were in many ways a golden age for the intergovernmental lobby. Federal aid to states and cities rose steadily during that time, reaching $91.5 billion by 1980—just over 25 percent of total state and local fiscal outlays. The passage of the general revenue sharing program in 1972 was perhaps the crowning achievement of these organizations. By contrast, the Reagan-Bush years were a time of declining political influence for the intergovernmental lobby. It was not able to prevent the elimination of the general revenue sharing program and the urban development action grants, and it could not overcome a slowdown in federal funds for housing, transportation, and many social programs.

With the election in 1992 of former Arkansas governor Bill Clinton to the presidency, the intergovernmental lobby hoped for more productive relationships with the federal government. Indeed, the cabinet appointments of former governors Richard Riley (South Carolina) and Bruce Babbitt (Arizona) and former mayors Federico Peña (Denver) and Henry Cisneros (San Antonio) were seen as hopeful signs. Yet Clinton's early focus on cutting the budget deficit made it clear that expansive new programs to assist state and local governments would not be priorities of his presidency. As discussed earlier, however, along with the Republican Congress elected in 1994, the intergovernmental lobby did succeed in 1995 in passing the Unfunded Mandates Reform Act, making it more difficult for Congress to impose costly mandates and certain conditions of grants-in-aid on state and local governments.

FEDERALISM IN ACTION

Two recent issues provide excellent examples of federalism in action and illustrate many of the concepts discussed in this chapter: the minimum allowable age for alcohol consumption, and the proper role of governments in water control and management.

FINDING INFORMATION ABOUT STATE AND LOCAL GOVERNMENTS

Have you ever wanted some information that you thought a state government agency could probably provide, but you didn't know where to write or call? Or perhaps you've faced a similar situation when you wanted to register a complaint to a local official or to investigate the possibility of a summer job—or a career—in government.

Virtually every state and city, as well as many counties and other municipalities, has an annual handbook that describes all the government offices and agencies, lists every officeholder and agency head, and provides information about the judicial system. Variously called "blue" or "red" or "green" books (from the color of the volume's cover), legislative manuals or registers, directories, and yearbooks, these volumes contain detailed information and helpful addresses. Typical features of a state handbook include photographs, brief biographies, and the addresses of the governor, the lieutenant governor, all members of the state legislature and judiciary, department and agency heads, and county and city legislators and officials;

detailed information on the state's congressional delegation; the state constitution; names of state party officials; names of press corps members; and a list of the state bird, tree, song, and the like.

Most handbooks are authorized publications. The official *New York State Red Book*, for example, has been published annually since 1892. It is authorized by concurrent resolutions of the state senate and assembly. The *Illinois Blue Book* and the *Connecticut Register* and *Manual* are the responsibility of those states' secretaries of state. The *Directory of Oklahoma* is published by the Oklahoma Department of Libraries, and the *Nebraska Blue Book* is compiled by the clerk of the legislature.

Any college or university library is likely to have the handbook for its own state and municipality. Larger libraries usually have the handbooks for their own states and municipalities and often have them for neighboring states. Business and reference libraries generally have handbooks for most of the states.

Setting the Minimum Age for Alcohol Consumption

For most of the nation's history, individual states have assumed the authority to set rules and regulations concerning the sale and use of beer, wine, and liquor—including the minimum age required for purchase and consumption.[25] Before 1984, twenty-eight states had established minimum ages below 21 for the purchase of some or all categories of alcohol. The national government had provided grants to states for the purpose of developing programs to reduce drunk driving but had not formulated policy in this area.

In the early 1980s, however, as drunk driving began to arouse public concern and as grassroots organizations such as MADD (Mothers Against Drunk Driving) were formed, national officials became more interested in the problem. In 1982 President Reagan appointed a commission to examine the drunk-driving issue. In its report, released in 1983, the commission recommended that each state establish 21 as the minimum age for the possession of alcohol *and* that federal grants for road construction projects be denied to states that did not comply with the age recommendation. Although the second recommendation proved controversial, it eventually became the means by which the national government exerted authority in an area previously reserved to the states.

FEDERALISM AND SAME-SEX MARRIAGE

Representative Barney Frank (D-Massachusetts): We are talking here about a desperate search for a political issue. . . . Nobody has come to me and said, "Gee, Congressman, I've been married for seven years and now my marriage is threatened because two women have fallen in love a couple of blocks away."

Representative Henry J. Hyde (R-Illinois): There is a moral issue. . . . People don't think that the traditional marriage ought to be demeaned or trivialized by same-sex unions.[1]

This emotional exchange between one of the few openly gay members of Congress and one of the leading congressional conservatives on moral issues took place on the floor of the House of Representatives on May 30, 1996. It was part of a debate over a bill called the Defense of Marriage Act, which was intended to register the opposition of the federal government to marriages between persons of the same sex. Although many people see same-sex marriage as an issue of justice or of sexual morality, the way it suddenly entered the political arena in the mid 1990s made it a lively issue in the field of federalism as well.

The immediate issue arose from a court case in Hawaii, where three homosexual couples who each wished to be legally married sued in Hawaiian state court to overturn Hawaii's law prohibiting marriage between persons of the same sex. In 1993, Hawaii's Supreme Court issued a statement indicating that unless the state could show a compelling reason why it should rule otherwise, the court would hold the law unconstitutional. Then, presumably, couples of the same sex could be issued valid marriage licenses, making Hawaii the first state to legalize same-sex marriages—and possibly thereby legalizing them in other states as well.

Although many politicians undoubtedly had strong views on the subject, same-sex marriage became a subject of congressional debate largely because 1996 was a presidential election year. With polls showing that Americans overwhelmingly opposed such marriages, some Republicans seized on the issue as a way to embarrass President Clinton. Clinton had been on record for years as opposing same-sex marriages, but

he had been hurt at the start of his presidency by his support for the right of homosexuals to serve openly in the military, and Republicans hoped they could damage him further with the same-sex marriage issue.

Introduced by Senator Don Nickles of Oklahoma and Representative Bob Barr of Georgia (both Republicans), the Defense of Marriage Act passed both houses of Congress by wide margins and was signed into law by President Clinton. It authorizes states to refuse to legally recognize same-sex marriages performed in other states. In addition, it withholds from married gay and lesbian couples the federal tax, welfare, pension, health, immigration, and survivors' benefits that are available to married heterosexual couples.

Opponents of the legislation argued that it violated the Constitution, specifically the "full faith and credit" clause, which reads, "Full faith and credit shall be given in each state to the public acts, records, and judicial proceedings of every other state." In legal terms, this language means that each state must accept as valid the public acts, statutes, and records of every other state and must enforce the civil judgments of the courts of other states.

In general, the "full faith and credit" clause has been interpreted to require states to recognize as valid marriages that are valid under the laws of another state. Some opponents of same-sex marriage thus feared that gay and lesbian couples from all over the nation might travel to Hawaii to get married (as many heterosexual couples do now) and return to their home states, which would then have to recognize the marriages as legally valid.

There is, however, one recognized exception to the general rule requiring states to honor and recognize legal actions of other states. The courts have ruled that the paramount interests of an individual state—as reflected in its traditions, laws, customs, notions of justice, and moral attitudes—may on occasion outweigh the full faith and credit mandate. A valid marriage in one state may not have to be accepted in another state if such recognition would run counter to the clearly expressed public policy of that state. Bigamous or polygamous marriages, for example, are explicitly prohibited by law in most states.

An Atlanta couple celebrate their ceremony of commitment to each other. Some supporters of same-sex marriage argue that society has an interest in promoting stable relationships among homosexuals just as it does among heterosexuals. But opponents say government should continue to provide a privileged legal status to the heterosexual nuclear family.

As of 1996, however, only a few states actually had laws on the books explicitly prohibiting same-sex marriages. (In addition to Hawaii, they included Indiana, Louisiana, Maryland, New Hampshire, Texas, Utah, and Virginia.) Presumably these states could not have been forced to validate same-sex marriages, but other states possibly could.

The same-sex marriage issue raises interesting questions about the obligations states have to each other in our federal system. Federalism is more than just a way of describing the relationship between the national government and the states. It describes the relationships between and among the states as well. Obviously cooperation among the states is essential if the nation is to survive. The Framers recognized this by including in the Constitution provisions, found primarily in Article IV, that deal with the obligations and responsibilities states have to each other. They prevent states from discriminating against citizens of other states, guarantee freedom of movement from one state to another, and ensure that states recognize as valid the laws and public acts of other states. The "full faith and credit" clause cited above is one of these provisions.

To get more information about this issue or to become involved on one side or the other, contact one of the following groups:

Supporting legalization of same-sex marriage:

Human Rights Campaign
1101 14th Street NW, Suite 200
Washington, D.C. 20005
ph: (202) 628-4160
fax: (202) 347-5323
e-mail: hrc@hrcusa.org

Opposing legalization of same-sex marriage:

Family Research Council
700 13th Street, Suite 500
Washington, D.C. 20005
ph: (202) 393-2100
fax: (202) 393-2134
e-mail: frc@sojourn.com

[1]*New York Times*, May 31, 1996, p. A18.

SOURCE: For background on the federalism aspect of the issue, see John P. Feldmeier, "Federalism and Full Faith and Credit: Must States Recognize Out-of-State Same Sex Marriages," *Publius: The Journal of Federalism* (Fall 1995), 107–126.

Congressional opposition centered on the issue of states' rights. New Hampshire senator Gordon Humphrey asked, "Who are we, the national legislature, who have done a perfectly abysmal job of managing our own business, to tell the state legislatures . . . how to conduct their business?"[26] In a similar vein, Montana senator Max Baucus said, "The real issue is whether the Federal Government should intrude into an area that has traditionally and appropriately been left to the States and force them into accepting its solution to the problem of drunk driving."[27]

However, the majority of the members of Congress did not share this view, and in 1984 the National Minimum Drinking-Age Act was enacted into law. Reflecting on the act's possible usurpation of state authority, President Reagan commented that "the problem [of drunk driving] is bigger than the individual States. It's a grave national problem, and it touches all our lives. With the problem so clear-cut and the proven solution at hand, we have no misgivings about this judicious use of federal power."[28]

The National Mimimum Drinking-Age Act specified that larger proportions of highway funds would be denied to states the longer they delayed in establishing the required minimum age. The effectiveness of this provision is illustrated by the fact that by 1993 all states had raised to 21 the minimum age for buying liquor.

As explained earlier in this chapter, federal regulatory activities of this type are called *crossover sanctions*: the federal government threatens to withhold funds in one program area (in this case, highway monies) to achieve policy objectives in another area (in this case, the minimum age required for alcohol purchase and consumption). The growth of federal grant programs in recent decades and the increased reliance of state and local governments on these grants has made crossover sanctions a potent policy tool. The national government has used it successfully to achieve uniform state policies in areas such as highway beautification and energy conservation as well as in establishing a uniform minimum drinking age.

The Control and Management of Water Resources

Water is the nation's most precious natural resource, and its management—the authority to store, use, and transport it—provides an excellent example of the politics of policy making in a federal system. For decades the national, state, and local governments have debated their proper roles in managing the nation's water supplies. One long-time observer of water policies stated, "Two of the most difficult problems with which people in the United States must live [are] water [and] federalism."[29]

Initially, states exercised almost exclusive authority in this area. Even before 1900, however, many states in the West, where the climate is generally dry and water scarce, sought assistance from the national government in developing a regional policy of sound water conservation and management. At first the national government responded to their request by ceding federally owned land to the states, which sold the land and used the proceeds to develop their own water policy programs. But although millions of acres of federal land were turned over to the states, a viable, comprehensive policy for water resource management never emerged.

Responding to increased needs, Congress passed the Reclamation Act of 1902, which created a fund from the sale of federal lands that was to be used to build irrigation projects. Participating farmers were to repay the cost of the projects in interest-free installments; this money would then be used to fund more projects. A central issue in the passage of the Reclamation Act was the involvement of the national government in water policy, an area previously left to the states. Some observers believed that the national government was overstepping the bounds of its

Grassroots organizations like Mothers Against Drunk Driving helped bring national attention to the issue of driving while intoxicated. MADD lobbied for stricter laws and harsher penalties, and eventually the federal government threatened to withhold highway monies from states that did not raise the minimum drinking age to 21. President Reagan had "no misgivings about this judicious use of federal power."

legitimate authority. A speaker addressing the National Irrigation Congress in 1906 set forth this position:

> Any plan or scheme that seeks to transfer the control and administration of irrigation affairs, from the several States to the general government at Washington, is regarded as an encroachment upon the rights of the State and an interference with individual prerogative acquired under local custom and law, and meets with more or less hostility on the part of those largely interested in irrigation affairs.[30]

Others, however, believed that the national government not only *should* be involved in water policy but should assume *even greater* responsibility. Representative George Ray of New York complained that the Reclamation Act "surrenders all control" and amounts to a "robbery or looting of the Treasury of the United States."[31] The vote on the bill reflected strong regional differences, with western states favoring it and northeastern states opposing.

In the twentieth century a number of court decisions have strengthened the role of the national government in water management. In 1908 the Supreme Court ruled that traditional state control over water policy was mitigated by treaties and agreements made at the national level. In 1963 it added that national interests in water policy extended to federal establishments such as national recreational areas and national forests. Thirteen years later the Court extended the sphere of national influence to include groundwater withdrawals that affect water levels on federal lands, and more recently to groundwater on nonfederal lands.

In pursuing water-related projects, the national government has spent billions of dollars on dams, ports and harbors, reservoirs, irrigation efforts, and hydroelectric power plants. These projects provide significant "pork-barrel" opportunities for members of Congress to benefit their own districts, and they often become—or at least seem—very important to the economic health of particular areas. Therefore, attempts to end or cut back on such projects frequently meet intense political opposition.

President Jimmy Carter experienced such opposition in 1977 when he tried to change the direction of national water policy to focus less on the construction of massive projects and more on the less costly policies of conservation and water resource management. Carter's proposals encountered considerable hostility in regions that depended on large-scale federally funded construction projects. Governor Allen Olson of North Dakota argued that failure to fund expanded water projects in his state would result in "irreparable harm to the state of North Dakota," and Wyoming governor Ed Herschler called the Carter proposal a "complete strangulation of the western states."[32] As a result of this statement, no major water policy initiatives were approved during the Carter years.

Carter's successor, Ronald Reagan, was more supportive of traditional water construction projects despite the considerable budget pressures he faced while in office. In 1986, with strong presidential support, Congress passed a water resource bill authorizing the expenditure of $16 billion in water projects. For the first time, however, state and local governments were required to pay significant portions (in some cases almost half) of the cost of constructing new projects.

In recent years, appropriations for water resource projects have been relatively noncontroversial. In November 1995, President Clinton signed a bill appropriating almost $20 billion for energy- and water-related projects. As is typically the case, the bill included billions of dollars for numerous dam, beach erosion, navigation, and flood control projects spread over numerous states and congressional districts (including an expensive project in Kansas, the home state of Bob Dole, then serving as Senate Majority Leader). Despite the emphasis on budget cutting by the new Republican majority in Congress, Representative Frank Riggs (R-California) commented, "There was enough [state and local projects] in there to effectively dissipate any momentum to kill the bill."[33]

The nation's evolving water management policy illustrates some of the lasting tensions between the national government and state and local governments in the American federal system. The national government was slow to become involved in an area that was viewed as an exclusive concern of state and local governments. But over the years, often responding to regional demands, the national government has become a more influential player.

The issue of water policy also illustrates the way spending by the national government influences relations between levels of government in a federal system. Once the national government becomes involved in a policy area and billions of federal dollars are committed to projects in particular localities, states, and regions, it may be politically difficult for the national government to retreat from its involvement—even when the initiative for reduced involvement comes from the national government itself.

SUMMARY

Throughout the nation's history there have been conflicts over the meaning of federalism and the proper division of power and responsibility among federal, state, and local governments. During the period following ratification of the Constitution, those who favored more power and responsibility for the national government were opposed by those who sought to protect and enhance the rights of individual states. Those with a nation-centered view believed that the Constitution was applicable to the American people as a whole. Those with a state-centered view believed that the Constitution was a compact among the states and that the states themselves were the legitimate center of power and authority. Advocates of states' rights argued that if the national government overstepped its legitimate boundaries, its acts should be null and void; this position is known as the *doctrine of nullification.*

The conflict over national supremacy versus states' rights intensified along with opposition to slavery, finally culminating in the Civil War. After the war, nullification theory was discredited and a new relationship known as *dual federalism* emerged. It recognized separate and distinct spheres of authority for the national and state governments. During this period much of the debate over federal-state relations centered on the proper role of Congress in regulating the nation's commerce. The Supreme Court invalidated a number of regulatory actions by Congress on the grounds that they usurped state authority.

The Great Depression of the 1930s ushered in a period of *cooperative federalism*, which stressed a partnership and a sharing of functions, responsibilities, and programs between the states and the national government. This era was marked by increased use of *grants-in-aid*, programs through which the national government shared its fiscal resources with state and local governments. By 1960 there were about 132 grant programs, with most of the grants made for specific purposes defined by Congress. The number of grants increased dramatically during the 1960s, especially as part of President Johnson's Great Society social programs.

After 1968, however, President Nixon's *new federalism* deemphasized the use of grants for specific purposes and focused instead on large grants in general policy areas. These gave the recipient governments greater discretion in the expenditure of funds and decreased the national government's control. During the Reagan administration there was a slowdown in the rate of increase in the funding of grant programs, but under President Bush spending began to rise faster again.

For much of the past half-century, Supreme Court rulings have been interpreted by many as eliminating—or at least significantly reducing—state and local sovereignty. But within recent years some Court decisions seem to have restored a measure of state and local independence. Moreover, the Republicans who won control of Congress in the 1994 elections mounted a strong effort to return to the state and local governments many responsibilities that had been assumed by the federal government in recent decades, such as welfare, job training, and Medicaid. These shifts suggested a trend toward a new era in intergovern-mental relations, which some have called *devolution federalism.*

In its attempts to regulate states and localities, the national government may issue direct orders, preempt state and local activities, or use grants-in-aid to encourage certain activities and discourage others. Occasionally the national government issues direct orders, such as antidiscrimination and environmental regulations, that local governments must comply with or else face civil or criminal penalties. Preemption removes a certain policy area, such as regulation of copyrights or cable television rates, from state authority. *Partial preemption* occurs when the national government establishes policies and delegates the responsibility for implementing them to state and local governments, provided that they meet certain conditions or standards.

A more common approach to regulation is the use of grants-in-aid. Grants have been used to fund projects and efforts in a wide variety of areas, ranging from mass transportation to nutrition programs for the elderly. National influence over state and local policies is accomplished through the conditions and requirements that recipients must satisfy in order to receive the aid. *Crosscutting requirements* apply across the board and deal with issues such as environmental protection and labor standards. *Crossover sanctions* impose national sanctions in one area to influence state or local policy in another.

Historically, there have been three types of grants. *Categorical grants* are made for specific purposes defined by Congress and give the recipient states and localities little discretion in terms of how the money is to be spent. *Block grants* allow appropriated funds to be used in broad policy areas, with state and local officials determining how the money is actually spent. *General revenue sharing*, which existed from 1972 to 1986, was a system by which federal funds were allocated to state and local governments to be used for virtually any purpose, provided that the money was not spent in a discriminatory manner.

Grants may also be categorized by their criteria for distribution. *Formula grants* are distributed according to a formula that is applied proportionally to all eligible recipients. *Project grants* are those for which potential recipients must apply directly to the agency responsible for administering the grant; the agency determines which proposals are to be funded and at what level.

Some states and regions receive considerably higher per-person allocations of grant monies than do others.

As a result, controversies and conflicts sometimes arise over the regional distribution of grant funds. In particular, officials in Frostbelt states and in Sunbelt states often clash over the formulas for distribution of federal funds.

State and local governments naturally attempt to influence the adoption and distribution of federal grants. The term *grantsmanship* refers to efforts by local officials to maximize federal grants received and to influence the interpretation of grant rules in ways that are favorable to their locality. State and local governments have also organized an *intergovernmental lobby* to press for more federal aid, see that grants are designed to meet their needs, and keep abreast of new rules and regulations.

KEY TERMS

doctrine of nullification
dual federalism
cooperative federalism
grants-in-aid
new federalism
devolution federalism

partial preemption
crosscutting requirements
crossover sanctions
categorical grant
block grant

general revenue sharing
formula grant
project grant
grantsmanship
intergovernmental lobby

RESOURCES

SCHOLARLY STUDIES

Conlan, Timothy. *New Federalism: Intergovernmental Reform from Nixon to Reagan.* Washington, D.C.: Brookings Institution, 1988. A thorough account of events in American federal relations focusing especially on the presidencies of Richard Nixon and Ronald Reagan. The author presents an interesting analysis of the "politics" of intergovernmental relations during those years.

Hamilton, Christopher, and Donald T. Wells. *Federalism, Power, and Political Economy.* Englewood Cliffs, N.J.: Prentice-Hall, 1990. A contemporary overview of federalism, suggesting that conflicts between the states and the national government are central to politics and economics in America.

Kincaid, John, ed. *American Federalism: The Third Century.* Annals of the American Academy of Political and Social Science. Newbury Park, Calif.: Sage, 1990. A collection of essays by scholars examining various aspects of federalism in the 1990s, including fiscal roles, finance, regulation, and court decisions.

Nice, David C., and Patricia Fredericksen. *Federalism: The Politics of Intergovernmental Relations.* 2d ed. Chicago: Nelson–Hall, 1995. A good textbook on federalism, with a useful look at various models of federal systems as well as a discussion of interstate relations.

Peterson, Paul E. *The Price of Federalism.* Washington, D.C.: Brookings Institution, 1995. An excellent examination of contemporary political debates in the federalism arena, with special focus on the policy consequences of "devolution."

Peterson, Paul E., Barry G. Rabe, and Kenneth K. Wong. *When Federalism Works.* Washington, D.C.: Brookings Institution, 1987. An examination of the operation of nine federal programs in education, health, and housing. The study attempts to assess why some federally sponsored programs work well and others do not.

Riker, William H. *The Development of American Federalism.* Boston: Kluwer Academic Publishers, 1987. A collection of essays addressing various aspects of federal relations. The book presents an especially interesting look at institutions such as Congress, the presidency, and the military in a federal context.

Swartz, Thomas R., and John E. Peck. *The Changing Face of Fiscal Federalism.* Armonk, N.Y.: M. E. Sharpe, 1990. A collection of essays examining federalism from a fiscal perspective, focusing primarily on the Carter, Reagan, and Bush presidencies. The book looks especially at the "winners" and "losers" in the changing system of federal finance.

Walker, David B. *The Rebirth of Federalism*. Chatham, N.J.: Chatham House Publishers, 1995. An excellent brief overview of the most important aspects of American federalism. The book presents an especially insightful look at the various stages of development of the American federal system.

LEISURE READING

Caro, Robert. *The Power Broker: Robert Moses and the Fall of New York*. New York: Vintage Books, 1975. A biography of Robert Moses, master planner and builder of New York City in the 1930s and 1940s, with a special focus on his use of the intergovernmental grant system to supplement the city's budget in accomplishing his goals.

Moynihan, Daniel P. *Maximum Feasible Misunderstanding*. New York: Free Press, 1970. A critical look at the implementation of the community action programs of the 1960s. Moynihan explores in particular the problems of implementing and evaluating programs whose objectives are unclear and contradictory.

Rivlin, Alice. *Reviving the American Dream*. Washington, D.C.: Brookings Institution, 1992. An interesting and provocative look at contemporary issues of federalism, focusing especially on a proposed realignment of responsibilities. Rivlin proposes that states assume proportionately more of the responsibility for such activities as education, highways, and job training and that the national government do likewise for welfare, Social Security, and health care.

Sanford, Terry. *Storm over the States*. New York: McGraw-Hill, 1967. Presents the perspective of a state governor operating in the American federal system.

Wills, Gary. *Explaining America: The Federalist*. New York: Penguin Books, 1981. An interesting look at the political philosophies of Alexander Hamilton and James Madison, with particular attention to their ideas on federalism.

PRIMARY SOURCES

The Budget of the United States. Washington, D.C.: U.S. Government Printing Office, annual. Provides budgetary information on intergovernmental programs and changes in the system.

Statistical Abstract of the United States. Washington, D.C.: Bureau of the Census, annual. Provides detailed statistics, often on a state-by-state basis, for a range of government and policy areas.

ORGANIZATIONS

Advisory Commission on Intergovernmental Relations, 800 K Street, N.W., Washington, DC 20575; phone (202) 653-5540; fax (202) 653-5429; e-mail ir002529@interramp.com. A government commission that publishes useful studies and reports on various aspects of American federalism. Especially useful is its annual report, *Significant Features of Fiscal Federalism*, which presents detailed fiscal information on numerous intergovernmental programs and issues.

American Society for Public Administration, 1120 G Street, N.W., Washington, DC 20005-2885; phone (202) 393-7878; fax (202) 638-4952; e-mail dcaspa@ix.netcom.com. A scholarly organization focusing on many aspects of American federalism. Especially useful is its journal *Public Administration Review*, which contains articles dealing with the funding, administration, implementation, and evaluation of intergovernmental programs.

Center for the Study of Federalism, 1616 Walnut Street, Temple University, Philadelphia, PA 19103; phone (215) 204-1480; fax (215) 204-7784; e-mail v2026r@vm.temple.edu. An interdisciplinary educational and research institute located at Temple University. Its publication, *Publius: The Journal of Federalism*, is an excellent source of scholarly research dealing with federal issues.

Civil Rights and Liberties

I n the late 1980s school officials in Vernonia, a small logging community in Oregon, noticed a sharp increase in drug use and disciplinary problems among their students. Student athletes, in the officials' view, not only were among the users but were actually leaders of the drug culture. As a result, in 1989 the school board approved a policy under which athletes had to sign a form consenting to drug testing and obtain the written consent of their parents as well. At the beginning of the season in each sport, every athlete playing that sport was tested for drugs.

Then, throughout the season, 10 percent of the athletes were randomly selected to be tested each week.

When the parents of James Acton, a 12-year-old seventh grader, sued the Vernonia School District over the constitutionality of the drug-testing policy, a federal district court rejected their claim that it violated the Fourth Amendment's guarantee against "unreasonable searches and seizures." But a federal court of appeals reversed that ruling, and school officials appealed to the Supreme Court. Lawsuits challenging similar drug-testing programs adopted by other schools and colleges throughout the country had resulted in conflicting rulings in state and federal courts. It was therefore important for the Supreme Court to resolve the controversy.

Not only students but also public employees have increasingly been required to submit to random drug testing since the 1980s. Whereas proponents of testing insist that it is a necessary part of the country's "war on drugs" and important to ensuring the health and safety of students, employees, and the general public, opponents counter that it violates individuals' right of privacy as well as the guarantee against "unreasonable searches and seizures." Typically, they point out, a search requires a showing of "probable cause," or at least a "reasonable suspicion," that a person is engaged in illegal activities. Random drug testing, however, requires no such showing.

Political controversies such as the one over drug testing of students eventually find their way to the Supreme Court. The Court decides only important cases, and most have a political dimension. They involve people or institutions that are in conflict with one another or with the government. When that conflict enters the judicial arena, it concerns rules of law and how those rules are interpreted. The law may be the Constitution, statutes, or prior rulings known as precedents. In any case, it is for the courts to resolve the legal issue. Their judgments often have widespread implications, affecting not only the individuals in a specific case but the society as a whole. In this sense, courts interact with and affect the political environment.

Prior to ruling on drug testing in public schools, the Supreme Court had approved a drug-testing program for federal employees, in *National Treasury Employees Union v. Von Raab* (1989), as well as mandatory drug tests for railroad workers involved in serious accidents, in *Skinner v. Railway Labor Executives' Association* (1989). Both of those cases had sharply divided the justices. And by a 6-to-3 vote in *Vernonia School District 47J v. Acton*, the Court reversed the appeals court's decision and upheld the school district's policy.

In his written opinion explaining the reasoning of the Court's majority, Justice Antonin Scalia cited as precedents those earlier decisions upholding the drug testing of public employees. In addition, he emphasized that students are subject to the supervision of teachers and have fewer constitutional protections than adults. Since every student athlete was tested for drugs, he reasoned, school officials were not being arbitrary in choosing whom to test, and students' expectations of privacy were less because all athletes were tested.

By contrast, in a dissenting opinion on behalf of herself and two others, Justices John Paul Stevens and David H. Souter, Justice Sandra Day O'Connor wrote that the Court's majority wrongly minimized students' privacy interests and the constitutional requirement for probable cause for government searches. In her words, "The population of our Nation's public schools, grades 7 through 12, numbers around 18 million. By the reasoning of today's decision, the millions of these students who participate in interscholastic sports, an overwhelming majority of whom have given school officials no reason whatsoever to suspect they use drugs at school, are open to an intrusive bodily search."

T he controversy over drug testing in public schools illustrates how civil rights and liberties are linked to larger political struggles. Interest groups on both sides of the controversy were mobilized and divided over the competing values at stake. Even the justices disagreed with each other when deciding *Vernonia School District*. The Court is a political institution, and its rulings respond to and may invite political conflicts. Civil rights and liberties ultimately depend not only on the Court's rulings but also on the achievement of political consensus in the country.

RIGHTS, LIBERTIES, AND CONSTITUTIONAL POLITICS

One of the great ongoing struggles in American politics involves the protection of civil rights and civil liberties. **Civil rights** are rights, such as the right to vote, that government may not categorically deny or infringe on because of an individual's race, gender, ethnicity, or various other characteristics. **Civil liberties** are freedoms that government must respect, such as the freedom to think, express oneself, and act in a manner that conforms to one's beliefs and values.

The government has not always respected every individual's civil rights and liberties. For example, women, African Americans, and other minority groups have been discriminated against, and for much of American history so-called subversive political ideas and speech have been punished. As a result, American politics has been animated by political struggles aimed at guaranteeing equal civil rights and liberties for all people.

Political struggles over civil rights and liberties stem from the competing demands for majority rule and for individual or minority rights. We have seen already how difficult it is to have a government based on majority rule that also respects the rights of individuals and minorities. Conflicts between the majority and minority often arise over issues such as free speech, school prayer, the rights of those accused of crimes, abortion, and the rights of homosexuals. Resolving those disagreements is crucial to the stability and vitality of the political system.

Conflicts over civil rights and liberties can be traced back to the development of guarantees for individual rights in England. The Magna Carta (1215), the Petition of Right (1628), and the English Bill of Rights (1689) recognized the equality of individuals before the law and placed certain limitations on government power. Together with the philosophical tradition of unalienable natural rights, those basic charters inspired America's founders when they drafted the Declaration of Independence, the Constitution, and the Bill of Rights. The core idea of these documents is that all people enjoy certain rights and liberties that are essential to their personal freedom and well-being and to their equality before the law.

The Constitution itself was viewed by some as a bill of rights. Alexander Hamilton argued that individuals' rights and liberties would remain secure because the powers of the national government were limited to those expressly granted to it in the Constitution. In addition, he said, the states would continue to safeguard civil rights and liberties because the states were closer to the people and directly accountable to them. But the Anti-Federalists, who feared that the national government would not only usurp the powers of the states but also deny individuals their rights and liberties, were not persuaded. To ensure that their concerns were satisfied, they made the addition of the first ten amendments to the Constitution—that is, the **Bill of Rights**—more or less a condition for its ratification in Massachusetts, Virginia, and New York. Their fears were probably well founded, since the 1787 Constitution contained only five provisions that directly protected civil liberties. In any case, however, all the states ratified the Bill of Rights in 1791.

James Madison, the principal drafter of the Bill of Rights, had also sought to include protection for individuals' "rights of conscience" and limitations on the powers of the states to deny civil rights and liberties, but Congress rejected those proposals. Initially, then, the guarantees of the Bill of Rights were viewed as limitations only on the federal government, not on the states. Congress assumed that the states would ensure individuals' civil rights and liberties under their own constitutions, but these varied widely in their safeguards. As a result, the Supreme Court finally *nationalized* the Bill of Rights, making its guarantees applicable to the states as well as to the federal government by construing them to be included in the Fourteenth Amendment's guarantee of "due process of law." The nationalization of the Bill of Rights has involved the Court in political controversy, because it expanded the judiciary's supervision over state legislation and made the Court a powerful arbitrator in the struggle for civil rights and liberties.

We now turn to the functions of the Supreme Court as an arbitrator of civil rights and liberties. How has it sought to balance individual rights against societal interests? In particular, how has it interpreted the constitutional guarantees of the rights of the accused? And what about other rights, such as the right of privacy, that are not explicitly mentioned in the Constitution? (In the next chapter we take up issues of political freedom—the freedoms of speech, press, and religion—along with the quest for equality and the elimination of racial and nonracial discrimination.)

THE NATIONALIZATION OF THE BILL OF RIGHTS

The guarantees in the Bill of Rights are stated in broad terms. The First Amendment is the only one that specifically singles out the national government in its provisions, which prohibit Congress from passing laws establishing religion and from denying the free exercise of religion and the freedoms of speech, press, and assembly. Nevertheless, the view that the first ten amendments limited the powers *only of the national government* prevailed until the twentieth century. This view was well stated in Chief Justice John Marshall's ruling in *Barron v. Baltimore* (1833). By grading streets and diverting some streams, the city of Baltimore had created soil deposits that made Barron's wharf unusable. Barron therefore sued the city for depriving him of his property without "just compensation" and "due process of law," as stated in the Fifth Amendment. But the suit was invalid unless the Fifth Amendment was found to apply to states and localities, not just to the federal government. In ruling that it did not apply, Marshall pointed out that the language of the First Amendment and the history of the adoption of the Bill of Rights demonstrated that the purpose of the entire Bill of Rights was to guard against, as he put it, "encroachments of the general government—not against those of the local governments."[1]

But with the adoption of the Fourteenth Amendment in 1868 there was a new basis for applying the Bill of Rights to the states. Indeed, one of the motives of Congress at the time was to overturn Marshall's decision in *Barron*.[2] Like the Fifth Amendment, the Fourteenth contains a due process clause, but that clause specifically limits the power of the states: "No State shall make or enforce any law which shall abridge the privileges or immunities of citizens of the United States; nor shall any State deprive any person of life, liberty, or property, without due process of law; nor deny to any person within its jurisdiction the equal protection of the laws."

Immediately after the adoption of the Fourteenth Amendment, lawyers tried to convince the Supreme Court that the Fourteenth Amendment "incorporated" or "absorbed" the guarantees of the Bill of Rights and applied them to the states. Yet with one exception, the Court refused to go along with that argument in the nineteenth century. The exception came in 1897, when the Court held that the concept of eminent domain, which is contained in the Fifth Amendment's guarantee that private property shall not be taken "without just compensation," also applies to the states.

In a revolutionary decision in 1925, however, the Court ruled in *Gitlow v. New York* that a major provision of the First Amendment (the guarantee of the freedoms of speech and press) applies to the states. Justice Edward T. Stanford simply announced that "for present purposes we may and do assume that freedom of speech and press, which are protected by the First Amendment from abridgement by Congress, are among the fundamental personal rights and 'liberties' protected by the due process clause of the Fourteenth Amendment from impairment by the States."[3] In the 1930s and 1940s the Court applied the remaining First Amendment guarantees—those dealing with religion and the right of assembly—to the states on a case-by-case basis. But the Court remained reluctant to apply to the states the rest of the

Bill of Rights, particularly the rights of the accused contained in the Fourth through Eighth Amendments.

During the 1960s, however, when the Court was headed by Chief Justice Earl Warren, a liberal, it selectively incorporated the other principal guarantees of the Bill of Rights into the Fourteenth Amendment's due process clause and made them applicable to the states (see Table 4-1).[4] In addition, in 1965 it found a "right of privacy" (which is not specifically mentioned in the Constitution) and applied it to the states under the Fourteenth Amendment. By the 1970s all the major provisions of the Bill of Rights had been held to apply to the states. The only ones that do not apply are the right to keep and bear arms (Second Amendment); the provision against the quartering of troops in private homes (Third); the provision for grand jury indictments (Fifth); the right of a jury trial in civil cases (Seventh); and the provision that the other enumerated rights "shall not be construed to deny or disparage others retained by the people" (Ninth).

The Court's nationalization of the Bill of Rights, particularly the guarantees pertaining to criminal justice and the rights of the accused, sparked a major and continuing controversy in American politics. In 1968 Richard M. Nixon based his successful presidential campaign on attacking the Court's rulings on criminal justice and calling for a "return to law and order in the country." And throughout the 1980s the

TABLE 4-1	THE NATIONALIZATION OF THE GUARANTEES OF THE BILL OF RIGHTS	

YEAR	GUARANTEE AND AMENDMENT	CASE
1897	Eminent domain (V)	*Chicago, Burlington & Quincy Railroad v. Chicago*
1925	Freedom of speech (I)	*Gitlow v. New York*
1931	Freedom of press (I)	*Near v. Minnesota*
1932	Right to counsel in *capital* cases (VI)	*Powell v. Alabama*
1934	Free exercise of religion (I)	*Hamilton v. Regents of the University of California*
1937	Assembly and petition (I)	*DeJonge v. Oregon*
1947	Establishment of church and state (I)	*Everson v. Board of Education of Ewing Township*
1948	Public trial (VI)	*In re Oliver*
1949	Unreasonable searches and seizures (IV)	*Wolf v. Colorado*
1961	Exclusionary rule (IV)	*Mapp v. Ohio*
1962	Cruel and unusual punishment (VIII)	*Robinson v. California*
1963	Right to counsel in all criminal cases (VI)	*Gideon v. Wainwright*
1964	Compulsory self-incrimination (V)	*Malloy v. Hogan*
1965	Confrontation of witnesses (VI)	*Pointer v. Texas*
1965	Right of privacy[a]	*Griswold v. Connecticut*
1966	Trial by impartial jury (VI)	*Parker v. Gladden*
1967	Right to a speedy trial (VI)	*Klopfer v. North Carolina*
1968	Jury trial in nonpetty criminal cases (VI)	*Duncan v. Louisiana*
1969	Double jeopardy (V)	*Benton v. Maryland*
1972	Right to counsel in all cases involving a jail term (VI)	*Argersinger v. Hamlin*

[a]The right of privacy is not enumerated in the Bill of Rights, but the Supreme Court found it in the "penumbras" or "shadows" of the provisions of the First, Third, Fourth, and Fifth amendments.

THE DEBATE OVER THE EXCLUSIONARY RULE

Few stances taken by the Supreme Court engender more debate and political controversy than the exclusionary rule, intended to ensure police compliance with the requirements of the Fourth Amendment. First set forth by the Court in *Weeks v. United States* (1914), the rule forbids prosecutors in a trial from introducing evidence that police have obtained by "unreasonable searches and seizures." In 1961 the Court held that this rule applies to state as well as to federal law enforcement officials.

Critics argue that its price is too high—that too many criminals can and do go free as a result of mistakes or misconduct by the police. Instead of forbidding the use of illegally obtained evidence at trial, they contend, the courts should hold police criminally liable and award civil damages for illegal searches. Defenders of the exclusionary rule counter that few police officers are prosecuted for such violations and that most could not afford to pay civil damages. In addition, they point out that the only way to protect personal autonomy and privacy, the core values of the Fourth Amendment, is to deter police misconduct by enforcing the rule.

In two 1984 rulings, *United States v. Leon* and *Massachusetts v. Sheppard*, the Court cut back on—but stopped short of overturning—the exclusionary rule. The case involving Alberto Leon began in 1981, when a confidential informant told a police officer in Burbank, California, that two individuals whom he knew as "Armando" and "Patsy" were selling cocaine and methaqualone at their home. The informant gave the police their address but also claimed that they generally kept only small quantities of drugs there, storing the rest at another location. The police began an investigation and staked out the residence of Armando Sanchez, who had previously been arrested for possessing marijuana,

and Patsy Stewart, who had no prior criminal record.

During the course of the investigation the officers saw a car belonging to Ricardo Del Castillo, who had previously been arrested for possessing fifty pounds of marijuana, arriving at Sanchez's house. The driver entered the house and left shortly thereafter with a small paper bag. A check of Del Castillo's probation records led the police to Alberto Leon. Leon had been arrested in 1980 on drug charges, and one of his companions informed the police that he was heavily involved in the importation of drugs into the United States.

One day during their surveillance of Sanchez and Stewart, police officers saw them boarding separate flights to Miami, Florida; they later returned to Los Angeles together. They were stopped at the airport and consented to a search of their luggage. A small amount of marijuana was discovered, but they were allowed to leave the airport.

On the basis of this and other investigations, a judge granted the police a warrant to search the residences of Sanchez, Stewart, and Leon for a long list of items related to drug trafficking. The search produced a large quantity of drugs, and all three were subsequently indicted by a grand jury and charged with conspiracy to possess and distribute cocaine and other drugs.

Leon's attorney filed a motion to suppress the evidence seized in the search on the grounds that the police had failed to fully establish "probable cause" for the issuance of a warrant, as required under the Fourth Amendment. A district court judge granted the motion, and a federal appellate court subsequently affirmed that ruling. The Reagan administration appealed the appellate court's ruling and asked the Supreme Court to decide "whether the Fourth Amendment exclusionary rule should be modified so as not to bar the admission of evidence seized in rea-

Justice Department pressed, often unsuccessfully, for the Court to overturn some of the most controversial rulings on the rights of the accused that had been handed down in the 1960s. The Reagan administration, for example, asked the Court to overturn its earlier rulings upholding the use of the exclusionary rule under the Fourth Amendment. The **exclusionary rule** requires that evidence illegally obtained by police in violation of the Fourth Amendment's requirements for searches and

With a suspected drug dealer in handcuffs, police in Bridgeport, Connecticut, begin their search for evidence. In recent years the legal rule that such evidence must be excluded in court if the search is found constitutionally improper has come under increasing legal and political pressure.

sonable, good-faith reliance on a search warrant that is subsequently held to be defective."

The Supreme Court granted review in the *Leon* case along with another, *Massachusetts v. Sheppard* (1984). In the *Massachusetts* case, police had made an arrest using the wrong form of warrant, one normally issued for searches for controlled substances instead of for arrests. A judge had signed the warrant after finding that the police had established probable cause in their application, even though they had used the wrong form because it was a Sunday and their office had run out of the correct forms.

In both cases the Supreme Court held that the police had acted in "good faith," that their warrants were valid, and that, therefore, the evidence discovered by their searches could be used at trial. Subsequently, in *Arizona v. Evans* (1995), the Court extended this exception to the exclusionary rule in holding that police acted in "good faith" when they searched a car on the basis of an incorrect computer record indicating that there was an outstanding warrant for the driver's arrest.

The debate over the exclusionary rule is certain to continue, and the rule may eventually be abandoned. The Court has become more sympathetic to society's interests in law enforcement and in not penalizing police for good-faith mistakes.

Discussion Questions

1. What are the arguments for and against the Supreme Court's enforcement of the exclusionary rule under the Fourth Amendment?
2. Should the Supreme Court balance the rights of the accused against victims' rights and law enforcement interests? If so, on what basis does the Bill of Rights authorize the Court to balance competing interests such as these?

seizures be excluded (prohibited from being introduced) at trial. Critics of the rule argue that it often allows guilty people to go free and does not deter police misconduct. Although the Court made exceptions to the application of the exclusionary rule, it nevertheless refused to abandon the rule in all criminal cases. (This controversy is the subject of the Case Study above.)

The controversy over rulings upholding the rights of the accused stemmed not only from the Court's giving priority to individuals' rights over society's interests in law enforcement and crime control but also from its involvement in matters that had traditionally been the responsibility of the states. State court judges, police, and prosecutors resented the Supreme Court's supervision of their decisions and the imposition of requirements contained in the Bill of Rights on their criminal-justice procedures. Indeed, in 1958 thirty-six state chief justices issued a report protesting the Court's "erosion of the federal system."[5]

The intensity of the opposition partially explains why guarantees of the Bill of Rights were *selectively* applied on a case-by-case basis, rather than being extended all at once as some justices wished. Members of the Supreme Court disagreed over the extent to which they should defer to state courts and how and which guarantees of the Bill of Rights should be applied to the states.

Although controversy continues, the Supreme Court is unlikely to overturn its rulings applying the Bill of Rights to the states. However, under its last two Chief Justices, Warren Burger and William Rehnquist, the Court has increasingly given greater weight to states' law enforcement interests when balancing them against individual rights.

CIVIL RIGHTS AND CRIMINAL JUSTICE

Americans enjoy a great number of civil rights and liberties that limit the coercive powers of government. Some are a result of both the Supreme Court's interpretation of the Constitution and congressional legislation designed to ensure equal access to justice and equality before the law. Others are contained in state constitutions and bills of rights. Many, such as due process of law and freedom from unreasonable searches and seizures, are rooted in principles that originated in the English common law—judge-made law in England—and are embodied in the guarantees of the Bill of Rights. The following discussion examines the provisions of the Bill of Rights that limit the powers of state and federal governments in criminal procedures and law enforcement. These provisions are listed in the box on page 104. The major stages in the criminal-justice process are presented in Figure 4-1.

Due Process of Law

Under the due process clauses of the Fifth and Fourteenth Amendments, no person shall be deprived of "life, liberty, or property, without due process of law." But what is **due process**? What "process" is "due"?

Those are vexing questions, for the concept of due process is broad and elusive. It can be traced back to the English Petition of Right and then even further back to the Magna Carta, where it originally meant simply "the law of the land." Due process, as Justice Felix Frankfurter once explained, "is compounded of history, reason, the past course of decisions, and stout confidence in the strength of the democratic faith which we profess. Due process is not a mechanical instrument. It is not a yardstick. It is a delicate process of adjustment inescapably involving the exercise of judgment by those whom the Constitution entrusted with the unfolding of the process."[6]

As Frankfurter's statement suggests, many complex elements enter into due process. To understand this issue more clearly, it is helpful to think of due process as being divided into two basic kinds: procedural and substantive.

Procedural due process   **Procedural due process** is concerned with *how* the law is carried out—whether by police, judges, legislatures, or administrative agencies. Although procedural due process often pertains to the specific rights and pro-

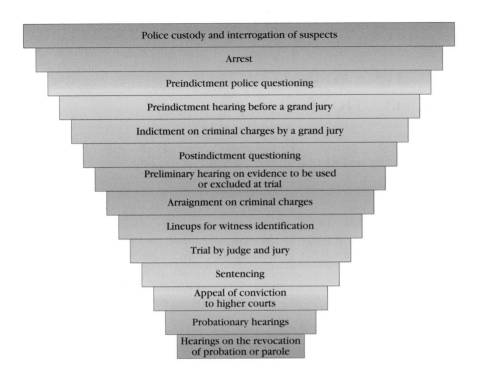

Police custody and interrogation of suspects

Arrest

Preindictment police questioning

Preindictment hearing before a grand jury

Indictment on criminal charges by a grand jury

Postindictment questioning

Preliminary hearing on evidence to be used
or excluded at trial

Arraignment on criminal charges

Lineups for witness identification

Trial by judge and jury

Sentencing

Appeal of conviction
to higher courts

Probationary hearings

Hearings on the revocation
of probation or parole

FIGURE 4-1
The criminal-justice
process.

cedural guarantees mentioned in the Bill of Rights, the Supreme Court has also sought to enforce a more general standard of fairness in criminal procedures and law enforcement. In *Rochin v. California* (1952), for example, the Court reversed the conviction of Antonio Richard Rochin for selling and possessing narcotics. Police with no arrest or search warrant had broken into Rochin's home and found him in bed, where he immediately swallowed two morphine capsules that were on a table next to the bed. The police attempted to make him cough up the evidence, repeatedly kicking him and trying to make him gag. Finally they took him to a hospital and ordered a doctor to pump his stomach. At Rochin's trial the prosecution introduced the regurgitated morphine as evidence. In an opinion for the Supreme Court overturning Rochin's conviction, Justice Frankfurter observed that the conduct of the police "shocks the conscience. . . . Due process of law [means that] convictions cannot be brought about by methods that offend 'a sense of justice.' "[7]

The Court has held that some laws are unconstitutional because they are overly broad or *void for vagueness*. For instance, laws that made it a crime to treat the American flag "contemptuously" have been struck down because they do not make clear exactly what is permitted and what is prohibited and thus give arbitrary and unfair discretion to prosecutors, judges, and others who carry out such laws. In general, the Court holds that "[a] statute which either forbids or requires the doing of an act in terms so vague that men of common intelligence must necessarily guess at its meaning and differ as to its application, violates the first essential of due process."[8]

During the 1960s and 1970s, the Court greatly expanded the requirements of procedural due process by applying them to administrative agencies and other government institutions. For example, it held that individuals must be given some kind of hearing or opportunity to challenge the termination of welfare benefits; student suspensions from school; and the disconnecting of electric, gas, and water services by public utilities.[9] In the 1980s and 1990s, however, the Court became more conservative and more sensitive to societal interests as opposed to the interests of individ-

103

INDIVIDUALS' RIGHTS AND SAFEGUARDS IN CRIMINAL PROSECUTIONS

The Bill of Rights guarantees certain limitations on the power of government in criminal procedures and law enforcement.

1. The right to be secure in one's person, house, papers, and effects against unreasonable searches and seizures. (Fourth Amendment)
2. The issuance of a search warrant or an arrest warrant only with probable cause, supported by oath or affirmation, and particularly describing the place to be searched and the person or things to be seized. (Fourth Amendment)
3. Indictment by a grand jury for a capital or an otherwise infamous crime. (Fifth Amendment)
4. Immunity against double jeopardy. (Fifth Amendment)
5. A privilege against self-incrimination. (Fifth Amendment)
6. The right to be informed of the nature and cause of an accusation. (Sixth Amendment)
7. The right to a speedy and public trial, by an impartial jury. (Sixth Amendment)
8. The right of accused people to confront witnesses for and against them. (Sixth Amendment)
9. The right to be represented by counsel in criminal cases. (Sixth Amendment)
10. The prohibition of excessive bail, excessive fines, and cruel and unusual punishment. (Eighth Amendment)

uals demanding a fair hearing. It has resisted further expansion of the concept of procedural due process and has also let stand certain criminal convictions even though the accused's rights were not fully honored because some "harmless error" was made by the prosecution at the trial.[10]

Substantive due process　**Substantive due process** is concerned with the subject matter of a law, regulation, or executive order; it places limitations on *what* government may do. The Court looks at the substance of the law itself, why it was enacted, and whether it is "unreasonable," "irrational," or "arbitrary" in light of the concept of due process and other constitutional guarantees. Because the Court may overturn laws, substantive due process is highly controversial. As Justice Oliver Wendell Holmes once observed, the Court becomes a "super-legislature" by imposing its own view of the reasonableness of a law and overturning the will of elected legislators.

In the late nineteenth and early twentieth centuries, the Court was dominated by conservatives opposed to most social welfare legislation. During this period it often used substantive due process to strike down government regulation of economic relations, including laws that governed the prices of goods and the wages and hours of workers. It did so on the basis of a "liberty of contract," which, though not specifically mentioned in the Constitution, the Court found to be implicit in the concept of due process. Between 1897 and 1937, over two hundred state and federal laws were overturned as unreasonable and infringing on the liberty of contract.

This use of substantive due process to promote the interests of business became a major political issue—particularly when the Court invalidated much of the early

New Deal economic legislation of the 1930s, which was intended to alleviate the effects of the Great Depression. In 1937, President Franklin Roosevelt retaliated. He proposed that the number of justices be increased from nine to fifteen so that he would be able to appoint new justices and thereby secure a majority willing to uphold his New Deal program. Although his opponents denounced him for trying to "pack" the Court, the Court at that point handed down a series of decisions—which humorists called "the-switch-in-time-that-saved-nine"—abandoning its use of substantive due process and liberty of contract. Since 1937, no economic regulation has been struck down on the grounds of substantive due process.

More recently, however, the Court has employed substantive due process to overturn laws infringing on noneconomic civil liberties. Notably, in the 1965 case of *Griswold v. Connecticut*,[11] the Court invoked the right of privacy under the Fourteenth Amendment's due process clause to overturn a law prohibiting the use of contraceptives. In its highly controversial 1973 ruling in *Roe v. Wade*, the Court went even further by striking down most laws forbidding abortion. It did so on the basis of the right of privacy and a balancing of the interests of women against the interests of the state. (See the Hot-Button Issue box on pages 106–107.)

Since *Roe*, however, a more conservative Supreme Court has been reluctant to rely on substantive due process to protect or extend benefits to individuals. Indeed, the two dissenters in *Roe*, Justices Rehnquist and White, protested specifically against the Court's revival of the doctrine. Although Rehnquist's view did not prevail in *Roe*,

Justices Oliver Wendell Holmes (left) *and Louis D. Brandeis* (right), *the two "great dissenters," were among the Court's most respected justices. Holmes had fought in the Civil War and served on the Court from 1902 to 1932. Brandeis was the first Jewish justice and served on the Court from 1916 to 1939. Both were progressive legal thinkers, and when they were on the Court together they frequently dissented together.*

PRO-CHOICE, PRO-LIFE, PROLONGED

When the Supreme Court handed down its watershed ruling on abortion in *Roe v. Wade* (1973), the issue of abortion was elevated to the national political agenda. After *Roe*, states could no longer outlaw all abortions or impose criminal penalties on doctors who perform medically safe abortions. The Court declared that during the first trimester (about three months) of a pregnancy women have the right to decide whether to continue or to terminate it. During the second trimester, states may regulate the conditions under which abortions are performed, but only to safeguard the health of the mother and the unborn. In the third trimester, the Court decided, states' interests in preserving the life of the unborn become compelling, and they may limit—even ban—abortions except when necessary to save the mother's life.

Until the mid-nineteenth century, most states had permitted abortions before the quickening, or first movement, of the fetus, and an abortion at a later stage of pregnancy was usually considered only a minor offense. After the Civil War, however, states gradually began to toughen their laws. By 1910 every state except Kentucky had made abortion a felony. After the sexual revolution of the 1960s, women's groups began pressuring states to liberalize their abortion laws. Prior to *Roe*, fourteen states had done so to permit abortions when the woman's health was in danger, when fetal abnormality was likely, or when the woman was a victim of rape or incest. Four of these states had also repealed all criminal penalties for abortions done in early pregnancy. Thus the legal status of abortion had returned to about where it was a century earlier.

Roe sparked a heated controversy that mobilized opponents of abortion and led to the formation of numerous anti-abortion groups, including the National Right-to-Life Committee—the largest and most influential such organization in the country. The Court's ruling also left numerous questions unanswered and afforded ample opportunities for noncompliance. Although most states adopted new laws in conformity with *Roe*, others sought to limit the availability of abortion by such means as withholding Medicaid funds and denying the use of public hospitals for the procedure. Likewise, Congress passed several laws restricting the availability of abortion and barring the use of federal funds for programs in which it is presented as a method of family planning.

Although public opinion on the issue did not divide neatly either along partisan lines or into "pro-life" and "pro-choice" camps, by the 1980s the Court's ruling on abortion had become an issue in electoral politics as well. Republican platforms endorsed by Ronald Reagan and George Bush supported a constitutional amendment "to restore protection of the right to life for unborn children." Moreover, Reagan and Bush made opposition to abortion a criterion for their appointments to the federal judiciary, including the Supreme Court; and their Justice Departments encouraged and joined in litigation that might undercut and ultimately lead to the reversal of *Roe*. The Democrats, meanwhile, increasingly took on the role of champions of a woman's right to abortion, a stance reflected in their party platforms. Abortion became an issue not only in presidential elections but in races for Congress, governorships, and state legislatures. The identification of the Republican party with the anti-abortion position helped to win the support of many religious conservatives for Republican candidates, but it also alienated many women from the party and contributed to a widening "gender gap" in partisan preferences.

Interest groups on both sides of the controversy held rallies for their supporters, lobbied Congress and state legislatures, and entered into litigation challenging or defending more restrictive abortion laws. Extreme anti-abortion groups, such as Operation Rescue, picketed abortion clinics and blockaded their entrances; even more extreme opponents bombed clinics and fatally shot two doctors and several other people involved in performing abortions. But most in the pro-life movement remained peaceful and lawful in competing for influence with pro-choice groups.

As the Supreme Court's composition changed in the 1980s and early 1990s, speculation mounted that *Roe* would be overturned. Despite six appointments to the Court by presidents Reagan and Bush, however, a bare majority of the justices upheld the "essence of *Roe*" in *Planned Parenthood of Southeastern Pennsylvania v. Casey* (1992).

Flowers left on the steps of a Brookline, Massachusetts, abortion clinic memorialize two employees murdered by an abortion opponent in 1994. Despite occasional violent incidents, however, most pro-life advocates remain peaceful in their protests.

On the other hand, the majority in *Casey* did uphold most of Pennsylvania's restrictions on access to abortions. According to the decision, women seeking abortions must be informed by doctors about fetal development, then give their consent (minors must obtain parental consent), and then wait at least 24 hours before having the abortion. The majority also imposed certain reporting and public disclosure requirements on doctors who perform abortions; however, it struck down a requirement that married women notify their husbands of their desire to obtain an abortion, because that requirement potentially exposed women to violence and economic duress. In sum, a bare majority reaffirmed *Roe* while rejecting much of the analysis on which it was based. States may not completely ban abortions, but the Court signaled that it would uphold restrictions that do not "unduly burden" women seeking abortions.

With the 1992 election of Democratic president Bill Clinton and his appointment to the Court of Justices Ruth Bader Ginsburg and Stephen Breyer, it became even more unlikely that *Roe* would be overruled. Still, interest groups on both sides remain active, and the controversy is not likely to vanish from

American politics—at least in the foreseeable future. In 1996, religious conservatives pressured Republican presidential candidates to take a strongly pro-life stance and blocked Republican moderates from weakening the anti-abortion plank in the party platform. The same year, Congress approved legislation directly banning certain late-term abortions. Clinton vetoed the bill, and Congress failed to override his veto, but Republican presidential nominee Robert Dole tried to use the issue against him in the 1996 election campaign.

To get more information about this issue, or to become involved on one side or the other, contact one of the following groups:

National Abortion Rights Action League Foundation
1101 14th Street, N.W.
Washington, D.C. 20005
(202) 973-3000

National Right to Life Committee
419 7th Street, N.W.
Washington, D.C. 20004
(202) 626-8800
http://www.nrlc.org/nrlc

in 1989 he persuaded a bare majority of the justices to hold (in *DeShaney v. Winnebago County Department of Social Services*[12]) that social workers were not accountable for violating a 4-year-old boy's constitutional rights. The social workers had failed to protect the child from repeated beatings by his father that left him brain-damaged, even though on occasion they had taken him into custody as a precaution against his father's abuse. In his opinion in the case, Rehnquist wrote that the Fourteenth Amendment's due process clause does not guarantee a child a substantive right that requires social workers to ensure his or her safety. This ruling underscores the Court's refusal to further expand substantive due process.

In sum, whereas liberals attacked the pre-1937 Court for imposing its own values (in economics) under the doctrine "liberty of contract," conservatives criticized the post-1937 Court for doing precisely the same thing (in moral standards) through its application of the "right of privacy." The use of substantive due process will always be hotly contested because it pits the Court against the forces of the majority. Indeed, any time the Court sides with the individual or with a minority against the state or society, its decisions are likely to be controversial.

Freedom from Unreasonable Searches and Seizures

Like many other rights, the freedom from "unreasonable searches and seizures" provided for in the Fourth Amendment is rooted in the history of the English common law and the American colonial experience. The principle that people should be "secure in their persons, houses, papers, and effects" was well expressed in a speech by William Pitt the Elder:

> The poorest man may in his cottage bid defiance to all the force of the Crown. It may be frail; its roof may shake; the wind may blow through it; the storms may enter, the rain may enter—but the King of England cannot enter; all his forces dare not cross the threshold of the ruined tenement.[13]

Yet during the colonial period, royalist judges issued *writs of assistance* or *general warrants*, which allowed British authorities to search and ransack homes. The purpose of the Fourth Amendment was to prevent such intrusion—to forbid police from conducting "arbitrary," "unreasonable," and "general" searches and seizures.

The key to this protection is the requirement that a magistrate issue a warrant before a search or an arrest can be made. To obtain a warrant, the police must swear under oath that they have "probable cause" for its issuance, and the warrant must describe the specific places that will be searched and persons or things to be seized. The police are barred from conducting more wide-ranging searches.

Exceptions to the warrant requirement may be allowed when the arrest is made in a public place, when the police are in "hot pursuit" of a suspect, or when someone's life is in danger. Even when the police arrest or "seize" a person in a public place, they must still have *probable cause* to believe, or a *reasonable suspicion*, that the person had committed or was about to commit a crime. In *California v. Hodari D.* (1991), however, the Rehnquist Court held that police may chase a person even without probable cause or reasonable suspicion.[14] Hodari D., a teenager standing with others on a streetcorner at night, ran away at the sight of an undercover police car. The police then chased him and recovered a piece of crack cocaine that he had thrown away, and the crack was used as evidence at trial against him. Even though the police had not had a basis for questioning or detaining Hodari D. before he threw away the crack, the Court held that, for the purposes of the Fourth

Amendment, he had not been "seized." When the police arrest a person, moreover, they may search him or her as well as whatever area and items are in "plain view."

The provisions of the Fourth Amendment apply not only to people's houses but also to their apartments, their offices, and (under some circumstances) their cars and other personal effects, such as clothing and luggage. In general, the Court has held that the amendment "protects people, not places" and applies in cases in which the Court deems someone to have a "reasonable expectation of privacy."

In response to the growth of government and the rise of the administrative state, in which government agencies regulate virtually every kind of activity, the Court has ruled that in some circumstances administrative officials (such as housing inspectors and agents of the Occupational Safety and Health Administration) must obtain a warrant before searching a home or business without the owner's consent. However, in 1985 the Court upheld a school principal's warrantless search of a student's purse and locker, and two years later it upheld the warrantless search of an employee's office by her supervisor. As discussed at the beginning of this chapter, in the 1989 cases of *National Treasury Employees Union v. Von Raab*[15] and *Skinner v. Railway Labor Executives' Association*[16] the Court upheld, respectively, drug testing of federal employees and alcohol testing of employees involved in serious accidents. And in 1995, in *Vernonia School District 47J v. Acton*,[17] the Court held that student athletes may be subjected to random drug testing. The Court has also ruled that individuals do not have reasonable expectations of privacy and Fourth Amendment protection against warrantless searches of papers or records held by third parties such as banks, accountants, and lawyers; of garbage in trash cans; or of the interior and contents of cars. Nor does the Fourth Amendment protect individuals against police helicopters flying over their property in search of marijuana plants.

Other threats to personal privacy posed by new technologies and changing law enforcement techniques have been addressed by the Court as well. The use of wiretaps, electronic eavesdropping devices, and secret television cameras could not, of course, have been foreseen by the drafters of the Fourth Amendment. When initially confronted by the issue of whether wiretapping constituted an "unreasonable search and seizure" in the 1928 case of *Olmstead v. United States*, a bare majority of the Court said no.[18] Chief Justice William Howard Taft reasoned that the Fourth Amendment protects individuals only against the seizure of physical objects and actual physical entry into their premises; it does not protect them against the tapping of telephone wires. But forty years later, in *Katz v. United States* (1967), the Court reversed itself. It held that police must obtain a search warrant before conducting wiretaps—even wiretaps placed in public telephone booths—because the amendment safeguards individuals' "reasonable" and "legitimate expectations of privacy."[19] Subsequently, in the Crime Control and Safe Streets Act of 1968, Congress established federal guidelines for the use of electronic surveillance by law enforcement officials and forbade any unauthorized person from tapping telephones and using other kinds of electronic listening devices.

Government Interrogations and the Right to Counsel

Individuals enjoy a number of rights under the Fifth and Sixth Amendments, which bar the government from coercing confessions and forcing the disclosure of incriminating evidence. One of these, known as the privilege against **self-incrimination**, may be traced to the seventeenth century, when ecclesiastical courts in England forced confessions from religious dissenters through torture. In response to criticism

THURGOOD MARSHALL: LIBERAL LANDMARK

The first African American to sit on the Supreme Court, Thurgood Marshall was nominated to the high bench by President Lyndon B. Johnson in 1967. His appointment symbolized the politics of the times. A Democratic president and a Democratic Congress had recently pushed through the first major civil rights legislation in more than a century, striking down barriers and expanding opportunities for minorities and women. Marshall's career stands as a larger-than-life metaphor for that controversial period in American politics.

In fact, Marshall had earned a place in history even before his appointment to the Supreme Court. After attending Lincoln University and Howard University Law School, he led the National Association for the Advancement of Colored People (NAACP) Legal Defense and Education Fund in the 1940s and 1950s. As a lawyer for the NAACP, he argued before the Supreme Court—and won—the watershed 1954 school desegregation case *Brown v. Board of Education of Topeka, Kansas*, along with twenty-eight other cases that extended protection to individuals and minorities.

During his twenty-four years on the Court, Marshall sat through a sharp rightward turn in its direction. He had come aboard at the height of a liberal-egalitarian revolution in constitutional law forged by the Court under Chief Justice Earl Warren. Between 1961 and 1969, over 76 percent of its rulings each term took a liberal direction. During the next seventeen years under Chief Justice Warren Burger, the Court's rulings were liberal less than 50 percent of the time.

Republican president Ronald Reagan's choice of three conservative justices, as well as his elevation of William Rehnquist to Chief Justice, consolidated the counterrevolution on the Court. By the late 1980s, Marshall had become increasingly isolated in defending the Court's role as a guardian of civil liberties and civil rights. He warned that the country's "war on drugs," for example, must not come at the sacrifice of basic liberties. Moreover, he implored the Court to take the burden of *Brown* seriously in the face of failed efforts to achieve integration in many schools across the country.

Yet a critical mass on the bench was no longer sympathetic. When the old warrior retired in 1991, the

As he announced his resignation, Justice Marshall sat under a portrait of the first Chief Justice, John Jay. Asked why he was retiring, the 82-year-old Marshall replied forthrightly: "I'm old! I'm old and I'm falling apart!"

Rehnquist Court was poised to overturn landmark decisions on affirmative action and to limit lower federal courts' role in overseeing school desegregation efforts. The Senate confirmation of Bush nominee Clarence Thomas to fill the "black seat" on the Court did little to hearten Marshall.

The Supreme Court's last uncompromising champion of liberalism died on January 24, 1993, marking the end of an era in constitutional law and politics.

SOURCE: Based on David M. O'Brien, "The Triumph of the Right," *Los Angeles Times*, June 30, 1991, M1.

of this practice, the privilege against self-incrimination was incorporated into the English common law.

The privilege, or right, against self-incrimination is a fundamental principle of an **adversary** (or **accusatory**) **system** of justice. In such a system people are not required to prove their innocence and may not be forced to testify against themselves; in the American adversary system, the government has the burden of proving guilt and may not compel a defendant to testify at all. In contrast, under the **inquisitorial system** used in France and other European countries, the accused person is presumed guilty, interrogated by magistrates and required to answer their questions, and denied many of the other rights afforded under an adversary system.

Although the Fifth Amendment protection against self-incrimination literally applies only during criminal trials, it has been extended to protect individuals who are summoned to appear before other government institutions and agencies. It may be invoked in the proceedings of grand juries, congressional and state investigatory committees, and some administrative agencies. Individuals cannot lose their government employment because they claim the privilege before a disciplinary board. But individuals may invoke the privilege only when their disclosures would in fact prove incriminating, not merely embarrassing.

The privilege against self-incrimination may be waived by an individual who is offered a **grant of immunity** by a prosecutor, grand jury, or congressional investigatory committee; such a grant must be approved by a judge. Grants of immunity are offered when the government is more interested in obtaining information about some criminal activity, such as drug trafficking, than in prosecuting a particular individual. In exchange for immunity from subsequent prosecution (which would be based directly on the incriminating testimony), the witness may no longer claim the Fifth Amendment or refuse to testify.

The Supreme Court has also sanctioned the practice of **plea bargaining**, in which an accused person, in order to obtain probation or a reduced sentence, pleads guilty to a lesser offense than the one with which he or she was originally charged. In exchange for the lighter sentence, defendants who plea-bargain must surrender their constitutional rights against self-incrimination, as well as their right to a speedy and public jury trial and to confront witnesses against them. Plea bargaining is advantageous for the government as well as for the accused because it eliminates the time and cost of going to trial. Approximately 90 percent of all guilty pleas in American courts result from plea bargains that are struck between the accused and the prosecution.

The most controversial extension of the protection against self-incrimination is the Supreme Court's use of it to limit police interrogations of criminal suspects. For years the Court reversed convictions that were based on coerced confessions and police brutality. But this practice meant that the Court had to examine all the circumstances in each case to determine whether the accused's rights had been violated, and it provided little guidance for the police and added to the Court's workload by increasing the number of criminal appeals.

To clarify and safeguard the rights of the accused, in the 1960s the Court handed down several landmark rulings that had wide-ranging consequences for the criminal-justice system. In *Escobedo v. Illinois* (1964) it held that whenever a person becomes the primary suspect in a criminal investigation, he or she has the right to request the assistance of counsel.[20] A year earlier, in *Gideon v. Wainwright* (1963), it had ruled that any individual accused of a criminal offense but too poor to hire a lawyer has the right to a court-appointed attorney.[21] Both cases acknowledged that

THE *MIRANDA* WARNINGS

1. You have the right to remain silent and refuse to answer questions. Do you understand?
2. Anything you do say may be used against you in a court of law. Do you understand?
3. You have the right to consult an attorney before speaking to the police and to have an attorney present during any questioning now or in the future. Do you understand?
4. If you do not have an attorney available, you have the right to remain silent until you have had an opportunity to consult with one. Do you understand?
5. If you cannot afford an attorney, you have the right to have one appointed for you. Do you understand?
6. Now that I have advised you of your rights, are you willing to answer questions without an attorney present?

without the assistance of counsel, individuals may not fully understand their rights and may be intimidated by police and by the judicial process itself.

Subsequently, in *Miranda v. Arizona* (1966), Chief Justice Earl Warren sought to establish objective standards for determining whether confessions were coerced.[22] Ernesto Miranda, a 23-year-old indigent with a ninth-grade education, had been arrested and charged with kidnapping and raping an 18-year-old girl on the outskirts of Phoenix, Arizona. At the police station the rape victim identified Miranda in a police lineup; two officers then took him into a separate room for interrogation. At first denying his guilt, Miranda eventually confessed and wrote out and signed a brief statement admitting and describing the crime. After his trial and conviction Miranda's attorneys appealed, contending that the use of a confession obtained during police interrogations, in the absence of an attorney, violated Miranda's Fifth Amendment right to remain silent. The Court agreed, holding that confessions cannot be introduced at trial unless the police had initially informed the suspect of his or her constitutional rights. This procedural safeguard is known as the **Miranda warnings**.

Like the rulings on the exclusionary rule, the *Miranda* decision has been widely criticized for "handcuffing" the police and making law enforcement more difficult. The Court has become more sensitive to these concerns and—although it is unlikely to overturn the *Miranda* decision—has recognized certain exceptions and modified its enforcement of the *Miranda* warnings. In 1989, for example, it ruled by a bare majority that police no longer have to use the precise language of the *Miranda* warnings (see the box at the top of this page) when informing suspects of their rights under the Fifth Amendment.[23]

Escobedo, Gideon, Miranda, and other rulings were crucial to ensuring individuals' Sixth Amendment right to counsel and to achieving equality before the law for rich and poor citizens alike. Subsequent decisions held that the right to counsel applies to virtually every stage of the criminal-justice process—from initial police interrogations and preliminary hearings, through trials and sentencing, to the first appeals of convictions and sentences. Only when individuals do not face the possibility of imprisonment has the Court held that they have no right to a court-appointed attorney. Still, the Court's rulings protecting the rights of the accused

Ernesto Miranda

THE RIGHTS OF THE ACCUSED IN COMPARATIVE PERSPECTIVE

Even among democratic countries, the United States stands out in the degree of protection given to the rights of individuals suspected of or charged with crimes. Although the legal systems of major Western European countries, for example, provide some protection against coerced confessions and arbitrary searches and seizures, this protection does not extend as far as the protections accorded to Americans under the Fourth and Fifth Amendments to the Constitution.

A privilege against self-incrimination was recognized in English courts as early as the seventeenth century as a legacy of the Middle Ages. However, the British Parliament and the courts have rejected an exclusionary rule for the failure of police to warn suspects of their right to remain silent. Moreover, the Criminal Justice and Public Order Act, which went into effect in 1995, further removed many of the protections afforded by the right to silence. Notably, prosecutors and judges may now imply to juries that suspects who refuse to testify in their own behalf are guilty. England also does not have an exclusionary rule for evidence obtained from illegal searches. Confessions obtained by police coercion are inadmissible in court, but otherwise police may obtain incriminating evidence by any means, even theft.

France, Germany, and Italy are all civil law countries in which police, prosecutors, and judges have extensive investigatory powers. Still, each country has recognized—to different degrees—an exclusionary rule for the failure of police and judges to warn criminal suspects of the right to remain silent.

In France, since 1897 the courts have held that those suspected of a crime need not be warned of their rights to remain silent and to speak with counsel until their first appearance before a magistrate, rather than at the earlier stage of police interrogations. Thus police and magistrates need not advise suspects of the right to silence until they have a strong case against them. Once a suspect receives the warning, however, any incriminating statements made afterwards are excluded as evidence.

In Germany, a right-to-silence warning was guaranteed—but only in limited circumstances—under the Code of Criminal Procedure of 1877. The code provided that "[t]he accused is to be asked whether he wishes to respond to charges" and required judges to give suspects that warning, but it did not require police or prosecutors to do so. In 1964, the German legislature revised those provisions to require that the accused be informed of the rights to silence and to counsel at the first hearing before police, prosecutors, and a judge. Trial judges have discretion in excluding confessions as evidence, based on the circumstances in which they were made.

In Italy, a right-to-silence warning is required at every stage of the judicial process in order to protect individuals' right against self-incrimination. Even suspects who are questioned but not arrested are entitled to the rights to silence and counsel, although they need not receive a warning of the right to silence. Italian courts also require the exclusion as evidence not only of statements obtained prior to the warning of a right to silence but also of other types of evidence obtained illegally by police.

SOURCE: David M. O'Brien, *Constitutional Law and Politics*, vol. 2, *Civil Rights and Civil Liberties* (New York: Norton, 3d ed., 1997).

remain controversial. For one thing, law enforcement officials resent the Court's second-guessing their operations. For another, the Court's decisions may make law enforcement efforts more costly and difficult, because police must follow the Court's guidelines. Moreover, guilty individuals are sometimes allowed to go free as a result of the Court's decisions. Finally, many people have little sympathy for those who are *accused* of crimes, even though they may be innocent, and it is sometimes hard to see that the Supreme Court's rulings are in fact designed to safeguard the presumption of innocence.

The Right to a Fair Trial

When a criminal case goes to trial, a number of other safeguards come into play to ensure that the accused gets a fair trial. In addition to being guaranteed the assistance of counsel, accused individuals are guaranteed the *right to be informed of the nature and cause of the accusation* against them. It is the responsibility of the prosecutor—the attorney representing the government and the public—to bring the charges. Usually this is done through an indictment by a grand jury. A **grand jury** is composed of twelve or more citizens who, first, hear the government's charges against a suspect on the basis of a preliminary presentation of the evidence and, then, may approve an **indictment**, a written statement of the charges or offenses for which the accused will stand trial. Not all states require grand jury indictments, however. About half permit the prosecution to present a **bill of information**, a document specifying the charges and evidence against an accused, to a judge at a preliminary hearing. The accused's attorney may then seek to exclude particular evidence from being used at the defendant's trial.

At trial, the prosecution presents the evidence against the defendant, and the latter's attorney presents evidence in his or her defense. In criminal cases, defendants have the right to be tried by a **petit jury**, traditionally consisting of twelve persons selected by the judge and the prosecution and defense attorneys from members of the community. The jury determines the guilt or innocence of the accused. In some

In this typical courtroom, the jury listens intently as the judge interrupts a witness and opposing attorneys wait to resume their arguments. The adversary system is time-consuming and costly, but it is the heartbeat of the American judicial system. It also gives citizens the opportunity to participate by serving on juries.

jurisdictions the jury also determines the penalty or sentence to be imposed on a person who has been convicted of a crime; in other jurisdictions the judge does this.

During the trial the defendant has the *right to confront witnesses*. After the prosecution introduces witnesses and questioning designed to prove the defendant's guilt, the defendant (or the defense attorney) may question these witnesses to try to persuade the judge and jury that their testimony is unreliable. In addition, the defense may call its own witnesses to challenge the prosecution's case or establish the defendant's innocence; the prosecution in turn may question these witnesses. This confrontation—or "fight"—between advocates is the essence of an adversary system of justice. It is derived from the Anglo-Saxon substitution of trials for private out-of-court battles. Judge Jerome Frank, a sharp critic of abuses of the adversary process, provides a classic description of why he nevertheless believes that confrontation remains crucial to ensuring a fair trial:

> Many lawyers maintain . . . that the best way for a court to discover the facts in a suit is to have each side strive as hard as it can, in a keenly partisan spirit, to bring to the court's attention the evidence favorable to that side. . . . We obtain the fairest decision "when two men argue, as unfairly as possible, on opposite sides," for then "it is certain that no important consideration will altogether escape notice."[24]

A particularly vexing issue for the Court in recent years has involved the right of defendants to confront their accusers in court in cases of alleged rape and sexual abuse of children. In *Michigan v. Lucas* (1991) the Court upheld a state "rape shield" law requiring that evidence of a defendant's sexual conduct prior to the alleged offense be barred at trial unless the defendant is given notice of its introduction at least ten days prior to the trial.[25] In two earlier cases the Court had ruled that defendants on trial for sexually abusing children do not have an absolute right to confront their accusers face to face and that states may shield alleged victims by introducing the children's testimony through the use of videotaped statements or closed-circuit television. Then, in *White v. Illinois* (1992), the Court unanimously held that in trials involving charges of sexual abuse of children the Sixth Amendment permits the introduction of the alleged victim's testimony made to police and doctors, and the Court rejected the claim that an accused has a right to confront the child-victim as a witness at trial.[26]

Moreover, criminal suspects may not be subject to **double jeopardy**—that is, after an acquittal they may not be retried for the same offense in the same court, whether state or federal. However, they may be tried in both state and federal courts for an offense that violates both state and federal laws.

The Sixth Amendment requires the federal government to give a person accused of a crime *a speedy and public trial before an impartial jury*, and the Seventh Amendment guarantees the right to a jury trial in civil cases involving controversies concerning amounts that exceed $20. These provisions for jury trials are based on the English common law principle that a trial by a jury of one's peers is the surest way to safeguard against arbitrary and vindictive prosecutions. They may temper the enforcement of unpopular and outdated laws, and they serve as a hedge against a corrupt or overzealous prosecutor and a biased or eccentric judge.

The Sixth Amendment does not explain what constitutes a speedy trial, but Congress has done so. Under the Speedy Trial Act of 1974, a person who is arrested must be charged with a specific crime within thirty days, arraigned ten days later, and tried by a jury within two months of arraignment. In major metropolitan areas, those

The trial of O. J. Simpson for the murders of his ex-wife and a friend riveted—and divided—the nation, raising troubling questions about the influence on the criminal justice system of race, celebrity, money, and the media. After Simpson's acquittal, juror Brenda Moran held a press conference to explain the verdict.

requirements are not always met because of the large number of criminal cases, procedural delays requested by defendants, and the frequency of plea bargaining.

Although trials have historically been public, widespread newspaper and television coverage of sensational trials may create a conflict between the defendant's right to a fair trial and the claims of reporters to freedom of the press. Defendants often claim that pretrial and trial publicity prejudices judges and juries, but reporters counter that closed judicial proceedings deny them their rights under the First Amendment. Today fair trial/free press controversies, with few exceptions, are resolved in favor of open trials. Only in extraordinary circumstances may pretrial hearings and trials be closed to the press and the public, or may prosecutors, defense attorneys, and witnesses be forbidden to talk with reporters about the trial.[27] In 1981 the Supreme Court approved the use of cameras in the courtroom as long as they are not disruptive.[28] Television coverage of criminal trials is regulated by each of the states. The Supreme Court, however, refuses to allow television coverage of its own proceedings.

Judges may employ a number of safeguards and remedies to protect the rights of the accused against the effects of prejudicial publicity. If pretrial publicity can reasonably be expected to threaten the chances of obtaining an impartial jury, the defendant may ask for a change of venue—that is, for the trial to be moved to another locality where there has been less publicity. When the jury is being selected, the defendant's attorney may question potential jurors about the publicity and their views of the defendant; on the basis of that questioning, the attorney may ask the judge to disqualify them. In addition, during the trial the jurors may be sequestered and forbidden to read or watch news coverage of the trial. Finally, a judge may declare a mistrial if any of the safeguards are violated, and a defendant always retains the right to appeal a conviction on the grounds that prejudicial publicity prevented a fair trial.

Juries must be not only impartial but representative of a fair cross-section of the community. This does not mean, however, that defendants are entitled to a jury that includes members of their own race, gender, religion, or national origin or one that is representative of the proportions of such groups in the community. Rather, the defendant's rights and those of potential jurors are considered to be denied only if members of a particular group are denied the opportunity to be selected for jury service.[29]

Traditionally, juries have been made up of twelve members, and to convict a defendant they had to agree unanimously that the prosecution had proved guilt "beyond a reasonable doubt." The standard of "proof beyond a reasonable doubt" applies for all criminal cases tried in federal courts and in state criminal cases, but some states have adopted smaller juries and permit nonunanimous verdicts in order to reduce the costs of conducting jury trials. The Supreme Court has upheld juries with as few as six persons in civil and criminal cases—except cases involving the death penalty—in state courts.[30] And it continues to require a unanimous verdict by six-member juries, although nonunanimous verdicts have been approved for juries with more than six members.[31]

Outside the Florida prison where serial killer Ted Bundy was about to be executed, supporters of capital punishment waited, half hoping to see the lights dim as the current was delivered to the electric chair. There was a moratorium on executions in the late 1960s and early 1970s, but the number of executions has steadily increased since the late 1980s. The United States is one of the few industrialized nations that still impose the death penalty.

After trial and conviction, the accused is sentenced. In federal and most state courts the laws provide for a range of terms of imprisonment for particular offenses, and judges and juries have some discretion in sentencing within that range. The federal government and some states, however, have systems of **determinate sentencing** by which a mandatory length of imprisonment is specified for each offense.

The only limitation on sentencing and punishment provided in the Constitution is the Eighth Amendment, which forbids the levying of "excessive fines" and the inflicting of "cruel and unusual punishment." According to the Supreme Court, the ban on cruel and unusual punishment limits sentencing in two ways. First, it prohibits barbaric forms of punishment, such as torture and unnecessary infliction of pain. Second, it forbids punishment that is grossly disproportionate to the crime committed.

These broad standards do not always provide clear guidelines in particular cases. In 1910, for instance, the Court struck down a law providing for twelve years of hard labor for anyone convicted of falsifying a government document. But in *Rummell v. Estelle* (1980) it upheld a life sentence imposed on an individual for three thefts that totaled $289.[32] Rummell had refused to plea-bargain, and because he insisted on a trial, the prosecution charged him under the state's criminal-rehabilitation statute, which imposed a mandatory life sentence on anyone convicted of three felonies. Subsequently, though, the Court found that a life sentence without the possibility of parole was excessive for a person convicted of writing a $100 bad check.[33]

In the past few decades a major controversy has centered on whether the death penalty is a cruel and unusual punishment and hence unconstitutional. Justice William J. Brennan Jr. maintained that it is, arguing that whenever the state takes a life, it violates the fundamental principle of respect for human dignity embedded in the Constitution. Chief Justice Rehnquist countered that capital punishment was permissible when the Constitution was drafted and that state legislatures, not the courts, should decide whether the death penalty should be imposed.

In an important ruling in *Furman v. Georgia* (1972), a bitterly divided Court held that the death penalty is not cruel and unusual punishment but that there must be precise standards for imposing it in order to minimize the potential for injustice and ensure the equal protection of the law.[34] Without standards for guiding a jury's discretion in imposing death sentences, the Court said, some individuals convicted on the basis of similar facts and offenses could be executed whereas others might not. *Furman* essentially invalidated most of the capital punishment laws in effect at that time. Within the next decade, however, thirty-six states redrafted their laws and reintroduced the death penalty.

When reviewing challenges to these new laws, the Court ruled that capital punishment may be imposed only in cases involving murder and not in those involving rape or other crimes unrelated to murder.[35] It also overturned laws requiring mandatory death sentences for certain crimes, including the killing of police officers. States are required to specify the circumstances (such as the age or role of the accused and the circumstances of a murder) that allow a judge and jury to sentence the accused to death rather than to life imprisonment. Moreover, juries must be allowed to consider all mitigating factors when deciding whether to impose the death penalty.

In 1989, on the other hand, the Court held that states may execute convicted murderers who are mentally disturbed or retarded and those who are minors, age 16 or older. In general, under Chief Justice Rehnquist the more conservative Supreme

Court has become less willing to overturn death sentences, and the number of executions has increased dramatically in the 1990s. In addition, some states (such as New York) that had abolished or limited capital punishment have reenacted and expanded death penalty laws.

RIGHTS AND LIBERTIES VERSUS ECONOMIC INTERESTS

The Supreme Court assumed the role of "guardian of civil rights and liberties" after 1937. Before then, it was preoccupied with protecting economic and property interests. With the gradual nationalization of the Bill of Rights, the Court began devoting more attention to cases involving civil rights and liberties and the equal protection of the law, abandoning its role as a champion of economic interests. As a result, a **judicial double standard** evolved. Since 1937 the Court has upheld, under the Fourteenth Amendment's due process clause, virtually all legislation regulating economic interests. But it has given greater scrutiny to, and has often invalidated, legislation that impinges on individuals' civil rights and liberties.

The Court's role as a guardian of individual rights is illustrated by the attention given to the special problems of indigents in the criminal-justice system. Beginning with the ruling in *Gideon v. Wainwright* (1963), in which the Court stated that people have the right to a court-appointed attorney if they are too poor to hire their own, the Court has sought to ensure equal access to justice in several areas. Convicted defendants who are too poor to hire lawyers must be given transcripts of their trials so that they can prepare appeals.[36] If sanity is an issue in the defense, states must provide access to a psychiatrist.[37] Prison officials must also provide an "adequate law library" so that prisoners may make a "meaningful appeal."[38] And indigents may not be held beyond the maximum term or imprisoned solely because they cannot pay fines.[39]

In addition to enforcing the guarantees of the Bill of Rights, the Court has struck down numerous laws that infringe on rights and liberties not specifically mentioned in the Constitution. The Court's application of the *right of privacy* in overturning laws forbidding abortions remains perhaps the most controversial of these actions. But the right of privacy actually embraces a broader concept, "the right to be left alone." As Justice Louis Brandeis put it:

> The makers of our Constitution undertook to secure conditions favorable to the pursuit of happiness. They recognized the significance of man's spiritual nature, of his feelings and of his intellect. . . . They conferred, as against the Government, the right to be left alone—the most comprehensive of rights and the right most valued by civilized men.[40]

Accordingly, the Court has sought to ensure various other constitutionally protected privacy interests, such as the right of *associational privacy*—that is, the right to form and join groups and organizations of one's own choosing.[41] The Court has also defended privacy interests in a person's home, papers, property, and effects as protected by the Fourth Amendment's guarantee against "unreasonable searches and seizures," as well as privacy interests under the Fifth Amendment's privilege against self-incrimination. It has not, however, extended the right of privacy to cover all matters of personal autonomy. In *Bowers v. Hardwick* (1986), for instance, it rejected the claims of a homosexual that laws prohibiting sodomy between consenting adults violate the constitutional right to privacy.[42]

The Court has enforced as well other rights that are not specifically mentioned in the Constitution. In 1969, for instance, it struck down a one-year residency require-ment for the recipients of state welfare benefits. It did so on the grounds that indi-viduals have a fundamental *right to travel* from one state to another, while acknowl-edging that the federal Department of State may regulate their international travel.

The Court's exercise of its supervisory powers over civil rights and liberties is likely to remain controversial. Its post-1937 double standard of protecting civil rights while not scrutinizing laws that infringe on economic interests has been widely crit-icized. Still, the Bill of Rights contains explicit language that guarantees a variety of civil rights and liberties; only the Fifth Amendment mentions economic interests, in providing that a person may not be deprived of "life, liberty, or property" without the due process of law and that private property may not be taken "for public use with-out just compensation." The Court has shown little willingness to expand protection of economic interests under the due process clause or to return to its pre-1937 defense of property rights and economic liberty.[43] It has been more willing, however, to scrutinize land use laws and environmental regulations under the "taking clause" of the Fifth Amendment, which prohibits governments from taking private property for public use without providing just compensation. In *Nollan v. California Coastal Commission* (1987), for example, it struck down regulations that required owners of beachfront property to provide public access across their land as a condition of obtaining building permits.[44]

The Court's enforcement of the guarantees enumerated in the Bill of Rights is, in James Madison's words, "an auxiliary precaution" against the tyranny of the majority. As Justice Robert H. Jackson eloquently observed:

> The very purpose of a Bill of Rights was to withdraw certain subjects from the vicissitudes of political controversy, to place them beyond the reach of majorities and officials and to establish them as legal principles to be applied by the courts. One's right to life, liberty, and property, to free speech, a free press, freedom of worship and assembly, and other fundamental rights may not be sub-mitted to vote; they depend on the outcome of no elections.[45]

Because the Court has the task of enforcing the guarantees of the Bill of Rights, it often thwarts the will of the majority and becomes the center of political contro-versy. Yet the Court accomplishes little unless its rulings have the support of other branches of government and, ultimately, command a national consensus. In Chief Justice Edward White's words, "The Court's power rests solely on the approval of a free people."[46]

SUMMARY

Civil rights and liberties are guaranteed in the Bill of Rights and other legislation. Yet they often become matters of intense political debate and conflict. When the Supreme Court hands down controversial rulings on civil rights and liberties, it invites larger political struggles between competing interest groups. Ultimately, civil rights and liberties depend not only on the Court's rulings but also on the achievement of political consensus.

Civil rights are rights, such as the right to vote, that

government may not categorically deny or infringe on because of an individual's race, gender, ethnicity, or var-ious other characteristics. *Civil liberties* are freedoms that government must respect, such as the freedom to think, communicate, and behave in a manner that con-forms to one's beliefs and values. Political struggles over civil rights and liberties stem from the competing demands for majority rule and for individual or minor-ity rights.

During the struggle over ratification of the

Constitution, the Federalists argued that it would protect individuals' rights and liberties because the powers of the national government were limited to the powers expressly granted to it. The Anti-Federalists believed that this protection was not sufficient. Their concerns resulted in the passage of the *Bill of Rights*, the first ten amendments to the Constitution. Initially the guarantees contained in the Bill of Rights were viewed as limitations only on the federal government, not on the states. But because the state constitutions varied widely in their protection of individual rights and liberties, the Supreme Court eventually nationalized the Bill of Rights—that is, made its guarantees applicable to the states as well as to the federal government. The due process clause of the Fourteenth Amendment specifically limited the power of the states. Until the middle decades of the twentieth century, however, the Supreme Court did not use this clause to apply the guarantees of the Bill of Rights to the states. By the 1970s, all the major provisions of the Bill of Rights had been held to apply to the states.

The nationalization of the Bill of Rights was highly controversial. The guarantees pertaining to criminal justice, such as the *exclusionary rule* (which excludes evidence obtained in violation of the Fourth Amendment), were subjected to especially severe criticism.

Under the due process clauses of the Fifth and Fourteenth Amendments, no person shall be deprived of "life, liberty, or property, without due process of law." There are two kinds of *due process*. *Procedural due process* is concerned with how law is carried out. *Substantive due process* is concerned with the subject matter of a law, regulation, or executive order.

One area in which the Supreme Court has been particularly active is the Fourth Amendment freedom from "unreasonable searches and seizures." Holding that the amendment "protects people, not places," the Court has extended its provisions to cover not only people's houses and apartments but also their offices, cars, and personal effects. It has also addressed the threat to personal privacy posed by new technologies, ruling that the police must obtain a warrant before conducting wiretaps.

Individuals enjoy a number of rights under the Fifth and Sixth Amendments, which bar the government from coercing confessions and forcing the disclosure of incriminating evidence (*self-incrimination*). The privilege against self-incrimination is a fundamental principle of an *adversary* (or *accusatory*) *system* of justice, in which the government must prove that an accused person is guilty. In contrast, in an *inquisitorial system* an accused person is presumed guilty. An individual who accepts a *grant of immunity* from prosecution or *plea bargaining* to obtain probation or a reduced sentence waives the privilege against self-incrimination.

The most controversial aspect of the protection against self-incrimination is its use to limit police interrogations of criminal suspects. In 1966 the Supreme Court ruled that confessions cannot be introduced as evidence at trial unless the suspect had originally been informed of his or her constitutional rights by the police. This procedural safeguard is known as the *Miranda warnings*. Related Court rulings require that suspects be allowed to request the assistance of counsel and that criminal suspects who cannot afford counsel be assisted by court-appointed attorneys.

Accused individuals are guaranteed the right to be informed of the nature and cause of the accusation against them. Usually this is done through an *indictment* by a *grand jury*, but in some states the prosecution may present a *bill of information* to a judge at a preliminary hearing. In criminal cases, defendants have the right to be tried by a *petit jury*; during the trial, the defendant has the right to confront and question witnesses for the prosecution. The Sixth Amendment also requires the federal government to give the accused a speedy and public trial.

Widespread newspaper and television coverage of sensational trials may create a conflict between the defendant's right to a fair trial and reporters' claims to freedom of the press. In such cases the defendant may ask for a change of venue, or jurors may be sequestered during the trial. In extreme cases the judge may issue a gag order forbidding the prosecution, counsel, and witnesses from talking to reporters about the trial.

Criminal suspects who have been acquitted may not be subject to *double jeopardy* in the same court. However, they may be tried in both federal and state courts for an offense that violates both federal and state laws.

In federal and most state courts, judges and juries have some discretion in sentencing; however, federal drug laws provide for, and some states have systems of, *determinate sentencing* that specify a mandatory length of imprisonment for each offense. The Eighth Amendment forbids "cruel and unusual punishments," including punishment that is grossly disproportionate to the crime. A major controversy of recent decades centers on whether the death penalty constitutes cruel and unusual punishment.

Since 1937 a *judicial double standard* has evolved by which the Supreme Court has upheld virtually all legislation regulating economic interests but has invalidated much legislation impinging on individuals' civil rights and liberties. In addition to enforcing the guarantees of the Bill of Rights, the Court has struck down laws that infringe on rights and liberties not specifically mentioned in the Constitution, such as the right of privacy.

KEY TERMS

civil rights
civil liberties
Bill of Rights
exclusionary rule
due process
procedural due process
substantive due process

self-incrimination
adversary (accusatory) system
inquisitorial system
grant of immunity
plea bargaining
Miranda warnings
grand jury

indictment
bill of information
petit jury
double jeopardy
determinate sentencing
judicial double standard

RESOURCES

SCHOLARLY STUDIES

Abraham, Henry J., and Barbara Perry. *Freedom and the Court*. 5th ed. New York: Oxford University Press, 1994. A highly readable and enjoyable survey of the Supreme Court's rulings in the areas of civil liberties and civil rights.

Berns, Walter. *The Death Penalty: Cruel and Unusual Punishment*. New York: Basic Books, 1979. A provocative argument for the imposition of capital punishment, based on society's moral outrage at heinous crimes.

Black, Charles L. Jr. *Capital Punishment: The Inevitability of Caprice and Mistake*. New York: Norton, 1974 (rev. ed., 1982). A classic and provocative condemnation of the death penalty, based on the inevitability of injustice in its imposition.

Cortner, Richard C. *The Supreme Court and the Second Bill of Rights: The Fourteenth Amendment and the Nationalization of Civil Liberties*. Madison: University of Wisconsin Press, 1981. A detailed discussion of the cases in which the Supreme Court has applied the guarantees of the Bill of Rights to the states.

Craig, Barbara, and David M. O'Brien. *Abortion and American Politics*. Chatham, N.J.: Chatham House, 1993. A case study of the controversy over abortion and how it has played out in the courts, the states, Congress, the executive branch, public opinion polls, and the activities of pro-life and pro-choice interest groups.

Kalven, Harry Jr., and Hans Zeisel. *The American Jury*. Chicago: University of Chicago Press, 1986. A comprehensive study of the history of the jury system and its impact on American law.

Schwartz, Herman, ed. *The Burger Court Years*. New York: Viking, 1987. A fascinating collection of essays assessing the Burger Court years and their legacy for civil rights and liberties in a number of important areas.

LEISURE READING

Baker, Liva. *Miranda: Crime, Law and Politics*. New York: Atheneum, 1983. A detailed history of the watershed ruling in *Miranda v. Arizona* and of the controversy and debate sparked by that ruling.

Garrow, David J. *Liberty and Sexuality: The Right to Privacy and the Making of* Roe v. Wade. New York: Macmillan, 1994. An exhaustive account of the background for the Supreme Court's declaration of a constitutional "right of privacy" and its extension to protect a woman's right to have an abortion.

Irons, Peter. *The Courage of Their Convictions*. New York: Penguin Books, 1990. Tells the stories of several individuals who took their cases all the way to the Supreme Court and describes the impact of the

Court's rulings on their lives and on the course of constitutional law.

Lewis, Anthony. *Gideon's Trumpet.* New York: Random House, 1989. An excellent introduction to the judicial process in a case study of the landmark ruling that extended the Sixth Amendment's right to counsel to state courts.

PRIMARY SOURCE

Schwartz, Bernard, ed. *Roots of the Bill of Rights: An Illustrated Source Book of American Freedom.* 5 vols. New York: Chelsea House, 1981. A comprehensive collection of primary documents bearing on civil rights and liberties.

ORGANIZATION

United States Civil Rights Commission, 1121 Vermont Avenue, N.W., Washington, DC 20425; (202) 376-8312. A government agency authorized by Congress to study and recommend changes in laws bearing on civil rights and liberties.

Issues of Freedom and Equality

PREVIEW

■ Freedom of religion: separation of church and state; freedom of religious exercise

■ Freedom of speech and press: protected, unprotected, and symbolic speech; speech-plus-conduct; freedom of association

■ The quest for equality: the extension of voting rights; redistricting and equal representation; ending racial discrimination; nonracial discrimination; affirmative action and reverse discrimination

O utside the 1984 Republican National Convention in Dallas, Gregory "Joey" Johnson and other members of the Revolutionary Communist Youth Brigade held a rally in protest of the Reagan administration's policies toward Latin America and its support of the contras in Nicaragua. After a march through the streets, Johnson set fire to an American flag while the crowd chanted, "America, the red, white, and blue, we spit on you." Police officers moved in and arrested Johnson.

During Johnson's trial his attorney argued that like the Vietnam War protesters of the 1960s and 1970s, Johnson had burned the flag as a form of political expression, a form protected by the First Amendment guarantee of freedom of speech. Nevertheless, Johnson was convicted of violating a Texas law forbidding abuse and destruction of the American flag. He appealed to the Texas Court of Criminal Appeals, which reversed his conviction on First Amendment grounds. The ruling was then appealed to the Supreme Court by the state's attorney general in *Texas v. Johnson* (1989).

For protest as well as for patriotism, the American flag provides one of the most potent political symbols in the United States. The Supreme Court has often been involved in controversies over the flag. One of the issues that has come before the Court is the authority of government to require participation in symbolic acts honoring the flag; another is the legitimacy of punishing those who abuse the flag as a way of expressing their political views. In 1943, for example, the Court struck down a law requiring children in public schools to salute the flag at the beginning of each schoolday. In this case the Court upheld the claim of a Jehovah's Witness that the law denied his First Amendment rights by forcing his children to worship a graven image in violation of their religious beliefs. Subsequently the Court overturned the conviction of a protester who had burned the flag, of an individual who had worn a small flag on the seat of his pants, and of a student who had hung a flag upside down with a peace symbol attached to it from the window of his dormitory room.

Despite the more conservative composition of the Court in the late 1980s, it again upheld the First Amendment protection of political expression in *Texas v. Johnson*. The Court struck down the Texas law as well as laws in forty-seven other states that made it a crime to desecrate the American flag. In the opinion announcing the majority's decision, Justice William J. Brennan wrote, "if there is a bedrock principle underlying the First Amendment, it is that the Government may not prohibit the expression of an idea simply because society finds the idea itself offensive or disagreeable."[1]

President George Bush immediately denounced the Court's ruling. "Flag burning is wrong—dead wrong," exclaimed Bush, continuing to sound a theme of his 1988 campaign.[2] In the aftermath of the Court's ruling, numerous congressional leaders in both parties joined the president in calling for a constitutional amendment to reverse the Court's judgment. Instead, Congress passed the Federal Flag Protection Act of 1989, which authorized the prosecution of individuals who desecrate the American flag. That law was immediately challenged, and was overturned by the Court in *United States v. Eichman* (1990).[3] Following the ruling, another attempt to overturn the Court's ruling by means of a constitutional amendment failed. The House of Representatives voted 254 to 177 in favor of the amendment—34 votes short of the required two-thirds needed to propose a constitutional amendment. The proposed amendment also fell 9 votes short of a two-thirds majority in the Senate.

Flag desecration quickens the pulse of American politics. Most Americans agree that it is wrong, and few actually burn the flag. But the ruling in *Texas v. Johnson* illustrates the difficult role the Supreme Court plays in safeguarding the rights of minorities and those who express unpopular views. It also illustrates the controversy and opposition the Court is likely to generate when it takes a position that supports those who speak or behave in a manner that the majority finds objectionable. Finally, it demonstrates that the Court cannot avoid political issues as it fulfills its government role as an interpreter of the Constitution.

Among the political freedoms that are essential to free government are those that James Madison called "the equal rights of conscience"—the freedom of religion and the freedoms of speech and press. Under the First Amendment, individuals are equally free to worship or not to worship according to their own conscience and to express their opinions as they please. But these basic freedoms are not (and cannot be) absolute. Individual and societal interests often collide—for example, in disputes over prayer in public schools and the advocacy of unpopular ideas like revolution. As in other areas of public policy where the interests of the majority and a minority clash, the Supreme Court must draw lines between permissible and impermissible restrictions on individual freedoms. In drawing those lines, the Court has historically sought to ensure that freedoms are enjoyed equally by all citizens.

We focus in this chapter on the fundamental freedoms of religion and expression, as well as on the quest for greater equality. How has the Supreme Court defined the boundaries of those freedoms in response to major political controversies and shifts in public opinion? And what has been the Court's special role in applying the Fourteenth Amendment to eliminate racial and nonracial discrimination and to achieve equal voting rights and greater access to the political process for all people?

Many of the people who settled in the American colonies were escaping from religious persecution and state churches in England and on the European continent. Although some colonists professed support for religious freedom, the colonies as a whole were far from tolerant of religious diversity. Most provided financial support to an established religion and required holders of public office to adhere to it. Catholics, Jews, and atheists, as well as Protestants belonging to nonestablished sects, were excluded from office and sometimes persecuted.

By the time the Constitution was ratified in 1789, religious freedom and tolerance had become more accepted. Four of the original thirteen colonies never had established churches, and three others abandoned their establishment practices during the American Revolution. After the Revolution the remaining six (now states) gradually accepted religious diversity and evolved from sponsoring particular churches to providing support for all Protestant or Christian faiths.

In the original Constitution, Article VI indicated that the founders deemed freedom of religion a fundamental political freedom. Article VI provides that "no religious test shall ever be required as a qualification to any office or public trust under the United States." With the adoption of the Bill of Rights, the First Amendment provided a broader and more explicit statement: "Congress shall make no law respecting an establishment of religion, or prohibiting the free exercise thereof." Note that the amendment provides a dual protection for religious freedom. First, the **establishment clause** expressly forbids the creation of a national religion; it separates church and state. Second, the **free exercise clause** guarantees that individuals may worship as they please.

The oldest synagogue in the United States, built in 1763 in Newport, Rhode Island. Jews, Catholics, atheists, and members of Protestant denominations other than the one established by law could not hold public office in most of the thirteen colonies and were sometimes persecuted. In Rhode Island, however, religious freedom was guaranteed from the colony's beginning.

These two provisions raise more vexing questions than they settle about the scope of religious freedom. Does the Amendment forbid the establishment of a national church but allow the states to sponsor particular religions? Does any state aid to religious schools constitute an establishment of religion, or do only certain forms of aid do so? Religious *beliefs* are protected, but how far may states go in prohibiting certain religious *practices*, such as the use of poisonous snakes in religious services? And what should be done when the provisions for separation of church and state and for free exercise of religion conflict?

Separation of Church and State

According to James Madison and Thomas Jefferson, the establishment clause embodies "a high wall of separation" between church and state. This was the view taken by the Supreme Court in *Everson v. Board of Education of Ewing Township* (1947), in which it ruled that the principle of separation applies to the states no less than to the national government. In this case the Court held that a state must be "*neutral* in its relations with groups of religious believers and nonbelievers" but that religious organizations may benefit from government programs that have a clearly secular purpose. The Court approved New Jersey's providing free bus rides to schoolchildren regardless of whether they were attending public schools or private religious schools. As Justice Hugo Black explained:

> The "establishment of religion" clause of the First Amendment means at least this: Neither a state nor the federal government can set up a church. Neither can pass laws which aid one religion, aid all religions, or prefer one religion over another. Neither can force nor influence a person to go or remain away from church against his will or force him to profess a belief or disbelief in any religion. No person can be punished for entertaining or professing religious beliefs or disbeliefs, for church attendance or nonattendance. No tax in any amount, large or small, can be levied to support any religious activities or institutions, whatever they may be called, or whatever form they may adopt to teach or practice religion.[4]

Critics of the wall-of-separation theory argue, however, that the Court has gone too far in its emphasis on strict neutrality, which they contend has actually led to state hostility toward religion. In their view, the government is forbidden not from aiding religion but only from showing *favoritism* toward any particular religion.[5] The controversy over religious establishment came to a head in 1948 in a case involving a "released-time" program for religious education, in which children in public schools could attend one-hour classes of Protestant, Catholic, or Jewish instruction during school hours and in the school building. The Court held that this program violated the wall-of-separation doctrine that organized religion in the public schools establishes religion over nonreligion. But in a second "released-time" case a few years later, the Court allowed children to have the option of attending classes in religious instruction held *off* the school grounds.

Despite the Court's decisions, and its distinction between religious activities held in public schools or away from them, many schools chose to interpret the ruling narrowly by arguing that it applies only to formal instruction in a religion. This argument was used to defend a practice that had become customary in many schools: requiring children to begin the schoolday with a prayer. In time, however, this practice was also challenged, in the landmark cases of *Engel v. Vitale* (1962) and *Abington School District v. Schempp* (1963).[6] In *Engel*, at issue was the New York

FINDING SUPREME COURT DECISIONS

Cases pending before the Supreme Court are analyzed in *Preview of United States Supreme Court Cases*, published regularly during each Court term by the Public Education Division of the American Bar Association. Each discussion summarizes the issues, facts, background, significance, arguments (for and against), and amicus briefs (for and against) for each case. *Preview* is an excellent source for clearly written descriptions of the cases awaiting decision; it can be found in law and research libraries.

Once a case has been decided, the justices issue their opinion. The final draft is given to the reporter of decisions—the Court official responsible for overseeing the publication of opinions. The reporter adds a headnote at the beginning summarizing the decision and adds a list at the end of how each justice voted. When a decision is announced, 275 copies (called "bench opinions") are made. They are distributed to the news media and other interested parties. One copy is immediately sent to the Government Printing Office, which prints several thousand copies (called "slip opinions") for immediate distribution, primarily to federal and state courts and agencies and to the public. Finally, the decision, along with any corrections from the slip-opinion version, is incorporated by the Government Printing Office into the formal record of Supreme Court decisions, *United States Reports*.

When a Supreme Court decision is referred to, or cited, in a formal text, a specific format is followed. Court citations always begin with the names of the parties to the case, starting with the appellant (the person or party bringing the case), followed by *v.* (meaning "versus," or "against"), followed by the name of the appellee (the person or party responding)—all usually underscored or italicized. Next comes the volume number of *United States Reports* in which the decision appears, followed by the page number on which the decision begins. Next, if a specific quotation from the decision is being cited, the word *at* and the page number of the quote appear. In parentheses following the page number is the year in which the decision was made. For example, the case *McCulloch v. Maryland*, 17 U.S. 316 at 317 (1819), is found in volume 17 of *United States Reports* starting on page 316, with the particular quote cited appearing on page 317; the decision was made in 1819.

Information about Supreme Court decisions can also be found in commercial publications such as *Supreme Court Reporter, United States Law Week*, and *United States Supreme Court Reports, Lawyer's Edition*. In addition, computerized legal databases such as LEXIS contain Supreme Court decisions. Sources like these are found in all law libraries and in many research libraries.

State Board of Regents' recommendation for the daily recital in the public schools of a brief nonsectarian prayer: "Almighty God, we acknowledge our dependence upon Thee, and we beg Thy blessings upon us, our parents, our teachers, and our country." *Schempp* involved a challenge to the required recital of the Lord's Prayer in schools in Pennsylvania and Maryland. In both cases the Court found that the "high wall of separation" had been breached by these religious activities.

The Court's rulings were widely criticized at both the state and the national levels, and numerous constitutional Amendments designed to overturn them were introduced in Congress. Although those attempts failed, state and local governments found ways of evading the decisions. By 1983 almost half the states had enacted laws permitting voluntary moments of silence or prayer in public schools. Opponents claimed that children were being subjected to peer pressure to conform and that children's rights under the free exercise clause were being violated, and in 1985 the Court overturned Alabama's law because it required a "moment of silent meditation or *prayer*" and did not have a clear secular purpose. But some of the written opinions in this case seemed to indicate that a majority of the justices might be willing to uphold laws that do not mention prayer but merely allow for moments of silent meditation and religious reflection.[7] Nonetheless, in *Lee v. Weisman* (1992) the Court held that prayers during a high school graduation ceremony run afoul of the First Amendment's establishment clause.

In recent years the Court has moved somewhat away from enforcement of a "high wall of separation" and has adopted instead an "accommodationist" or "preferential-ist" approach to church-state relations. Chief Justices Warren Burger and William Rehnquist, among others, have championed this interpretation of the First Amendment, which holds that government may aid or extend benefits to religion as long as it does not prefer one religion over another. In advancing this view, the Court has evolved a three-part test. If a law or program is to avoid violating the estab-lishment clause, (1) it must have a *secular legislative purpose*, (2) its *primary effect* must neither advance nor inhibit religion, and (3) it must *avoid excessive govern-ment entanglement with religion*.

Under the "accommodationist" approach, the Court must draw some very fine lines in determining what the establishment clause forbids and permits. In 1984, for example, the Court split 5 to 4 in upholding the display of a crèche during the Christmas season by the city of Pawtucket, Rhode Island. Chief Justice Burger's opin-ion for the majority interpreted the crèche as a secular, not a religious, symbol and found no excessive government entanglement with religion.[8] However, in 1989 the Court reconsidered the circumstances under which local governments may display a crèche and a Jewish menorah. Again splitting 5 to 4, the justices held that the dis-

December forces delicate decisions on local officials and often on courts, who must determine if Christmas trees, crèches, and other seasonal symbols on government property violate the First Amendment. In 1995 the Supreme Court ruled that the Ku Klux Klan had to be allowed to erect a cross on the lawn of the statehouse in Columbus, Ohio, for four days during the Christmas season. But the story did not end there, as anti-Klan protesters knocked the cross over into the mud.

play of a crèche *inside* a city office building violates the establishment clause, but they upheld the display of a menorah next to a Christmas tree *outside* a county office building. The crucial difference, in the view of the majority, was that the display of the crèche inside a public building suggested that the government was endorsing a particular religion, but the exterior display suggested that the government was promoting peace and religious freedom.[9]

The Court thus has taken an ambivalent position. On the one hand, it holds that the First Amendment forbids state-sponsored school prayer, the posting of the Ten Commandments in classrooms, and laws banning the teaching of evolution or requiring instruction in "creation science." On the other hand, it permits the study of the Bible and religion as part of secular education in public schools.[10] And in some circumstances it has approved loans of books and other services from public schools to private religious schools, exemption from real estate taxes on property owned by religious schools, and tax deductions for parents who send their children to parochial schools.

In general, the Court tries to distinguish between legitimate state aid to students, even those in sectarian schools, and illegitimate state sponsorship of religion. In *Witters v. Washington Department of Services for the Blind* (1986), for example, it approved a state's giving higher-education grants to blind students even though one recipient, Larry Witters, chose to study at a Christian college. According to Justice Thurgood Marshall, the state's grant program did not violate the establishment clause because it had a secular purpose, and denying a grant to Witters would violate his right of free exercise under the First Amendment. Likewise, in *Rosenberger v. Rector and Visitors of the University of Virginia* (1995) the Court held that the university could not deny funds used for extracurricular student activities to a Christian student group that published a newspaper. Funding for the newspaper did not violate the establishment clause, Justice Anthony Kennedy held, and the university's denial of funding infringed on the Christian students' First Amendment rights of free speech and religious exercise.[11]

Freedom of Religious Exercise

The free exercise clause embodies the principle of government neutrality with respect to the religious convictions held by individuals and to the ways in which they act on those convictions. Religious *beliefs* may never be prescribed or coerced by the state; for example, people may not be required as a condition of government employment to take an oath that they believe in God. But in some circumstances the government may regulate and even ban *actions* or *practices* that grow out of those beliefs, as well as require actions that offend beliefs.

Basing its decisions on the distinction between beliefs and practices, the Supreme Court has sought to ensure religious freedom by enforcing a **secular regulation rule**. This rule requires that all laws must have a reasonable secular purpose and that they must not discriminate on the basis of religion. But the rule also means that people may not claim exemption from reasonable government regulations on religious grounds, because that would amount to religious favoritism and would violate the establishment rule. In *Reynolds v. United States* (1879), for instance, laws forbidding polygamy were upheld over the objections of Mormons, even though at the time the practice was part of Mormon religious beliefs.[12] Subsequently the Court ruled that states may require schoolchildren to have smallpox vaccinations, denying claims for exemption by Christian Scientists.

The Court has also upheld laws restricting the sale of pamphlets and books in

Although the Supreme Court exempted the Amish from sending their children to school after the eighth grade because of their unique religious and cultural beliefs, in Minnesota v. Hershberger *(1990) it held them responsible for complying with highway safety and other generally applicable laws.*

public buildings, dismissing objections by the Hare Krishna that such sales are part of their religious rituals. It has ruled that the Amish may be required to pay Social Security taxes even though doing so is contrary to their faith. And it has upheld "blue laws" requiring businesses to close on Sundays, despite claims that Sunday closing could cause economic hardship to members of religious groups that observe their Sabbath on Saturday, such as Orthodox Jews. In all these cases the Court has argued that the state, because of its obligation to protect the health and well-being of all citizens, may limit practices that might adversely affect society.

Clearly, such decisions can create tensions, and the Supreme Court has not always sided with the state. It has ruled, for instance, that parents have the right to send their children to religious schools instead of to public schools, as long as those schools are certified by the state. Nor may children in public schools be forced to salute the American flag if doing so violates their religious convictions (as it does those of Jehovah's Witnesses). In *Wisconsin v. Yoder* (1972) the Court even ruled that the Amish may not be required to attend school beyond the eighth grade because such a requirement would contradict their religious beliefs and cultural practices.[13] Because society needs for all children to have a minimum level of education, however, it may require education up through the eighth grade.

Recently the Court has signaled that it may no longer exempt religious minorities from generally applicable laws. In *Employment Division, Department of Human Resources of Oregon v. Smith* (1990), the Court abandoned the so-called balancing test it had previously used in such cases, which weighed the free exercise claims of individuals against the regulatory interests of states in an effort to decide which should be given priority. The case involved two Native Americans' claims that in denying them unemployment compensation, Oregon had violated the free exercise clause.[14] Both had been fired from their jobs because they took peyote (an intoxicating drug produced from mescal cacti) during religious ceremonies of the Native American Church. Although they did not contest their employers' right to fire them, they did argue that because their firing resulted from their religious beliefs and practices, the Court's prior rulings forbade the state from denying them unemployment compensation. But the Court abandoned these precedents and rejected their claims. This decision was so controversial, however, that a wide range of religious groups

ANIMAL SACRIFICE

As the American population has grown increasingly diverse in culture and religion in recent years, courts have had to grapple with new issues arising out of the First Amendment's provision that "Congress shall make no law . . . prohibiting the free exercise [of religion]." At issue in *Church of Lukumi Babalu Aye v. City of Hialeah* (1993), for example, was the constitutionality of a city ordinance prohibiting animal sacrifice in religious ceremonies. Attorneys for the church claimed that the ordinance violated the First Amendment by effectively barring the practice of Santeria. Practiced in the Caribbean and in parts of the United States by Cuban refugees, Santeria involves the sacrifice of animals at birth, marriage, and death rites, as well as in ceremonies to cure the sick and to initiate new members. An estimated 50,000 to 60,000 followers of Santeria live in southern Florida.

In challenging the ordinance, the attorneys argued that because the state of Florida does not bar the killing of animals, Hialeah was discriminating against a religious minority. After all, Florida allows hunting, fishing, and trapping; medical research that results in the death of animals; the sale of lobsters to be boiled alive; and the practice of feeding live rats to pet snakes. In this case the Supreme Court held that states and localities, while permitting other forms of killing of animals, may not then ban sacrifices or ritual killings. Such laws, the Court ruled, lack a compelling state interest and abridge the freedom of religion.[1]

[1]*Church of the Lukumi Babalu Aye v. City of Hialeah*, 508 U.S. 502 (1993).

A follower of Santeria—a mixture of African ritual, Voodoo, and Catholicism—with a ram about to be sacrificed as part of a Santeria service in Miami Beach. In 1992, the Supreme Court ruled that states and localities may not prohibit the killing of animals as part of religious rites.

---

persuaded Congress to override it with the Religious Freedom Restoration Act of 1993. That law reestablished the earlier standard that government may not burden the free exercise of religion unless it has a "compelling interest" and adopts the "least restrictive means" of advancing that interest.

In these and other cases (see the Constitutional Conflict box above), the Court has avoided trying to define religion. The First Amendment does not protect only traditional or orthodox religions; rather, it guarantees the right of each person to define his or her own religious beliefs. And that is the greatest guarantee of religious freedom. For as Justice Robert H. Jackson so eloquently put it, "If there is any fixed

star in our constitutional constellation it is that no official, high or petty, can prescribe what shall be orthodox in politics, nationalism, or religion, or other matters of
opinion, or force citizens to confess by word or act their faith therein."[15]

FREEDOM OF SPEECH AND PRESS

The freedom of speech and press is often called the "preferred freedom" because it
is integral to the politics of a constitutional democracy. Campaigns, elections, and
government accountability to the people would have little value without free and
uncensored exchanges of opinion. In Justice William J. Brennan's words, the First
Amendment registers "a profound national commitment to the principle that debate
on public issues should be uninhibited, robust, and wide-open, and that it may well
include vehement, caustic, and sometimes unpleasantly sharp attacks on government
and public officials."[16]

In fact, however, the broad protection accorded freedom of speech and press
today is a product of Supreme Court rulings in only the past forty years. Prior to
Gitlow v. New York (1925)[17] the First Amendment did not apply to the states, and censorship of unpopular and subversive ideas was common. Before the Civil War, aboli-
tionist literature was confiscated and burned by authorities in both the North and
the South. Thereafter, many states passed laws forbidding obscene and indecent publications, a category that was interpreted to include such now classic works as James
Joyce's *Ulysses*, Henry Miller's *Tropic of Cancer*, and Theodore Dreiser's *An
American Tragedy*. Beginning in the late nineteenth century, fears of the spread of
subversive ideas and doctrines—anarchism, socialism, communism—led to a rash of
prosecutions during World War I and again during World War II.

The prevailing view of the First Amendment throughout the nineteenth century
was that it incorporated freedoms inherited under the English common law. In
this view the Amendment required only that there be *no prior restraint* on
publications—in other words, censorship *before* publication was prohibited.
Although that remains an important guarantee, there was no protection against *subsequent punishment*; books could be banned and newspapers closed. Moreover,
under English law, individuals could be prosecuted for **seditious libel**—that is, for
defaming or criticizing the government or its officials.

Most of the founders' generation accepted this view of freedom of speech and
press. Indeed, only a few years after the Bill of Rights was adopted the Federalist
Congress passed the Sedition Act of 1798, making it a crime to "utter false, scandalous
and malicious" statements about the government. It did so in order to silence its
Jeffersonian critics. But when prosecutions were brought under the act, there was a
violent public reaction. After his election in 1800, President Jefferson pardoned those
who had been convicted under the act, and it expired in 1801.

James Madison, the author of the First Amendment, insisted that it embodied
greater protection than the mere requirement of no prior restraint. But not until after
World War I did the Supreme Court begin to articulate the constitutional principles
and rules that ensure freedom of speech and press today.

Protected Speech

The First Amendment guarantee of free speech and press is not self-interpreting. The
Court must give it meaning by developing tests or standards that define the scope of
protected speech and press. The **clear and present danger test**, perhaps the
Court's best-known test in this area, was formulated by Justice Oliver Wendell

Holmes in *Schenck v. United States* (1919). In that case the Court upheld the conviction of Charles T. Schenck under the Espionage Act of 1917 for urging resistance to the draft and distributing antidraft leaflets during World War I. Schenck's antidraft advocacy at a time of war constituted, in the Court's view, "a clear and present danger" to the country. In Justice Oliver Wendell Holmes's familiar words:

> The character of every act depends upon the circumstances in which it was done. . . . The most stringent protection of free speech would not protect a man in falsely shouting fire in a theater and causing a panic. . . . The question in every case is whether the words used are used in such circumstances and are of such a nature as to create a clear and present danger that they will bring about the substantive evils that Congress has a right to prevent. It is a question of proximity and degree.[18]

Despite the Court's ruling against Schenck, the clear and present danger test was formulated as a broad measure to protect individuals against prosecution for unpopular ideas. Majorities may be tempted to suppress minority views, but "the theory of our Constitution," Holmes contended, is that government has no power to say what is true or false. Each individual has the right to express his or her own beliefs.

In the 1920s, however, the Court was unwilling to go along with Holmes's position affording protection for unpopular speech. Instead, it relied on the common law "bad tendency" doctrine. Under this doctrine the test used by the Court was whether speech tends to corrupt public morals, incite crime, and disturb the public peace. In 1925, when upholding the conviction of Benjamin Gitlow under New York's criminal anarchy statute (Gitlow had published a book calling for a Russian-type revolution in New York), the Court maintained that as long as the law against it was reasonable, **subversive speech** could be punished.

Once the World War I hysteria over subversive political speech subsided, however, the Court greatly expanded the protection of free speech, acknowledging it as a "preferred freedom." Basically, this meant that the Court gave special scrutiny to laws limiting freedom of speech and took on the task of ensuring the rights of those who, in Justice Hugo Black's words, "are helpless, weak, outnumbered, or . . . are nonconformist victims of prejudice and public excitement."

In the aftermath of World War II, the perceived threat of international communism ushered in the cold war and led to further censorship of views that were considered subversive. The Court again cut back on the protection accorded free speech; it upheld the Alien Registration Act of 1940 (the Smith Act), the first federal legislation restraining political speech since the ill-fated Sedition Act of 1798. This ruling came in the case of *Dennis v. United States* (1951), in which the Court upheld the convictions of eleven leaders of the American Communist party for advocating the overthrow of government, even though they had not done anything illegal other than teach and advocate communism. In this decision a majority of the justices reinterpreted the clear and present danger test. The question in every case, stated Chief Justice Fred Vinson, was always "whether the gravity of the 'evil,' discounted by its improbability, justifies such invasion of free speech as is necessary to avoid the danger."[19] Vinson left no doubt that the threat of *international* political events warranted the convictions under the Smith Act.

The two dissenters in the *Dennis* ruling, Justices William O. Douglas and Hugo L. Black, vehemently protested the Court's recasting of the clear and present danger test into a test that upheld the suppression of speech. Douglas pointed out that the convictions were for the *mere advocacy* of communist doctrines; there was no evidence that the Communist party was in fact conspiring to overthrow the govern-

Justice Hugo Black

ment violently, and books advocating communism could be found in public libraries. For his part, Justice Black championed an "absolutist interpretation" of the First Amendment. He summarized his position as follows:

> I read "no law abridging" to mean *no law abridging*. The First Amendment, which is the supreme law of the land, has thus fixed its own value on freedom of speech and press by putting these freedoms wholly "beyond the reach" of *federal* power to abridge. . . . Consequently, I do not believe that any federal agencies, including Congress and this Court, have power or authority to subordinate speech and press to what they think are "more important interests."[20]

Although Justice Black was unable to persuade his fellow justices to accept this absolutist position, the Court gradually expanded First Amendment protections in a series of rulings beginning in the late 1950s.[21] By 1969, in the case of *Brandenburg v. Ohio*, it took the position that only the advocacy of immediate, violent, and illegal action may be subject to criminal prosecution. The *Brandenburg* decision illustrates the premium now placed on First Amendment values and how far the Court is willing to go in protecting freedom of speech.

Charles Brandenburg, the leader of a Ku Klux Klan group, had been arrested, tried, and convicted under Ohio's criminal syndicalism statute for "advocate[ing] . . . the duty, necessity, or propriety of crime, sabotage, violence, or unlawful methods of terrorism as a means of accomplishing industrial or political reform" and for "voluntarily assembl[ing] with any society, group, or assemblage or persons formed to teach or advocate the doctrines of criminal syndicalism." Standing before a burning cross, Brandenburg had addressed a small rally of hooded men, some of whom carried firearms, declaring (among other things) that if the president, Congress, and the Supreme Court continued "to suppress the white, Caucasian race, it's possible that there might have to be revengenance taken."[22] Brandenburg unsuccessfully appealed his conviction to a state appellate court and then to the state supreme court, which denied review. When he appealed to the United States Supreme Court, however, the justices unanimously voted to overturn his conviction and to strike down Ohio's law as an unconstitutional violation of the First Amendment.

Speech that has **social redeeming value**, because it addresses matters of public concern, is now fully protected. The government may neither exercise prior restraint on nor subsequently punish individuals for speech or publications that touch on political, scientific, literary, or artistic matters. Even speech that might threaten national security is protected. In 1971, at the height of the Vietnam War, the Court rejected the Nixon administration's attempt to prevent the *New York Times* and the *Washington Post* from publishing excerpts from the *Pentagon Papers*, a 47-volume documentary history of America's involvement in the war that had been classified as top secret. In this watershed ruling, the Court maintained that the government "carries a heavy burden" of justifying its attempts at censorship.[23]

Determining what speech has social redeeming value, however, is often politically controversial. The interests of communities in discouraging certain types of speech conflict with those of individuals who claim that the First Amendment protects their right of self-expression. In the late 1980s and the 1990s, for example, more than thirty states, as well as numerous localities, colleges, and universities, enacted "hate-crime" and "hate-speech" laws. St. Paul, Minnesota, made it a crime to place on public or private property a burning cross, swastika, or other symbol likely to arouse "anger, alarm, or resentment in others on the basis of race, color, creed, religion, or gender." But the constitutionality of that ordinance was challenged by Robert A. Vicktora, who along with several other white youths burned a cross after midnight on the lawn of the only African-American family in his neighborhood. In *R.A. V. v. City of St. Paul, Minnesota* (1992), the Supreme Court ruled that the ordinance violated the First Amendment because it punished certain kinds of speech on the basis of their content. Writing for the Court, Justice Antonin Scalia observed that "the First Amendment does not permit St. Paul to impose special prohibitions on those speakers who express views on disfavored subjects."[24]

In *Wisconsin v. Mitchell* (1993), however, the Court upheld laws that give defendants longer prison terms if they commit crimes that are determined to have been motivated by racial, religious, or gender bias. In that case, an African American who said "go get that white boy" and then assaulted the individual received a four-year instead of a two-year prison sentence under Wisconsin's prison-enhancement statute for so-called hate crimes.[25]

Unprotected Speech

The broad protection afforded the freedoms of speech and press is not absolute. In *Chaplinsky v. New Hampshire* (1942), which upheld the conviction of Chaplinsky for calling a police officer "a goddamned racketeer," Justice Frank Murphy explained the Court's rationale for defining some categories of speech as unprotected and outside the scope of the First Amendment:

> There are certain well-defined and narrowly limited classes of speech, the prevention and punishment of which has never been thought to raise any Constitutional problem. These include the lewd and the obscene, the profane, the libelous, and the insulting or "fighting" words—those which by their very utterance inflict injury or tend to incite an immediate breach of the peace. It has been well observed that such utterances are no essential part of any exposition of ideas, and are of such slight social value as a step to truth that any benefit that may be derived from them is clearly outweighed by the social interest in order and morality.[26]

Historically, there have been only four categories of unprotected speech: obscenity, libel and slander, fighting words, and commercial speech. Yet defining standards for each category has proven extraordinarily vexing.

Obscenity For centuries, **obscenity** has been subject to government censorship, but defining what is obscene has been a persistent problem. Prior to *Roth v. United States* (1957), federal courts permitted state and local governments to ban even major literary works under an English common law rule set forth in 1868. Known as the *Hicklin* rule, it permitted the banning of books on the basis of isolated passages that might tend to "deprave and corrupt those whose minds are open to such immoral influences." This was a very broad standard and, as Justice Felix Frankfurter put it, would eliminate virtually all literature "except that only fit for children."

In the *Roth* decision the Court held that obscenity is "not within the area of constitutionally protected speech," but it also rejected the *Hicklin* rule for determining what is obscene. Justice Brennan, in his opinion for the Court in *Roth*, announced a new test: "whether to the average person, applying contemporary community standards, the dominant theme of the material taken as a whole appeals to prurient interests."[27] Basically, the *Roth* test meant that only hard-core pornography was outside the scope of First Amendment protection. But the justices remained unable to agree on how to define obscenity. That problem led Justice Potter Stewart to confess that although he could not define it, "I know it when I see it."

The *Roth* ruling ignited considerable political controversy because it appeared to open the floodgates for purveyors of pornographic materials. Presidential commissions studied the problem, and state and local law enforcement agencies sought tougher standards. Under pressure to overturn *Roth*, the more conservative Court of the 1970s redefined the basis for determining whether material is obscene. In *Miller v. California* (1973), the Court stipulated three tests for judging allegedly obscene material: (1) whether the average person, applying local community standards, would find that a work, taken as a whole, appeals to a prurient interest; (2) whether the work depicts in a patently offensive way sexual conduct specifically defined as "obscene" in law; and (3) whether the work, taken as a whole, lacks "serious literary, artistic, political, or scientific value."[28]

Although many law enforcement agencies thought the *Miller* decision gave them broader power to prosecute purveyors of obscenity, the Court subsequently reaffirmed that only hard-core pornography lies outside the First Amendment's protection. The use or public display of "four-letter words" may not be banned.[29] However, students in public schools may be disciplined for the use of indecent as well as obscene language.[30] Furthermore, states may forbid the sale of pornographic materials to minors (those under the age of 18), completely ban pornography depicting minors,[31] and prohibit sexually explicit live entertainment and films in bars.[32] In addition, municipalities may use exclusionary zoning to regulate the location of adult bookstores and theaters.[33]

The Federal Communications Commission (FCC), which regulates the broadcast media, also has the power to prohibit indecent and obscene language on the airwaves. The FCC was given this power in 1934 because radio, television, and other electronic media were considered a scarce public resource that should be licensed and regulated in the public interest. In 1978, in a case initiated by the FCC, the Court ruled that comedian George Carlin's monologue "Filthy Words" (about seven words that could not be said on radio or television) could be banned because children and unsuspecting listeners otherwise could not be completely protected from "patently offensive, indecent material presented over the airwaves."[34] However, eleven years later the Court struck down a congressional statute authorizing the FCC to ban telephone "dial-a-porn" services and held that only hard-core obscene messages may be so outlawed. A major unsettled controversy revolves around access to indecent and obscene materials available on the Internet.

Long synonymous with sin, the Times Square neighborhood of New York City may soon be sanitized. Wanting to "clean up" Times Square and stop the spread of sex-oriented businesses into residential areas, Mayor Rudolph Giuliani pushed through zoning changes to break up concentrations of such establishments and confine them to isolated commercial districts. Similar restrictions elsewhere have been upheld by the Supreme Court.

Libel and slander In legal terms, **libel** is false statement of fact about a person or defamation of his or her character by print or by visual portrayal on television. **Slander** is such a statement or defamation by speech. Both damage an individual's reputation by holding the person up to contempt, ridicule, and scorn, and both may be subject to civil lawsuits.

Under the Sedition Act of 1798, seditious libel was a crime that carried a sentence of up to five years' imprisonment. But as noted earlier, there was widespread public outcry over the prosecutions under the act, and in *New York Times Co. v. Sullivan* (1964) the Court expressly noted that criminal libel is inconsistent with the values of the First Amendment.[35] Today all libel cases are civil actions—that is, suits for compensatory and punitive damages (monetary awards). Compensatory damages are based on an individual's actual financial losses as a result of being libeled, such as loss of employment or income. Punitive damages aim to punish wrongdoers by making them pay for their victims' mental suffering and for the damage done to their victims' reputations. Because awards for punitive damages are based on a jury's subjective view of the injury, they may be very large. For example, a former beauty contest winner who sued *Penthouse* magazine received $1.5 million in compensatory damages and $12.5 million in punitive damages.

The landmark ruling in *New York Times Co. v. Sullivan* established the standards for determining when public officials and public figures may recover damages. Such individuals must prove "actual malice"; they must show that statements about them were made with knowledge of their falsity or with reckless disregard of their truth or falsity. This standard makes it exceedingly difficult for public figures to win libel awards. By contrast, private individuals, those who neither hold public office nor have wide reputations and have not been thrust into the limelight, may recover damages on a lesser standard. They simply must show that the statements were false and that the publisher was negligent in its reporting.

The Court's standards make it relatively easy for private individuals to bring libel suits to trial, and when juries rule in their favor, they tend to make large awards. But in about two-thirds of the cases the awards are later reduced or overturned by appellate courts. Some critics contend that the Supreme Court has made it too difficult for public officials and public figures to win libel cases. Publishers, on the other hand, claim that the law of libel has a chilling effect on freedom of the press. They frequently face high court costs in defending their publications, and reporters and editors may be challenged to justify their editorial decisions.

The Court, nevertheless, has tried to maintain a line that will ensure robust exchanges of opinion, sharp public criticism of those in the public eye, and freedom of the press. In a 1988 decision it reaffirmed the principles established in the *Sullivan* case, holding that they apply to satires and cartoons as well as to stories and reporting. The Court's decision in *Hustler Magazine v. Falwell* reversed a lower court's $200,000 award to the Reverend Jerry Falwell for "emotional distress" caused by a parody portraying him as having committed incest with his mother in an outhouse.[36] It did so because the characterization was not presented as factual truth and thus actual malice could not be shown.

Fighting words So-called **fighting words** (described by Justice Murphy in the *Chaplinsky* case, page 137) have been held to be unprotected speech because they are likely to incite violence or lead to a breach of the peace and public order. In recent years, however, the Court has reversed every conviction for controversial or "fighting" words. So it is uncertain that any prosecution under this category of unprotected speech would be upheld.

Commercial speech   Advertising or **commercial speech** was for many years deemed to be outside the scope of First Amendment protection, ostensibly because it does not bear on political matters. In addition, governments have important interests in regulating some kinds of advertising. The Court still upholds regulations aimed at ensuring truth in advertising, but it also recognizes that in some cases the public's interests in obtaining information may justify extending First Amendment protection to commercial speech. Accordingly, it has overturned state and local laws forbidding the advertising of the price of prescription drugs, routine legal services, the availability of abortion services, and some other kinds of professional services. In addition, the Court has ruled that corporations' advertisements, newsletters, and mailings are protected under the First Amendment.[37]

Symbolic Speech, Speech-plus-Conduct, and Freedom of Association

Besides extending First Amendment protection to virtually all forms of *pure speech*, the Supreme Court has ruled that certain other kinds of expression are protected by the First Amendment because they involve the communication of ideas. These include symbolic speech, speech-plus-conduct, and the freedom of association.

Conduct that involves the communication of political ideas, often as a protest, is known as **symbolic speech**. The Court has held, for example, that wearing a black armband in school,[38] displaying a red flag,[39] and turning the American flag into a

In the 1970s the Supreme Court overturned state and local laws that had long prohibited the advertising of legal and other professional services.

peace symbol in order to protest the Vietnam War[40] are protected forms of expression under the First Amendment.

Speech-plus-conduct also involves the communication of ideas, but the ideas are conveyed through marching, picketing, and holding sit-ins on sidewalks and streets and in other public areas. Protection for these kinds of expression is rooted not only in the First Amendment's guarantee of free speech but also in its provision for freedom of association and "the right of the people peaceably to assemble, and to petition the government for a redress of grievances."

In public places such as streets and parks, individuals have the right to engage in political activities subject only to *reasonable time, place*, and *manner* restrictions. Thus cities may limit the hours that parks may be used or the times that sound trucks may travel the city streets. In 1989, for example, the Court upheld a New York City ordinance requiring the use of the city's sound system and city engineer for all concerts held in Central Park. Time, place, and manner restrictions must apply equally and not discriminate against particular kinds of political expression.

The protection accorded to the **freedom of association** is broader than that accorded to the freedom to organize rallies and peaceful protests. It also includes the right to join political parties and religious, economic, and other kinds of organizations. As a result, the disclosure of an organization's membership list cannot be compelled by election officials[41] or by legislative investigating committees.[42] Nor may individuals be dismissed from employment because of their political associations[43] or be required to disclose their associations in order to gain admission to the bar.[44]

However, the Court has ruled that the freedom of association may be limited in

In February 1960 a group of African-American students from North Carolina A&T College, who had been refused service at a lunch counter reserved for white customers, staged a sit-down protest at Woolworth's in Greensboro, North Carolina. These three stayed seated throughout the day. Civil rights activists often used such protests, and the litigation they sparked, to desegregate public accommodations.

certain ways when there are overriding societal interests in doing so. It has upheld the Hatch Act of 1940, which forbids federal employees from actively campaigning in elections and assuming leadership positions in political parties.[45] Such federal and state laws have been found to be a reasonable way of ensuring a neutral civil service. The Court has also held that the right of association of members of an all-male club was outweighed by a state law prohibiting gender discrimination in public and private organizations.

By protecting the rights of individuals and minorities to express their political views through marches, pickets, and other kinds of demonstrations, the Court has challenged the views of the majority and invited more political controversy. Yet in defending the right to express unpopular views, it ensures the freedom of public discussion and debate that is essential to democratic self-governance and a free society.

THE QUEST FOR EQUALITY

The concept of equality and equal freedoms for all citizens is mentioned in neither the Constitution nor the Bill of Rights. Nevertheless, it is the bedrock of a political system based on the consent of the governed. The Declaration of Independence was emphatic about equality of political freedoms: "We hold these truths to be self-evident: That all men are created equal; that they are endowed by their Creator with certain unalienable Rights." But not until 1868, with the ratification of the Fourteenth Amendment, did the Constitution expressly provide that no person shall be deprived of "the equal protection of the laws." Achieving that equality in practice has proven to be extraordinarily difficult. There remains no greater struggle in American politics than the struggle to guarantee all citizens their basic civil rights without discrimination due to their race, religion, national origin, or sex. That struggle reflects the impact of social movements and the increasing diversity of American society on the politics of government (see Figure 5-1).

In 1870, Mrs. D. S. Sonnesberger became the first woman voter in Jackson County, Wyoming. Women found it easier to win suffrage in the West, partly because the more voters a territory had, the sooner it could become a state.

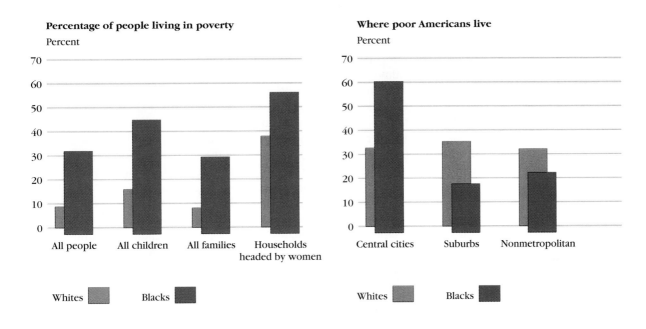

Percentage of people living in poverty
Percent
70
60
50
40
30
20
10
0
All people
All children
All families
Households headed by women
Whites
Blacks
Where poor Americans live
Percent
70
60
50
40
30
20
10
0
Central cities
Suburbs
Nonmetropolitan
Whites
Blacks
Black workers' earnings
Dollars in earnings (per $1000 for whites)
1000
900
800
700
600
500
400
300
200
100
0
1939
1949
1959
1969
1979
1989
Black men
Black women
Positions held by women
Percent
70
60
50
40
30
20
10
0
Professional
Managerial
Technical
Blue collar
Military officers
Enlisted personnel
Among white workers
Among black workers

Figure 5-1

Some measures of comparative socioeconomic status in the United States.

Source: Andrew Hacker, *Two Nations: Black and White, Separate, Hostile, Unequal* (New York: Scribner's, 1992), 100, 101, 105. Copyright © 1992 Andrew Hacker. Reprinted with permission of Scribner, a Division of Simon & Schuster.

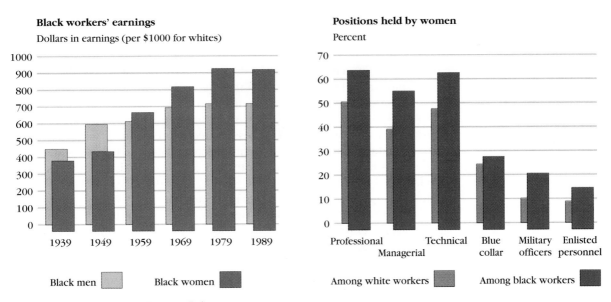

The Extension of Voting Rights

The narrow victory of General Ulysses S. Grant in the 1868 presidential election convinced the Republican party that to maintain its control of Congress it needed the votes of African Americans. So it proposed the Fifteenth Amendment (ratified in 1870), which forbade the abridgment of any citizen's right to vote "on account of race, color, or previous condition of servitude."

Although the amendment did not mention discrimination on the basis of gender, some women hoped that they might win **suffrage**, or the right to vote, in federal elections by claiming that this right was guaranteed by the Fourteenth Amendment's clause forbidding the abridgment of any citizen's "privileges and immunities." Susan B. Anthony gave this as her defense when she was prosecuted for casting a ballot in a federal election in 1872, but the argument was rejected by a federal court. In 1875 the Supreme Court dashed the hopes of a woman who sought to vote in a Missouri election when it held that "the Constitution of the United States does not confer the right of suffrage upon anyone."[46] By 1913, only nine states allowed women to vote.

Political pressure in support of women's suffrage mounted during World War I as large numbers of women entered the work force and contributed to the war effort. In 1918 President Woodrow Wilson endorsed women's suffrage, and during the next year Congress submitted to the states a constitutional amendment granting women the right to vote. The Nineteenth Amendment was ratified in 1920.

Although African Americans were guaranteed the right to vote by the Fourteenth and Fifteenth Amendments and many were elected to office in the South during Reconstruction, white-dominated state governments and party organizations soon erected barriers such as poll taxes and literacy tests. Poll taxes required a payment in order to vote and thereby discouraged the poor from voting. Likewise, literacy tests were used in the South to discourage African Americans from voting by requiring them to first answer questions—often obscure questions—about American law and politics. By the turn of the century, African Americans were effectively disenfranchised.

In 1937 the Supreme Court ruled that poll taxes did not violate the Fourteenth and Fifteenth Amendments, a decision that sparked a campaign to get the states and Congress to abolish poll taxes. The campaign had considerable success in the states; by 1960, only Alabama, Arkansas, Mississippi, Texas, and Virginia retained poll taxes. Congress finally banned poll taxes in federal elections with the Twenty-Fourth Amendment, ratified in 1964, and two years later the Court decided that the Fourteenth Amendment's equal protection clause forbids poll taxes in state elections.

Among the goals of the civil rights movement of the 1950s and 1960s was the elimination of all barriers to voting rights for African Americans (see the box on page 145 for a chronology of the civil rights movement in those decades). Rev. Martin Luther King Jr. launched voter registration drives in the South, where there was widespread and often violent resistance. Congress passed civil rights acts in 1957 and 1960, but they proved ineffective in ending the discriminatory practices that discouraged African Americans from voting. Not until the Voting Rights Act of 1965 was suffrage for African Americans effectively guaranteed.

The Voting Rights Act bans the use of literacy tests or tests for educational achievement and understanding, as well as requirements that voters prove "good moral character" or present certificates verifying their qualifications, in any state or locality where less than 50 percent of the citizens of voting age were registered on November 1, 1964, or voted in an election that November. Moreover, it authorizes the U.S. Civil Service Commission to appoint federal examiners to register voters

Chronology of the Civil Rights Movement, 1954–1968

May 1954
The Supreme Court hands down its decision in *Brown v. Board of Education*, declaring racial segregation in public schools unconstitutional. This is a major victory for the National Association for the Advancement of Colored People (NAACP), which has been challenging the constitutionality of racial segregation in the courts for almost twenty years.

December 1955
African Americans boycott the bus company in Montgomery, Alabama, to protest racial segregation. Dr. Martin Luther King Jr. is a leader of this boycott and subsequent protests.

September 1957
President Dwight D. Eisenhower sends National Guard troops to Little Rock, Arkansas, to enforce the desegregation of Central High School.

February 1960
At a lunch counter in Greensboro, North Carolina, African-American college students stage the first sit-in to protest racial segregation in public accommodations.

May 1961
African Americans begin "freedom rides" by attempting to sit in the sections of interstate buses reserved for whites. There is widespread violence, buses are burned, and United States marshals must restore order in some parts of the South.

September 1962
The effort to enroll James Meredith as the first African American to attend the University of Mississippi leads to violence.

April 1963
Police turn attack dogs and fire hoses against African Americans who attempt to hold a public demonstration in Birmingham, Alabama.

June 1963
Medgar Evers, state chairman of the NAACP in Mississippi, is murdered in Jackson.

August 1963
Civil rights leaders organize a major march in Washington to push for passage of civil rights legislation as committees of the Senate and House are debating what eventually will emerge as the Civil Rights Act of 1964.

June 1964
Three civil rights workers are murdered in Neshoba County, Mississippi.

July 1964
The first of many ghetto riots by African Americans starts in Harlem, New York City. During the summer, riots erupt in other cities around the country.

January 1965
King starts the first of a series of protest marches in Selma, Alabama. In February and March, marchers are attacked by police.

August 1965
Inner-city riots erupt in Los Angeles and Chicago.

June 1966
James Meredith is shot during a protest march in Mississippi.

Summers, 1966 and 1967
Ghetto riots erupt in Chicago, Cleveland, New York, and more than sixty-five other cities.

April 1968
King is murdered in Memphis, Tennessee, setting off another wave of riots.

where the attorney general deems it necessary for the enforcement of the Fifteenth Amendment.

Because it limits the powers of the states to determine the qualifications for voting, the Voting Rights Act has remained controversial. However, the Supreme Court affirmed its constitutionality in 1966, and the act has been extended several times since then. It was last extended by Congress in 1982 and is not scheduled to lapse until 2007. The major provisions of voting and other civil rights legislation are shown in the box on page 147.

Redistricting and Equal Representation

Besides striking down poll taxes and other barriers to exercising voting rights, the Supreme Court has become involved in issues of **redistricting**, that is, redrawing the boundaries of legislative districts. Traditionally, the courts avoided districting issues on the grounds that they involve "political questions," which must be resolved by legislative bodies. However, in a landmark decision (*Baker v. Carr*, 1962)[47] the Court ruled that such controversies contain issues of fairness and justice that open them to judicial review as well.

The issues of fairness and justice to which the Court referred pertain to the relationship between population and representation. In a democracy all voters must be equal; one person's vote cannot count for more than another's. Yet representation is decidedly unequal when members of the House of Representatives or members of state legislatures represent districts with different numbers of residents, a condition that was prevalent in many states after the Civil War. In most cases, rural districts enjoyed representation equal to or even greater than urban areas, even though their populations were smaller. For example, the Court's ruling in *Baker v. Carr* involved

(Left) *The march from Selma, Alabama, to the state capitol in Montgomery on March 7, 1965, marked a turning point in the civil rights movement. At issue were discriminatory voter registration practices in the South. After marchers had twice been beaten back by mounted police and three civil rights workers had been murdered, Dr. Martin Luther King Jr. led about 25,000 on the final march.* (Right) *The events in Selma helped Democratic president Lyndon B. Johnson push the Voting Rights Act of 1965 through Congress, and King was among those invited to watch him sign the act into law.*

MAJOR PROVISIONS OF CIVIL RIGHTS LEGISLATION

1957
The Civil Rights Commission is created, and trying to prevent a person from voting in federal elections is made a crime.

1960
The Department of Justice is authorized to appoint federal referees to investigate allegations of the denial of African Americans' voting rights, and using interstate commerce to threaten or carry out a bombing is made a criminal offense.

1964
Legislation bars certain devices and literacy tests that were used to deny voting rights to African Americans; forbids discrimination on the basis of race, color, religion, or national origin in public accommodations such as restaurants, motels, lunch counters, gas stations, theaters, stadiums, and boardinghouses with more than five rooms for rent; authorizes the Department of Justice to bring lawsuits to compel the desegregation of public schools; forbids discrimination in employment on the grounds of race, color, religion, gender, or national origin in all businesses employing fifteen workers or more; authorizes the cutting of federal funds from any program that discriminates on the basis of race, color, religion, or national origin.

1965
Legislation authorizes the appointment of voting examiners to supervise federal, state, and local elections in areas where discrimination is determined to have been practiced or where less than half of the voting-age residents were registered to vote on November 1, 1964, or voted in the 1964 presidential election.

1968
Legislation bans discrimination in the sale and rental of most housing, except by private owners who sell or rent their homes without the use of a real estate agent.

a challenge to the districting of Tennessee's state legislature. Despite growing urbanization and population changes over a sixty-year period, Tennessee had not changed the boundaries of its legislative districts since 1901. As a result, the population ratio between urban and rural districts in the state was more than 19 to 1. Charles Baker and several other citizens claimed that urban residents were being denied the equal protection of the law under the Fourteenth Amendment and asked the Court to order state officials to hold either an at-large election or an election in which legislators would be selected from constituencies with equal populations in accordance with the 1960 federal census.

When the Supreme Court granted review in *Baker v. Carr*, it faced two central issues: (1) whether the malapportionment of a state legislature is a "political question" and therefore "nonjusticiable," or not subject to judicial review, and (2) the merits of Baker's claim that individuals have a right to equal votes and equal representation. With potentially broad political consequences, the case divided the Court. Four justices believed that the case presented a nonjusticiable political question, four thought that the issue was justiciable and were prepared to address the merits of the case, and the remaining justice considered the issue justiciable but did not want to address the merits of the case. As a consequence, the Court's majority opinion was limited to the jurisdictional question: Was districting an issue that courts could decide? The Court's answer was yes.

In two subsequent cases in the 1960s, the Court did rule on the merits of this issue, applying the principle of **one person, one vote** to congressional districts and to state legislative districts. This principle requires that the weight of a vote cast in each election district (and usually the total population in each district) must be roughly equal. In the 1970s and 1980s the Court extended the rule to virtually all local elections as well.

The Court's rulings meant that district lines for congressional, state, and local elections must be redrawn every ten years, after the national census, to ensure equal representation. This redistricting requirement has made the American electoral process at all levels more open, accessible, and democratic. It has also made redistricting a partisan issue that reemerges every ten years.

When congressional district lines were redrawn following the 1990 census, racial and ethnic issues also came to the fore. Citing a provision of the 1982 Voting Rights Act and several Supreme Court decisions, the Justice Departments of both the Bush and the Clinton administrations pressed state legislatures to create more so-called minority-majority voting districts, in which a majority of the voters were African Americans or Hispanics. As a result, the number of minorities elected to the House of Representatives more than doubled. Because African Americans and Hispanics tend to vote heavily Democratic, however, their heavy concentration in certain districts made other, "whiter" districts more likely to elect Republicans and thus provided an overall Republican advantage. White Democrats in some southern states challenged the constitutionality of such "racial gerrymandering," and in *Miller v. Johnson* (1995) a bare majority of the Court agreed that racial gerrymandering violates the Fourteenth Amendment's equal protection clause and ruled that race may not be the sole or primary factor in congressional redistricting.[48]

Ending Racial Discrimination

Despite the Fourteenth and Fifteenth Amendments (as well as the Thirteenth, which prohibited slavery), new barriers to racial equality emerged in the late nineteenth century in the form of so-called **Jim Crow laws**, which separated the races in public transportation and accommodations and discriminated against African Americans in other ways. Moreover, segregation persisted in housing, education, and employment and was permitted by the Supreme Court. In 1883 the Court struck down as unconstitutional the Civil Rights Act of 1875, which had forbidden discrimination in public accommodations such as hotels, theaters, and railroad carriages. According to the Court, Congress had exceeded its power under the Fourteenth Amendment by prohibiting *private* individuals from discriminating; the amendment, in the Court's view, forbade only *state* discrimination.

Subsequently, in the case of *Plessy v. Ferguson* (1896), the Court affirmed the **separate but equal doctrine** by upholding Louisiana's law requiring separate but equal facilities for the races in railroad cars.[49] Although it struck down laws specifically denying or limiting the right of nonwhites to acquire property, it upheld until 1948 the enforcement of **restrictive covenants**, that is, contracts in which property owners agree not to sell or lease their property to members of certain racial or religious groups.

Beginning in the 1930s, individuals and organizations such as the National Association for the Advancement of Colored People (NAACP) began filing lawsuits to force the end of racial segregation in housing, education, and employment. Like the other branches of government, the Court was slow to respond to these demands. Not until 1954 did it step firmly into the racial discrimination controversy with its landmark decision in *Brown v. Board of Education of Topeka* (1954).[50] In that case

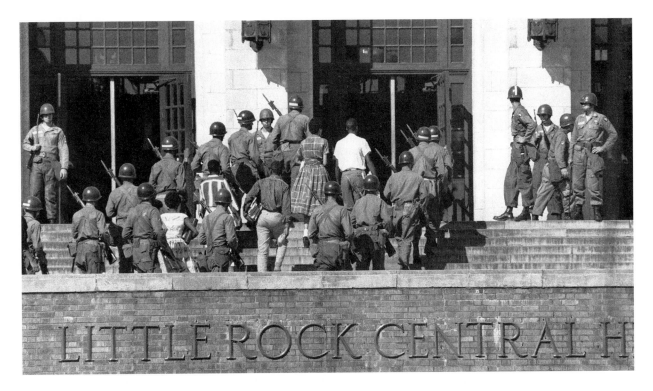

In 1957, when Arkansas governor Orval Faubus defied a court order to integrate the state's public schools and refused to guarantee any student's safety, Republican president Dwight D. Eisenhower reluctantly sent troops to Little Rock Central High School to ensure order.

the Court finally rejected the separate but equal doctrine, holding that racially segregated public schools violated the equal protection clause of the Fourteenth Amendment.

Even in *Brown*, the Court was reluctant to press too hard too quickly for desegregation; the justices knew how much political controversy their ruling would stir. It was another year before the Court handed down its remedial decree stating that school boards must proceed with "all deliberate speed to desegregate public schools at the earliest practical date."[51] The decree of "all deliberate speed" was a compromise between requiring precise deadlines for school desegregation and simply allowing states and localities to comply with *Brown's* mandate at their own discretion.

In fact, the *Brown* decision and its enforcement decree did meet with massive resistance, in the form of widespread evasion, occasional violence, and even a year-long shutdown of an entire school system. The vagueness of the phrase "with all deliberate speed" actually served to justify noncompliance; progress toward achieving integrated schools was deliberately slow and uneven. In addition, President Dwight Eisenhower refused to use the power of the executive branch to ensure compliance until he was forced to send the National Guard to quell resistance to the desegregation of Central High School in Little Rock, Arkansas, in 1957. Eisenhower sent the troops not because he favored the Court's ruling but because it was the law of the land. In the decade following the *Brown* decision, less than 2 percent of all African-American students in the South attended desegregated schools, and there was virtually no effort to achieve desegregation in the North and West.

The major advance in ending racial segregation, not only in education but in housing and employment, came after the passage of the Civil Rights Act of 1964. Title VI of this act forbids schools from discriminating "on the ground of race, color, or national origin in any program or activity receiving federal assistance." Besides authorizing the withholding of federal funds from schools that discriminate, the Department of Justice was authorized to enforce the act and the mandate of *Brown*. Title II of the act forbids discrimination in public accommodations—inns, hotels, restaurants, theaters, and the like—and Title VII makes it illegal for employers in any business or industry with fifteen or more employees to discriminate on the basis of race, color, national origin, religion, or sex. Subsequent amendments extended all parts of the act to forbid discrimination based on gender and age, as well as discrimination against those with disabilities and against Vietnam veterans.

By the late 1960s the Supreme Court also made it clear that it would no longer abide delays in complying with *Brown's* mandate. In proclaiming that "continued operation of racially segregated schools under the standard of 'all deliberate speed' was no longer permissible," the Court stated that school districts had to "terminate immediately dual school systems based on race and operate only unitary school systems."[52]

During the 1970s, 1980s, and early 1990s, the issue of bringing an end to segregated schools was replaced by the issue of achieving integrated schools. This was a particularly troublesome question in the North and West, where schools were segregated as a result of housing patterns (**de facto segregation**), not because of

On September 13, 1974, helmeted police lined the streets of South Boston as school buses, escorted by motorcycle police, carried African-American students to South Boston High School. Many communities that were under court orders to achieve integrated schools in the 1970s experienced widespread boycotts and sporadic violence. In the late 1990s, about five hundred public school districts remain under federal judicial supervision as they try to achieve and maintain integrated schools.

laws and official policies (**de jure segregation**). One device for overcoming de facto segregation is busing children to schools they would not ordinarily attend. Although busing can be a means of achieving integrated schools, it violates the tradition of neighborhood schools, creates lengthy travel for some students, and sometimes increases racial tensions within schools.

The Court's position on busing is clear: it has upheld the power of federal judges to order busing *within* school districts but not *between* them as a remedy for segregated schools. In *Milliken v. Bradley* (1974), for instance, the Court held that lower federal courts could not order the busing of schoolchildren to and from Detroit's overwhelmingly black inner-city school district and fifty-one predominantly white suburban school districts.[53] Given the racial composition of many school districts, this position has not enabled proponents of integrated public schools to achieve their goal. However, it may have contributed to the movement of white families from the cities to suburban neighborhoods to escape busing.

More than forty years after the landmark ruling in *Brown v. Board of Education*, approximately 500 school desegregation cases remain in the lower federal courts around the country. Most involve the issue of whether school systems have eliminated vestiges of past discrimination.

In *Freeman v. Pitts* (1992) the Supreme Court held that lower federal courts may withdraw from their supervision of desegregation efforts once school districts have complied with desegregation orders, even if their schools remain racially imbalanced due to housing patterns and other socioeconomic factors.[54] At the same time, in *United States v. Fordice* (1992) the Court held that Mississippi's admission and funding policies for its state colleges and universities perpetuated racial segregation and had failed to achieve a system of racially integrated higher education.[55] In *Missouri v. Jenkins* (1995), however, the Court reiterated its view that lower federal courts should disengage from desegregation efforts.[56] In that case, the Court held that a federal judge had gone too far in ordering the school district in Kansas City, Missouri, whose enrollment is over 90 percent African-American, to create magnet schools with special educational opportunities in order to attract white students in surrounding suburbs. Together, these decisions recognized both the importance of equal opportunities in education and the limitations of what courts and local school boards can do in areas that remain or are becoming racially segregated due to housing patterns and population changes.

Nonracial Discrimination

All legislation and government policy, by its very nature, discriminates because it confers burdens or benefits on some groups and not on others. For example, most states require that individuals be at least 16 years old and pass a driving test before they can operate a motor vehicle. From the standpoint of civil rights, the question is whether laws and regulations are reasonable and do not unfairly discriminate against particular groups.

When considering challenges to law and policy under the Fourteenth Amendment's equal protection clause, therefore, the Supreme Court must decide whether the discrimination is invidious and unconstitutional. During the mid-1950s and the 1960s, the Court evolved a two-tier approach to applying the equal protection clause. When reviewing challenges to legislation that deals solely with economic matters, it uses a **minimal scrutiny test**, meaning that it simply looks to see whether the legislation in question has a rational basis. Using this test, the Court has

RUTH BADER GINSBURG: JUSTICE FOR WOMEN

Appointed to the Supreme Court in 1993 by President Bill Clinton and confirmed by a 96-3 vote in the Senate, Justice Ruth Bader Ginsburg was the second female, sixth Jewish, and 107th member of the Court. When announcing her nomination, Clinton called her "the Thurgood Marshall of the women's movement," and "neither liberal nor conservative" but instead a moderate and well-respected jurist who would be a "force for consensus building" on the Court.

Prior to her appointment to the Court, Justice Ginsburg served for thirteen years on the Court of Appeals for the District of Columbia Circuit. Before that she taught at the law schools of Columbia and Rutgers universities and served as general counsel for the American Civil Liberties Union.

In the 1970s Ginsburg was at the forefront of the women's movement in law. She not only wrote frequently on women's rights, but she argued six gender discrimination cases before the Supreme Court and won five of them. During one case, Justice William Rehnquist asked her why women were not content now that Susan B. Anthony's face was on a coin. Ginsburg passed up the bait, but what she almost replied, she said later, was "No, your Honor, tokens won't do."

Justice Ginsburg has been one of the most articulate advocates of the view that the equal protection clause of the Fourteenth Amendment forbids gender-based discrimination. As she told Senator Arlen Specter during her confirmation hearings,

The framers of the Fourteenth Amendment meant no change . . . at all in the status of women before the law, but in 1920, when women achieved the vote, they became full citizens. And you have to read this document as a whole— changed, as Thurgood Marshall said, over the years by constitutional amendment and by judicial construction. . . . I remain an advocate of the equal rights amendment, I will tell you, for this reason: because I have a daughter and a granddaughter, and I would like the legislature of this country and of all the states to stand up and say, "We know what that history was in the nineteenth century, and we want to make a clarion call that women and men are equal before the law, just as every modern human rights document in the world does since 1970." I'd like to see that statement made just that way in the Constitution.

In 1996, Ginsburg articulated these feminist principles again in her majority opinion for the Court in

Bill Clinton and Ruth Bader Ginsburg walk along the colonnades at the White House as they head for a news conference where the president nominated Ginsburg to the Supreme Court.

United States v. Virginia, which held that as a state college the Virginia Military Institute could not exclude women from admission. In her decisions Ginsburg has generally sided with the Court's moderate to liberal wing, which also includes Justices John Paul Stevens, David Souter, and Stephen Breyer.

Born in Brooklyn, New York, in 1933, Justice Ginsburg received her B.A. from Cornell University and attended Harvard and Columbia law schools, where she received her LL.B. and J.D. degrees. She then clerked for a federal district court judge. But even after her clerkship year in 1961, no law firm in New York would hire her—because she was a woman and a mother. As a result Ginsburg spent several years doing legal research before assuming a teaching position at Rutgers.

SOURCE: Quotations from David Margolick, "Trial by Adversity Shapes Jurist's Outlook," *New York Times*, June 25, 1993, A19; and "Excerpts from Senate Hearing," *New York Times*, July 22, 1993, A20.

not struck down any federal or state economic legislation under the equal protection clause since 1937.

When legislation is based on a "suspect classification" or denies individuals their "fundamental rights," the Court uses a **strict scrutiny test** for determining its constitutionality. The strict scrutiny test puts the burden of proof on the state, which must demonstrate a "compelling interest" to justify the law or policy in question. Suspect classifications include race, nationality, and alien status. Because those characteristics are immutable—individuals cannot choose or change their race or nationality—laws that impose burdens or deny benefits on the basis of them invariably fail to pass the Court's strict scrutiny test.

In the past two decades the Court has confronted an increasingly broad range of claims of nonracial discrimination, including claims of discrimination based on gender, age, and wealth. In response to these new challenges the Court has created a third, intermediate test—the **strict rationality test**, also known as the **exacting scrutiny test**. It has done so primarily because a majority of the justices have refused to consider gender a "suspect classification" under the Fourteenth Amendment, even though it is an immutable characteristic.

Under the strict rationality test, legislation must in a reasonable way further some legitimate government policy. Such a standard is necessarily more subjective or flexible than strict scrutiny. For example, gender-based discrimination has been approved by the Court in cases challenging an all-male military draft,[57] the enforcement of statutory rape laws against males but not females,[58] the sale of 3.2% beer to males (but not females) under the age of 21,[59] the assignment of female guards in prisons,[60] and the denial of health benefits to women who miss work because of pregnancy leaves.[61] On the other hand, the Court has struck down laws discriminating against women in cases involving the denial of benefits for dependents of female (but not male) military personnel,[62] and the denial of seniority status to women who take pregnancy leaves from work.[63] Moreover, in 1986 the Court unanimously agreed that female employees could sue employers for sexual harassment under the Civil Rights Act.[64] Finally, in 1991 the Court overturned a fetal protection policy of Johnson Controls, a Milwaukee-based manufacturer of automobile batteries. Under Johnson Controls' policy, fertile female employees were barred from certain jobs that exposed them to high levels of lead, which can pose severe health risks to developing fetuses. The Court struck down that discriminatory policy as a violation of the rights of women under the Civil Rights Act of 1964 and the Pregnancy Discrimination Act of 1978.[65]

The case study on page 154 discusses the battle over whether women should be admitted to Virginia Military Institute, a struggle that led to a landmark Supreme Court decision in 1996.[66]

Age discrimination in employment is another area in which the Court has encountered claims of invidious discrimination. Responding to pressure brought by groups of senior citizens and to demographic changes in the American population, Congress prohibited age discrimination under the Age Discrimination in Employment Act of 1967, which was amended in 1975 and 1978. The Supreme Court has upheld several claims under this legislation. However, the Court has found no constitutional objection to a state law requiring police officers to retire at the age of 50. Nor did the Court find any constitutional violation on the basis of age when, in *Gregory v. Ashcroft* (1991), it upheld a Missouri law requiring state judges to retire at 70.[67]

In other areas of nonracial discrimination—where benefits for illegitimate children or welfare benefits, for example, are at issue—the Court also applies its exacting scrutiny test, taking each case on its own merits. Basically, the Court tries to bal-

WOMEN AND VMI

At least until recently, the Virginia Military Institute (VMI) was perhaps best known for a former faculty member, General Stonewall Jackson, who led his students into battle in the Civil War. By 1989, when it celebrated the 150th anniversary of its founding as the first state military college in the nation, the school that supplied the Confederate army with some of its youngest soldiers had long been racially integrated. But VMI remained all-male, employing a rigorous "adversative" military type of training system that aims at graduating "citizen soldiers, educated and honorable men" suited for leadership in both civilian and military life.

In 1990, however, the U.S. Department of Justice sued VMI and the state of Virginia on behalf of a female high school student who wanted to attend VMI. The Department argued that gender-based discrimination in state colleges, like racial discrimination in public schools, violates the Fourteenth Amendment's guarantee of equal protection. A federal district court disagreed. It found that VMI had a unique history and set of traditions that the admission of women would destroy. In addition, the court concluded that VMI's "adversative" model of education was "simply inappropriate for the vast majority of women." But a federal court of appeals overruled that decision and ordered Virginia either to admit women into VMI or to create a separate and comparable institution providing females with a military type of education.

The state responded by designing and funding the Virginia Women's Institute for Leadership at the all-female Mary Baldwin College, a private college. A task force headed by the dean of Mary Baldwin determined that the mission of the institute would be to have its female students pursue the same goals as those pursued at VMI: education, military training, mental and physical discipline, character development, and leadership skills. However, the task force also concluded that these goals could be better achieved by designing a program that deemphasized VMI's harsh "adversative" methods.

When the Mary Baldwin plan was announced, it was immediately challenged in court by the Department of Justice and a number of women's organizations, which argued that the program was simply not comparable to VMI's in terms of training and educational methods. Furthermore, they pointed out, it denied women the advantages of VMI's network of thousands of loyal and influential alumni. A district court nevertheless upheld the plan, and a federal appellate court agreed. The Department of Justice appealed to the U.S. Supreme Court.

In June 1996, the Supreme Court handed down its decision in *United States v. Virginia*. By a 7–1 vote, with Justice Clarence Thomas not participating because his son was attending VMI, the Court held that the creation of a separate program was not an adequate remedy for the constitutional violation of VMI's discriminating against women. In the majority opinion, Justice Ruth Bader Ginsburg observed that the Mary Baldwin program was not equal to that of VMI in terms of rigor, funding, or prestige. Her opinion also emphasized Virginia's and other states' historical discrimination against women. In a long, angry dissent, Justice Antonin Scalia countered that

ance the interests of government against the claims of individuals to equal protection of the law, and the results are sometimes unpredictable.

Affirmative Action and Reverse Discrimination

Affirmative action in education and employment has been especially controversial. Designed to help women and members of minority groups advance in areas in which they have historically been discriminated against, **affirmative action** originated with Lyndon Johnson's Democratic administration in 1964–1965. Affirmative action

Stonewall Jackson's statue looks down on VMI cadets being put through their paces. In response to a lawsuit seeking to end its all-male admissions policy, the school argued unsuccessfully that its harsh "adversative" program was inappropriate for women.

Court had no business invalidating VMI's long all-male tradition. He also warned that single-sex private colleges might now face legal challenges because most of them receive substantial funding, along with tax breaks, from state and federal governments.

Deciding against an effort to make VMI a private college, in September its governing board voted 9–8 to admit women beginning in 1997—but said they must meet exactly the same standards as male cadets, including crew cuts. VMI's South Carolina counterpart, The Citadel, where a woman had enrolled briefly several years earlier after a court battle, had announced two days after the Supreme Court ruling that it would begin admitting women.

Discussion Questions

1. To what extent is sex discrimination comparable to racial discrimination?
2. Should single-sex state colleges be permitted, as Scalia maintains, or not, as Ginsburg ruled?
3. What do you think of government funding and tax breaks for single-sex private colleges?

programs give special consideration to women and minorities in, for example, admission to college and promotion in the workplace. Consequently, these programs have been attacked for practicing **reverse discrimination**—that is, for penalizing whites and males in violation of their rights under the Fourteenth Amendment's equal protection clause. Critics argue that what affirmative action does is move beyond the principle of **equality of opportunity** in education and employment in an effort to ensure **equality of result**.

During the presidencies of Richard Nixon, Gerald Ford, and Jimmy Carter, affirmative action programs were promoted and defended by their administrations. Under Ronald Reagan and George Bush, on the other hand, the Department of Justice

AFFIRMATIVE ACTION/NEGATIVE REACTION

Following the Republican takeover of both houses of Congress in the 1994 elections, Republican strategists promised to make affirmative action a "wedge issue" dividing the electorate in the 1996 presidential election. In their campaign speeches, leading contenders for the party's presidential nomination declared their opposition to giving any preference to women or minorities in college admissions or in hiring and promotions in business. Some of these politicians, such as Kansas senator Robert Dole and California governor Pete Wilson, were once supporters of affirmative action programs. Others, including Texas senator Phil Gramm and journalist Patrick Buchanan, had long opposed affirmative action as a denial of individual rights in favor of "group rights." They portrayed all affirmative action programs as "quotas" and as "reverse discrimination," contending that they necessarily elevate less qualified women and minorities above more qualified white males. In response to growing political pressure, President Bill Clinton was forced to qualify his own defense of such policies.

Historically, affirmative action programs were developed with the support of both Democratic and Republican presidents. Following the enactment of the Civil Rights Act of 1964, which prohibited discrimination in employment and education, Democratic president Lyndon Johnson signed an executive order requiring federal contractors to "take affirmative action to ensure that applicants are employed, and that employees are treated during employment, without regard to race, color, religion, sex or national origin." In 1966 a federal court ordered the first race-conscious hiring program, intended to recruit African Americans into a New Orleans union that was all-white and had for decades excluded minorities. Under Johnson's successor, Republican president Richard Nixon, the Department of Labor adopted the so-called "Philadelphia plan" requiring federal contractors to analyze their work force in terms of gender and race and to set goals and timetables to end underrepresentation of women and minorities.

The affirmative action programs that began under Johnson and Nixon were expanded by Republican president Gerald Ford and Democratic president Jimmy Carter. Today there are over 160 federal programs, involving tens of billions of dollars in government contracts and affecting a quarter of all businesses. Similar programs have been enacted in all fifty states and by thousands of local governments. In the 1970s, the University of California adopted the first affirmative action program for college admissions.

The 1970s, however, also saw the beginning of organized opposition to affirmative action, a movement that grew throughout the 1980s. During the administrations of Republican presidents Ronald Reagan and George Bush, the Department of Justice opposed affirmative action and, in cases like *City of Richmond v. J. A. Croson*, rather successfully urged lower courts and the Supreme Court to limit those programs. In 1995 California governor Pete Wilson spearheaded a drive culminating in a bitter fight that ended the University of California's historic program. The same year the Supreme Court ruled, in *Adarand Constructors, Inc. v. Pena*, that such programs must be narrowly tailored to remedy past discrimination. In 1996, a federal appellate court struck down the minorities admission policy for the University of Texas Law School. And in the 1996 election California voters approved a state constitutional amendment designed to ban almost all affirmative action programs in employment, education, and contracting by state and local governments.

In the face of the Supreme Court's ruling in *Adarand* and Republican threats to capitalize on the issue in the 1996 presidential election, President Clinton in 1995 undertook a review of all federal affirmative action programs. After a five-month study he announced a "mend it, don't end it" policy and issued an executive order directing all departments to review their programs in light of four tests. "Any program must be eliminated or reformed," according to Clinton's executive order, if it creates a quota, creates preferences for unqualified individuals, creates reverse discrimination, or continues after its equal opportunity purposes have been achieved. In addition, the Clinton administration's Department of Justice issued guidelines for agencies to reexamine affirmative action programs in light of the *Adarand* ruling.

Students at the University of California at Berkeley demonstrate against the 1995 decision by the university's Board of Regents to end affirmative action in admissions, hiring, and contracting.

The controversy is not likely to go away in the near future. Opponents argue that even if affirmative action programs were once justified, they have outlived their usefulness. Supporters counter that discrimination against women and minorities persists, along with a need for greater diversity in education and employment. For example, they point to studies showing that in the early 1990s no more than 3 percent of the employment discrimination cases brought in federal courts were for reverse discrimination; the vast majority were for discrimination against women and minorities. Moreover, African Americans remain more than twice as likely as whites to be unemployed, and salaries for whites remain higher; in 1993, according to the Bureau of Labor Statistics, the median weekly paycheck of whites was $478, compared with $370 for African Americans and $355 for Hispanics. And in spite of affirmative action programs, the percentage of minorities in construction unions, for instance, has declined over the last decade.

For these reasons even some Republican governors, such as William Weld of Massachusetts and George Voinovich of Ohio, favor continuing their states' affirmative action programs. General Colin Powell and other prominent black Republicans have also publicly defended affirmative action. Although the party's 1996 platform called for an end to such programs, after Dole won the presidential nomination he largely avoided raising the issue during the general election campaign, except during a late (and unsuccessful) effort to save his chances in California.

The issue is complex in a number of ways. In addition to the arguments already mentioned, for example, supporters of affirmative action often question how accurately standardized tests can predict an employee's or student's performance. For their part, some opponents contend that because policies are perceived as giving preference to minorities, they inevitably stigmatize individuals as inferior in their own minds as well as in those of others. Some people have suggested basing affirmative action in college admissions on economic status rather than race. Although this criterion is more difficult to assess, it might satisfy many opponents of race-based plans without significantly changing the pool of people eligible for affirmative action.

Further complicating the political debate are the varying ways in which pollsters pose questions about affirmative action. An overwhelming majority of the public opposes giving "preferences to unqualified individuals." At the same time, a majority favors programs that "fight discrimination," "promote equal opportunity," and "treat everyone fairly." A smaller percentage supports giving "special treatment" to women and minorities and quotas are overwhelmingly opposed. In short, as Alexis de Tocqueville observed in the nineteenth century, Americans remain very individualistic: they want individuals to be treated equally and fairly, and they also respect individual merit.

lenged the constitutionality of such programs. Subsequently, Bill Clinton ordered that federally sponsored policies be reviewed in an effort to narrow their scope and end those that had achieved their goals. Regardless of which party has controlled the executive branch, however, affirmative action programs adopted at the state and local levels have been bitterly contested in the courts.

Defenders of affirmative action argue that because women and members of minority groups were previously denied equal opportunities in education and employment, they frequently do not have the education, training, or seniority necessary for some jobs and promotions, and judging them by the criteria used to judge white males will perpetuate their disadvantage. Critics, however, claim that affirmative action programs go too far in the pursuit of greater equality. To support this position, critics often rely on the words of Justice John Marshall Harlan in his dissenting opinion in *Plessy v. Ferguson* (1896): "Our Constitution is color-blind and neither knows nor tolerates class among citizens."[68]

When confronted with challenges to affirmative action programs, the Supreme Court initially was as sharply divided as the rest of the country. One of the most important cases was *Regents of the University of California v. Bakke* (1978).[69] Alan Bakke, a white who had been denied admission to the medical school at the University of California at Davis, contended that his application had been rejected because the school set aside 16 out of 100 admissions for African Americans, Chicanos, Asians, and Native Americans—groups that had previously been underrepresented in the student body. He claimed that this policy violated his rights under the Civil Rights Act and the Fourteenth Amendment, because some of the minority students admitted under the school's affirmative action program had grade-point averages and test scores lower than his.

The Court agreed in part with Bakke. The majority opinion stated that *quota systems* (programs that set aside a precise number of openings for minorities) like the one at the University of California are unconstitutional. At the same time, however, the Court upheld the constitutionality of affirmative action programs that consider race as one among many factors in student admissions.

Affirmative action programs in employment have proven even more divisive. In 1979 the Court ruled that employers and labor unions may agree to adopt private affirmative action programs despite the objections of white members of the union. In the following year it upheld Congress's power to set aside 10 percent of federal funds for public works projects to be used to pay for supplies and services provided by minority-owned businesses. The Court's decisions offered little clear guidance for policy makers, however, since in every case the justices split 5 to 4 or 6 to 3, with those in the majority often disagreeing on why they should uphold or strike down particular programs. Still, in three out of four rulings during the 1980s the Court upheld the constitutionality of affirmative action programs, basing its decisions on its exacting scrutiny test. Programs aimed at promoting African Americans and other minorities and women over white employees with more seniority have proven particularly troublesome. The Court was unable to establish a principle for judging the constitutionality of such programs. From 1984 to 1987 it upheld some programs and struck down others.

By 1989, however, changes in the composition of the Court resulted in a conservative majority inclined to oppose most affirmative action programs. In *City of Richmond v. J. A. Croson* (1989) the Court struck down a program in Richmond, Virginia, that required nonminority building contractors to subcontract 30 percent of all city-awarded projects to minority-owned businesses.[70] This set-aside quota was as much a way to help black construction companies penetrate the local building industry as it was a remedy for past discrimination. Half of Richmond's population was black, but minority-owned firms had won less than 0.6 percent of the $25 million awarded in city contracts in the preceding five years.

In announcing the Court's ruling, Justice Sandra Day O'Connor noted that Richmond's affirmative action program was not narrowly targeted to the city's African Americans, because minority-owned businesses from all over the country were eligible to bid on projects. The ruling held that state and local governments may no longer adopt affirmative action programs unless they are designed specifically as remedies for past discrimination in denying opportunities for African Americans and other minorities.

J.A. Croson was a major break with prior rulings because the Court abandoned its use of the exacting scrutiny test for upholding affirmative action programs and signaled that henceforth the tougher strict scrutiny test would be employed. Under this standard, states and localities must have a "compelling interest" in adopting any program that discriminates on the basis of race, regardless of whether that discrimination is for the purpose of conferring benefits, rather than burdens, on racial minorities and women. This decision threw into question the constitutionality of hundreds of state and local affirmative action programs and has forced city governments and state legislatures to redraft their laws in anticipation of further challenges.

One year after *J. A. Croson*, however, a bare majority of the justices upheld affirmative action programs adopted by the *federal* government and approved by Congress. In *Metro Broadcasting, Inc. v. Federal Communications Commission* (1990), the Court upheld the FCC's policy of giving preferences to minority owners of broadcast companies when awarding licenses to operate television stations.[71] The FCC had adopted its affirmative action policy to promote the public's interests in broadcast diversity, and the Court ruled that Congress, on the basis of its power as the national legislature, could authorize the FCC to do so. More generally, the Court held that Congress may enact affirmative action programs on the basis of its constituional powers to "provide for the general welfare" and to enforce the equal protection guarantee of the Fourteenth Amendment.

The decision in *Metro Broadcasting*, however, was overturned in *Adarand Constructors, Inc. v. Pena* (1995). Writing for the Court, Justice O'Connor held that the strict scrutiny test applies to affirmative action programs adopted by the federal government, no less than to states and localities as in *J.A. Croson*. In *Adarand*, Justice O'Connor found that a set-aside program for minority-owned subcontractors in federal highway construction violated the equal protection clause of the Fourteenth Amendment.[72]

Along with the ruling in *J.A. Croson*, in the late 1980s, the Court handed down several other decisions that made it much more difficult for women and minorities to prove discrimination in the workplace and, at the same time, made it easier for white males to attack affirmative action programs in the courts. Those rulings sparked a bitter debate in Congress and between Congress and the administration of George Bush over whether and how to override the Court. After a two-year battle, Congress passed and President Bush signed into law the Civil Rights Act of 1991, which overturned twelve Supreme Court rulings.

The major provision of the act returned to employers who are sued for discrimination the burden of proving that their hiring practices are "job-related to the position in question and consistent with business necessity."[73] The act also expanded the coverage of the 1866 Civil Rights Act to bar discrimination in all phases of employment, not just in hiring practices;[74] and extended protection against discrimination based on race, religion, gender, and national origin to employees of United States companies who are stationed abroad.[75] In addition, Congress reversed four other rulings that had made it more difficult for African Americans and women to prove discrimination in employment[76] and had made it easier for whites to challenge court-ordered affirmative action programs.[77]

The Civil Rights Act of 1991 also, for the first time, allows women, members of religious groups, and people with disabilities, along with racial minorities, to sue for monetary damages for intentional discrimination. However, the Democratic majority in Congress had to compromise with their Republican colleagues and President Bush to win passage of the law. For example, it put a cap of $300,000 on the amount of damages that women and members of nonracial minority groups may win in discrimination suits, whereas there is no limit on awards that members of racial and ethnic minority groups may receive.

As the controversy over affirmative action programs shows, political struggles over civil rights and liberties usually involve more than a conflict between an individual and the state. They often reflect deeper divisions in society and competing interests in how to balance liberty and equality that must be reconciled over time.

SUMMARY

Individual freedom and the quest for equality often collide and become the focus of political struggles and competing political movements, which in turn put pressure on government. The Supreme Court plays an important role in responding to political controversies over issues of freedom and equality. In drawing lines that define those freedoms, the Court has historically sought to ensure that those freedoms are enjoyed equally by all citizens.

The First Amendment provides a dual protection for religious freedom. The *establishment clause* forbids the creation of a national religion, and the *free exercise clause* guarantees that individuals may worship as they please. In 1947 the Supreme Court took the view that the establishment clause embodies "a high wall of separation" between church and state; it ruled that the government must maintain strict neutrality on matters involving religion. Critics claimed that this neutrality amounted to state hostility toward religion, and in recent years the Court has moved toward an "accommodationist" approach. This approach involves a three-part test. If a law or program is to avoid violating the establishment clause, (1) it must have a secular legislative purpose, (2) its primary effect must neither advance nor inhibit religion, and (3) it must avoid excessive government entanglement with religion.

Under the free exercise clause, religious beliefs may not be prescribed or coerced by the state, but in some circumstances the government may regulate or ban religious practices. The Court's *secular regulation rule* requires that all laws have a reasonable secular purpose and not discriminate on the basis of religion. But individuals may not claim exemption from permissible government regulations on religious grounds.

The First Amendment also guarantees freedom of speech and press. Before 1925, however, the First Amendment was viewed as requiring only that there be no prior restraint on publications; individuals had no protection against subsequent punishment for what they said or wrote. In particular, they could be prosecuted for *seditious libel*—defaming or criticizing the government. After World War I, the Supreme Court began expanding the protection accorded freedom of speech and press. Under the Court's *clear and present danger test*, speech is not protected if it creates a danger of serious consequences. At first this doctrine was applied to any *subversive speech* (such as advocating the overthrow of government), but gradually the Court modified the doctrine so that only the advocacy of immediate, violent, and illegal action may be subject to criminal prosecution. Speech that touches on political matters or has *social redeeming value* because it addresses matters of public concern is now fully protected.

Historically, there have been four categories of unprotected speech: obscenity, libel and slander, fighting words, and commercial speech. Identifying *obscenity* has been a persistent problem for the Supreme Court. In *Miller v. California* (1973) it stipulated three tests for judging allegedly obscene material: (1) whether the average person, applying local community standards, would find that a work, taken as a whole, appeals to a prurient interest; (2) whether the work depicts in a patently offensive way sexual conduct specifically defined as "obscene" in law; and (3) whether the work, taken as a whole, lacks "serious literary, artistic, political, or scientific value."

Libel is false statement of fact about a person or defamation of character by print or by visual portrayal on television. *Slander* is false statement or defamation of character by speech. In the past, *fighting words* were unprotected speech because they are likely to lead to a breach of the peace and public order, but in recent years the Court has struck down all convictions on these grounds. *Commercial speech* (advertising) was until recently deemed to be outside the scope of First Amendment protection, but the Court has overturned laws forbidding advertising of certain kinds of professional services.

The Court has ruled that certain other kinds of expression are protected by the First Amendment. These include *symbolic speech*, the communication of political ideas through flags, armbands, and other symbols; *speech-plus-conduct*, in which ideas are conveyed through marching, picketing, and the like; and *freedom of association*, which includes the right to join political parties and religious, economic, and other kinds of organizations.

With the ratification of the Fourteenth Amendment in 1868, the Constitution expressly provided that no person shall be deprived of "the equal protection of the laws." However, it has been extremely difficult to achieve that equality in practice. *Suffrage* was extended to African Americans with the ratification of the Fifteenth Amendment in 1870, but devices such as poll taxes and literacy tests were adopted to prevent them from voting. Most women did not gain the right to vote until the ratification of the Nineteenth Amendment in 1920. In the middle decades of the twentieth century, most formal obstacles to voting by African Americans were removed, but not until the enactment of the Voting Rights Act of 1965 was suffrage for African Americans effectively guaranteed.

Another area involving the equal protection of the laws is *redistricting*, that is, redrawing the boundaries of legislative districts. Under the principle of *one person, one vote*, the weight of votes cast in different election districts must be roughly equal; therefore, district lines must be redrawn every ten years on the basis of census results.

Other barriers to equal protection of the laws take the form of racial and nonracial discrimination. Racial segregation by *Jim Crow laws* became commonplace in the decades following the Civil War. In *Plessy v. Ferguson* (1896) the Supreme Court upheld the *separate but equal doctrine*, and until 1948 it upheld the enforcement of *restrictive covenants*. The separate but equal doctrine was overturned in *Brown v. Board of Education of Topeka* (1954), but not until passage of the Civil Rights Act of 1964 was there a sustainable effort by the federal Justice Department to effectively enforce desegregation.

During the 1970s, 1980s, and early 1990s, efforts were made to overcome school segregation caused by housing patterns (*de facto segregation*), not by law (*de jure segregation*). Efforts to integrate the public schools through such devices as busing have had limited success.

When considering issues of discrimination, the Court uses a *minimal scrutiny test* to review legislation dealing with economic matters, but it uses a *strict scrutiny test* to review matters involving individuals' fundamental rights. When considering claims of nonracial discrimination, it uses a *strict rationality*, or *exacting scrutiny, test*. Under this test, legislation that discriminates on the basis of gender, age, or wealth is unconstitutional unless it furthers some legitimate government policy in a reasonable way.

Affirmative action is a policy designed to help women and minority groups advance in areas in which they have historically been discriminated against. The goal of affirmative action programs is to move beyond *equality of opportunity* to *equality of result*. Critics claim that such programs are a form of *reverse discrimination*. During the 1980s the Supreme Court tended to uphold the constitutionality of affirmative action programs. In the early 1990s, however, it handed down several decisions that made it harder for women and minorities to prove discrimination in the workplace and easier for white males to attack affirmative action programs in the courts. The Civil Rights Act of 1991 overturned some of those rulings and required employers to prove that their hiring practices are not discriminatory.

establishment clause
free exercise clause
secular regulation rule
seditious libel
clear and present danger
    test
subversive speech
social redeeming value
obscenity
libel
slander

fighting words
commercial speech
symbolic speech
speech-plus-conduct
freedom of association
suffrage
redistricting
one person, one vote
Jim Crow laws
separate but equal doctrine
restrictive covenants

de facto segregation
de jure segregation
minimal scrutiny test
strict scrutiny test
strict rationality, or exacting
    scrutiny, test
affirmative action
reverse discrimination
equality of opportunity
equality of result

RESOURCES

SCHOLARLY STUDIES

Edsall, Thomas, and Mary Edsall. *Chain Reaction: The Impact of Race, Rights, and Taxes on American Politics.* New York: Norton, 1992. A provocative study of how the civil rights era has affected American politics in the 1990s.

Graham, Hugh Davis. *The Civil Rights Era: Origins and Development of National Policy, 1960–1972.* New York: Oxford University Press, 1992. A fine historical analysis of the civil rights movement and its impact on American politics.

Levy, Leonard W. *Emergence of a Free Press.* New York: Oxford University Press, 1985. A rich account of freedom of speech and press during the founding period.

Lewis, Anthony. *Make No Law: The Sullivan Case and the First Amendment.* New York: Random House, 1992. An insightful analysis of the Supreme Court's landmark ruling on libel and subsequent decisions in the area.

Peltason, Jack W. *Fifty-Eight Lonely Men: Southern Federal Judges and School Desegregation.* Urbana: University of Illinois Press, 1971. A study of the efforts of federal district court judges to enforce the ruling in *Brown v. Board of Education* in southern states.

LEISURE READING

Friendly, Fred W. *Minnesota Rag: The Dramatic Story of the Landmark Supreme Court Case That Gave New Meaning to Freedom of the Press.* New York: Random House, 1982. A thorough account of *Near v. Minnesota* (1931), the ruling that prohibited prior restraints on newspapers.

Kluger, Richard. *Simple Justice.* New York: Knopf, 1976. A definitive and readable story of the Court's school desegregation decision in *Brown v. Board of Education* (1954).

Rembar, Charles. *The End of Obscenity.* New York: HarperCollins, 1968. The story of the struggle to persuade the Supreme Court to broaden First Amendment protection, told from the perspective of a lawyer involved in several of the leading obscenity cases in the 1960s.

PRIMARY SOURCES

O'Brien, David M. *Constitutional Law and Politics: Civil Rights and Civil Liberties.* 3d ed. New York: Norton, 1997. A comprehensive collection of the Supreme Court's most important rulings on civil rights and liberties. Also contains introductory essays on the history and politics of the Court's interpretive decisions regarding the Bill of Rights and the Fourteenth Amendment.

Schwartz, Bernard, ed. *Statutory History of the United States: Civil Rights.* 2 vols. New York: Chelsea House, 1970. A useful and comprehensive collection of the federal laws and other congressional materials and documents related to civil rights and liberties.

ORGANIZATION

U.S. Civil Rights Commission, 1121 Vermont Avenue, N.W., Washington, DC 20425; (202) 376-8312. A government agency authorized by Congress to study and recommend changes in laws bearing on civil rights and liberties.

Political Socialization and Participation

PREVIEW

■ Political socialization: changes over the life cycle; party affiliation; major political events; agents of political socialization; attitudes and behavior

■ Political participation: ways of participating; who participates; political participation and public policy

Bill Clinton's first brush with national politics came in July 1963, when he was an Arkansas delegate to Boys Nation, the annual civics celebration for high school juniors sponsored by the American Legion. The high point of the week was a trip to the White House, where President John F. Kennedy would briefly address the delegates. David Maraniss, a reporter and Clinton biographer, describes that day:

It got quiet inside the Boys Nation buses as they pulled through the White House gate from the South. . . . Bill Clinton was at the front of the first bus. He wanted a prime spot in the Rose Garden. . . . [After some brief remarks, Kennedy moved to the audience.] . . . As the president walked toward them, the boys surged forward. Clinton was the first to shake his hand. The sixteen-year-old from Hot Springs lost his breath, his face contorted in what he would later call "my arthritis of the face." The Boys Nation photographer was nearby, snapping away.

The next morning, their last in Washington, they returned from a day at the FBI and the Capitol to find a bulletin board . . . cluttered with photographs taken during the week by a Legion photographer. Each picture was numbered so that the boys could order copies. They mobbed the board, writing down their selections. Along with an overwhelming feeling that in Washington he had seen the career he longed for, Bill Clinton brought home a captured moment bonding his joyous present with his imagined future.

A year later, when Clinton went back to Washington to begin college at Georgetown University, he was on something of a political losing streak. He was determined to reverse his political fortunes, and though he was a Southern Baptist at cosmopolitan, Catholic Georgetown, he began immediately to run for freshman class president. Maraniss describes that campaign:

Clinton had lost two elections in a row—to Jack Hanks, Jr., of Texas for the Nationalist party vice-presidential nomination at Boys Nation, and to Carolyn Yeldell for senior class secretary at Hot Springs High. In both cases he had run for offices below his aspirations and therefore had done so halfheartedly. Now he would run as hard as he could. Within a few days of settling in Room 225 he had been off and running for president of the freshman class. [Tom] Campbell helped him distribute leaflets and [Thomas] Caplan advised him on speeches, but Clinton ran his own show. His candidacy was nonideological, and he developed a platform of dry moderation. He called for better communications through a campus government newsletter and referendum powers for the student body. "I believe this is a possible platform," he assured potential voters. "The feasibility of every plank has been carefully examined."

Every voting bloc in the East Campus electorate was carefully examined as well. In surveying the political landscape, Clinton learned that student politicians from Long Island tended to dominate. Another Long Island power play was taking shape, with a slate of freshman candidates that included Glen Pallen of Garden City for president, Judi Baiocchi of Manhasset for secretary, and Paul Maloy of Manhasset for treasurer. Campbell could help Clinton cut into Pallen's Long Island vote. Clinton saw great potential support among the women at the language institute, especially after he talked one of them out of running against him. He mimeographed his platform and signed copies by hand while eating breakfast. And then he set out to meet every voter on the East Campus. John Dagnon across the hall, another non–Long Islander, was running for treasurer against Maloy, and formed an informal alliance with Clinton[,] accompanying him around the dorms at night, going door to door. . . .

On Halloween Eve, Clinton was elected president of the freshman class. He took office with a phalanx of Long Islanders, who were somewhat surprised to find him in their midst. "Bill Clinton[,] who looks and sounds like an amiable farm boy, is the latest to ascend to that position of status supremacy known as freshman class president," the next issue of *The Courier* proclaimed.[1]

The losing streak was over.

Americans learn about and participate in politics in different ways and for different reasons. No one, not even a future president, is born political—at least not in the sense that understanding of the political system and interest in public affairs are genetic traits. Our interest in politics is inspired by our family, our friends, and our life experiences; if and when that interest has been established, we must learn how to function politically.

For most of us, these experiences do not include shaking hands with a president, much less becoming one. For some people, in fact, political interest never develops even to the point of voting. For others, it leads to active kinds of involvement like signing a petition, donating to a candidate, joining a political interest group, or participating in a protest demonstration. And for those like Clinton, it reaches a level that makes them want to actually become part of government—the structure that tries to resolve the conflicting demands that politics produces.

This chapter explores the processes by which Americans become—or do not become—political. It considers how we orient ourselves to the American political culture and political system and then examines how we participate—or why we do not participate—in politics and government. The chapter concludes by describing the constraints we encounter and the choices we make as participants in politics.

POLITICAL SOCIALIZATION

Political socialization is the ongoing process by which individuals acquire the information, beliefs, attitudes, and values that help them comprehend the workings of a political system and orient themselves within it. Through political socialization,

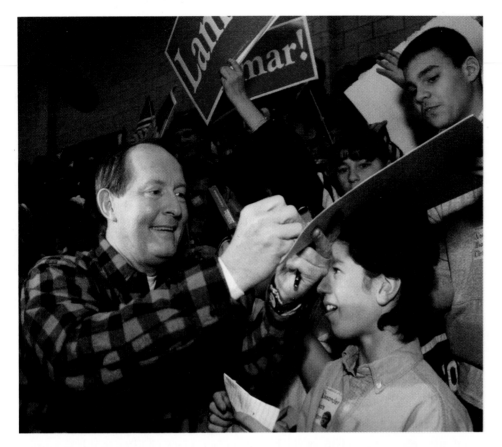

*Clad in his trademark lumberjack plaid shirt, Republican presidential hopeful
Lamar Alexander signs autographs at a New Hampshire junior high school shortly
before the state's 1996 primary. Earlier, he had won a mock election among the
students. As children enter adolescence, they become aware of the conflict inherent
in politics and the need to position themselves politically.*

people learn to be **citizens**, or members of a political society. The study of political
socialization casts light on citizens' feelings and concerns about their government
and the politics of their country; it also reveals how individuals' attitudes and beliefs
affect their participation in the political process. For example, a Native American girl
coming of age on a reservation in New Mexico is likely to perceive the political
world and orient herself to it quite differently than a prep school girl growing up in
Westchester County, a wealthy enclave north of New York City. And both their
"takes" on politics and government probably vary a good deal from that of a boy
from small-town Arkansas in the 1960s.

Studying political participation helps in comprehending broad patterns of behavior within a political system. Just as a chemist would find it essential to identify the
characteristics of molecules before explaining chemical elements, so it is important
to explore the characteristics of American citizens before trying to describe and
explain the politics of American government. Later chapters look at group and mass
political behavior; here the focus is on individuals and the way they become
citizens.

You should be aware, however, that political socialization and political participation are complex topics.[2] Human motives in general are difficult to penetrate and

explain. Furthermore, much of the research on political socialization focuses on children and how they learn about the political universe and develop a sense of their own place within it. But children lack the cognitive and expressive skills necessary to permit sophisticated inquiry into their socialization processes. As a result, research on individual political behavior is still shot through with large areas of uncertainty. Although consensus has emerged on some aspects of how socialization occurs and participation patterns unfold, many issues remain controversial.

Changes over the Life Cycle

Political socialization is an endless process, in which people keep learning as their life experiences accumulate and their circumstances change. The values and skills they acquire early in life may not be adequate for their needs later in life. Thus they refine their attitudes and values throughout their lives in response to the new needs they develop and the new information they acquire.

No one is sure exactly how early political socialization begins, but by the second grade many children already possess some knowledge and ideas about the political system in which they live. At this age, most of them are aware of the existence of a government and are able to identify two important authority figures: the president of the United States and the police officer. They may also be familiar with political symbols such as the flag, the national anthem, and George Washington. Most American children, for example, learn to recite the Pledge of Allegiance before they have any idea what its words mean.

In the preadolescent period, the majority of American children develop positive feelings about their nation's government and its leaders. Most see the police officer as a helper and protector, and the president as a good and wise person who is interested primarily in the welfare of the nation. In fact, many children in this age group compare the president to their father and place the president near the top of their list of favorite people.

The positive character of most children's early perceptions of the American political system is important because it facilitates the bonding between citizen and government that is essential to the government's legitimacy, the citizens' belief in its right to rule. If citizens do not believe that a government is legitimate, they are unlikely to participate faithfully in its processes or support its decisions. In the United States there is widespread acceptance of the legitimacy of the government. Most children become patriotic before they have acquired enough information to explain the loyalty they feel. Although these strongly positive feelings tend to be modified as children grow older, they play an important role in the maintenance and stability of the American political system by securing the support of most of its citizens early in their lives.

The political socialization of girls differs from that of boys. In most families in which both parents are present, children of both sexes perceive their father as the more relevant political role model and as the more knowledgeable parent on political matters. Even though the mother talks more often with children about such matters as sex, religion, and study, the father usually has the advantage when the topic is politics. In addition, the early socialization of children has long emphasized the public roles of males and the private roles of females.[3] This reinforcement of the association between men and politics helps explain why men historically have participated in politics at higher levels than women. Recent research indicates, however, that gender-based differences in political socialization are diminishing. American

GLORIA STEINEM: FEMINIST FOUNDING MOTHER

Political activist and writer Gloria Steinem first came to public notice as a voice for the newly emerging women's movement in 1963 with the publication of her exposé article, "I Was a Playboy Bunny." From that beginning Steinem rose to national prominence as a political feminist. In 1971, along with Betty Friedan, Bella Abzug, and Shirley Chisholm, Steinem founded the National Women's Political Caucus (NWPC), an organization dedicated to encouraging women to run for public office.

In 1972, Steinem became the founding editor of *Ms.* magazine. Within a year *Ms.* had attained a circulation of 500,000. Many of today's most significant women's issues—equal pay, reproductive freedom, maternity leave, date rape, sexual harassment—were first identified and discussed in the pages of that publication. In a very real sense, *Ms.* raised the consciousness of an entire generation of women. But because advertisers were reluctant to appear in a "radical" magazine, Steinem spent most of her time on the road, speaking on campuses and in towns and cities around the country to raise money. She still found time to write trenchant articles and books, most notably a collection of essays called *Outrageous Acts and Everyday Rebellions*, first published in 1983.

Steinem remains an editorial consultant to *Ms.* She is also very active as a lecturer, organizer, and spokesperson for the feminist movement and issues of equality. Over the years she has helped to found the *Ms.* Foundation for Women, Voters for Choice, the Women's Action Alliance, and the Coalition of Labor Union Women.

Recently Steinem has come to take a wider view of feminism, tying it to larger questions of self-esteem and self-knowledge for both women and men. "Progress for women," she says, "lies in becoming more assertive, more ambitious, more able to deal with conflict. Progress for men will lie in becoming more empathetic, more compassionate, more com-

Gloria Steinem, long-time activist and leader in the women's movement, expanded her definition of politics to include the Washington Mall and the shopping mall. "Politics also may be who's doing the dishes," she says.

fortable working inside the home."[1] Her book *Revolution from Within: A Book of Self-Esteem* (1992), explores these issues.

Although she has now slowed the pace of her public appearances, Steinem has hardly given up on organized feminism. She frequently points out that the issues first raised by feminists in the early 1970s are still in the news today—but as national, not feminist, issues. We will know progress has been made, says Steinem, "when young men on campuses get up and ask as much as young women do, 'How can I combine a career and family?'"[2]

[1]Interview in *Esquire*, quoted in *Current Biography* entry.
[2]*USA Today* magazine interview, August 1989.

families today are far more varied than ever before in form and function, and gender roles are far less rigid than in the past.

As children move into adolescence, their perceptions of the political world become more sophisticated. They begin to recognize that there is more to government than presidents and police officers; they become aware of Congress, courts, cabinet members, and the distinctions among various levels of government. Also emerging at this point is a sense of the conflict that pervades politics. As children begin to recognize that individuals may take sides in disagreements among candidates, political parties, and interest groups on controversial issues, they are confronted by the need to choose a side, to position themselves within the political universe. This is a critical stage in the process of political socialization, because it shapes the lifelong attitudes of many Americans.

Party affiliation   One of the most important of these choices is that of an affiliation with a political party. In the United States, citizens do not join a party in the way that they join a club or a church. They make no formal profession of membership, they receive no membership card, and they are not required to pay dues. What they tend to do instead is simply to identify with a particular political party (or, in many cases, to identify themselves as independents). Because the political party identification that begins for many children in elementary school structures their orientation to politics throughout their lifetimes, party identification is an important concept in American political analysis.

In the early elementary grades, many children have a notion of the existence of Republicans and Democrats and can identify themselves with one party or the other. Several studies done in the 1960s found that more than half of the fifth-graders questioned had a party preference. By the twelfth grade, according to another study, almost two-thirds of a national sample had a preference. Subsequent research has

Political attitudes take root early, and even schoolchildren often identify with a particular party. But they have little understanding of ideological differences until adolescence. After that, their political attitudes and patterns of participation may last a lifetime.

indicated that larger numbers of children than was the case in the 1950s and 1960s are identifying themselves as independents or adopting no partisan preference.[4]

As you might expect, most of these early partisan attachments are based on very little substantive knowledge. Children who identify themselves with a political party or as independents usually cannot express an ideological or issue-based explanation for their choice. In some cases they can cite a prominent political personality: they have identified with Republicans, for instance, because they admire former president Ronald Reagan or because they dislike something they have heard about President Bill Clinton. Few, however, are able to go beyond a superficial knowledge of individual political figures in explaining their preference for a particular party. Awareness of substantive differences between the parties rarely comes before the last years of elementary school, and even then less than 10 percent of children can make distinctions based on issues or ideology.[5] Not until high school do most people acquire an understanding of the substantive differences between political parties.[6]

Political cynicism   Along with the increase in knowledge about politics and partisanship that occurs in the adolescent years comes a modification of the positive attitudes held in earlier years. Teenagers' political views become more realistic, and teens begin to perceive political figures in less heroic terms as they begin to understand the complexities and controversies of politics. It is also during the teenage years that most people begin to perceive government as a constraint on personal behavior by means of local curfews, minimum ages for driving and drinking, and school attendance requirements.

Cynicism in political attitudes tends to develop in early adulthood and to increase, in varying degrees, throughout the remainder of life. This delayed development is not surprising, for children and adolescents are not asked to participate in American politics. With adulthood comes broader exposure to the daily realities of politics, government, and public policy, as well as the first significant opportunities to participate in politics. Although some adults remain unaffected, for many this new perspective on the political world yields diminishing faith in the effectiveness of political institutions and decreasing trust in political leaders and their motives.

Major political events   The acquisition of political attitudes and attachments is further complicated by the major political events that occur during a person's lifetime. Each generation of Americans is exposed to a different set of stimuli because each lives through a different period of history.

Major events, especially those occurring during the formative years, may have a lifelong impact on the generation that experiences them. For example, the generation of southern whites who came of age during and immediately after the Civil War mostly learned to view Republicans as the villains of that war and as "carpetbaggers" who rode roughshod over the South during Reconstruction. Their allegiance to the Democratic party was tighly forged as a result. Similarly, the generation of Americans who reached adulthood during the Great Depression of the 1930s tended to blame the Depression on Herbert Hoover and the Republicans and to attach their loyalties to the Democrats. In both cases, party loyalties remained in place long after the passing of the events that created them. The New Deal generation, for instance, remained a core component of the Democratic party for many decades after Franklin Roosevelt's first election to the presidency in 1932.

People who have come of age politically since the 1960s have been affected less by any single major event than by the general movement away from strong political

THE POLITICS OF A GENERATION: THE BABY BOOM

The year 1947 saw the beginning of a demographic development that will deeply influence American life and politics well into the twenty-first century. Although it was not much noticed at the time, Americans began to have babies by the millions.

In 1940 the median age at first marriage was 24.3 for men and 21.5 for women. By 1947 the medians had dropped to 23.7 and 20.5, and in 1956 they bottomed out at 22.5 and 20.1. With the marriages came babies. In 1940, 2.6 million babies were born in the United States. In 1945 there were 2.9 million. By 1947 the number of births had grown to 3.8 million, and it stayed over 3.6 million until the end of the baby boom in the mid-1960s. From 1953 through 1963, on average 4.2 million babies were born every year in the United States.

This was the baby boom, and it produced the largest population cohort in American history. The effect on public life was dramatic. As the oldest baby boomers reached school age in the early 1950s, an unprecedented wave of school construction began, with major impacts on government budgets and tax rates. By 1965 the pressure of local school budgets had grown so great that the federal government began to provide aid to education for the first time. By 1979 a new cabinet-level Department of Education had been created to supervise the myriad programs that had grown up in the wake of that initial decision.

As family size grew during the 1950s and 1960s, the demand for more and larger houses grew as well, accelerating the move to the suburbs and the decline of the tradition of the multigenerational extended family living under one roof. Not only were there a lot of baby boomers, but they had access to more disposable income than any previous generation. Those with products to sell took notice. As the baby boomers reached puberty and early adulthood, they quickly became the favorite target of mass marketers,

Bill and Hillary Rodham Clinton are the first baby boomers in the White House.

inspiring fads like hula hoops and coonskin caps and trends like rock-'n'-roll music, informal dress, and a preference for television over books.

As the baby boomers passed through the crime-prone years of adolescence, crime rates shot up. As they finished high school in record numbers, they inspired unprecedented demands for college education. As they reached working age, they required more new jobs than the economy had ever before produced. As their incomes grew to the highest levels in history, they created a vast new market for consumer electronics, luxury cars, pricey restaurants, and other amenities of the good life. And as they age, they will blaze yet another trail into the golden years. By the year 2035 almost one-fourth of the United

States population will be over age 65—more than double the current figure. Demand for retirement housing, medical care, and a cure for Alzheimer's disease will grow apace.

To an extent rarely encountered before in American politics, the baby boomers have gone their own way. Probably it is not surprising that a generation so large would have so many diverse impulses. This was not only America's largest generation but also its freest: free from the pressure to conform that had characterized the generations of the two world wars, free—because of the invention of the birth control pill and the availability of abortion—from the inevitability of unwanted children, free from the imperative felt by earlier generations to help support financially marginal family members, and free from the need to participate in politics in order to get what they wanted. The baby boomers forged their own identities. Some fought in the Vietnam War; others protested against it. Some joined the civil rights movement; others rioted in urban ghettos. Some became the first in their families to go to top colleges or work in top firms or start their own companies. Others became homemakers, farmers, or factory workers, as their parents had been. More than any previous generation, they had the power, the means, and the opportunity to make their own life choices. And they made them.

In 1968 the first of the baby boomers became eligible to vote. (The voting age was still 21.) Baby boomers represented less than 10 percent of the potential electorate in that election. By 1972, however, with the voting age lowered to 18, baby boomers made up more than 20 percent of the potential electorate. By 1976 their percentage had grown to more than one-third, by 1984 to half, and by 1992 to almost 60 percent.

By virtue merely of their strength in numbers, baby boomers have had the potential to be the controlling force in American politics. But they haven't become so, because they have resisted traditional forms of political organization—especially strong loyalty to a political party. To date, baby boomers have been less likely than members of other generations to vote and less likely to identify strongly with either major political party. This generation, notes political scientist Paul Light, has been less a kingmaker than a heartbreaker—a reliable source of support for no party or candidate or broad-based political movement.

The baby boomers' political diversity reflected their cultural and economic diversity. And thus they became a great frustration to national and local political leaders even as they themselves became those leaders. There was no herding, and often no leading, the baby boomers. They resisted traditional calls to political action and political loyalty. They turned inward to their own cultural, racial, and economic groups and found little reason to work hard at bridging the differences (and sometimes the hostilities) among those groups. Since the baby boomers came of political age, the United States has become more difficult to govern than at any time in the twentieth century.

Discussion Questions

1. How would you characterize the political attitudes and opinions of the baby boomers you know, perhaps including your parents?
2. Did any single political event, on the order of the Great Depression or the Civil War, affect the political party loyalties of the baby boomers?
3. Do you think the baby boom generation will pass on its own complex pattern of political socialization and participation to its children?

Source: Paul C. Light, *Baby Boomers* (New York: W. W. Norton, 1988), 144–145.

party orientations that has been characteristic of this period. The effects of the Vietnam War, the Watergate and Iran-contra affairs, and other political scandals and failures have combined to create a trend toward alienation—or at least disconnection—from politics. At the same time, the organization of political campaigns has shifted away from the political parties. Even though some young people have found themselves attracted to charismatic political figures (such as Ronald Reagan in the 1980s and Bill Clinton in the 1990s), that attraction has not appeared to translate into deep and abiding loyalty to a particular political party. The large number of young and middle-aged adults who now think of themselves as political independents is not surprising, since they came of age at a time when political parties may have appeared irrelevant in shaping their political interests.[7] (See the Case Study about the baby boom generation on pages 172–173.)

Agents of Political Socialization

How do young Americans acquire their information and attitudes about politics? Two theories have been proposed.[8] According to one theory, individuals are taught most of what they come to know and feel about politics by **agents of political socialization**, that is, people and institutions with an active interest in influencing their beliefs. The other theory suggests that individuals themselves have considerable autonomy in acquiring the political information they find useful and the political attitudes they find comfortable. Actually, the two theories are not necessarily at odds. In American society, as in every other society, certain agents do attempt to socialize young people to accept and adapt to the prevailing political culture. But American society also gives young people ample opportunities to shape their own political socialization through independent acquisition and evaluation of political information.

The family   The family remains a potent agent of political socialization in the early years. At least until children begin school, most of them spend most of their waking hours in contact with one or more members of their family. Even during the years that children do attend school, the family normally remains an important reference point.

However, although parents are in an unusually good position to influence their children's political attitudes, they do not always make their influence felt. Studies have indicated that the potential for family influence is likely to be realized only when three conditions are met: (1) a close relationship among family members, (2) significant agreement among adults in the family on political values and attitudes, and (3) frequent communication of those values and attitudes to the child. Thus, if both parents are active Republicans or Democrats who discuss politics frequently at home, their son or daughter is much more likely to adopt their views and their partisan preferences than if they were not interested in politics or disagreed with each other on fundamental political matters.

Most studies have found that the development of party identification is the area in which the family has the greatest influence. Statistically, there is a close connection between the party identification of children and that of their parents, especially if the parents' identification is strongly felt.[9] Table 6–1 indicates some of the dimensions of this relationship. It shows, for example, that among students whose parents were strong Democrats, 89 percent thought of themselves as Democrats as well. Conversely, for those whose parents were strong Republicans, 84 percent said that they too were Republicans.

In the past several decades, old notions about the role of the family as a socializ-

TABLE 6-1	STUDENT AND PARENT REPORTS OF PARTY IDENTIFICATIONS (IN PERCENT)						

	PARENTS LABEL THEMSELVES						
STUDENTS LABEL THEMSELVES	**Strong Dem.**	**Weak Dem.**	**Ind. Dem.**	**Ind.**	**Ind. Rep.**	**Weak Rep.**	**Strong Rep.**
Democrat	89	71	53	33	17	14	8
Independent	8	18	37	51	37	13	9
Republicans	3	11	10	16	46	73	84

Source: Richard G. Niemi, How Family Members Perceive Each Other *(New Haven, Conn.: Yale University Press, 1974), 59. Copyright © 1974. Reprinted with permission of the publisher.*

ing agent have become increasingly suspect as American families have undergone dramatic changes. Most of the research on this subject was carried out before the large-scale entry of women into the work force and the explosive increase in the divorce rate among younger couples. Fewer young Americans than ever before grow up in families in which the parents remain married and the mother does not work outside the home. Projections suggest, for example, that more than half of all children born in the early 1980s will become part of a single-parent family before they reach the age of 18.[10] Consequently, the family is a less potent source of political attitudes and orientations than it was when children spent more time with both of their parents than they often do now.

The family that demonstrates together is more likely than not to keep demonstrating together. Children are most apt to absorb the family's political attitudes when they are young and when those attitudes are expressed clearly and frequently.

Most children first come into contact with the political world through patriotic rituals in school, like the Pledge of Allegiance to the flag and the observance of national holidays. But schools have less impact on political socialization than one might expect.

Schools   Schools have many of the same advantages that families do as potential influences on the political socialization of children. They occupy a good many of the child's waking hours, and they are expressly designed as instruments of instruction. Indeed, much of this instruction is aimed specifically at informing children about the American political system and guiding them to become good citizens. If only because schools provide children with many kinds of socializing experiences, one might expect them to play a significant role in political socialization as well. But most of the evidence indicates that they do not.

Studies of the impact of school civics courses have consistently shown how little impact such courses have on either the knowledge or the attitudes of the students exposed to them.[11] Nor is there significant evidence that teachers are likely to have much independent impact on their students' political attitudes.[12] A lot of ritualistic patriotic activity takes place in schools: saluting the flag, celebrating national holidays, singing patriotic songs, and so on. During the Persian Gulf War, for example, students in public schools wrote letters and sent food to American soldiers, festooned their buildings with yellow ribbons, and joined vigorously in the patriotic fervor of the moment. But although such activities may reinforce children's support for the political system, they do not appear to have a lasting impact on adult attitudes or political behavior.

Rather than having much independent impact on political socialization, it seems, schools tend to complement other, more important socializing forces in a child's life. Since public education in the United States is locally controlled, teachers and curricula usually reflect, within certain broad limits, the prevailing values of the community in which a school is located. For many decades after the Civil War, for example, southern schoolteachers often referred to that conflict as the War of Northern Aggression. Today, in school districts close to military bases or defense manufacturing plants, patriotism is usually given greater emphasis in the curriculum than it receives in districts where military influence is absent. It would be unusual indeed to find local public schools fostering values that were at odds with popular beliefs in their communities, and this congruence of values helps explain why schools rarely have much independent effect on the political socialization of a community's children.

By equipping people to comprehend and participate in the political world, however, schools have traditionally influenced political socialization in a more indirect way. The more formal education people obtain, the better informed they are likely to be about politics, the greater their interest in politics is likely to be, and the more likely they are to take part in political activities.[13] Thus people who are well educated may be better equipped to direct their own political socialization than those who are not.

Peers Peer groups share some of the advantages of families and schools in influencing the political socialization of individuals. In some ways, in fact, their advantages are even greater. Interaction with a peer group usually persists into adulthood as exposure to family and school declines. Most people are members of peer groups throughout their lives (although the composition and character of those groups may change) and tend to be receptive to communications received from them. In fact, people are often much more attentive and accommodating to members of peer groups than they are to those in their schools or families.

When peer groups actively engage in political discussions or activities, they are likely to be very influential in shaping the political orientations of their members. A classic study of this phenomenon was conducted at Bennington College in the 1930s.[14] A substantial majority of the students in the study became politically liberal during their college years, even though many of them came from families with quite conservative views, and the study indicated that interaction with peers had been the major cause of the change. When most of the students were reinterviewed twenty years later, the researchers found that in an overwhelming proportion of cases the effects of peer interaction during their college years had persisted over time—that is, their ideological liberalism had remained intact. Other studies of schoolchildren in Detroit and in high schools across the country have confirmed how significant peer groups are in forming and solidifying certain political attitudes.[15]

The mass media Anyone who has grown up in the contemporary United States would naturally expect the communications media, especially television, to have a significant impact on the way citizens come to perceive their political environment. After all, Americans spend a great deal of time watching television—nearly 50 hours per week in the average household. Adults also pay some attention to the print media: more than half of all households receive at least one newspaper a day, and many adults scan or peruse several magazines each week. Increasingly, Americans are turning to the Internet, as well, as a source of news and information.[16]

However, the evidence that the media play a significant role as political socializing agents is mixed. Recent studies have indicated that television is an important source of news and political knowledge for young people and for immigrants, helping those new to the political system to get their bearings and orient themselves in partisan or ideological debates. Subsequently, however, people tend to sustain and enlarge their political interests by turning to newspapers and other print media. In

*Bull sessions in the dorm may make a big difference in the world. Over the long
term, peer groups often have more impact than families on individuals' political
attitudes. Television is a major source of political news, but plays a lesser role in
shaping political attitudes and ideologies.*

this regard, television can be seen as important in helping to politically socialize
people who are not yet ready to use print media for this purpose.[17] In any event,
little evidence suggests that any medium people use to obtain political information
has much independent effect on their political attitudes. In other words, most
people's opinions are not altered significantly by their exposure to the mass media.

One explanation for this finding is that most people use the media primarily for
entertainment; viewing or reading material with specific political content consumes
only a small portion of the time that they spend with their television set or daily
newspaper. Indeed, a significant number of Americans have little more than a
peripheral interest in politics, a fact clearly reflected in the way they use the communications media. Furthermore, most people who do watch or read political programs or articles tend to gravitate toward those that support their existing views and
partisan preferences. Psychologists refer to this phenomenon as **selective perception**. Conservative citizens, for instance, are likely to read newspaper columns by
conservatives William F. Buckley Jr. and George Will or to listen to radio programs
hosted by Rush Limbaugh or Oliver North, whereas liberals are likely to read
columns by liberals Michael Kinsley or Mary McGrory and avoid talk radio, where
liberal hosts are in short supply.

But even if the mass media do not seem to shape partisan or ideological preferences to any significant extent, they may affect political socialization in another,
perhaps more profound way. Some recent studies have suggested that the cumulative effect of television watching may be to increase disaffection and cynicism
among Americans. The lengthening of election campaigns combined with extensive
television coverage often leads to boredom rather than to heightened interest, and
intensive scrutiny of political scandals and the private lives of public officials
inevitably makes American leaders seem less heroic than they often appeared in the

days before television.[18] During the 1992 primary campaign in New Hampshire, for example, no single story received more coverage than Gennifer Flowers's allegations of Bill Clinton's marital infidelity. The accumulation of such stories tends to reduce support for the political system and esteem for its leaders.

Such findings are especially noteworthy because in the political socialization of younger Americans, increasing reliance on television now often substitutes for the role that parental communications once played. Political scientist Paul Light has written, for example, that "television became a new social parent. . . . Recall the question of why parents did not pass on their party loyalty to their children. Perhaps one answer is that TV got in the way."[19]

Secondary groups Americans start joining organizations in early childhood and continue to do so throughout their lives. Sociologists refer to groups that people join voluntarily as **secondary groups**, in contrast to the primary groups, such as the family or cliques at school, in which there is close person-to-person interaction. Typical of the secondary groups to which Americans belong are professional associations, social or service clubs, labor unions, and political action organizations.

Membership in a group may have some effect on an individual's political socialization if three important conditions are met: (1) the individual identifies closely with the group's values or objectives; (2) those values or objectives relate directly to some aspect of politics; and (3) the group engages in promotional activities designed to inspire specific political attitudes or actions on the part of its members. In recent years, for instance, the Roman Catholic Church and some fundamentalist Protestant sects have made aggressive efforts to get the federal and state governments to prohibit abortion. The efforts of these church groups have had an impact on both the attitudes and the political activity of some of their members, stimulating or solidifying their personal opposition to abortion and inspiring them to engage in political action to change public policy on the issue.

On the other hand, a good many of the secondary groups that Americans join— the bridge club, the bowling league, the volunteer fire company—do not engage in political activity and provide little inspiration for their members to do so. Even groups with specific political objectives, such as the National Conservative Political Action Committee or the liberal People for the American Way, can rarely take credit for affecting the political socialization of their members. Rather, they tend to attract people who already share the group's objectives and values—indeed, who join for precisely that reason. Usually a secondary group does not cause a change in the attitudes or activity of an individual so much as it provides an outlet for personal beliefs that are already well formed.

Traditionally, secondary groups have played a major role in supporting and strengthening party affiliation. If an individual was inclined by parental influence and other forces to identify with the Democratic party and then joined a labor union that was closely linked with the Democrats, membership in the union would tend to strengthen the individual's bond with the party. But the solidarity and appeal of many of the large groups that once served as building blocks of American politics is in decline. A leading political reporter, E. J. Dionne, has noted:

> the party system of the New Deal was relatively stable because definable groups voted together and largely held together, even in bad times. Now, almost everything conspires against group solidarity. Unions are in trouble. . . . New jobs in the service industry promote individualism. The decline of the small town and the old urban ethnic enclaves . . . further weaken social solidarity.[20]

An important consequence of these trends is that secondary groups no longer reinforce party identification in the way they once did. Such groups can, however, affect political participation in important ways, as indicated later in this chapter.

Attitudes and Behavior

As noted earlier, political socialization is a dynamic process, one that continues throughout the life cycle. Although important aspects of belief systems and political attitudes begin to take shape before adulthood, these are not immutable. But neither do they change easily; alteration of political attitudes formed in the preadult years requires exposure to potent stimuli in adulthood. And because those stimuli appear only infrequently, attitudes formed early in life usually remain at the core of a person's belief system.

Involvement in political activities, however, is another story. The evidence examined here suggests strongly that preadult experiences have a much greater impact on adult political attitudes (what we think) than on political behavior (how we act). To a certain extent, of course, childhood learning will contribute to an adult's predisposition to engage actively in political behavior, but so too will the situations and problems that people encounter in their adult lives. Even those with little predisposition to engage in political activity and with little confidence in their own political skills may become deeply involved in issues that affect them directly and inspire them to active political involvement: the discovery of a toxic contaminant in their water supply, the desire to improve the quality of their children's schools, a neighborhood effort to prevent the construction of a new highway.

POLITICAL PARTICIPATION

Political participation is a critical ingredient in a successful democracy. To use the language of Abraham Lincoln, government cannot be "for the people" if it is not also "of the people and by the people." Specifically, the public must participate in policy making enough to ensure that public policy accurately reflects both the intensity and the direction of popular concerns. But participating in politics and government is not easy. It takes time and energy; it requires knowledge of political and government processes; and it requires that people feel that their political activity will make a difference.

Some people participate; others do not. Some people participate extensively, others only minimally. Why? Part of the answer comes from variations in the socialization patterns discussed earlier. Part also results from differences in opportunities or incentives to participate, from external factors that have a direct effect on people's lives. Three important aspects of political participation are (1) the ways in which Americans most commonly participate in political life, (2) the characteristics of those who participate and those who do not, and (3) the impact of participation on public policy.

Ways of Participating

Political participation encompasses a variety of activities. Some, such as running for political office, are very demanding. Others, such as voting, require only minimal amounts of time and knowledge. Between these extremes is a wide range of other activities.

Campaign activity   Short of getting elected to office oneself, securing the election of people who share one's views is probably the most direct way to get those views embedded in public policy. Participating in a political campaign is not difficult if a person has the desire to do so. The vast majority of campaign workers are volunteers, and political candidates are always glad to get help. Campaign activity may consume a lot of time, but the amount of time invested is usually up to the volunteer. Although broad experience in politics may be useful in a campaign, it is not a prerequisite. Some people support candidates with their money as well as, or instead of, their time. Increasingly, in fact, financial contributions to candidates are coming to replace volunteered time as a meaningful form of political participation.[21]

Much campaign work still requires only the ability and the willingness to stuff envelopes, make phone calls, or distribute campaign literature. What campaign activity does require is political interest: the participant must care about the outcome of the race and believe that one candidate is better than the others. The fact that so many Americans have never participated in campaign activities (see Table 6-2) suggests that even this level of interest is not very common. Indeed, much current research suggests that levels of political interest are in decline in the United States, especially among the young.[22] Because of their mobility and willingness to do the menial work of politics, young people normally constitute the core of campaigns, but in recent decades disaffection with conventional politics has kept many young people away. This helps explain why campaign activity is a relatively rare form of political participation.

Voting   Voting is widely regarded as the simplest form of political activity. Not surprisingly, therefore, it is also the form that is engaged in most frequently; in fact, it is the only political activity in which many Americans participate regularly. Nevertheless, as Table 6-2 indicates, more than one-fourth of the American people do not even identify themselves as regular voters.

Why do people not vote? Some say that they lack time, interest, or motivation. Historically, registration requirements in many states (discussed in Chapter 10) have

TABLE 6-2	**AMERICAN CITIZENS ACTIVE IN VARIOUS FORMS OF POLITICAL PARTICIPATION, 1968–1992 (IN PERCENT)**						
TYPE OF ACTIVITY	1968	1972	1976	1980	1984	1988	1992
Voted[a]	76	73	72	71	74	70	75
Worked for party or candidate	6	5	4	4	4	3	3
Attended rallies or meetings	9	9	6	8	8	7	8
Tried to persuade others how to vote	33	32	37	36	32	29	38
Wore campaign button, displayed bumper sticker	15	14	8	7	9	9	11
Contributed money to campaign	9	10	16	8	13	9	6

[a]These are self-identified voters. This figure generally exceeds the percentage of eligible adults who participate in any single national election.

Source: Data for 1968-1980 are adapted from David B. Hill and Norman R. Luttbeg, Trends in American Electoral Behavior *(Itasca, Ill.: Peacock, 1983), 99. Data for 1984-1992 are adapted from the National Election Studies.*

Distance Voting

Election day. All over America, lines wind languidly around firehouses, schools, and other public buildings as citizens wait to vote. It's a tradition as old as the Republic: going to the polls with your neighbors to choose political leaders.

But these days, some jurisdictions are moving away from that old tradition by experimenting with a new form of election: voting by mail. In this system, all citizens vote as if by absentee ballot. They get a paper ballot from their local voting clerk, fill it out, and mail it in by a fixed deadline, so that the votes can be counted by election day. The states of Washington and Oregon have already begun to experiment with voting by mail; Oregon used it in a special election in 1996 to select a United States senator after long-term incumbent Bob Packwood resigned.

More experimental is the approach of electronic voting, whose advocates argue that citizens should be permitted to vote by indicating their choices on their own computers or on computers in public places. There might be electronic kiosks in shopping malls, for example, where citizens could use a touch screen to vote. These votes would be forwarded electronically to a central computer, where they would be automatically tabulated.

Proponents of distance voting make three arguments. First, it is logistically efficient and cost-effective. Local communities need not pay to staff polling places, and citizens need not spend significant amounts of time traveling to polling places and standing in line. Second, it permits more informed voting. Citizens can sit with their ballot and whatever infor-

mation they may have gathered to help them make intelligent choices; they are not hurried to vote quickly on an unfamiliar ballot or machine at the polling place. Third, and most important in the minds of its supporters, distance voting should increase participation. Because it is less time-consuming and requires less information about election procedures than voting at a polling place, it should encourage more voting from those who are easily daunted by the chore of going to a polling place. In the Oregon special election to replace Senator Bob Packwood in 1996—where mail ballots were the only way to vote—more than 66 percent of registered voters participated.

Not everyone, however, is enthusiastic about these changes in the way Americans vote. Some traditionalists worry that we will lose the ritual of voting, participation in which is itself a stimulus to voters. After all, some people just like to go to their local polling place to feel that they are participating in a time-honored rite of democracy. Other critics worry about fraud. How can we be sure, they wonder, that no one will vote more than once and that all ballots will actually be cast by a qualified voter? They especially worry about these problems if we move to electronic voting.

The debate is just beginning and will swell in future years as the technology for distance voting expands. How do you feel about these proposed changes? Will the quality of popular elections be improved or diminished if we begin to vote in our homes instead of at a polling place?

also been an impediment. Although much is made of the relatively low percentage of eligible Americans who vote (in comparison with rates in other democracies), there are a number of other ways to affect the political process—and even nonvoters may engage in them.[23]

Personal contacting   Some citizens directly contact a political figure or a public agency for the purpose of altering public policy. Sometimes the issue at stake may relate to the welfare of the community or the nation, but it is more likely to involve a personal concern or problem: the woman who appears at city council meetings to plead for better care of the gardens in a public park; the parents who contact state welfare agencies to get public support for their disabled child's training; the couple

THE ART OF PERSONAL CONTACTING

You've just learned that your state legislature is about to consider a bill to eliminate an agency that provides educational loans to college students. You have been borrowing money from the agency, and you doubt that you can stay in college if this funding source disappears. What can you do to prevent that?

You can, of course, try to vote for candidates for the legislature who will work to keep the agency open. But the next election is more than a year away, and the bill to close the agency is pending in the legislature now. You could write a letter to your local newspaper expressing your views on the topic. Your state representative might read it. Or maybe not. You could join with others and mount a demonstration outside the state capitol building.

Or you could try to make direct contact with your representative in the legislature and perhaps with other representatives as well. Personal contacting is one of the most effective ways to communicate with public officials. It permits you to communicate your message clearly. It allows public officials to ask you questions, and you to provide answers. It personalizes issues for busy public officials in a way that no other form of communication can.

But how do you go about this? The first task is to decide whom to contact. In general, two rules of thumb are helpful here. First, try to contact the officials who are most directly involved in the decision. If the bill is pending in a legislative committee, for example, members of the committee—especially the chair—would be appropriate people to contact. Second, contact people who represent you directly. For obvious reasons, representatives are always more sensitive to the views of their own constituents—the people who elect them to office.

So, then, how do you find out the names and addresses of relevant participants in a policy decision and your own representative? The telephone book is always a good place to start. Local phone books nearly always have "government pages" that indicate whom to call for specific concerns, and frequently they also have central numbers you can call for information about government. Remember, too, that with each passing week more and more of this information is available on the Internet, as state and local governments set up their own home pages to provide information about their decision-making processes and ways to access public officials.

Once you have the necessary names and addresses, what's the best way to make contact? The old reliable is a letter. To make quicker contact, you might send your letter by fax. If you choose to write, be sure to clearly state your reason for writing, the action you hope the recipient of your letter will take, and concise arguments in support of your position. Whenever possible, try to provide an honest statement of the impact of this policy on your life. What will happen to you if the education finance agency closes? Public officials have plenty of access to data; what they often lack is an understanding of how real people are affected by their policy choices.

A phone call to the official's office is another good way to make personal contact. Don't expect that you'll make immediate contact with the person you're calling—public officials are not usually sitting by the phone waiting for calls from citizens. Have your message prepared in advance; try to be brief, but be sure to make your point. And, again, try to personalize policy impacts as much as possible.

These days, many public officials also have electronic mail addresses. If it's possible, you might choose to deliver your message by e-mail. In general, the larger the jurisdiction of public officials, the less likely it is that they will actually read all the e-mail they get. So don't expect your United States senator to personally read e-mail sent to her office, but your state representative or city councilor might.

Often the most effective form of personal contacting is to meet with public officials face to face. You can do this at public hearings, by informing the body holding the hearing of your desire to testify. You can attempt to schedule a meeting with relevant public officials at their offices. Or you can catch a few minutes of conversation with officials after speeches or at local town meetings or other events scheduled to give them access to their constituents.

For those who wish to make direct contact with public officials, there are many options. One or more of them is sure to yield a hearing for your views.

Michigan Congressman John Conyers meets with constituents in his Washington office. Contacting your representatives directly is one of the most effective ways to make your political voice heard.

who contact local officials for assistance in getting a traffic light placed at a busy intersection where their child was hit by a car. A growing number of Americans now contact their local, state, and national representatives to try to influence those officials' votes on policy issues. In fact, Americans are more likely to engage in this form of political activity than are Europeans.[24]

Oddly enough, individuals who engage in personal contacting often do not think of themselves as politically active. Many of them, in fact, are not very interested in politics, especially partisan politics; personal contacting is their principal, often their sole, mode of political participation. However, because it requires considerable initiative as well as some knowledge and persistence on the part of the contacter, even in the United States most political participation beyond the act of voting takes the form of collective, rather than individual, action.

Cooperative activity   An American citizen who wants to influence public policy and who thinks about effective strategies for doing so is likely to calculate that his or her message will have more impact if it comes from an organized group rather than from a single voice. This belief is nothing more than the old law of politics that says there is strength in numbers. The greater the number of people who support a particular course of action, the greater is the likelihood that such a course will be pursued by public officials.

The emphasis on cooperative forms of political participation is evident at both the local and the national levels. In most communities, policy decisions are frequently influenced by the efforts of organized groups of citizens: the PTA working for increases in school budgets, the chamber of commerce trying to hold down the tax rate in order to attract new business investment, the city employees' union supporting candidates for local office who will vote for increases in salaries or benefits. Similarly, at the national level, most significant interests in American public life are now organized as groups with their own lobbyists in Washington. There are thousands of such organizations, reflecting interests as diverse as those of autoworkers, milk producers, the mentally retarded, summer camp operators, and importers of exotic animals. Interest groups are a commanding presence in contemporary American politics, and we look at their role more closely in Chapter 8.

Cooperative activity requires more initiative than voting but less than personal contacting. Although those who engage in it may have considerable knowledge, at least about the issues that concern the groups in which they participate, a high level of information is not a requirement; in fact, for many people the combination of high interest and low information is what motivates them to join a group and participate in its activities. In general, the number who do so is smaller than the number who vote but larger than the number who engage in personal contacting.[25]

Unconventional participation   Not all efforts at political participation follow the conventional channels described thus far. Some circumvent them and, therefore, may be termed **unconventional participation**. These include such activities as protest demonstrations, sit-ins, rent strikes, riots, and other forms of violence, including bombings, kidnappings, and assassinations.

Unconventional activities most often occur when individuals or groups of citizens do not know how to follow conventional participation channels or do not believe that they can influence public policy by going through those channels. In

During the Vietnam War, unconventional political strategies, some with tragic outcomes, were the only ones available to those who lacked the power to influence policy. On May 4, 1970, National Guardsmen fired tear gas into a crowd of war protesters at Kent State University. In the confusion that followed, the Guard panicked and fired live bullets at the students, killing four.

In the summer of 1963, people around the world saw clearly—many for the first time—how the white South, as exemplified by the Birmingham, Alabama, police, treated African Americans deemed to be out of line. As television viewers saw live pictures of police dogs being set on peaceful protesters, their understanding of segregation, of civil rights, and of civil disobedience changed forever.

many cases, they are frustrated or believe themselves powerless to compete effectively in conventional politics. A good example is student activism against the Vietnam War in the 1960s. Under the laws in effect at the time, most students could not vote. They did not have the money or the organizational skills necessary to establish effective national interest groups, nor did their individual contacts with government officials seem to produce much change in the conduct of the war. Consequently, many students chose to express their opposition to the war outside of the routine channels of political participation: in street demonstrations, mass marches, sit-ins, and other kinds of organized protest.

Protesting against the political system does not prevent later participation—even leadership—in the system. For example, the initial political participation of John Kerry, who later became a Democratic senator from Massachusetts, was as a young Vietnam veteran protesting that war. John Lewis, later a Democratic representative from Georgia, first gained public attention when he was clubbed by state troopers during a voting rights demonstration in Alabama in 1965. Like Kerry and Lewis, many current mayors, city councilors, and state legislators entered conventional politics only after using unconventional tactics.

Social scientists have little reliable data on the number of people who participate in unconventional political activities, but most analysts believe that it is not very large, perhaps 1 or 2 percent of the population. Among certain groups, however, the percentage may be substantially higher. One study in upstate New York found that less than 3 percent of white citizens had ever taken part in a street demonstration but that 11 percent of African-American citizens had done so.[26]

Moreover, because of their intensity and, in the age of television, their visibility, unconventional forms of participation may affect public policy more than one would anticipate from the proportion of people typically involved in them. During the civil rights movement of the 1950s and 1960s, only a small percentage of the American people—even of African Americans—participated personally in public protest activities, but those who did captured national attention and became important symbols of the issues involved. In the summer of 1963, for example, African-American citizens in Birmingham, Alabama, sat stoically on a sidewalk in nonviolent protest of the racial discrimination then embedded in the laws of that city and state. Public officials responded by assaulting the protesters with police dogs, cattle prods, and water from fire hoses. Although the number of people directly involved on either side was not large, Americans all over the country watched these events on television; the vividness of the pictures focused national attention on the civil rights issue and helped solidify support for the significant pieces of national civil rights legislation that were enacted in 1964 and 1965.

Nonparticipation   A sizable number of Americans do not participate in political activities at all. They do not vote regularly; they engage in no direct contacts with public officials; they are not members of any group involved in political action; and they do not participate in unconventional forms of political activity. They are politically inactive.

Among these inactive citizens are several different types of people: those who are elderly and infirm, mentally incompetent, or incarcerated in prisons or other confining institutions; those who live lives of poverty and desperation and lack the skills, confidence, or energy necessary to take part in political life; and those who believe that political life is inherently corrupt or unfair and inequitable. Still others are inactive because they are basically satisfied with their own lives and with the state of national affairs and see no reason to invest any time or effort in political activities directed at change.

Whatever their reasons, approximately one-fifth of American adults are politically inactive.[27] What does it say about democracy in the United States if one-fifth of its citizens take no active part in choosing their leaders or in shaping the public policies that affect their lives? Although many believe that so much nonparticipation threatens the vitality of the democratic process, others contend that as long as participation is possible and encouraged, the system meets democratic criteria. A democracy could become unstable and unworkable if everyone participated extensively at all levels and on most issues. Thus some level of nonparticipation may be necessary for stability and efficiency in public life.

Who Participates?

Answers to the question of who participates must be given with caution. Participation patterns are complex, and no simple formulation can adequately describe or accurately predict the participation level of all individuals. Citizens from all types of backgrounds are found among the most active segments of the population, but they are also found among the least active. The same is true of every category in between. Nevertheless, some patterns do exist, and examining these may shed light on the role of political participation in shaping American politics and public policy. Keep in mind, however, that these are broad patterns to which there are numerous exceptions.

The impact of socio-economic status   One of the most consistent findings of studies of American political participation is that participation correlates closely with an individual's **socio-economic status** (SES), or social and economic standing relative to other citizens. The higher one's SES, the greater is the likelihood that one will participate actively in politics. Most citizens who are active participants are well educated and well-off, and among the inactives and those whose only activity is voting are a disproportionate number with low levels of education and income.

What accounts for this strong correlation between SES and participation? An important recent study of a sample of more than 15,000 Americans led political scientists Henry Brady, Sidney Verba, and Kay Lehman Schlozman to propose what they call a "resource model of political participation." They argue that three resources are essential for political activity—time, money, and civic skills—and that these critical resources are distributed unequally among groups defined by SES. By definition, those higher on the SES ladder have more money; because they are well educated, they are also likely to have acquired more knowledge about the workings of the political system (that is, civic skills). Free time, on the other hand, is not related to SES but to other variables such as having a job, a spouse, or children at home. Nevertheless, even in this area higher-SES people are more likely to apply whatever time they have to political activities because they typically have higher levels of political interest. To put the point another way, political interest plays an important part in engaging people in those forms of participation that require time as a resource (campaign work, board membership, and attending meetings).[28]

The relationship among interest, participation, and SES is not very surprising. Because of their greater knowledge of politics, higher-SES individuals are more likely to follow political issues on television and in the press. Their higher levels of income may indicate that they have a substantial financial interest in many public policy decisions (taxes and investment regulations, for example). Most important, studies of political participation suggest that people of high socio-economic status tend to have higher levels of political efficacy.

Political efficacy is an individual's feeling that he or she can bring about a desired political outcome. Citizens with a high level of political efficacy feel that their participation in politics makes a difference, that engaging in political activity is likely to produce results. In contrast, those with low levels of efficacy feel that they are insignificant and that politicians are not going to pay any attention to them no matter what they do.

Other demographic correlates   No other demographic characteristic matches the impact of socio-economic status on participation, but several others appear to affect participation levels. Age is one. In general, young adults—particularly those under age 30—and people over age 65 are less likely to be active participants than are those in between. As Figure 6-1 indicates, participation levels tend to increase as one gets older, level off in middle age, and then drop as one moves into the traditional retirement years.

Race, gender, and religion are also factors in participation. African Americans, for example, are less likely than whites to be politically active, in part because they are overrepresented in the lower socio-economic status groups. Women are less likely to be active than men, although the gap between the sexes has been narrowing in recent years and has disappeared in voting participation.[29] And people who participate significantly in religious activities are more likely to be politically active than people who don't attend religious services regularly.

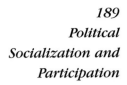

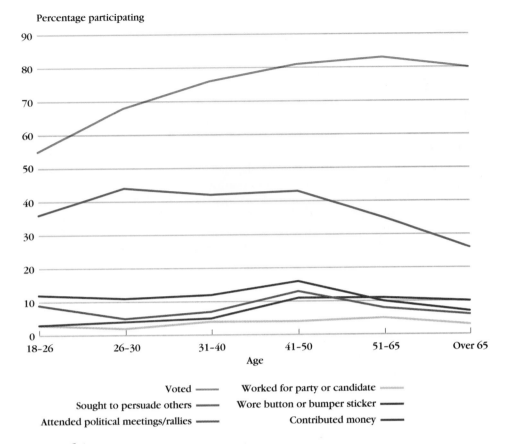

FIGURE 6-1

The Effect of Age on Political Participation.

SOURCE: American National Election Study, 1992.

The importance of mobilization   Several recent studies have sought to broaden our understanding of the dynamics of participation by emphasizing the importance of mobilization. People participate in political life, these studies suggest, not simply because they have essential resources or interests but also because someone asks or inspires them to. They are mobilized to participate.

Mobilization can be caused by an especially close election, high levels of spending or organizational activity by candidates, the presence of highly salient issues, or the activities of interest groups and other organizations. Political scientists Steven J. Rosenstone and John Mark Hansen argue forcefully in a recent study of political participation that

> Political participation arises from the interaction of citizens and political mobilizers. Few people participate spontaneously in politics. Participation, instead, results when groups, political parties, and activists persuade citizens to take part. Personal characteristics—resources, perceived rewards, interests, and benefits from taking part in politics—define every person's predisposition toward political activity. The strategic choices of political leaders—their determination of who and when to mobilize—determines the shape of political participation in America.[30]

Americans participate in policy making in many ways, at least on the local level. (Left) At town meetings on Nantucket Island, every citizen can discuss and vote on every issue in an almost pure democracy. (Right) Native American tribes have sovereignty in their own territories and make policy decisions at tribal councils like this Navajo "summit meeting" in New Mexico, which included neighboring tribal leaders, business executives, and politicians from nearby states.

Political Participation and Public Policy

Two important pieces of information emerge from this material on political participation: (1) the American people vary greatly in the extent to which they participate in political life, and (2) socio-economic status is the major cause of that variation. What are the implications of these findings?

Some have argued that the critical issue is whether everyone has the opportunity to participate. As long as this opportunity is widespread, they say, individuals are free to choose whether they will participate or not. And if policy decisions are made primarily by those who participate actively, that is alright as long as all citizens can participate when they choose. Those who question this view point out that there is an important difference between the legal right to participate in politics and actual possession of the skills and incentives necessary to do so. They argue that nonparticipation is rarely just the exercise of free choice, because those who participate less are usually disadvantaged in terms of information, political skills, and political efficacy.

If participants and nonparticipants were scattered randomly throughout the population, the actual level of participation might not make much difference in terms of public policy. But participation patterns are not random, and the political views of those who do participate are often quite different from the political views of those who do not.[31] To the extent that policy decisions are a response to what public officials hear from the public, that response is skewed toward the views of those who are most likely to make themselves heard: the active participants. Thus the haves tend to speak with a louder, steadier, and more influential voice than the have-nots, and they can perpetuate their advantage.

The policies of government result from the processes of politics. When some people participate and others do not, both process and policy are affected. The question of who participates and who does not directly and deeply affects the politics of American government.

Political socialization is an ongoing process in which individuals acquire the information, beliefs, attitudes, and values that help them comprehend the workings of a political system and orient themselves within it. Through political socialization, people learn to be *citizens*, or members of a political society.

Political socialization continues throughout the life cycle. The process begins early—many second-graders already possess some knowledge about the political system. During the preadolescent period, the majority of American children develop positive feelings about their government and its leaders. These feelings play an important role in the maintenance and stability of the political system.

During adolescence, children's perceptions of the political world tend to become more sophisticated. Adolescents begin to recognize that individuals may take sides in disagreements among candidates, political parties, and interest groups. They are confronted by the need to make choices, of which the most important is the choice of a party affiliation. By the time they reach twelfth grade a majority of American adolescents have a party preference, although in recent years an increasing number have identified themselves as independents.

Cynicism in political attitudes tends to develop in early adulthood and to increase throughout the remainder of the life cycle. The acquisition of political attitudes is further complicated by the major political events that occur during a person's lifetime, events that can affect the political orientation of an entire generation.

Agents of political socialization are groups and individuals from whom citizens acquire political information and learn political attitudes and values. The family is the dominant agent of political socialization in the early years, but the potential for family influence is likely to be realized only when there is a close relationship among family members, significant agreement among adults in the family on political values and attitudes, and frequent communication of those values and attitudes to the child. The development of party identification is the area in which the family has the greatest influence. With the increase in single-parent families, however, the family is becoming a less potent source of political attitudes.

Although much of a child's time is spent in school, schools play a limited role in political socialization.

Teachers and curricula tend to reflect the prevailing values of the community in which a school is located.

When peer groups actively engage in political discussions or activities, they are likely to be very influential in shaping the political orientations of their members. The mass media, in contrast, provide political information but do not have a significant effect on political attitudes. Most people tend to watch programs or read articles that support their existing political views, a phenomenon known as *selective perception*. But television viewing may affect political socialization in a broader sense by creating distrust and cynicism about politics, government, and political leaders.

Secondary groups such as professional associations and labor unions may affect an individual's political socialization if three conditions are met: (1) the individual identifies closely with the group's values; (2) those values relate directly to some aspect of politics; and (3) the group engages in promotional activities designed to inspire specific political attitudes or actions on the part of its members. Traditionally, a major impact of secondary groups has been to support and strengthen party affiliation, but this is less true today.

People vary greatly in the extent to which they participate in politics and in the types of activities in which they engage. The most common forms of political participation are campaign activity, voting, personal contacting, and cooperative activity.

Participation in political campaigns does not require skill or experience, but it does require political interest. Because levels of political interest have been declining in the United States, campaign activity is a relatively rare form of political participation. The most frequent form is voting, the only political activity in which many Americans participate regularly. Many people do not even vote, however, saying that they lack time, interest, or motivation or that registration requirements create an impediment.

Some citizens directly contact a political figure or public agency for the purpose of altering public policy; this may be their sole mode of political participation. But because personal contacting requires considerable knowledge and initiative, few Americans participate in this way. Citizens are much more likely to engage in cooperative activity designed to influence public policy, and organized groups are active at all levels of government.

Unconventional participation includes activities such as protest demonstrations and riots. These activities occur most often when individuals or groups do not know how to participate in conventional ways or do not believe that they will be able to influence public policy by going through conventional channels. Although they attract only a small proportion of citizens, unconventional forms of participation may have a significant effect on public policy because of their intensity and visibility.

About one-fifth of American adults do not participate in political activities at all. Nonparticipants are concentrated among the elderly; the mentally incapacitated and incarcerated; the poor; and those who believe that political life is corrupt or unfair.

Participation correlates closely with an individual's *socio-economic status* (SES), or relative social and economic standing. The higher one's SES, the greater is the likelihood that one will participate actively in politics. People with a high level of *political efficacy*—the belief that one has the capacity to bring about a desired political result—are also more likely to participate. Other demographic factors that affect participation levels are age, race, gender, and religion. In addition, participation is shaped by mobilization—the impact of issues and candidates, the closeness of elections, and the efforts of political parties and interest groups to engage and motivate citizen participation.

KEY TERMS

political socialization
citizen
agents of political socialization

selective perception
secondary group
unconventional participation

socio-economic status
political efficacy

RESOURCES

SCHOLARLY STUDIES

Abramson, Paul R. *Political Attitudes in America: Formation and Change*. San Francisco: Freeman, 1983. A comprehensive examination of what Americans believe and the factors that shape and alter those beliefs.

Conway, M. Margaret. *Political Participation in the United States*. 2d ed. Washington, D.C.: Congressional Quarterly, 1991. A recent survey of scholarship on many elements of political participation.

Greenstein, Fred I. *Children and Politics*. New Haven, Conn.: Yale University Press, 1965. An original and imaginative exploration of the ways in which children come to know and relate to the political world.

Newcomb, Theodore M. *Persistence and Change: Bennington College and Its Students After Twenty-Five Years*. New York: Wiley, 1967. A detailed study of attitudinal development in a group of students both during college and in subsequent years.

Rosenstone, Steven J., and John Mark Hansen. *Mobilization, Participation, and Democracy in America*. New York: Macmillan, 1993. An empiri-

cal argument focusing attention not simply on the predisposition of citizens to participate, but on the impact of efforts to mobilize them to do so.

Sigel, Roberta S., ed. *Political Learning in Adulthood: A Sourcebook of Theory and Research*. Chicago: University of Chicago Press, 1989. A compilation of some of the best research on political socialization.

Verba, Sidney, Kay Lehman Schlozman, and Henry Brady. *Voice and Equality: Civic Voluntarism in American Politics*. Cambridge, Mass.: Harvard University Press, 1995. A study of 15,000 Americans and the reasons for variance in their political participation patterns.

Verba, Sidney, and Norman H. Nie. *Participation in America: Political Democracy and Social Equality*. Chicago: University of Chicago Press, 1972. A landmark study of impressive scope, analyzing participation patterns in the United States.

LEISURE READING

Moody, Anne. *Coming of Age in Mississippi*. New York: Dell, 1992. Autobiographical writings of an African-American girl growing up in segregationist Mississippi.

Morris, Roger. *Richard Nixon: The Rise of an American Politician*. New York: Holt, 1991. A biography of the early life and initial political experiences of one of the dominant American political figures of the second half of the twentieth century.

Wills, Garry. *Reagan's America*. New York: Viking Penguin, 1988. Relates the impact of friends and events on the political development of the nation's fortieth president; includes a chapter on the legacy of the Reagan era.

PRIMARY SOURCES

Greenstein, Fred I., and Nelson Polsby, eds. *Handbook of Political Science*. Reading, Mass.: Addison-Wesley, 1975. Readings on topics in political science, with excellent essays on both political socialization and political participation.

Renshon, Stanley Allen, ed. *Handbook of Political Socialization*. New York: Free Press, 1977. A set of important articles about the study and substance of political socialization.

ORGANIZATIONS

Committee for the Study of the American Electorate, 421 New Jersey Avenue, S.E., Washington, DC 20003; phone (202) 546-3221; fax (202) 546-3571. A nonpartisan research group that studies issues involving low and declining voter turnout.

League of Women Voters of the United States, 1730 M Street, N.W., Washington, DC 20036; phone (202) 429-1965; fax (202) 429-0854; Internet http://www.electriciti.com/~/wvus/ A nonpartisan organization that works to increase participation in government.

Partnership for Democracy, 2335 18th Street, N.W., Washington, DC 20009; (202) 483-0030. A foundation that provides technical and financial assistance to grassroots citizen and community organizations concerned with public policy issues.

Public Opinion

D o you know who Norma McCorvey, Jack Kevorkian, and Greg Louganis are? Norma McCorvey is not well known to the American public, although she might be recognized by her pseudonym, Jane Roe. Dr. Jack Kevorkian is a retired pathologist who lives in Michigan. Greg Louganis won four gold medals in diving in the 1984 and 1988 summer Olympics. Each of these people has gained a degree of notoriety and, in doing so, has affected public policy. Their actions, the events they triggered, and the public's reaction to those events illustrate many of the characteristics of American public opinion today.

In 1970, McCorvey filed a lawsuit challenging the restrictive abortion law in her home state of Texas. Three years later, in *Roe v. Wade*, the Supreme Court invalidated that law and established standards for states that wished to limit access to abortion. McCorvey's involvement with the abortion issue continued after her successful suit, although the verdict came too late for her to terminate her own pregnancy. After having a baby and giving it up for adoption, she spent much of the next twenty-five years working with various feminist groups and abortion clinics, becoming a prominent symbol for the pro-choice movement.

When Operation Rescue, an antiabortion organization, moved its national headquarters next-door to a clinic in which McCorvey worked, she first ridiculed the group's director, Rev. Philip Benham. Eventually, however, she befriended him. A fundamentalist minister, Benham convinced her to change her views on abortion, her allegiances to the feminist movement, and, ultimately, her job. In 1995 she called a press conference to announce that she was going to work for Operation Rescue. Although McCorvey's former allies noted that her announcement seemed less than wholehearted in its opposition to abortion, it clearly came as a stunning public relations coup for pro-life forces.

Since 1990, Dr. Jack Kevorkian has been waging a personal campaign to legalize doctor-assisted suicides, a campaign in which he has helped numerous people, many of them terminally ill, to take their own lives. His actions have provoked a storm of protest. Reacting to those who believe assisted suicide to be murder, the Michigan legislature enacted a law in 1992 that made actions similar to those of Kevorkian a crime punishable by imprisonment. Although this law expired in 1994, Kevorkian was twice tried for suicides he assisted while it was in effect. In both cases, he was acquitted. After the Michigan Supreme Court ruled that even in the absence of a specific law, helping to end another's life is a crime under common law punishable by up to five years in jail, Kevorkian was tried in 1996 for two assisted suicides and again acquitted. He has continued to help sick people who wish to end their own lives.

The issue, however, remains hotly debated by religious, medical, and political leaders, and it has also become the subject of judicial interpretation. In 1996 federal appeals courts struck down a Washington state statute and parts of a New York state law that made assisting a suicide a felony. These decisions were accepted for review by the U.S. Supreme Court in its 1996–1997 term.

Greg Louganis has AIDS. He had it when he won gold medals in the 1988 Olympics, but he didn't tell anyone at that time, even after he had a minor accident in the preliminary competition in which he hit his head on the diving board and bled into the water. It was more than five years later that Louganis told the public about his infection, his sexual orientation (homosexual), and how he got the disease (unprotected sex). His announcement, which startled the sporting world after admissions by basketball star Magic Johnson and tennis great Arthur Ashe that they also had AIDS, refocused public attention on the disease and how it can be spread.[1]

It also raised a variety of contentious social issues. For example, after Johnson discovered that he was infected with the virus that causes AIDS, he retired from professional basketball in 1991. Four years later and still in good health, he rejoined his team with much fanfare for one season. Should he have been allowed to do so? Should those who test positive for the virus be allowed to engage in any activity in which physical contact occurs? Should restrictions be placed on certain individuals, such as health-care workers and prostitutes, if they are infected with the AIDS virus? Moreover, should public policy on AIDS emphasize prevention or finding a cure? Johnson, appointed to a presidential commission on the issue, resigned in protest of what he said was the Bush administration's failure to devote enough attention and money to the issue. Was the administration reflecting the public mood, or was Johnson?

Together, these three cases reveal a lot about the breadth, depth, and consistency of American public opinion. They also indicate the staying power of certain issues for relatively long periods of time. Some issues, such as abortion, generate widespread interest, are extremely divisive, and continue for many years. Others, such as assisted suicide, are also very emotion-laden but have not produced such clear-cut divisions of public feeling. Still others, such as AIDS, have produced sympathy for those affected, but also a backlash from those who see the disease primarily as a consequence of illegal or immoral behavior and thus may not be sympathetic to government funding. Whenever religion and morality intersect with public policy, the result is apt to produce intense feelings that make it difficult to arrive at a satisfactory solution. Such attitudes affect electoral and governing politics.

In some respects these three issues are exceptional, however, precisely because they arouse such strong emotions. Most issues do not. The dominant public mood is one of apathy. As a rule, people become concerned only when an issue "hits home"—*their* home.

The extent of the public's awareness of and interest in particular issues, the depth of its feelings about them, and the degree of public agreement or disagreement on them cannot help intruding on the politics of American government because that government is based on popular consent. They intrude on the electoral process when politicians constantly evaluate how their positions and actions will affect their opportunities for public office. They intrude on the process of government because public officials believe they have an obligation to be sensitive to the values, beliefs, and opinions of the population and to represent their political constituencies. They intrude on public policy in that public opinion plays a critical part in determining what government does and when and how it is done. Public opinion also provides an ongoing evaluation of how the political system is working and how government officials are performing.

What are the values, attitudes, and opinions of the American people? What policy issues do they consider most important, and how strongly do they feel about them? How can these opinions be determined? Those are the questions that need to be answered if public officials are to make responsive policy decisions.

In this chapter we examine the characteristics of public opinion and its distribution within society. We discuss how to determine public opinion through polling, what levels of information and range of attitudes and opinions people have, what aspects of public opinion are most critical to the operation of a democracy, and what impact these opinions have on the operation of politics and government.

THE NATURE OF PUBLIC OPINION

Public opinion consists of **opinions,** or judgments on current issues; **attitudes,** or broad orientations toward policy areas; and **values,** or basic ideals and beliefs. Figure 7-1 shows this configuration for the issue of abortion. Of the three components, opinions change most readily and values are the most stable. Values and attitudes help shape opinions. They provide a conceptual and perceptual lens through which to observe events and make judgments, and they help determine the **salience,** or importance, of issues.

Naturally, issues that touch on core values such as personal rights, political

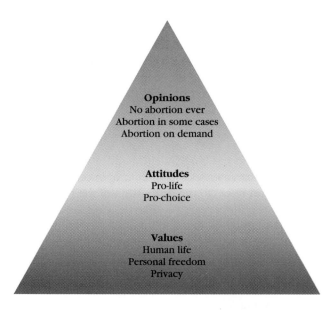

FIGURE 7-1
Public opinion on abortion.

Opinions
No abortion ever
Abortion in some cases
Abortion on demand

Attitudes
Pro-life
Pro-choice

Values
Human life
Personal freedom
Privacy

Images of war, famine, and other disasters stir strong emotions among the public, often helping to make these issues politically salient. Televised reports of atrocities during the civil war in the former Yugoslavia provoked public outrage in the United States and pressured the Clinton administration to do something to end the killing of innocent civilians.

equality, and national security elicit a stronger response than those that do not. For example, issues such as abortion, racial discrimination, and crime have been salient for years, even decades, whereas those that pertain to free trade or developing natural resources (off-shore oil drilling or lumbering in national forests) do not have the same staying power even though they may be politically divisive for short periods. Similarly, issues that have the most direct and immediate impact tend to be more salient than issues whose effect is indirect or potential. For example, in the 1980s United States policy toward Iraq was not of primary interest or concern to the American public; few Americans knew or cared that the United States had tilted toward Iraq in its war with Iran. However, after the Iraqi invasion of Kuwait in August 1990, United States policy toward Iraq became a salient issue. The perception that vital American interests were involved, the commitment of American troops to the Persian Gulf, and the outbreak of war brought the issue home to millions of Americans and has kept it there.

Characteristics

Policy makers commonly assess three characteristics of public opinion: direction, stability/fluidity, and intensity. **Direction** refers to the proportion of the population that holds a particular view. Evaluations of direction over time indicate the **stability** or **fluidity** of public opinion. Over the last three decades, for example, national surveys have asked the American people whether they support or oppose abortions. Their responses have been remarkably consistent (stable), as indicated in Figure 7-2a. There has been much more fluidity in the public's evaluation of the performance of individual presidents during their terms of office. Figure 7-2b shows the dramatic drop in George Bush's approval rating between the American victory in the

A. Support for legal abortion under different circumstances.

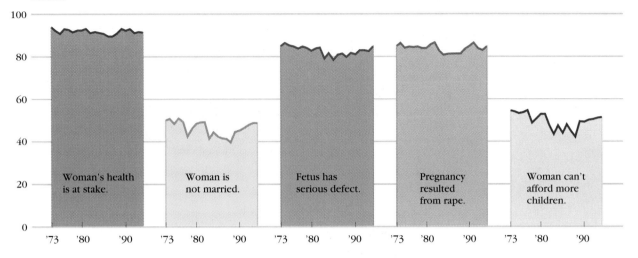

B. Approval of President Bush's performance.

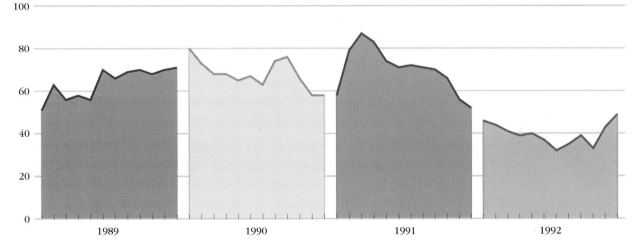

"Do you approve of the way George Bush is handling his job as president?"
(Bush: Final Job Approval Jan. 8–11, 1993 was 56%)

FIGURE 7-2

Stability and fluidity of public opinion.

SOURCE: For Part A: National Opinion Research Center surveys of adults nationwide. The questions were not asked every year. Results were provided by the Roper Center for Public Opinion Research © The Roper Center for Public Opinion Research, University of Connecticut, Storrs. Reprinted by permission as appearing in the *New York Times*, February 25, 1996, 4E. For Part B: *National Journal*, November 4, 1995. Copyright © 1995 by National Journal Inc. All rights reserved. Reprinted by permission. Update of Gallup polls by authors.

Persian Gulf War in early 1991 and his loss in the November 1992 election.

Intensity refers to the depth of feelings. Since opinions are easy to express, even without much information, intensity is a good indicator of whether people will act on the basis of their opinions. Naturally, the more intense people feel about an issue, the more likely they are to do something about it. A good illustration of the impact

| TABLE 7-1 | INTENSITY OF PUBLIC OPINION ON AIDS (PERCENTAGE RESPONDING) |

HOW WORRIED ARE YOU THAT AT SOME TIME IN THE FUTURE YOU, YOURSELF, MIGHT GET AIDS?

Responses	Percent*
Very worried	14
Somewhat worried	21
Not too worried	22
Not at all worried	42

*Percentages do not total 100 due to rounding.
Source: Theresa F. Rogers, Eleanor Singer, and Jennifer Imperio, "The Polls: Poll Trends—AIDS an Update," Public Opinion Quarterly 57 (Spring 1993): 92. American Association for Public Opinion Research, University of Chicago Press Journals Division. Reprinted by permission.*

of strong public opinion on public policy has been the success that opponents of smoking have had in restricting smoking in public places. Intensity is measured by asking people how strongly they feel about particular issues. Table 7-1 illustrates one response to a question designed to measure the intensity of feelings about contracting AIDS.

Distribution

On any issue, people with different backgrounds usually have different opinions. Table 7-2 indicates how various population groups differ on the issue of abortion. It should come as no surprise that women tend to be more supportive than men of the legal right to obtain an abortion in all cases, although it is interesting to note also that a slightly larger proportion of women than of men oppose any legalized abortion. What may be more surprising in this survey is the pro-choice orientation of Catholics, in view of their church's strong opposition to abortion.

In assessing public opinion, pollsters divide the population into three broad groups based on the relative level of information that people possess: the mass public, the attentive public, and opinion makers (see Figure 7-3). The **mass public** is the largest group (approximately 75 to 80 percent of the population), the least informed, and the most apathetic most of the time.[2] Because it is subject to the greatest swings in mood and shifts in opinion, it is also the most easily manipulated of the three groups—at least for the short periods when its attention can be directed toward public policy issues.

The second group is the **attentive public** (approximately 15 to 20 percent of the population). Better informed and more interested than the mass public, the attentive public comprises people who have a general awareness of issues, candidates and officials, and politically relevant events. They tend to have well-developed and consistent opinions on many issues, follow them in the news media, and discuss them with others. However, members of this group generally refrain from most political activities other than voting.

As its name suggests, the third group, the **opinion makers** (less than 5 percent of the population), consists of those who inform and shape the views of others. Their interest level, knowledge, and political activities set them apart. Included in this smallest group are party leaders, elected and appointed government officials, business executives, labor leaders, some members of the media, educational and religious leaders, and other interest group representatives. The opinion makers tend to hold the most consistent political beliefs.

FIGURE 7-3
Distribution of public opinion.

TABLE 7-2 | HOW GROUPS DIFFER ON ABORTION (PERCENTAGE RESPONDING)

WHICH COMES CLOSEST TO YOUR POSITION? ABORTION SHOULD BE . . .

	Legal in all cases	Legal in most cases	Illegal in most cases	Illegal in all cases
All voters	34	30	23	9
Said issue was important to their vote in 1992	34	11	27	26
Men	31	32	25	8
Women	37	28	22	10
Non-high school graduate	26	22	27	15
High school graduate	27	30	26	12
Some college	36	30	23	8
College graduate	35	31	23	7
Postgraduate education[a]	43	29	20	6
White	34	30	24	9
Black	38	29	17	9
Hispanic	31	26	25	16
Asian	22	30	27	13
Married	30	30	26	10
Single	43	29	18	7
Protestant	30	31	26	9
Catholic	30	29	26	10
Jewish	62	31	5	1
Born-again	13	19	41	24
Attend church weekly[b]	19	25	35	17
Democrat	40	31	17	7
Republican[c]	25	28	32	12
Independent	37	30	22	8
18–29 years[d]	41	27	21	8
30–44	34	32	23	8
45–59	31	31	26	9
60+	30	27	24	11

[a]Fifty-one percent of women with a postgraduate education compared with 36 percent of men with the same level of education said abortion should be legal in all cases.
[b]Sixty percent of those with no religion said abortion should be legal in all cases.
[c]Twenty-eight percent of Republican women compared with 23 percent of Republican men said abortion should be legal in all cases.
[d]Women in every age category under 60 were more likely than men to say abortion should be legal in all cases. Forty-four percent of 18- to 29-year-old women said abortion should always be legal; 37 percent of 18- to 29-year-old men did.

Source: Survey conducted on November 3, 1992, by Voter Research and Surveys for a consortium of the major news networks as appears in American Enterprise *4, No. 1 (January/February 1993): 103. Copyright © 1993, The American Enterprise. Distributed by The New York Times/Special Features. Reprinted by permission of The American Enterprise.*

The opinion makers, the attentive public, and the mass public differ not only in their level of information but in their political attitudes as well. In particular, political scientist Herbert McClosky found significant differences between elite and mass attitudes toward the principles and practices of democracy. Although most people value freedom of speech in the abstract, they differ about how that freedom should be applied. The elite (most of the opinion makers and some of the attentive public) express more support for individual civil liberties than does the mass public.[3]

Whereas the attentive and mass publics determine the direction and intensity of public opinion on a particular issue, the opinion makers define the alternatives, the specific policies that are considered, and the tone of public debate. That debate conditions the coverage that issues receive from the news media, which in turn can capture the attention of the mass public. For example, broad public concern over the role of the federal government and its ability to deal fairly, effectively, and efficiently with a range of social and economic issues set the tone for the 1994 and 1996 electoral campaigns by focusing attention on the size of the government, the scope of its responsibilities, and, specifically, its taxing, spending, and regulatory policies. The discussion on whether and for whom to lower taxes, how to achieve a balanced budget, and what controls (if any) should be placed on the issuance of federal regulations was structured by proposals emanating from the Republican leadership in Congress and from President Clinton.

DISCOVERING PUBLIC OPINION

How do policy makers discover what people think about an issue? They observe their behavior, monitor their communications, and ask them questions. However, some individuals in every group are more demonstrative and outspoken than others, perhaps because their opinions are more intense or because their personalities create a need for them to express themselves. Since it is important to determine the opinions of a range of people, not just those who are vocal, most policy makers survey the population as a whole. The most efficient way to do this is through **public opinion polls.**

Polls indicate the direction, the stability, and to some extent the intensity of public opinion prevailing at the time the polls are taken. Not only do they reveal which groups of people are most likely to support certain policies, be concerned about certain issues, and vote for particular candidates, but they can also indicate which issues do not generate much public interest or awareness and thus may not have to be addressed by public officials. During an election campaign, polls provide feedback to candidates about voters' concerns, their political attitudes, and their reactions to the symbols, issues, and images that the candidates are using. Indeed, this information is now available so quickly that candidates are able to assess the damage caused by an opponent's charges almost immediately and respond to them quickly. The failure to do so can be fatal, as Democratic presidential candidate Michael Dukakis found out in 1988 when he did not respond to Republican George Bush's charge that he was soft on crime, weak on defense, and out of step with basic American values. In 1992 and again in 1996, effective polling enabled Democratic candidate Bill Clinton to anticipate and reply to charges against him within twenty-four hours.

Polls cannot predict what opinions people will hold in the future, however, and that is why those taken several days before an election may not accurately forecast the results if a large number of voters make up or change their minds after the polls are completed. Voter preferences for Harry Truman in 1948 and Ronald Reagan in 1980 crystallized during the week before the election, confounding pollsters who had sampled opinion earlier. Morever, even if polls do accurately reflect public opinion, they may not be able to measure its intensity or the extent to which people might act on the basis of it. More often than not, polls are a snapshot that policy makers may consider, rather than a detailed guide for action.

GEORGE GALLUP: POLLING PUBLIC OPINION

The modern science of opinion polling reaches back to the 1920s and the pioneering work of George Gallup (1901–1984). In 1928, Gallup earned a Ph.D. at the University of Iowa with a dissertation in which he designed a method of gauging public opinion through the use of scientifically selected samples. Gallup showed that many polls then in existence inadvertently introduced distortions and bias by the way they selected respondents, but he argued that accurate, unbiased samples were possible through the use of statistical analysis. In other words, the responses of a few thousand randomly chosen respondents would accurately represent the views of the entire population. Putting theory into practice, Gallup founded the American Institute of Public Opinion in 1935 to provide polls commercially.

Gallup's work was viewed with considerable skepticism at first, even after he predicted the results of the 1934 congressional elections to within one percentage point. Two years later, he correctly predicted the results of the presidential election between Republican candidate Alf Landon and Democratic incumbent Franklin Roosevelt, whereas organizations that conducted larger but less scientific surveys did not. Gallup's success demonstrated the value of surveys in which respondents are selected randomly and gave scientific polling techniques greater credibility than they had previously enjoyed. Soon politicians were regularly commissioning polls to gauge public opinion on issues and candidates. Business also began to rely on polls as the basic framework of the new science of market research.

The hard-won acceptance of opinion polling suffered a major setback in the presidential election of 1948 when Gallup, along with most other pollsters, incorrectly predicted that Republican candidate Thomas E. Dewey, who was leading in the polls, would be elected. By concluding their polls ten days before the election, they failed to detect the late surge for Democratic incumbent Harry Truman, who eventually won a decisive victory. For months following this embarrassing faux pas, Gallup received letters

When George Gallup (seated) first began polling, he used a slide rule to calculate the proportion of the public that had responded in a certain way. Then it took about ten days to conduct a survey and analyze its results — a far cry from the daily polling and instant analyses that are possible today.

addressed to "Mr. Wrong." But he and his colleagues recovered from their mistake and have enjoyed an excellent record ever since. Today, polling is so widely used and apparently so accurate that it sometimes seems to substitute for the elections themselves.

Fifty years of polling millions of Americans taught George Gallup three lessons, he said: (1) the collective judgment of the American people is sound; (2) the public will make great sacrifices for the national good in times of crisis; and (3) the will of the people sooner or later becomes law.

SOURCES: *The Gallup Report* 241, October 1985; *New York Times*, obituary, July 28, 1984; Richard Reeves, "George Gallup's Nation of Numbers," *Esquire*, December 1983.

Election Polls

Speculating on electoral winners is as old as elections themselves, but formal attempts to forecast results have a shorter history.[4] In 1824 the Harrisburg *Pennsylvanian* conducted the first "straw" poll, asking its reporters to assess public support for the four candidates seeking the presidency. The equivalent of tossing a piece of straw into the air to gauge the direction of the wind, polls sample a small group of people to determine the attitudes of the electorate as a whole.

In presidential elections, the first prediction based on a national sample was made in 1892, when the *New York Herald* tallied polls collected by newspaper editors across the nation.[5] The largest and most comprehensive of the early national surveys were conducted by *Literary Digest,* a popular monthly magazine that mailed millions of ballots and questionnaires to people whose names appeared on lists of automobile owners and in telephone directories. In 1924, 1928, and 1932, the *Digest* poll correctly predicted the winner of the presidential election; in 1936, however, it did not. That year the poll forecast a huge victory for Republican candidate Alf Landon. Instead, Democratic incumbent Franklin Roosevelt won over 60 percent of the popular vote and swept all but two states.

What went wrong? The major flaw was that those who returned the ballots and questionnaires did not represent the electorate at large, because in 1936 automobile

The night of the 1948 election, early returns from the Northeast showed Republican Thomas E. Dewey in the lead. The polls had forecast a Dewey victory, and the Chicago Tribune, *which had endorsed Dewey, published its first edition under the headline that he had won. The morning after the election, President Truman happily showed off the* Tribune's *mistake during his victory speech.*

owners and telephone subscribers simply were not typical voters. Cars and phones had become semi-luxuries during the Depression, and those who could afford them were decidedly more Republican than the electorate as a whole.

While the *Digest* was tabulating its 2 million responses and predicting a Landon victory, a number of other pollsters were conducting more scientific surveys and correctly forecasting Roosevelt's reelection. The national polls of George Gallup and Elmo Roper differed from the *Digest* poll in two principal respects: they were considerably smaller, and they tried to approximate the characteristics of the entire population in their **sample**—that is, the portion of the population whose opinions were assessed.

As Gallup, Roper, and other pollsters refined their sampling techniques and established a record for accuracy, public confidence in election polling began to grow. That confidence was shattered again in 1948, however, when the major pollsters incorrectly forecast a victory for Republican candidate Thomas Dewey over Democratic incumbent Harry Truman. With Dewey leading by a substantial margin, the pollsters stopped conducting surveys several weeks before the election, reasoning that undecided voters would cast their votes along the same lines as those who had already decided. In fact, the late deciders, who made up 14 percent of the electorate, voted 3 to 1 for Truman.[6]

Pollsters were surprised again in 1980, when they correctly forecast a win for Republican presidential candidate Ronald Reagan but vastly underestimated the size of his victory. Having completed their final surveys four days before the election, most national polling organizations did not detect a late surge of support for Reagan. By interviewing until the eve of the election, pollsters working for both Republican and Democratic candidates discovered the Reagan surge and therefore provided a more accurate forecast.

The forecasting errors of 1948 and the underestimates of 1980 emphasize a principal limitation of polls mentioned earlier: they reflect opinion at the time the survey is taken but cannot predict future opinions. The closer to election day a poll is taken, the more accurate it is likely to be. However, the weakening of voters' ties to political parties and the inability to correctly anticipate who will actually vote have also impeded the accuracy of election forecasts. A good example of this problem occurred in the 1992 presidential election, when the Gallup poll underestimated the size of Ross Perot's vote by not properly allocating the vote of those who told the pollsters they were undecided at the end of the campaign. Gallup assumed that support for the independent candidate would decline among undecided voters, as it had done in 1980 for independent John Anderson. It did not do so in 1992, however.

Pollsters have responded to the challenge of voter indecision and volatility with improved surveying techniques that produce more consistently accurate results. Between 1936 and 1950, for example, the average error of the final Gallup poll was 3.6 percent. Between 1952 and 1960 the average error fell to 1.7 percent; between 1962 and 1970 it declined to 1.6 percent; and between 1972 and 1992 it decreased even further, to 1.4 percent.[7] How have these improvements in accuracy been achieved?

Sampling Theory

The main reason that polls have become increasingly accurate is improvements in the methods used to choose the sample. Since the objective of surveying is to generalize from a small number of people to the population as a whole, it is essential that the people interviewed be representative of that population. The odds of the sample being representative can be estimated when the sample is chosen through random selection techniques.

Random selection simply means that every element in the population (in this case, the eligible electorate) has an equal chance of being included in the sample, and the choice of any one element would not preclude the choice of any other. The *Literary Digest* sample of 1936 was not random. There was no way to determine whether the people interviewed were typical; as it turned out, they were not.

Since sampling is based on a mathematical theory of probability, the odds of being right or of being wrong can be calculated. In a random sample these odds are determined primarily by the size of the sample, not by the size of the population being sampled. Naturally, the more the sample approximates the size of the population, the more likely it is to be accurate and the more confidence can be placed in the results of the survey. The way to increase the accuracy of a sample, therefore, is to enlarge it. However, enlarging it adds to the cost of the survey. At some point a law of diminishing returns sets in: the gain in accuracy is small, but the increase in cost is considerable.

In assessing the results of a random sample, two factors must be considered: sampling error, and level of confidence. Both result from random selection itself and the odds of being wrong. **Sampling error** refers to the degree to which the sample could deviate from the population as a whole. Thus if a poll with a sampling error of ±3 reported that 50 percent of those surveyed thought the president was doing a good job, pollsters could generalize that anywhere from 47 to 53 percent of the entire population held that opinion.

Even within the range of sampling error, however, there is always a chance that the results of the sample (the findings of the survey) would not be accurate for the population as a whole; the smaller that chance, the greater is the confidence that one would have in the results. Most national surveys are based on a **level of confidence** of 95 percent, meaning that nineteen times out of twenty the results of the sample are probably within the range of its sampling error. But occasionally the results will not be. A Gallup poll reported in January 1996 that approval of President Clinton had fallen to 42 percent, whereas other polls conducted during the same period and using the same methods and questions found approval levels in the low 50s. One explanation of the difference would be chance error—that one chance in twenty that Gallup was wrong.

Dangers of Polling

Public opinion polls can provide a wealth of information—information that has immense value for candidates and public officials as well as for private groups that wish to influence government policy. However, anyone who bases decisions on the results of polls should be aware of their limitations. In addition to the possibility of incorrect assumptions, a sampling error, or outdatedness, polls may present an inaccurate picture because of the way their questions are worded, the way surveys are constructed, or the way responses are interpreted.

Bias can be introduced by using emotional or controversial words. For example, terms such as "pro-choice," "baby-killing," "rape," or "incest" in a question about abortion affect the response. So do phrases like "don't you believe?" "isn't it true?" and "most people believe, don't you?" Even slight changes in wording can produce large differences in responses. During the initial stages of the Bosnian peace keeping operation in 1995, two national surveys, one conducted by Gallup for CNN/*USA Today* and the other by CBS News, asked the questions shown in Table 7-3. What explains the differences in the responses? The wording in the Gallup poll did not mention the number of troops to be sent or their mission to enforce the accord; CBS News did.[8]

There are other dangers as well. Questions of the agree/disagree variety may be biased toward the "agree" response. The choice of closed- or open-ended questions also may affect the kinds of responses obtained. **Closed-ended questions** force a person to choose among a list of responses, whereas **open-ended questions** have no predetermined answer. Although responses to closed-ended questions can be categorized and analyzed more easily than open-ended responses, such questions lead people to express opinions on issues about which they have little or no information or do not feel strongly, or they may force responses into categories that do not accurately reflect the respondent's opinion.

The more closed-ended that questions are, the more likely they are to create this effect. For example, both the Gallup poll and the *New York Times*/CBS News poll wanted to determine how voters perceived George Bush and Bill Clinton during the summer of 1992. Gallup asked people simply if their opinion of each candidate was favorable or unfavorable, whereas the other poll gave two additional options: undecided, or hadn't heard enough to make a judgment. Gallup found that 40 percent had a favorable impression of Bush and 63 percent of Clinton, compared with 27 and 36 percent respectively for the *New York Times*/CBS poll.[9] The difference in the responses can be attributed, to some degree, to the format of the questions. How hard pollsters press those who indicate that they do not know the answer or do not have an opinion is another potential source of disagreement in polls, particularly between polls that otherwise seem comparable in content and time frame.

The order in which questions are asked also can affect the responses people give. Information included in the early questions may be used to answer later questions. Similarly, answers to the initial questions may affect answers to later questions, particularly if people try to be consistent in their answers.

In fact, the interview itself can affect the response. An interviewer who develops rapport with the respondent (the person being interviewed) may be able to elicit more information than can be obtained from an impersonal questionnaire. On the other hand, personal interviews also tend to encourage responses that are considered socially acceptable or desirable and to suppress those that are not. A good illustration of this tendency occurred during the nonpartisan primary in Louisiana in 1991, when the number of people who voted for David Duke, a former Grand Dragon of the Ku Klux Klan and supporter of Nazi ideology, was much higher than

TABLE 7-3	OPINION ON DEPLOYMENT OF UNITED STATES TROOPS TO BOSNIA	Favor	Oppose	Don't Know
Now that a peace agreement has been reached by all the groups currently fighting in Bosnia, the Clinton administration plans to contribute U.S. troops to an international peace-keeping force. Do you favor or oppose that? (Gallup for CNN/*USA Today*)		46	40	14
Do you favor or oppose sending up to **20 thousand** U.S. troops to Bosnia, as part of a NATO peace-keeping force, to **enforce** this peace agreement between Bosnia, Serbia, and Croatia? (CBS News)		33	58	9

the number who had told interviewers they would do so in surveys taken before the election.

There are other examples. More people regularly tell pollsters that they have voted than actually vote; similarly, more say that they have voted for the winner than actually do. To achieve a more accurate forecast of votes or more accurate information about other personal matters (such as income), pollsters usually use written ballots or questionnaires, which people are asked to complete and deposit in a closed container. Under these conditions, even the interviewer does not know their response.

Finally, error can also be introduced by the way survey results are interpreted. In early preelection polls, the candidates who tend to do best are those who are best known, not necessarily those who ultimately prove to be the most electable. Senator Gary Hart led all other Democratic presidential candidates in the December 1987 preelection poll in Iowa, even though he had only recently reentered the race after withdrawing in May following allegations of adultery. In the caucus election one month later, he finished in fifth place. The Hart example suggests that the interpretation of polls, and the prognoses that often follow from them, must be made with great care. The Practicing Democracy box on page 209 offers some guidelines for such interpretation.

PUBLIC KNOWLEDGE AND OPINIONS: WHO KNOWS WHAT?

The political opinions of the majority of the public rest on an extremely limited information base. Why are some people more informed, interested, and involved in political life than others? Why do some have more consistent political beliefs, look to gov-

Because of David Duke's past as a Nazi sympathizer and Grand Dragon of the Ku Klux Klan, many Louisianans were embarrassed to tell pollsters the truth—that they planned to vote for him for governor. People's tendency to say what they think they should causes particular problems in polls based on personal interviews.

INTERPRETING POLLS

Keep the following guidelines in mind when interpreting poll results:

1. Check the sampling error. If the margin for error exceeds the margin separating two responses, one response cannot be interpreted as more probable than the other. For example, if the random sampling error is ±4 percent and Candidate A leads Candidate B by 2 percent (say, 51 to 49), the contest is too close to call.

2. Determine whether the group sponsoring or conducting the poll has a vested interest in the results. Treat skeptically any findings disclosed by candidates, their organizations, and their supporters.

3. Examine the survey questions. Do the questions measure what the pollsters claim they do? Remember that the wording of the questions, their placement in the survey, and the responses permitted can all affect the results. Be sensitive to any positively or negatively valued buzzwords, symbols, goals, or names of individuals that may influence responses.

4. Check the time frame during which the poll was conducted. Have any events that might change respondents' opinions occurred between the time the poll was taken and the day the results were published? For example, a new candidate entering a campaign can affect the distribution of support among the other candidates.

5. Remember that random selection is the key to sampling accuracy. The results of surveys that do not use a random sample may be interesting or provocative, but they cannot be considered representative of the population as a whole. With this in mind you should discount polls, popular with some local media, that require respondents to telephone or mail in their responses. Such surveys usually only measure the preferences of people concerned enough to take the time and initiative to respond.

See the St. Martin's Student Survey of Political Attitudes for a guide on how to construct your own public opinion poll.

---

ernment for solutions to problems, or show greater tolerance of minority rights? The answer has a lot to do with their education, their ideology, and their understanding of democracy.

Characteristics of Public Knowledge

Lack of information Survey after survey conducted during the past thirty years has shown that the public is poorly informed about government officials and political issues. Not only do Americans know little about specific issues, but most people would be hard-pressed to name their representatives in Congress and their state legislature, much less recall the representatives' performance in office unless they have been involved in a scandal or abused their position. For example, a national poll conducted from November 28 to December 4, 1995, by the *Washington Post*, Kaiser Family Foundation, and Harvard University found that only 60 percent of those surveyed could name the current vice president of the United States, 53 percent the Speaker of the House, and 34 percent the Senate majority leader. Only one in four knew the length of a senator's term in office.[10] Some of the other results of the poll are shown in Figure 7-4.

Knowledge about entertainers in the movies and television tends to be greater than knowledge about most public officials, even the high-ranking ones. The same

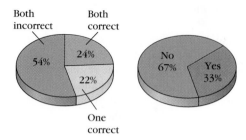

Q: Do you happen to know the names of the U.S. senators from your state, or not? What are their names?

Q: Do you happen to know the name of the person who serves in the U.S. House of Representatives from your congressional district, or not?

Both incorrect

Both correct

54%

24%

22%

One correct

No 67%

Yes 33%

FIGURE 7-4

How much do Americans know about their elected officials?

SOURCE: *Washington Post*/Kaiser Family Foundation/Harvard University national survey, conducted Nov. 28–Dec. 4, 1995, of 1,514 randomly selected adults as reported in the *Washington Post*, January 29, 1996, A6.

poll mentioned above found that only 6 percent of respondents knew the name of the Chief Justice. Even Justice Clarence Thomas, who was confirmed in a very controversial hearing shown on national television (a hearing that included explicit charges against him of sexual harassment), was known by only 30 percent. A national poll conducted in October 1995 found that only 17 percent of respondents could name three of the nine justices on the Supreme Court, but 59 percent could name the Three Stooges.[11]

Not only higher levels of education but also higher income is associated with greater political information. The relationship between income and information can be attributed in part to the demands of a professional or business life, which require that one be aware of what is going on in the political arena. The relationship may also be due to efforts to protect one's income or profession from those who might threaten it. In addition, education and income tend to be associated with each other. Better-educated people generally make more money, and those who make more money tend to be the better educated.

Age is also strongly associated with a person's level of information on political issues. As people get older, as they develop greater stakes in their community and profession, they become more aware of the effects of political decisions on their lives and well-being. As the number of government policies affecting senior citizens increases, older people have an incentive to remain informed and involved.

Generational differences may also be a factor. *The Pew Research Center for The People & The Press* analyzed historic polling data in 1990 and found that "Americans under 30 represented a generation that knew less, cared less, and read newspapers less than previous generations of young people." The Center's subsequent studies have confirmed this conclusion. They have found that only one out of five people between 18 and 29 pays close attention to the news.[12]

What implications does the low level of information have for the politics of government? For one thing, it gives government leaders more initial discretion in making policy decisions. With less direction from the public, they have more flexibility to fashion a solution. This is particularly evident in foreign affairs and in complex economic and technological issues such as telecommunications policy, nuclear energy, and biomedical research. In contrast, where the public is better informed, public officials have much less leeway. For example, in the 1995–1996 debate over

Republican plans to balance the budget by 2002, a public outcry against Medicare cuts forced congressional Republicans to change and eventually drop their proposals to increase premiums and limit spending.

Even in the absence of discernible public concern, government officials rarely have a blank check. Certain proposals cannot be enacted because they lie outside the values and beliefs of most people. For example, few considered a national health system run by the government, often referred to as "socialized medicine," to be a viable solution to recent health-care problems in the United States, even though it has been utilized in other Western democracies such as Canada, Sweden, and Great Britain.

Another consequence of limited public knowledge is that it tends to encourage short-term solutions. Not understanding the full complexity of issues, the public expects and demands results here and now. These demands are readily converted into political pressure on government officials for quick fixes rather than longer-term solutions.

A third implication of the low level of public information is that it seems to increase the power of interest groups and their leaders. When many people are uninformed and uninterested, opinion leaders—particularly those who represent large and powerful groups—exercise more clout. A poorly informed public is easier to manipulate.

Ambivalence   The consistency with which beliefs and opinions are held varies. People are often ambivalent about issues—they seem to talk out of both sides of their mouths. For instance, surveys of public opinion indicate that Americans want to protect and preserve their interests around the world but shy away from involving United States forces in that effort; they want to help those who cannot help themselves but are opposed to most government-run welfare programs at home or extensive foreign aid abroad; they believe in the sanctity of human life as well as the right of individual choice. This ambivalence stems in part from clashing values. Americans cherish numerous values such as liberty, equality, and opportunity. Unless they are able to order these values in terms of their relative importance, however, conflicts are likely to develop and persist.

One way to resolve such conflicts is to adopt a **belief system**, a set of related ideas that helps people understand and cope with the world around them and that also provides guidelines for behavior. Examples of a belief system include a religion (such as Christianity, Islam, or Judaism) or an ideology (such as communism or capitalism). Frequently, however, people do not accept all the tenets of a belief system; and they may adhere to religious, political, and economic belief systems that are not logically congruent, that do not easily mesh with one another. That is a major reason why public opinion often lacks consistency.

Education is a key variable in determining the consistency of someone's beliefs. People with more education tend to be more consistent in the political positions they take and the political beliefs they hold and express. Not only does education increase their awareness of issues, but it gives them the skills to think logically and spot inconsistencies in their beliefs.

Diversity   In addition to low levels of information and ambivalent attitudes, public opinion in the United States is characterized by diversity. That diversity reflects the heterogeneity of the population—its various subcultures, races, and levels of education and income. Table 7-4 illustrates these differences in opinion on a number of

TABLE 7-4

**DIVERSITY OF PUBLIC OPINION, 1994
(PERCENTAGE AGREEING)**

ISSUES*	GENDER		RACE		AGE			
	MALE	FEMALE	WHITE	NONWHITE	18–29	30–49	50–64	65+
1. Women and men should have equal roles.	—	—	70	73	81	76	68	51
2. The death penalty should be abolished.	13	23	15	38	18	18	20	18
3. Government should see to it that people have good jobs and an acceptable standard of living.	—	—	25	53	38	29	32	16
4. Government should improve the social and economic conditions of African Americans.	—	—	18	40	25	23	20	14
5. Government should provide fewer services to reduce government spending.	38	26	44	28	33	45	41	45
6. Welfare benefits should be limited to two years.	—	—	78	62	79	78	70	72
7. Prayers should not be allowed in public schools.	12	10	12	7	12	12	10	10
8. Immigration should be decreased.	64	66	66	59	68	64	67	65

—Indicates that data is not available.

*The questions put for each issue were these:

1. Recently there has been a lot of talk about women's rights. Some people feel that women should have an equal role with men in running business, industry, and government. . . . Others feel that a woman's place is in the home. . . . Where would you place yourself on this scale (1 . . . 7), or haven't you thought much about this? ("Percentage agreeing" is total of scaled responses 1–3.)

2. Do you favor or oppose the death penalty for persons convicted of murder?

3. Some people feel the government in Washington should see to it that every person has a job and a good standard of living. Others think the government should just let each person get ahead on his or her own. Where would you place yourself on this scale (1 . . . 7), or haven't you thought much about it? ("Percentage agreeing" is total of scaled responses 1–3.)

4. Some people feel that the government in Washington should make every effort to improve the social and economic position of African Americans. Others feel that the government should not make any special effort to help African Americans because they should help themselves. Where would you place yourself on this scale (1 . . . 7), or haven't you thought much about this? ("Percentage agreeing" is total of responses 1–3.)

contemporary issues. The table indicates the percentage of people who agree with each statement. Notice that education and income often vary directly with each other, and that significant generational differences exist between those in the youngest and oldest age groups on several issues. It is also interesting that opinion differences between the races tend to be greater than those between the genders.

The ambivalence and contradictions in people's attitudes and opinions can be very frustrating for policy makers who look to public opinion for guidance. What should public officials do, for example, when people demand deficit reduction and

TABLE 7-4

**DIVERSITY OF PUBLIC OPINION, 1994
(PERCENTAGE AGREEING)** *(continued)*

	EDUCATION				INCOME (IN THOUSANDS OF DOLLARS)			
ISSUES*	DROP-OUT	HIGH SCHOOL	SOME COLLEGE	COLLEGE GRAD.	UNDER 15	15–24	25–49	50+
1. Women and men should have equal roles.	51	63	79	83	59	70	73	76
2. The death penalty should be abolished.	26	14	17	21	25	21	15	14
3. Government should see to it that people have good jobs and an acceptable standard of living.	37	32	28	23	38	32	26	25
4. Government should improve the social and economic conditions of Africans Americans.	25	15	20	28	28	22	19	19
5. Government should provide fewer services to reduce government spending.	31	37	46	51	31	36	45	48
6. Welfare benefits should be limited to two years.	66	77	77	78	63	73	80	80
7. Prayers should not be allowed in public schools.	9	8	9	20	9	10	12	12
8. Immigration should be decreased.	66	75	63	54	65	69	66	63

5. Some people think the government should provide fewer services, even in areas such as health and education, in order to reduce spending. Other people feel it is important for the government to provide many more services even if it means an increase in spending. Where would you place yourself on this scale (1 . . . 7), or haven't you thought much about it? (Percentages are totals of responses 1–3.)

6. Another proposal is to put a two-year limit on how long someone can receive welfare benefits. Do you favor or oppose this two-year limit?

7. Which of the following views comes closest to your opinion on the issue of school prayer?
By law, prayers should not be allowed in public schools.
The law should allow public schools to schedule time when children can pray silently if they want to.
The law should allow public schools to schedule time when children, as a group, can say a general prayer not tied to a particular faith.
By law, public schools should schedule a time when all children would say a chosen Christian prayer.

8. Do you think the number of immigrants from foreign countries who are permitted to come to the United States to live should be increased a little, increased a lot, decreased a little, decreased a lot, or left the same as it is?

Source: The American National Election Studies, conducted by the University of Michigan, Center for Political Studies, Ann Arbor, Michigan. Data provided by the Inter-University Consortium for Political and Social Research, located at the University of Michigan, Center for Political Studies, Ann Arbor, Michigan.

lower taxes, but no reduction in levels of spending for specific programs? This is precisely what the American people said they wanted in the mid 1990s.[13]

Political Ideologies

As noted earlier, many people seek to orient themselves to the political world by adopting a system of beliefs called an ideology. A **political ideology** is a set of interrelated attitudes that shape judgments about and reactions to political issues.

PUBLIC OPINION DATA

What is the public's opinion on contemporary issues, and how can you find it out? The findings of national public opinion polls started to appear on the Internet in 1996. Among them are data provided by the Gallup Poll and *New York Times*/CBS News Poll. In addition to these national surveys, almost every website of a major news organization contains the findings of its latest polls.

If you want to research trends in American public opinion over time, the best places to locate these data are the archives at several universities. The Documents Center at the University of Michigan has the best collection of academic public opinion surveys, and the Roper Center at the University of Connecticut has a collection of survey data from all the major polling organizations, television networks, and major newspapers and magazines. However, much of the data at the university websites is available only to subscribers, those who pay a fee for access. Check with your instructor to see whether your school has subscriber privileges at one of these library data sites.

Here are some useful addresses:

CURRENT PUBLIC OPINION POLLSTERS

Gallup Organization
  http://www.gallup.com/
New York Times/CBS News Poll
  http://www.nytimes.com/library/politics/
  newspoll.html

SELECTED NEWS MEDIA SITES WITH POLLING DATA

AllPolitics (CNN, *Time* magazine, and other major news networks)
  http://AllPolitics.com/
American Voter '96 (*Congressional Quarterly*)
  http://voter96.cqalert.com/

ElectionLine (ABC News, *Newsweek*, and the *Washington Post*)
  http://www.electionline.com/
PoliticsUSA (*National Journal* and American Political Network)
  http://PoliticsUSA.com/PoliticsUSA/campaign96/

PUBLIC OPINION DATA LIBRARIES AND DATA ARCHIVES

Electronic Data Services (Columbia University)
  http://www.columbia.edu/acis/eds/
Inter-University Consortium for Political and Social Research (University of Michigan)
  http://www.icpsr.umich.edu/
National Election Studies (University of Michigan—Center for Political Studies)
  http://www.umich.edu/~NES/
Princeton Survey Research Center
  http://www.princeton.edu/~abelson/
Roper Center for Public Opinion Research (University of Connecticut)
  http://www.lib.uconn.edu/RoperCenter/
Social Sciences Data Center (University of Virginia Library)
  http://www.lib.virginia.edu/socsci/
Social Sciences Data Collection (University of California at San Diego)
  http://ssdc.ucsd.edu/
Statistical Resources on the Web—Political Science (University of Michigan)
  http://www.lib.umich.edu/libhome/Documents.center/stpolisc.html
Yahoo
  http://www.yahoo.com/

Ideologies provide a general stance toward the political system, a perceptual lens through which to view and evaluate events.

In the United States the two dominant political ideologies are **liberalism** and **conservatism**. Perhaps no two words in the English language have been used more often, and with less consistency, than *liberal* and *conservative*. What is the historical precedent by which these terms acquire meaning today?

During the Great Depression of the 1930s, when Franklin Roosevelt's administration decided to use the government as a massive force to restore the health of the economy, deep divisions emerged within America between those who supported and those who opposed the president's proposals. The liberals were those who supported Roosevelt's philosophy that the government can and should be used as a powerful force in achieving greater social and political equality and greater economic opportunity for all; the conservatives generally opposed Roosevelt's New Deal policies, believing that the intrusion of government threatened individual freedom and violated the basic tenets of the capitalistic system.

More recently, liberals have also supported government intervention to protect civil rights and promote equal opportunity for minorities who have not been afforded the same privileges and opportunities as the majority. But they have tended to oppose government actions that threaten to deprive people of their basic personal and political freedoms, particularly the freedom to deviate from social norms and to oppose government policies. In general, liberals have subscribed to a literal reading of the First Amendment, which states that Congress shall pass no law (and, by implication, the executive shall issue no regulation) that abridges freedom of speech, press, and religion and the right of people to assemble peaceably and "petition the government for a redress of grievances." Liberals' desire for greater social equality and personal freedom extends to foreign policy as well, where they have tended to favor policies of accommodation, reject the threat of force as an instrument of diplomacy, and support programs designed to help the economically and politically deprived.

Conservatives have tended to fear government involvement *more* in the economic sphere, particularly where such involvement places restrictions on the free-enterprise system, and *less* in the social realm, particularly in matters of law and order where individual behavior is constrained. They have usually voiced opposition to increased taxation, especially as a device to redistribute wealth. As proponents of private enterprise, conservatives prefer to keep capital in the hands of individuals and nongovernment groups, to be spent and invested as they see fit. They contend that a vigorous economy will generate solutions to many of the country's social ills. Compared with liberals, conservatives seem to be more satisfied with the status quo, more willing to accept economic and social inequalities as natural consequences of the human condition, and more resistant to large-scale social change.

Conservatives accept the notion of individual liberties, although they are less likely than liberals to permit behavior that deviates from social norms and community standards. They see the need for an ordered and stable society in which property is protected and entrepreneurship encouraged, and they contend that the government has a major responsibility for providing that protection as well as protection against external threats to the national interests and security of the United States. Since World War II, conservatives have generally supported a foreign policy based on military strength and the extension of aid, primarily military, to governments that are politically allied with the United States and in a position to strengthen American geopolitical interests.

Do people actually think along these ideological lines? Do they use liberalism and conservatism as a basis for formulating opinions and making decisions? The evidence suggests that they do. It also suggests that the more information people have, the more likely they are to maintain views on policy issues that are consistent with their ideological orientation.

Although that orientation does not dictate positions on issues for most people, it is a useful device for self-identification and for explaining and even rationalizing policy positions and candidate preferences. But whether ideology is the principal

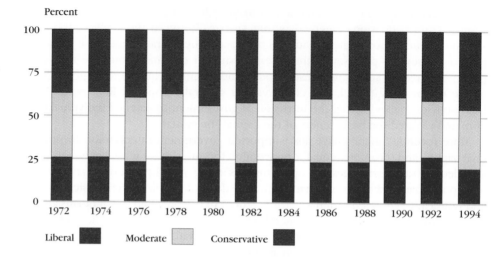

Percent

FIGURE 7-5

Percentage of Americans identifying themselves as liberal, moderate, or conservative, 1972–1994.

SOURCE: Analysis based on data from the American National Election Studies, conducted by the University of Michigan, Center for Political Studies, Ann Arbor, Michigan. Data provided by the Inter-University Consortium for Political and Social Research, located at the University of Michigan, Center for Political Studies, Ann Arbor, Michigan; and National Opinion Research Center, University of Chicago, general social surveys, for 1994.

reason for forming an opinion, taking a position, or arriving at a political judgment remains difficult to say. Studies conducted during the 1950s found little data to support the proposition that ideology affects voting for most Americans.[14] Studies conducted during the 1960s found some support for this proposition, with more than twice as many people explaining their voting choices in ideological terms in 1964 and 1968 as in 1956.[15]

Ideological awareness has continued to grow. In recent presidential elections there has been a strong association between ideological self-identification and voting patterns, although there is little evidence that ideology itself causes people to vote as they do.[16] Figure 7-5 identifies patterns of ideological self-identification from 1972 to 1994. Note that although conservatives have maintained an advantage over liberals throughout this period, that advantage increased markedly in the 1990s.

Who are the liberals and conservatives in the American electorate? According to statistics assembled by political scientists between 1982 and 1994 (see Table 7-5), men are more conservative than women, whites are more conservative than nonwhites, and older Americans are more conservative than younger Americans, although the differences here are not great.

The ideological orientation of the American electorate has had an impact on partisan politics. As Table 7-5 indicates, conservatives tend to ally themselves with the Republican party and liberals with the Democratic party. Ideology also affects policy making in that problems that are defined in ideological terms tend to be more difficult to resolve. Ideologues are not good compromisers. Although the ideological orientation of the American polity has shifted in a conservative direction during the 1980s and 1990s, the people continue to display considerable latitude in the application of their political views to the issues of the day. That is why American politics is characterized more by pragmatism than by rigid adherence to ideological beliefs.

Changes in public attitudes on some major economic and social issues have been influenced by shifting patterns in ideological identification. Since the mid 1970s the public has shown less support for large-scale government programs than it did during the previous two decades.[17] Cynicism toward the national government has increased. Government-run agencies such as the United States Postal Service, the Internal Revenue Service, the Bureau of Alcohol, Tobacco, and Firearms, the Federal Bureau of Investigation, the Central Intelligence Agency, and the Immigration and Naturalization Service have been the targets of much criticism, and there continue to be endless complaints about government regulations and paperwork. Within the social sphere, Americans—particularly young Americans—have become more tolerant of certain kinds of behavior, such as single motherhood and homosexuality, than they were in the past. But they are also more supportive of harsh penalties for criminal behavior, such as the death penalty for those who commit heinous crimes.

Democratic Beliefs

In addition to their varying levels of political knowledge and differing ideological perspectives, Americans hold a range of attitudes toward government, society, and the interaction between the two. These attitudes condition the kinds of issues public officials must consider and the range of options they can follow in dealing with them. In particular, attitudes have an impact in five areas that are critical to the operation of a democracy: the role of government, trust in public officials, political efficacy, support for democratic processes, and tolerance of others.

TABLE 7-5 **POLITICAL IDEOLOGIES: WHO HAS THEM? (PERCENTAGE AGREEING)**

	LIBERAL			MODERATE			CONSERVATIVE		
	1982	1992	1994	1982	1992	1994	1982	1992	1994
Sex									
Male	30	26	19	37	29	28	33	45	53
Female	29	30	21	42	34	40	29	37	39
Age									
18–29	31	32	25	43	35	35	26	33	40
30–49	35	32	24	36	26	30	29	43	46
50–64	23	21	14	44	33	35	33	46	51
65 and up	24	19	12	38	40	42	38	41	45
Race									
White	42	27	19	35	31	33	23	43	48
Nonwhite	25	36	26	42	37	48	34	28	27
Party									
Democrat	35	44	38	40	32	39	25	24	22
Republican	17	8	5	37	27	22	46	66	73
Independent	31	28	18	49	35	42	20	38	41

Source: The American National Election Studies, conducted by the University of Michigan, Center for Political Studies, Ann Arbor, Michigan. Data provided by the Inter-University Consortium for Political and Social Research, located at the University of Michigan, Center for Political Studies, Ann Arbor, Michigan.

The role of government   What do the American people see as the proper role of government? In the economic realm, support for government intervention to promote employment, control inflation, and foster growth has remained fairly consistent since the Great Depression. However, there has been disagreement over how much the government should be involved in the economy, and how much it should regulate economic activity. This disagreement is often couched in partisan and ideological terms, with Democrats and liberals supporting a larger government role than Republicans and conservatives.

In the realm of social issues, attitudes do not fit neatly into partisan categories, although they do divide along ideological lines. Liberals in general, and racial and ethnic minorities in particular, favor a more vigorous government role—promoting racial integration, voting rights, and equal opportunity programs—than do conservatives and whites. On issues where moral judgments come into play—pornography, obscenity, homosexual behavior, abortion—there also tends to be a liberal-conservative cleavage, with conservatives inclining more than liberals toward the imposition of community standards by government intervention.

Abortion is a particularly divisive social issue. Recent surveys indicate that age, education, and religion are the most important factors in explaining public attitudes on abortion. As a general rule, young people and those with more formal education favor the pro-choice position of legalized abortion in all cases more than do older people and those with lower educational levels. Of the religious groups, Catholics tend to support the pro-choice position of legal abortion in all or most cases almost as often as Protestants do, despite Church doctrine that opposes abortion. (See Table 7-2 on page 201.)

Trust in public officials   The question of what the government should do in certain policy areas becomes meaningless unless citizens can trust public officials to mean what they say, say what they mean, and do what they promise. Without trust, no government can operate successfully; without trust, the motives of public officials will always be suspect and their actions subject to misunderstanding and misinterpretation.

In the early 1970s, President Richard Nixon lost the trust of the American people when he attempted to cover up the involvement of his White House staff in the burglary of the Democratic National Committee at the Watergate office building. As a result, his power declined and he lost the ability to govern effectively. The Watergate scandal was one of a series of events, including the Vietnam War, that resulted in a steady decline of trust in the United States government by its citizens during the 1960s and 1970s. As the economy improved in the early 1980s, trust in government increased; but as Figure 7-6 shows, it leveled off by the middle of the decade. During the early 1990s (with the exception of brief periods such as those following the Persian Gulf War and the Oklahoma City bombing) it was on the decline once again, at least partly because of a series of incidents that revealed members of Congress and executive branch officials to be abusing the perquisites of their office. Disappointment at the performance of those in office, and particularly those in Congress, has also continued.

People tend to be less willing to give government officials leeway in developing policy if they have little trust in the ability of those officials to find acceptable solutions. A decline in trust also shortens the length of time the public is willing to wait for results. It increases cynicism and discourages the participation in the political process that is so important in a democracy.

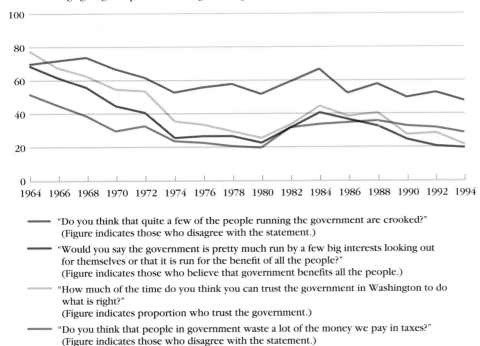

Percentage giving a response indicating trust in government

——— "Do you think that quite a few of the people running the government are crooked?"
(Figure indicates those who disagree with the statement.)

——— "Would you say the government is pretty much run by a few big interests looking out
for themselves or that it is run for the benefit of all the people?"
(Figure indicates those who believe that government benefits all the people.)

——— "How much of the time do you think you can trust the government in Washington to do
what is right?"
(Figure indicates proportion who trust the government.)

——— "Do you think that people in government waste a lot of the money we pay in taxes?"
(Figure indicates those who disagree with the statement.)

FIGURE 7-6

Trust in government, 1964–1994.

SOURCE: Analysis based on data from the American National Election Studies, conducted by
the University of Michigan, Center for Political Studies, Ann Arbor, Michigan. Data provided
by the Inter-University Consortium for Political and Social Research, located at the
University of Michigan, Center for Political Studies, Ann Arbor, Michigan.

Levels of trust are not uniform throughout the population. Young people traditionally exhibit more trust in government than their elders do. Although political
trust among young people declined during the late 1960s and early 1970s, by the
mid 1970s young people were again the most trusting of any age group, and they
have remained so since that time. Political trust is also generally greater among people with higher education; however, African-American college graduates have
been less trusting than African Americans who do not have a college education.

Trust also varies among racial groups, largely in response to their ability to identify with the policies of a particular president. For example, trust in government
among African Americans rose during the early 1960s but declined after Richard
Nixon became president in 1969. Conversely, when Jimmy Carter became president,
African Americans' trust increased but that of whites continued to decline. Political
trust among whites declined steadily from 1958 until 1980, rose slightly during the
Reagan presidency, but declined again in the early 1990s.

Declining trust has partisan implications as well. It has hurt the Democrats more
than the Republicans, since their rank and file are less trustful of government and
more critical of its performance.[18] Trust is a motivation for voting.

Not only are people less trusting of government, but they are less trusting of each
other. In 1964, approximately half of Americans believed that others could be
trusted most of the time. By the end of 1995, that percentage had dropped to 35.[19]

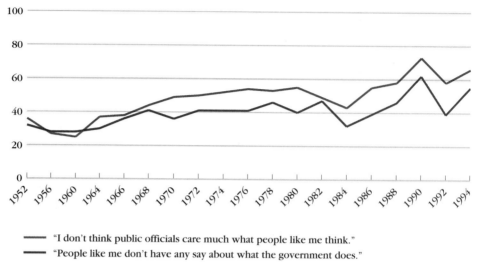

Percentage agreeing with the statement

——— "I don't think public officials care much what people like me think."

——— "People like me don't have any say about what the government does."

FIGURE 7-7

Political efficacy, 1952–1994.

SOURCE: Analysis based on data from the American National Election Studies, conducted by the University of Michigan, Center for Political Studies, Ann Arbor, Michigan. Data provided by the Inter-University Consortium for Political and Social Research, located at the University of Michigan, Center for Political Studies, Ann Arbor, Michigan.

Political efficacy For civic responsibility to be taken seriously, citizens must believe that they can make a difference, that they can bring about a desired political outcome. This belief, known as **political efficacy**, was discussed in Chapter 6. Like trust, political efficacy has declined in recent years; Figure 7-7 documents the drop.

Evidence of lower political efficacy can also be seen in the decreasing levels of voter turnout since the 1960s, when a little over 60 percent of the eligible population voted. During the 1970s and 1980s, that percentage declined to the point where barely more than half the electorate voted in the 1988 presidential election. Although turnout did increase to 55 percent in 1992, it was only in the range of 36 percent in the 1994 midterm elections and approximately 49 percent in 1996, the lowest level in a presidential election since 1924. A sizable proportion of American voters still apparently believes that their vote does not really matter.

As a group, both African Americans and Hispanics have a lower sense of efficacy than whites do. Their lower levels of education explain some of the difference, because studies conducted regularly since the 1950s have consistently found that education is correlated with higher levels of political efficacy. Yet the increase in educational levels in the general public has not resulted in an overall increase in political efficacy, nor has it led to an increase in the portion of the population that votes. Among the factors that contribute to lower efficacy today are the weakening of party loyalties, cynicism caused by the news media's attention to conflicts of interest and unethical behavior on the part of public officials, and the size and complexity of modern government and the average citizen's difficulties in dealing with it.

Trust and efficacy are related. People who trust government tend to feel that they can affect its decisions, whereas those who lack trust often feel helpless and become alienated and angry.[20] In the 1990s much of this anger has been directed against the federal government and those who run it. The vote against the presidential incum-

In the aftermath of the 1995 bombing of the federal office building in Oklahoma City, media attention to the strident antigovernment stance of paramilitary groups (left) and right-wing talk show hosts generated a public backlash against them. The show hosted by Gordon Liddy (right), who had demonstrated for viewers how to shoot to kill federal agents, was canceled by some stations.

bent in 1992 and against the Democrats (the party controlling Congress) in 1994 reflected much unhappiness with the way those in power were behaving and governing. More extreme manifestations of this anger have included the growth of private militia groups around the country and terrorist acts such as the 1995 bombing of the federal office building in Oklahoma City. Fueled by increasingly negative media coverage of government and hostile political rhetoric, particularly on talk radio, this alienation and anger can create conditions that undermine a democratic political system.

For such a system to exist and thrive, the people must value the rules of democracy—the principles and processes on which it is based. If people perceive the rules as unfair, they are unlikely to be content with electoral or policy decisions made in accordance with those rules, and they may choose not to abide by those decisions.

Levels of satisfaction with government vary with the culture of a society, its political tradition, and the stability of its government. Figure 7-8 shows how people in four European countries felt about their governments from the late 1970s to the early 1990s.

Support for democratic processes Fortunately, most Americans value the norms that underlie their political system.[21] Although they have been increasingly critical of their government, they strongly oppose taking violent actions against it, as can be seen in the reaction to the Oklahoma City bombing (see Figure 7-9). In fact, public support for the principles of majority rule and minority rights remains high.

Surveys conducted during the last two decades have also found greater tolerance for diverse groups and nontraditional behaviors, including changes in gender roles.

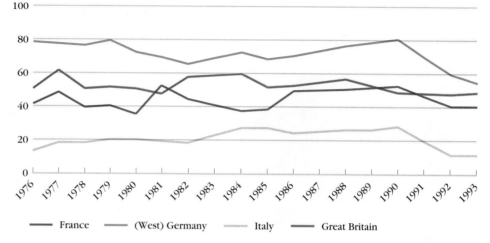

Question: "On the whole, are you very satisfied, fairly satisfied, not very satisfied, or not at all satisfied with the way democracy works in (your country)?" The lines on the figure represent the totals of those who answered "very satisfied" or "fairly satisfied." Before 1990, Germany included only West Germany.

FIGURE 7-8

Europeans' satisfaction with their government, 1976–1993.

SOURCE: Index to International Public Opinion Series, 1976–1994, Westport, Conn.: Greenwood Press, 1995.

In theory at least, people seem more willing today than they were in the past to tolerate homosexual behavior, accept women in what were traditionally considered male jobs, and vote for minority candidates for office. In practice, however, certain beliefs and affiliations (atheism, racism, communism, and Nazism, for example), certain forms of speech (obscenity, blasphemy, and speech that is perceived as sexual harassment), and certain kinds of behavior (desecration of patriotic symbols, lesbian motherhood, and interracial marriage) are not as readily tolerated.

How to prevent people from being intolerant of others is an extremely difficult problem. Attempts to protect minority rights by prohibiting discrimination have themselves become controversial. Consider free speech. Most Americans are taught that freedom of speech is a central element of their belief system and that it is protected by the First Amendment to the Constitution. Yet how tolerant are people of speech that contains objectionable ideas, fighting words, or racial or religious slurs? In the late 1980s, some colleges and universities created codes of conduct that punished those whose speech and actions denigrated or offended others, particularly women and certain minority groups. Proponents of these codes contend that some words constitute or can lead to behavior that violates people's rights, behavior that society has a right to prevent. However, critics contend that the codes establish what kinds of language and behavior are **politically correct** and limit individual rights protected by the First Amendment. Several codes have subsequently not met the test of constitutionality, and others have been modified or rescinded by the schools that issued them.

Tolerance of others   Tolerance is a learned behavior. It is influenced by family, school, community, and the many associations people have in the course of their

Q: Thinking about the overall goals and activities of armed private militia groups, would you say you support the armed private militia groups strongly, support them somewhat, oppose them somewhat, or oppose them strongly?

Q: On another subject, if you had to say, would you say you think of the federal government as your friend or as your enemy, or don't you think about it in those terms?

Q: Do you think it is ever justified for citizens to take violent action against the United States government, or not?

Q: I'm going to read a few statements. For each one, please tell me if you agree or disagree with that statement:

A. *People in this country are too quick to criticize the federal government.*

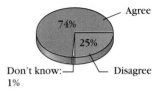

B. *The federal government is taking more and more rights and freedoms away from average citizens.*

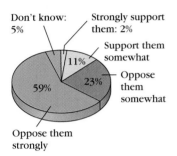

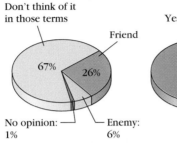

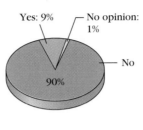

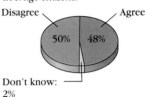

FIGURE 7-9
Government as friend or foe.

SOURCE: Laura Stanton, *Washington Post*/ABC News Poll, *Washington Post*, May 18, 1995, A1, A14.

daily lives. Once again, level of education seems to be the most important factor. The more education a person has, the more likely it is that he or she will be tolerant of those who are different.

How tolerant are the American people today? Figure 7-10 gives some indication of people's willingness to let others express their beliefs. Although Americans obviously have a way to go before they accept in practice what they preach in theory, they do seem to be more tolerant than in the past.[22] Whether that tolerance would continue to increase in the light of major economic, social, or political upheavals is difficult to say. The case of Germany during the 1930s and 1940s, when the Nazis gained control and tried to eliminate "non-Aryan" minorities, leftists, homosexuals, and various other groups, provides a thought-provoking example in view of the relatively high levels of education prevailing in that country at the time.

A considerable amount of research has focused on differences in beliefs and behavior between **elites**, or people in leadership positions, and the general population.[23] The key finding of this research is that elites tend to be more supportive of the political rights of others than is the general population (see Table 7-6). Does the fact that the average person is less tolerant than are the governing elites and less supportive of the norms and practices of democracy threaten the democratic character of the system? According to a group of scholars known as **democratic elitists**, the answer is no. As long as those in power make decisions and take actions in accordance with democratic principles, they argue, the character of the system is not threatened (although, obviously, public support of basic democratic values is still essential).[24]

Homosexuals should be allowed to . . .

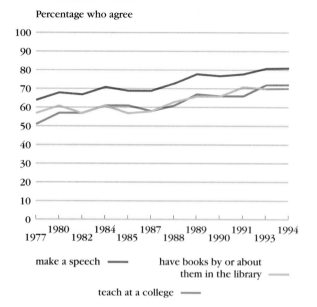

make a speech —— have books by or about
them in the library ——

teach at a college ——

Racists should be allowed to . . .

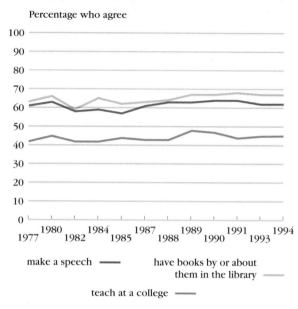

make a speech —— have books by or about
them in the library ——

teach at a college ——

Atheists should be allowed to . . .

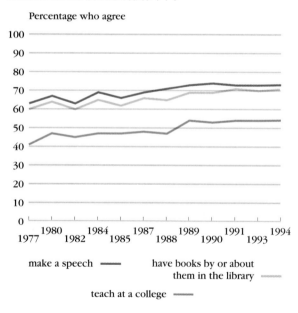

make a speech —— have books by or about
them in the library ——

teach at a college ——

Communists should be allowed to . . .

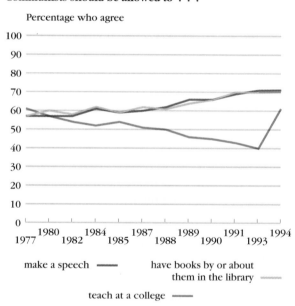

make a speech —— have books by or about
them in the library ——

teach at a college ——

FIGURE 7-10

Tolerance of homosexuals, racists, atheists, and communists.

SOURCE: General social surveys, National Opinion Research Center, University of Chicago, 1994.

Although tolerance of others' differences is a basic democratic principle, many Americans find it difficult to accept speech and behavior that conflicts sharply with their own values or those of the majority. Among actions that can still arouse strong passions are interracial dating, public nudity or cross-dressing, and disrespect for patriotic or religious symbols such as the flag or the cross.

Another factor that affects tolerance is personality. The need for a more structured and ordered existence makes some people less able to accept behavior that violates the norms of society than are others who can function in a looser, less structured environment. The term **authoritarian personality** is often used to describe people who are prone to doctrinaire views and willing to follow those who preach them. Their behavior pattern of dominance and submission is thought to compensate for deeply held feelings of insecurity.[25]

The impact of personality on tolerance is difficult to measure, although it is frequently used to explain behavior. In general, the less real and direct a perceived threat is, the more tolerant people are likely to be, regardless of their personality. When an issue becomes personal—particularly when it adversely affects one's job, property, or lifestyle—then it is more difficult for people to be tolerant.

TABLE 7-6	TWO VIEWS OF FREEDOM (PERCENTAGE AGREEING)	Elite	Non-elite
Books that preach the overthrow of the government should be banned from the library.		13	51
It is a good idea for the government to keep a list of people who take part in demonstrations.		17	50
When the country is at war, people suspected of disloyalty should be watched closely or kept in custody.		22	54
A teacher who refuses to salute the flag at a school assembly should be suspended or dismissed.		17	47

Source: Data from Herbert McClosky and Alida Brill, Dimensions of Tolerance *(New York: Russell Sage, 1983), 71, 109, 121, 153. Reprinted by permission of the publisher.*

PUBLIC OPINION AND GOVERNANCE

Regardless of what different groups of Americans believe about issues that are vital to democratic government, the general public does not dictate policy. It cannot. Relatively few people have the time, interest, or motivation to contact government representatives directly. Moreover, specific policy issues have minimal influence on the voting behavior of most Americans.

What is the role of public opinion in the determination of policy? It helps establish the salience of issues and, to some extent, identifies acceptable and unacceptable policy alternatives. For example, consider the drug problem. Policy options range from educational campaigns in schools, to methadone treatment centers for addicts, to criminal prosecution for those who sell illegal drugs. To date, however, the legalization of "hard" drugs has not been seen as a viable option because it conflicts with the public's strongly held view that these drugs are dangerous and their use should be discouraged.

A high level of public interest and concern indicates that an issue is important and, usually, that something must be done about it. If there is a dominant mood or opinion, public officials tend to follow it. Scholars who have studied opinion change and policy outcomes have found a correlation between the two;[26] they have also found that opinion change *precedes* rather than *follows* policy change, a pattern that one would expect in a democracy.[27]

For most issues, however, there is not a single dominant opinion but a variety of opinions. These opinions are developed, publicized, and communicated by the opinion makers, who have the skills, contacts, and motivation to try to convert them into policy decisions. Specific courses of action are more likely to be influenced by the interchange between opinion makers and government officials than by the general public. However, the values and beliefs of the people are still important because they set the parameters within which policy debate occurs and policy decisions are made.

Do officials respond to the public's opinions, or do they try to shape them? They try to do both. At the national level, government officials regularly make use of public opinion polls to discern the contours of political attitudes and the prevalent opinions of the day. In 1979 Jimmy Carter cited the results of a national survey conducted by his pollster, Pat Caddell, when he described the public mood as a malaise that needed to be cured. Throughout their presidencies, Ronald Reagan, George Bush, and Bill Clinton used surveys conducted for them or their parties to assess and react to the public mood. The Republican congressional leadership was heavily influenced by focus groups in drafting its 1994 Contract with America as well as in selling it, and particularly its proposal to cut the growth of Medicare, to the American people in the fall of 1995. On the basis of what they learned in the focus groups, Republicans described their changes not as cuts but as reforms to protect and preserve the Medicare system.

Because government officials have been extremely sensitive to public opinion, they have been accused of pandering to it and also of manipulating it to their advantage. Such accusations, however, do not take account of the fine line between leading and following. A good leader gets out in front, but not too far. Although Americans may fault their political leaders for failing to heed public opinion or to lead it, government officials still must make many of their decisions without knowing exactly how the public will react.

Moreover, effective policy may demand that decision makers do what they think is right and what will benefit the country the most in the long run, regardless of the public mood and the short-run consequences of a decision. But there is a danger here, too. American history is filled with examples of policies that failed or had to be curtailed because of lack of public support. Prohibition is one outstanding example; the Vietnam War and President Clinton's proposals to reform the health-care system are others.

Finally, what is the impact of public opinion on the politics of American government? The public's values and beliefs constitute the intellectual foundation on which the political system rests; the public's opinions frame the policy debate and influence the government's decisions. Those decisions, in turn, are continuously subject to public evaluation and reevaluation. Public opinion therefore is a critical component of democratic politics.

SUMMARY

Public opinion affects the politics of American government, as it should in a system based on popular consent. The politics of public opinion is evident in the stands candidates take, in the decisions officials make, and in the policy they establish for the country. Although the politics of public opinion influences the issues the government tackles and when and how it tackles them, public opinion does not usually dictate specific solutions. Rather, it sets the parameters within which policy debate occurs and contentious issues are resolved by those with the knowledge, power, and responsibility to do so.

The *opinions* (judgments on current issues), *attitudes* (broad orientations toward policy areas), and *values* (basic ideals and beliefs) of the public all impact on public policy. Of these components, opinions vary the most. They can be described in terms of their *direction* (the proportion of the population that holds a certain view), their *stability* or *fluidity* (whether or not a view changes over time), their *salience* (their importance), and their *intensity* (how strongly a view is held).

Opinion-holders can be categorized on the basis of the amount of information they possess. The *mass public* is the least informed, most apathetic, most easily manipulated, and the largest group. The *attentive public* is better informed and more interested, but it takes little political action beyond voting. These two groups determine how far the public is willing to go on an issue. *Opinion makers* are set apart by their interest, knowledge, and political activities. They shape specific policies, influence others, and inform public debate.

The most efficient way to discover what the public thinks is by conducting *public opinion polls*, or surveys that ask questions of a *sample* representing the population under study. Samples are *randomly selected*; that is, every element of the population under study has an equal chance of being included. In assessing the accuracy of a sample, pollsters consider two factors: *sampling error*, the degree to which the sample could deviate from the population as a whole; and *level of confidence*, the extent to which the results could be incorrect by chance.

Polls may be inaccurate because of how questions are worded, how surveys are constructed, or how responses are interpreted. Emotional or controversial words may introduce bias. The use of *closed-ended questions* (which force a choice from a list of items) or *open-ended questions* (which have no predetermined answer) may also influence responses, as may the order of the questions or the way an interview is conducted.

Most Americans are poorly informed about government and public policy. Education seems to be the key variable; those with more formal education tend to be better informed. Above-average income also correlates with higher levels of political information. And as people age, they become more aware of how political decisions affect them. A poorly informed public gives government leaders more flexibility in making policy decisions, but it also encourages short-term solutions and increases the influence of interest groups.

Because Americans are ambivalent about many issues, they often adopt a *belief system*, a set of simplified ideas that helps them understand and cope with the world. A *political ideology* is a belief system that shapes responses to policy issues and positions. The two dominant political ideologies in the United States are *liberalism* and *conservatism*.

Liberals tend to support government intervention in social and economic programs—especially to protect civil rights and promote equal opportunity—and to oppose government action that might deprive individuals of basic freedoms. Conservatives tend to oppose government involvement—especially in the economic sphere, contending that a free market produces the prosperity that solves many of the country's social ills; but they are more supportive of it to curb behavior that conflicts with the norms of society. Conservatives lean toward the Republican party, whereas liberals lean toward the Democratic party.

Although most Americans agree that government should promote employment, control inflation, and foster growth, they disagree over how extensive such involvement should be. Indeed, attitudes toward the overall role of government vary widely, as do levels of trust in public officials and levels of belief in *political efficacy*, the idea that political participation can make a difference. In general, however, the American public supports the concepts of democracy and the principles of majority rule and minority rights. It opposes violating the law and disobeying the government despite a trend of declining confidence in and increasing cynicism about government and the performance

and behavior of those who work in it. In terms of applying the principles of democracy and the rule of law, there is less agreement. Certain beliefs and affiliations, forms of speech, and types of behavior are not as readily tolerated as others. However, codes of conduct that attempt to establish the bounds of *politically correct* language and behavior have been criticized as violating constitutionally protected freedoms.

Tolerance seems to decline with age and to increase with education. Research also shows that *elites* (those who lead) support political rights for individuals more than does the general population (those who follow). *Democratic elitists* say that as long as those in power honor democratic principles, the system is not threatened. People with *authoritarian personalities* are very intolerant.

Public opinion does not dictate policy, but it does establish the salience of issues and set limits on acceptable policy alternatives. A high level of public interest indicates that an issue is important and requires action. But in most cases, no single opinion dominates. When many different opinions exist, policy is more apt to be produced by negotiations between opinion makers and government officials than by the general public.

KEY TERMS

public opinion
opinions
attitudes
values
salience
direction
stability
fluidity
intensity
mass public

attentive public
opinion makers
public opinion poll
sample
random selection
sampling error
level of confidence
closed-ended question
open-ended question
belief system

political ideology
liberalism
conservatism
political efficacy
politically correct
elites
democratic elitists
authoritarian personality

RESOURCES

SCHOLARLY STUDIES

Cantril, Albert H. *The Opinion Connection: Polling, Politics, and the Press*. Washington, D.C.: Congressional Quarterly, 1991. An introduction to the merits and pitfalls of polling and the application of polling to the political process.

Cook, Elizabeth A., Ted G. Jelen, and Clyde Wilcox. *Between Two Absolutes: Public Opinions and the Politics of Abortion*. Boulder, Colo.: Westview, 1992. Uses extensive survey data to analyze public opinion on this divisive and highly emotional issue.

Craig, Stephen C. *The Malevolent Leaders: Popular Discontent in America*. Boulder, Colo.: Westview,

1993. A study of the trends in and causes of public distrust in government.

Erikson, Robert S., Norman R. Luttbeg, and Kent L. Tedin. *American Public Opinion: Its Origins, Content, and Impact.* 4th ed. New York: Macmillan, 1991. An excellent summary of the literature on political opinion by three political scientists.

Erikson, Robert S., Gerald C. Wright, and John P. McIver. *Statehouse Democracy: Public Opinion and Policy in the American States.* New York: Cambridge University Press, 1993. A well-researched and well-documented correlation of public opinion and public policy in the fifty states.

Herbst, Susan. *Numbered Voices: How Opinion Polling Has Shaped American Politics.* Chicago: University of Chicago Press, 1993. A historical account of how polling data have come to play an important role in American politics.

Hunter, James Davison. *Before the Shooting Begins: Searching for Democracy in America's Culture War.* New York: Free Press, 1994. A contemporary study of public opinion on the abortion issue and the competing values on which that opinion is based.

McClosky, Herbert, and Alida Brill. *Dimensions of Tolerance: What Americans Believe About Civil Liberties.* New York: Russell Sage, 1983. A study of political beliefs that argues that tolerance is a learned behavior reinforced by group associations.

Sapiro, Virginia. *The Political Integration of Women.* Urbana: University of Illinois Press, 1984. A thorough analysis of the development of women's political consciousness in the 1980s.

Smith, Robert C., and Richard Seltzer. *Race, Class, and Culture: A Study in Afro-American Mass Opinion.* Albany: State University of New York Press, 1992. Examines racial attitudes and opinions within the African-American community and contrasts those attitudes and opinions with those of the white majority in the United States.

Stimson, James A. *Public Opinion in America: Moods, Cycles, and Swings.* Boulder, Colo.: Westview, 1991. Presents a theory of how public moods change and the impact of those changes on politics and elections.

LEISURE READING

Edsall, Thomas B., with Mary D. Edsall. *Chain Reaction: The Impact of Race, Rights, and Taxes on American Politics.* New York: Norton, 1992. A study of three divisive issues and their impact on contemporary American politics.

Harris, Louis. *Inside America.* New York: Vintage Books, 1987. A summary of a well-known pollster's findings about attitudes and beliefs in America, written in a lucid, tongue-in-cheek style.

Hoffer, Eric. *The True Believer.* San Bernardino, Calif.: Borgo Press, 1991. A provocative analysis of the psychological and social needs that underlie mass movements.

ORGANIZATIONS

The Gallup Poll, 53 Bank Street, Princeton, NJ 08540; phone (609) 924-9600; fax (609) 924-2584; Internet http://www.Gallup.com/

Inter-University Consortium for Political and Social Research, Institute for Social Research, University of Michigan, Ann Arbor, MI 48106; phone (313) 764-5494; fax (313) 764-8041; e-mail netmail @um.cc.umich.edu Internet http://www.icpsr.umich.edu/

Roper Center for Public Opinion Research, User Services Department, P.O. Box 440, Storrs, CT 06268; phone (203) 486-4440; fax (203) 486-6308; Internet http://www.lib.uconn.edu/RoperCenter/

Political Interest Groups

A mericans care about the environment, but they also care about the economy. In the last three decades these concerns and the interests that support them have continually clashed with one another. On one side are the environmental groups, such as the Sierra Club, the National Wildlife Federation, the Environmental Defense Fund, and the Natural Resources Defense Council; their allies from state and local governments; and concerned members of the scientific community. On the other side are various economic groups: trade associations such as the American

Manufacturers Association, the National Lumber Association, and the U.S. Chamber of Commerce; energy producers and consumers; and the workers who are employed in these industries.

In their battles over legislation to establish environmental standards and regulations to implement them, each side has developed a strategy for achieving its policy objectives. Each has worked with its own allies on Capitol Hill and in the executive branch. Each has tried to mobilize public support. And each has been involved in electoral politics, supporting like-minded candidates for office.

During the 1970s the environmentalists had the upper hand. Not only did they gain legislation to reduce pollution into the air, water, and soil, to protect endangered species, and to conserve and manage the nation's natural resources; they also saw the creation of the federal Environmental Protection Agency (EPA), charged with issuing regulations, monitoring activities, and prosecuting violators. In 1980, Congress even created a Superfund to help pay the costs of cleaning up sites contaminated with toxic wastes.

With the election of Ronald Reagan later that year, however, the fortunes of the environmental proponents began to change. The Reagan administration, more sympathetic to the economic concerns and wanting to decrease the federal government's regulatory activities, ordered the EPA to reduce its aggressive enforcement of environmental standards.

Moreover, Congress, particularly the Republican-controlled Senate from 1981 to 1987, resisted new and more far-reaching environmental legislation.

In 1986, environmental and economic groups began a major battle over clean air legislation, in which the economic forces were initially successful. With the backing of the Reagan administration, they prevailed on their congressional allies to block the bill in committee. But the battle resumed in subsequent Congresses, and by the end of the decade, growing environmental concern had generated sufficient political pressure to make the adoption of some legislation likely. Consequently, President George Bush, elected in 1988, proved far more sympathetic to such legislation than President Reagan had been. Changes in congressional leadership also contributed to a more favorable climate for enacting legislation.

During the first year of his administration, President Bush delivered a major speech on the environment. He later proposed a bill to tighten controls on utilities that burned soft coal and to institute new, tougher auto emissions standards. Praised at first by environmentalists and criticized by energy producers and users, his proposals became the focus of a new debate and provided the basis for a compromise in 1990, known as amendments to the Clean Air Act.

In politics, however, defeat is rarely final if the issue and the protagonists remain. This time it was the business community that took the lead, urging the president to avoid issuing stringent rules to implement the new law. In 1992, facing enormous political pressure from organized groups that had supported his administration, as well as a tough reelection campaign, Bush gave in to their demands. Although doing so failed to save his electoral fortunes, it was left to the Clinton administration to issue the regulations by which the 1990 law was to be effectively implemented.

But the pendulum has kept swinging. In 1993, President Clinton was forced to seek a compromise between loggers and environmentalists in the Northwest over the threat posed to the spotted owl, an endangered species, by continued logging in the forests it inhabited. After their victory in the 1994 elections, congressional Republicans tried to limit the EPA's regulatory clout by substantially restricting its authority to enforce parts of the Clean Air Act and the Clean Water Act. But divisions developed within the party. Moderate Republicans broke with their leadership and joined Democrats to strike the EPA restrictions. Powerful environmental interests lobbied against tying the hands of the EPA. With public opinion coalescing against them, the Republicans were also forced to restore funding they had initially proposed be cut from the agency's 1996 budget and to enact a law that requires state and local governments to inform people about health-threatening substances in their drinking water.

The clash over environmental issues illustrates the pervasiveness of interest group politics in practically all aspects of contemporary policy making, both foreign and domestic, and in all arenas of government from the legislative to the executive to the judicial. Whether the concern be clean air and water, wetlands, endangered species, private property rights, grazing and mining fees, pesticides, farm conservation, fishing, nuclear and chemical waste disposal, interstate garbage dumping, international trade, or the costs of toxic-waste cleanup, diverse groups cooperate with or contend against one another to influence government and affect public policy.

 he ebb and flow of interest group activity is another aspect of the politics of American government. This activity occurs within a political system that encourages people to organize to pursue their objectives and protects them when they do so, but also limits their activities by laws that establish the bounds of acceptable and nonacceptable behavior. Who wins and who loses these political battles, and to what extent, is determined by several factors: the size and clout of the groups, the political environment in which they must operate, and the partisan composition of government. Those groups that are best able to mobilize large coalitions, to shape and activate public opinion, and to gain access to and influence over those in power are apt to be most successful.

The struggle among groups is continuous, and it extends from the electoral to the governing arenas and within each of the branches of government. The objective is favorable public policy. The openness of the process to outside interests is consistent with democracy; the advantages certain groups have and the benefits they receive may not be. Therein lies the dilemma of interest group politics for a democratic society.

This chapter addresses the political dimensions of interest group activity and their impact on American government. It examines the composition of groups, the functions they serve, the methods they use, the ways in which they affect the electoral and governing processes, and the policy outcomes that result from their activity. In doing so, the chapter raises several fundamental questions about the role of groups in a democratic society. Do the unequal representation of people in groups and the unequal power that interest groups exercise within the political system undercut the democratic process? Do groups facilitate or impede the functioning of government? Does the struggle among groups adversely affect public policy, aiding special interests at the expense of the national interest, or does the pursuit of group interests somehow contribute to the common good?

INDIVIDUALS, GROUPS, AND SOCIETY

People join and participate in groups from birth to death. The family is the first and most basic social unit. As people get older, they associate with others by virtue of where they live, what they believe, and what they like to do. Neighborhood, religious, and recreational groups form the basis of these early associations. As a presidential candidate, Jimmy Carter referred to his various associations in describing himself to the American public: "I am a Southerner and an American. I am a farmer, an engineer, a father and husband, a politician and former governor, a planner, a businessman, a nuclear physicist, a naval officer, a canoeist, and, among other things, a lover of Bob Dylan's songs and Dylan Thomas's poetry."[1]

By providing a sense of community and security, groups contribute to a person's social identity and self-enhancement. They help people reinforce their values, clarify their goals, and identify their achievements. Belonging to a group can be a source of economic benefit as well; labor unions, business groups, and professional organizations regularly seek to promote the financial interests of their members. But groups also promote noneconomic interests such as the environment (Sierra Club), religious or ethical values (the Christian Coalition), ideological beliefs (the American Civil Liberties Union), or the welfare of particular groups of people (National Gay Rights Organization).

To achieve their objectives, groups have to become involved in the political and governing processes. Those that do are referred to as **political interest groups**. They have three primary characteristics: (1) shared interests and goals, (2) an organizational structure, and (3) a desire to influence public policy.

Unless a group involves itself in the political process in order to influence public policy, it is not a political interest group. The local bridge club, for example, is not a political interest group, whereas the American Farm Bureau Federation, the Teamsters Union, the National Rifle Association, and the American Political Science

In the mid 1990s, as the Clinton administration campaigned to reduce smoking by teenagers, the tobacco industry mounted a major advertising effort to assure the public that it, too, wanted to discourage young people from using its products. The industry's role in trying to head off restrictive laws on smoking has come under increasing criticism in recent years as an example of the disproportionate influence exerted on public policy by certain interest groups.

Association are. Institutions such as universities and corporations also get involved in political activities and are often referred to as *organized interests.* They may join together in associations such as the American Association for Higher Education to pursue their common interests. These associations often become active political interest groups.

Political interest groups differ from political parties in several ways. First, they tend to have a narrower membership base than parties—especially the major parties, the Democrats and the Republicans. In addition, political interest groups are more focused on policy issues than are political parties, which are concerned primarily with elections and, if they are successful, with the organization of government. Whereas parties take positions on a wide range of issues, most political interest groups focus their political involvement on those issues that directly relate to their interests. The National Rifle Association is concerned with the possession of firearms but not with farm subsidies, taxes, or abortion. The Republican party, however, has taken positions on all four issues.

In many ways, political interest groups supplement the role of political parties in the governmental process by representing and promoting interests on a wide range of public policy issues. Political interest groups broaden and strengthen the ties

Among the largest and most powerful political interest groups are those representing senior citizens, who have the time and money to ensure that their opinions are well articulated in government. Here they demonstrate on the steps of the Capitol against proposals to cut back the growth of the Medicare program.

between representatives and their constituents. However, they also heighten and extend the political struggle. Many diverse, overlapping, and conflicting groups compete for access and influence within government, within the parties, within the electorate, and increasingly, within the electoral arena.

Interest group formation is not uniquely American; in most democratic societies interest groups supplement political parties in making demands on government. However, the nature of the groups varies. The United States has a pluralistic system in which a variety of groups such as business, labor, and professional associations, even ethnic and racial organizations, flourish and compete with political parties for influence. In Germany and some of the countries of northern Europe, the groups are comparatively larger and more centralized than they are in the United States and often work in concert with political parties to affect government decision making. France and Italy have more groups than Germany, but many of them are under the tutelage of larger institutions such as the Catholic Church and the Communist or Socialist parties.[2] Canada, the United Kingdom, and Japan have multiple and diverse groups like those in the United States.

Regardless of how groups are organized, they compete with one another to influence politics and policy making. Some people believe that this competition is beneficial to a democratic society, that interest groups perform a useful and necessary function. Others are not so sure, fearing that groups promote their own interests at the public's expense. The automobile industry's objections to strict emissions standards, the National Rifle Association's campaign to protect and promote gun ownership, and the tobacco lobby's attempt to head off a ban on cigarette advertising are three illustrations of interest group positions and activities that some would regard as harmful to the general public. Does group activity aid or hurt the democratic process? It can do both, depending on how well groups represent the population as a whole, how effectively they exercise influence, and how much of that influence shapes public policy.

POLITICAL INTEREST GROUPS
AND DEMOCRATIC THEORY

Group activity is not, in and of itself, inconsistent with democracy. Political interest groups can educate people about their civic responsibilities. By increasing public awareness, providing an outlet for public expression, and encouraging participation in the political process, interest groups energize the political system, extend democracy, and channel self-interested behavior into legitimate and productive political activity. On the other hand, group activity can weaken democracy if the competition between groups is unbalanced—that is, if certain groups become dominant by virtue of their size, status, access to policy makers, or skills in influencing them. To illustrate, for years the American Medical Association (AMA) was the most powerful health-care group, and it used its power to prevent the development of programs that it viewed as a threat to private medical practice in the United States. But as other health-care professionals and citizen activists organized and lobbied for new policies and more government involvement in health care, the AMA's influence over this area of public policy began to erode.

Domination by political interest groups is precisely what James Madison feared and why he defended the Constitution in *The Federalist, No. 10.* He argued that people naturally pursue their own interests. If given the freedom to do so, they form *factions* (Madison's term for political interest groups) that have the potential to gain power, control the government, and make policy in their own interests. The dilemma for Madison was to maintain freedom for individuals to join groups and for groups to pursue their own interests while at the same time controlling the harmful effects of their behavior on society.

Madison saw the structure designed by the framers of the Constitution as an effective way to resolve this dilemma. In his view, the representational character of the system refined and distilled public passions, and separate institutions checking and balancing one another decreased the likelihood that a single group—even if it were in the majority—could control the government. For these reasons, Madison lauded and defended the republican form of government created by the Constitution as infinitely better than a direct democracy in which the majority would rule. He also believed that the large size of the country would act as a hedge against a large faction gaining control.

Another problem, one that Madison did not address, is that struggles among groups tend to encourage compromises in policy. Though necessary in a large, pluralistic society like that of the United States, compromises entail the risk of producing wishy-washy policies that do not alienate powerful groups but do not solve difficult problems either. The 1990 amendments to the Clean Air Act mentioned at the beginning of this chapter and the 1996 agreement on drinking water standards are two examples of the kind of compromises that democratic governments make when trying to devise solutions to social and economic problems.

In short, the actions of political interest groups in a democratic system cut two ways. Political interest groups add a dimension to representation or detract from representation, depending on how well they reflect the interests and needs of the general public. Similarly, they can make governing easier or more difficult, depending on how well their interests and needs are transformed into policies.

The consequences of interest group activities for American politics and government are examined later in this chapter. First, however, it is necessary to look at the interest group phenomenon itself: why groups have developed and how they have evolved in the United States, what resources are available to them, and what are the ways in which they have sought to affect public policy.

THE ORIGINS AND DEVELOPMENT
OF POLITICAL GROUPS

In the last several decades, there has been a surge in the activity of political interest groups. Why? What causes these groups to be created? Why have some flourished and others faded quickly from the scene?

Theories of Group Formation

One of the first political scientists to address these questions was David Truman.[3] Writing in the 1950s, Truman postulated that major disturbances within the political environment produce conditions that encourage group activity.[4] He reasoned that people whose interests are adversely affected by these conditions will band together to improve their lot. In the process, he suggested, they will frequently turn to the government for help.

Truman went on to argue that the creation and activity of political interest groups spurs other people to organize to promote their interests. The process of competitive mobilization that is initiated generates additional group formation and activity, until at some point a balance among groups is achieved and the activity stabilizes. The equilibrium lasts until a new disturbance reactivates the cycle.[5]

Truman's **disturbance theory** assumes the existence of an active and informed citizenry that has the will and the capacity to organize and pursue its interests and redress its grievances. A problem not addressed by disturbance theory, however, is that people do not all have the same will and capability to organize themselves; some have greater incentive to do so than others. The differences in people's incentives led economist Mancur Olson to suggest that the principal incentives for joining a group are the **selective benefits** that people receive from being members.[6] If the benefits of membership were generally available to people who did not join, there would be little incentive to join. Olson's logic is borne out by the fact that the American Association of Retired Persons, in addition to working for the collective good of Americans over fifty, offers its members a variety of individual benefits such as insurance, mutual funds, credit cards, travel services, and a mail order pharmaceutical service.

A problem with Olson's theory of selective benefits, however, is that it does not appear to be equally applicable to all types of groups. As might be expected, people who join economic groups tend to be more motivated by direct economic benefits than are those who join issue-oriented or ideological groups. Indeed, the motive for joining a pro-life or pro-choice group is very different from the motive for joining a labor union or business association.

Another political scientist, Robert Salisbury, used the analogy of the marketplace to explain why some groups prosper and others do not. A group that has a valuable product and is able to promote it, he suggested, will probably be successful in creating and maintaining its organization. Salisbury saw the group's leaders—or entrepreneurs, as he called them—as holding the key to this success.[7]

Of course, the resources available to the founders of various groups are not equal. In another influential study of interest groups, Jack Walker argued that group formation and activity, particularly in contemporary times, are closely tied to the nature of a group's financial base. Start-up funds need to be sufficient to begin the group and support its operations. At least initially, Walker noted, these funds must be obtained from outside the membership base, although over time the membership may be able to sustain itself financially.[8]

Not only do groups try to influence what the government does, but the government itself stimulates group formation, mobilization, and activities as a consequence of new legislation and regulations.[9] As Walker pointed out, more than half the groups representing senior citizens were organized after the passage of the Medicare legislation and the Older Americans Act in 1965.[10]

When all these theories are put together, they do not yield a single explanation of why groups develop. Rather, various factors seem to be conducive to their origination, continuation, and ongoing activities. These include a discernible interest by the public, an interest that is affected by conditions in the social and economic environment; an incentive for joining and a benefit (not necessarily an economic one) for remaining a member; and leaders who are able to articulate and communicate this benefit to those who desire it. The communication task often requires a strong financial base. When these conditions are present, groups are likely to flourish.

The Evolution of Political Interest Groups

Although political interest groups have existed throughout the nation's history, their development has occurred in waves (lending support to Truman's disturbance theory). The first of these waves occurred prior to the Civil War, from 1830 to 1860, and saw the formation of groups ranging from the anti-immigration, anti-Catholic Know-Nothings of the 1830s and 1840s to the antislavery abolitionists of the 1850s.

In the second wave of group activity, during the 1880s, industrialization and unsettled labor conditions prompted the formation of unions like the American Federation of Labor and the Knights of Labor. Another spurt took place from 1900 to 1920, with the creation and expansion of national business and trade associations like the U.S. Chamber of Commerce, the National Association of Manufacturers, the American Medical Association, and the American Farm Bureau Federation. Such large groups were made possible by a technological revolution that facilitated rapid nationwide communications.

After 1920, activity by political interest groups continued to expand, but the next sustained period of growth did not begin until the 1960s. This new surge of group formation and activity has continued for three decades. In addition to the proliferation and professionalization of groups formed to pursue economic interests (such as business, labor, and trade associations), this period saw the rapid rise of idea and issue groups focusing on political beliefs and fundamental values. (The main categories of political interest groups are listed in Table 8-1 on pages 240–241.) Idea and issue groups include public interest groups such as Common Cause and Public Citizen (one of citizen-activist Ralph Nader's organizations); civil rights groups such as the Congress of Racial Equality and La Raza; and environmental, education, and other issue advocacy organizations.

Why have political interest groups become so numerous since 1960? One major reason is the growth of federal programs and regulatory activities prior to and during this period, which encouraged those whose economic interests were affected to become more involved in the political process so as to protect and expand programs that benefit them. Farmers wanted to maintain high commodity prices or get crop subsidies; laborers tried to preserve and increase minimum wages and job benefits and to improve their working conditions; senior citizens sought to make sure that Social Security and Medicare payments would not diminish. The list of groups wishing to protect their piece of the action has expanded in tandem with the expansion of government in the domestic sphere.

The publicity given to the dissident political movements of the 1960s also con-

RALPH NADER: IN THE PUBLIC INTEREST

In 1964, Ralph Nader, a young attorney on the staff of the U.S. Department of Labor, produced an exhaustively detailed legislative report on highway safety. The next year, that report was expanded into a book, *Unsafe at Any Speed,* a scathing indictment of the design practices of the American automobile industry. In his book Nader alleged that dangerous design flaws, not poor road conditions or bad judgments on the part of drivers, were responsible for many serious highway accidents.

Nader's treatise generated strong public support for passage of the Traffic and Motor Vehicle Safety Act of 1966. During hearings on the bill, the president of General Motors admitted that private detectives had been hired to investigate and discredit Nader. Transformed by this revelation into a folk hero, Nader quickly became the leader of a growing national consumer-rights movement.

He recruited hundreds of young lawyers and activists to his new research organization, the Center for the Study of Responsive Law. "Nader's Raiders," as they soon came to be called, investigated a wide range of public interest issues; the investigations helped lead to mandatory automobile safety features such as seat belts and shatterproof glass, to the creation of the Environmental Protection Agency in 1970 and the Occupational Safety and Health Administration (OSHA) in 1976, and to passage of the Freedom of Information Act in 1974. The placement of air bags in automobiles was also a consequence of his organization's efforts.

In recent years Nader, who is known for his ascetic lifestyle, has continued his active involvement on a host of public policy issues. He strongly objected to the congressional pay raise in 1993 and has been a strong proponent of term limits for members of Congress. He has even proposed compulsory voting to force government to be more responsive to *all* citizens. In economic policy, he has opposed the agreements negotiated by the Clinton administration to promote freer trade on the grounds that they do not adequately protect U.S. safety standards and environmental concerns. He has also vigorously denounced legislation that eliminates the 55-mile-per-hour speed

For more than thirty years Ralph Nader has spearheaded efforts to make consumer products and work environments safer, government more responsible to citizens, and citizens more involved in government. In 1996 he entered the electoral arena as a protest candidate, when the Green party nominated him for president.

limit on interstate highways, arguing that it will increase the number of traffic deaths and injuries.

Nader-inspired organizations such as Public Citizen, Congress Watch, Public Interest Research Groups in twenty-six states, the Disability Rights Center, the Center for Auto Safety, the Freedom of Information Clearinghouse, and the Equal Justice Foundation carry on the fight for consumer rights, corporate and government accountability, and citizen activism. Although Nader's critics contend that his work has provided a bonanza for liability lawyers and that some of these organizations' activities have been funded by the very same lawyers, his supporters point to the money and lives of average citizens that he has saved and to the increased levels of public participation he has generated.

TABLE 8-1	POLITICAL INTEREST GROUPS
BASIC TYPE	**SPECIFIC GROUPS**
Economic	
Business	American Newspaper Publishers Association
	U.S. Chamber of Commerce
	National Association of Manufacturers
	National Federation of Independent Businesses
	Tobacco Institute
	United Ship Owners of America
Labor	AFL-CIO
	American Federation of Teachers
	International Brotherhood of Teamsters
	International Longshoremen's Association
	NFL Players Association
	National Association of Government Employees
Agriculture	American Farm Bureau Federation
	American Feed Industry Association
	National Corn Growers Association
	National Grange
	National Milk Producers Federation
	National Turkey Federation
Other professional associations	Institute of Electrical and Electronic Engineers
	National Association of Professional Insurance Agents
	National Health Lawyers Association
	National Society of Fund Raising Executives
	Reserve Officers Association
Noneconomic	
Public interest	Common Cause
	Congress Watch
	Friends of the Earth
	League of Women Voters
	March of Dimes
	Public Citizen
	United States Public Interest Research Group

tributed to the increase in group activity. By demonstrating the dramatic impact that organized political activism could have on public policy, the civil rights struggles and the protests against the Vietnam War became models for others who felt that government was not being responsive to their needs and interests, such as environmentalists and consumers, or those who were adversely affected by changes in public policy. Organizations opposed to established policies sprang up across the political spectrum. Business groups extended their efforts to resist policies that increased their costs or restricted their freedom to do business, and conservative groups became more active and successful in opposing the government's increasing economic intervention and social welfare programs.

Technology played a part as well. Faster and cheaper means of mass communication such as WATS lines, fax machines, computerized mailings, and now e-mail and home pages on the Internet have made it possible for organizations to reach out and broaden their membership, raise more money, and more effectively promote issues and mobilize grassroots activities. Moreover, the potential membership base of many

TABLE 8-1	POLITICAL INTEREST GROUPS *(continued)*
BASIC TYPE	**SPECIFIC GROUPS**
Noneconomic	
Single-issue	American Civil Liberties Union
	American Rifle Association
	National Abortion Rights League
	National Coalition to Ban Handguns
	National Committee to Preserve Social Security and Medicare
	National Organization for the Reform of Marijuana Laws
	National Right to Life Committee
Ideological	Americans for Democratic Action
	The Conservative Caucus
	Liberty Lobby
	People for the American Way
	National Center for Policy Alternatives
Civil rights	American Arab Anti-Discrimination Committee
	Anti-Defamation League of B'nai B'rith
	Association for Retarded Citizens of the United States
	National Association for the Advancement of Colored People
	National Council of La Raza
	National Organization for Women
Religious	American Jewish Conference
	Christian Coalition
	National Conference of Catholic Bishops
	National Council of Churches
Government	Council of Large Public Housing Authorities
	National Association of Counties
	National Association of State Boards of Education
	National League of Cities
	National Governors Association

public interest, citizen, and consumer advocacy groups has grown greatly since World War II because of the increasing proportion of the population with some college education, who are more likely to see the value of joining and supporting these organizations.[11]

A final factor contributing to the expansion of group activity has been changes in the nature and rules of the political system—notably, the fragmentation and weakening of political parties, the increasing orientation of elections toward candidates rather than party affiliations, the adoption of laws regulating contributions and expenditures, and the opening of the legislative process to public scrutiny. These changes have made candidates for office more solicitous of group support and public officials more sensitive to organized interests.

The proliferation of groups has transformed the politics of American government, making it more pluralistic and more responsive to outside pressures and turning the nation's capital into a city of lobbyists and public relations specialists. The number of Washington-based groups, government relations offices of major corporations,

At some point, almost every group with a cause goes to Washington to "petition the Government for a redress of grievances." One of the most impressive gatherings took place on August 28, 1963, when Martin Luther King Jr. led a march to promote civil rights. With the Lincoln Memorial as a backdrop, King intoned the speech that instilled the phrase "I have a dream . . ." in the American consciousness.

and lobbyists, lawyers, and others involved in public affairs has mushroomed in recent years. More than 11,000 companies in the United States and abroad now have representation in Washington.[12]

Consider the trade associations, for example. In 1971 only 19 percent of them had headquarters in Washington; twenty years later roughly one out of three was located in the nation's capital.[13] Ten years ago there were approximately 10,500 people working for organizations in Washington whose principal objective was to influence the government's decisions on public policy; today that number approaches 15,000. These include about 5,000 officers of trade and professional associations and labor unions; 1,500 corporate representatives; 2,500 advocates of particular causes or issues; 3,000 lawyers representing clients in legal or regulatory matters or registered as lobbyists or foreign agents; 2,500 public relations consultants and lobbyists; 200 officials of political action committees; and 350 policy experts associated with think tanks.[14] Approximately 12,000 organizations and individuals have registered as lobbyists under the 1995 lobbying disclosure law, which now requires registration on the part of those who devote at least 20 percent of their work to representing clients before Congress or the executive branch.[15]

In fact, there are so many lobbyists today that they have formed their own associations to lobby on their behalf—organizations such as the American League of Lobbyists and the National Association of Business Political Action Committees. These groups have been extremely active in opposing bills to limit the tax deductions for business expenses, such as taking public officials to lunch or inviting them to attend conferences at the lobbyist's expense.

The objective of all these lobbying groups is to influence government decisions in ways that protect or promote their own or their clients' interests. To do this, lobbying groups need to know what is happening, how it affects them, and what they can

INTEREST GROUPS

Do you believe in the legalization of marijuana? How about euthanasia? Do you want to volunteer for the American Heart Association? the Red Cross? Or do you want to join a group that protects the welfare of animals, the environment, or the right to own a gun? These are all part of the diverse world of interest groups, or subjects that have inspired the formation of an interest group. Interest groups can be either political or nonpolitical, but they are all great avenues to becoming involved in local or national civic life. The Internet provides a useful way to find out about a group as well as to get up-to-the-minute information on its activities.

A growing number of interest groups have home pages on the World Wide Web. However, it is often difficult to find them—even some of the most politically active. For instance, it is almost impossible to find the e-mail address of Common Cause (75300.3120@compuserve.com) simply by surfing the Net. Here are some tips on how to easily access the interest group of your choice:

YAHOO—A GUIDE TO THE WWW
HTTP://WWW.YAHOO.COM/GOVERNMENT/POLITICS/
INTEREST GROUPS

Several search tools can be used to locate interest groups in cyberspace, but *Yahoo* is a particularly useful, well-organized one that includes "gopher" and "ftp" sites as well as World Wide Web sites on its menu. In *Yahoo*, look for interest groups first under the general category of "Interest Groups." Under the title "Government/Politics/Interest Groups/Public Interest Groups," you will find many political organizations as well as a long list of other groups.

When a group does not fit the category of interest group on the Internet, try looking under specific subjects. For example, the American Heart Association is not listed under "Interest Groups" but it is listed under "Health/Medicine/Cardiology." The Hemp Industries Association is listed under "Business and Economy" only, but its goal, stated on its home page, is clearly political—"to seek to remove a number of the arbitrary barriers that have been imposed on the industry by governmental regulation." Similarly, the Christian Coalition is listed under the entry "Society and Culture/Religion/Organizations/Christianity," even though the site (like the coalition itself) seems heavily involved in political activism.

Don't be discouraged if you can't find the interest group you are looking for. Just call the organization you want to learn about—it may be in the process of getting plugged into the Internet, or already there in a place you hadn't thought to look.

---

do about it. In fact, the desire for information is a principal reason for the vastly increased presence of so many organized interest groups in Washington; staff members spend much of their time and energy simply finding out what is going on or is likely to occur. This monitoring function is as important as lobbying itself, because groups may not even be aware that they have an interest that requires their involvement until a congressional committee holds a hearing or an agency proposes a new regulation.[16] Edward Laumann and David Knoke report the case of a lobbyist for a trade association reading the *Federal Register*, which publishes new government regulations, and discovering, much to his dismay, that the Federal Aviation Administration (FAA) was about to issue a rule requiring detailed flight plans from noncommercial pilots:

> The trade association director muttered, "We've got a problem," and spent a frantic morning on the phone alerting his group's membership to apply pressure on the FAA to set aside the regulation. The executive realized that once detailed flight plans were on record with the FAA, the open-disclosure provisions of the Freedom of Information Act would allow anyone to learn where his member

companies' planes were flying on their aerial explorations for oil, gas, and minerals. The alert director's quick mobilization of collective response saved the corporations potentially millions of dollars worth of secret data that might have fallen into the hands of their competitors.[17]

Once organizations determine that they have a discernible interest in an actual or a projected government decision, they try to affect that decision. What are their sources of influence? Why are some successful and others not?

SOURCES OF GROUP INFLUENCE ON PUBLIC POLICY

All groups are not equally influential. Their power varies according to a number of factors: their size, the composition of their membership, their unity and sense of purpose, their leadership, and the resources at their disposal. Their goals are also a factor, because goals that are grandiose or lie outside the mainstream of public norms, values, or beliefs (the legalization of narcotics, for example, or the establishment of socialized medicine) are not likely to be achieved. Among interest groups, then, some begin with a considerable advantage.

Consider the factor of size. Groups with a large membership such as the American Association of Retired Persons (AARP), with over 33 million members, or the American Automobile Association (AAA), with about 31 million, exercise influence by virtue of their numbers. However, larger groups are more likely to be plagued by internal divisiveness, and issues that are salient to some of their members are less important to others. As a result, dissension may dissipate the group's impact or even discourage it from taking a position.

Large labor unions like the AFL-CIO, business federations like the U.S. Chamber of Commerce, and groups like the National Organization for Women are others that fall into this category. Although their leaders are interested in numerous public issues, their members are united on only a few of them. Business groups and labor groups each unify (usually in opposition to each other) on bread-and-butter issues

Success need not depend on numbers for groups whose followers care enough about their cause. For the 2.5 million members of the National Rifle Association, "stick to your guns" is both the style and the goal. Here Marion P. Hammer, the first woman president in the NRA's 125-year history, sounds the call to arms at the group's 1996 national convention.

such as the minimum wage, health benefits, job security, and working conditions; but their members divide on social issues such as affirmative action. For women's groups, the issues that are most likely to produce a consensus include equal employment opportunity and equal pay, reproductive rights, and child care; for senior citizens they include health and retirement benefits.[18] Smaller organizations, such as the Milk and Ice Cream Association, the National Association of Home Builders, and the National Bankers Association, have a narrower membership base and fewer policy interests, but there is greater consensus among members about which issues are salient. Unity brings strength to the smaller interest groups.

A related factor is emotional intensity. To some extent, depth of feeling can compensate for lack of numbers. For years the National Rifle Association's membership was less than 2.5 million, yet it was able to derail federal gun control legislation.[19] Success has also been experienced by organizations with even smaller memberships, such as the American Civil Liberties Union, in protecting First Amendment rights.

Emotional intensity raises the salience of issues such as abortion and school prayer. But intensity expressed by all sides in an issue may also have the effect of making the problem more difficult to resolve in a manner that satisfies any of them. President Clinton found this out the hard way when he raised the question of whether homosexuals who acknowledge their sexual orientation should be permitted to serve in the military. He proceeded to irritate all the groups that were concerned with this issue: the gay and lesbian community, the military, and various religious groups.

The geographical distribution of a group's members, and their social and professional status, also affect its influence. Groups that are geographically concentrated, such as federal government workers, may exercise a great deal of local power but tend to have much less national influence. On the other hand, large groups with a dispersed membership, such as the National Education Association (NEA), the American Medical Association (AMA), and the American Bar Association (ABA), can be influential on many levels of government. These organizations have also benefited from the professional prestige and social standing of teachers, doctors, and lawyers, respectively.

Financial resources are very important, too, not only for staffing an organization and keeping the members informed but also for lobbying and supporting candidates for office. The Planned Parenthood Federation of America, a group that has been active in the abortion controversy, had a budget of over $405 million in 1995.[20] The American Heart Association, a major combatant against smoking, had a budget of almost $252 million, of which a third was spent on public education.[21] The AARP spent $358.5 million in 1994, of which $35.1 million was devoted to lobbying activities, including political research.[22] Each of these groups employs a large administrative staff. Their extensive resources enable them to engage in a variety of political activities.

The better the financial resources a group has, the more likely its communications facilities will be state-of-the-art. At the U.S. Chamber of Commerce, for example, a satellite television system links the group's national office to its state and local affiliates around the country. A toll-free telephone number allows its members to talk with public officials who are interviewed on its satellite broadcasts or on the television news programs that it regularly sponsors in most media markets. Moreover, the organization maintains a computerized fax network that reaches 42,000 business owners who are members of the Chamber, publishes a magazine with a circulation of over 850,000, and regularly uses these means to mount grassroots campaigns to affect congressional consideration of public policy issues.[23]

Many large political interest groups have both an elected leadership to establish policy and an administrative staff to run the organization. Often, however, the administrative staff, with its professional expertise and day-to-day involvement, assumes de facto policy leadership, defining the group's positions on issues and working to get them adopted by Congress and government agencies.

For organizations with staffs in Washington, an important source of influence is contact with people "in the right place" in government. Washington is full of former members of Congress and former executive branch officials, including senior White House aides, who represent organized interests in the private sector—a practice referred to as **revolving door politics**. Former top-level Department of Defense officials, both military and civilian, may be found working for major government contractors or even for foreign governments. Conversely, federal regulatory agencies are often composed of people who have worked in the industries they are charged with regulating. It is the personal contacts within the relevant government agencies that enhance an interest group's ability to influence those agencies.

Some political interest groups have benefited from a lack of effective opposition. Traditionally, producers (such as automobile manufacturers, pharmaceutical companies, and dairy farmers) have been better represented and more successful than the consumers of their products. Other groups have gained or lost credibility as their claims, interests, and objectives came to coincide or conflict with public moods, attitudes, and beliefs. The tobacco industry is a good example. It exerted considerable influence when most adult Americans smoked, but research findings that smoking can cause heart disease and lung cancer have put the industry on the defensive, leaving it less able to influence public policy decisions than it was decades ago. In contrast, groups such as the American Heart Association and the American Cancer Society now have a major impact on public policy on food processing, product labeling, and smoking.

ELECTORAL ACTIVITY

How do political interest groups influence the politics of American government? A group that is interested in influencing public policy has three electoral options. It can support specific candidates either in an election or when the president proposes a nomination to the Senate. In some states it can also introduce a recall petition to remove elected officials. A recall election occurred in California in 1995 when Los Angeles County voters removed a representative to the state legislature who had been elected as a Republican but switched to independent, thereby denying the Republicans a majority in the lower chamber. The third option, permitted by some states but not the national government, is to petition to get policy initiatives directly on the ballot, usually by obtaining the signatures of 10 percent of the voters in the most recent statewide election. Citizens groups that favor term limits for legislators and groups supporting and opposing homosexuals' rights have actively used the initiative petition route to achieve their policy objectives.

Political interest groups have become extremely active in political campaigns. Before the 1970s, groups channeled most of their campaign activity through the Democratic and Republican party organizations, which exercised more control over nominations and general election campaigns than they do now. Indeed, federal legislation prevented corporations and labor unions from making direct contributions to political campaigns, so they had to work within the parties to exert influence. Today the nomination process is less subject to the dictates of party leaders and more a product of activities initiated by candidates and regulated by government. Laws that limit private contributions, subsidize presidential elections, and require candidates to report revenue and expenditures govern the financial environment in which federal elections occur.

The vehicles for reaching voters have evolved as well. Radio and television have become the principal media through which elections are observed, perceptions formed, and candidates judged. Computerized mailings have also assumed considerable importance, being used for soliciting financial contributions, shaping candidates' images, and generating popular support. Together these communications media have reshaped the electoral process, often outside the rubric of the parties and their organizations. They have provided both incentives and opportunities for political interest groups to affect the elections.

The law does not allow business organizations, labor unions, or other interest groups to make direct contributions to candidates for national office. But it does allow them to form groups among their employees, stockholders, or members to do so. Known as **political action committees (PACs)**, these groups solicit voluntary contributions and use the money to influence political campaigns and policy outcomes. PACs can contribute up to $5,000 to individual candidates (except for the major parties' presidential and vice presidential nominees), spend an unlimited amount of money independently in support of or in opposition to candidates, and educate, mobilize, and register voters on behalf of candidates. And there are even ways to circumvent the contribution limits. In one such technique, called **bundling,** a PAC solicits donations for a group of candidates but requests that the checks be made out directly to specific candidates, not to the PAC. It then bundles together the checks for each candidate and sends them to the candidates. This technique was pioneered by Emily's List, a PAC that solicits contributions for women candidates.

In addition to contributing to federal candidates, PACs can contribute to state and local candidates and political parties in an effort to turn out a large vote. The opportunity to affect who wins and who loses provides a powerful incentive for PACs to organize and participate in the electoral process, and they have done so in a big way.

One particularly active goup in recent years has been the gambling industry. Desirous of legislation that permits legalized gambling, PACs created and financed by the industry contributed millions of dollars to congressional candidates in the mid 1990s and many millions more to state legislative candidates. In Florida alone, they spent $16.5 million in the 1993–1994 election cycle in an unsuccessful effort to win approval for casino gambling in that state.[24]

Types of PACs

Most PACs are composed of people who have formal affiliations with an established organization, such as employees of a corporation or members of a union or trade association. These are known as *connected* PACs. Examples include the RJR Nabisco PAC, the AFL-CIO PAC, the Association of Trial Lawyers of America PAC, the National Association of Realtors PAC, and the NRA Political Victory Fund. *Nonconnected* PACs, which are composed of people who are not connected to such organizations but share the same interests in public policy issues, include groups such as the Committee for an Effective Congress, the National Right to Life Political Action Committee, and the English Language Political Action Committee as well as election-oriented or candidate-oriented groups such as GOPAC, Emily's List, and the Fund for a Democratic Majority. (See the Case Study about GOPAC on pages 248–249.)

THE GOPAC CONTROVERSY

One of the most successful and controversial of the nonconnected PACs has been GOPAC. Founded in 1978 by Delaware governor Pierre S. (Pete) du Pont IV and nineteen other Republican governors, GOPAC took as its primary goal to identify and assist Republican candidates in their campaigns for state and local offices. The objective was to build a Republican "farm team" on the state and local level in order to develop a strong national party from the ground up.

In 1986, Representative Newt Gingrich, a history professor at West Georgia College and subsequently Speaker of the House, took over as chairman of GOPAC. He invigorated and reoriented the organization, using its resources to recruit and train Republican candidates as well as to promote conservative causes and ideology. In 1993 and 1994, GOPAC ran thirty-eight training seminars for congressional, state, and local Republican candidates. Campaign professionals provided instruction on how to start a campaign, exploit an opponent's weaknesses, obtain money from PACs in Washington, and even use particular words when appealing for votes. These sessions were seen as instrumental in the party's success during the 1994 midterm elections. Almost half of the newly elected Republican representatives in 1994 were the products of the GOPAC recruitment and strategy.

Since May 1994, however, GOPAC has been mired in controversy. The Federal Election Commission (FEC) charged that it failed to register as a PAC when it first began supporting candidates for national office, that it has failed to disclose all of its contributors and the size of their contributions, and that the contributions from individual donors exceeded legal limits. A federal court acquitted GOPAC of the first charge in 1996, ruling that its activities in the 1990 election, which included mailings urging voters to elect a Republican majority to Congress, did not constitute evidence that it was trying to influence specific federal elections. GOPAC subsequently registered with the FEC in 1991. There have also been allegations that contributions to state and local candidates in 1990 were not reported as required by some states.[2]

Another charge concerns the disclosure of contributors, which federal law requires. GOPAC has refused to list its contributors prior to 1991. Since then it has reported only some of its contributors and their contributions, the percentage that the PAC claims has been spent on federal elections.

The size of the contributions and the benefits that contributors received for their money have also raised questions. Although federal law limits an individual's contributions to a particular PAC to $5,000 a year, GOPAC solicited and received much larger con-

Before becoming Speaker of the House, Newt Gingrich taught a college course that was made available nationwide through satellite and videotapes. Production and broadcasting costs were subsidized by an educational foundation that in turn received financial support from the Republican-sponsored group GOPAC. Critics charged that because the course lectures and readings promoted Gingrich's conservative ideology, the GOPAC support violated the foundation's tax-exempt status; such foundations are not allowed to engage in political activities.

tributions in the form of "soft money," that is, funds to support voluntary efforts to get out the vote. Political parties have regularly solicited this type of contribution, but PACs have not. The largest contributor has been businessman Terry Kohler, who with his wife gave $715,457 to GOPAC from 1985 to 1994 and an additional $70,000 in early 1995. Other benefactors from 1985–1993 include investment counselor Owen Roberts ($324,513), investor Richard Gilder Jr. ($310,000), and Roger Milliken, chief executive officer of Milliken & Co. ($255,000).[3]

The issue is not only the size of these contributions but also the question of whether large contributors receive special treatment for their money. For example, in a 1990 letter to Gingrich, Miller Nichols noted that he had contributed $50,900 to GOPAC (as well as contributing to Gingrich's campaign funds in 1988 and 1991), and he requested that Gingrich look into federal regulations on asbestos, which he said were costing his company millions of dollars. Gingrich promised to do so and did. In a letter dated April 24, 1991, Gingrich raised the issue of "the crisis of asbestos litigation" with the administrator of the Environmental Protection Agency, William K. Reilly, creating at the very least the appearance of impropriety.[4]

Finally, GOPAC has also come under criticism for providing financial support to a tax-exempt foundation that promoted conservative causes and educational programs with which Gingrich was heavily involved.[5] The foundation helped set up and publicize the course, "Renewing American Civilization," that Gingrich taught at colleges nationwide through a satellite hookup and videocassettes. Here the issue is whether GOPAC money violated the foundation's nonpartisan status; if so, then contributions to the foundation by private individuals (which supplemented the goals of GOPAC) should not have been tax-deductible. The foundation was disbanded in 1995 after the Republicans succeeded in achieving their objective of gaining control of both houses of Congress.

In addition to the FEC, the House Ethics Committee has also been investigating these charges. A special counsel, originally appointed by the committee to look into whether the tax-exempt foundation improperly funded Gingrich's college course, in September 1996 broadened its investigation to include the allegations that GOPAC received illegal contributions and that its donors received favorable treatment in return for their gifts. Gingrich strongly denied that any improprieties had occurred, but his testimony before the committee was also being examined for possible untruthfulness or withholding of information.

Discussion Questions

1. Should PACS be required to reveal the sources and sizes of their contributions, or does such a policy violate an individual or group's right to privacy?
2. Should people and organizations doing business with the government or directly affected by government decisions be prevented from contributing money to campaigns, organizations, or even programs and causes associated with public officials involved in these decisions?
3. What distinguishes a nonpartisan, educational organization from a partisan one? Is it the content of the subject matter or the viewpoint of the subject matter that it promotes? Can and should our tax laws make this nonpartisan/partisan distinction?

[1]GOPAC is an acronym for GOP Action Committee. GOP stands for Grand Old Party, a nickname (first used in the 1870s) for the Republicans.

[2]"New Questions on Donations Made by GOPAC," *New York Times*, April 22, 1996, B8.

[3]From GOPAC donor list as it appears in "Top 10 Contributors," *Los Angeles Times*, January 29, 1995, A23.

[4]Ruth Marcus and Toni Locy, "FEC Says GOPAC Aided Gingrich Race Despite Law," *Washington Post*, November 30, 1995, A16; Marcus and Locy, "GOPAC Donor Sought Aid from Gingrich," *Washington Post*, December 1, 1995, A1 and A8.

[5]Reporter Ruth Marcus reported that documents released by the Federal Election Commission showed that the foundation was administered by the same people who ran GOPAC and that it rented space from GOPAC, received contributions from GOPAC charter members, and borrowed at least $45,000 from GOPAC, Ruth Marcus, "GOPAC Used Foundation to Fund Cable TV Series," *Washington Post*, December 12, 1995, A8.

Of these types of PACs, those representing businesses and those falling into the nonconnected category have grown most rapidly in recent years (see Figure 8-1). They have also tended to raise and spend the most money. Table 8-2 indicates which individual PACs spent the most during recent elections.

A third type of PAC, called a *leadership* PAC, differs from the other two in that it is created not by a group but by an individual, largely to enhance his or her political stature and clout. Various presidential aspirants and members of Congress who aspire to leadership positions have established such PACs, and their number is growing. Under the current campaign finance laws, a PAC enables a "leader" to raise and spend more than he or she could raise acting as an individual.[25] Money from PACs can be used to give political contributions to others, thereby making new friends and creating new debts that can be collected in the future, but it also can be used to support the promotional activities of candidates as they travel about the country making speeches, holding news conferences, and appearing at other events—all designed to give them visibility.

Spending by PACs

Where does PAC money go? That question is fairly easy to answer because PACs are required to report their receipts and expenditures to the Federal Election Commission, a government agency. At the national level most of the money goes to incumbents, primarily because they have the power to make decisions on public policy that affect the interests of contributing PACs and their constituents.

The large contributions from health-care PACs illustrate this phenomenon. From 1985 to 1995, PACs representing the health insurance industry gave $25.5 million to members of Congress and political parties, and PACs representing doctors and other health-care professionals gave $23.1 million. Contributions increased dramatically during the period in 1993 when Congress was debating health-care reform and Medicare reform. Table 8-3 indicates the principal beneficiaries of this largesse. Note

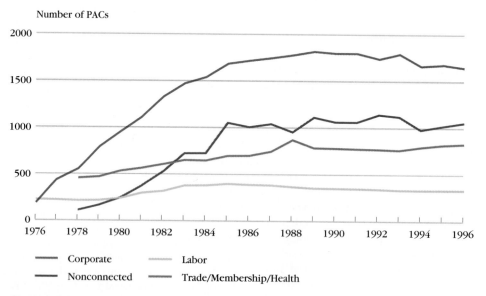

FIGURE 8-1

The growth of PACs, 1976–1996 (July 1).

SOURCE: Federal Election Commission, *Record*, September 1996, 7.

TABLE 8-2	TOP CONTRIBUTORS AMONG POLITICAL ACTION COMMITTEES, 1993–1996

1993–1994

POLITICAL ACTION COMMITTEE	TOTAL CONTRIBUTIONS TO FEDERAL CANDIDATES
United Parcel Service	$2,647,113
American Federation of State, County, & Municipal Employees	$2,529,682
Democratic/Republican/Independent Voter Education Committee (PAC of the International Brotherhood of Teamsters)	$2,487,152
American Medical Association	$2,386,947
National Education Association	$2,260,850

1995–JUNE 30, 1996

Democratic/Republican/Independent Voter Education Committee	$1,584,710
Association of Trial Lawyers of America	$1,552,975
International Brotherhood of Electrical Workers	$1,321,600
American Federation of State and County Municipal Employees	$1,311,222
United Auto Workers	$1,293,775

Source: Federal Election Commission.

that with one exception (Newt Gingrich), the major recipients in the House of Representatives were all Democrats. Most of the recipients were members of key committees that deal with health care or taxation.

PACs did not always give primarily to incumbents. When they were first created, in the 1970s, they gave money to candidates who were most sympathetic to their interests and needs; business PACs gave mostly to Republican candidates and labor PACs to Democrats, the party that controlled Congress at that time. During the 1980s, however, Democratic congressional leaders applied pressure on business leaders to allocate more of their PAC contributions to Democratic incumbents, who controlled the House of Representatives. They warned these PACs that if they wanted to maintain their access and get a fair deal, they should support those who

TABLE 8-3	THE TOP 10 RECIPIENTS OF HEALTH-CARE PAC MONEY, 1985–1995

1. Rep. Fortney "Pete" Stark (D-California)	$ 284,250
2. Rep. Richard A. Gephardt (D-Missouri)	268,513
3. Rep. Charles B. Rangel (D-New York)	264,315
4. Sen. John H. Chafee (R-Rhode Island)	253,658
5. Sen. Daniel Patrick Moynihan (D-New York)	219,655
6. Rep. Robert T. Matsui (D-California)	215,902
7. Rep. Henry A. Waxman (D-California)	213,050
8. Rep. Sam Gibbons (D-Florida)	212,000
9. Rep. Newt Gingrich (R-Georgia)	205,045
10. Sen. Orrin G. Hatch (R-Utah)	204,592

Source: Washington Post, December 1, 1995, A25.

have the power to hear them out and make decisions. The business PACs complied; they became the House Democrats' largest financial backers, giving them even more money than their labor counterparts did in the 1980s and early 1990s.

Then came the Republicans' surprising victory in the 1994 midterm elections. The GOP reaped the financial benefits, as business and trade association PACs reverted to their natural ideological leanings and gave more of their contributions to Republican members of Congress.[26] Before the election they had given the bulk of their money to Democratic incumbents. According to a Republican analysis of the top 400 PACs, Republican candidates received only about one-third of their donations from PACs in 1993–94, but a little more than half in 1995.[27] Overall, their PAC contributions more than doubled during this period, while the Democrats' contributions declined (See Figure 8-2.) Ironically, it was the House Democrats who had voiced the most opposition to efforts to reform campaign finance laws by limiting or eliminating PAC contributions when the issue came before Congress in 1994. Not surprisingly, when the Republicans controlled Congress, many of them—particularly their leadership—opposed changing the law.

PACs play a more important role in congressional politics than they do in presidential politics. Within Congress, PAC money is more critical for members of the House of Representatives than for members of the Senate and, as noted previously, more important for incumbents than for challengers. At the presidential level, PAC contributions account for a very small percentage of the total contributions candidates receive in their quest for their party's nomination. In 1992 they accounted for less than 1 percent. In 1996 they were approximately 1.1 percent of total revenues (including matching funds); Dole received the most, amounting to about 2.7 percent of his total revenues.

As noted earlier, no PAC contributions are permitted to be given to major-party candidates in presidential elections, but the grassroots activities and voluntary efforts of PACs can be a vital supplement to a campaign. In 1996, for example, organized labor waged a $35 million "nonpartisan" voter education campaign that was aimed at turning out a sizable pro-labor vote. A special assessment of $1.80 on each of the 13 million union members in the United States was made to raise money for radio and television commercials and for training and organizing a rank-and-file grassroots movement. Officials of the campaign concentrated their efforts in seventy-five congressional districts that had a large union membership. Since the majority of these districts were represented by Republicans and labor has traditionally backed Democrats, the Republicans naturally saw the "nonpartisan" campaign as blatantly partisan and even instituted legal action in an unsuccessful attempt to prevent it.

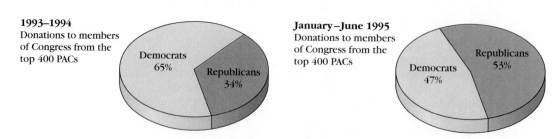

1993–1994
Donations to members of Congress from the top 400 PACs

Democrats 65%
Republicans 34%

January–June 1995
Donations to members of Congress from the top 400 PACs

Republicans 53%
Democrats 47%

FIGURE 8-2
PAC giving to members of Congress, 1993–1995.

SOURCE: National Republican Campaign Committee as reprinted in the *Washington Post*, November 27, 1995, A9.

PACs: Pro and Con

The increasing involvement of PACs in the electoral process has generated considerable criticism and led to proposals for reform. The criticism has stemmed in part from the pressure that has been placed on people to make "voluntary" contributions—pressure that can be seen in the following memo sent by a corporate executive to his company's managers in 1992:

> It is very important for us to have our views heard by congressmen, senators, and staffers within the government. Without the chance to tell our story on a wide range of issues, we cannot influence the decisions made. We have a broad range of customers: Air Force, DOD, NASA, DOE, etc., so there are many committees and people that need to hear our story.
>
> Access to these people is not theoretically bought, but if you want to see them in a timely manner, it is expected for us to make a contribution to their campaign funds. . . .
>
> Corporations cannot provide these funds by law, but their employees can. The PAC is merely a bank account funded by salaried employees that provides these "access" funds. . . .
>
> Contribute! Consider it a premium on an insurance policy on our business.[28]

In addition to the pressure on donors, critics contend that PACs exercise undue influence on public officials. Since PACs have contributed disproportionately to incumbents, it is natural to infer that they are seeking to obtain the sympathetic ear of those who are already in power. Not only does PAC money gravitate toward incumbents, but it goes disproportionately to party leaders and the chairs of committees and subcommittees, because PACs believe that these individuals have the most power to help or hurt the interest group. These patterns raise the suspicion that the more money a candidate receives from a particular PAC, the more difficult it will be for that person to make independent decisions about the PAC's issues once in office.

This distribution of funds would not elicit so much objection were all segments of society equally represented by PACs, but they are not. Corporate and trade association PACs are more numerous and raise and spend more money than their chief adversaries, the labor PACs. And all three groups raise and spend much more than consumer groups. Similarly, nonconnected and ideologically conservative PACs have been more active and more successful fund-raisers than have their liberal opponents.

In any event, although the charges of undue influence may be true, it is very difficult to know for certain the reasons that legislators make particular decisions. Potential influences range from their own partisan and ideological orientations, to their personal views, to the pressures exerted by constituents and political interest groups (including PACs). Nevertheless, groups that can gain a better hearing for their case and make a more compelling argument unquestionably have an advantage over others. One expert, Frank Sorauf, argues that this advantage is greatest "in the narrower, less salient issues that escape party, presidential, or popular attention."[29]

Other political scientists have also found a relationship between money and influence. For example, Richard L. Hall and Frank W. Wayman studied the participation of members of the House of Representatives on three committees in three issue areas (milk price supports, job training, and natural gas deregulation). They found that the more a PAC had given to committee members, the more time and effort those members devoted to the PAC's issues. As Hall and Wayman concluded, although PAC money may not have bought votes, "it apparently did buy the marginal time, energy, and legislative resources that committee participation requires."[30]

Another controversial aspect of PACs is their effect on political parties. Most political scientists believe that PACs hurt parties. In addition to siphoning funds away from them, PACs encourage policy-oriented candidates who may not have a history of party involvement or allegiance, and they promote their own relatively narrow agendas. These activities detract from the ability of the parties to take consistent positions on a broad range of issues, to attract candidates who support those positions and are willing to toe the party line, and to hold candidates responsible for how they perform once they gain office.

Proponents of PACs, in contrast, note that PACs help finance elections, thereby reducing the burden on taxpayers and the general public; they increase knowledge of the issues among their members and the public at large; and they encourage people to vote and to participate in the electoral process in other ways. These activities contribute to the functioning of a democratic society. Moreover, by supporting candidates who are sympathetic to their points of view and are in a position to help them achieve their policy objectives, PACs link the public with its representatives—another important objective of democracy. Finally, proponents point out that group association and election activity are protected by the First Amendment to the Constitution.

Nonetheless, there have been frequent proposals to reform the system and limit the influence of PACs. Recent proposals have included imposing spending limits on congressional candidates, lowering or eliminating the amount of money PACs are allowed to contribute to campaigns, and even providing public funding as is done in presidential elections.

LOBBYING

Once an election is over, what can a group do to ensure that its point of view is forcefully presented when issues of concern arise on Capitol Hill or in a state legislature? It can **lobby**, a term that describes the behavior of people who accost their elected representatives in the lobbies of legislatures and other government buildings and try to persuade them how to vote on an issue. Unfortunately, the word also suggests some of the seamy sides of representation, and it is often associated in the public's mind with illegal and unethical behavior in politics.

Lobbyists do indeed congregate in and around legislative lobbies, but they do much more than that. Their principal function is to provide public officials with information to influence their opinions and positions. Although lobbyists can use a variety of positive and negative inducements in this effort, they must be careful not to exceed the bounds of what officials consider proper conduct or to make permanent enemies. Moreover, because lobbyists typically deal with the same officials again and again, they take care to see that the information they provide is correct. Lobbyists believe that their ability to persuade is directly related to their credibility; they fear that if they mislead, either purposely or accidentally, their information and arguments will always be viewed skeptically by those they are trying to influence.

Types of Lobbying

Lobbying can take many forms: a memo or statement to a public official indicating a group's position, a trip by influential constituents to Washington to plead an organization's case, or a public relations campaign in which millions of people participate and millions of dollars are spent. In general, however, lobbying techniques may be divided into direct and indirect types (see Figure 8-3). In direct lobbying, group rep-

Lobbyists are a common sight lined up outside the door of the House Ways and Means Committee room as they wait to buttonhole key legislators and plead in their clients' interests. This corridor is known as "Gucci Gulch" because of the expensive Italian shoes that lobbyists favor.

resentatives themselves contact public officials; in indirect lobbying, they encourage others to do so. Whether direct or indirect, lobbying activity has the same goal: to influence the decisions of public officials and thereby affect public policy in a manner that accords with the group's interests.

Lobbyists attempt to influence the policy process directly by testifying at public hearings and by providing detailed policy statements, briefings, and supporting material to public officials and their staffs. Sometimes they even draft proposed bills or regulations for use by a committee considering legislation or an agency attempting to implement it. Even when lobbyists do not testify or prepare position papers, they make a point of attending hearings when proposals in which they are interested are being considered.[31]

Examples of interest groups using these direct methods to affect policy deliberations abound at the national and state levels. Following the Supreme Court's *Webster* decision in 1989, which opened the door to legislative consideration of the abortion issue at the state level, pro-choice groups drafted bills that would protect abortion rights, and pro-life organizations proposed legislation that would prohibit abortion after the twentieth week of pregnancy. Both sides issued public statements and provided officials at all levels of government with research and data to support their positions.

These same groups have been active in indirect lobbying as well, writing speeches for their sympathizers to deliver and instituting grassroots campaigns to build support for their side within the general public—particularly among people

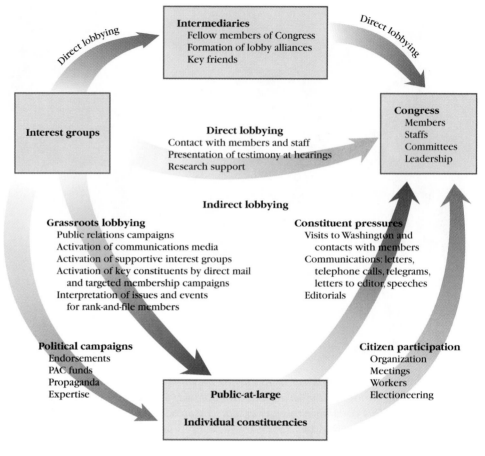

Intermediaries
Fellow members of Congress
Formation of lobby alliances
Key friends

Direct lobbying

Direct lobbying

Interest groups

Congress
Members
Staffs
Committees
Leadership

Direct lobbying
Contact with members and staff
Presentation of testimony at hearings
Research support

Indirect lobbying

Grassroots lobbying
Public relations campaigns
Activation of communications media
Activation of supportive interest groups
Activation of key constituents by direct mail
and targeted membership campaigns
Interpretation of issues and events
for rank-and-file members

Constituent pressures
Visits to Washington and
contacts with members
Communications: letters,
telephone calls, telegrams,
letters to editor, speeches
Editorials

Political campaigns
Endorsements
PAC funds
Propaganda
Expertise

Citizen participation
Organization
Meetings
Workers
Electioneering

Public-at-large

Individual constituencies

FIGURE 8-3
Direct and indirect lobbying.

SOURCE: William J. Keefe, Henry J. Abraham, William H. Flanigan, Charles O. Jones, Morris S. Ogul, and John W. Spanier, *American Democracy: Institutions, Politics, and Policies,* 2d ed. (Chicago: Dorsey Press, 1986), 259, modified by the author. Copyright © 1986 Dorsey Press. Reprinted with permission.

who feel strongly about the issue and are likely to communicate their feelings to those in government. Computer technology makes it possible to precisely target large groups and quickly generate letters to them to raise money, solicit member-ships, and mobilize support for a particular policy.

Direct mail, particularly as used by fundraiser Richard Viguerie, has been the major reason for the financial success of conservative groups in the past twenty-five years. Viguerie put together over three hundred mailing lists with the names of more than 25 million contributors to various conservative causes. Not only were these individuals likely donors for fundraising drives, but they also constituted a large num-ber of potential activists for the causes themselves. As Viguerie has noted, "Raising money is only one of several purposes of direct-mail advertising letters. A letter may ask you to vote for a candidate, volunteer for campaign work, circulate a petition among your neighbors, write letters and postcards to your Senators and Congressmen, urging them to pass or defeat legislation, and also ask you for money to pay for the direct-mail advertising campaign."[32]

One of the most recent targets of Viguerie's campaign has been senior citizens who have joined the AARP, an organization that Republicans perceive as supporting liberal, big-government policy, especially programs that aid the elderly. To be successful, targeted mail must gain the immediate attention of those to whom it is directed. The senior citizens who were the targets of the AARP-related campaign received letters with a scary warning on the envelope that dire consequences would result from proposed changes to the Social Security system.[33]

Grassroots campaigns have been in vogue for some time, but now interest groups have begun to engineer these campaigns for their own purposes. This practice is known as **astroturfing**, a name that conveys the artificiality or deceptiveness of the public response that such a campaign creates.

A good example of astroturfing was the successful effort by the lobbying industry itself to kill a lobbying reform bill at the end of the Democratic-controlled 103rd Congress. The bill, which would have restricted the amount of gifts, trips, and meals members of Congress could receive from lobbyists, contained a provision requiring representatives of all organizations trying to affect public policy to register as lobbyists and provide information about their organization. Fearing that this provision would adversely affect groups sympathetic to their beliefs and interests, especially religious organizations, House Republicans mounted a grassroots effort to defeat the bill. More than 300 religious and conservative organizations received a faxed alert from the Republican leadership, describing the potential dangers of the legislation and urging them to mobilize their members against it.

Joined by several liberal groups such as the American Civil Liberties Union (who saw the requirements as an infringement of First Amendment rights) and business, labor, and trade groups (who had initially been willing to accept the legislation but jumped on the opposition bandwagon when they realized its potential), the coalition was able to slow down the bill's progress in a Senate that had previously been supportive of it. The Republicans then instituted a filibuster, and the Democrats were unable to stop it. The lobbyists had effectively defeated lobbying reform, but only for one year. In 1995 a new bill was passed that broadened the definition of a lobbyist and strengthened the requirement to register. It did not, however, require that the cost of grassroots lobbying be reported, and it exempted organizations that spend less than $20,000 on lobbying during a six-month period.

Astroturfing is frequently generated by advocacy advertising, such as that engaged in by the health insurance industry to defeat the Clinton administration's health-care reform proposal in 1994. Another illustration of advocacy advertising was the campaign sponsored in 1994–1995 by Citizens for a Sound Economy, a group that received major financial support from private industry. (Its name suggests a public interest organization, but it is not.) The group ran a series of television commercials ridiculing the size of judicial awards given to people who had successfully sued companies for negligence. Its *cause célèbre* was a woman who spilled hot coffee on herself, sued the McDonald's restaurant from which she purchased it, and received a multimillion-dollar award.[34]

Industry groups that direct, fund, and profit from an astroturfing campaign often try to hide their involvement so as to create the impression that the movement is public-spirited, not privately motivated. Thus when the American Tort Reform Association mounted a highly successful campaign to reform liability laws on the state and federal level—making it more difficult and less profitable for individuals to sue builders, manufacturers, or service providers—they publicized the community groups such as the little leagues and school boards that supported their coalition, not the large manufacturers, insurance companies, and retail chains that provided the money and would be the primary beneficiaries of the legislation.

A related tack is to point to a common enemy to generate public support. When President Clinton vetoed product liability legislation that Congress had enacted in 1996, critics immediately charged that he was beholden to trial lawyers who had contributed heavily to his campaign and who opposed the limits on monetary awards.

Radio is another medium that has been used extensively in recent years to activate the public. In 1993, for instance, conservative talk-show hosts and Christian fundamentalist ministers employed this medium to rally opposition to President Clinton's proposal to permit homosexuals to serve openly in the military. Telephone calls to the White House averaged 50,000 a day, ten times their normal volume, during the brief period when the issue was a prime focus of public attention. At the height of the controversy, members of Congress received over half a million letters in a single day!

Targets of Lobbying

Most Americans tend to equate lobbying with efforts to influence the legislative process. However, any experienced lobbyist knows that this process is only one part of the government, and that it is not always the most important or most pertinent part for a particular group on a particular issue. At the national level, the president has an active role in the legislative process and the executive agencies have a great deal of discretion in the administration of the laws. Moreover, the courts have the power to interpret and, in some cases, invalidate laws passed by Congress. At the state level, similar patterns of interaction and spheres of influence are evident. What determines the best place for a group to lobby, and what kinds of activities are most successful in different branches or levels of government?

Legislatures Sometimes getting legislation passed is vital to a group's interests. This was the case in 1979 when the Chrysler Corporation asked the federal government to guarantee the repayment of loans that the corporation wished to obtain from banks and that it needed to stay in business. No federal agency had the power to grant such guarantees without a legislative mandate. Congressional action is also required when industries seek import tariffs to protect domestic manufacturers against foreign competition, when exporters wish to sell advanced technology, or when public interest groups want to open government deliberations and documents to the public view (through so-called sunshine laws). And when the banking industry seeks to modify regulations on how much capital banks must hold or the conditions under which they may engage in interstate banking, specific provisions must be written into new legislation.

Legislators are relatively easy to lobby. They are open and accessible; as elected representatives they have to be sensitive to outside pressures, particularly when those pressures come from their constituencies. Lobbyists can also provide things that legislators need and want as they carry out their legislative responsibilities: information about how legislation will affect their constituents, political support for the legislation, and financial backing in the next election. For these reasons lobbyists are generally welcome or at least tolerated in the halls of legislatures and in lawmakers' offices.

How successful lobbyists are in getting what they want from legislators is another matter. The main challenge facing those who hope to influence legislative bodies is the relatively large size of most legislatures and consequently the large number of members who must be contacted and persuaded. It takes time, which costs money. A second problem, particularly at the national level, stems from the degree of activity and number of groups interested in any particular issue. Legislators must deal with a variety of issues and be receptive to a range of special pleaders, and thus lobbyists are rarely alone in presenting their position or unified in the advice they give. Normally, they meet with opposition from other lobbyists.

Sometimes "buttering up" is almost a literal description of a lobbyist's job. Here Senator Larry Craig (R-Idaho) attends an "ice cream social" sponsored by the International Dairy Foods Association at the Capitol.

The proliferation of lobbying has resulted in coalition building among diverse political interest groups. The formation of alliances in support of and in opposition to clean-air and clean-water laws (described at the beginning of this chapter) illustrates the alliance making that regularly occurs among groups with similar interests and objectives. To cite another example, even before President Clinton proposed his health-care reform package to the nation, health-care groups began to form alliances in support of or opposition to his plan.

A third limitation on the ability of lobbyists to get their way is the fact that legislators frequently behave as if they do not owe lobbyists anything. They may use the professional and personal services provided by lobbyists (such as legislative research, political support, financial contributions, electoral endorsements, and grassroots activity) without promising anything in return. They may also accept invitations to participate in (and relax at) conventions held in plush resorts, with the lobbying organization picking up the bill.

In fact, legislators can even pressure firms to change their lobbyists. After the Republicans took control of Congress in 1995, the House Republican leaders adopted a "K Street strategy" to "encourage" groups to replace their Democratic lobbyists with Republicans. (The name refers to the street in Washington on which many corporations, trade associations, and the lobbyists who represent them have offices.) According to the *Washington Post,* House Majority Whip Tom DeLay suggested to one corporate CEO that if his company wanted to get in to see DeLay, it needed to hire a Republican.[35] In short, legislators are able to affect and manipulate the behavior of those who attempt to manipulate them, thereby undercutting the lobbyists' influence on legislative outcomes.

The executive branch   Chief executives—the president and the state governors—and their administrative agencies have also become a major focus of lobbying activities. As in the legislature, lobbying in the executive branch is viewed as legitimate and is usually not discouraged. Indeed, lobbyists and executive branch officials tend to have mutual needs and interests. Whereas interest groups desire access, visibility, and support for their objectives, chief executives and their administrations require political allies within the public arena. Particularly at the national level, where political parties are weak, interest groups can be mobilized to build support for the president's programs.

Lobbying the lobbyists is not a recent phenomenon for presidents. In 1978 an office, known as public liaison, was created in the White House to orchestrate the activity of interest groups in support of the administration's key priorities as well as to serve these groups' political, policy, and membership needs.[36] Each administration has used this office as well as other senior aides to maintain ties with important and powerful groups. In courting corporate America, for example, the Clinton administration has invited business leaders to the White House for briefings, small dinner parties with the president, and formal state dinners. Thomas "Mack" McLarty, a former Arkansas oil executive who was Clinton's first chief of staff and later presidential counselor, has served as one of the president's principal links to the business community; another was Commerce Secretary Ron Brown, who led several delegations of American executives on trade missions abroad before his death in an airplane crash on a trade mission to Croatia in 1996.

In addition to trying to influence policy making in the executive branch, interest groups try to shape the content and application of rules governing policy implementation. Indeed, most executive agencies are required to publish proposed regulations and hold public hearings on them to solicit input from the interested public.

Moreover, lobbyists specializing in executive branch activities frequently have served in the very departments and agencies they seek to influence. They know how the game is played, who the principal players are, and which arguments and information are apt to be most persuasive.

Groups may also try to influence the selection of political appointments. For example, the Christian Coalition, the Family Research Council, various pro-life groups, and other conservative organizations that opposed Clinton's nomination of Dr. Henry Foster to be surgeon general testified against the nomination in Senate hearings and mounted considerable public opposition. In contrast, most agricultural interest groups were delighted with the selection of former Kansas congressman Daniel Glickman to be secretary of agriculture.

The judiciary   The judicial arena is also a focus of group activity, since political interest groups that have little or no hope of achieving their ends through the legislative and executive processes often turn to the courts for help. How do groups lobby the judicial branch? One way is through the selection of judges. Although the judicial selection process, particularly at the federal level, is often portrayed as nonpolitical, partisan considerations are almost always involved in the nomination and confirmation processes. The vast majority of federal judicial nominees are of the same partisan affiliation as the president. Although most are confirmed by the Senate without much challenge, occasionally a nominee provokes considerable controversy and lobbying of senators by interest groups. This was the case when federal judges Robert Bork (1987) and Clarence Thomas (1991) were nominated to fill vacancies on the Supreme Court; Bork was rejected, and Thomas was barely confirmed. (The conflicts over these nominations are described in Chapter 15.)

Another way to influence the judiciary is through litigation. For those who wish to prevent a hostile majority from depriving them of what they consider their basic rights, the courts are a last resort. Business groups, for instance, have regularly appealed to the courts to invalidate government attempts to regulate their operations. In the early part of this century, they successfully challenged state and national laws that limited the hours employees could work and established the minimum wage they could be paid. Today business groups continue to contest restrictions on how they do business, including regulations on health, safety, and environmental concerns and even personnel practices such as hiring, firing, and promoting.

The area of civil rights also provides many illustrations. The landmark school desegregation case of *Brown v. Board of Education* (1954) was brought in the absence of legislation because a law making segregation illegal was unlikely to be enacted by Congress or southern state legislatures in the 1950s. Similarly, groups have gone to court to require state-supported military colleges such as the Citadel and Virginia Military Institute to admit women. (The VMI lawsuit is discussed in Chapter 5.)

In addition to instituting legal challenges, an interest group may file an **amicus curiae** ("friend of the court") **brief**. This is a legal argument that a group makes to influence a decision on a pending case. For example, over one hundred different groups filed briefs with the Supreme Court in connection with *Regents of the University of California v. Bakke* (1978), a case dealing with the issue of whether states or the federal government could require affirmative action programs to make up for past discrimination. "Friends of the court" in this case included such diverse organizations as the American Federation of Teachers, the American Indian Bar Association, the American Jewish Congress, the NAACP Legal and Educational Fund, the United Farm Workers, and the United Mine Workers. Eleven years later the Court received seventy-eight amicus briefs in the case of *Webster v. Reproductive Health Services*; of these, forty-six favored the Missouri abortion law that was at issue in the case, and thirty-two opposed it. Similarly, over one hundred organizations and groups filed amicus briefs in the case of *Planned Parenthood of Southeastern Pennsylvania v. Casey*, which was decided by the Supreme Court in 1992. These briefs debated issues ranging from when life begins, to the legislative history of abortion in America, to the constitutionality of the *Roe v. Wade* decision.

Efforts to influence the justices by means of legal arguments have been supplemented by more visible demonstrations of public support. One pro-choice group organized a campaign to send a million postcards to the Supreme Court. Both sides on the abortion issue have engaged in extensive media campaigns, including full-page advertisements in newspapers that the justices were likely to read, such as the *Washington Post* and the *New York Times*. There have even been demonstrations outside the Supreme Court building when the major abortion cases were argued and when the decisions were announced.

Public rallies, private correspondence, and media advertising obviously serve the interest groups' needs for visibility and public education (and, indirectly, for their own fundraising), but whether these activities have much impact on Supreme Court decisions is questionable. However, the Court is not oblivious to the outside world. In their 1989 and 1990 opinions stating that burning the American flag is a form of protest protected by the First Amendment to the Constitution, the justices went to great lengths to explain their decisions in anticipation of an adverse public reaction—even though the Court is not expected to follow or conform to popular opinion when interpreting the law.

Changes in Lobbying and Lobbyists

As American society grows more pluralistic, many new groups are seeking to influence government. Lobbying activities have increased manyfold, not only in Washington, D.C., but in most state capitals as well. Foreign interests have also found new ways to be represented.

Before the 1980s most non-American companies used the commercial sections of their countries' embassies to promote their interests. Although embassies still provide their nationals with diplomatic and consular services, foreign governments and corporations have increasingly turned to American firms to represent them in the United States. And they turn to people with the experience and contacts to do so: former government officials. A 1992 report by the General Accounting Office found that eighty-two former executive officials, legislators, and senior congressional staff members who had left their posts between 1986 and 1992 were working as lobbyists or representatives for foreign interests.[37]

Whether by such insiders or others, foreign representation by Americans in Washington is extensive. Between 1988 and 1995, Japanese interests used more than 160 public relations lobbying firms and individual consultants to look out for their concerns.[38] The governments and corporations of Japan, the United Kingdom, Canada, Germany, France, and Mexico spend the most on these activities in Washington.[39] Their spending has encouraged others to present their side as well. To counter Canada's influence on American public opinion, the government of Quebec retained three Washington firms and spent $350,000 to present the case for secession.[40] Canada spent $50 million to promote the U.S.–Canadian Free Trade Agreement while Mexico spent nearly $40 million to promote the North American Free Trade Agreement (NAFTA). In 1995 the National Council of Resistance in Iran and both combatants in the dispute in Northern Ireland hired companies in the United States to represent them, promote their positions, and improve their public images.[41]

Large expenditures by foreign governments, political groups, and private companies raise serious questions about how much non-Americans should be permitted to influence public policy in the United States. In response to these concerns, President Clinton requested all major appointees in his administration to promise that they would *never* represent foreign interests after they left government.

While becoming more diverse in its participants, the lobbying business has also become more specialized. Lawyers and law firms are still major players, but public relations, issues management, and accounting firms are increasingly active. Some of the largest firms, often referred to as "supermarkets," offer a wide variety of services, ranging from lobbying to coalition building, grassroots development, media consultation, fundraising, events planning, issue research, and public opinion polling. Most large political interest groups regularly employ specialists in these areas in addition to their own public relations professionals.

Legal changes have affected lobbying as well. Sunshine laws mandating that congressional committee meetings and executive agency deliberations be open to the public have forced lobbyists and decision makers to operate in the public spotlight much of the time.[42] New ethics and finance laws have imposed more stringent requirements on public officials who interact with lobbyists, and the news media also report more on improprieties. In one highly publicized incident during the 102nd Congress (1990–1992), five senators were accused of using their influence to obtain special favors for the Lincoln Savings and Loan Bank of California, owned by Charles H. Keating Jr.

There are many other examples of abuses. To cite just one, in 1995 a scheme was revealed in which a grassroots lobbying firm hired to generate opposition to a telecommunications bill Congress was considering sent letters and telegrams to members from constituents who had no knowledge of "their" communications. The campaign was supposed to work as follows. People were to be called on the telephone, read a script describing the legislation, and asked whether or not they were for it or against it. Those who answered "correctly" were to have letters or telegrams sent to their member of Congress (and at no cost to them). However, thousands of letters carried the names of people who were not consulted. In one case a congressman received a letter from himself, or at least from a constituent with the same name as his but with a bogus address. Another member of Congress, from Chicago, received a letter from a dead constituent; the next day he got another letter from the same (apparently persistent) deceased person.[43] The publicizing of these unethical activities has led to demands for more stringent regulation of lobbying.

Regulation of Lobbying

Some activities by lobbyists and those they lobby, such as the letter scheme or the buying and selling of influence through campaign contributions and gifts, are obviously illegal.[44] In other cases, behavior may be legal but inconsistent with the principles of a democratic political system, in which the influence of the wealthy should be no greater than that of the poor. Such practices include offering honoraria to government officials for speeches (this is now illegal) or selling tickets to party or candidate fundraisers or meetings with members of Congress in which issues are debated and legislative strategy is planned. In 1993, for example, Republican House members invited lobbyists to a retreat and charged each $6,000 for the privilege of attending. Not to be outdone, the Democrats invited many of the same lobbyists, and others who would pay, to purchase tables or seats at dinners featuring the president, cabinet members, and prominent Democratic legislators. Two years later both parties raised the ante. For a "soft-money" contribution of $100,000 or more, donors would be invited to special events with a party's elected officials, including the Democratic president and vice president and the Republican Speaker of the House and Senate majority leader. Each party raised well over $100 million in this effort. One such gift, a $425,000 contribution to the Democratic National Committee by an Indonesian couple, drew attention during the 1996 election campaign when Republicans charged—and Democrats denied—that it had influenced the Clinton administration's policies toward Indonesia on trade and human rights.

Over the years there have been numerous attempts to control lobbying activities. The Federal Regulation of Lobbying Act, enacted in 1946, required that anyone hired by someone else for the principal purpose of lobbying Congress must register and file a financial report. When this law was challenged as placing undue restrictions on constitutionally protected activity, the Supreme Court upheld it but interpreted the registration provision very narrowly. Consequently, many lobbyists who worked on behalf of American companies and causes did not feel compelled to register. However, those representing foreign governments and companies had to do so with the Justice Department.

In 1995 Congress tightened the registration and reporting requirements. It enacted legislation that broadened the definition of lobbying to include not only direct contact with government officials but also the preparation of information to influence those officials. Those who spend at least 20 percent of their time lobbying members of Congress, their staffs, and executive branch officials are required to register and report the identity of their clients, the issues on which they were involved, and the amount of money they were paid for their services. In addition, the law precludes members of Congress, their staffs, and presidential appointees from earning outside income, although income derived from educational activities such as teaching or writing is excluded as long as these activities are not performed during government time. Presidential appointees may not accept gifts or even a free meal. However, finger food at a reception attended by twenty-five people or more is all right. The law goes so far as to prohibit the director and deputy director of the office that represents the United States in trade negotiations with other countries from *ever* representing foreign interests after they leave public service.

Other legislation has been directed at establishing guidelines for ethical behavior by current and former public officials. The Ethics in Government Act of 1978 was designed to prevent conflicts of interest that impair the ability of government officials to act in the public interest. Among other provisions, it prohibits former mid- and high-level officials from lobbying an agency on "any particular matter" of "direct and substantial interest" to that agency for one year after leaving office. Similarly, there is a one-year ban on lobbying Congress that applies to former members. President Clinton asked his appointees voluntarily to extend the one year limit to five years and, as noted previously, never to represent foreign interests. The 1978 legislation also barred former executive branch officials from representing anyone on any issue on which they were directly involved while in government.

There still is considerable controversy not only about the effectiveness of these laws but even about their desirability. Is it necessary to encourage ethical conduct in and after public office? Proponents argue that it is; they note that the careers of public officials often begin and end in the private sector, creating a need for rules that prevent private gain at public expense. Others, however, fear that the requirements

Both Michael Deaver (top), *deputy chief of staff for President Reagan, and Lyn Nofziger* (bottom), *a head of the administration's political office, used their White House contacts after leaving government and were accused of violating ethics rules. Deaver was convicted of lying to Congress about his lobbying efforts; Nofziger, also convicted of improper activities, won acquittal on appeal.*

for financial disclosure, the limits placed on private employment after government service, and the restriction of foreign representation may keep some of the best-qualified people out of government.

CONSEQUENCES OF THE GROUP STRUGGLE

What are the consequences of the American system of interest group representation? Does it have an impact on national policy? Does it diminish government's ability to pursue nationwide policies and long-term interests and favor those with narrower, more immediate, and direct appeal?

When resources are limited, it is almost inevitable that some people will benefit more than others. In 1960, E. E. Schattschneider suggested that the beneficiaries of the struggle among political interest groups are the people in higher socio-economic brackets—those with the most money, the best organizations, and the greatest influence.[45] Most citizens can never be adequately represented, Schattschneider believed; if they were, the system would become hopelessly stalemated.[46]

Today, almost four decades later, there are many more organized interests, but the system still favors the "haves" in the sense that it is resistant to large-scale policy change. Moreover, corporations, educational institutions, and local governments still outnumber public interest and consumer groups and have a larger and more pronounced presence in Washington. They have more resources to hire high-powered lawyers, lobbyists, and public relations firms, which they believe give them greater ability to influence policy makers' decisions.

How effective are political interest groups in actually affecting policy outcomes? This depends on how much competition there is among groups within a particular policy sphere and on who will benefit from and who will pay for a new policy. In general, if there is little competition, an interest group seeking change will be more likely to get what it wants than if there is much competition among groups with comparable resources. A good example of a noncompetitive situation is "pork-barrel" legislation (such as agricultural price supports, military bases, medical research grants, or public works projects), in which the benefits are concentrated but the costs are widely dispersed. In such a situation those who stand to gain a lot from creation of the programs or a lot to lose from their elimination have much more incentive to organize and try to influence policy than do those who will pay or save a relatively small amount as a result of the change.

But if there is competition between groups (such as over pollution standards between environmental and energy groups, or over highway speed limits between motorists and truckers on one hand and the insurance industry on the other), there may be a standoff until the competitors can make a deal (as in the case of clean air) or until one side wins (as in the case of removing the national speed limit of 55 miles per hour on interstate highways). In general, the American system puts the burden on those who wish to change policy, not those who wish to maintain it.

Change *is* possible, but it is usually incremental; and it is often the product of strong political leadership, most often but not exclusively emanating from the White House. In the 1960s, presidents Kennedy and Johnson refocused public policy with their New Frontier and Great Society programs designed to provide direct and indirect aid to those in the lower socio-economic groups. In the 1980s, President Reagan sought to reverse these policies, reducing the federal government's role in social and economic policy. He did so despite pressure from interest groups that had benefited from these programs and had organized to protect their benefits. In the 1990s, President Clinton proposed streamlining the federal government and reforming the nation's health-care and welfare systems although powerful forces prevented him from achieving many of his legislative objectives. In turn, congressional Republicans offered their own comprehensive plans to balance the budget and devolve many federal government responsibilities onto the states, but they too were forced to modify or abandon some of their proposals in the face of strong pressure from constituents and opposition from the president.

In short, organized interests try to influence what government does, but their influence may be offset or deflected by other interests, the public mood, or skilled political leadership. Thus political interest groups do not usually dictate policy, but they certainly influence it, especially in a government system designed to respond to public pressures.

SUMMARY

The politics of interest groups stems from their orientation toward promoting the interests and beliefs of their members. Within a heterogeneous society, interests and beliefs will naturally conflict. So when groups try to influence public policy, they will struggle with others who have different, even competing, objectives. This struggle is played out in the electoral and governing arenas and among and within the three branches of government. Interest group politics is the inevitable consequence of a political system based on popular consent, which permits individuals to organize and petition their government to alter public policy or leave it in place.

The activity of *political interest groups* can strengthen the democratic process by educating people about their civic responsibilities, increasing public awareness, providing an outlet for public expression, and encouraging participation in the political process. However, it can also produce consequences that are not nearly as beneficial. If certain groups come to dominate decision making, they will shape policy in their interests. If they cannot do so, if struggles among competing groups persist, the result may be compromises that are necessary in a pluralistic society but that sometimes bring less-than-ideal solutions to the problems at hand.

Although political interest groups have existed throughout the nation's history, they have undergone their greatest development since the middle of the twentieth century. The rapid increase in the number of interest groups after 1950 was spurred by the growth of government programs and regulatory activity and by the political movements of the 1960s and 1970s. Changes in the political system, especially in the

nature of parties and elections, also contributed to the increase in group activity.

Several factors affect the ability of interest groups to shape public policy: their size, the extent to which their members hold unified views, and the intensity of these views. In addition, groups that are geographically concentrated tend to exercise more power locally than nationally, and organizations of professionals derive influence from their members' prestige and financial resources. A group's influence is also affected by its leadership and by the contacts those leaders have with people in positions of power.

Before the 1970s, much of the electoral activity of political interest groups was funneled through the Democratic and Republican party organizations. Today the nomination process is less subject to the influence of party leaders; interest groups have greater incentives and opportunities to impact nominations, influence the positions of candidates and parties, and affect election outcomes.

Nonparty groups known as *political action committees (PACs)* solicit contributions from their members and make donations to candidates. They also engage independently in other campaign activities to support or oppose particular candidates. The amount of money spent by PACs has led some observers to conclude that public officials are bound to be influenced by their contributions. They point out that most PAC money goes to incumbents, especially party leaders and committee chairs. Another criticism of PACs is that they weaken the political parties by siphoning funds away from them and encouraging policy-oriented candidates who may lack allegiance to their party and its positions. Proponents of PACs respond that these groups help finance elections, increase public knowledge of the issues, and encourage voting. Besides, such contributions are currently legal, and electoral activity is protected by the Constitution.

Lobbying is the practice of providing government officials with information designed to influence their opinions and decisions on current issues. Lobbyists can influence the legislative process directly by testifying at public hearings, providing policy statements to legislators, and drafting proposed bills. Increasingly, they also launch public relations campaigns to influence the decisions of government officials.

Lobbyists' targets include not only legislatures but also the executive branch and the judiciary. Interest groups lobby executive officials and agencies to gain access, visibility, and support for their interests. In exchange they offer their members' political support for the administration, its personnel, and its policies. In addition to attempting to influence the formulation of policy, groups try to shape the content and application of rules governing its implementation. In the judicial arena, groups may try to influence the selection of judges, bring lawsuits if they are unable to achieve their ends through the legislative and executive processes, or file *amicus curiae briefs* in support of positions in pending cases.

In recent years there have been a number of changes in the nature of lobbying. The amount of lobbying activity in Washington, D.C., and in state capitals has increased dramatically. Foreign companies and governments regularly hire American firms to represent them. The lobbying business has also become more specialized, with law firms being joined by public relations, issues management, and accounting firms. Sunshine laws force lobbyists to operate more in public view, and new ethics and finance laws and regulations have imposed stringent requirements on public officials who interact with lobbyists or become lobbyists after they leave office.

The extent to which political interest groups actually affect policy outcomes is largely determined by the degree of competition among groups in a particular policy area and by the distribution of benefits and costs among them and the general public. If there is little competition, a concerned group is in a better position to get what it wants, particularly if costs are distributed widely among the population. If there is competition between groups, and the groups represent equally powerful constituencies, there may be a standoff or a compromise producing incremental policy change. In either case, the basic orientation is toward the maintenance of the status quo unless and until outside forces and strong political leadership combine to create a majority constituency for policy change.

KEY TERMS

political interest group
disturbance theory
selective benefits

revolving door politics
political action committee (PAC)
bundling

lobbying
astroturfing
amicus curiae brief

RESOURCES

SCHOLARLY STUDIES

Clawson, Dan, Alan Neustadtl, and Denise Scott. *Money Talks: Corporate PACs and Political Influence.* New York: Basic Books, 1992. A contemporary account of corporate political action committees and their impact on American politics.

Heinz, John P., Edward O. Launmann, Robert L. Nelson, and Robert H. Salisbury. *The Hollow Core: Private Interests in National Policy Making.* Cambridge, Mass.: Harvard University Press, 1993. An empirical study of the relationship between interest groups and public policy, focusing on four domestic policy areas: agriculture, labor, health, and energy.

Lowi, Theodore. *The End of Liberalism: Ideology, Policy, and the Crisis of Public Authority*. 2d ed. New York: Norton, 1979. A classic analysis and criticism of interest group politics in America.

Petracca, Mark P., ed. *The Politics of Interests: Interest Groups Transformed*. Boulder, Colo.: Westview, 1992. An up-to-date collection of case studies and research on interest groups and their impact on the American system.

Rothenberg, Lawrence S. *Linking Citizens to Government: Interest Group Politics at Common Cause*. New York: Cambridge University Press, 1992. A comprehensive case study of the public interest group Common Cause: its composition, organization, decision-making processes, and impact on public policy.

Schlozman, Kay L., and John T. Tierney. *Organized Interests and American Democracy*. New York: HarperCollins, 1990. A comprehensive text about interest groups and their impact on the American system, based in part on interviews with 175 Washington representatives of major organizations.

Walker, Jack L. Jr. *Mobilizing Interest Groups in America: Patrons, Professions, and Social Movements*. Ann Arbor: University of Michigan Press, 1991. Pointing out that all interest groups in the United States are not equally represented, the author discusses the disparity as well as the forces behind the expansion of interest groups at the national level.

LEISURE READING

Birnbaum, Jeffrey H. *The Lobbyists: How Influence Peddlers Get Their Way in Washington*. New York: Random House, 1992. The author, a reporter for the *Wall Street Journal*, provides a behind-the-scenes account, focusing on the 1990 budget process, of how corporate lobbyists use money, information, and pressure to try to get their way.

Birnbaum, Jeffrey H., and Alan S. Murray. *Showdown at Gucci Gulch*. New York: Vintage, 1987. Two journalists describe how lobbyists tried to influence the Tax Reform Act of 1986.

Luker, Kristin. *Abortion and the Politics of Motherhood*. Berkeley: University of California Press, 1984. A balanced and lucid study of the abortion issue, based on over two hundred interviews with pro-life and pro-choice activists.

Wolpe, Bruce C. *Lobbying Congress: How the System Works*. Washington, D.C.: Congressional Quarterly, 1990. A "how-to" guide with case studies.

PRIMARY SOURCES

The Capital Source: The Who's Who, What, Where in Washington. Washington, D.C.: The National Journal, semiannual publication. A reference book, published twice a year, that lists people, positions, addresses, and telephone and fax numbers for government officials, media correspondents, interest groups, think tanks, and others doing policy research, consultation, and lobbying.

Encyclopedia of Associations. 3 vols. Detroit: Gale Research, annual. A comprehensive listing of organizations by type and geographic area.

The Washington Representatives. Washington, D.C.: Columbia Books, annual. A listing of Washington representatives, clients, and their areas of principal legislative and regulatory concerns.

Zorack, John L. *The Lobbying Handbook*. Washington, D.C.: Professional Lobbying and Consulting Center, 1990. A comprehensive guide for lobbyists that includes appropriate federal regulations, lobbying strategies, maps of congressional buildings, and the procedures of Congress.

ORGANIZATIONS

Common Cause, 2030 M Street, N.W., Washington, DC 20036; phone (202) 833-1200; fax (202) 659-3716; e-mail: 75300.3120@compuserve.com A self-described citizens' lobby, concerned with issues of governance such as campaign finance, lobbying practices, federal government salaries, and the availability of government information.

Federal Election Commission, 999 E Street, N.W., Washington, DC 20463; phone (800) 424-9530 (information division); flashfax (202) 501-3413; Internet http://www.fec.gov Collects, analyzes, and sends out information on election laws, contributions, and other campaign activities; releases annual reports as well as election summaries.

National Abortion Rights Action League, 1156 15th Street, N.W., Suite 700, Washington, DC 20005; phone (202) 973-3000; fax (202) 273-3096. A pro-choice group that lobbies legislatures, brings court cases, and mounts public relations efforts.

National Right to Life Committee, Inc., 419 7th

Street, N.W., Suite 500, Washington, DC 20004; phone (202) 626-8800; fax (202) 737-9189; Internet http://www.nrlc.org/nrlc   A pro-life group that lobbies legislatures, brings court cases, and mounts public relations efforts.

Office of Public Liaison, The White House, 1600 Pennsylvania Avenue, N.W., Washington, DC 20500; phone (202) 456-2930; fax (202) 456-6218; no direct e-mail. Handles the president's relations with organized political interest groups, including servicing their needs, keeping track of their positions, and trying to mobilize them behind key presidential initiatives.

Political Parties

All political parties claim to support policies that are in the interests of the country. They differ, however, over which policies should be pursued, at what cost, and at whose expense. Moreover, Republicans and Democrats tend to approach the problems of cost and benefits in different ways.

Ever since the New Deal era of Franklin Roosevelt, Democratic politicians and their core constituency—made up of middle- and lower middle-class voters, organized labor, and ethnic and religious minorities—have

looked to the national government to rectify social and economic inequities by providing services directly to people who need them: subsidies to farmers, welfare to the poor, and pensions and health-care benefits to the elderly. To pay for these programs they have also supported a progressive tax system, in which the wealthy pay comparably more. They have not been reluctant to use the federal government to impose guidelines on the states and private sector to ensure that certain standards are met.

The Republicans have taken a different tack. Believing the free enterprise system with its internal competition and private ownership to be the key to the country's economic and social well-being and political vitality, they have been leery of any policy that takes money out of the private sector (such as increased taxes) or any program that competes with it (such as public health and welfare programs), or any government rules that increase the costs of conducting business. The Republican core constituency—made up of middle- and upper middle-class voters as well as the well-to-do, business entrepreneurs and executives, and white Protestants—has been largely sympathetic to this perspective and critical of big government, particularly the government in Washington and many of its domestic programs.

Translating this perspective into a coherent set of policy proposals, Republican candidates for the House of Representatives in 1994 publicly subscribed to a "Contract with America," which consisted of ten legislative proposals designed to balance the federal budget, reduce taxes, and devolve federal government responsibilities onto the states. The Contract became the Republicans' agenda, and after winning a majority of seats in both houses of Congress, the House enacted most of the items in the Contract, but the Senate did not.[1] More individualistic by tradition, less responsive to the mood of the electorate in any one election, and lacking personal commitments by its Republican members to support the Contract, the Senate moderated some of the House's proposals and rejected others.

But the legislation still had to circumvent another hurdle—President Clinton. Wanting to please his party's electoral and congressional constituencies and to protect policy initiatives achieved during the first two years of his administration, the president vetoed or threatened to veto the Republicans' proposals for deep spending cuts in education, health, and welfare programs. He also opposed large tax cuts for the wealthy.

Compromise is essential in a system of government in which rivalry between legislative and executive branches is accentuated by partisan differences. Indeed, political considerations contributed to a desire for compromise on the part of all three of the leading figures in the conflict. House Speaker Newt Gingrich, the author of the Contract with America, wanted a legislative record to demonstrate that the Congress could function effectively under Republican leadership. Senate Majority Leader Robert Dole also wanted a record on which he and his party could run in 1996; his presidential candidacy was initially predicated on the claim that he was the most experienced Republican and the one who had exercised successful political leadership. As for Clinton, a compromiser by nature, he too had much at stake in working out a deal to keep the government running and to demonstrate his success in moderating what Democrats referred to as the "extremist Republican agenda."

But rank-and-file leaders of both parties, and particularly members of the House, were more resistant to change their positions. Freshman House Republicans felt that the Speaker had given away too much; they pressured him to stand fast for the proposals in the Contract, particularly a balanced budget and tax cuts. On the other side, House Democrats, perceiving a public that increasingly shared their opposition to massive government spending cuts and reductions in Medicare, saw confrontation as the most likely strategy to regain control of the House in 1996. Thus they urged the president not to cave in, and they unified behind his leadership.

The result of these diverse political pressures was a no-win standoff in which small compromises were made to keep the government operating and Clinton finally agreed to major cutbacks in welfare programs, but the larger debate over the size and role of the national government was not resolved. That debate continued into the 1996 election campaign.

In that campaign, Republicans argued that the changes they had initiated would be threatened by the election of more congressional Democrats and the reelection of President Clinton. Their party platform, campaign rhetoric, and appeals to their electoral coalition were designed to contrast their vision of a smaller, less obtrusive, national government and the less fettered operation of a free enterprise system with "the failed liberal Democratic policies of a bygone era." In contrast, the Democrats staked out a more centrist and populist position, lauding their traditional goals of greater economic and social equality but acknowledging that some of the programs designed to achieve these goals needed to be reformed. They claimed they represented mainstream America against conservative extremists who had captured the Republican party. Voters responded by reelecting both Clinton and a Republican Congress—leaving the highly partisan spirit of the previous four years likely to continue for the foreseeable future.

Differences over what the government should do, whether the national government or the states should be primarily responsible for the health, welfare, education and safety of citizens, how much should be spent on these activities, and where the funds should come from reveal much about the character of political parties in the United States: their differing constituencies, philosophies, and policies. They also reveal some similarities between the parties, especially in their appeal to those without strong partisan allegiances.

American political parties operate within a framework defined by public opinion. To be successful, they must be sensitive to the continuities and changes in that opinion. Because they have diverse constituencies, their policy positions must be sensitive to that diversity but at the same time articulate a coherent set of positions. This is not easy to do, as the Republicans discovered in 1996 as they struggled to reach an acceptable compromise on their platform's abortion stand. The Democrats had similar difficulties in the past on civil rights. Individualism and diversity characterize American parties and the politics that they generate.

The politics of parties conditions all aspects of their activity, from elections to the making and implementation of public policy. The political interests that bind the parties and their candidates provide citizens with a basis for deciding for whom to vote; these interests also help public officials decide what policies to pursue when representing their constituents; and finally, they help provide continuity and support for the policy itself. If politics is a struggle for position, power, and policy, parties are a vehicle by which that struggle is carried out. In this way they enhance the accountability of those in office, helping the public to hold them responsible for their successes or failures.

This chapter explains how political parties influence the political environment in which they operate. After describing the nature of parties in the United States, it traces their evolution from the period after the Republic was founded to contemporary times: their composition, organization, and influence on elections, government, and public policy.

PARTIES AND PARTISANS

A **political party** is an organization whose goal is to win elective office in order to influence the policies of government. It is composed of three interacting groups of supporters, or **partisans**: professionals, candidates and elected officials, and rank-and-file supporters (see Figure 9-1).

Professionals, the smallest group, are employed by the party. For them, it is an organization to which loyalty is owed, for which work is performed, and from which compensation is received. That work includes raising money, mobilizing sympathizers, developing positions, projecting images, making appeals, and continuing traditions. In performing these functions, party professionals compile and maintain lists of rank-and-file supporters, provide liaison to elected party leaders at all levels of government, coordinate party activities, and handle the administrative chores of running a large organization.

For members of the second group of partisans—candidates for public office and elected officials—the party is a source of funds and services. Simply running as a Republican or a Democrat activates the support of a sizable portion of the electorate, something that running as an independent does not automatically do. Most candidates need that support to win office, and a party needs to have its partisans in office if it is to influence public policy.

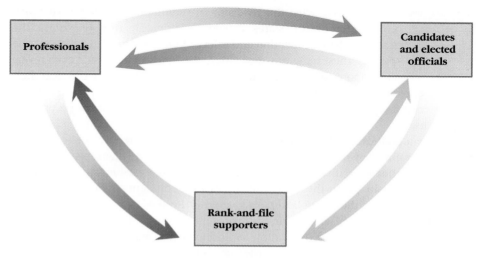

FIGURE 9-1

The composition of political parties.

SOURCE: Adapted from Frank J. Sorauf and Paul Allen Beck, *Party Politics in America*, 7th ed. (New York: HarperCollins, 1992), 11. Copyright © 1992 by Frank J. Sorauf and Paul Allen Beck. Reprinted by permission of Addison-Wesley Educational Publishers.

Whereas professionals and candidates both carry the party's banner, the rank-and-file supporters are more difficult to identify. In the United States these partisans rarely carry membership cards or attend political meetings. They may not even vote. In most cases, all they have to do is think of themselves as partisans or state that they are partisans when they participate in a party's primary election.

Partisanship is a lens through which political events can be judged and electoral choices made. The more strongly people feel about a party, the more likely they are to vote, and to do so in a way that supports their party's candidates and its policy positions.

THE NATURE OF AMERICAN PARTIES

In the United States, the party system developed after the Constitution was ratified and the government began to function. It has been primarily a two-party system; one of two major parties has usually held the support of a majority of the electorate. Although third parties have not played as important a role, they have existed for almost as long as the major parties have.

Major Parties

The two major American parties share characteristics that distinguish them from the major parties in other democratic political systems: they are more diversified in composition, decentralized in structure, and generally pragmatic in their approach to policy making. In fact, the composition and orientation of the parties help explain the character of the American political system. The United States has maintained a two-party system primarily because its major parties have been inclusive in their membership, wide-ranging in their political beliefs, and nonideological in their approach to government and public policy. In contrast, political parties in multiparty systems such as those of France, Israel, Italy, and Russia tend to be more exclusive in composition, narrowly focused on policy issues, and ideological in orientation.

What explains the character of the major parties in America? Part of the explanation has to do with the federal system of government. The Constitution vests substantial powers and responsibilities in the states, including the conduct of elections for all federal and state officials. In fact, except for the election of the president and vice president, all elections in the United States are for state or local officials or for state representatives to Congress. The party system reflects this decentralized federal structure. Candidates are recruited at the state or local level and are responsive primarily to their own constituencies. At the national level, the major parties consist of representatives of the fifty state parties; at the state level, they consist of local party representatives. This parochialism affects the policy positions that parties take and the decisions that their elected officials make.

The decentralized and inclusive nature of the major parties is reinforced by another characteristic of the American electoral system. Most officials are chosen in a district in which only one candidate is elected (known as a **single-member district**); there is no prize for coming in second. As a result, each candidate must try to obtain a majority (more than half the votes) or a plurality (more votes than any other candidate) within the district, and candidates of smaller parties have little chance of winning. Members of the British House of Commons are also chosen in single-member districts. However, in Britain the national party leaders designate the candidates, whereas in the United States they are chosen mainly by party supporters in state and local primaries and caucuses. Hence the parties must be receptive to a variety of candidates from different districts.

Countries such as France, Germany, and Spain, as well as some states and cities in the United States, have electoral systems in which several candidates are elected from the same district (known as a **multi-member district**), with the winners being determined by the proportion of the votes they or their party receives. In elections decided by proportional voting, there is an incentive for candidates to affirm their party's positions, downplay their own personal beliefs, and appeal to their party's rank and file for support. As a consequence, candidates selected in multi-member districts tend to be more loyal to their party and its ideological perspective than are those chosen in single-member districts. A multi-member district system also encourages more parties to run candidates, since to win they need not finish first but only make a strong showing.

Since the United States encompasses a large geographic area with a highly diverse population, its major parties must be broad-based and adopt positions that are acceptable to as much of the electorate as possible. Hence the parties' policy positions tend to be in the mainstream of public attitudes and opinions, and when they are not, that itself becomes an issue as it was for Republican Barry Goldwater in 1964 and Democrat George McGovern in 1972.[2] Their ideological orientations—Goldwater was very conservative and McGovern very liberal—resulted in high rates of defection by party supporters, who voted for the candidate of the other party.

Another, related reason for the pragmatic, moderate approach that major parties have assumed during most of their existence in the United States is the consensus among the electorate on basic political values. This consensus about the goals of government and the objectives of public policy is shared by the leaders and the rank and file of both parties; where they disagree is on the means to achieve these goals, that is, the specific policy solutions. Thus, for example, the major parties in the

United States are divided not over the question of whether there should be equal opportunity but over programs, such as affirmative action, that are designed to achieve that goal.

Minor Parties

Minor parties have been a part of the American political landscape since 1831, when a small party known as the Anti-Masons held a national convention to nominate candidates and propose a set of governing principles. Minor parties have come and gone quickly since then. But some of the shortest-lived have exerted the greatest influence by getting one or both of the major parties to address their concerns. In general there have been three basic types of minor parties in American history: ideological, issue, and candidate-oriented. The latter are of more recent origin. (See Table 9-1 for a list of some of the most significant minor parties.)

Of the three, **ideological parties** have had the greatest staying power but the least political impact. (In multiparty systems they often have a greater impact be-

---

TABLE 9-1　　**TYPES OF MINOR PARTIES**

IDEOLOGICAL PARTIES		
Party	**Life Span**	**Platform**
Socialist party	1901–	Replacement of much private enterprise with a worker-run state
Communist party	1924–	Overthrow of capitalism and establishment of a socialist state
Libertarian party	1971–	Opposition to most government regulation and, particularly, to state-sponsored social programs

ISSUE PARTIES		
Party	**Life Span**	**Platform**
Free Soil party	1848–1852	Opposition to the extension of slavery to new territories
Know-Nothing party	1854–1856	Opposition to immigration
Greenback party	1876–1884	Inflationary paper money to raise the prices of farm products
Populist party	1892–1908	Inflationary monetary policy through the free coinage of silver; government ownership of railroads; direct election of senators; graduated income tax

CANDIDATE-ORIENTED PARTIES		
Party	**Life Span**	**Platform**
Progressive party: Theodore Roosevelt	1912	Antitrust laws; direct primary; unemployment insurance
American Independent party: George Wallace	1968–1972	Opposition to civil rights legislation; hawkish stance on Vietnam War
National Unity party: John Anderson	1980	Independent, nonideological, moderate leadership
United We Stand America: H. Ross Perot	1992–1996	Deficit reduction; streamlining of government; citizen activism
Reform Party: H. Ross Perot	1995–	Deficit reduction; government reform; citizen participation

"Segregation now, segregation tomorrow, segregation forever," Governor George Wallace promised Alabamians in 1963. When he ran for president on the American Independent Party ticket in 1968 (there wasn't "a dime's worth of difference" between Democrats and Republicans, he said), he got almost 10 million popular votes (and 45 electoral votes) promoting states' rights rather than overt segregation. In 1972, two days after he was shot while campaigning in Maryland, he won the Democratic primaries there and in Michigan. But he was paralyzed below the waist and did not try again to win the presidency.

cause their support is needed to form a majority in the legislature; examples include the religious parties in Israel and the Free Democratic party in Germany.) Ideological parties in the United States, such as the Socialists, the Communists, and the Libertarians, have advocated a new way of thinking about the relationship between government and society, a set of ideas that differ significantly from those of the major parties. Because their beliefs lie outside those of mainstream America, however, their followings have been loyal but not large.

Issue parties have had more political success. Created out of dissatisfaction with one or both of the major parties when they ignored an important issue or took an unpopular stand, these parties have sought to get the major parties to change their ways. They have done so largely by attracting support for their own candidates, thereby reducing the electoral coalitions of the major parties. Although issue parties have not usually managed to get their candidates elected, they have drawn attention to their interests, reduced the vote going to the major parties, and forced one or the other to take the actions or support the positions that prompted their protest in the first place.

In 1892, for example, the Populist party supported farmers, miners, and small

Ross Perot (right) *with former Colorado governor Richard Lamm at the 1996 convention of the Reform party, where the two competed for the party's presidential nomination. Perot, a billionaire businessman who had founded and funded the party as a vehicle for his own presidential candidacy, used his control of its machinery to easily brush off Lamm's challenge.*

ranchers who favored the unlimited coinage of silver and government regulation of commerce when both major parties rejected these positions. The Democrats subsequently adopted a "free-silver" policy. Another issue party, but one that was more candidate-oriented, was the Progressive (Bull Moose) party. Unhappy with President William Howard Taft and hoping to reform the electoral process, a group of Republicans split from their party in 1912 and nominated former Republican president Theodore Roosevelt. The split within the Republicans enabled Democratic candidate Woodrow Wilson to win the presidency with only 42 percent of the popular vote.

Although issue parties have continued to emerge from time to time, in recent decades they have become heavily candidate-oriented, dominated by individuals who have used them as vehicles for promoting themselves and their own policy agenda. A good example is the party created from the organization that H. Ross Perot established for his presidential campaign of 1992. It was Perot's decision to create the new party, which, not surprisingly, adopted many of his policy positions such as reducing the budget deficit and reforming the campaign finance system.

Perot's success in creating a national organization and in obtaining 19 percent of the 1992 presidential vote has encouraged others to consider running as independents. In 1994, independent Angus King was elected governor of Maine, and independent Bernard Sanders was reelected to Congress from Vermont. The movement to draft General Colin Powell as a presidential candidate in 1996, even before he identified himself as a Republican, is another example of the trend toward the personalization of American politics, which reflects the electorate's unhappiness with the candidates, policies, and performance of the two major parties.

In surveys conducted throughout most of the 1990s, a majority of Americans favored the formation of a third party that would run candidates for office, although a somewhat smaller percentage indicated that they would actually vote for its candidates.[3] When pressed, however, people also said that a third-party presidential candidate would have serious problems with Congress, would generate more political conflict than currently exists, and would not facilitate the process of government.[4]

For minor-party candidates, the two-party tradition has generated legal obstacles to getting on the ballot and obtaining sufficient funds to run a viable campaign. Most states require that new parties must obtain the signatures of a specified percentage of registered voters to appear on the ballot and that they do so many months in advance of the election. For the 1996 election in California, for example, 89,006 voters (0.60 percent of the registered voters in the state) had to register as members of a new party or 147,238 had to sign a petition more than one year before the election. In Ohio, 33,463 new party registrants (0.54 percent of registered voters) were required.[5] In 1995, Perot's party garnered enough signatures to qualify in California but not in Ohio. When a party does not obtain sufficient signatures to get on the ballot, its candidates can still obtain ballot access but they must do so individually by petition. At the very least, such requirements involve much arduous grassroots activity, usually at a considerable expense.

Third parties are also disadvantaged at the presidential level by the mechanics of the Electoral College, which benefits candidates who can win a statewide popular vote. Even if a third-party candidate could win enough electoral votes to prevent either major-party candidate from getting a majority, the next step in the process, in which the House of Representatives must determine the winner, also favors major-party candidates because almost all the representatives are aligned with one of the major parties. These election rules also create a powerful psychological disincentive to voting for minor party candidates, since in all likelihood such a vote will be "wasted"; it will not directly determine the winner.

In addition, third parties also operate from a financial disadvantage. Their presidential candidates do not automatically receive government funding unless they have received at least 5 percent of the vote in the previous election, but they are still subject to the limits on individual and group contributions during the campaign. The only way to skirt these limits is for candidates to use their own money, as Perot did in the 1992 general election (and as Steve Forbes did in the 1996 Republican nomination campaign). In 1996, however, Perot accepted $29 million in government funds and supplemented it by soliciting private contributions. He could spend only $50,000 of his own money on his campaign.

A BRIEF HISTORY OF THE TWO-PARTY SYSTEM

American political parties have changed significantly over the years. That evolution has been influenced not only by the federal character of the political system in the United States but also by major events such as the Civil War, the recession of the early to mid 1890s, and the Great Depression of the 1930s. How the parties reacted to these conditions, how they proposed to deal with the attendant economic and social problems, and whom they appealed to for support have all affected the composition of the parties and their success or failure in winning elections and governing the country. The following discussion traces the history of American political parties from the beginning of the Republic to the contemporary period. The six stages during which the composition of the parties shifted significantly, with new partisan majorities being formed, are illustrated in Figure 9-2.

The Development of National Parties, 1789–1824

Parties are not mentioned in the Constitution and did not exist prior to its adoption and the presidency of George Washington. They came into being largely to support or oppose this first administration's policies: the assumption by national government of the Revolutionary War debt, the taxation of imported goods to protect domestic

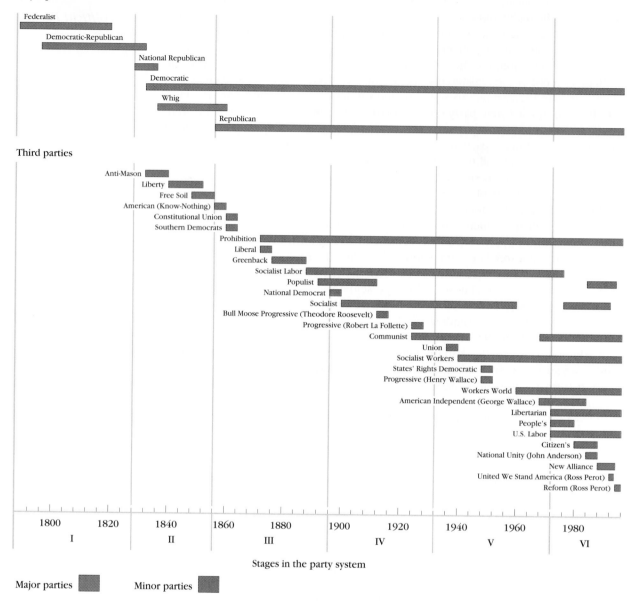

Major parties

Third parties

Stages in the party system

Major parties   Minor parties

FIGURE 9-2

American political parties since 1789.

SOURCE: Congressional Quarterly Guide to U.S. Elections, 3rd ed. (Washington, D.C.: Congressional Quarterly 1994), 258. Updated by the authors.

industry, and the establishment of a national bank to regulate currency. In general, Washington's supporters included commercial interests—merchants, manufacturers, bankers, creditors, and speculators—whereas farmers, laborers, debtors, and other less advantaged members of society opposed him. Those who saw their interests adversely affected by Washington's policies turned to Thomas Jefferson, who had resigned from his cabinet position to lead the loyal opposition.

The political groupings that emerged during this period also differed in their foreign policy orientations. Those who backed the administration, the so-called **Federalists,** tended to be more pro-British; they supported the treaty that Ambassador John Jay had negotiated to end the official state of hostilities between Britain and its former colonies. Jefferson's supporters, known as **Democratic-Republicans** or simply Republicans, opposed it.[6] Although the Jay Treaty was ratified by the Senate, it engendered a partisan debate and vote, the first party vote in Congress.

Partisanship was evident in the elections of 1796 and 1800. In fact, so unified were the Republicans in the presidential election of 1800 that all the electors who were Republican partisans voted for the two Republican candidates, Jefferson and Aaron Burr. The result was a tie that forced the House of Representatives, still controlled by the Federalists, to choose between the two Republicans.[7] By 1800 these two parties were competing within most states and at the national level.[8]

Neither the Republicans nor the Federalists enjoyed much popular backing; their most active supporters were primarily elected officials and people who desired public office. Of the two parties, however, the Federalists had the narrower base. Concentrated in the Northeast, they tended to be people with property, high social status, and considerable political influence. Unable and seemingly unwilling to broaden its appeal, the Federalist party declined rapidly as a competitive force after 1800. Its demise was accelerated by the War of 1812, in which some of its New England supporters allegedly undermined the United States war effort and expressed sympathy for the British.

The Republicans professed more confidence than the Federalists in the common people. Blessed with a succession of prestigious presidential candidates—the so-called Virginia dynasty of Jefferson, James Madison, and James Monroe—they were able to expand their base, becoming the majority party by 1800 and the only national party by 1820. The last Federalist candidate for president ran in 1816 and received only a handful of electoral votes.

The early party system contributed to the nation's evolving political tradition in several important respects. By channeling the debate about how the nation should develop, what role the government should play in that development, and which national policies should be pursued, it provided a mechanism for resolving differences of opinion about public issues. In addition, it created an institutional means for recruiting public officials and for influencing their policy judgments. Finally, it forced candidates to be sensitive to public opinion and public officials to represent their constituents' interests.

The Regionalization of Parties, 1828–1852

By the mid 1820s, the Republicans had become victims of their own success. Without a rival party, they split into feuding factions. In the election of 1824, five Republican candidates campaigned for the presidency. Two dominant groups emerged: one, the National Republicans, supported John Quincy Adams; the other, the Democratic-Republicans, backed Andrew Jackson. After Jackson won a plurality of votes in the Electoral College and was defeated by a vote in the House of Representatives, he organized a broad-based political coalition and engaged in grassroots campaigning that led to his election four years later.

The 1828 election was the first in which the electors in a majority of the states were chosen in direct popular elections. Besides accelerating the movement toward popular election of the president, Jackson's victory spurred a shift of power from the national government to the states. The congressional party caucus, which had been used to nominate presidential and vice presidential candidates between 1800 and 1824, was replaced by national nominating conventions controlled by state party leaders. Increasingly, members of Congress owed their nomination and election to their state party and its leadership.

Jackson's new electoral coalition also changed the landscape of American politics. His principal backing came from economically disadvantaged groups: small farmers and newly enfranchised voters in the West and South, along with Catholics and new immigrants in the East. Known simply as the **Democrats,** Jackson's following soon dominated the Democratic-Republican party, which dropped "Republican" from its name.

A new party, the **Whigs,** emerged in opposition to Jackson. A diverse group composed of prosperous farmers in the South and West, commercial interests in the East, and antislavery advocates in the Northeast and Appalachia, the Whigs held themselves together in national campaigns by running military heroes as candidates.

The policies of these new parties reflected their bases of support. Jackson's Democrats advocated an agrarian society in which the national government had a limited role and greater economic opportunities were available for the average person. In contrast, the Whigs, like their Federalist predecessors, envisioned a more industrial society in which a strong central government promoted policies designed to stimulate economic development.

By 1840 the Democrats and Whigs were competitive national parties. For the first time there was two-party competition in the South and West, and there were no regions of one-party domination as there had been in prior decades and would be again.[9] With heated competition, voter participation soared; it reached a high of approximately 80 percent of eligible voters in the 1840 presidential election, nearly double the highest rate attained earlier.[10]

Three minor parties also emerged during this period. The Anti-Masons, mentioned earlier, favored protectionist economic policies and government-sponsored internal improvements, such as roads and canals. The Liberty party opposed the existence of

When Andrew Jackson won the presidency in 1828, his supporters took it as a victory for the common people. They thronged to his inauguration in Washington and followed him back to the White House, where they celebrated for three days. It was a raucous party. This drawing shows a similar event on February 22, 1837, shortly before Jackson left the White House. His supporters hacked off huge chunks of a 1,400-pound cheese that was kept in the vestibule. By one contemporary account, "the air was redolent with cheese, the carpet was slippery with cheese."

Abraham Lincoln won the presidency for the Republicans in 1860 with under 40 percent of the popular vote but a majority in the Electoral College. Created out of various factions opposed to slavery and its expansion in the territories, the Republican party stood for national unity during the Civil War; it emerged from the war as the dominant party.

slavery, and the Free Soil party opposed the extension of slavery into the western territories and the influx of new immigrants into the country. Although none of these parties could generate much popular support or staying power, together they revealed growing discontent within the two major parties. This discontent was to lead to the breakup of the two-party system during the prelude to the Civil War, and to the system's eventual restructuring during and after the conflict.

The Civil War and Its Aftermath, 1856–1892

The new Republican party was organized in 1854. Its constituents included disillusioned Whigs, who feared and opposed new immigrants; Anti-Masons; Free Soilers; and others opposed to slavery (abolitionists) or its expansion (white laborers, small farmers, and some entrepreneurs). In 1856 the **Republicans** ran their first presidential candidate, John C. Frémont, who did surprisingly well. Although he was not elected, he received 40 percent of the vote.

By 1860 the Democrats had split over slavery, with northern and southern factions each running their own presidential candidate. The Whigs, controlled by antislavery forces, lost their support in the South and suffered so many defections in the North over the immigration issue that they were no longer a viable political force. With the opposition divided, the Republican candidate, Abraham Lincoln, won the 1860 election with only 39.8 percent of the popular vote, the smallest winning percentage in history.

Out of the turmoil created by the Civil War, Reconstruction, and the rapid expansion of industrialization, new partisan coalitions emerged. The Republicans evolved from their beginnings as a party of small business, labor, and farmers into a party that was increasingly dominated by big business. Banking and commercial interests also influenced the northern wing of the Democratic party, but its southern wing remained controlled by the white supremacists who sought to reimpose the pre–Civil War social and economic structure in the South. African Americans were effectively disenfranchised in the South following the withdrawal of federal troops in 1876.

Minor parties, such as the agricultural Greenback party and the urban Socialist Labor party, organized to appeal to farmers and workers whose grievances had not been adequately addressed by the major parties. In addition, new parties opposing the consumption of alcohol (the Prohibition party) and favoring more participation by the people in government (the Populist party) emerged. (The Prohibition party, which still exists, is the oldest third party in the United States.[11])

The Republican Era, 1896–1928

A recession in 1893, during the Democratic administration of Grover Cleveland, led to a shifting of political forces that culminated in a realignment of the major parties' electoral coalitions. At the turn of the century, the Republicans emerged as the majority party. They gained adherents in the Northeast and Midwest, whereas the Democrats lost them in these areas. In the grain-producing states of the prairies and the silver-mining states of the Rockies, on the other hand, the Democrats picked up support, largely on the basis of the "free-silver" policy discussed earlier and advo-

William Jennings Bryan electrified the 1896 Democratic National Convention with his famous "cross of gold" speech. The gold standard had divided the party and the country, as farmers and laborers, unable to pay their debts in gold, urged the free and unlimited coinage of silver. Taking up their cause, Bryan implored convention delegates not to "crucify mankind upon a cross of gold." His speech so moved the delegates that he was nominated for president not only in 1896 but again in 1900 and in 1908. Each time, however, he lost the election.

cated by William Jennings Bryan, the unsuccessful Democratic candidate for the presidency in 1896, 1900, and 1908. The South remained staunchly Democratic. Thus partisan conflict during this period took on a regional coloration. There were also divisions along ethnic and religious lines, with the newer wave of immigrants (largely Catholics and primarily from southern and eastern Europe) affiliating with the Democratic party, whereas those who had immigrated earlier (largely Protestants from northern Europe) turned to the Republicans.

Smaller parties that appealed to the plight of industrial workers in the cities, such as the Socialists and Communists, also gained a foothold during this period. The Progressive party, which had developed out of the Populist party, supported Theodore Roosevelt's Bull Moose candidacy against Republican incumbent William Howard Taft and Democratic candidate Woodrow Wilson in 1912. Although Wilson won, Roosevelt received the largest share of votes (27.4 percent) of any third-party candidate in American history.

In general, however, the Republican party and its northern European, Protestant constituency dominated national politics until the 1930s. During the period from 1896 to 1928 the Democrats controlled Congress for only six years and the White House for only eight. In the 1920s, however, the flow of new immigrants, combined with unpopular Republican policies (particularly Prohibition), led urban-based ethnic groups to enlarge the Democrats' electoral base. In 1928, the Democrats won a majority of the vote in the large cities for the first time since the Civil War.

The Roosevelt Realignment, 1932–1968

In the 1932 election, which occurred during the greatest economic depression in the nation's history, the Republicans suffered the loss of the presidency to Franklin Roosevelt along with major losses in Congress, as the Democrats expanded their support among white southerners and Catholics and gained support from organized labor. By 1936, when Roosevelt was reelected to the second of his four terms, African Americans had abandoned the party of Lincoln for the party of Roosevelt. Jewish voters, attracted by the president's anti-Nazi foreign policy, also shifted their allegiance to the Democrats. And although the Republicans retained their hold on northern Protestants, the Democrats made inroads among them as well, particularly those in the lower socio-economic groups. The electorate thus was divided along economic class lines: less prosperous voters were more likely to be Democratic, and more prosperous ones Republican. The exception to this pattern was in the South, where regardless of their socio-economic status most voters maintained their Democratic loyalties.

The economic division between the parties became evident in the policy perspectives they adopted. Since Roosevelt's New Deal policies, the Democrats have generally believed that the government should play an important role in solving the nation's economic and social problems, whereas the Republicans have been more leery of government involvement, particularly national efforts to regulate private industry and expand social services. The Republicans have tended to look to private enterprise for economic and even social solutions.

It is difficult to say precisely when the Roosevelt realignment that gave the Democrats a secure hold on the allegiance of a majority of voters was completed. But after World War II, the party's electoral coalition was strained by divisive new issues such as civil rights, American military involvement in Korea and then Vietnam, the deterioration of the nation's cities, and the associated problems of crime and drugs. These issues weakened the loyalties of some of the party's supporters and allowed the Republicans to attract new voters and to encourage older ones to split their ticket and vote for more Republican candidates. The Democrats lost their dominance at the presidential level in 1968, and their status as the majority party eroded even further after that.

The discontent generated within the Democratic party, combined with the growth of the Republican party, created a fluid political environment in which minor parties with new policies, ideologies, and candidates emerged to challenge the major parties. Since 1948 there have been twelve new or newly reconstituted minor parties, although few of them have commanded the allegiance and electoral support of a significant portion of the electorate for any length of time and only two of their presidential candidates—George Wallace in 1968 and H. Ross Perot in 1992—have received a sizable vote. Wallace won 13.5 percent of the popular vote and 46 electoral votes, and Perot received 18.9 percent of the popular vote but no electoral votes. (In 1996, Perot garnered 8.5 percent of the popular vote and no electoral votes.)

The Contemporary Dealignment and Potential Realignment, 1972–Present

The character of the Democratic coalition built during Franklin Roosevelt's presidency has undergone major changes since that period. One of the most significant and enduring of these changes has been the defection of white southerners, who had supported the party since the Civil War. The seeds of this defection were sown in 1948, when the Democratic National Convention adopted a strong civil rights plank in its party platform and some southern delegates walked out and later supported J. Strom Thurmond's splinter-party candidacy. In the 1960s the exodus of white southerners from the party accelerated with the advocacy of school desegregation, civil rights legislation, and other social programs by presidents John F. Kennedy and Lyndon Johnson. Since 1970 the party's nomination of liberal presidential candidates and its adoption of liberal campaign platforms have continued to alienate this group. Even moderate southern Democrats such as Jimmy Carter and

Maintaining his ties with the Hispanic community, an important component of his electoral coalition, Bill Clinton speaks at a Mexican Independence Day celebration during his 1992 campaign.

Bill Clinton were unable to win a majority of the white vote in the South, although with the help of African Americans Carter did win a majority of the total southern vote in 1976. Clinton did not, however, in either of his elections.

The Democrats have also suffered declining support from several other key groups of the New Deal coalition. Organized labor, for example, remains Democratic, but the decreasing proportion of blue-collar workers (especially union members) in the population has made labor a smaller and hence less important component of the electorate. Catholic identification with the Democratic party has also weakened, although Catholic backing of Clinton increased from 1992 to 1996.

On the other hand, the Democrats have continued to benefit from the support they receive from minority groups, notably African Americans and Hispanics. With the exception of those of Cuban descent, who tend to be Republican, African Americans and Hispanics overwhelmingly think of themselves as Democrats and vote for Democratic candidates at all levels of government. Relatively low socio-economic status has worked to reinforce the Democratic inclinations of many of these minority voters, but it has also lowered their turnout at the polls. Demographic differences in the parties are revealed in Table 9-2.

Since 1980, discernible differences have developed in the partisan identities and

TABLE 9-2	DEMOGRAPHY OF DEMOCRATS AND REPUBLICANS IN THE MID 1990S (PERCENTAGE)		
	Republican	**Democrat**	**Independent**
National	30	31	39
Sex			
Male	31	26	43
Female	28	37	35
Age			
18–29 years	29	26	45
30–49 years	30	29	41
50–64 years	30	33	37
65 & older	29	42	29
Region			
East	27	31	42
Midwest	29	29	42
South	31	34	35
West	31	30	39
Race			
White	34	26	36
Nonwhite	11	52	33
Black	6	62	28
Education			
College grad.	35	28	37
Some college	31	29	40
H.S. grad.	29	32	39
Less than H.S. grad.	22	38	40
Family Income			
$75,000 & over	42	24	34
$50,000–74,999	37	27	36
$30,000–49,999	32	29	39
$20,000–29,999	27	33	40
Under $20,000	22	38	40

Source: "Republicans: A Demographic and Attitudinal Profile," The Pew Research Center For The People & The Press, August 7, 1996, 7–9.

voting patterns of men and women: women are more likely than men to identify with the Democratic party, and men are more likely than women to prefer the Republican party. In presidential voting, this "gender gap" reached its maximum in 1996, when men voted for Dole over Clinton by 44 to 43 percent whereas women backed Clinton by 54 to 38 percent.[12] The gender gap has tended to be larger among whites than among nonwhites, larger among better educated and wealthier voters than among less advantaged groups, and larger among unmarried people than among married ones.

Another important shift in the partisan electoral coalitions has been the movement of new voters, particularly youth. After being more Democratic than their elders for several decades, younger voters (those age 18 to 29) began to change their political allegiances, ideological orientations, and voting patterns in the 1980s. They became more conservative than the general public on a host of economic and social issues and more Republican in their voting behavior, supporting Ronald Reagan in 1980 and 1984 and George Bush in 1988. During this decade a majority of the younger voters entering the electorate also identified with the Republican party. However, the 18- to 29-year-old voters returned to the Democratic fold in 1992 and have remained there. In 1996 this age category provided Clinton and Democratic congressional candidates with stronger support than did any other.[13]

In light of these shifts, how can the Democratic party's electoral coalition be described today? The Democrats have become a diverse party in which ethnic and racial minorities constitute core constituencies and women—especially younger single women—increasingly do as well. Although they still receive overwhelming support from those with the lowest incomes and those who live in central cities, the relatively small size of these groups and their lower turnout at the polls make them less important components of the total electorate than they were in the past. Some of the other traditionally Democratic-oriented groups, such as union members and Catholics, also provide less support than in the past, and a majority of southern whites seem to have deserted the party altogether. Clearly, the Democrats' New Deal coalition has eroded.

As for the Republicans, in the last three decades they have gained adherents, probably more from new voters than from a wholesale shift of existing ones. As an electoral coalition, Republicans have become more white, more male, and more suburban. While gaining support in the South and Southwest, they have lost support in the Northeast. While they have maintained the traditional loyalties of white Protestants, they have gained support from Protestant fundamentalists who backed Democratic candidates through 1976. The core constituency of the contemporary Republican party thus consists of members of racial and religious majorities and higher socio-economic groups. (See Figure 9-3.)

What conclusions can be drawn about the parties today? The old electoral coalitions have changed and, in the case of the Democrats, weakened to the point where they have lost their partisan advantage. Indeed, by the end of the 1980s the major parties were at or near parity, with an increasing portion of the electorate identifying themselves as independent.

It is clear that a partisan **dealignment**—a weakening of the attachments that people feel toward political parties—has been occurring over the last thirty years. This dealignment has led more people to think of themselves as independents and vote more for the candidate and less for that candidate's partisan affiliation. It is not nearly as clear, however, whether a *realignment* has occurred or is occurring.

A **realignment**—a shifting in the partisan attitude of the electorate—normally occurs over a series of elections and is characterized by changes in the allegiances of some existing voters from the majority party to the minority party and by the development of preferences for the new emerging majority party among many new

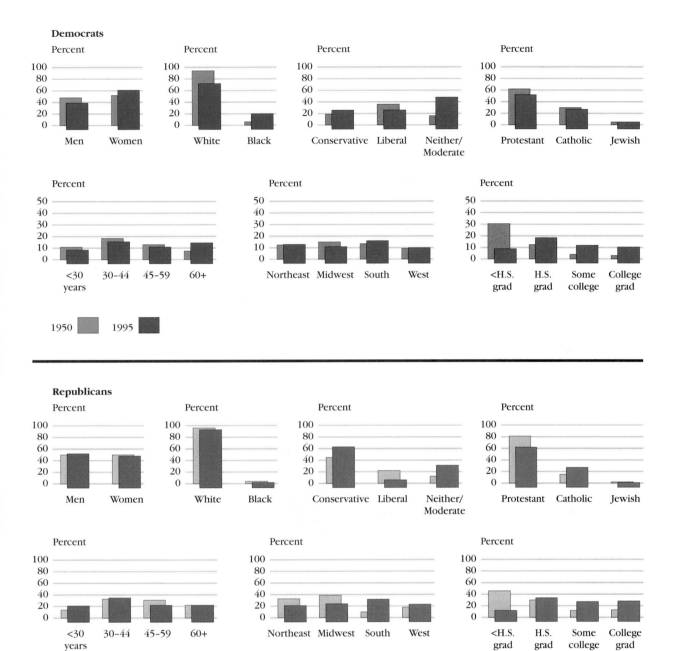

FIGURE 9-3

Profile of the Democrats and Republicans, 1950 and 1995.

SOURCE: Surveys by the Gallup Organization, latest that of January–October, 1995, as appears in *American Enterprise*, January/February 1996, 94-95.

ONWARD CHRISTIAN SOLDIERS: FIGHTING FOR THE SOUL OF THE REPUBLICAN PARTY

Their battle began during the Reagan years, and it is still being waged today. An army of believers, for the most part Protestant fundamentalists, they wish to shape public policy in their own image and on the basis of their own values. Organized by groups such as the Moral Majority and its successor, the Christian Coalition, the so-called Christian right has been trying with varying success to gain effective control over state and national Republican party organizations in order to recruit its own candidates, highlight its own issues, and promote its own policy agenda.

Opposing them are much of the Republican establishment, the party's moderate wing, and those conservatives who are primarily concerned with economic and national security issues. During the Reagan years, as the Christian right was beginning to organize, the schism between the two sides was not nearly as deep as it is today. Although President Reagan's programs were oriented toward revitalizing the economy and rebuilding defense, he articulated the social values and beliefs of his religious constituency, which overwhelmingly supported him in 1980 and 1984.

The Christian right, which also voted solidly (81 percent) for George Bush in 1988, became increasingly dissatisfied with his administration as it progressed even though Bush continued to stress the family and community values that were important to these religious believers. In 1992, this dissatisfaction manifested itself in the electoral support that Pat

Christian fundamentalists have exercised increasing influence on Republican party politics. Although they supported George Bush in 1992 and Bob Dole in 1996, they forced the party to take very conservative positions in its platform, especially on social issues such as abortion, school prayer, and homosexuality. Here Dole speaks to a 1995 convention of the Christian Coalition, a gathering also addressed by most of his rivals for the Republican presidential nomination.

voters. With the exception of white southerners, who have switched their partisan allegiances from Democratic to Republican, wholesale shifts from one electoral coalition to another have not occurred. Nor have overwhelming proportions of young voters aligned themselves with one party.

Shifts in partisan attitudes *have* produced a more volatile electorate, however, one on which neither party can depend as confidently as before. These shifts have also contributed to the decline in the party's influence over its candidates, the electorate, and elected officials. If a partisan realignment does occur, it is likely to be characterized by weaker partisan attachments than occurred during the last realignment in the 1930s. This would make it a less important influence on the

Buchanan, a Roman Catholic, received from "born-again" Christians in his challenge to Bush for the Republican nomination; in the debate over the Republican platform, in which the positions of the Christian right were adopted; and in the substantial decline in the religious right's vote for Bush in the 1992 election.[1] With Bush's defeat and with the Republicans remaining a minority in Congress, control of the party was up for grabs.

By 1993, the Christian right had a new political opponent in Bill Clinton, a president who was hostile to much of their policy agenda and whose secular and pragmatic views, not to mention his alleged extramarital affairs, were antithetical to many of their beliefs, values, and norms of behavior. Fueled by talk radio, sermons, and a well-organized, well-funded, well-led public relations campaign, groups such as the 1.7-million-member Christian Coalition grew increasingly active in state and national Republican politics, mobilizing upwards of 4 million voters who were sympathetic to their values, beliefs, and policy positions. According to a group of political scientists who have studied the Christian movement in politics, the turnout of evangelical Christians in 1994 may have been a factor in thirty Republican victories in the House.[2] Almost one out of every four Republican votes in 1994 came from an evangelical Christian, compared with only 7 percent for the Democrats.[3]

By 1995, the coalition was heavily involved in Republican party politics, forcing the party's presidential candidates to indicate their approval of its positions on abortion, school prayer, homosexuality, and a variety of other family and social issues. With the exception of Senator Arlen Specter, who campaigned against the religious right, every one of the other candidates appeared before the Christian Coalition's annual convention in September 1995 to express his ideological solidarity with the group. When Colin Powell announced that if he ran for president it would be as a moderate Republican, the leaders of the Christian right led the criticism of him.[4] When Republican moderates proposed to change the party's pro-life platform position and include a reference to tolerance of other views, coalition leaders strongly objected and rallied their troops to defeat the changes. Clear policy differences between the parties and their candidates on most social issues kept the coalition solidly in the Republican camp during the 1996 election campaign.

[1] A majority of evangelical Christians still supported his candidacy, however. Mitofsky International, "Religious Americans in Politics," *American Enterprise*, November/December 1995, 20.
[2] John C. Green, James L. Guth, Lyman A. Kellstedt, and Corwin E. Smidt, as quoted in "Religious Voters in 1994," *American Enterprise*, November/December 1995, 20.
[3] Mitofsky International, 1994, as appears in *American Enterprise*, November/December 1995, 20.
[4] Entrance polls at the beginning of the Iowa caucuses indicated that of the 35 percent of the Republican participants who identified with the religious right, 42 percent said they supported Buchanan compared with only 19 percent supporting Senator Robert Dole. "Entrance Poll Results," *Washington Post*, February 13, 1996, A6.

political process than other realignments have been. If people have less confidence in parties and weaker partisan allegiances, then their affiliation is not likely to matter as much.

PARTY ORGANIZATION

In the decentralized organization of the major political parties, power is dispersed (see Figure 9-4). Separate structures at the national, state, and local levels operate largely independently of one another. Each exercises autonomy over its nominations and campaigns as well as over the election of its own officials.

The National Level

At the national level, parties have traditionally been weak. Even when parties first emerged and power was centralized in Congress, there was no effective party organization beyond the informal congressional caucuses that met to decide whom their electors should vote for in the Electoral College. Only after national conventions replaced the congressional caucuses did the parties establish national committees to make arrangements for the conventions and coordinate national campaigns more effectively. The Democratic National Committee was organized in 1848, the Republican National Committee in 1856. Initially each was composed of an equal number of representatives from each state party. The Republicans have maintained this principle of equal representation, but the Democrats have not. In addition, each party has increased the size of its national committee to include state party chairs and, in the case of the Democrats, other elected and appointed party leaders.

Both national committees used to operate more like confederations of state parties than like independent entities. The Democrats no longer do so. They now provide representation to the states on the basis of their population and their past support for Democratic candidates, a change that has given larger states like California, New York, and Texas much more influence on the national committee.

Both parties have also increased their national administrative apparatus. Prior to World War I neither party had a headquarters, a staff, or a full-time paid chairperson.[14] Today both have all three, and their large staffs and budgets expand even further during election years.

The chair of the national committee is its chief public spokesperson and liaison to elected officials and party leaders. The chair also oversees the party's administrative operation, although sometimes day-to-day responsibilities are performed by an executive director if the chair holds another position, usually that of an elected official. For example, this is the way that Senator Chris Dodd and Donald Fowler divided

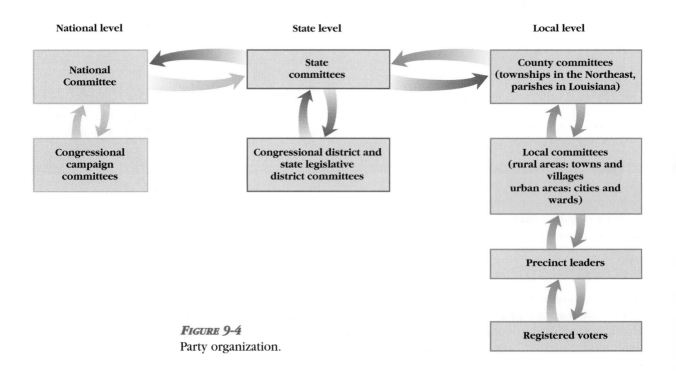

FIGURE 9-4
Party organization.

their responsibilities after they were appointed general chairman and national chairman, respectively, of the Democratic National Committee in 1995.

Generally speaking, the national parties direct the bulk of their energies to presidential campaigns. They raise and dispense funds, identify and target voters, survey and communicate with the public, develop policy positions, and generate partisan appeals. They also provide assistance directly to candidates as well as to state and local party organizations.

The Republicans have led the Democrats in those activities. During the 1970s they aggressively expanded their fundraising and technical services while the Democrats, saddled with a divided party and a sizable debt from their 1968 presidential campaign, were unable to do so. In the 1980s the Democrats began to emulate the Republicans in providing some of these benefits for their candidates, but they still lag in fundraising and campaign support. During the 1993–1994 election cycle the Republican party committees at the state and national levels raised almost twice as much as their Democratic counterparts. The parties raised even larger sums during the 1995–1996 election cycle.[15]

The national parties' fundraising activities have been reinforced by the success of their congressional campaign committees, which raise money for the reelection of their legislators and for the recruitment and training of challengers to take on incumbents of the other party. Congressional campaign committees have become a powerful political force, contributing to the reelection of congressional candidates and to their independence from the party's national committee.[16]

In addition, the major parties have established elaborate in-house media facilities that can be used by their candidates and elected officials. The Republicans produce a regular one-hour television program that is transmitted via satellite to stations around the country, and both parties have engaged in generic television and radio advertising to promote their policy positions. They have also devoted considerable resources to surveying public opinion.

Another development that has strengthened the national Democratic party has been changes in that party's rules for the selection of delegates to nominate its presidential and vice presidential candidates. Beginning in the 1970s and continuing into the 1990s, a series of party commissions have reformed the delegate selection process and, with the approval of the national committee, have tried to impose these reforms on the state parties. The new rules deal with the issues of who can participate in party primaries and caucuses, when these contests can be held, how the delegates to the Democratic National Convention are apportioned among states and other units, and for whom they can vote.

Both the Democrats' nationalization of party rules and the centralization of fundraising and campaign services by both parties have significantly increased the influence that national party organizations have on their state and local affiliates. Nevertheless, the national organization does not control the selection of any of the party's nominees, the platforms on which nominees run, or the conduct of political campaigns.[17] In 1994, for example, it was GOPAC, not solely the Republican National Committee and Congressional Campaign Committee, that sparked the recruitment, campaigns, and policy positions of Republican candidates for the House of Representatives (see Chapter 8, pp. 248–249).

As the national party organizations have become more important, groups within the parties have become more active. Caucuses representing women, ethnic minorities, gay and lesbian activists, and others have striven for greater visibility as well as for more influence on the party on their issues. Pro-life and pro-choice advocates have been active within both major parties. In addition, more broadly focused pol-

Christopher Dodd (top) *and Haley Barbour, general chairmen of the Democratic and Republican national committees, respectively.*

icy groups have also tried to affect the general orientation of their parties' programs. One such group, the Democratic Leadership Council, created in the mid 1980s to advocate a more conservative agenda than the one articulated over the last thirty years by most Democratic presidential candidates and congressional leaders, received considerable attention and became more influential when one of its organizers and early chairs, Bill Clinton, was elected president. The Progressive Policy Institute, a research organization associated with the Leadership Council, has had some success in influencing the policy positions of the Clinton administration. Similarly, the Christian Coalition exercised considerable influence on the 1996 Republican presidential nomination process, including the party platform.

The State Level

Some of the developments that have changed national party organizations have also affected their state counterparts. The organizational structure of many of them has been strengthened, and their operations have been institutionalized. Most state parties now have a permanent staff. Their fundraising capabilities have been substantially improved, their operating budgets have increased, and their ability to train and assist candidates in the general election has been enhanced.[18] In general, state Republican parties have done a better job of organizing and raising money than have their Democratic counterparts.[19]

The strengthening of state party organizations has not been easy. For one thing, the growth of primary elections, which make it easier for candidates to get on the ballot and encourage candidates to mount their own campaigns and make their own appeals to voters, has made it more difficult for state party leaders to exercise control over the nomination process. Similarly, the influence of television as a vehicle for communicating to the electorate has weakened the capacity of parties at all levels to control the message their candidates present to the voters. Moreover, the growth of the civil service system at all levels of government has reduced the patronage powers of party leaders and elected officials.

State party structures are decentralized. In most states there is a party committee composed of representatives from different geographic subdivisions, usually counties. State party committees vary in size, composition, and function. Some elect their members in primary elections, others in local caucuses, and still others at state conventions. Because most state party committees meet infrequently, the chair has considerable discretion in the conduct of party affairs. In only a few states, however, is the position of chair a full-time paid job. Turnover is high: state chairs average less than three years in office.[20]

State chairs play a variety of roles. Some serve as the principal link between a high-ranking elected official (such as the governor or a powerful big-city mayor) and the state party organization. Others exercise influence on their own in the absence of such an official. In addition, chairs often serve as spokesperson for their party.

Electing candidates to state and national office remains the primary goal of state parties, although they get involved in a variety of activities, ranging from taking official positions on salient issues, to holding meetings and conventions, to conducting fundraising and membership drives. State parties recruit potential nominees and help them with their campaigns. Like the national parties, state parties in recent years have improved their capacity to raise money, compile lists of voters, and provide organizational support to candidates. In fact, national party fundraising activities have benefited state party organizations by giving them the task of distributing a substantial portion of the funds raised to candidates within their states. All these developments have strengthened the state parties and increased their electoral impact. They have not, however, eliminated the need for candidates to obtain funds on their own, build their own grassroots organizations, or hire their own campaign consultants.[21]

The Local Level

Local parties also have their own organizations built around geographic subdivisions, usually counties or cities. The county or city organization is made up of representatives from still smaller units, called wards or precincts. Usually the key figure in directing the party's efforts is the chair of the county committee or the mayor of the town or city, assisted by precinct captains and ward leaders.

It was primarily at the local level, particularly in cities, that political organizations referred to as *machines* (because of the effectiveness of their operation) and party leaders referred to as *bosses* (because of their near-total control over party affairs) flourished during the second half of the nineteenth century and the first half of the twentieth. For their members, many of whom were newly arrived immigrants, these organizations provided help in securing jobs, obtaining housing, learning English, and, more generally, becoming integrated into the life of American cities. In exchange for this help, the machine got their votes.

The machines weakened and eventually lost their hold over city politics as a result of several factors. Not only did immigrants gradually become assimilated into American society, but urban governments expanded their social and economic services, reducing the need for those provided by parties. Also, a civil service system based on merit gradually replaced a political appointment system based on partisanship. Other political reforms, such as the direct primary, reduced the power of party leaders to control nominations. Today only a few strong party machines, such as the Cook County Democratic organization in Chicago and the Nassau County Republican organization on Long Island, New York, still operate much as the old-style machines did, using patronage to secure the loyalty of a cadre of workers and political supporters.

Local party organizations tend to be loosely structured. Most of their leaders and workers are volunteers; there may be no paid staff. Most of their activities, like those of the state parties, are organized around election campaigns: arranging fundraising

Strong local party leaders have become the exception rather than the rule. Chicago mayor Richard Daley Jr. and New York senator Alfonse D'Amato are two exceptions. Daley (left), *who followed in his father's footsteps as mayor and head of the city's Democratic organization, and D'Amato* (right), *a product of the Nassau County Republican organization, continue to exercise considerable clout within their state and national parties.*

events, contributing money to candidates, and publicizing themselves and their candidates through media advertising, press releases, telephone campaigns, and the distribution of campaign literature. The local organization also maintains lists of registered voters and organizes get-out-the-vote campaigns.

Local campaign activity has increased in recent years. Some of the increase seems to be the result of greater competition between the parties at the local level. In areas where such competition is weak, there is less incentive for the parties to mount a strong campaign. For years, local party organizations in the South were less active than those in the Northeast, the Midwest, or the Pacific Coast, because they had less competition. But Republican gains in the South over the last three decades have forced Democratic party organizations there to take their membership-building and campaign activities more seriously.[22]

In recent years the power of ethnic and racial minorities in local parties has grown substantially. Beginning in the 1970s and continuing into the 1990s, African Americans, Hispanics, and Asian Americans have won control of local party organizations in areas where they are a dominant population group. This control has enabled these minorities to nominate and elect candidates sensitive to their needs, many of whom are themselves minorities. The gains of these groups, especially in many of the nation's largest cities, mirror those of European immigrants a half-century earlier, particularly the Irish and Italians. Women too have seen increased electoral success at local as well as higher levels of government.

PARTIES AND ELECTIONS

Parties are election oriented: their principal function is to get their candidates into office. To do this, they need to influence the electoral process. Today the parties exercise less influence over the conduct of elections—the nomination of candidates, the structure of the campaign, and the vote itself—than they did three or four decades ago, but they still remain an important factor.

Getting Out the Vote

Until about a hundred years ago, the methods used by parties to get out the vote were often sneaky if not downright dishonest. Parties printed and distributed the ballots, listing only their own candidates, and paid people to take time off from work to vote. Because voting was open and public, enormous pressure was exerted on people to vote for the party's ticket. Allegations of fraud against the parties for registering ineligible voters, stuffing ballot boxes, and miscounting the results were frequent.

Toward the end of the nineteenth century, fraudulent activity was reduced by the passage of state laws that governed the conduct of elections. Uniform procedures for voting were established: standard ballots, designed by state officials, were introduced, as was the requirement for secret voting. Today punch cards and voting machines have replaced paper ballots at election polls, reducing fraud and making it possible to determine the outcome of elections quickly and accurately. (New technology may eventually permit electronic voting from home, as discussed in the box on page 182.) States have enacted laws for the registration of voters, the oversight of the vote, and the designation of the official results. Boards of elections monitor these activities and provide information to the public. These laws have forced the parties and their candidates to compete more honestly, although they have not eliminated all questionable activities.

GETTING INVOLVED IN PARTISAN ACTIVITIES

The easiest way to get involved in a political party is to join the chapter of the Young Democrats or Young Republicans at your school. At some schools there may also be affiliates of other parties, such as the Libertarians, the Green party (in California), and the Socialist Workers. If there is no party chapter at your school, it is relatively easy to organize one.

Both major national parties have a youth division with a staff to coordinate activities with the party's college and university chapters around the country. The national parties also have speaker's bureaus, run campaign seminars, and organize volunteers for campaigns and elections.

But joining a party's college chapter is not the only way to get involved. Most state and local parties need a lot of help during campaigns, mostly with fundraising, grassroots organizing, and get-out-the-vote activities. (You can find party headquarters through the local phone directory.) Because candidate organizations do

much the same thing, parties compete with them for volunteers. The advantage of working with a party at the local or state level is that you come in contact with a variety of campaign workers and candidates. The disadvantage is that the campaign is not likely to garner as much public attention as national campaigns.

During nonelection periods the parties have less need of help, but there are still jobs associated with party meetings, ongoing fundraising, and membership solicitation.

There are opportunities at the national level as well, but you usually have to be in Washington to take advantage of them. The Republican and Democratic National Committees always have need of volunteers. You can contact the Republican committee on the Internet at http://www.rnc.org and the Democratic committee at http://www.democrats.org. Here are some of the telephone numbers (all in area code 202) you can call for specific offices at the national party headquarters.

	Republican	Democrat
Main Number	863-8500	863-8000
Chairman	863-8700	863-8148
Treasurer	863-8720	863-7147
Counsel	863-8638	863-7110
Communications	863-8614	488-4048
Press Secretary	863-8550	863-8151
Political/Campaign Director	863-8600	863-7112
Research Director	863-8666	479-5130
Finance Director	863-8720	863-7187
Membership/Marketing	863-8630	863-7121
Fax	863-8820	863-8081

Primary Elections

Party organizations have been affected by other changes in the electoral process as well. Chief among these has been the evolution of the nomination process.

When the congressional caucus system for nominating presidential and vice presidential candidates began to break down in the 1820s, it was replaced by state and national party conventions that were usually controlled by party leaders. Local

HEMAL VAIDYA: YOUNG PARTISAN

The translation of my Indian last name is "doctor." But even though family history and genetics suggested a career in medicine or the natural sciences, my abilities and pursuits have led to a much different result: studies at Georgetown's School of Foreign Service and the London School of Economics, a degree in politics, extensive experience on Capitol Hill, and aspirations of a career in public service.

I should note that for years I thought my political career had been doomed in the third grade. I lost the race for class representative to a peer who was more popular with the female voters, through on the day of the vote I had given a clearly superior speech on how I would extend the recess hour and abolish homework were I elected. Political leadership, I soon learned, involved forging a consensus among all segments of society and tackling problems with knowledge and truthfulness.

I began to see this leadership in practice during my internship with Senator Paul S. Sarbanes of Maryland in the spring of 1993, just after President Clinton's inauguration. As an intern and research assistant, I was first overwhelmed by the sheer volume of calls and letters the Senator received from his constituents—whose purposes ranged from seeking redress from an intolerant landlord to voicing support or opposition to American involvement in the former Yugoslavia. As a result of this communication between the Senator and his constituents, I observed that a significant bond exists between the people of our country and their chosen leaders. Even if people called or wrote to dis-

agree with a politician's view or an administration's policy, they were actually taking part in our political process, and they looked to their elected officials for a solution.

After my internship with Senator Sarbanes, I realized that to contribute meaningfully to the betterment of our society, I would need to learn more about our political process. The Democratic National Committee (DNC) has been a particularly apt place wherein I could learn the dynamics of party politics and develop my career. During the summer of 1993, I pursued an internship that focused on constitutional functions of the Democratic party—from learning the history and methodology of the party's charter and bylaws to working on the site selection process for the 1996 Democratic National Convention. In June 1994, I became the youngest person ever to be named the DNC's Assistant Director of Party Affairs and Delegate Selection, in which capacity I work with state Democratic parties to design and implement their presidential primary or caucus.

The culmination of our party's presidential nominating process is, of course, the Democratic National Convention. For the 1996 convention, I played the roles of both a political administrator and a student. As a DNC staffer, I focused most of my work on the convention's standing committees—platform, rules, and credentials. Each of the committees had testimonial hearings at which key constituencies, voters, and supporters of the presidential campaign voiced their concerns and presented issues on which they felt the

precincts chose delegates to county conventions, which in turn chose delegates to state conventions, which in their turn chose nominees for state office and delegates to the national nominating conventions. However, this system was neither as representative nor as receptive to popular control as it appeared to be. Party leaders could use their clout to affect the choice of delegates and influence their behavior at the conventions. Not only did the nomination process minimize the impact of the party's rank and file, but in areas of one-party dominance, it effectively denied a voice to supporters of the minority party. The nomination was, in effect, the election.

The capacity of the system to be manipulated by party leaders, combined with the selection of unpopular, unimaginative, and in some cases unethical candidates, led to demands for reform. At the beginning of the twentieth century, the

Hemal Vaidya (right) *with Donald Fowler, national chairman of the Democratic National Committee, in front of the party's national headquarters in Washington.*

Democratic party should articulate a stance. The committees then presented their reports to the full convention for consideration and approval.

As in previous conventions, much of the negotiating for platform positions and rules procedures occurred behind the scenes. In this regard, I learned *how* the process works while I worked closely with different groups to facilitate a smooth process.

Certain intangibles, such as these negotiations and working with the press corps and so many interests, can be fully appreciated only after experiencing the process. At times, I feel that I am treading in uncharted waters because of my age. Many in the political world, particularly those who organize the conventions, feel that one has to earn his or her battle scars before making a meaningful contribution to the process. I have often tried to challenge this notion by showing that one can do both.

As a young individual working through his first full presidential cycle, I have seen the immense preparation and organization needed to run a nationwide effort. Literally each aspect of our party's positions and strategies is carefully deliberated with the aim of contributing toward a better America. My experiences at the DNC have also underscored the importance of working with others toward a common goal. Politics has often been labeled the art of compromise, but people in politics should also be true to their own values. While working with members of the White House, elected officials, and political activists, I have realized that I am pursuing my own beliefs and values.

Although I have not pursued the medical or scientific profession that my name had suggested, in choosing a life of public service I can still play a role in my community and country akin to that of a physician. A physician is, after all, a care giver and servant of the community. After almost three active years in politics, I hope that I can convince others that a career in public service aspires to the same ideal.

Progressive movement responded to these demands by urging a direct primary election in which the rank-and-file supporters of a party would choose the party's nominees. In 1904, Florida became the first state to hold such an election. Others followed suit. By 1916 twenty states had some type of primary; by the mid 1950s most of them did. In 1976, Indiana became the last state to adopt this method of nominating candidates for state office.

Primaries are more democratic than multi-staged delegate selection processes because they allow more people to participate. However, even in primaries those who participate may not be an accurate reflection of the general electorate or even the party as a whole. The better-educated, higher-income, more professional supporters of the party tend to be overrepresented.

Primaries have not only improved participation; they have also affected representation. In areas in which the parties are competitive, primaries have generally improved representation and have often heightened competition between parties. In areas dominated by a single party, however, primaries have had the opposite effect, decreasing competition and working to perpetuate the dominance of the majority party.[23] In such areas ambitious politicians generally seek nomination by the majority party, for winning its primary is tantamount to winning the general election.

Primaries have also encouraged a different type of candidate, one who can appeal to the party's rank and file and not simply to its leadership. In this way, primaries have encouraged factions built on personal followings. They have also made it more difficult for parties themselves to maintain consistent policy positions, because the parties can no longer control who is nominated or what appeals those nominees make.

Modern Campaigns

Campaigns are important. Without a strong campaign, it is difficult for a challenger to gain sufficient recognition to defeat an incumbent; without a strong campaign, it is difficult for candidates of parties who do not command the loyalties of a majority or plurality of the electorate to overcome this disadvantage; without a strong campaign, it is even difficult for a candidate to win an open seat or a nonpartisan election.

The demands of modern campaigning, and particularly the increased use of television and other electronic media, have reduced the traditional role of parties as the principal link between candidates and voters. Since candidates need to raise much of their own campaign money and discern public opinion, they have increasingly turned to a new group of professionals who have rivaled and in many instances replaced party pros as campaign strategists and technical advisers. As explained in Chapter 8, changes in the campaign finance law have increased the influence of PACs and encouraged candidates to seek money and organizational support from them. Parties and PACs have spent approximately the same amount in elections since 1978.

Professional campaign consultants and interest group leaders not only compete for influence in the campaign; they continue to vie for the candidate's ear after the election is over. In this way they challenge party leaders and their organizations. Nonetheless, parties remain viable in and valuable to the electoral system and the organization and operation of government.

PARTIES AND GOVERNANCE

Despite its emphasis on elections, the party's ultimate objective is to control the machinery of government so as to influence the formulation of public policy in accordance with the interests and needs of its supporters. These interests and needs are articulated by the party in its quadrennial platform, by its candidates during the campaign, and by its leaders and elected officials during nonelection periods.

Determining the Party's Positions

A **party platform** is a formal statement of beliefs, opinions, and policy stands tied together by a set of underlying principles based on the party's ideological orientation. It is drafted by a platform committee composed of delegates to the party's national convention and then approved (occasionally with modifications) by the convention itself. Over the years the platforms of the two major parties have differed significantly, despite the common allegation that there is not a "dime's worth of difference" between them. Between 1944 and 1976, for example, more than two-thirds of the pledges made in each party's platform were not made in the other's.[24]

The sharpest distinctions between Democrats and Republicans have been evident in relation to the economy, welfare, and social and cultural issues where the Democrats favor greater government involvement on economic issues and the Republicans support government-imposed community standards on social issues such as abortion, prayer in school, and homosexuality. Foreign affairs did not produce many clear-cut or consistent differences between the two parties until the 1990s, when partisan divisions have become evident in the debates over the role and participation of the United States in peacekeeping operations led by international and regional organizations such as the United Nations and NATO.

Differences between party platforms are important because elected officials do attempt to redeem the promises they and their parties make. One study of party platforms and campaign promises made during presidential election campaigns between 1960 and 1984 found that presidents "submitted legislation or signed executive orders that are broadly consistent with about two-thirds of their campaign pledges."[25] Of this legislation, a substantial percentage was enacted into law, ranging from a high of 89 percent of that proposed during the Johnson administration to a low of 61 percent of that proposed during the Nixon years.[26]

More recently Newt Gingrich, the leading architect of the Republicans' 1994 Contract with America, pledged to vote on the proposals within it during the first 100 days of the new Congress if his party won control of the House of Representatives. It did; and as Speaker, Gingrich made it a point to redeem this pledge in less than 100 days.

Converting Positions into Public Policy

The successful conversion of a partisan agenda into legislative enactments and executive actions is an important measure of **responsible party government**, that is, holding the party accountable for its platform and the promises made by its candidates for national office.[27]

Officials who abandon their party's positions may jeopardize the benefits they receive from their party's leaders—such as legislative committee assignments and presidential support. However, this is often not a very serious risk to run, as indicated by what happened to Phil Gramm when he was a Democratic representative

Members of the platform committee at the 1996 Republican National Convention. After they adopted a platform endorsing very conservative policy positions, the party's presidential nominee, Bob Dole, announced that he did not consider himself bound by it.

PROMISES AND PERFORMANCE: DO PLATFORMS MATTER?

Every four years at their national nominating conventions, the two major parties articulate their philosophy, goals, and positions on the issues of the day. In developing their platforms, both parties appoint a committee, composed of representatives of the candidates who are seeking the party's presidential nomination and other party leaders and officials, to draft a document for approval by the convention.

Despite the conventional wisdom that platforms are forgotten once the campaign is over, elected officials do have a relatively good record of meeting their pledges. Although approximately three-fourths of a party platform consists of high-sounding rhetoric, about one-fourth of it contains fairly specific promises that successful congressional and presidential candidates try to redeem.

Here are some of the domestic policy positions adopted by the Democrats in 1992. Note how many of them have become national policy in the years following the Democrats' victory.

1. *New jobs.* The platform pledged to create jobs through investment in infrastructure, conversion of defense facilities to civilian use, and a national information network. Although no specific jobs bill was enacted into law, money for

vocational education was authorized in the 1993 education bill. The Republicans attempted to eliminate money from President Clinton's vocational education program in 1995, but a veto threat reduced substantially the amount of money they proposed to cut.

2. *Deficit reduction.* The Democratic platform proposed to achieve this objective through spending cuts, reducing the administrative costs of government, adopting a strict "pay-as-you-go" rule for noninvestment spending, and increasing taxes on the rich. The Clinton administration submitted a legislative plan that included these measures. In 1993 it succeeded, although barely, in getting Congress to enact legislation that promised to reduce the budget deficit by half over a period of five years through cuts in spending programs and administrative costs as well as income tax increases that primarily affected the wealthy and a small gasoline tax increase. Two years later, a Republican Congress proposed tax cuts, deeper spending cuts, and cutbacks in entitlement programs for those on welfare and those over 65 (Medicare). Welfare reform was enacted into law, but changes in Medicare were not.

from Texas. As a member of the House budget committee, Gramm supported the budget proposals of the Reagan administration in 1981 to reduce domestic spending and allegedly conveyed the content of confidential Democratic discussions to the Republicans. The Democratic leadership punished him by denying him a seat on the Budget Committee in the next Congress. Gramm responded by switching parties and winning reelection as a Republican, an example that was not lost on subsequent party leaders. In 1995, when Senator Mark Hatfield of Oregon broke ranks to oppose a major Republican proposal (a constitutional amendment to require a balanced federal budget), a party caucus that considered his actions did nothing.

A party organization has limited leverage over public officials, regardless of their partisan affiliation. The heterogeneous nature of the major parties and their decentralized structures result in policy positions that are not equally attractive and salient to all candidates and officeholders. Moreover, platforms become dated over time.[28] Although legislators of both parties maintain committees and caucuses to define partisan policy positions, during nonelection years the parties have had dif-

3. *Education.* The platform promised to expand Head Start and children's health and nutrition programs; to make college education affordable to all qualified students by revamping the student loan program and instituting a program of national service by which loans could be partially or fully paid off; and to allow students more choice in selecting public schools within a school district but not provide government credits or vouchers for students to attend private schools. The administration succeeded in its attempts to revise the student loan program and enact a national service program, although not of the magnitude the president had initially proposed. In 1995–1996 the Republican Congress reduced funding for these programs; it debated but did not enact a school voucher program for the District of Columbia.

4. *Health care.* A major plank in the platform and a major priority of the Clinton administration was to reform the health-care system by controlling costs and making health care affordable and accessible to *all* Americans. However, the administration's proposal for comprehensive national health-care reform died in the Senate in 1994. In the 104th Congress, the Republicans proposed comprehensive changes in Medicare and Medicaid, but Congress enacted only modest programs to expand the availability of private health insurance and to require insurers to pay for at least 48 hours of hospital care for women giving birth.

5. *Abortion.* The platform stated the right of every woman to choose abortion, consistent with the guidelines set forth by the Supreme Court in *Roe v. Wade*, regardless of her ability to pay, and supported a national law to protect that right. No such law was enacted. However, by executive memorandum the president rescinded prohibitions made by previous administrations with respect to abortion counseling, fetal tissue research, and the performance of abortions at military hospitals at private expense. The 104th Congress voted to prohibit certain late-term abortions, but Clinton vetoed the bill.

Platforms of the major parties are available from national committee headquarters: Republican National Committee, 310 1st Street, S.E., Washington, DC 20003, (202) 863-8500; Democratic National Committee, 430 S. Capitol Street, S.E., Washington, DC 20003, (202) 863-8000.

ficulty articulating and promoting stands on issues. An exception was the Republicans' Contract with America, which served as a basis for the 104th Congress's legislative agenda.

Finally, in the United States system of different branches of government sharing powers, there may not be one controlling party. Control of the legislative and executive branches by opposite parties has been the rule, not the exception, since 1968, a period during which the public has made significant demands on government. In such a situation, credit or blame for inaction is difficult to assess. Thus, party is but one influence among many on public policy.

Partisan Influence on the Legislature

Parties shape the structure and operation of Congress, as they do those of most legislatures. The vote on legislative leadership occurs along party lines: the Speaker of the House and the Senate majority leader are chosen on straight party votes. In addition, the majority party controls committees, recruits most of the staff, and influences rule making, personnel, and policy matters.

Although the effect of partisanship on substantive matters varies with the issue, it tends to be greater than any other factor in affecting the outcome of voting in Congress at the final stage of deliberation.[29] For example, from 1954 through 1986 a majority of Republicans opposed a majority of Democrats on an average of 43.2 percent of the roll-call votes in the House and 42.9 percent of those in the Senate.[30] Since that time the parties have become even more unified, with partisan majorities opposing each other on an average of 57.6 percent of all roll calls in the House and 49.1 percent in the Senate.[31] (See Table 9-3.)

A continuing difficulty for the parties, however, is that there are few sanctions they can impose on members who refuse to support the party's position. Unlike their counterparts in the United Kingdom, for example, where members of Parliament who do not support their party may be denied the opportunity to run for reelection, party leaders in the United States cannot control or in some cases effectively influence the nomination, campaign, and election of those who wear the party label, although they may exercise leverage over the financial resources candidates can receive. Hence the ability of the leadership to affect legislative decision making rests primarily on persuasion. In situations where constituency, executive, or other strong pressures push against the party's position, however, persuasion may be difficult. The increase in the minimum wage that was approved by Congress in 1996 is a good example. In their opposition to the bill, conservative House Republican leaders tried to keep more moderate Republicans in line by indicating their willingness to accept an increase if small businesses were exempted. Nevertheless, in light of public opinion polls favoring an increase, enough Republicans voted with the Democrats to defeat the exemption and then to approve the bill.

Partisan Influence on the Executive and Judiciary

Traditionally, chief executives perform a number of functions that may be subject to party influences. They set the agenda for public debate, choosing which initiatives they wish to emphasize. They nominate certain people to high-level executive positions and, in the federal government, to judicial positions as well. They even exercise some discretion over the performance of government services. In each of these activities they are affected by partisan considerations, but they also influence those considerations.

Even if a president, governor, or mayor does not hold a formal position within a party, he or she is considered to be the party's leader at the national, state, or local level. As such, a chief executive can make policy decisions and personnel choices (including the choice of national committee chair) and also have an impact on a party's financial and electoral support. Some choose not to do so, however.

Presidents in particular have neglected their parties in recent years because of the time and energy that partisan activities involve. Presidents can sometimes afford to do so because, unlike prime ministers, their position in power is not based solely on their continuing partisan support. In 1995 the British prime minister, John Major, actually resigned the leadership of the Conservative party after receiving criticism from some of its members. Reelected by a large vote, Major subsequently solidified his position as party leader and prime minister.

American presidents often cause divisions within their own party by taking a stand that is unpopular with some of their own partisans, as George Bush did when he supported a tax increase in 1990 and Bill Clinton did when he supported free trade agreements in 1993–1994. These divisions reduce presidents' political capital

| TABLE 9-3 | PARTY UNITY VOTES[a] |

YEAR	HOUSE	SENATE	YEAR	HOUSE	SENATE	YEAR	HOUSE	SENATE	YEAR	HOUSE	SENATE
1954	38%	47%	1965	52%	42%	1976	36%	37%	1987	64%	41%
1955	41	30	1966	41	50	1977	42	42	1988	47	42
1956	44	53	1967	36	35	1978	33	45	1989	55	35
1957	59	36	1968	35	32	1979	47	47	1990	49	54
1958	40	44	1969	31	36	1980	38	46	1991	55	49
1959	55	48	1970	27	35	1981	37	48	1992	64	53
1960	53	37	1971	38	42	1982	36	43	1993	65	67
1961	50	62	1972	27	36	1983	56	44	1994	62	52
1962	46	41	1973	42	40	1984	47	40	1995	73	69
1963	49	47	1974	29	44	1985	61	50			
1964	55	36	1975	48	48	1986	57	52			

[a]Percentage of roll-call votes in which a majority of Republicans opposed a majority of Democrats.

Source: Congressional Quarterly, *January 27, 1996, 244.*

and may weaken them in subsequent elections. Indeed, the costs of neglecting or dividing a party can be significant even for presidents who ran as outsiders and did not depend on members of Congress to get elected, because they do need congressional support to govern effectively.

Legislators are likely to support a chief executive of their own party because they and the chief executive share similar goals and objectives. Their political fates are also usually bound together. A good example was the support that many Democratic members of Congress gave President Clinton on his deficit-reduction plan even though it contained tax increases and spending cuts opposed by some of their constituents. On this issue, which came to a vote in the first year of his administration, Democrats saw Clinton's popularity and programmatic success as tied to their own. That support waned several months later, however, when the president's health-care proposal failed to achieve a consensus among congressional Democrats. In general, being popular with the public helps presidents gain and maintain congressional support, particularly from members of their own party who have political incentives to oppose them.

The electoral fates of the legislature and executive are not as closely linked as they once were, however. Presidential "coattails," to which candidates of the president's party may cling during presidential elections, have gotten shorter.[32] And presidents have even less influence over the election of fellow partisans during nonpresidential elections and practically no influence over nominations other than their own at any time. In 1986 a popular president, Ronald Reagan, campaigned actively for the reelection of eight Republican senators. Although he helped them raise money and may have increased the size of their vote, six of them lost. Reagan's experience indicates the very limited ability of contemporary presidents to share their popularity with candidates of their own party.

Chief executives have some rewards that they can bestow on partisan supporters, rewards such as patronage appointments, campaign resources, and media exposure. On the other hand, an unpopular president or governor hurts the party and can affect the success of legislators running on the same ticket in the next election. In 1994, for example, many conservative and some moderate Democrats "jumped ship," distancing themselves from President Clinton and the liberal policies that were associated with his administration.

Partisanship is an important consideration in the appointment of federal judges and some state judges, and partisan divisions are evident even in states where judges are selected on the basis of merit alone.[33] However, the influence of party on judicial decision making is more difficult to discern. Although studies have found that Republican and Democratic judges differ on certain types of issues, these studies have not been able to determine whether the differences are a result of partisanship or differing values, ideology, and judicial philosophy.[34]

Moreover, the mores of judicial decision making require judges to make their decisions on the basis of law, not politics, although personal and partisan factors may intrude on these decisions. The sentence given to a person convicted of a heinous crime could affect a state judge's reelection; the determination of whether a redistricting plan accords with federal guidelines could affect a party's chances in the next election. Nonetheless, partisan considerations do not affect the judiciary in the same way they affect the legislative or executive branches.

The political party is thus an instrument for governance although it does not control government. What it does is link institutions on the basis of common ideas and overlapping interests and promote cooperation through a system of rewards and occasional sanctions. Parties help produce an agenda and contribute to consensus building within institutions and among the general public. In theory this linkage between politics and government also contributes to public accountability, although weak party discipline and separate institutions that may be controlled by different parties make that accountability harder to achieve in practice. Nevertheless, the performance of a party's public officials affects the election prospects of others who run on the same party label.

The crucial relationship between party and government puts a premium on building and maintaining party unity. Only by converting public choices into coherent partisan positions can the parties minimize internal struggles and thereby maximize their chances of winning. Party unity also facilitates governance. It promotes accountability by making it easier for the public to allocate responsibility for the government's decisions and actions. That is why political parties are an important component of a democratic system and why partisan politics are essential to its operation.

SUMMARY

Partisan activities organize the politics of American government. They do so through the electoral process, in which parties nominate candidates for office, help provide resources for their campaigns, mobilize their supporters, and turn out the vote. They do so through the process of government, in which parties influence the selection of public officials from legislative elections to executive and judicial appointments; develop policy positions in campaign platforms and proposals; and build support for these positions within and outside the government. Partisan activities also provide continuity in personnel and policy and accountability for performance in office. In this sense, they are critical to the strength and vitality of the American political system.

The nature of the major American parties—diversified in composition, decentralized in structure, and usually pragmatic in approach—sometimes generates as much politics within them as between them. Thus parties are not only the vehicles *through which* the principal functions of democracy (that is, elections and policy making) are exercised; they are also the organizations *in which* each of these activities occurs. Together with minor parties that have narrower constituencies, more focused policy agendas, and, in recent years, more of an orientation toward candidates, the major American political parties present a broad structure in which candidates compete, issues are debated, and policy is pursued.

In the United States, political parties are almost as

old as the Republic itself. They began to take shape during the administration of George Washington. The first parties, the *Federalists* and the *Democratic-Republicans* (or Republicans), had little popular support. By the 1820s one of them, the Federalists, had faded from the scene and the other, the Republicans, split into feuding factions, one of which formed the coalition that succeeded in electing Andrew Jackson president in 1828. Jackson's followers became known as the *Democrats* and were opposed by a new party known as the *Whigs*.

In 1854 the party known today as the *Republicans* was organized. When the Democrats split over the slavery issue in 1860 and the Whig party collapsed, Republican candidate Abraham Lincoln was elected president. Originally composed of small-business owners, laborers, and farmers, the Republican party increasingly became influenced by big business. At the turn of the century, economic conflict between rural and urban interests culminated in a partisan *realignment* that made the Republicans dominant in national politics for the next three decades, until the election of Franklin Roosevelt in 1932.

During the Great Depression of the 1930s the electorate divided along economic class lines with less prosperous voters more likely to be Democratic and more prosperous voters more likely to be Republican. The Democrats expanded their support among white southerners and racial and religious minorities. Since the end of the 1960s, the Democratic New Deal coalition has frayed but not completely disintegrated. The Republicans have gained adherents, and the proportion of voters considering themselves independent has also risen. Today the parties are at rough parity with one another, each commanding the allegiance of approximately the same percentage of the electorate.

The weakening of the Democratic coalition has been the result of several factors: the defection of southern whites to the Republicans, the decline in the proportion of Catholics who regularly support Democratic candidates, and the reduction in the blue-collar labor vote within the electorate as a whole. Democrats have retained the support of African Americans and most Hispanic groups. Republicans have profited from the increasing numbers of white-collar workers and from the support they have received from Christian fundamentalist groups. In recent years a gender gap has also appeared, with women more oriented than men toward the Democratic party and its candidates, and men more inclined than women to vote Republican.

Parties' hold on the voters has also been reduced as partisan loyalties have become less intense. Although a partisan *dealignment* has clearly occurred in recent decades, it is less clear whether there has been a realignment, a large-scale shifting of partisan preferences.

At the national level, the parties direct the bulk of their energies to presidential campaigns. They raise funds, target voters, communicate with the public, develop policy positions, and provide assistance to candidates. National party organizations have become more important in recent years with the development of their fundraising capabilities and the Democrats' nationalization of party rules for the presidential nomination. The centralization of fundraising has also strengthened state party organizations, particularly during campaigns.

State parties focus on electing candidates to state and national office; they also raise funds, take official positions on salient issues, and recruit potential nominees. At the local (county or city) level, parties are active primarily during election campaigns, especially where there is real competition between them.

A primary objective of parties is to get their partisans in office. To do so, they concentrate their efforts on the electoral process. One of the major changes in this process has been the democratization of party nominations. With the goal of stimulating rank-and-file participation, the parties have turned increasingly to primaries as the mechanism for selecting their nominees. This has had the effect of reducing the influence of party leaders over the choice of their nominees.

The advent of primaries, however, has not been the only factor that reduced the influence of parties. The growth of the mass media has also affected the traditional role of parties as the link between candidates and voters; and the use of sophisticated techniques, such as polling, has led to the rise of a new group of professionals who compete with party professionals to influence campaign strategy. These changes have weakened the ability of the parties to control the electoral process as they did in the past.

Parties become involved in the electoral process to get their candidates into office. Their ultimate goal is to affect public policy in accordance with the principles, beliefs, and interests of their partisans. Every four years, as part of their national conventions they adopt a *party platform* that articulates their philosophy and policy positions on the important issues of the day. In addition, in 1994 the Republican candidates for the House of Representatives agreed on a common platform that they called their *Contract with America*, campaigned on it, and sought to implement it once elected.

Parties shape the structure and operation of most legislatures, and partisanship carries more weight than any other factor in affecting the outcome of voting. However, there are few sanctions that parties can impose on elected officials who do not support their positions. As a result, their ability to affect legislative decision making rests primarily on persuasion, consensus building, and popular support.

Chief executives—presidents, governors, and mayors—are considered their party's leaders on the national, state, and local levels and are expected to make policy decisions and personnel judgments that reflect the party's positions. Executives who disregard their party once in office may have difficulty governing effectively. Partisanship is a major factor in the appointment of the federal judiciary and some state judges, but it has a less direct impact on judicial decision making than on decision making in the legislative and executive branches. The political party contributes to government by promoting cooperation and enhancing the accountability of government to the people. People know whom to blame if the party in control of government doesn't live up to public expectations. Accountability is more difficult to assess when control of government is divided.

KEY TERMS

political party
partisan
single-member district
multi-member district
ideological party
issue party

Federalists
Democratic-Republicans
    (Republicans)
Democrats
Whigs
Republicans

dealignment
realignment
party platform
responsible party government

RESOURCES

SCHOLARLY STUDIES

Abramson, Paul R., John H. Aldrich, Phil Paolino, and David W. Rohde. "Third-Party and Independent Candidates: Wallace, Anderson, and Perot." *Political Science Quarterly* 110 (Fall 1995), 349–367. A recent article that explains why it is so difficult for third-party and independent candidates to win presidential elections.

Beck, Paul Allen, and Frank J. Sorauf. *Party Politics in America.* 8th ed. New York: HarperCollins, 1996. A recent revision of a highly regarded text on political parties.

Cotter, Cornelius P., James L. Gibson, John F. Bibby, and Robert Huckshorn. *Party Organizations in American Politics.* Pittsburgh: University of Pittsburgh Press, 1989. A comprehensive study of party organizations in the states.

Gillespie, J. David. *Politics at the Periphery: Third Parties in Two-Party America.* Columbia: University of South Carolina Press, 1993. An examination of third parties in America, investigating their history, types, and usefulness.

Herrnson, Paul S. *Party Campaigning in the 1980s.* Cambridge, Mass.: Harvard University Press, 1988. Provides evidence of the strengthening of national party influence on electoral campaigns.

Key, V. O., Jr. *Southern Politics.* Knoxville: University of Tennessee Press, 1984. The classic study of southern politics from the end of the Civil War until the middle of the twentieth century.

Pomper, Gerald M. *Passions and Interests: Political Party Concepts of American Democracy.* Lawrence: University Press of Kansas, 1992. A study that focuses on the role of American political parties in theory and practice in the democratic process.

Shafer, Bryon E., and William J. M. Claggett. *The Two Majorities: The Issue Context of Modern American Politics.* Baltimore: Johns Hopkins University Press,

1995. An empirical study of public opinion that supports the thesis that Americans' political preferences remain relatively stable and consistent with the two major parties' political ideologies.

Wattenberg, Martin P. *The Decline of American Political Parties, 1952–1992.* Cambridge, Mass.: Harvard University Press, 1994. A concise, well-written account.

LEISURE READING

O'Connor, Edwin. *The Last Hurrah.* Boston: Little, Brown, 1985. One of the best novels on urban politics, telling the story of an old-style Irish politician's final attempt to win reelection against a modern media candidate.

Warren, Robert Penn. *All the King's Men.* New York: Bantam, 1990. A fictionalized account of southern politics, Louisiana-style, based on the story of Huey Long's reign as Democratic party boss.

Williams, T. Harry. *Huey Long.* New York: Vintage, 1981. A wonderfully written biography of Louisiana's most influential and colorful political leader.

PRIMARY SOURCES

Johnson, Donald Bruce, ed. *National Party Platforms.* 2 vols. Urbana: University of Illinois Press, 1978. A collection of the platforms of the major and minor parties from 1840 to 1976.

Maisel, L. Sandy, ed. *Political Parties and Elections in the United States.* 2 vols. New York: Garland Publishing, 1991. An encyclopedia that contains short essays on all aspects of parties, their history, and their candidates.

ORGANIZATIONS

Democratic Congressional Campaign Committee and Democratic Senatorial Campaign Committee, 430 S. Capitol Street, S.E., Washington, DC 20003; DCCC phone (202) 863-1500, fax (202) 485-3512, no e-mail; DSCC phone (202) 224-2447, fax (202) 485-3120, Internet http://www.dscc.org/d/dscc.html These committees raise and distribute funds for Democrats who seek election or reelection to the House of Representatives and the Senate, respectively.

Democratic National Committee, 430 S. Capitol Street, S.E., Washington, DC 20003; phone (202) 863-8000, fax (202) 863-8174, Internet: http://www.democrats.org This committee, supported by a large staff, makes and implements policy and personnel decisions for the Democratic party.

National Republican Congressional Committee, 320 1st Street, S.E., Washington, DC 20003; phone (202) 479-7000, fax (202) 863-0693, no e-mail. National Republican Senatorial Committee, 425 2nd Street, N.E., Washington, DC 20002; phone (202) 675-6000, fax (202) 675-6058, no e-mail. These committees raise and distribute funds for Republicans who seek election or reelection to the House of Representatives and the Senate, respectively.

Republican National Committee, 310 1st Street, S.E., Washington, DC 20003; phone (202) 863-8500, fax (202) 863-0693, Internet: http://www.rnc.org This committee, supported by a large staff, makes and implements policy and personnel decisions for the Republican party.

Senate Democratic Policy Committee, S-118 Capitol Building, Washington, DC 20510; phone (202) 224-5551; no fax: e-mail; info@dpc.senate.gov comments and questions postmaster@dpc.senate.gov This committee establishes policy for the Democratic party in the Senate.

Senate Republican Policy Committee, 347 Russell Office Building, Washington, DC 20510; phone (202) 224-2946, fax (202) 224-1235, e-mail webmaster@rpc.senate.gov This committee establishes policy for the Republican party in the Senate.

Campaigns and Elections

O n March 6, 1991, President George Bush delivered an address to Congress in which he declared that the United States and its allies had been victorious in the Persian Gulf War. The first public opinion poll following Bush's speech revealed that almost 90 percent of the American people approved of the job he was doing as president. But less than two years later, in November 1992, Bush was defeated in his quest for reelection, receiving just 38 percent of the vote.

On January 21, 1993, Bill Clinton was sworn in as president. The first

Democrat to be elected since 1976, he was also the first president since Jimmy Carter whose party controlled both houses of Congress. In his inaugural address, Clinton promised to end the legislative gridlock that had gripped the Bush years. He also proposed new Democratic policies for old problems: "to end welfare as we know it," to reform lobbying and campaign finance, to promote investment, to reduce crime, to improve education, to clean the environment, and to end discrimination on the basis of sexual orientation. And that was not all. His three principal legislative priorities were to stimulate the economy, reduce the federal budget deficit, and reform health care.

Two years later, only a few of those proposals had become public policy. Some had been defeated in Congress; others were modified by Congress. Of the president's major priorities, his stimulus plan was killed by a filibuster in the Senate, his deficit reduction plan was passed narrowly after being completely overhauled, and his health-care proposal died in the legislature. With his party divided, his White House staff an embarrassment, his wife a polarizing figure, and his administration marred by allegations of illegal and unethical behavior, the president's performance in office was disapproved of by almost as many as had approved of it during his first two years in office.

Congress was also in bad repute. The Democratic leadership's inability to transform the legislature into an effective policy-making institution and to prevent its members from engaging in self-interested and self-aggrandizing behavior led to increasing public dissatisfaction and anger with the government in general and with Clinton and the Democratic Congress in particular. The voters responded the first chance they had: in November 1994 they elected the first Republican Congress since 1954. In their Contract with America, the Republicans promised to do things differently; but within one year the level of public dissatisfaction rose again, and this time the Republicans were the principal target.

How could a governor from a small state with no experience in Washington and little national exposure, such as Bill Clinton, a candidate with considerable personal vulnerabilities, defeat an incumbent president who had successfully prosecuted one war and presided over the end of another, the cold war? How could little-known Republican challengers, campaigning in local areas with a national program, do so well against an entrenched Democratic party that had been in power for forty years? How could these very same Republicans so quickly become the objects of public unhappiness? And then how could public opinion change again so quickly that in 1996 both President Clinton and the Republican congressional majority were reelected? The answers lie in the rules under which nominations and elections are conducted, in the advantages the system gives to incumbents, and in the turbulent contemporary political environment.

During the nomination period the rules and procedures prescribed by the political parties favor those candidates with the best organization and the most money. In 1992, these were George Bush and Bill Clinton and the congressional incumbents of both parties. In 1994 and in 1996, the insiders again had the advantage. Clinton was not challenged for the Democratic nomination, and Robert Dole, Senate majority leader, started off as the odds-on favorite for the Republican nomination and easily won it.

In the general election the system also usually favors the incumbents—candidates who are well known, have had contact with voters, and have done favors for them. This was the case in 1992 and 1996 for most members of Congress, but it was not for the Democrats in 1994.

The political environment is another key factor in determining an election's outcome. In the early 1990s, the public mood shifted from euphoria over victory in the Persian Gulf War to pessimism over the economy, social conditions, and the country's future direction, then to anger over alleged abuses by public officials in Congress and the executive branch and frustration over government's inability to address pressing national issues. These attitudes proved fatal to President Bush in 1992 and to Democrats in 1994. But in 1996 the public was more contented. People perceived the economy to be stronger; they saw themselves as better off than they were four years earlier; and more saw their country moving in the right direction. Under these circumstances, incumbents of both parties benefited.

T
he elections of the 1990s are prime examples of a dynamic political process at work, of candidates who defied initial odds and an electorate that reconsidered its early impressions and reevaluated its performance judgments, of effective versus ineffective campaigns, and of the powerful impact of perceptions of economic and social conditions on voting behavior. These are some of the key features of American electoral politics. The elections also demonstrate the principal way in which voters hold those in government accountable for their decisions and actions and, by their voting behavior change the direction of government and its public policy.

This chapter discusses these and other political aspects of the electoral process. It first looks at the relationship between elections and democracy and then focuses on the American voter, on who votes and why. Finally, it examines the stages of the electoral process, campaign strategy and tactics, election returns, and the implications of elections for government and public policy.

ELECTIONS AND DEMOCRACY

Elections are a mechanism for making important political choices. They frame policy debate, select public officials, and influence the decisions of those officials. Such functions are essential for a democratic government because they establish and reaffirm popular control.

If elections are to link the people to their representatives, they must meet three criteria: universal suffrage, meaningful choice, and political equality. **Universal suffrage** means that all citizens who are responsible for their own actions are permitted to vote in order to protect and promote their own interests.[1] If some people are denied the right to vote, their ability to influence the decisions of public officials will be reduced. Effective representation and electoral power go hand-in-hand.

Meaningful choice implies that there is some opportunity to select among different options. This criterion requires a minimum of two candidates whose views are not identical and who have sufficient resources to present their beliefs to the public. It also implies that the voters have an opportunity to make that choice, that elections are structured in such a way that people can easily and effectively choose among competing candidates.

In rendering a judgment on election day, the votes of all those who choose to participate should be equal. Application of this principle of **political equality** requires that the majority rule, that the candidate with the most votes win.

For the electoral process to work, candidates for office must communicate with the public. In presidential elections, the televised "debate" has become one of the principal forums in which the major contenders try to put themselves and their ideas forward. Although candidates tend to respond in set patterns to questions rather than debating each other, these debates are important because more people watch them than any other campaign event.

Why do the losers accept such a result? Because the democratic system protects the losers as well. It does so by obligating the winners to govern by the rule of law. The law contains provisions and safeguards that protect all members of society against arbitrary and capricious actions by those in power. One of the most important of these safeguards is the electoral system itself, particularly the regularity and frequency of elections.

Each of these democratic criteria seems logical, straightforward, and noncontroversial; yet each has generated considerable conflict. In the United States much of the conflict has turned on the issue of suffrage—the question of who may vote. Another problematic issue is how to structure the election so as to ensure meaningful choice. Rules governing voter registration, ballot access, vote challenges and recounts, even the hours and places for voting—all shape how well elections convert public opinion into choices that reflect that opinion. Yet another controversy, in recent years, has concerned the application of the principle of equality. Should individual candidates have the right to spend their own money and utilize their own resources during a campaign? Or does this right violate a basic democratic assumption that no person or group should exercise greater influence in an election simply on the basis of wealth?

Suffrage: Who Can Vote?

The framers of the Constitution struggled with the problems of participation and representation. In theory, they favored a government of, by, and for the people. In practice, they feared that the self-interested behavior of the general public could lead to what James Madison referred to as a "tyranny of the majority."

One way to prevent such a tyranny was to restrict suffrage—that is, to limit the right to vote. Such restrictions, however, would not have been consistent with the political rights defined in the Declaration of Independence or with the preamble to the Constitution. Moreover, they would have jeopardized the ratification of the Constitution. So the framers took another tack by designing a system to represent three different constituencies: (1) the nation (president and vice president), (2) the states (Senate), and (3) the people (House of Representatives). To avoid the potentially divisive issue of who would be eligible to vote, they made the states responsible for resolving that question, retaining for Congress the power to legislate on these matters if it desired.

Initially most states required property ownership as a condition of voting. Since property was owned primarily by white men, this requirement effectively disenfranchised women and racial minorities. Some states imposed an additional requirement: belief in a Christian God.

In the early nineteenth century, pressure developed to expand the franchise—to enable more people to vote. By the middle of the 1830s, property ownership and religious beliefs had been dropped as qualifications for voting in most states. However, gender and racial barriers remained, and it took the enactment of constitutional amendments to remove them. The Fifteenth Amendment, ratified in 1870, abolished race, color, and national origin as qualifications for voting, at least in theory. In practice, formal and informal restrictions effectively prevented large-scale voting by African Americans in the South for another hundred years. The Nineteenth Amendment, ratified in 1920, prevented states from denying women the right to vote. Moreover, the Twenty-Sixth Amendment, ratified in 1971, required states to extend this right to citizens 18 years of age or older. Each of these amendments was passed as a result of successful struggles in the public arena—that is, political

For many decades, the extension of suffrage to women met considerable resistance. After the Civil War, women who demanded voting rights were depicted as mannish, even lewd. In this Currier and Ives print, The Age of Brass *(1869), women wear men's hats, smoke cigars, expose their legs, and look downright nasty. The one man on the scene holds a baby, a sign of frightful role reversals to come if women should get the same rights as men.*

struggles—by those who favored the expansion of suffrage against those who wanted to maintain the status quo. (The debate over lowering the voting age to 18 is described in the Case Study on page 316.)

The restrictions on suffrage, which prevented the United States from achieving the goal of political equality, benefited those in power, generally the more well-to-do members of society. They made challenges to those in power more difficult, especially at the state and local levels. As suffrage was gradually extended, however, these consequences were also gradually reversed. As women and minority groups increased their representation in government, policies that benefited these newest members of the electorate were enacted and implemented. The party system became more competitive at all levels of government, and within the parties there were more opportunities for the rank and file to be heard and to influence the selection of nominees.

Meaningful Choice: How Are Elections Structured?

In the early days of the republic, the states had extensive authority to determine the conduct of federal elections. Subsequently, constitutional amendments and congressional statutes limited that discretion—particularly the right to set qualifications for voting and, more recently, the procedures for voter registration. Nevertheless, state laws that control ballot access, electoral challenges, and even the time, place, and manner of voting continue to have an important impact on the electoral process.

Electoral choice is affected by the rules for getting on the ballot. States can make it tough or easy to run for office. They can impose residence requirements on can-

THE 18-YEAR-OLD VOTE

Americans take it for granted today that any citizen who is 18 years of age and older should have the right to vote. But thirty years ago that was not the case. States used to set their own minimum age for voting, and most required that their citizens be 21 years of age or over.

There was not much support to establish a national minimum voting age of 18 until the development of massive opposition to the Vietnam War in the late 1960s, when "conscription without representation" became an issue. If men were old enough to be drafted into the armed services and sent to fight in Vietnam, putting their lives on the line in the process, it was argued, then they were old enough to choose the public officials responsible for this policy. The increasing educational levels among younger people and the desirability of expanding the electorate in a democracy were other reasons offered for lowering the voting age.

Nonetheless, considerable opposition remained. Proponents of states' rights, particularly those in the South, contended that the establishment of national voting qualifications denied the states their constitutional right to set the voting age. Others believed that younger Americans were not sufficiently mature, responsible, or informed to vote. Some even felt that allowing 18-year-olds to vote could adversely affect public policy by, for example, creating pressure to lower the drinking age (which also varied from state to state) or encouraging candidates to make unrealistic promises as a means of gaining votes in certain elections, such as those for school boards.

The good news is that these fears have not been realized since the Twenty-Sixth Amendment—which established 18 as the age at which states must permit their citizens to vote—went into effect on July 1, 1971. The bad news is that relatively few 18- to 21-year-olds actually do vote (see Figure 10-1, page 324). In fact, this group has had the lowest percentage of voter registration and turnout of any age cohort within the population. This fact alone leads to a number of serious questions about our youngest voters:

Discussion Questions

1. In retrospect, were the principal arguments put forth by the proponents of the Twenty-Sixth Amendment valid?
2. Why do you think people between the ages of 18 and 21 do not exercise their right to vote with nearly the same regularity as do those in other age groups?
3. Does the lower voter participation of those between 18 and 21 years of age confirm the allegation that younger people are less informed, interested, and responsible? Are they turned off to democracy?
4. What about you? Have you registered and voted? Why, or why not?

didates, make them pay a filing fee, and require them to obtain the signatures of a certain number or percentage of registered voters before their names can be placed on the ballot. The more rigorous these requirements are, the fewer the candidates and the greater the party's control over its nominees. H. Ross Perot's United We Stand and Reform parties encountered this difficulty in 1992 and 1996. His organization spent considerable time and money collecting signatures simply to get on the ballot.

The authority of the states to conduct general elections extends to primaries as well. The type of primary, the date for holding it, the requirements for entering it, and the rules for determining the winner are all established by state laws. In some cases these laws have elicited considerable controversy, particularly when they conflict with national party rules. In other cases they have worked to the advantage of candidates who have the backing of state party leaders and their organizations. New York State, for example, required Republican presidential candidates to obtain the

HOW TO REGISTER TO VOTE

Since 1995 the federal "motor-voter law" has required states to permit people to register to vote by mail or when applying for a driver's license. The Federal Election Commission has designed a single national registration form, which is reproduced below. In addition to motor vehicle offices, the form should be available at other state offices, such as those that dispense welfare, aid people with disabilities, or supervise elections. Forms can also be obtained at military recruitment offices.

If you have any problems obtaining a voter registration form, contact the Federal Election Commission at (800) 424-9530; the staff should be able to tell you where and how to obtain the mail-in form and where to send it when you have completed it.

General Instructions

Who Can Use this Application

If you are a U.S. citizen who lives or has an address within the United States, you can use the application in this booklet to:

- Register to vote in your State,
- Report a change of name to your voter registration office,
- Report a change of address to your voter registration office, or
- Register with a political party.

Exceptions

Arkansas, by law, cannot accept this form until after Jan. 1, 1996.
New Hampshire town and city clerks will accept this application only as a request for their own absentee voter mail-in registration form.
North Dakota does not have voter registration.
Virginia, by law, cannot accept this form until after Jan. 1, 1996.
Wyoming will not let you use this application for registering to vote in that State.

Please do **not** use this application if you live outside the United States and its territories and have no home (legal) address in this country, *or* if you are in the military stationed away from home. Use the Federal Postcard Application available to you from military bases, American embassies, or consular offices.

How to Find Out If You Are Eligible to Register to Vote in Your State

Each State has its own laws about who may register and vote. Check the information under your State in the State Instructions.
Note: All States require that you be a United States citizen by birth or naturalization to register to vote in federal and State elections.
Also Note: You **cannot** be registered to vote in more than one place at a time.

When to Register to Vote

Each State has its own deadline for registering to vote. Check the deadline for your State on the last page of this booklet.

How to Fill Out this Application

Use both the Application Instructions and State Instructions to guide you in filling out the application.
First, read the Application Instructions. These instructions will give you important information that applies to everyone using this application.
Next, find your State under the State Instructions. Use these instructions to fill out Boxes 6, 7, and 8. Also refer to these instructions for information about voter eligibility and any oath required for Box 9.

How to Submit Your Application

Mail your application to the address listed under your State in the State Instructions. Or, deliver the application in person to your local voter registration office.

If You Were Given this Booklet in a State Agency or Public Office

If you have been given this booklet in a State agency or public office, it is your choice to use the application or not.
If you decide to use this application to register to vote, you can fill it out and leave it with the State agency or public office. The application will be submitted for you. Or, you can take it with you to mail to the address listed under your State in the State Instructions. You also may take it with you to deliver in person to your local voter registration office.
Note: The name and location of the State agency or public office where you received the application will remain confidential. It will not appear on your application. Also, if you decide not to use this application to register to vote, that decision will remain confidential. It will not affect the service you receive from the agency or office.

Voter Registration Application
For U.S. Citizens

You can use this form to:
- register to vote
- report that your name or address has changed
- register with a party

This space for office use only.

Please print in blue or black ink

1 Mr. Mrs. Miss Ms. | Last Name | First Name | Middle Name(s) | (Circle one) Jr Sr II III IV

2 Address (see instructions)— Street (or route and box number) | Apt. or Lot # | City/Town | State | Zip Code

3 Address Where You Get Your Mail If Different From Above (see instructions) | City/Town | State | Zip Code

4 Date of Birth Month / Day / Year | 5 Telephone Number (optional) | 6 ID Number (see item 6 in the instructions for your State)

7 Choice of Party (see item 7 in the instructions for your State) | 8 Race or Ethnic Group (see item 8 in the instructions for your State)

9 I swear/affirm that:
- I am a United States citizen
- I meet the eligibility requirements of my state and subscribe to any oath required.
(See item 9 in the instructions for your state before you sign.)
- The information I have provided is true to the best of my knowledge under penalty of perjury. If I have provided false information, I may be subject to a fine or imprisonment or both under Federal or State laws.
Please sign full name (or put mark) ↓
Date: Month Day Year

10 If the applicant is unable to sign, who helped the applicant fill out this application? Give name, address and phone number (phone number optional).

Fold here

Please fill out the sections below if they apply to you.

If this application is for a **change of name**, what was your name before you changed it?

A Mr. Mrs. Miss Ms. | Last Name | First Name | Middle Name(s) | (Circle one) Jr Sr II III IV

If you were registered before but this is the first time you are registering from the address in Box 2, what was your address where you were registered before?

B Street (or route and box number) | Apt. or Lot # | City/Town | State | Zip Code

If you live in a rural area but do not have a street number, or if you have no address, please show on the map where you live.

- Write in the names of the crossroads (or streets) nearest to where you live.
- Draw an X to show where you live.
- Use a dot to show any schools, churches, stores, or other landmarks near where you live, and write the name of the landmark.

NORTH ↑

C Example | Route #2 | Grocery Store | Woodchuck Road | Public School | X

To Mail:
1. Address the back of this application (see address under your state).
2. Remove plastic strip below.
3. Fold form at middle and seal at top.
4. Put on a first-class stamp and mail.

signatures of 1,250 voters or 5 percent of the registered Republicans in *each* of the thirty-one legislative districts in which they wished to run slates of delegates. This requirement advantaged state party leaders who control the field organization that can be used to obtain the necessary signatures. Other candidates have to create such an organization on their own.[2]

In two landmark decisions, *Cousins v. Wigoda* (1975) and *Democratic Party of the U.S. v. La Follette* (1981), the Supreme Court held that the parties may determine their own rules for delegate selection and refuse to seat delegates at their national conventions who are not chosen in accordance with those rules. Despite these rulings, however, increased popular participation in the nomination process has weakened the ability of party leaders and organizations to select candidates for office. As a result, the responsiveness of many elected officials to the constituencies that elected them has increased, but in a way that fragments rather than concentrates political power. This may produce a more democratic political system, but it also produces a more divided government.

Political Equality: The Issue of Money in Elections

The criterion of making sure that all citizens have an equal voice and vote in the electoral process has generated a decades-long debate over campaign finance, and specifically over whether the American tradition of unrestricted private funding of political campaigns undercuts the basic principles of a democratic electoral process. Before the mid 1970s, campaigns were financed entirely by individual contributions. Both parties depended on a small number of wealthy donors for much of their funding.[3] As campaign expenditures increased, primarily as a result of rising media costs (primarily for television advertising), questions began to be raised about the connection between giving and governing. Did the wealthy exercise disproportionate influence? What did they get for their money? Could elected officials be responsive to large donors and to the general public at the same time? Did the high costs of running discourage qualified individuals from seeking office? These questions have persisted into the 1990s.

Congress debated these issues, and in 1971 and again in 1974 it enacted legislation to limit campaign spending and provide government support for presidential nomination and election campaigns. The Federal Election Campaign Act required public disclosure of all contributions and expenditures above a certain amount and created the Federal Election Commission to monitor activities and oversee compliance. Parts of this legislation were highly controversial. In particular, some saw the limits on contributions as a restraint on freedom of speech. In *Buckley v. Valeo* (1976) the Supreme Court took the middle ground. Arguing that personal expenditures can be a form of expression but that campaign finance can be regulated, the Court upheld the right of Congress to restrict the amount that individuals and groups could contribute to candidates in any federal election, but not the amount they could spend *independently* on behalf of those candidates.

Even after the Court's decision, however, partisan debate over the law continued. Republicans were generally opposed to it for practical as well as philosophical reasons. Not only did they believe that limits on individual contributions denied their party its traditional financial advantage, but some of them also objected to the very idea of government subsidies, arguing that the government should not support semipublic political organizations. Democrats, in contrast, contended that such support for parties and their nominees was a legitimate function of government and that equalizing the amount of money candidates had available to them would produce a more democratic result.

The campaign finance legislation did correct some problems it was designed to address. The wealthy can no longer exercise direct and disproportionate influence on an individual election contest unless they happen to be candidates themselves: there are no effective limits on what a person can contribute to his or her own campaign (unless the person is running for the presidency and accepts federal funding)[4]. The size of a contribution and the name of the contributor are now part of the public record, and the news media regularly report this information. Finally, at the presidential level there is greater opportunity for candidates of both parties, even those who lack national recognition, to obtain at least some minimal financial support with the help of government matching funds and grants.

The legislation has had several unintended consequences, however. Most federal funds and some private contributions go directly to the candidates, not to the party. As a result, candidates are forced to create and use their own campaign organizations rather than relying on the party's. Thus the legislation has contributed to factionalism within the parties and has reduced the parties' influence over the campaigns of their own candidates.

Another problem for the parties has been the growth of political action committees (PACs), which the legislation not only permits but encourages (see Chapter 8). The Supreme Court decision that allows PACs to spend an unlimited amount on their own on behalf of candidates also reduces the parties' influence over the electoral process. In 1979 Congress reacted to the parties' plight, as well as to a decline in voter turnout, by amending the law to permit them to raise and spend unlimited funds on efforts to encourage people to register and to vote. These so-called soft-money expenditures, which have created a huge loophole in the limits on contributions and expenditures, have been substantial in recent years. In 1992 they were reported to the Federal Election Commission as $51.4 million for the Republicans and $36.3 million for the Democrats; in 1994 the figures were $55.4 million (Republicans) and $47.8 million (Democrats); in 1995 they were $33.7 million and $25 million, respectively. For the first 6 months of 1996, they exceeded $83.9 million for the Republicans and $70.3 million for the Democrats.[5]

Not only have soft-money contributions increased, but the ways in which they are currently being used to circumvent party and candidate spending limits in the election have also been imaginatively expanded. When Robert Dole reached his expenditure limit after effectively securing the Republican presidential nomination in 1996, his campaign was supplemented by a $20 million preconvention advertising campaign orchestrated by the Republican National Committee and funded largely with soft money. The Democrats were already engaging in a similar effort on behalf

After winning renomination in Chicago, President Bill Clinton and Vice President Al Gore campaign by bus in Illinois. Campaign finance legislation has had the unintended effect of forcing candidates to create and use their own campaign organizations. In this way they have become increasingly independent of party control.

MONEY AND CAMPAIGNS

An initial intent of the campaign finance legislation enacted by Congress in 1971 and 1974 was to limit campaign contributions so that the wealthy would not exercise disproportionate influence. A second goal was to level the playing field for candidates, providing more equal opportunities for those who sought federal office. Giving the public more timely and accurate information about the financial aspects of the campaign, the sources and amounts of money contributed and the ways in which it was spent, was a third objective.

Unfortunately, these goals have not been achieved to the extent that the architects of the legislation hoped. Loopholes have permitted skillful politicians and their campaign advisers to circumvent the law easily. One such loophole was created by the Supreme Court's decision in 1976 that contributions to candidates could be limited but independent expenditures on behalf of them could not be. This decision gave advantage to wealthy individuals, particularly those who chose to be candidates themselves, and to well-financed groups, such as business, labor, and trade association PACs. A second loophole became evident after Congress amended the Federal Election Campaign Act in 1979 to permit unlimited amounts of money to be raised and spent in educational efforts to get people out to vote, the so-called soft money provision. This loophole was widened by the Federal Election Commission's and the judiciary's interpretation of educational efforts to include any appeal that did not express support or opposition to specific candidates for federal office.

Other consequences of the legislation that have resulted in inequities stem from the ability of PACs to raise and spend large amounts of money, particularly on congressional races; the ability of incumbents to use their offices to gain recognition, money, and other electoral advantages and carry them over from one election to another; and the failure to adjust the contribution limits, especially those that pertain to individuals, for inflation.

Congress first considered reforming the law only a few years after it was enacted. And it has been considering it ever since then, but to no avail. President Carter proposed spending limits and public funding for congressional elections. Others have suggested that PAC contributions be further restricted or prohibited; that limits on personal donations be increased; that incentives be created for voluntarily limiting spending, such as free television time and low-cost mailings; that candidates be required to raise more than half their campaign money from the congressional district or state in which the election is held; and that soft money be curbed or eliminated.

The closest any of these proposals came to becoming law was in 1991, when Congress enacted legislation to create voluntary limits for congressional elections, public funding for candidates who abided by these limits, and curbs on soft-money expenditures. President Bush vetoed the legislation, believing that it

of the Clinton-Gore ticket. In this manner, both parties saved their hard money, which was strictly limited, for the general election and raised and transferred soft money to their state affiliates to use for targeted advertising. The circumvention of the campaign finance law has led to persistent calls for reform, calls which Congress has acknowledged but not acted upon. (See the Hot-Button Issue box above.)

To summarize, who votes, what choices they have, and how much influence they exert over election outcomes are all critical issues. Elections that maximize voter participation, voter choice, and voter influence reaffirm the principle of popular control of government and the practice of holding public officials

benefited the Democrats at the expense of the Republicans.

Campaign finance became an issue in the 1992 presidential election, with third-party candidate Ross Perot calling for reform as a major priority and Bill Clinton promising to approve a law similar to the one Bush had vetoed. Nonetheless, in 1993–94 the Democratic-controlled Congress did not act on Clinton's promise. When the Republicans took over in 1995, the debate continued, and bipartisan legislation was introduced, but it too failed. The issue moved into the 1996 election campaign, with both Democrats and Republicans complaining that the other was violating the law. Campaign finance reform remains a hot-button issue for the 105th Congress.

What is the problem with reforming the campaign finance system? A simple answer would be that the people who must change the law, members of Congress and the president, are the very ones who stand to lose the most. As Senator John McCain, (R-Arizona) noted in a speech in support of a reform proposal in 1996, PACs gave incumbents $59.2 million in 1995, compared with $3.9 million to challengers.

Although maintaining political advantage is a principal issue, and perhaps the most important, it is not the only one. Many people argue that campaign contributions and expenditures are constitutionally protected forms of free speech. Moreover, in an era of tight budgets and increasing campaign costs, there is also the problem of who should pay the costs if political activists or the wealthy are not to do so. Should it be the taxpayers? The mass media? Voter turnout is also related to campaign costs. If spending is restricted, campaigns will not reach as many voters, and turnout may suffer, a danger in a democracy.

What do you think should be done about the problem, and how would you go about building support for your proposal?

To get more information about the issue or to become involved on one side or the other, contact one of the following groups:

Supporting campaign finance reform:

Common Cause
2030 M Street, N.W.
Suite 300
Washington, D.C. 20036
phone (202) 833-1200
fax (202) 659-3716
e-mail 75300.3120@compuserve.com

Opposing campaign finance reform:

National Association of Business PACs
801 North Fairfax Street
Suite 215
Alexandria, VA 22314
phone (703) 836-4422

accountable for their actions and decisions. Elections that limit these criteria do not.

THE AMERICAN VOTER

Who *can* vote and who *does* vote are two different questions. The expansion of suffrage has made the American political system more democratic—at least in theory. In practice, however, there has always been a gap between eligible voters and actual voters, a gap that has traditionally been widest for newly enfranchised voters. Table 10-1 indicates the magnitude of this gap.

TABLE 10-1   SUFFRAGE AND TURNOUT

Year	Total Adult Population (Including Aliens)[a]	Total Presidential Vote	Percentage of Adult Population Voting
1824	3,964,000	363,017	9
1840	7,381,000	2,412,698	33
1860	14,676,000	4,692,710	32
1880	25,012,000	9,219,467	37
1900	40,753,000	13,974,188	35
1920	60,581,000	26,768,613	44
1932	75,768,000	39,732,000	52.4
1940	84,728,000	49,900,000	58.9
1952	99,929,000	61,551,000	61.6
1960	109,672,000	68,838,000	62.8
1964	114,090,000	70,645,000	61.9
1968	120,285,000	73,212,000	60.9
1972	140,777,000	77,719,000	55.5
1976	152,308,000	81,556,000	53.5
1980	164,595,000	86,515,000	52.6
1984	174,447,000	92,653,000	53.1
1988	182,600,000	91,602,291	50.2
1992	187,033,000	104,552,736	55.9
1996	196,507,000	95,800,000[b]	48.8

[a]Restrictions based on sex, age, race, religion, and property ownership prevented a significant portion of the adult population from voting in the nineteenth and early twentieth centuries. Of those who were eligible, however, the percentage casting ballots was often quite high, particularly during the last half of the nineteenth century.

[b]Unofficial returns based on total estimated vote.

Source: Population figures for 1824 to 1920 are based on estimates and early census figures that appear in Neal R. Pierce, The People's President *(New Haven, Conn.: Yale University Press, 1979). Copyright © 1979. Reprinted with the permission of the publisher. Population figures from 1932 to 1984 are from the U.S. Department of Commerce, Bureau of the Census, Statistical Abstract of the United States (Washington, D.C., 1987), 250. Figures for 1988 and 1992 were compiled from official election returns published by the Federal Election Commission. Unofficial returns are estimated for 1996 by Curtis B. Gans, director of the Committee for the Study of the American Electorate.*

What explains the gap between those who can vote and those who actually cast ballots? Part of the answer may have to do with the time required for people to develop the interest, knowledge, and incentive to vote. Women, for example, received the right to vote in 1920 but voted at a lower rate than men until 1986. Similarly, African Americans in the southern states effectively gained the ability to vote in the mid 1960s, but their rate of participation still lags behind that of whites.

TABLE 10-2   EDUCATION AND VOTING TURNOUTS, 1982–1994

Years of Education	1982	1984	1986	1988	1990	1992	1994
Less than high school	43%	57%	38%	50%	30%	51%	36%
High school graduate	56	66	48	62	44	71	54
Some college	66	78	56	78	53	84	61
College graduate	77	91	72	92	67	93	78

Source: Data from American National Election Studies, conducted by the University of Michigan, Center for Political Studies, Ann Arbor, Michigan. Data provided by the Inter-University Consortium for Political and Social Research, located at the University of Michigan, Center for Political Studies, Ann Arbor, Michigan.

TABLE 10-3

THE REPUBLICAN ELECTORATE, 1996 (PERCENTAGES)

PERCENT OF TOTAL VOTE		VOTED FOR			
		DOLE	BUCHANAN	FORBES	OTHER
	Total vote, 28 states (millions)	6.6	2.7	1.5	1.1
	Age				
10	18–29 years	52	25	12	11
30	30–44 years	50	25	12	11
28	45–59 years	52	24	13	11
32	60 and older	65	18	10	7
	Education				
3	Without a high school diploma	49	24	8	19
20	High school graduate	57	27	9	7
30	Some college	54	24	11	11
27	College graduate	55	20	13	12
19	Some postgraduate education	39	12	10	39
	Party affiliation				
4	Democrats	61	21	10	8
21	Independents	41	28	15	16
75	Republicans	29	29	11	31
	Those who describe themselves as				
2	Very liberal	45	19	10	26
7	Somewhat liberal	53	19	14	14
33	Moderate	59	16	13	12
37	Somewhat conservative	59	20	11	10
21	Very conservative	44	38	9	9

Source: This table constructs a Republican primary electorate from exit polls conducted in twenty-eight Republican primary states from February through March 26, 1996, by Voter News Service, New York Times, March 31, 1996, 7. Copyright © 1996 by The New York Times Company. Reprinted by permission.

Turnout

The motivations for voting are complex. They have to do with interest in the campaign, concern about the outcome, feelings of civic responsibility, and a sense of political efficacy.[6] Generally speaking, people who identify with a political party are more strongly motivated to vote than those who do not. They tend to have more interest in the campaign, more knowledge about the candidates and issues, and more concern about the outcome of the election.[7]

Demographic characteristics also contribute to political involvement. Of these, the most important is education: the more educated a person is, the more likely that person will vote.[8] Education enhances one's ability to understand the issues, to follow the campaign, and to discern the difference between the candidates' positions. More education also usually leads to higher income, which in turn may increase a person's perceived stake in the outcome of elections.[9]

These differences are starkly revealed in Tables 10-2 and 10-3. Given the effects of education and income on voting, it is a little surprising that from 1960 to 1990 the electoral turnout decreased even though education and income levels for the population increased. To understand why this has occurred, it is necessary to look at other factors that affect the vote.

One of these factors is age. Studies have shown that the youngest group of eligi-

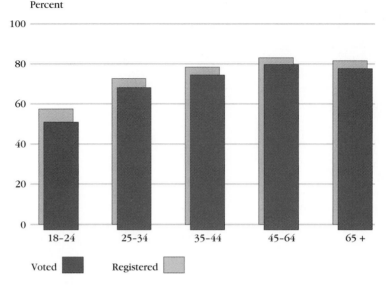

FIGURE *10-1*

Age and voting, 1992.

SOURCE: Data from the American National Election Studies, conducted by the University of Michigan, Center for Political Studies, Ann Arbor, Michigan. Data provided by the Inter-University Consortium for Political and Social Research, located at the University of Michigan, Center for Political Studies, Ann Arbor, Michigan.

ble voters, those under the age of 30, vote less regularly than do people in the middle age groups (see Figure 10-1). Older people—those over age 75—also are less likely to vote. Among the young, greater mobility, weaker partisanship, and a less developed sense of community contribute to lower rates of participation, whereas poor health and decreased interest are the major reasons for lower turnout by senior citizens. Demographic trends that have resulted in larger proportions of younger and older voters undoubtedly helped to reduce voting turnout during the period 1960-1990, but these trends do not fully explain the decline because all age groups have experienced lower turnout.

Another contributing factor has been the public's increasingly negative feelings about the performance of those in government, feelings that have led to greater apathy, more cynicism, and lower efficacy (see Chapters 6 and 7). A study of voting behavior by three political scientists, Paul R. Abramson, John H. Aldrich, and David W. Rohde, found that 62 percent of the decline in turnout can be attributed to the combined effects of weaker partisan affiliation and feelings of decreasing political effectiveness.[10] Negative political advertising may have produced a similar effect, reducing the appeal of candidates running for office and thus decreasing the motivation to vote for them.

This discussion of voter motivation may suggest why turnout declined from 1960 to 1990 and again in 1994 and 1996, but it does not explain why turnout increased in 1992. Factors unique to the 1992 election appear to be more directly responsible for the 5 percent increase in turnout from the previous presidential election. People seemed to be more aware of the issues and more concerned about them in 1992 than they were in 1984, 1988, and 1996. That concern, undoubtedly aroused by the recession, generated a higher-than-normal vote. In addition, the candidates, primarily H. Ross Perot, may have provided greater incentive. Perot's independent candi-

Discrimination in registration and voting practices persisted long after ratification of the Fifteenth and Nineteenth Amendments. African Americans had little recourse in states where segregationists controlled the dominant Democratic party. In protest, Fannie Lou Hamer and others founded the Mississippi Freedom Democratic party and tried to get seated in place of the regular Mississippi delegation at the 1964 Democratic National Convention. At first they were denied admission, but after a struggle, Ms. Hamer took one of the two at-large seats they were given. After Congress enacted the Voting Rights Act in 1965, the federal government was required to intervene in counties where large numbers of citizens were not registered.

dacy seemed to energize those who were most angry and frustrated with the major parties and their nominees. Had Perot not run, many of the 19.7 million people who voted for him in 1992 would probably have stayed at home. The percentage of Democrats who voted in that election was also slightly higher than in previous years, although the percentage of Republicans who voted declined.[11] Finally, there was the campaign itself, especially the candidates' use of television talk shows to reach and motivate a portion of the electorate usually less affected by traditional campaign events.

Who votes is as important a question to a democracy as *who is eligible to vote.* The answer not only indicates the extent to which the ideal of equal participation and influence is being achieved but also reveals levels of satisfaction and dissatisfaction among the population. It forecasts how representative the government is likely to be and which segments of the society are likely to benefit the most.

Turnout has partisan implications as well. The Republican party, composed of a larger proportion of well-educated, high-income, white-collar workers, usually gets a greater percentage of its adherents to vote than does the Democratic party. The higher Republican turnout has helped that party counter the Democrats' advantage in number of registered voters. In contrast, during the 1980s, lower turnout among

Television talk shows have become popular venues for candidates. Larry King Live *on CNN certainly helped H. Ross Perot's 1992 presidential bid. When Perot announced that he might run if enough people wanted him, the CNN switchboard was flooded with favorable calls—and he ran. Talk-show campaigning probably enhances voter turnout and affects voting behavior because it reaches many people who might otherwise pay little attention to the campaign.*

younger voters hurt the Republicans more than the Democrats, because newer voters identified more with the Republicans than with the Democrats during this period.

In 1992 the turnout among those who identified themselves as Republicans, (82 percent) was only marginally higher than among Democrats (80 percent), according to data from the American National Election Studies. But in 1994 it was substantially higher, contributing to the GOP's victory in the congressional elections. Republican congressional candidates received 70 million votes in 1994 (36 percent of the voting-age population), compared with only 60 million four years earlier. The Democratic vote was only marginally larger in 1994, by 130,000 votes.[12]

Would the results of recent presidential elections have been different if everyone voted? Political scientist Ruy A. Teixeira contends that they would not. He argues that nonvoters typically have much weaker partisan ties than do voters and therefore would be more likely to be influenced by general perceptions of the candidates than by partisan inclinations. He speculates that their vote would probably reflect the vote of the electorate as a whole, and he supports his argument with surveys of nonvoters that have been taken after presidential elections.[13]

Voting Behavior

Although *who* votes obviously influences the outcome of the election, so do the political attitudes and social groupings of the electorate. Voters do not come to an election with a completely open mind; they come with preexisting beliefs and attitudes. Of these, the most important is partisan identification.[14] A majority of the electorate still identifies with a political party, a commitment that is relatively stable and has both direct and indirect influences on voting.

As noted in Chapter 6, people develop political attitudes early in life and generally maintain and strengthen them as they get older. Although partisan attitudes can change, they are less likely to vary than positions on issues and perceptions of candidates. Moreover, when people do drop their partisan identity, they are more likely to think of themselves as independents than as supporters of another party, and they are still more likely to vote for candidates of their former party than for those of other parties. Actually, not only do two-thirds of those who claim to be independent lean toward one party or the other, but these *independent leaners* often vote in a more partisan fashion than do people who continue to claim a weak partisan allegiance.[15] Thus partisan predispositions directly affect the vote of those who feel strongly about their party and its candidates, and they indirectly affect the vote of those who feel less strongly but still tend to view their party's nominees more favorably than they view the opposition.[16]

Party identification is important because it provides a framework for analysis; it offers cues for evaluating the candidates and their stands. In general, the less that is known about the candidates, particularly those who are running for state or local office, the greater is the influence of party, because it becomes the primary factor that people consider in deciding how to vote. In contrast, at the presidential level more information is usually available to voters, such as the experience, character, leadership potential, and issue positions of the candidates.

Today about two-thirds of American voters consider themselves either Democrats or Republicans, compared with the three-fourths who identified with one of the two major parties in 1952. Not only does a smaller proportion of the electorate identify with the major parties, but the strength of their partisan attitude has also weakened. The result has been more **split-ticket voting**—that is, voting for candidates of different parties on the same ballot—and more emphasis on candidates' personal characteristics and less on their party affiliation. The weakening of partisan allegiances also tends to make deciding whom to vote for harder for many people. As a consequence, they tend to make their voting decisions later in the campaign. According to data from the American National Election Studies, 46 percent of the voters in the 1992 presidential election made their decision after the political conventions were over.

Group orientations can also influence voting. Most people see themselves as members of groups. To the extent that groups believe their interests are best served by particular parties, candidates, or issues, they will tell their members how to vote in a given election.

Group associations generate pressures that find expression in the political process. These pressures may reinforce partisan inclinations, or they may undermine them by creating cross-pressures that give mixed signals to voters.[17] In the 1980s, for example, the partisan identities of white blue-collar workers oriented them toward the Democrats and that party's stands on economic issues. Yet their dissatisfaction with the Democratic party's positions on welfare, law and order, and defense and national security issues, combined with their unhappiness with the presidency of Jimmy Carter, led many to support Ronald Reagan in 1980 and 1984. They did, however, return to the Democratic fold in 1992 and stayed Democratic in 1996.[18]

Another group of people whose association produces voting cohesion are white born-again Christians. From the New Deal era of the 1930s until 1978, this group supported Democratic candidates. In 1976, Jimmy Carter, himself a born-again Christian, received a majority of the vote of this group. In 1980, however, born-again Christians deserted the Democratic party over social issues: they opposed the Democrats' liberal positions on abortion, homosexuality, and the feminist movement and sided with the Republicans' emphasis on traditional family values and community standards. And they have remained Republican. In 1992, George Bush received

Large events that take on great emotional and symbolic impact can affect voting behavior. Jimmy Carter's defeat in 1980 was due in part to the crisis that followed the capture of a group of American diplomats in Iran. Carter's inability to free the hostages became a metaphor for his weak leadership and a failed presidency.

the support of 61 percent of this group, his largest and most cohesive voting bloc; in 1994 born-again Christians voted 3 to 1 for Republican candidates.[19] In 1996 they also voted Republican, with 65 percent of them supporting Robert Dole.

Cross-pressures delay voting decisions. Voters who feel these pressures tend to decide later in the campaign whether to vote and, if so, for whom. To minimize the impact of cross-pressures, parties and candidates go to great lengths to coordinate their messages and target them to specific electoral constituencies.

The candidates themselves and the issues of the day also affect how people vote. Voters' perception of candidates have become more important in recent years, largely because of the greater use of television, which tends to emphasize personality and leadership at the expense of substantive policy issues. The specific issues that affect voting behavior vary with the election, the constituency, and the candidates. Whether issues—be they jobs, crime, education, environment, health, or national security—are salient depends on four factors: (1) how much attention they receive from the media, (2) how directly they affect voters, (3) how much the candidates differ on them, and (4) voters' awareness of candidates' differences.[20] Thus important public concerns, particularly those that relate to fundamental values and needs (individual well-being, personal safety, economic prosperity), may not be campaign issues unless the public perceives that the candidates and their parties approach them in different ways.

The more direct the perceived impact of the issue, the more likely it is to have a discernible electoral impact. In the 1980s the recurring budget deficit was a theoretical concern for most Americans, one that had a minimal electoral impact. However, increasing taxes to reduce the deficit was a very real issue, one that had discernible electoral consequences. Walter Mondale's promise to raise taxes to help reduce the deficit hurt his candidacy in 1984, whereas George Bush's promise not to do so helped his in 1988 and hurt him four years later after he had to break it. By 1992 the deficit, along with an economy in recession, had become the key issue. Similarly, low public esteem for Congress was not a major election issue in the 1980s but by the 1990s it had become one, magnified in part by the attention given to institutional deadlock between Congress and the presidency, to the pay raise voted by Congress for itself, and to scandals involving abuse of post office and banking privileges by members of the House of Representatives.

In short, in every election there are multiple influences on voting. Because these influences, either singly or together, can affect the outcome of the election, candidates and parties try to shape them by designing a campaign strategy that puts their best case to the voters, one that emphasizes their own strengths and their opponents' weaknesses. *Campaigns do matter.* A single campaign may be too short a period to change attitudes or alter associations, but it is long enough to affect perceptions and influence voting. At least this is what the candidates and their campaign managers believe as they prepare for the election.

How do people weigh various factors in arriving at their decisions, and what questions do they try to answer? Political scientists have proposed two models of voting: retrospective voting and prospective voting. **Retrospective voting** is based on an assessment of the past performance of the parties and their elected officials in the light of the promises they made, political events that have occurred, and the conditions that currently exist.[21] In this model, voters base their judgment on their accumulated political experience, asking themselves, "Am I better off now than I was when the other party and leaders were in power?" In contrast, **prospective voting** anticipates the actions of candidates once they assume office. Voters compare their own values, beliefs, and opinions with those of the candidates and parties; then they base their judgment on their sense of which party and which candidates are likely to benefit them the most after the election.

The retrospective and prospective models are theoretical formulations of the thought processes that people go through when they decide how to vote. In practice, voters undoubtedly do both; they look backward and forward to arrive at their electoral judgments. They evaluate the candidates and their parties and how well they have done largely on the basis of how good or bad conditions seem to be. If the economy is strong, society appears harmonious, the nation feels secure, and government seems to be functioning normally, people assume that their leaders—particularly the president—must be doing a good job. If conditions are not favorable, they tend to blame those in power, especially the president. This judgment—how conditions are and who is responsible for them—is part of the voting decision, but not the only part. Voters must also anticipate which of the candidates and parties, given the record of the past, is likely to do better in the future. Thus both retrospective and prospective analyses help people arrive at the rationales they use for their voting decisions.

THE ELECTION CAMPAIGN

Every candidate's objective is to win, to convince voters that she or he is the most qualified and will do the best job. The campaign is the mechanism used to achieve this objective. Frequently, candidates must conduct two campaigns: one to gain their party's nomination, and another to compete in the general election. Because they are conducted at different times under different rules, appeal to different electorates, and often emphasize different issues, positions, and leadership traits, these campaigns are quite different.

Of the two, the nomination campaign has changed the most during the twentieth century. Formerly an internal matter decided by party leaders, the quest for nomination today occurs within the public arena, usually in primary races among self-declared aspirants for office. Candidates are selected on the basis of their appeal to primary voters. If successful, they must run again in the general election, refocusing their campaign and broadening and moderating their message for the entire electorate. In doing so, they may have to soften their partisan rhetoric, reposition themselves toward the center of the political spectrum, and stress those issues and personal traits that will attract the votes of independents, supporters of the other party, and partisans of their own party who did not vote for them in the primaries.

The quest for office is also conditioned by the rules that govern the election, the environment in which the election occurs, and the electorate to which the candidates must appeal. Of these, the economic and social environment is the most vari-

(Above) *In 1968, with Democrats bitterly divided over the Vietnam War, thousands of antiwar protesters clashed with police outside the party's convention hall in Chicago. The ugly televised spectacle alienated many voters and helped to doom the chances of Democratic presidential nominee Hubert Humphrey.* (Right) *In 1996, unified behind the reelection of President Bill Clinton, the Democrats returned to Chicago for the first time since 1968—and this time demonstrations were few and peaceful, leaving officers assigned to convention duty with little to do.*

able factor, changing from election to election. The rules are more predictable, but they too have changed, particularly those that pertain to the presidential nomination process. The electorate is stable but not static, as we noted in Chapter 9.

The Presidential Nomination Process

In theory, national nominating conventions still designate the major parties' nominees for president and vice president and formulate the platforms on which they will run. In practice, party activists have the greatest influence on those judgments. The movement toward increased popular control of the nomination process came during the 1970s, when the Democratic party revised its rules for delegate selection to its nominating convention in order to encourage greater public participation and more equitable representation of rank-and-file voters.

These changes made primary elections the preferred mode of selection. Today approximately three-fourths of the delegates pledged to particular candidates at both the Democratic and the Republican national conventions come from states that hold some form of primary. All of the remaining Republican pledged delegates and some of the remaining Democratic ones come from states that utilize a multistage party **caucus.** In addition to the pledged delegates, the Democrats choose a number of unpledged delegates from among the party's elected and appointed leaders; in 1996 these **superdelegates,** as they are called, constituted about 18 percent of the total number of delegates who attended the Democratic convention.

Another major objective of the rule changes was to more accurately reflect popular preferences in the selection of delegates. That is why the Democrats adopted the principle of **proportional voting,** in which delegates are awarded to each candidate in a primary or caucus in proportion to the number of popular votes the candidate receives. To be eligible for delegates, however, a candidate must receive a minimum percentage of the total vote, or *threshold,* usually 15 percent. Initially the Democratic party also established quotas, specifying that minorities and women had to be represented on the state delegations in proportion to their numbers within the state. Protests over the quotas, which were deemed inconsistent with the principle of personal choice and majority rule, led the Democrats to eliminate them and adopt affirmative action guidelines for designated minority groups while continuing to require that the delegates be equally divided between men and women.

The Republicans have not imposed similar national rules on their state parties except for a prohibition against discrimination. Nevertheless, state Republican parties operate under rules that have increased rank-and-file participation and have broadened representation at their conventions. The chief difference is that the Republicans permit states to have **winner-take-all voting.**

In a winner-take-all system, the candidate or the delegates (if they run separately) with the most votes win and the losers get nothing. Such a system benefits front-running candidates and puts them in a position to lock up the nomination earlier than Democratic candidates usually can. Ronald Reagan in 1980, George Bush in 1988, and Robert Dole in 1996 all benefited from winner-take-all voting. For example, in 1988 Bush won 59 percent of the popular vote in states holding some type of winner-take-all primary on the first Tuesday in which a large number of states held their nominating contests. But Bush won 97 percent of the delegates selected in these states, giving him an insurmountable lead over Dole, his principal rival. Eight years later Dole took advantage of his front-runner status to perform a similar feat against his principal rivals.

The changes in the way the parties select their delegates have resulted in greater public involvement in the nomination process. In 1968, before the reforms, only 12 million people participated. Four years later that number rose to 22 million. By 1988, with two contested nominations, it was almost 37 million, the highest primary turnout in history.

Turnout declined in 1992 and 1996. Approximately 20 million people voted in the 1992 Democratic primaries, but only 10.8 million in 1996, when President Clinton had no major opposition. On the Republican side, in both years the turnout was about 13 million. It was higher in the early contests, before front-runners George Bush and Robert Dole had effectively wrapped up their party's nomination, than in the later ones.[22]

Although a larger portion of the electorate is now involved in the nomination process, primary voters are not equally distributed among all segments of society. Generally speaking, better-educated, higher-income, older party members participate more frequently than do younger people with less education and lower incomes. Racial minorities in particular have tended to be poorly represented among those who vote in primary elections, although Jesse Jackson's campaigns for the Democratic nomination in 1984 and 1988 generated a higher turnout of African Americans than in previous campaigns. Table 10-3 (on page 323) presents a demographic profile of the 1996 Republican primary voters.

Representation at the nominating convention has also improved for various groups within the parties. The percentages of delegates who are women or minorities have increased significantly since 1968 (see Table 10-4). But even though conventions are demographically more representative of the American electorate, they are not necessarily ideologically more representative. Studies of recent convention goers have found Republican delegates to be more conservative and Democratic delegates more liberal than their party's rank-and-file members and much more conservative or liberal than the electorate as a whole (see Table 10-5).[23] The stronger ideological position of the delegates may explain why recent party platforms have contained unequivocal stands on controversial issues such as abortion, taxes, capital punishment, the balanced budget, and Equal Rights amendments,[24] positions that many of the party's rank and file—and even the presidential nominees—may not accept.

The changes in rules have affected party leaders as well, by reducing the leaders' ability to choose delegates and influence delegates' behavior at the convention. The greater openness of the nominating process and increased participation by the rank and file have encouraged people who had not been party regulars in the past to become involved. They have also forced candidates and the delegates who support them to depend less on the party apparatus and more on their own organizing skills.

On balance, the rules for delegate selection have led to an increase in the number of candidates and to the creation of separate candidate organizations. Even incumbents may face opposition, as did Gerald Ford in 1976, Jimmy Carter in 1980, and George Bush in 1992.

The trend toward greater popular control of the nomination process has taken its toll on the parties. It has encouraged interests within the parties to organize, make demands, and exert influence on the selection process and the platform. It has made it harder for the party to project a unified appeal to the voters. It has also made governing more difficult by creating pressures on those in power by groups whose support was critical to their electoral success. A case in point was the gay and lesbian community's financial backing of Bill Clinton during the 1992 Democratic primaries. At a major fund-raiser a thankful Clinton promised to end discrimination

| TABLE 10-4 | | THE DEMOGRAPHY OF NATIONAL CONVENTION DELEGATES, 1968–1996 (PERCENTAGES) | | | | | | | | | |

THE DEMOGRAPHY OF NATIONAL CONVENTION DELEGATES, 1968–1996 (PERCENTAGES)

	1968		1972		1980		1988		1996		ALL REG. VOTERS (1996)
	DEM.	REP.	DEM.	REP.	DEM.	REP.	DEM.	REP.	DEM.	REP.	
Women	13	16	40	29	49	29	48	33	57	39	52
African Americans	5	2	15	4	15	3	23	4	21	2	11
Under age 30	3	4	22	8	11	5	4	3	4	2	16
Median age (years)	(49)	(49)	(42)	—	(44)	(49)	(46)	(51)	—	—	—
Lawyers	28	22	12	—	13	15	16	17	—	—	—
Teachers	8	2	11	—	15	4	14	5	—	—	—
Union members	—	—	16	—	27	4	25	3	34	2	11
Attended first convention	67	66	83	78	87	84	65	68	60	55	—
College graduate	19	—	21	—	20	26	21	32	27	37	19
Postgraduate[a]	44	34	36	—	45	39	52	34	45	36	11
Protestant	—	—	42	—	47	72	50	69	—	—	—
Catholic	—	—	26	—	37	22	30	22	—	—	—
Jewish	—	—	9	—	8	3	7	2	—	—	—

[a]Includes those in the category of college graduates.

Source: CBS News Delegate Surveys, 1968 through 1980. Warren J. Mitofsky and Martin Plissner, "The Making of the Delegates, 1968-1980," Public Opinion (December-January 1980): 43. Data reprinted with permission of CBS, Inc. and The American Enterprise Institute for Public Policy Research, Washington, D.C. 1988 data supplied by CBS News from its delegate surveys and reprinted with permission of CBS News. 1992 data in the New York Times, July 13, 1992, B6, the Washington Post, August 16, 1992, A19, and survey data supplied by the Republican National Committee. Data for 1996 from Washington Post/ABC News surveys as appearing in the Washington Post, August 10, 1996, M8, and August 25, 1996, M4.

against homosexuals in the military, a promise that was to cost him dearly as president. His attempt to fulfill it diverted attention from his principal priorities, encountered widespread opposition, enabled Republicans to label him a liberal, and forced him to accept a compromise that satisfied virtually no one and made him look weak.

Preconvention strategy and tactics   In the past, entering primaries was optional for leading candidates and necessary only for those who lacked party support. Today everyone must do it. No longer can an acknowledged political leader sit on the side-

THE IDEOLOGY OF NATIONAL CONVENTION DELEGATES, 1980–1996 (PERCENTAGES)

	1980		1984		1988		1992		1996		ALL VOTERS IN 1996
IDEOLOGY	DEM.	REP.	DEM.	REP.	DEM.	REP.	DEM.	REP.	DEM.	REP.	
Liberal	46	2	48	1	43	0	47	1	43	0	16
Moderate	42	36	42	35	43	35	44	28	48	27	47
Conservative	6	58	4	60	5	58	5	70	5	66	32

Source: CBS News Delegate Surveys, 1976 through 1980. Characteristics of the public are average values from seven CBS News/New York Times polls, 1980. Warren J. Mitofsky and Martin Plissner, "The Making of the Delegates, 1968-1980," Public Opinion (December-January 1980): 43. Data reprinted with permission of CBS, Inc. and The American Enterprise Institute for Public Policy Research, Washington, D.C. 1984 and 1988 data for delegates and public supplied by CBS News from its delegate surveys and reprinted with permission of CBS News. 1992 data published in the New York Times, July 13, 1992, B6, and the Washington Post, August 16, 1992, A19. 1996 data obtained from New York Times/CBS News Polls as appearing in the New York Times, August 26, 1996, A12.

lines and wait to be drafted by party leaders and rank-and-file supporters (as William Jennings Bryan was in 1896 by the Democrats, and Wendell Willkie in 1940 and General Dwight Eisenhower in 1952 were by the Republicans). Presidential aspirants now have to create a movement on their own behalf, raise their own money, build their own organizations, hire their own consultants, and actively campaign for many months, even years, to obtain the nomination.

Campaigns usually start well before the first caucuses and primaries are held, because candidates need to do well in these early tests of their appeal to voters. George McGovern got the earliest start, beginning his successful quest for the 1972 Democratic nomination in January 1971. Phil Gramm was the first candidate for the 1996 Republican nomination, announcing his candidacy in February 1995; other aspirants quickly followed suit. By early summer, more than a year before the Republican convention, ten candidates had officially thrown their hats into the ring for the Republican nomination. The first contests have assumed great importance because of the attention they attract from the news media and the momentum they can generate.

Even candidates who do not stand a realistic chance of winning their party's nomination will run in the early contests to take advantage of the news media coverage. An example is Pat Buchanan's challenge to George Bush in 1992. Angela Buchanan, the candidate's sister and campaign manager, articulated Buchanan's strategy for the New Hampshire primary, traditionally the first in the nation:

> Winning New Hampshire was never in the cards, but New Hampshire would give us momentum maybe to carry it though Georgia and then possibly an outside chance, in our wildest dreams, to make it through Super Tuesday. Winning New Hampshire for us was just doing well. It was doing better than it was perceived we would do. . . . What we needed to do was make certain that those expectations were kept as low as possible.
>
> So we were up there saying, geez, you know, we're at nine. We hope to get to the teens. One of the Bush people made the mistake of saying "They won't break 30."[25]

Buchanan actually received 34 percent of the vote. However, a glitch in the early exit polls announced by the media on the night of the election elevated his percentage even higher, thereby further embarrassing the president before a large viewing audience and enhancing Buchanan's credibility in the process. In the 1996 New Hampshire primary Buchanan received the most votes, 27.4 percent of the total. There were seven other candidates running.

One reason for beginning so far ahead of the nomination is that it takes time to raise the money needed for a serious campaign. Millions of dollars are necessary to build an organization, pay its expenses, move around the country, and project an appeal. Financial pressures have forced candidates to devote much of their time to fundraising, especially since individual donors cannot contribute more than $1,000 and groups more than $5,000.

Successful fundraising long in advance of the first contests is particularly significant for those who do not begin the quest for their party's nomination with a national reputation, such as Michael Dukakis in 1988, Bill Clinton in 1992, and all the Republican contenders in 1996 except Dole. The ability to raise relatively large amounts of money early provides an edge in gaining recognition and getting a message across.[26]

The increasing use of the mass media, particularly television, by aspirants for their party's nomination has also upped the financial ante. Television time is not

How to Find Information About Federal Elections

The Federal Election Commission (FEC) is a good source for a variety of information about campaigns and elections for federal offices, including regulations, forms, schedules, and any legal actions the commission initiates or advisory opinions it offers. Because its mission is to provide information about these activities to the general public, the commission offers a large number of services for little or no charge. The monthly newsletter *Record*, which lists press releases and other published FEC reports, should be available in your college library. If it is not, you may obtain a free subscription by calling the FEC's public records office at (800) 424-9530. Copies of the documents listed can be obtained at little or no charge by calling or by writing the FEC at 999 E St. N.W., Washington, D.C. 20463.

If you are in a hurry, the documents can be faxed to you at government expense. All you have to do is call (202) 501-3413 using a touch-tone phone. (The system operates 24 hours a day.) You will be asked for the identification numbers of the documents you want, your fax number, and your telephone number. The documents will then be quickly faxed to you, usually within hours.

You can also obtain these documents on the Internet. The FEC also has a home page (**http://www.fec.gov**), which has several menu options. For example, a *Citizens Guide to Contributions and the Law* contains highlights from various FEC publications and a guide to using the FEC's public records office and its on-line Direct Access program, as well as summaries, charts, and graphs of presidential and congressional financial campaign information that are updated monthly. News releases and media advisories are also available at this Web site. You can even obtain information on how to register to vote in your state and a national registration voting form.

If you have any questions about the kind of information the FEC has available, and you do not want to use the Internet, you can call the FEC's public information office at (800) 424-9530.

---

cheap. In New Hampshire in 1992, the cost of a single 30-second commercial on a major station in Manchester during prime time was $1,000. Design and production expenses also have to be factored into the total cost. Yet candidates feel they have no choice but to take to the airwaves, since more and more people obtain their information about the campaign from the electronic media. An additional problem is that an increasing number of states have moved their caucuses or primary toward the front end of the nomination period. In 1996 this so-called "front loading" reached new heights: more than 70 percent of the Republican delegates were selected in a 44-day period from mid February to the end of March. To run effectively in so many contests so close together, where there is too little time to make many personal appearances, candidates need to wage costly media campaigns.

In addition to media, the expenses of building a campaign organization and conducting public opinion polls have increased the financial burden on candidates in recent elections. Candidates can no longer depend solely or primarily on state party leaders to deliver the vote. However, the activities and organization of the state leaders, particularly governors, can be important and are often crucial. Bush cultivated and benefited from this support in 1992, as did Dole in 1996.

Immediately following the 1994 elections, Dole's staff communicated with

*Televised debates can help candidates gain public attention if they can distin-
guish themselves from their opponents. Here some of the Republican hopefuls
get ready for a debate before the 1996 New Hampshire primary. Although a
huge family fortune and the flat tax issue helped Steve Forbes (second from right)
win a few primaries, no challenger succeeded in knocking out front-runner
Robert Dole.*

Republican governors, promising them the senator's support for the early enactment
of legislation to end unfunded federal mandates on the states and to replace entitlement programs such as Medicaid and welfare programs with block grants. Dole eventually received the endorsement of 21 of the 31 Republican governors even before
the primaries got under way, including New Hampshire's Steve Merrill and New
York's George Pataki. He followed up these endorsements by holding fund-raisers in
those states in which governors backed him, thereby enhancing his financial advantage as well. In New York the entire party apparatus supported Dole, retaining an
antiquated election law that made it difficult for other Republicans to challenge him
in that state's primary.

With intentions clear, money in hand, and an organization in place, a candidate
then must ascertain public sentiment, appeal to it, and, if need be, manipulate it.
This is often done through public opinion polling. Here is how Clinton's pollster,
Stan Greenberg, described early polling results for the 1992 campaign:

> In September we did some initial research in New Hampshire. Interpretations
> of the results of that research led us into this race. We concluded that the nor-
> mal assumption that the New Hampshire primary electorate is liberal and that a
> moderate candidate would not face good prospects was wrong-headed. But,
> more importantly, voters didn't care about ideology; they did not respond to
> anything we tested about "a new kind of Democrat"; . . . the bread and butter
> issues were all New Hampshire voters wanted to hear about.[27]

Another device that is frequently used to explore the public mood is the focus group—a collection of individuals who are brought together and asked to discuss and respond to a variety of real and hypothetical situations involving candidates, issues, and ideology. Information gleaned from focus groups can be extremely helpful in creating and adjusting a campaign appeal. For example, focus groups were used extensively by candidate Bill Clinton in 1992 to gauge voter reaction to the allegations about his character and to his response to those allegations. (House Republicans also used such groups in 1994 to design their Contract with America.) Candidates who cannot afford to conduct polls or focus groups may find themselves at a comparative disadvantage. They are forced to guess what is on the voters' minds and whether their appeals are being well received.

Assessing public opinion is also important because in building an electoral coalition, a candidate has to tailor messages to specific groups within the party. For example, in the 1996 Republican nomination contest Phil Gramm trumpeted his credentials as an economic and small-government conservative, presenting himself as the heir to the economic philosophy of the Reagan administration. Dole, previously viewed as a moderate, also stressed his conservatism on a number of fronts, criticizing the movie industry for its depictions of sex and violence, pledging his support for a law to make English the official language of the United States, and promising to support school prayer and oppose abortions. Steve Forbes, appealing to anti-tax sentiment, focused on replacing the progressive income tax with a flat tax; Lamar Alexander, seeking the anti-Washington vote, said he would return power to the people and their elected representatives; Richard Lugar stressed his experience in foreign affairs; Arlen Specter criticized the views and positions of the Christian right; and Pat Buchanan used strident rhetoric to underline his social conservatism and neo-isolationism.

Although polls can track public reactions and help guide candidate appeals, they cannot substitute for an effective campaign. Even with the most accurate polls in hand, candidates still need to make critical tactical decisions about how and where to use their resources. If they are not well known, their initial goal must be to gain recognition. To do this, they have no choice but to compete in the early contests. Doing well in those races will provide them with opportunities they would not otherwise have. Doing poorly, however, will terminate their candidacy.

Those who are better known have greater flexibility and are also in a better position to take advantage of their reputation and political influence to build a strong organizational and financial base. In 1988, for example, George Bush built what his campaign manager referred to as a "firewall" in the South by raising more money, collecting more endorsements, creating larger state organizations, and running more television advertisements than any of his Republican opponents. The "firewall" was intended to cement his initial advantage, preventing his campaign from collapsing if he lost one or more of the early contests (he did lose in Iowa) and putting him in an almost unassailable position if he won them. Bill Clinton pursued much the same strategy in 1992, as did Robert Dole in 1996, helped by their superior organizational support and fundraising capabilities.

One of the distinctive aspects of recent nomination campaigns has been the propensity of candidates, particularly Democrats, to circumvent the national news media whenever possible. They do so in a variety of ways, such as distributing videotapes and providing satellite feeds to local television stations. In 1992 nearly one-half of the local television news stations conducted interviews with the candidates for their party's nomination, mostly via satellite, compared with only 20 percent four years earlier.[28] Even incumbents have engaged in this form of campaigning

CANDIDATE CLINTON: STRATEGIES FOR SUCCESS

As candidates and their advisers plan their quest for a party's presidential nomination, they have to begin by taking into account whether or not the candidate is seen as the front-runner, since that perception dictates how the campaign itself has to begin. Bill Clinton's campaigns for the 1992 and 1996 Democratic presidential nominations provide good illustrations of the alternative opening strategies this consideration imposes, as well as examples of some of the specific strategic approaches that candidates use today.

Clinton did not begin as a front-runner for the nomination in 1992, but he emerged as one before the first primary in New Hampshire. Initial preparation for the first Clinton campaign began in the fall of 1991. A major decision early in the planning was to cast Clinton as a national (rather than regional) candidate who would emphasize middle-class values and interests. To set the thematic structure of the campaign, he gave three major speeches on economic, domestic, and foreign policy at his alma mater, Georgetown University in Washington, D.C.

New Hampshire posed a difficult challenge for the candidate, who was competing against both a regional favorite, former senator Paul Tsongas of Massachusetts, and a Vietnam War hero, Senator Bob Kerry of Nebraska. Clinton's advisers assumed he would be in third place for most of the New Hampshire campaign, hoped that he would pick up strength toward the end by stressing economic issues, but were ready to move quickly to other primaries regardless of the result.[1]

To the dismay of the Clinton campaign, however, allegations of marital infidelity and draft dodging surfaced in the month prior to the New Hampshire vote, dominated headlines, and forced Clinton to defend himself. It was decided to tackle the infidelity issue immediately, with the candidate and his wife appearing on the popular television-magazine program *60 Minutes*. In his brief appearance, Clinton admitted that he and his wife had had marital difficulties but said these difficulties were a thing of the past. The campaign's quick televised response to the accusations limited their political fallout. Even though the draft-dodging charges were not handled nearly as well nor as quickly, the character issue that had forced

A politician's private life has become public business, as Bill Clinton found out in 1992 when Gennifer Flowers accused him of having been her lover for twelve years. Clinton denied the charge, but the "character issue" remained an albatross around his neck as president.

Gary Hart to end his candidacy four years earlier did not prove fatal to Clinton. In fact, on the night of the New Hampshire vote, campaign spokespersons actually turned the issue and its electoral ramifications to Clinton's advantage, referring to their candidate as the "Comeback Kid" and describing his second-place finish as if it were a victory.

Having successfully survived New Hampshire, the campaign next had to blunt any momentum that Tsongas might have built by coming in first in that state. The strategy was to beat him in the Georgia primary (which had been moved forward a week at the request of the Clinton campaign) as well as in Colorado. Both objectives were achieved. With the help of Georgia's Democratic governor, Zell Miller, and his political organization, Clinton easily won that state. By focusing on the issue of nuclear energy, of concern to Colorado Democrats, Clinton provided an opportunity for former California governor Jerry Brown to defeat Tsongas there. Only in Maryland did Tsongas win. The split verdict broke Tsongas's momentum and positioned Clinton perfectly for the southern "Super Tuesday" primaries, in which he crushed his opponents and amassed a large delegate lead.

Fresh from the victory on Super Tuesday, the Clinton campaign moved to the Midwest, to Illinois and Michigan. Clinton's superior organization and financial position made him the favorite in both states, and by winning them he became the prohibitive favorite for the nomination. They did not end his campaign, however. Although Brown's refusal to bow out did not threaten Clinton's nomination, his criticism affected Clinton's stature in the eyes of the voters. His image was severely damaged in the New York primary, which Clinton won. National polls indicated that 60 percent of those surveyed believed that Clinton did not possess the honesty and integrity to be president. To counter this perception, the Clinton campaign reintroduced the candidate to the electorate in a series of biographical television commercials depicting the hardships that Clinton encountered while growing up and ultimately surmounted in his rise to political prominence. These commercials, combined with talk-show appearances in which Clinton reminisced about his upbringing, gradually muted his negative image.

The development of H. Ross Perot's presidential campaign and the decision by the Republicans to attack Perot in June and July enabled Clinton to get back on his feet before the Democratic National Convention. An important component of Clinton's strategy during this period was to ignore Perot in the hopes that the Republicans would destroy him and/or that he would destroy himself. Again, that part of the strategy proved correct. Clinton's popularity was building as he approached the convention, which nominated him on the first ballot with minimum opposition from Brown.

In 1996, as the incumbent, Clinton faced no real challenge for the nomination. Nonetheless, his campaign strategists saw the nomination period as an opportunity to lay a foundation for the general election.

A key element in this plan was keeping the Democratic party united by discouraging any would-be challengers who wished either to defeat Clinton or to use the nomination process to further their own political agenda. The president did this by quickly and aggressively pursuing a fundraising goal of raising the maximum allowed by law. Not only did this activity dry up Democratic money for anyone else, but it provided a war chest to use for advertising and voter registration efforts. (Ronald Reagan had adopted a similar strategy in 1984.) In addition, White House aides put pressure on Democratic governors and state parties to discourage them from conducting straw polls or other events that would give a would-be opponent a chance to embarrass the president. Facing only token opposition in the primaries, the president was free to use the money he raised during the prenomination period to improve his image, highlight his issues, and refine his message for the general election.

The advertisements began to be aired in the summer of 1995, almost a year and a half before the election. Targeted toward key battleground states in the Midwest and California, and funded largely by the party, the commercials were designed to preempt Republican criticism as well as emphasize the president's major themes of education, the environment, and health care, especially for senior citizens. They used excerpts from his well-received 1995 State of the Union address to place Clinton in a setting that emphasized the status of his office.

With a very compact general election campaign of about 9 weeks, the Clinton campaign anticipated that the bombardment of messages every night on television and radio would effectively cancel each other out, muting the impact of the campaign on most voters. They thus anticipated that the election would be decided *before* the nominating conventions, not *after* them. Their nomination strategy, based on this assumption, was to present a clear, consistent, centrist message, one that lauded the administration's achievements, presented him primarily as a president, not as a politician, and labeled his Republican opponent as a candidate from the past.

[1]Stan Greenberg, quoted in Royer, ed., *Campaign for President: The Managers Look at '92* (Hollis, N.H.: Hollis Publishing Co., 1994), 34.

despite their ability to make news as president and their campaign's ability to buy air time.

Candidates are also taking increasing advantage of free television time on national talk-entertainment shows. In 1992 Clinton appeared on 21 of these programs from January to July, and Perot, once he got into the race, was on 4.[29] Jerry Brown, one of Clinton's rivals for the Democratic nomination, made the most extensive use of radio talk shows. In doing so, he always repeated his 800 telephone number to raise money and solicit volunteers, a device Perot used as well when he launched his presidential campaign.

National nominating conventions   After the delegates have been selected, the national nominating conventions are held. The conventions decide on the party's rules, choose its presidential and vice presidential nominees, and adopt the party platform. Despite the conventions' political rhetoric, today they actually decide little that has not been preordained by the delegate selection process. Nevertheless, they do serve several important purposes. They reward the party faithful—activists who were involved in the delegate selection process, those who have toiled for the party, and elected officials, party leaders, and other prominent individuals who desire public recognition and political support. They unify groups that have been divided by the nomination process, stimulating them to pull together during the election campaign. Finally, they constitute a massive public appeal by the parties on behalf of their candidates in the general election.

It was women and children first at the Republican and Democratic national conventions in 1996, as both parties aimed to showcase their concern for American families. The Republicans, facing a serious "gender gap" in support for presidential candidate Robert Dole, featured New York congresswoman Susan Molinari (left), a 38-year-old mother of a two-month-old baby, as keynote speaker. Dole's wife, Elizabeth (right), charmed delegates and television viewers with her talk-show-style walk on the convention floor. The Democrats countered with First Lady Hillary Clinton, well known as an advocate for women and children, whose speech made frequent reference to her daughter, Chelsea.

Satisfying the first of these purposes has not been too difficult. Conventions are large public events, and party leaders and activists regard them as the place to be. Cities compete vigorously to host them, even though it is a logistical nightmare to seat, feed, house, transport, and protect so many people. In 1996 approximately 25,000 delegates, alternates, media representatives, and invited guests and visitors attended the Democratic convention in Chicago; and about 20,000 went to the Republican convention in San Diego.

As for the second purpose, conventions can be divisive before they become unifying. During a long nominating process, policy disagreements are voiced and personal animosities aired. If the nomination is in doubt, these divisions are exacerbated and the front-runner must try to generate a **bandwagon effect** that induces uncommitted delegates and those pledged to other candidates to get on board. To create this effect, the front-runner's organization must defeat any motion, procedural or otherwise, on any issue that raises doubts about who the eventual winner will be. No concessions can be made until the nomination is secured.

In 1976 President Gerald Ford, challenged by Ronald Reagan, successfully employed the bandwagon strategy. His organization pressured Republican delegates to defeat a change in party rules that would have required presidential nominees to disclose their choice for vice president before the convention voted for the presidential candidate. Ford's victory on this key procedural vote indicated that he had the necessary votes to win the nomination.

If the nomination is a foregone conclusion, as it has been in recent years, there are incentives for all participants to accommodate one another. The winner needs a unified party and support in the general election. The losers need to save face, maintain their influence, and position themselves for the next election or for appointment to high public office if the party's nominees for president and vice president win the election. Usually the losers are willing to get behind the successful candidate in exchange for something—for example, a chance to be heard during prime viewing hours at the convention, to have their most cherished positions included in the platform, or to obtain changes in the rules for the next go-round. Defeated presidential candidates Jesse Jackson and Pat Buchanan were invited to address national conventions that nominated their opponents. In 1992, however, Buchanan's speech was extremely controversial, containing very harsh rhetoric that appeased delegates who were unhappy with Bush but alienated moderate Republicans and independents. Republican convention planners did not repeat the same mistake in 1996. Buchanan did not speak, and those who did echoed a moderate theme.

The third purpose of conventions, to enhance the party's public image and improve its chances in the election, is often the most difficult to achieve because the interests of the party and those of the news media are often in conflict. Both seek to entertain as well as inform. But whereas the party is trying to present a unified front by scripting the convention proceedings to make them appear interesting and favorable to the party's image—in effect, to conduct a huge pep rally—the media are looking for news, not theater. In 1992, the conservative coup d'état at the Republican convention was the big news, in contrast to the near-unanimity at the Democratic one. In 1996 there was little "hard news" at either major-party convention. As a consequence, the amount of network news coverage declined, as did the number of viewers.

Conventions are one of many stimuli that voters receive during the election campaign. They occur at the midpoint of the process—at the end of the nomination period and the beginning of the general election campaign, months before the final vote. Although they generate more concentrated coverage than any other event to that point, frequently consuming more television time than the rest of the campaign, their impact on the vote is difficult to measure. Political scientists have suggested three major effects of conventions on voters. They heighten interest, thereby potentially increasing turnout. They arouse latent attitudes, thereby raising awareness of the partisan issues. They color perceptions, thereby affecting the electorate's judgments about the candidates, the parties, and their positions.[30] Studies have also found that people who watch the conventions tend to make their voting decisions early in the campaign. About one in five says that she or he does so at the time of the nominating conventions.[31]

The Presidential Election

Whereas the nomination process has undergone many changes in recent decades, the general election process has not. The presidential election still occurs within the context of the Electoral College system.

When the framers of the Constitution fashioned the system for choosing the president and vice president, they rejected the idea of a direct popular vote, preferring instead an indirect method in which a group of **electors** would choose the president. Their plan was to have states choose electors in any manner they desired. The electors, equal in number to the total number of senators and representatives from a state, would meet as the **Electoral College** and exercise their own judgment in selecting the president and vice president. It was expected that they would select the most qualified candidates, not necessarily the most popular ones.

Today electors are no longer chosen directly by state legislatures; they are chosen by the electorate of each state. When that electorate votes for president, it actually selects electors who are pledged to a particular presidential candidate. Moreover, the electors who are chosen no longer make an independent judgment but instead cast their votes for the candidate of their party.

In all but two states, Maine and Nebraska, the candidate who wins the most popular votes receives *all* of the state's electoral votes.[32] This winner-take-all method of voting in the Electoral College is known as the **general ticket system**. A majority of the votes in the Electoral College, 270 out of 538, is needed to win. A candidate can win a majority in the Electoral College and thus be elected president without winning a majority or even a plurality of the total popular vote. This situation has occurred twice: in 1876 and 1888 (see the box on page 343).

If no candidate wins a majority in the Electoral College, the House of Representatives selects the president; voting takes place by state, with each state's delegation having one vote. It is thus possible for the candidate with the most votes in the Electoral College to lose the presidency in the House. That is what happened in 1824 to Andrew Jackson, who led in both popular and electoral votes in a four-way race but did not have a majority of electoral votes. According to the Twelfth Amendment to the Constitution, when the House selects the president it must choose from among the three candidates with the most electoral votes. This provision eliminated Henry Clay, the Speaker of the House at the time of the 1824 election, who had come in fourth. Clay threw his support to the second-place finisher, John Quincy Adams, who won in the House. It was alleged at the time that Clay backed Adams in exchange for a promise of appointment as secretary of state; although Clay vigorously denied the charge, Adams did subsequently appoint him to that position.

If no vice presidential candidate receives a majority in the Electoral College, the Constitution puts the responsibility for choosing a vice president on the Senate. In

THE ELECTION OF THE LOSER

Presidential candidates who received the most popular votes were defeated in the Electoral College in 1876 and 1888. And it could happen again.

The election of 1876 was marred by illegal voting and ballot fraud, especially in many of the southern states. Separate slates of Republican and Democratic electors, both claiming to have been duly elected, were filed from Florida (4), Louisiana (8), and South Carolina (7). The Republicans, who controlled the three state legislatures, contended that the Democrats had forcibly prevented African Americans from voting. The Democrats alleged that many nonresidents and nonregistered people had voted. In addition, one Republican elector in Oregon was challenged on the grounds that he held another federal position at the time and hence was ineligible to be an elector.

Three days before the Electoral College vote was to be officially counted, Congress established a commission to examine and try to resolve the disputes about the electors. The commission was to consist of fifteen members: ten from Congress (five Republicans and five Democrats) and five from the Supreme Court. Four Supreme Court justices (two Republicans and two Democrats) were designated commission members by the congressional act, and they were to choose a fifth justice. It was expected that they would select David Davis, a political independent; but on the day the commission was created, Davis was appointed to the United States Senate by the Illinois legislature. The justices then chose Joseph Bradley, an independent Republican. Bradley sided with his party on every issue. By a strictly partisan vote, the commission validated all the Republican electors, thereby giving Rutherford B. Hayes a one-vote margin of victory in the Electoral College. Hayes, with nearly a quarter of a million fewer votes than Samuel J. Tilden, the Democratic candidate, was elected president.

The other election in which the winner of the popular vote lost in the Electoral College occurred in 1888. Benjamin Harrison, the Republican candidate, had 95,096 fewer popular votes than did Grover

Rutherford B. Hayes (R)   *Samuel J. Tilden (D)*

Cleveland, the Democratic candidate. However, Cleveland had only 168 electoral votes compared with Harrison's 233, so Harrison was elected president. Cleveland's loss of Indiana by about 3,000 votes and New York by about 15,000 led to his defeat.

Although all other leaders in the popular vote have won a majority of electoral votes, shifts of just a few thousand popular votes in a few states could have altered the results of other elections, notably in 1860, 1892, 1916, 1948, 1960, 1968, and 1976. Not only could the results of these elections have been affected by very small voter shifts, but in 1948, 1960, 1968, and 1992 there was the further possibility that the Electoral College itself would not have been able to choose a winner. In each of these elections, third party candidates or independent electoral slates threatened to secure enough voters to prevent either of the major candidates from obtaining a majority. Close competition between the major parties combined with a strong third party movement provides the Electoral College with its most difficult test.

SOURCE: Stephen J. Wayne, *The Road to the White House, 1996* (New York: St. Martin's Press, 1996), 17–18.

fact, the Senate has chosen a vice president in this manner only once. In 1837, because of a personal scandal, Richard Johnson, Martin Van Buren's running mate, fell one vote short of a majority in the Electoral College. The Senate elected him anyway.

The structure and operation of the Electoral College give the largest states disproportionate influence in presidential elections because they have the most electoral votes and cast those votes as a bloc. By giving an advantage to the large states, the Electoral College benefits groups that are concentrated in those states and tend to vote cohesively: these include such groups as Jews, Hispanics, and African Americans living in urban areas. The Electoral College also favors the very smallest states, those with four electoral votes or less; these states gain more influence than they would from a direct popular vote.[33]

Presidential candidates take the Electoral College into account when planning their strategy for the general election. Their primary objective must always be to win a majority of the college, not necessarily a majority of the popular vote. To do this, they need to concentrate much of their resources in the large industrial states with the most electoral votes, because failure to win a majority of these states makes it extremely difficult to put together a winning coalition. In building their electoral coalitions, candidates begin with states where they are strong, try to add states in which they have some support, and compete in most of the large states regardless of the odds.

Since the establishment of their current coalition during the 1930s, the Democrats have focused on the northeastern and midwestern states. New York, Pennsylvania, Ohio, Illinois, Michigan, and Missouri form the core of this geographic coalition. With many of their support groups concentrated in these large states, the Democrats have traditionally needed to win fewer states than the Republicans to gain an Electoral College victory.

A shift in population and electoral votes to the southern and western states, however, has made it more difficult for the Democrats to win a majority of the Electoral College. In the last eight presidential elections only the District of Columbia, with 3 electoral votes, has voted Democratic all eight times, and only Minnesota, with 10 electoral votes, has voted Democratic in seven of them. On the other hand, ten small states outside the South, which currently have a total of 52 electoral votes, have voted for the Republican candidate in each of the last eight presidential elections. When the southern states, which have become increasingly Republican, are added to this list, the Republicans begin the campaign with a considerably larger geographic core than do the Democrats.

The Republicans were able to take advantage of this core in the 1980s, but in the 1990s they were not. Bill Clinton won several southern states in both 1992 and 1996. Moreover, the Democrats have become increasingly competitive in New England, continue to do well in the Middle Atlantic region, and have maintained or expanded their support on the Pacific Coast, including California, whose 54 electoral votes alone provided Clinton with one-fifth of the 270 necessary to win. These developments leave the main battleground states in most presidential elections in the Midwest.

Today, neither party seems to have a lock on the Electoral College vote. In the 1984 election, Republican Ronald Reagan won every state except Minnesota and the District of Columbia, giving him a landslide majority of 525 to 13 in the Electoral College. In 1988 George Bush won 41 states, with 426 electoral votes, to only 9 states and the District, with 111 electoral votes, for Democrat Michael Dukakis. But in 1992, Clinton won 32 states and the District, with a total of 370 electoral votes, and Bush took only 18 with a total of 168 electoral votes. In 1996, Clinton won 31 states and the District to Robert Dole's 19, but he increased his Electoral College majority to 379 votes versus Dole's 159. (See the Electoral College maps on pages 358–359.)

In addition to the Electoral College, the incumbency factor is usually important in the presidential election. Of the fifteen presidents who sought reelection in the twentieth century, ten won. Franklin D. Roosevelt was reelected three times. However, between 1976 and 1992 three out of four incumbents who ran for reelection lost. They suffered from increasingly negative media coverage of the presidency, an increasingly hostile public mood toward government, the weakening of party allegiances and divisions within the parties' electoral coalitions, and the persistence of adverse economic and social conditions. These factors were muted in 1984 and 1996 by the perception of growing prosperity and the absence of a threat to the national security. Being an incumbent is an advantage in good times.

Incumbency is a two-edged sword, which can both strengthen and weaken a president's claim to leadership. Incumbency usually helps presidents demonstrate those traits deemed essential for the office: experience, knowledge, direction, decisiveness, and forcefulness. But it also highlights character weaknesses, such as inconsistency, indecisiveness, or inability to stand up to opposition or to demonstrate empathy. Presidents can use their position to gain media attention, promote policies, affect events, and dispense favors. But they also are subject to more critical media scrutiny than other politicians, get blamed for conditions and events they cannot foresee or control, and are often accused of having political motivations for whatever they do.

Nonpresidential Nominations

Some of the changes that have affected presidential selection have affected the election campaigns for other offices as well. The nomination process, especially, has changed. There are now more contested nominations within the parties, and more people are likely to vote in them, particularly when they occur in presidential election years. Fundraising has become a necessity for most candidates; the mass media have become the principal communication link for reaching large numbers of voters.

The level of competition varies, however. There tends to be more competition where the two parties are evenly matched than where they are not, more competition for open seats than for seats held by an incumbent who is seeking reelection, and more competition where the party organization is not supporting a particular candidate than where it is.[34]

The competition, in turn, affects voter turnout.[35] Contested primaries naturally attract more voters than uncontested ones. Even so, only a minority of the electorate (about 30 percent) regularly participates in these nonpresidential nomination contests. The smaller the turnout, the greater the impact a strong party organization has, because it can identify and mobilize electoral support for its preferred nominees.

The strategy and tactics for nomination campaigns are similar for national, state, and local offices. The principal differences in these contests involve the cost of the campaigns, the use of media, and the ability to employ sophisticated campaign techniques, including public opinion polling. Most money tends to be spent in races for governor and United States senator. These statewide nomination campaigns are also likely to depend more on visual media, primarily television, to convey a message. Because of the cost of buying television time, candidates for other state and local offices have to rely more on radio and print journalism and try to generate more coverage on local news. Similarly, public opinion surveys, a staple for presidential, senatorial, and gubernatorial candidates, are too expensive for most other candidates, who must depend more on their own impressions, instincts, and skills.

All elections except for the presidential election are conducted by the states according to state law. This law establishes the districts in which elections are held and the rules and procedures by which they are conducted and the winners determined. Of these factors, the process and product of districting can be especially controversial.

The legal environment: reapportionment and redistricting The Constitution requires that seats in the House of Representatives be redistributed among the states every ten years on the basis of the national census. The stakes are high in this redistribution, known as **reapportionment**, since it may affect not only the number of congressional representatives a state has but also the amount of federal aid it receives. Which states gain and lose representation as a consequence of reapportionment may also affect the partisan balance or control of Congress.

Whether or not the number of congressional seats allocated to a state changes, after each census the state legislature may have to redraw the boundaries of the state's congressional and other legislative districts to reflect geographic shifts in population within the state. This process is known as **redistricting**. The party in control of the legislature naturally uses its power to draw the districts in such a way as to maximize its political advantage.[36] This practice is often referred to as **gerrymandering**, a term coined in 1812 or 1813 to describe the shape of a particular legislative district in Massachusetts during the governorship of Elbridge Gerry. The district, which looked a little like a salamander and was dubbed a "Gerry-Mander," is shown in Figure 10-2.

Gerrymandering is a powerful political tool.[37] In states where one party is clearly dominant and refuses to change the legislative district borders, the only way the party out of power can effect a change is to gain control of the legislature. But because of the way the district lines are drawn, it cannot gain control of the legislature without a large influx of new voters who favor its candidates and positions. Therefore, changes in the partisan composition of an electorate are slow to be reflected in the composition of its government.

The significant political ramifications of the census help explain why the count has been subject to challenge. After the 1990 census, several cities, states, and citizen groups alleged that several million people, primarily in the inner cities, had been missed. They were unable to convince the census bureau to adjust its population count, however, or to get the courts to force the agency to do so.

For most of American history, states enjoyed complete discretion in districting. Beginning in the 1960s, however, a series of judicial decisions set limits on that discretion. One limitation concerns the size of the population within a district. In the case of *Wesberry v. Sanders* (1964), the Supreme Court held that all congressional districts within a state must be approximately equal in population, so that no individual voter will be overrepresented or underrepresented. To do otherwise, the Court said, would be inconsistent with the principle of **one person, one vote**. Today the populations of congressional districts within a state usually cannot vary by more than 1.5 percent. However, from one state to another, the populations of districts can vary considerably. Montana, for example, has one at-large congressional district with about 850,000 people; Wyoming has one with 475,000 people. The average congressional district is almost 600,000.

From the 1930s through the 1980s, the principal beneficiaries of gerrymandering were the Democrats, who used it to preserve their dominance of both state legislatures and the House of Representatives. A good example of the successful use of partisan gerrymandering occurred in California after the 1980 census gave that state

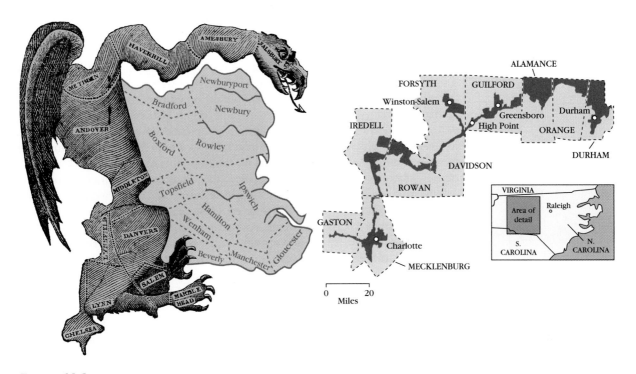

FIGURE 10-2
The first gerrymandered congressional district *(left)*, and one of the most recent, North Carolina's 12th congressional district, which was invalidated by the Supreme Court in 1996 *(right)*.

SOURCES: Data for Massachusetts from Library of Congress; for North Carolina from *New York Times*, July 29, 1993, A12.

additional House seats. The Democratic state legislature blatantly redrew the districts to their party's advantage, and the Democratic governor, Jerry Brown, signed the legislation. The Republicans protested, but to no avail. In Indiana, however, a Republican legislature and governor turned the tables on the Democrats and gained congressional seats for their party as a result of redistricting. The Democrats took the issue to court and lost, but in the process the Supreme Court ruled in the case of *Davis v. Bandemer* (1986) that partisan gerrymanders are justiciable issues—that is, they are subject to adjudication by the courts. This decision thrust the courts into the politics of redistricting.

After the 1990 census, federal judges played an active role in resolving redistricting disputes. At that time a majority of the federal judiciary had been appointed by presidents Reagan and Bush, so the judges' decisions tended to be more favorable to redistricting plans designed by Republican-controlled legislatures than to Democratic-sponsored ones.[38]

The Republicans were also aided in the early 1990s by the creation of congressional districts, largely in the South, in which a majority of voters were members of racial or ethnic minorities. Amendments to the Voting Rights Act of 1965 encouraged states to draw congressional district lines in such a way as to increase the possibility that minority candidates would be elected. The law gives the Justice Department the responsibility and authority to make sure that they do so. This discretion was utilized by both the Bush and the Clinton administrations to force states to create so-called majority-minority districts in which racial and ethnic minorities were concentrated. Their motives were different, however. The Clinton administration simply needed to respond to its African-American and Hispanic constituencies, which wanted a chance to elect more of their own members as representatives. Although the Bush administration also wanted to show that it cared about minorities, by concentrating Democratic voters in majority-minority districts it gained the added benefit of improving the chances of Republicans winning other districts. In fact, in gaining control of Congress in 1994, House Republicans picked up 19 seats in the South. One estimate was that the creation of 8 new seats to which African Americans were elected also resulted in a gain of 15 seats by the Republicans.[39]

The new majority-minority districts came under considerable criticism and legal challenges as "racial gerrymandering," because many of them were irregularly shaped, to say the least. (One of the districts created in North Carolina, shown in Figure 10-2, followed a narrow 160-mile course along an interstate highway.) In 1995 and 1996, a 5-to-4 majority of the Supreme Court ruled that no districting plan in which race was the dominant factor could meet the standards and conditions the Court has held to be required by the equal protection clause of the Fourteenth Amendment. The Court's decisions, which invalidated a majority African-American district in North Carolina and three Texas districts in which African Americans or Hispanics were the majority, had significant political ramifications. They opened all of the districts specifically designed to augment minority representation under the Voting Rights Act of 1965 to challenge by the white majority. They also gave the courts the last word on the matter.[40]

When the Georgia legislature was unable to agree on a redistricting plan in 1995, for example, a three-judge panel of a federal district court imposed a plan that eliminated two of the state's three districts in which African-American voters were in the majority. Not only did this dismay civil rights advocates but it also scared Republicans, who feared that they might lose some of their newly won congressional seats if the proportion of minority voters in those districts increased substantially. Only in North Carolina were these fears realized in 1996, as Republicans lost two seats there but held on to their other southern seats and picked up additional ones. Most of the new minority House members were also reelected from their reconfigured districts.

The institutional environment: the incumbency advantage?   Partisan gains from redistricting are reinforced in large part by incumbency. Incumbency provides recognition, which in turn generates support. Barring a high level of public dissatisfaction, the electorate is more likely to vote for candidates that it knows than for those it does not, and challengers are usually not nearly so well known.

Incumbents can also use the perquisites of their office to help themselves get reelected. The availability of staff, travel funds, and free mailings gives incumbents a head start and at the same time discourages qualified people from challenging them.[41] In addition, they have a fundraising advantage: potential contributors see incumbents as better able to help them because of their established position in government. The ability of incumbents to raise money, combined with the high costs of running (particularly for statewide office), also discourages would-be challengers. Thus those who oppose incumbents are often placed in a catch-22 situation: they cannot obtain sufficient funds, coverage, or voluntary support because their chances are not viewed as promising, and they cannot improve their chances without the necessary funds, coverage, and voluntary support. One byproduct of this predicament is an increase in the number of challenges by wealthy individuals with little political experience; another is the tendency of the party out of power to run its strongest candidates in districts where an incumbent is not seeking reelection.

The advantages of incumbency vary with the position. In general, the more visible and less service-oriented the office, the more vulnerable is the incumbent. United States senators and governors fit into this category. Their prestigious offices are more likely to attract strong challengers than are other legislative and executive positions. Moreover, their statements and policies are apt to receive the most public attention and, perhaps as a result, generate the most controversy. In contrast, members of the House of Representatives have tended to be more secure, at least until the 1990s. Although most enjoy relatively high name recognition in their districts, their role in the legislative process generally receives little scrutiny. Moreover, they can use their offices to perform constituency services, which enhance their personal reputations while downplaying any of their ideological convictions that may conflict with those of their constituents.

During the 1980s, over 90 percent of incumbents in the House of Representatives were renominated and reelected, compared with less than 80 percent of those in the Senate. In the early 1990s, when public frustration with government and the self-interested behavior of those in office reduced the power of incumbency, the reelection rate for House incumbents declined. But even with the shift in partisan control of Congress in 1994, the incumbency reelection rate was still relatively high, and it remained so in 1996. The incumbents who tend to be most vulnerable are freshmen who won their seats by narrow margins. Of the 70 Republicans who were first elected in 1994, 13 were defeated in 1996. The extent of the incumbency advantage in Congress is indicated by the data in Table 10-6.

In addition to its effect on individual candidates, the incumbency advantage works to perpetuate the ruling group within all levels and branches of government, be that group defined in partisan, demographic, or ideological terms. This advantage is one of the reasons that women, who constitute a majority of the population and vote at the same rates as men or even higher rates, have not achieved elective office in anywhere near the proportion that men have. Table 10-7 indicates the percentages of women in elective national, state, and local offices.

TABLE 10-6	CONGRESSIONAL INCUMBENCY AND REELECTION, 1980–1996					
	INCUMBENTS RUNNING IN GENERAL ELECTION		**INCUMBENTS DEFEATED IN GENERAL ELECTION**		**PERCENTAGE SUCCESSFUL**	
YEAR	**HOUSE**	**SENATE**	**HOUSE**	**SENATE**	**HOUSE**	**SENATE**
1980	398	29	31	9	90.7	55.2
1982	393	30	29	2	90.1	93.3
1984	409	29	16	3	95.4	89.6
1986	393	28	6	7	98.0	75.0
1988	408	27	6	4	98.3	85.2
1990	406	32	15	1	96.0	96.9
1992	348	27	24	4	93.1	85.2
1994	382	26	35	2	91.0	92.0
1996	361	20	21	1	94.2	95.0

Source: Norman J. Ornstein, Thomas E. Mann, and Michael J. Malbin, Vital Statistics on Congress, *1991-1992 (Washington, D.C.: Congressional Quarterly, 1992), 58-59; updated by the authors. Reprinted by permission of Congressional Quarterly, Inc.*

TABLE 10-7 **PERCENTAGES OF WOMEN IN ELECTIVE OFFICE**

LEVEL OF OFFICE	'75	'77	'79	'81	'83	'85	'87	'89	'91	'93	'94	'95
U.S. Congress	4	4	3	4	4	5	5	5	6	10	10	10
Statewide Elective	10	10	11	11	11	14	14	14	18	22	23	26
State Legislatures	8	9	10	12	13	15	16	17	18	21	21	21
County Governing Boards	3	4	5	6	8	8[a]	9	9[b]	NA	NA	NA	NA
Mayors and Municipal Councils	4	8	10	10	NA	14	NA	NA	NA	NA	NA	NA

[a]1984
[b]1988

Source: Copyright 1995, Center for the American Woman and Politics (CAWP), National Information Bank on Women in Public Office, Eagleton Institute of Politics, Rutgers University. Reprinted by permission.

The political environment: volatility and hostility   As noted in Chapter 9, the partisan disposition of the electorate, although relatively stable, does change over time. These changes have worked to reduce and now to eliminate the Democrats' partisan advantage within the electorate. Allegiances to parties have weakened, more people identify themselves as independents, and there is more split-ticket voting. All these changes have made the political environment more variable and volatile.

As mentioned in the discussion of presidential incumbency, public mistrust of government and disappointment with those in power have also affected the political environment. The movement for term limits, the defeat of prominent incumbents, and the growth of independent candidacies and political movements are products of this mood. So too has been the relatively large number of incumbent members of Congress who have chosen to retire rather than seek reelection in 1994 and 1996. To some extent the success of congressional challengers without Washington experience in the 1990s has also been a consequence of this hostile political environment.

Midterm Elections

Midterm elections, the congressional elections held in the even-numbered years between presidential elections, tend to work to the disadvantage of the party that controls the White House. Since the Civil War the president's party has lost seats in the House of Representatives in every midterm election except 1934, the election that occurred in the midst of the Great Depression. In some years these losses have been significant: 1946, 1958, 1966, 1974, and 1994. In only two of them, however (1946 and 1994), has control of Congress actually changed from one party to the other, in both cases going from a Democratic to a Republican majority.

Why does the president's party lose at midterm? Some analysts believe that it has to do with the previous presidential election, in which the victorious candidate sweeps into office fellow party members who come from marginal congressional districts, that is, districts that can be won by either party. In the midterm elections, without the president running, there are no "coattails" to help members of the president's party. Besides, some voters who supported the winning candidates for president and Congress will have become alienated by the decisions they made in office.

Moreover, with the president's coattails being no threat, the outparty can usually attract stronger candidates and raise more money than it can when the president is running for reelection. The Republicans accomplished this feat in 1994 with aggressive recruiting of their congressional candidates. The magnitude of Republican gains is indicated in Appendix E.

Organization and Strategy

Although candidates conduct their own campaigns, they tend to use similar types of campaign organizations and strategies. The components of a campaign organization are dictated by the functions that have to be performed: raising and spending money, traveling and giving speeches, monitoring opinion and creating an image, formulating and targeting a message, and meeting with the media and mounting efforts to get out the vote.

In developing and implementing a strategy, candidates must design and project a basic appeal. The appeal indicates the reasons why people should vote for them. Partisanship plays a major role in the appeal, especially for the candidate of the dominant party in the area. In articulating partisan themes, candidates normally stress issues that conjure up positive associations with their party and have the most direct impact on constituents, such as jobs, taxes, and crime and other social issues. Negative images of the opposition party are also part of most campaign messages. Democratic candidates refer to the Republicans as the party of the rich, the party of big business, the party that is insensitive to the plight of the less fortunate. Republicans, in turn, describe the Democrats as the party of big government, big spending, and big taxes.

Traditionally, foreign affairs have not played as large a role as domestic affairs in most campaigns, even at the national level. However, in recent elections the impact of foreign policy on the economy, on international politics, and on leadership itself has been sufficient to force candidates for national office to address international matters such as United States military and economic aid to other countries, peacekeeping operations, open markets and free trade, and even issues such as human rights. In 1980 the presence of American hostages in Iran was a major issue. In 1984 the arms race and funding for the Reagan administration's Strategic Defense Initiative ("Star Wars") were of concern. In 1988 attention shifted to arms control. The end of the cold war and concern about a range of domestic issues have muted the impact of foreign policy since the 1980s.

How do candidates demonstrate their qualifications for the positions they seek? Incumbents point to their experience, their record, and their performance in office. Challengers describe their own potential and criticize their opponents' record. In an election in which none of the candidates is an incumbent, experience in other public offices or, occasionally, other types of work may be cited as qualifications. Increasingly, neophyte candidates for major positions such as senator or governor engage in extensive media advertising to gain public recognition, exploit their strengths and their opponents' weaknesses, and build support for their candidacy.

In the end, the object is to amass a winning coalition. Beginning with a core of strong party loyalists, candidates need to hold on to their weaker partisan supporters, attract independents, and gain some support among members of the opposition party. This is why candidates of the dominant party have traditionally emphasized their partisan affiliation and those of the other major party have stressed their leadership abilities and issue positions when appealing to independent voters and weak party supporters.

In many local governments in the United States, officials are chosen in nonpartisan elections in which issue positions and candidate images are the central elements

CHRISTINE TODD WHITMAN: NEW JERSEY'S TAX-CUTTER GOVERNOR

Republican Christine Todd Whitman was elected the 50th governor of New Jersey on November 2, 1993. Her victory over Governor James J. Florio was noteworthy in two respects: first, she became the first candidate to defeat an incumbent New Jersey governor in a general election; and second, she became the first female governor in the history of the state.

On January 24, 1994, Whitman emerged into the national spotlight when she delivered the nationally televised Republican response to President Bill Clinton's State of the Union address. Traditionally, the opposition party's response to the State of the Union message had been delivered by party leaders in Congress. Whitman was chosen because the Republican party wanted to stress the devolution of power from Washington to the states.

Whitman's political career began in 1982 when she was elected to the Somerset County Board of Chosen Freeholders. She was reelected in 1985. In 1988, she was appointed by Governor Thomas H. Kean as president of the New Jersey Board of Public Utilities. Resigning that position in 1990 to run for the United States Senate, she came close to unseating Democratic incumbent Bill Bradley.

Whitman's 1993 gubernatorial campaign was run on a platform of cutting taxes and reducing the size of government. As governor, she kept her promise by pushing a 15 percent tax cut through the legislature in her first year in office. Whitman also reduced the huge budget deficit left by her predecessor by setting aside less money for pension and health-care costs for retirees and by tapping into surpluses built up in a variety of special state funds.

Although critics called this move a fraud that could shift billions of dollars of obligations onto future generations, Whitman argued that the pensions were overfunded.[1] She has also been criticized for reducing the budget of New Jersey's environmental office and easing regulations on toxic waste cleanup.[2]

Public opinion polls in 1994 indicated that Whitman was the most popular first-year governor in modern New Jersey history. Her management style and competence won her respect and admiration from her fellow Republicans and her Democratic critics alike. In 1994 gubernatorial elections, her policy approach of cutting taxes and reducing the size of government was embraced by Republican candidates nationwide.

Despite her fiscal conservativism, Whitman is moderate on social issues. She was one of the founders of Republicans for Choice and in 1996 led efforts to soften the Republicans' pro-life platform position on the abortion issue. She also opposed the congressional Republicans' welfare plan as too severe.

Some people attribute Whitman's popularity more to her political style than to her policy achievements. In sharp contrast to many politicians from both parties who thrive on generating controversies, she has practiced a kind of politics of consensus. Her administra-

of the campaign. Party labels are not used and, in fact, the leading contenders may all be associated with the same party. Thus they have to distinguish themselves in other ways.

ANALYZING THE ELECTION RESULTS

When the campaigns are over and the voters have made their decisions, political pundits, media analysts, party officials, and the winning and losing candidates dissect and evaluate the election. This analysis is important for several reasons. It helps the winners define and claim their electoral mandate—what the people want them to do. It helps the losers know why they lost and, equally important, what they

tion has been politically and socially diverse. A few of the high-ranking officials she appointed were Democrats, among them her welfare commissioner and a top budget officer. Her press secretary was a political independent; her secretary of state was an African-American woman; and she also appointed the first African American to the State Supreme Court.

Whitman's Republican loyalty and interest in politics run in her family. Her father, Webster Todd, was chairman of the New Jersey Republican party in the 1960s and 1970s; and her mother, Eleanor Todd, and grandmother were Republican national committeewomen. She has followed in their footsteps.

A few months before his death, former president Richard M. Nixon, a New Jersey resident, suggested in a conversation with commentator William Safire that the Republicans needed a woman such as Whitman on the ticket for the 1996 presidential election. And when he was Senate Majority Leader, Robert Dole once confirmed: "She'd certainly be on anybody's short list [for vice president]." After Dole had clinched the 1996 Republican presidential nomination, however, Whitman called him to say she had no interest in being his running mate and would prefer to continue as governor of New Jersey.

[1] Lisa Belkin, "Keeping to the Center Lane," *New York Times Magazine*, May 5, 1996, 66.
[2] Ibid., 81.

Christine Todd Whitman delivers her 1995 State of the State address to the New Jersey legislature. As a fiscally conservative, socially moderate, and personally popular woman governor of a major state, she has been prominently mentioned as a future presidential or vice presidential candidate.

might do to win the next time around. For other observers, it helps to clarify the meaning of the election, obviously an important concern for a government based on popular consent.

Most interpretations of elections have focused on the presidency. The midterm election of 1994 is an exception. The magnitude of the Republicans' victory at the national and state levels generated more than the usual amount of interest and led many to view the results in national rather than local terms.

To understand who voted for whom and why, researchers conduct surveys in which voters are asked to identify the principal reasons for their choices and how they feel about the candidates and issues. The two most frequently cited surveys of this sort are the large exit polls conducted for the major news networks, newspa-

TABLE 10-8 **PORTRAIT OF THE ELECTORATE, 1988–1996 (PERCENTAGES)**

	1996 TOTAL	1988		1992			1996		
		BUSH	DUKAKIS	CLINTON	BUSH	PEROT	CLINTON	DOLE	PEROT
Total vote:		53	45	43	38	19	49	41	8
Men	48	57	41	41	38	21	43	44	10
Women	52	50	49	46	37	17	54	38	7
Whites	83	59	40	39	41	20	43	46	9
Blacks	10	12	86	82	11	7	84	12	4
Hispanics	5	30	69	62	25	14	72	21	6
Asians	1	—	—	29	55	16	43	48	8
Married	66	57	42	40	40	20	44	46	9
Unmarried	34	46	53	49	33	18	57	31	9
18–29 years old	17	52	47	44	34	22	53	34	10
30–44 years old	33	54	45	42	38	20	48	41	9
45–59 years old	26	57	42	41	40	19	48	41	9
60 and older	24	50	49	50	38	12	48	44	7
Not high school graduate	6	43	56	55	28	17	59	28	11
High school graduate	24	50	49	43	36	20	51	35	13
Some college education	27	57	42	42	37	21	48	40	10
College graduate or more	43	56	43	44	39	18	47	44	7
College graduate	26	62	37	40	41	19	44	46	8
Postgraduate education	17	50	48	49	36	15	52	40	5
White Protestant	46	66	33	33	46	21	36	53	10
Catholic	29	52	47	44	36	20	53	37	9
Jewish	3	35	64	78	12	10	78	16	3
White born-again Christian	17	81	18	23	61	15	26	65	8
Union household	23	42	57	55	24	21	59	30	9
Family's financial situation compared with four years earlier									
Better today	33	—	—	24	62	14	66	26	6
Same today	45	—	—	41	41	18	46	45	8
Worse today	20	—	—	61	14	25	27	57	13

pers, and wire services on election day (see Table 10-8) and a smaller but more comprehensive pre- and postelection survey conducted by the National Election Center at the University of Michigan for scholars across the country. Interpretations of these data often produce mixed messages, but they do suggest the dominant issues, images, and partisan allegiances that seem to have shaped the retrospective and prospective judgments of the electorate.

The Presidential Election

In 1976 it was the Watergate scandal, President Ford's pardon of Richard Nixon, and a shaky economy that contributed to challenger Jimmy Carter's victory. That Carter himself was a southern Democrat, a moderate, and a Washington outsider at a time

TABLE 10-8 **PORTRAIT OF THE ELECTORATE, 1988–1996 (PERCENTAGES)** *(continued)*

	1996 TOTAL	1988 BUSH	1988 DUKAKIS	1992 CLINTON	1992 BUSH	1992 PEROT	1996 CLINTON	1996 DOLE	1996 PEROT
Family income									
under $15,000	11	—	—	59	23	18	59	28	11
$15,000–$29,999	23	—	—	45	35	20	53	36	9
$30,000–$49,999	27	—	—	41	38	21	48	40	10
$50,000 and over	39	62	37	39	44	17	44	48	7
$75,000 and over	18	—	—	36	48	16	41	51	7
$100,000 and over	9	65	32	—	—	—	38	54	6
From the East	23	50	49	47	35	18	55	34	9
From the Midwest	26	52	47	42	37	21	48	41	10
From the South	30	58	41	42	43	16	46	46	7
From the West	20	52	46	44	34	22	48	40	8
Republicans	35	91	8	10	73	17	13	80	6
Independents	26	55	43	38	32	30	43	35	17
Democrats	39	17	82	77	10	13	84	10	5
Liberals	20	18	81	68	14	18	78	11	7
Moderates	47	49	50	48	31	21	57	33	9
Conservatives	33	80	19	18	65	17	20	71	8
Employed	64	56	43	42	38	20	48	40	9
Full-time student	—	44	54	50	35	15	—	—	—
Unemployed	36	37	62	56	24	20	49	42	8
Homemaker	—	58	41	36	45	19	—	—	—
Retired	—	50	49	51	36	13	—	—	—
First-time voters	9	51	47	48	30	22	54	34	11

Notes: Data for 1988 based on surveys of 11,645 voters conducted by the *New York Times* and CBS News. Data for 1992 collected by Voter Research and Surveys and based on questionnaires completed by 15,490 voters leaving 300 polling places around the nation on Election Day. Data for 1996 collected by Voter News Service and based on questionnaires completed by 16,627 voters. Those who gave no answer are not shown. Dashes indicate that a question was not asked or a category was not provided in a particular year. "Born-again Christian" was labeled "born-again Christian/fundamentalist" in 1992 and "fundamentalist and evangelical Christian" in 1988. In 1996, "Employed" includes only those employed full time; all others are listed as unemployed.

Source: New York Times, *November 28, 1993, B9, and November 10, 1996, 28. Copyright © 1993 by The New York Times Company. Reprinted by permission.*

when insiders were viewed with suspicion helped him defeat the incumbent Republican president.

When Carter sought reelection four years later, however, being a Democrat, a southerner, a moderate, and an incumbent was not enough. Poor performance ratings overcame the advantage that partisanship and incumbency usually bring to the president of the dominant party. The first time Carter ran for president, he had been judged on the basis of his *potential* for office; the second time, he was judged on his *actual* performance in office, and that judgment was harsh. The vote for Carter fell below his 1976 totals in every single state.

Ronald Reagan was the beneficiary of the electorate's decision that Carter did not deserve another four years as president. By 1980 it was Reagan, not Carter, who voters believed had the greater *potential* for leadership. That potential was the primary reason he won: not his ideology, policy positions, or personal appeal.

Four years later it was a different story. Then Reagan's personal appeal, policy successes, and strong leadership contributed to his victory. Voters rewarded him for what they considered a job well done. Although they had voted *against* Carter in the previous election, they voted *for* Reagan in 1984.

This trend of retrospective voting continued in 1988. George Bush won because the electorate evaluated the Reagan administration positively, associated Bush with that administration, and concluded that he—not his Democratic opponent, Michael Dukakis—would be better able and more likely to maintain the good times and the policies and leadership that produced them. Bush's favorable image and Dukakis's negative one seemed to reinforce this judgment.

Analysis of the 1992 election also suggests that it was a retrospective vote, but one that worked to the president's disadvantage. An unhappy electorate turned Bush out of office because they were disgruntled about his leadership, his economic policies, and a myriad of other domestic problems. Although people had serious reservations about Bill Clinton's character and lack of national experience, they still saw him as more likely to effect change, particularly with respect to the economy. And the economy was the most important issue for a majority of voters. Thus Clinton won despite his personal vulnerabilities.

The mood of the country also provided the climate that permitted the independent candidacy of H. Ross Perot to get off the ground. Tapping the anger and frustration of the voters, Perot promised to do something about the problems of the deficit, the faltering economy, and a deadlocked and out-of-touch government. His straight talk and unconventional campaign, targeted to those who were "sick and tired" of the way things were going—those who had lost confidence in the major parties and their candidates—won him almost as many votes among independents as Clinton and Bush got (see Table 10-8, pages 354–355). However, Perot failed to persuade enough Republicans and Democrats to support his candidacy. His failure to do so attests to the difficulty that independent candidates face with the American electorate and in the Electoral College. Perot won no states and received no electoral votes despite the fact that he received 19 million popular votes.

By 1996, the economy was stronger, crime had decreased, and the nation remained at peace—all conditions that favor incumbents. Voters responded accordingly, reelecting the Democratic president and the Republican congressional majority. Clinton won more popular and electoral votes than in 1992, although the regional composition of his vote remained essentially the same. Despite misgivings about some aspects of the president's character—notably his honesty, his ideological leanings, and his willingness to stand up for his beliefs—voters saw him as more caring, more in touch with the times, and more visionary than his Republican opponent, Robert Dole. In comparison to 1992, the population groups that shifted most strongly toward the president were women, who responded to his pledges to preserve federal social welfare programs and to strengthen government support for families, and voters under age 30. Dole, in his fourth campaign for national office, and Perot, in his second, also suffered from no longer being new faces to which voters could look for a fresh alternative to the incumbent. As the candidate of the newly organized Reform Party, Perot drew less than half the number of votes he had in 1996.

In short, the 1996 election was a referendum on the Clinton presidency, and Clinton won. Not only did the electorate evaluate his first term favorably, but they saw the president as more capable than either of his major opponents of understanding and handling the challenges of the late 1990s and, in his words, "building a bridge to the twenty-first century."

Midterm Elections

Most midterm elections do not lend themselves to a single interpretation, although the results of those elections—that is, the composition of the new Congress—affect public policy for the country as a whole. Even though the news media read into the election certain national trends and issues, the dominant concerns for most voters most of the time are local personalities, parties, and constituency-related issues.

The midterm elections of 1946 and 1994 were different. In 1946, the voters reacted against sixteen years of Democratic control, against a Democratic president, Harry Truman, who was not perceived to be of the same stature as his much revered predecessor, Franklin Roosevelt, and against various scandals that had marred the Truman presidency.

In 1994, the voters protested against Democratic leadership. They reacted against a Democratic president who had not lived up to expectations, to a Democratic Congress that seemed unable or unwilling to follow his lead, to a Democratic party internally divided over a multitude of issues, and to a Democratic philosophy of government that seemed out of tune with the public's antigovernment, anti-Washington mood.

ELECTIONS AND GOVERNANCE

Elections influence what government does, particularly in the year following the election. That is why understanding the meaning of the election is so important. Contrary to popular belief, campaign promises and party platforms do get translated

Republican presidential candidate Robert Dole campaigns at the 1996 Veterans of Foreign Wars convention. Dole, who had been severely disabled by wounds he suffered in World War II, tried to make an issue of President Clinton's avoidance of military service during the Vietnam War, but with little apparent success. Voters seemed satisfied with Clinton's performance in office and rewarded him with another term.

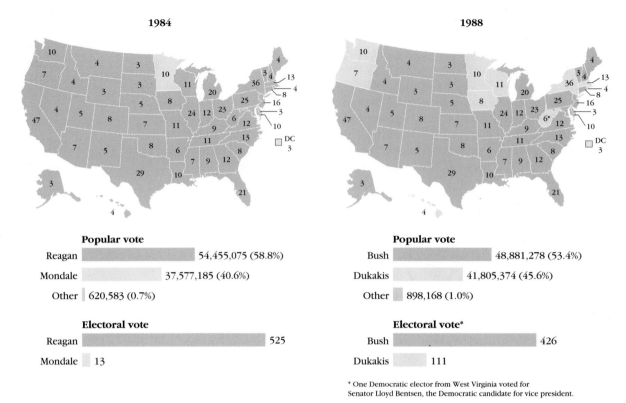

1984

1988

Popular vote

Reagan 54,455,075 (58.8%)
Mondale 37,577,185 (40.6%)
Other 620,583 (0.7%)

Electoral vote

Reagan 525
Mondale 13

Popular vote

Bush 48,881,278 (53.4%)
Dukakis 41,805,374 (45.6%)
Other 898,168 (1.0%)

Electoral vote*

Bush 426
Dukakis 111

* One Democratic elector from West Virginia voted for
Senator Lloyd Bentsen, the Democratic candidate for vice president.

FIGURE 10-3

The Electoral College vote, 1984–1996.

SOURCES: Data for 1984 and 1988 adapted from "America at the Polls 2: The Vote for President, 1968–1984," *Congressional Quarterly Almanac,* as it appeared in the New York Times, November 4, 1992, B13. Data for 1992 adapted from *Congressional Quarterly,* November 7, 1992, 3549. Reprinted by permission of Congressional Quarterly, Inc. Data for 1996 from *Newsday,* November 7, 1996, A39.

into public policy. Media scrutiny, frequent elections, and the desire to be reelected provide incentives for redeeming campaign promises and staying responsive to the electorate.

On the other hand, elections are rarely clear mandates, even though public officials may claim them. A poll taken before the 1994 elections found that even of those respondents who planned to vote Republican, only about 25 percent knew anything about the Republicans' Contract with America.[42] Moreover, Republican senators did not as a group declare their allegiance to the Contract as their House counterparts had done.

A mixed judgment is not unusual. People vote for the same candidate for different reasons, and they vote for different candidates for the same reason. They also vote for many different officials. As a consequence, the results of the election may yield seemingly contradictory messages. Differing national, state, and local constituencies also tend to produce outcomes that mirror the political system's decentralization and diversity more than a dominant public mood. Perhaps this is why divided partisan control at the national level has been the rule, not the exception, since 1968. Separate institutions and divided control of them has made governing more difficult precisely because the Republicans and Democrats have different and often competing priorities and policy agendas.

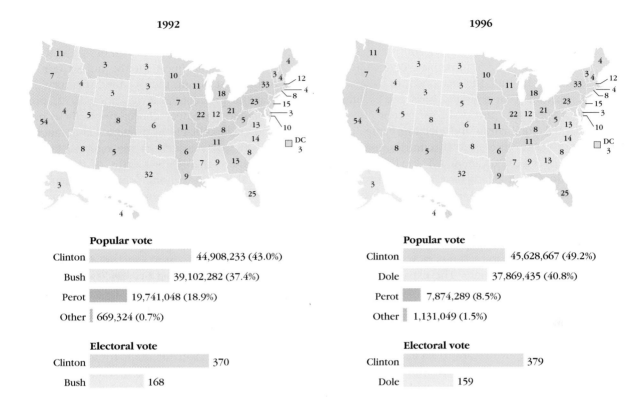

1992

1996

Popular vote

Clinton — 44,908,233 (43.0%)

Bush — 39,102,282 (37.4%)

Perot — 19,741,048 (18.9%)

Other — 669,324 (0.7%)

Electoral vote

Clinton — 370

Bush — 168

Popular vote

Clinton — 45,628,667 (49.2%)

Dole — 37,869,435 (40.8%)

Perot — 7,874,289 (8.5%)

Other — 1,131,049 (1.5%)

Electoral vote

Clinton — 379

Dole — 159

Finally, the length of the electoral process and the promises made by candidates to obtain and retain office have increased public expectations of government performance and, at the same time, made those expectations harder to meet. Today's successful candidates usually owe less to their party leaders and organizations than to themselves, their campaign organizations, and their constituencies. Once in office and over time, they tend to behave independently, guided more by the people who elected them than by their party's official position on current issues. At the national level, especially, this has produced more elected public officials who wish to lead and fewer who are willing to follow them.

SUMMARY

Electoral politics are the foundation upon which a democratic political system rests. They frame policy debate, determine legislative and top executive officials, and influence the decisions these officials make as well as the initial agenda they pursue. In this way electoral politics shape the who, when, and what of American government. It would be difficult to conceive of how representative government could function and public policy be formulated without regular elections, competing candidates, and partisan divisions.

Yet in the early years of the nation, suffrage was extremely limited. It took three amendments to the Constitution to remove racial and gender barriers to voting and extend *suffrage* to all citizens 18 years of age and older.

States still establish the rules and procedures for the conduct of elections. The more rigorous these requirements are, the lower voter turnout is likely to be. State laws also govern primary elections. If these laws conflict with party rules, the Supreme Court has held that parties may determine and enforce their own rules for delegate selection.

In recent years one of the critical issues concerning the democratic character of elections has been money. Congress has sought to regulate contributions and expenditures through the enactment of campaign finance legislation. That legislation has placed limits on campaign spending, provided government support for presidential nomination and election campaigns, and required public disclosure of contributions and expenditures over a certain amount. These laws, which may have reduced but clearly have not eliminated the disproportionate influence of the wealthy on the electoral process, have also contributed to factionalism within the parties and reduced the parties' influence on candidates.

Elections are critical for a democracy, but so is the participation of the electorate. The expansion of suffrage increased the number of eligible voters, but not the percentage of those who actually vote. Turnout declined from 1960 to 1990, went up in 1992, but declined again in 1994. Among the factors that have contributed to lower turnout are weakening party identification, mobility among younger voters, and the growing number of elderly people with poor health and less interest in politics. Government scandals have also increased the apathy and cynicism of the electorate.

The principal demographic characteristics that relate to voting are education, socio-economic status, and age, all of which correlate with one another. Older, better-educated, and higher-income people tend to vote more often and thus are in a better position to influence policy makers than are those who are younger and less educated and have lower incomes—people with greater needs that government could address. Voter turnout also varies with partisanship, interest in the election, concern over the outcome, sense of civic responsibility, trust in government, and political efficacy. People who identify strongly with a political party, follow the election, and care who wins will vote more often than those who lack these motivations.

Party identification is particularly important because it provides a framework for analysis and offers cues for assessing the candidates and their stands. Group associations influence voting because they generate cross-pressures that find expression in the political process—and that may reinforce or undermine partisan inclinations. The candidates and the issues also affect how people vote.

Candidates and parties contrive their campaigns to affect the electorate's judgment. There are usually two campaigns: one is to gain a party's nomination and, if that is successful, the other is to win the general election. Of the two, the quest for the nomination has changed the most during the twentieth century, particularly at the presidential level. Since 1972, presidential nominees have been chosen primarily by party activists and sympathizers in primaries and caucuses rather than by party leaders at the national convention. Today more than three-fourths of the pledged delegates to the national nominating conventions are chosen in state primary elections, with the remainder being chosen in multistaged party *caucuses*. The Democrats also designate party leaders and elected officials as *superdelegates*.

Modern presidential campaigns usually start well before the first caucuses and primaries are held. One reason for this is that it takes time to raise the money needed for a serious campaign. Millions of dollars are needed to build an organization, pay for television time, conduct public opinion polls, and develop voter appeals. Another reason for competing in the early contests is that there are more of them. The presidential selection process has become heavily front loaded, and candidates have no choice but to enter these early primaries and caucuses to gain recognition and win delegates.

The national nominating convention formally decides the party's rules, chooses its presidential and vice presidential nominees, and approves its election platform. Usually the nominees have been preordained by the delegate selection process. In cases in which the nomination is in doubt, the front-runner tries to generate a *bandwagon effect*, inducing uncommitted delegates and delegates pledged to other candidates to join the winning team. An important function of the convention is to unify groups that have been divided by the nomination process and launch the general election campaign with a broad national appeal.

The president is actually chosen by a group of *electors*, meeting as the *Electoral College*. The voters in each state select a group of electors equal in number to the state's senators and representatives; these usually vote as a bloc for the presidential and vice presidential candidates who have won the popular vote in the state. Candidates take the Electoral College into account when devising their campaign strategy. Democrats and Republicans try to expand their geographic base by concentrating their campaigns in the states with the largest populations, to which the Electoral College system gives disproportionate influence.

Some of the changes that have affected the presidential selection process have affected nonpresidential selection as well. Primaries have become the route to nomination at most levels of government. These primaries have led to more competition within the parties and have left them more factionalized. To win the nomination, candidates must build their own organization, raise their own money, design their own strategy, and mount a campaign that appeals to those partisans who are most likely to participate.

The rules and procedures governing the general election have also changed, particularly as they apply to *redistricting*. Every ten years the seats in the House of Representatives are redistributed on the basis of the national census. Because of this *reapportionment* and population shifts within states, legislatures may also have to redraw the boundaries of congressional and other legislative districts so that the population of each district within a state remains approximately equal. *Gerrymandering*, the practice of redistricting in such a way as to favor the party in power, is still common. However, the creation of districts to benefit candidates of racial and ethnic minorities has been successfully challenged in court in recent years.

For members of Congress, being in office is usually advantageous for staying in office. The services incumbents provide to their constituencies and the recognition they have affect the amount of money they can raise, which in turn helps them in seeking reelection. Although the president's party normally loses congressional seats in midterm elections, Democratic incumbents suffered more losses than usual in 1994, when their party lost control of both houses of Congress for the first time in forty years.

Who wins does matter in terms of what government does, particularly in the year following the election. Most elections are referendums on the people and the policies of those in power. The electorate evaluates how the government has worked and credits or blames those in office.

Elections are important because they provide an agenda of priorities as well as a potential coalition of supporters. It is up to those in power to convert that agenda into a series of proposals and mobilize a coalition to support them. They usually claim an election mandate to do so.

KEY TERMS

universal suffrage
meaningful choice
political equality
split-ticket voting
retrospective voting
prospective voting

caucus
superdelegate
proportional voting
winner-take-all voting
bandwagon effect
elector

Electoral College
general ticket system
reapportionment
redistricting
gerrymandering
one person, one vote

RESOURCES

SCHOLARLY STUDIES

Abramson, Paul R., John H. Aldrich, and David W. Rohde. *Change and Continuity in the 1992 Elections*. Washington, D.C.: Congressional Quarterly, 1994, and volumes for previous elections. A thorough analysis of the vote in presidential elections.

Campbell, Angus, Philip E. Converse, Warren E. Miller, and Donald E. Stokes. *The American Voter*. Chicago: University of Chicago Press, 1980. A classic study that postulates a theory of voting behavior that is still applicable. Not easy reading, but worth the effort.

Jacobson, Gary C. *The Politics of Congressional Elections*. 3d ed. New York: HarperCollins, 1991. A thorough analysis of the impact of party, incumbency, money, and other factors on the outcome of congressional elections.

Maisel, L. Sandy. *Political Parties and Elections in the United States.* New York: Garland Publishing, 1991. A two-volume encyclopedia on parties and their candidates.

Nie, Norman H., Sidney Verba, and John R. Petrocik. *The Changing American Voter.* Cambridge, Mass.: Harvard University Press, 1980. A skillful examination of voting patterns.

Rosenstone, Steven J., and John M. Hansen. *Mobilization, Participation, and Democracy in America.* New York: Macmillan, 1993. A comprehensive study of political participation. The authors suggest that economic interests may be less important motivating factors than moral values and ideological perspectives.

Sorauf, Frank J. *Inside Campaign Finance: Myths and Realities.* New Haven, Conn.: Yale University Press, 1992. A good source of information about campaign finance.

Wattenberg, Martin P. *The Rise of Candidate-Centered Politics.* Cambridge, Mass.: Harvard University Press, 1991. An examination of presidential elections during the 1980s and their increasing candidate orientation.

Wayne, Stephen J. *The Road to the White House, 1996.* New York: St. Martin's Press, 1996, postelection edition, 1997. A nuts-and-bolts description of the arduous quest for the nomination and the general election.

Wolfinger, Raymond E., and Steven J. Rosenstone. *Who Votes?* New Haven, Conn.: Yale University Press, 1980. An attempt to answer the questions of who votes and why by examining the impact of socioeconomic status, age, sex, political culture, and state laws on voter turnout.

LEISURE READING

Anonymous [Joe Klein]. *Primary Colors.* New York: Random House, 1996. A fictionalized account of the 1992 Clinton campaign.

Cramer, Richard Ben. *What It Takes: The Way to the White House.* New York: Random House, 1992. A highly readable journalistic account of the candidates in 1988, with emphasis on their motivation and drive for the presidency.

Crouse, Timothy. *The Boys on the Bus.* New York: Ballantine, 1986. A not-so-flattering account of the

press corps's coverage of the 1972 presidential campaign.

Matalin, Mary, and James Carville with Peter Knobler. *All's Fair: Love, War, and Running for President.* New York: Random House, 1994. Two senior Bush and Clinton campaign managers give their behind-the-scenes account of the 1992 presidential election and their romance.

White, Theodore H. *The Making of the President, 1960.* New York: Atheneum, 1989. A classic description of the Kennedy-Nixon race by a journalist who observed the campaign and the candidates up close.

Woodward, Bob. *The Choice.* New York: Simon & Schuster, 1996. An inside account of the beginning of the 1996 presidential campaign by a well-known journalist who had access to most of the principals and their aides.

PRIMARY SOURCES

Guide to U.S. Elections. 3d ed. Washington, D.C.: Congressional Quarterly, 1994. A collection of statistical data on elections for Congress, the presidency, and governorships as well as information on parties.

Scammon, Richard, ed. *American Votes.* Washington, D.C.: Congressional Quarterly, 1955–present. Official election statistics compiled on a state-by-state basis for every election since 1954.

ORGANIZATIONS

House Oversight Committee, 1309 Longworth Office Building, Washington, DC 20515; phone (202) 225-8281, fax (202) 225-9957; Internet http://www .house.gov/cho/ Holds hearings on legislation dealing with the electoral process and publishes transcripts of them; oversees the Federal Election Commission.

Federal Election Commission, 999 E Street, N.W., Washington, DC 20463; phone (800) 424-9530, fax (202) 219-3880, Internet http://www.fec.gov Issues a monthly newsletter, press releases, and various other reports in addition to its public computer file on campaign expenditures for all national campaigns.

Inter-University Consortium for Political and Social Research, University of Michigan, Ann Arbor, MI 48104; phone (313) 763-5010, fax (313) 764-8041,

Internet http://www.icpsr.umich.edu/ Has conducted national surveys during presidential and congressional elections since 1952 and disseminates data to scholars for analyses of voting behavior.

League of Women Voters, 1730 M Street, N.W., Suite 1000, Washington, DC 20036; phone (202) 429-1965, fax (202) 429-0854, Internet http://www.lwv.org/ Provides information to voters on election rules and procedures at the national, state, and local levels; also provides information on candidates' positions.

Senate Committee on Rules and Administration, 305 Russell Office Building, Washington, DC 20510; phone (202) 224-6352, fax (202) 224-3036, Internet http://www.senate.gov/committee/rules.html Holds hearings on legislation dealing with the electoral process and publishes transcripts of them; oversees the Federal Election Commission.

Politics and the News Media

T he first bomb went off in Chicago in 1978. A security guard was hurt, but no one was killed. The second exploded a year later at nearby Northwestern University, injuring a graduate student. The third explosion occurred on an airline flight originating in Chicago. Constructed in a similar manner, the bombs seemed to suggest that a serial bomber was at work. When the fourth went off in Chicago in 1980, injuring the president of United Airlines, the FBI dubbed its investigation of the case UNABOM after the apparent targets, universities and airlines.

The bombings continued but spread beyond the Chicago area to Vanderbilt University and the University of California at Berkeley. The first fatality occurred in 1985, when a person was killed outside a computer store in Sacramento, California, to which a bomb was mailed. No one claimed responsibility for any of these blasts, and the FBI had few solid leads. In 1993, after explosions occurred again at UC Berkeley and at Yale University, injuring two faculty members, the *New York Times* received a letter from an alleged anarchist group, the Freedom Club, claiming that it had set off the bombs. More letters, threats, and bombs followed—all widely publicized by the news media. By this point, the FBI had put together a profile of the culprit, who appeared to be a well educated man, perhaps with a graduate degree in engineering or mathematics, who had a grudge against modern industrial society and those who contributed to it.

In 1995, after a threat to bomb a plane at Los Angeles International Airport was made, the *New York Times* and the *Washington Post* each received a 56-page manifesto entitled "Industrial Society and Its Future." Along with this document, the author sent a letter promising to end the bombings if the newspapers published his essay. The promise placed the newspapers and law enforcement officials in a dilemma. Publication of the document could be viewed as a victory for the "Unabomber" and might encourage others to engage in similar illegal activities or threats to public security in order to gain a podium for their views. On the other hand, the bombings, which had killed three people, injured many others, and caused widespread public anxiety, might cease. After considerable debate and with no apparent break in the case, the newspapers decided to produce a joint publication that was printed and distributed by the *Post* in September 1995. The Unabomber had achieved his principal objective, the dissemination of views criticizing modern technology, and had done so with the help of the news media. Were they now accomplices in the crimes?

But the communication intended to warn of technology's evils soon became technology's captive. Long after copies of the manifesto had disappeared from newsstands, it continued to circulate on the Internet, kept alive by a Unabomber cult that regularly exchanged information about their mysterious, inventive, "hero." It was on the Net that David Kaczynski read portions of the Unabomber's views, which he concluded bore a remarkable resemblance to his brother's thoughts and writings. After much soul-searching, Kaczynski alerted federal authorities to the similarities. Theodore Kaczynski was arrested on April 3, 1996, at his primitive cabin in the mountains of Montana and charged with the bombings. A search of the cabin found three typewriters that officials believe he had used to write his letters to the newspapers, addresses for the mail bombs, and the manifesto itself.

Thus the media, responsible in large part for the publicity the Unabomber received for his actions, threats, and beliefs, were also responsible for providing the information that may have ultimately resulted in his capture. Obviously, the dissemination of information is a critical function of the press in a democratic society. However, by reporting an event, the media can become part of it, influencing the very story they cover. That happened with the Unabomber, and it wasn't the first time—nor will it be the last.

The Unabomber case also illustrates the delicate relationship between the news media and government in the United States. In fact, it was somewhat unusual in that two major newspapers cooperated with a government agency to try to work out a course of action that would best serve the public interest. More commonly, the American media consider that they best serve this interest by taking an adversarial, critical stance toward the people and institutions of politics and government. Especially in recent decades, this role has often had a significant impact.

The exposure of the White House connection to the Watergate burglary during the Nixon administration, the reporting of atrocities during the Vietnam War, the nightly television news program on the captivity of American diplomats held hostage in Iran, the revelation of arms sales to Iran, and, later, the diversion of funds to rebels fighting the Marxist government in Nicaragua—all helped focus public attention on major problems, forced government officials to react to those problems, and set off a series of decisions and actions that ultimately affected government, public policy, and the political environment.

The news media affect the politics of American government in a variety of ways: they focus attention on salient issues; create a time frame in which those issues are addressed; influence the content, tone, and parameters of public debate; and convey and evaluate the decisions and actions of those in power. Thus they play two critical roles for democratic government: they constitute principal vessels through which information is transmitted, and they influence that very information and how people may react to it by the manner in which they report it. In this sense the news media continually affect the reality they purport to describe and assess. That is why they are often referred to as the fourth branch of government.

This chapter examines the news media and their impact on American politics. The first section discusses the role of media in a democratic society, and the second reviews the conditions under which media can exist and flourish and the protections provided by the United States Constitution for a free press. The evolution of the media in America from print to electronic formats to the computer age of the Internet is the subject of the third section. The fourth section examines the media's coverage of American politics, primarily elections: its orientation, its content, and its impact. The fifth turns to coverage of government and reexamines the issues of orientation, content, and impact. In the final part of the chapter, the cumulative effect of the news media on the political system is assessed.

NEWS MEDIA IN A DEMOCRATIC SOCIETY

Newspapers, radio, and television are essential for a democracy. They are a vital link between the people and their public officials. They provide information and analysis about policy issues; they also sensitize those in government to public opinion, enabling policy makers to respond to the needs and desires of the population. Moreover, the news media play an important role in reporting and evaluating the decisions of government, a role that is critical for holding those in power accountable for their decisions and actions.

To perform those functions adequately the news media need to operate freely, with as few restrictions as possible on their collection and dissemination of infor-

The value of a free press for a democracy lies in its revelation of truth. But the media can also create perceptions of problems where none may exist. In January 1992, George Bush vomited and nearly fainted at a state dinner in Japan. The problem was a stomach virus, but rumors persisted that the president was more seriously ill. Were the media performing a critical public service by giving this event such detailed coverage?

mation. They need to be a "marketplace of ideas," a forum in which the truth will emerge. In a government based on the consent of the governed, such a forum is essential not only for discerning truth but for evaluating the performance of public officials.

In authoritarian political systems, news media have a different function. Far from criticizing the government, they are its biggest booster, buttressing those in power by transmitting their claims and projecting their images and messages to the people. In such systems even entertainment programming contains information that government wishes to convey.

In a democracy, those in power also wish to announce their achievements and publicize their successes, and the job of the news media is to report what they say and do. But the media also function as watchdogs, presenting other information and perspectives to the general public. The watchdog role of spotlighting and criticizing government policies and activities results in an interdependent but often adversarial relationship between the news media and those in positions of authority or those who wish to be. Despite the problems it creates, the tension generated by this relationship is essential to the maintenance of a free and democratic political system in which the government and the governed are permanently linked through open discussion and public criticism.[1]

The source of this tension varies with the issue, however. Sometimes it is a constitutional or legal question—freedom of the press versus the rights of individuals and groups, and the needs of government. Sometimes tension arises from a clash between candidates' attempts to shape their own images and the media's desire to uncover the "truth" about them. In other cases the problem is the mixed messages given by an administration's presentation of its major achievements and media coverage of that administration's principal failures. Tension is also evident within government itself—in the give-and-take between some policy makers' right to know and the need of others in their official positions to protect confidentiality and maintain national security. Even the attention given to personalities versus that given to issues has sparked debate about how well informed the citizenry actually is or can be and how well the news media are doing their job and meeting their public responsibilities.

FREEDOM OF THE PRESS

The First Amendment to the Constitution guarantees freedom of the press, but the Supreme Court has *not* held that freedom to be absolute. The Court has ruled that freedom of the press must be balanced by the rights and needs of others in society—individuals, groups, even the government. For the news media, the basic rights are to obtain information, to structure and analyze it, and to print, air, or otherwise transmit it. For others, the basic rights include the rights to privacy, truthfulness, and fairness.

A Free Press Versus the Rights of Others

Where should the line be drawn between freedom of the press and protection for individuals and society as a whole? The news media have a right to collect, evaluate, and disseminate information about public officials so long as that information is truthful, but they may not legally publish or broadcast information that they know to be false. The information reported can be personal so long as it bears some relationship to the conduct of public affairs. However, the news media have no right to invade the privacy of nonpublic figures, nor can they violate laws that prevent the dissemination of material harmful to national security. Each of these areas gives rise to potential conflicts between basic rights, conflicts that find their way into politics and may ultimately have to be settled by the courts.

Libel and slander   By what standard should the press be held responsible for falsehoods, printed or broadcast, that cause a person harm? As explained in Chapter 5, fallacious written statements or visual representations may constitute *libel*; oral statements, including those made on television or radio, may constitute *slander*. Those who make, print, and air such statements can be sued for damages by those who believe that their reputations have suffered as a result.

The Supreme Court has ruled that two different standards of proof should be applied to such suits, depending on whether or not the plaintiff is a person widely known to the public. If a newspaper prints something about you that is totally unfounded and untrue, all you need to prove is that the publisher did not exercise reasonable care in determining the truth; this lack of care is termed *negligence*, and you would be entitled to a retraction and, perhaps, monetary damages. If you were a public figure, however, the burden of proof would be tougher. You would have to demonstrate not only that the statement or story was false but that the publisher knew it was false and published it anyway; this behavior is termed *actual malice*.

The distinction between negligence and actual malice was made to protect debate on controversial issues and to keep public officials accountable. If falsity alone were the principal standard, those in the communications business might be reluctant to print, air, or transmit anything that was the least bit doubtful or controversial. They would play it safe, and this policy would work to the advantage of those in power by shielding them from outside scrutiny.

Coverage of criminal trials   A criminal act is news. But how the news is presented can affect the impartiality of a jury. Jurors need to have open minds and must base their decision only on the evidence and testimony presented during the trial in the court. When there is a lot of publicity before or during a trial—as was the case with the Watergate and Iran-contra scandals and the 1995 bombing of the federal

Believing that no jury in Oklahoma could give an impartial verdict on Timothy McVeigh (in orange shirt) and Terry Nichols, the two men charged with the 1995 bombing of the federal office building in Oklahoma City, a judge moved their trial to Denver. Courts must constantly balance the media's right to publicize crimes against the rights of those who may be unfairly harmed by the coverage.

office building in Oklahoma City, and as often happens in cases involving heinous crimes such as murder or rape—obtaining a fair trial may be difficult because of the adverse publicity. That is why defense attorneys may ask for a change of venue, which moves the trial away from the area in which the crime occurred.

According to the Supreme Court, restricting press access to the trial is the least tolerable method of ensuring that the treatment of defendants will be fair and impartial. Before judges can close the trial to the media, they must try to ensure a fair trial by other means. These include issuing so-called gag orders that prohibit out-of-court statements by witnesses, lawyers, or court officials.[2] Judges can also sequester the jury, that is, isolate them from information presented outside the courtroom.

The issue of the media's right to cover the courts versus defendants' rights to a fair trial is a perennial one and may become an even greater concern as television coverage increases. In fact, more states now permit television coverage of criminal and civil trials such as the O. J. Simpson murder trial, which was covered live by the Cable News Network (CNN). At least one cable channel now provides an endless diet of live and taped courtroom trials.[3]

Confidentiality of news sources   Should journalists be forced to disclose information or identify sources that may be needed in a criminal trial or other judicial proceeding? Journalists often claim that the First Amendment exempts them from having to reveal confidential sources so as to ensure that they are able to obtain critical information. Those in the news media fear that if the identity of sources who request anonymity is not protected, sources will be reluctant to provide information that could be used against them.

However, the Supreme Court has ruled that journalists are not privileged, that they must respond like other citizens when they are subpoenaed for information. (See the Constitutional Conflict box on page 371.) To counter the effects of this ruling, many states have passed **shield laws** that give journalists some protection against forced disclosure, similar to protections enjoyed by doctors, lawyers, and members of the clergy.

Government restrictions   Sometimes the executive branch tries to restrict what the media report. During the Persian Gulf War in 1991, for example, journalists' access to the battle area was limited, and information about operations was not released until it could no longer threaten the success of the operation or the lives of those involved. Even in peacetime the government uses a classification system to restrict access to information that could damage national security if it became public. Since government officials may classify more material than necessary, the news media as well as scholars and other students of government face an ongoing problem of obtaining information that they believe they need and have a right to know.

Congress addressed this problem in 1966 when it enacted the Freedom of Information Act. Designed to facilitate access to government documents, this law places the burden of showing why a document must remain classified on the government. (Some ways to use the act are described on pages 372–373.) However, the news media have not used this law very much because of the long time it takes to process the requests and because "leaks" by people within the government usually constitute easier, quicker, and cheaper sources of information.

In 1976, Congress enacted legislation requiring that the meetings of many federal agencies and some congressional committees be open to the public; in 1995, the House of Representatives modified its rules to require open committee sessions except when national security issues are involved. Despite the legislation, however,

PROTECTION OF SOURCES

Frequently the news media report activities that violate the law, activities that the government has the right and the responsibility to prevent. In many cases, information about illegal activities comes from sources who wish to remain anonymous for fear of reprisal or punishment. Protecting the confidentiality of their sources is a traditional and necessary obligation of reporters, who believe that without such protection people would be reluctant to blow the whistle on others.

Reporters are not the only ones who claim a privilege of confidentiality: doctors, lawyers, and members of the clergy make similar claims. But how far should a privilege of confidentiality extend? President Clinton initially claimed a lawyer-client privilege when he refused to release information about notes taken at a White House meeting pertaining to his and his wife's involvement in the Whitewater development failure. After the Senate threatened to obtain a subpoena for the information, he backed down. Should those with knowledge of potentially harmful or illegal actions, including presidents, be required to inform authorities who have the responsibility to investigate, prevent, or punish such activity? Should reporters, for example, be exempt from grand jury inquiries?

The Supreme Court answered these last two questions in the case of *Branzburg v. Hayes* in 1972. In this case, a reporter who had written about the illegal manufacture and use of drugs in a local community was summoned to appear before a grand jury. He appeared in court but refused to reveal the identities of those involved. The state court ordered him to do so, and the Supreme Court by a narrow margin sustained the state court's ruling. The Court majority argued that freedom of the press did not exempt reporters from the normal obligations of citizenry, and these include responding truthfully to grand jury inquiries about alleged criminal activities.

In reaction to this and subsequent decisions affirming the government's right to require the news media to reveal their confidential sources, some states enacted so-called shield laws to protect the anonymity of news sources. The Supreme Court has acknowledged that Congress also has the power to enact a shield law.

government decision making is not always visible to the public, nor are deliberations that go on behind the scenes easy to re-create or verify.

To prevent the publication or broadcasting of information that it believes would be harmful to the national security, the government occasionally tries to obtain restraining orders from the courts. This action is known as **prior restraint**. Although the Supreme Court has upheld the concept of prior restraint, it has been reluctant to approve it in practice. For example, in 1971 President Nixon tried to prevent the *New York Times*, the *Washington Post*, and other newspapers from publishing portions of a classified history of United States policy during the Vietnam War (the *Pentagon Papers*). By a 6-to-3 vote in the case of *New York Times v. United States*, the Supreme Court ruled against the government and allowed the information to be published.

Regulation of Radio and Television

Because the airwaves are considered to be public property, regulation of the electronic media is more extensive than regulation of the print media. Broadcasters are given licenses to use the airwaves only if they agree to operate in the "public interest, convenience, or necessity." The agency responsible for regulating the electronic

USING THE FREEDOM OF INFORMATION ACT AND THE PRIVACY ACT

Did you ever wonder about what government officials considered when they made important decisions or whether certain groups were given greater access than others or more information on policy that affected them? What about the various investigations in which the government has engaged under the guise of promoting national security or maintaining law and order? Has this information been used to create a file on you or someone you know, or a group that you are considering joining? Now you can find out.

Journalists, students of government, even ordinary citizens can use the Freedom of Information Act and the Privacy Act to obtain copies of government reports, memorandums, and files. The Freedom of Information Act (FOIA), enacted in 1966, requires agencies and departments of the executive branch of the United States government to provide the fullest possible disclosure of information to the public. The Privacy Act of 1974, a companion to FOIA, provides safeguards against invasions of individuals' privacy through the misuse of records by federal agencies. The Privacy Act allows most individuals to gain access to federal agencies' records about themselves and to seek to change any incorrect or incomplete information.

Both laws make federal agencies accountable for information disclosure policies and practices. Although neither law grants an absolute right to examine government documents, both laws establish the right to request records and to receive a response to the request. If a record cannot be released, the requester is entitled to be told the reason for the denial and has the right to appeal the denial and, if necessary, challenge it in court.

Often the most difficult part of obtaining information under the provisions of the FOIA and the Privacy Act is determining which agency has the records. There is no central government records office that handles all FOIA requests, nor is there a central index of federal government records about individuals. To find the correct agency, you must consult a government directory such as the *United States Government Manual* or a commercially produced directory such as *Information USA*. Both are found in virtually every college library. The next step is to write a simple letter to the agency's head or to its FOIA or Privacy Act officer. The letter should contain three important elements. First, state that the request is being made under the FOIA or Privacy Act (or both). Second, identify as clearly as possible the records that are being sought. Finally, include the name, address, and signature of the requester. There is no need to explain the reason for the request. Anyone can write a request letter; there is no need for a lawyer to be involved.

Federal agencies are required to respond to FOIA requests within ten working days, with actual disclosure of the requested information to follow promptly thereafter. Agencies may charge fees for processing some requests, particularly if the requester is going to use the information for commercial purposes. The fees are often reduced or waived for small requests made by individuals seeking information for personal or scholarly use.

The disclosure requirements of the FOIA do not

media is the Federal Communications Commission (FCC), which licenses stations, oversees their technical operations, and investigates citizens' complaints. The FCC rarely decides to revoke a broadcaster's license; rather, it imposes fines and warnings on broadcasters that do not serve the public interest.

The FCC has at times enforced three rules that affect the coverage of politics: the fairness doctrine, the equal time rule, and the right of rebuttal. The **fairness doctrine** required that discussions of important public issues be aired and that conflicting sides of an issue be presented. Under this rule, when the president gave a political address on radio and television, a representative of the party out of power was

apply to elected officials of the federal government, including the president, vice president, senators, and representatives; to the federal judiciary; or to state or local governments (all states and some localities, however, have passed laws similar to the FOIA). Moreover, under the FOIA an agency may withhold some types of information, such as that which is classified for national security or needs to be kept confidential for the conduct of an agency's business.

SOURCE: Sample letters adapted from letters that appear in *Civics for Democracy: A Journey for Teachers and Students* by Katherine Isaac, published by the Center for Study of Response Law and Information, Washington, D.C. ©Essential Books, 1996. Reprinted by permission.

permitted to give a response, usually for the same amount of time. The FCC suspended the use of the fairness doctrine in the late 1980s.

The **equal time rule** requires any broadcaster that allows a candidate for public office to appear on the station, or that carries advertising for that candidate, to provide other candidates for the same office with similar opportunities. Prior to 1983 this rule applied to all candidates, including those of minor parties. The FCC subsequently allowed radio and television stations some flexibility in staging debates (which are considered news events) and determining which candidates to invite to them. News shows and coverage of news events have been exempt from the equal

'INDECENCY' ON THE INTERNET

The virtual explosion in use of the Internet in recent years, and particularly its accessibility to children, have raised concerns about the availability of sexually explicit images and texts from private home pages and consumer on-line services. In 1996, Congress reacted to these concerns by tacking on a provision to the omnibus telecommunications bill that was enacted in that year. This part of the legislation, known as the Communications Decency Act, banned the dissemination of "indecent" material on the Internet and established penalties of prison terms and large fines for violators.[1]

Civil libertarians, medical educators, and companies offering on-line and computer services immediately objected. They argued that the enforcement of the law would have a chilling effect on Internet communications, placing the government in the position of censor with public officials determining what is or is not indecent. For example, would a medical journal that depicted parts of the human anatomy or discussed the transmission of AIDS through heterosexual or homosexual relations be subject to prosecution under the law? Critics also contended that text permitted in print or images permitted in a movie could be banned on the Internet, thereby creating a dual standard for different means of communication.

Proponents of the legislation, however, saw things differently. They noted the current restrictions on television broadcasting that provide for family programming during certain hours and require warnings prior to the airing of shows containing dialogue or images that some might find offensive. They also pointed to new requirements in the telecommunications law that broadcasters rate the content of their programming and that new televisions sold in the United States contain a device, known as a "V chip," that allows parents to prevent certain programs from being viewed on their own televisions. Besides, they argued, doesn't Congress have a right, even a duty, to make public policy that reflects community standards and the wishes of the majority?

The clash between individual rights and community standards is an ongoing one, and the arena of free speech is one in which it often occurs. In the case of the Communications Decency Act, the courts acted quickly, clearly, and decisively. A three-judge federal panel in Philadelphia ruled unanimously that key elements of the law that pertained to indecent material were unconstitutional. The court reasoned that the law was too sweeping; that there were other ways, short of government censorship, in which parents could control objectionable material on the Internet; and, finally, that information on the Internet had to be afforded at least as much protection under the First Amendment as printed matter. (Calling attention to the new communications technology, the court distributed its decision on a compact disk and published it on its

time rule. Application of this regulation during the 1980 and 1984 presidential campaigns meant that Ronald Reagan's old movies could not be shown on television because his opponents could have demanded and received equal time.

The **right of rebuttal** was established by the Supreme Court in the landmark case of *Red Lion Broadcasting Co. v. FCC* (1969). In this case a liberal author whose book about conservative senator Barry Goldwater was criticized by a conservative preacher asked for equal and free time to reply to his critic. The Court agreed, ruling that individuals or groups whose honesty, integrity, or character has been attacked during a broadcast, or a candidate whose opponent has been endorsed by a station, has a right of rebuttal.

The fairness doctrine, the equal time rule, and the right of rebuttal can be justified on grounds of equity. From the perspective of the news media, however, the regulations are restrictive and costly to broadcasters. Because they require that more

Despite arguments that children should be protected from the kind of material accessed by this Carnegie-Mellon University student, a federal law banning the dissemination of "indecent" text and images on the Internet failed to survive its first court challenge.

own bulletin board on the Internet.) The Justice Department immediately appealed the decision to the Supreme Court.

Do you think the court decision was the correct one, and if so, was it for the right reasons? Can or should indecent material be prevented from being disseminated on the Internet? If so, how would you define such material, and how would you prevent it from being disseminated?

To get more information about this issue or to become involved on one side or the other, contact one of the following groups:

Supporting the Communications Decency Act:

National Law Center for Children and Families
4103 Chain Bridge Road
Suite 410
Fairfax, VA 22030-4105
(703) 691-4626
e-mail 104134.3110@compuserve.com

Opposing the Communications Decency Act:

Center for Democracy and Technology
1634 Eye Street, N.W.
Suite 1100
Washington, DC 20006
(202) 637-9800
Internet http://www.cdty.org/

[1]The law did not address the issues of obscenity and pornography, which are already banned and which the Supreme Court has held are not protected by the First Amendment guarantees of freedom of speech and freedom of the press.

time be devoted to public programming, they may lead to a reduction in revenue from advertising, a serious problem for businesses that seek to make a profit. As a consequence, the fairness doctrine resulted in bland news coverage; the equal time rule, in little or no time given to any candidate (because of the requirement to provide time to *all* candidates); and the right of rebuttal, in the avoidance of critical commentary.

Another media-related issue that has generated controversy has been the portrayal of what critics call immoral, antisocial behavior in the form of rap music lyrics; threatening, inflammatory rhetoric on radio talk shows; and depictions of sexually explicit and violent behavior in television shows, video games, and movies and on the Internet.[4] In each of these areas, voluntary attempts to regulate such expression have not satisfied those who find such words and presentations undesirable and unacceptable in the public arena. In 1996, Congress enacted legislation that requires broadcasters and cable networks to rate their programming on the basis of its sexual content and degree of violence; it also requires that new television sets contain a computer chip that allows people to block out programs that exceed a certain rating. Congress has also restricted the depiction of pornographic material on the Internet, but a federal court declared parts of the law unconstitutional. (See the Hot-Button Issue box on pages 374–375.)

The Profit Motive

The vast majority of media in the United States are and always have been privately owned and operated.[5] This is not surprising in view of the strength of the free-enterprise system and the suspicion with which Americans have traditionally viewed government-owned and -operated media. Although some public support has been provided to the Corporation for Public Broadcasting and to the United States Information Agency (USIA) for its worldwide radio and television networks, that support has been modest and is declining.[6]

Not only are the news media private, but they are big business. Approximately 1,550 papers are published daily in the United States.[7] Most of the large ones (those with circulations over 100,000) are part of newspaper chains such as Gannett, Knight-Ridder, and Times Mirror; the ten biggest chains account for more than half of the daily newspaper circulation in the United States and are expanding their share of the market. The largest, the Gannett Company, publishes more than ninety newspapers with a daily circulation of over 6 million. Newspaper chains maintain their own news bureaus, which distribute reports, features, and news analyses to member papers. Their editors determine what material provided by the bureau gets published.

A concentration of news organizations is evident in the television industry as well, where the three major commercial networks (ABC, CBS, and NBC) and the cable news network (CNN) dominate national news. There are independent local stations and a few small independent networks, but the resources they have devoted to national news have been limited. With relatively few reporters, camera crews, and producers, these and other stations are forced to follow the lead of the major networks for national news. Not surprisingly, there is a tendency toward "pack journalism," as reporters focus on the same events, often in the same way.

Another trend in contemporary media communications is the development of giant conglomerates, companies that own and operate a combination of newspapers and radio and television stations. Three of the largest are Disney, which controls Capital Cities/ABC; Time Warner, which owns Turner Broadcasting and NBC; and Westinghouse Electric, which purchased CBS.

One reason for the concern about concentrated ownership relates to the lack of diversity in news coverage. Another pertains to bias, that is, to the perception that coverage is unfair and prejudicial. In fact, a large portion of the public believes that the news media do not deal fairly with all sides, that they favor some groups over others.[8]

Some critics place the blame for this perceived bias on the news industry itself.[9] They contend that the news giants do not put as many resources into investigating and reporting wrongdoing by companies with which they do business as they do into investigating and reporting problems that these companies may encounter with the government. Another frequently heard complaint is that the news media have a tendency to give more favorable treatment to those who are sympathetic to their pro-business orientation than to those who are not.[10] Whether or not these allegations are correct, they do raise the issue of how the profit-making orientation of the media affects their capacity to report the news fairly, accurately, and critically.

Profit-making media must capture and maintain as large an audience as possible. That is how they make money. To attract and maintain such an audience, they must provide a product that people want; they must please their readers, listeners, or viewers or face the risk of losing them. Their dilemma is how to meet market demands by satisfying their audience and simultaneously fulfill their role in a democracy, particularly if the majority of people do not desire much information about, or critical evaluations of, politics and government.

For the most part, the news media have attempted to resolve this dilemma by making the news entertaining. They emphasize action rather than ideas, politics rather than policy, people rather than organizations and processes. They focus on conflict, drama, and the human dimension because these aspects of the news spark public interest. Moreover, to save time and money (which are valuable commodities in a private-enterprise system) they may become overly dependent on a few sources and fail to devote sufficient resources to verifying the information they receive, much less providing alternate perspectives. These practices, conditioned by economic pressures, can undercut the democratic process, making the news media imperfect instruments for performing their important educational and informational roles.

A BRIEF HISTORY OF THE NEWS MEDIA

The tension between democratic goals and economic interests is apparent in the history of the news media in the United States—a history marked by professional change, economic competition, and technological advances.

Newspapers

In 1690, Benjamin Harris of Boston published what many experts consider the first newspaper in North America: *Publick Occurrences, Both Foreign and Domestick*. Only one issue was printed, however; the paper contained news that colonial authorities viewed as offensive, so Harris was barred from publishing it again. Several newspapers that followed *Publick Occurrences* contained only "safe" news. James Franklin changed all this in 1721, when he began publishing the *New England Courant*, which was critical of the colonial authorities. They responded to the negative publicity by obtaining a court order forbidding Franklin from publishing the *Courant* without their approval. To evade the order, he named his younger brother Benjamin as the paper's official publisher. Subsequently Benjamin Franklin moved to Philadelphia and took over the *Pennsylvania Gazette*, which became the best-known and most profitable newspaper in the colonies.

During the Revolutionary War, newspapers became more numerous and politically polarized. Most supported the revolution and became important sources of propaganda, reprinting many revolutionary treatises such as the Declaration of Independence and Thomas Paine's *Common Sense* and *Crisis* papers. The politicization of the press did not end with the war. The debate between the Federalists and the Anti-Federalists continued, with the most eloquent defense of the Constitution, *The Federalist Papers*, written by Madison, Hamilton, and Jay for publication in newspapers.

The press of this period was not only highly partisan but also shrill, subjective, and argumentative. The primary aim was to convince readers of the merits of a particular position or action, not to report the news objectively. In 1798 a Federalist Congress passed the Sedition Act, under which "false, scandalous, or malicious" articles about the government were considered a crime. Directed at critics of President John Adams's administration, the law engendered considerable criticism and was allowed to lapse in 1801 after Thomas Jefferson's Democratic-Republican party gained control of the executive and legislative branches.

Newspapers at this time were not aimed at the masses; they were written for the upper class, and their content was primarily business and political news. But their audience and content began to change during the 1830s, when technological improvements, a growth in literacy, and the movement toward greater public involvement in the democratic process all contributed to the development of the penny press—that is, newspapers that sold for a penny. These were oriented toward the less prosperous members of society, and they provided readers with interesting and lively content—local news, human interest stories, and accounts of crime and violence.

Not all the newspapers aimed at the general public were sensational. In 1841, Horace Greeley founded the *New York Tribune*. Greeley appealed to the intelligentsia; he also used his paper to promote various causes and crusades. In 1851, Henry Raymond founded a paper with a similar orientation and appeal, the *New York Times*, which in the twentieth century became the most highly respected and authoritative American newspaper.

The penny press revolutionized American journalism. Newspapers began to rely on advertising rather than on subscription revenue as their primary source of income. To attract advertisers, they had to have a larger number of readers. To attract readers, their content had to be different and eye-catching. As a result, there was a change in what was reported and how it was reported.

Prior to the development of the penny press, news was rarely "new" or exciting; many stories were weeks old before they appeared in newspapers and were simply rewritten or reprinted from other newspapers. When more newspapers became targeted at a general readership, a higher premium was put on gathering news quickly and reporting it in an engaging, easy-to-read manner. The invention of the telegraph helped make it possible for an emerging Washington press corps to communicate information about government to the entire country.

Between 1850 and 1900, the number of daily newspapers grew from 254 to 2,226, and circulation rose from 758,000 to 15,102,000. Sensationalism and aggressive crusading began to dominate the news, giving rise to what came to be known as **yellow journalism** (a term that had its origin in a battle for the rights to a popular comic strip, "The Yellow Kid").

In fact, Joseph Pulitzer, who bought the *New York World* in 1883, used yellow journalism to build the paper's circulation into the largest in America. Pulitzer's main audience was the large immigrant class in New York. His paper's stories on crime and sex, stunts like sending a reporter around the world, and crusades against the horrible conditions of sweatshops and tenements became the prototype for other large-circulation dailies such as William Randolph Hearst's *New York Journal*. Hearst and the *Journal* are most famous for their involvement in the Spanish-American War. Before the start of the hostilities, Hearst deliberately stirred up public sentiment in support of the war; once the war broke out, he covered it aggressively and sensationally.

In the early 1900s the number of daily newspapers started to decline. The economics of publishing, which made it essential to achieve lower unit costs and higher advertising revenues by increasing circulation, caused many newspapers to fold or

"Extra" editions of William Randolph Hearst's New York Journal *carried banner headlines about the sinking of the American battleship* Maine *in Havana harbor in 1898.
The paper sensationalized the story and even offered a reward of $50,000 for the
identity of the perpetrators. This so-called yellow journalism helped push the United
States into the Spanish-American War.*

merge with their competitors. Less competition and more consolidation has resulted
in the growth of newspaper chains. By 1996, only four daily newspapers had circulations of over 1 million, and the number of daily newspapers had decreased to
approximately 1,500. (Table 11-1 lists the dailies with the largest circulation.) The
proportion of the population reading newspapers on a regular basis remains large,
however, although not as large as the proportion who watch television news regularly. (See Table 11-2.)

One recent development has been the growth of national newspapers such as the

TABLE 11-1	DAILY NEWSPAPERS WITH THE LARGEST CIRCULATION[a]
Wall Street Journal	1,763,140
USA Today	1,523,610
New York Times	1,081,541
Los Angeles Times	1,012,189
Washington Post	793,660
New York Daily News	738,091
Chicago Tribune	684,366
Newsday (N.Y.)	634,627
Houston Chronicle	541,478
Detroit Free Press	531,825
Dallas Morning News	500,358

[a]Circulation as of September 1995.

Source: Editor and Publishers International Yearbook, *1996.*

Wall Street Journal and *USA Today* and the national and regional distribution of large metropolitan dailies such as the *New York Times*, *Los Angeles Times*, *Washington Post*, and *Miami Herald*. These metropolitan papers feature a larger amount of national and international news than do most other American dailies, whose coverage is oriented toward their own cities or areas. Some of the metropolitan papers also provide more in-depth discussion of policy issues.

Electronic Media

Radio   The first radio station began operating in 1920, and radio remained the principal electronic medium from the 1920s to the 1950s. Dominated by the major national networks, CBS and NBC, it broadcast entertainment and news programs to a national audience. At first, radio stations did not provide regular news coverage, but they excelled at covering special events as they were happening. The 1924 presidential election was the first to be reported on radio; the conventions, major speeches, and election returns were broadcast to a national audience. During the 1928 election, both major presidential candidates (Herbert Hoover and Alfred E. Smith) spent campaign funds on radio advertising.

Radio soon became the most important medium for reporting fast-breaking news stories. Whereas the speed with which newspapers could bring current events to readers was limited by the time required for printing and delivery, a radio station could have a story on the air in a matter of minutes.

In addition to being faster, radio had the advantage of being better able to convey the excitement and color of a scene. Radio also became extremely effective at reporting foreign news. Correspondents like H. V. Kaltenborn and Edward R. Murrow provided excellent coverage of the events that led to World War II, and during the war, they and other correspondents reported regularly from battlefields in Europe and Asia.

Politicians soon became aware of the power of radio to transmit ideas. Franklin Roosevelt was the first president to use it effectively to appeal directly to the people and mobilize support for his political agenda. Roosevelt's "fireside chats" fostered a personal relationship between the president and the public, and his technique became the model for his successors in the White House.

Although radio lost its national audience to television in the 1950s, it did not fade away. Instead, stations began broadcasting specialized programming aimed at smaller, local, homogeneous audiences. Today there are more radio stations operating than in radio's supposed "glory days" in the 1940s.[11] One factor that has kept radio flourishing has been the increasing amount of time Americans spend in their

---

TABLE 11-2	**REGULAR NEWS READERS, WATCHERS, AND LISTENERS IN WESTERN EUROPE AND NORTH AMERICA (PERCENT)**							
	CANADA	FRANCE	GERMANY	ITALY	MEXICO	SPAIN	GREAT BRITAIN	UNITED STATES
Read newspapers regularly	66	47	63	56	72	70	74	71
Watch television news regularly	83	84	79	91	92	91	86	85
Listen to radio news regularly	62	57	58	34	63	46	57	52

Source: Based on a survey prepared by the Times Mirror Center for the People and the Press and conducted during January 1994. The results were published in Mixed Message About Press Freedom on Both Sides of Atlantic, *Times Mirror Center for the People and the Press, March 16, 1994, 28–29.*

In his famous fireside chats on radio, President Franklin Roosevelt reached millions of listeners and built support for his policies. A president's role as "communicator-in-chief" has become critical, as more and more citizens get their information from electronic media rather than the printed press.

cars; unlike reading or watching television, listening to the radio is not difficult or dangerous to do while driving.

Because it is relatively cheap and accessible and can be targeted to different types of audiences, radio remains a major communications medium for candidates seeking public office and officials and organizations wishing to affect public policy. President Reagan used radio effectively to deliver policy statements on Saturdays, a practice that has been continued on this generally slow news day by presidents Bush and Clinton. The 1990s have also seen the expansion of talk radio, where listeners are encouraged to telephone the host with questions and comments. Many of the people who host such shows have strong ideological convictions that they share, usually with like-minded listeners. Rush Limbaugh, G. Gordon Liddy, Michael Reagan, and Oliver North have reached large audiences with their anti-Washington, anti-liberal, anti-Clinton rhetoric.

Television After World War II, television quickly transformed the American public into a large viewing audience. In 1950, only 9 percent of the households in the United States had televisions; ten years later, that percentage had grown to 87; by 1980, it had reached over 98 percent. Today almost 80 percent of American households have at least *two* television sets. Moreover, the average length of time that a television set is turned on each day has risen from approximately 4 hours in 1950 to about 7 hours today, with the average person watching over 900 hours per year. Figures 11-1 and 11-2 document the dominance of radio and television as primary sources of communication.

When television started to dominate the American media, three networks—ABC, CBS, and NBC—began to dominate television. During this formative stage, most of the commercial stations in the United States were affiliated with one of these three networks, which provided them with the bulk of their entertainment programming and national news.

Television featured daily newscasts almost from the outset, but its political impact was initially felt more strongly through its coverage of special events. For example, televised coverage of the Senate hearings on organized crime in 1950–1951 had a

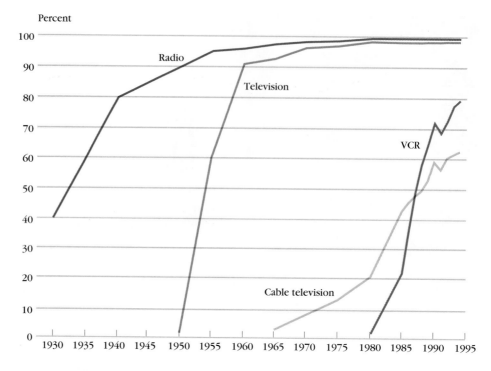

FIGURE 11-1

Households with radios, televisions, cable television, and VCRs, 1930–1994.

SOURCE: Samuel Kernell, *Going Public*, 2d ed. (Washington, D.C.: Congressional Quarterly, 1993), 108; updated by authors. Reprinted by permission of Congressional Quarterly, Inc. Data from 1991 to 1994 from *Statistical Abstract of the United States* (Washington, D.C., 1995), 571.

dramatic impact. Public awareness of organized crime increased; and the chairman of the committee that conducted the inquiry, Senator Estes Kefauver (D-Tennessee), became a national hero and a presidential candidate as a result of his television exposure. Kefauver's rise to prominence demonstrated the potential of television as a vehicle for increasing name recognition and enhancing personal image. It soon became a major medium through which campaigns were directed and elections observed.

In presidential elections, the effect of television was felt as early as 1952. The most important news event of that campaign was a speech by General Dwight Eisenhower's running mate, Richard Nixon. Accused of obtaining secret campaign funds in exchange for political favors, Nixon defended himself in a national television address. He denied accepting contributions for personal use, accused the Democratic administration of President Harry Truman of being soft on communism, criticized his Democratic opponents in the presidential campaign, and vowed that he would never force his children to give up their dog, Checkers, who had been given to the Nixons by political supporters. The emotion of the speech, and particularly the reference to Checkers, generated a favorable public reaction, ended discussion of the campaign funds, and kept Nixon on the Republican ticket.

Paid television advertising by the political parties also first appeared during the 1952 election. The marketing of candidates on television revolutionized the electoral

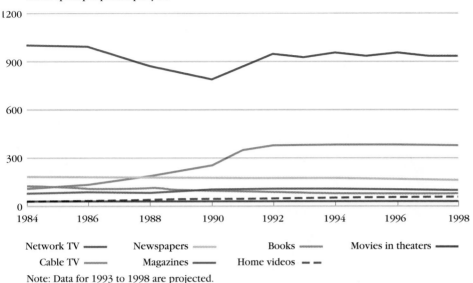

Hours spent per person per year

Network TV ——	Newspapers -----
Cable TV ——	Magazines ——
Books -----	Movies in theaters ——
Home videos -- --	

Note: Data for 1993 to 1998 are projected.

FIGURE 11-2
Media use by consumers, 1984–1998.

SOURCE: U.S. Bureau of the Census, *Statistical Abstract of the United States, 1995*, 115th ed. (Washington, D.C., 1995), 568, Figure 18.1.

process, particularly the strategy and tactics of campaigning. It enabled candidates to craft their own image and challenge the images of their opponents.

Over the next two decades television's power to shape personal images was demonstrated repeatedly. In 1954 it contributed greatly to the downfall of Senator Joseph McCarthy (R-Wisconsin), who had made a name for himself by charging that communists had infiltrated the government, particularly the State Department, and the military. During eight weeks of televised hearings by McCarthy's committee into possible communist influence in the Army, the public was able to view and evaluate (negatively, as events proved) the senator's unsubstantiated charges and browbeating of witnesses and others who denied his allegations.

Another example of the power of television came during the four debates held in 1960 between the two major presidential candidates, Senator John F. Kennedy and Vice President Richard M. Nixon, especially the first debate. In that confrontation the vice president appeared pallid; the color of his suit blended into the background; he seemed to need a shave; and he shifted nervously in his seat with his eyes darting back and forth. He did not look nearly as good as he sounded. In contrast, Kennedy appeared fresh; his clothes made him stand out; and his facial expressions and gestures came across well on television. Those who heard the debate on radio judged Nixon the winner; those who saw it on television were more impressed by Kennedy. The television exposure that both candidates received during the debates contributed to Kennedy's narrow victory.

Television coverage of the civil rights movement, particularly the 1963 protest staged in Birmingham, Alabama, by Dr. Martin Luther King Jr., and the reaction to it by the white police (with attack dogs, water cannons, and cattle prods), created unforgettable images for viewers. For much of the public, television provided the

In the first televised presidential debate, Senator John Kennedy (left) *took the offensive—gesturing, speaking quickly, spouting statistics, and pledging to "get the country moving again." The camera caught qualities that people seek in a president—strength, knowledge, and determination; in contrast, it revealed a cold, distant, nervous Richard Nixon* (right). *The debates vastly improved Kennedy's public image and contributed to his victory in 1960.*

evidence that justified the struggle for civil rights. Coverage of the Vietnam War, the first "living-room war," provides another vivid illustration of the power of television news on public opinion. Nightly pictures of the pain and suffering of the victims of the war, including American military casualties, and persistent, critical evaluations of the progress of the war by correspondents in the field of operations had a powerful cumulative effect on the public's conscience and helped turn national sentiment against the war.

The decade of the 1960s also saw the increasing importance of television network news and the growth of a large Washington press corps. In 1948, NBC and CBS began airing 15-minute evening newscasts. By 1963, the national news was extended to a half-hour. Since that year, Americans have cited television as their principal and most believable source of news (see Table 11-3).[12]

Television affected the print media as well. Since television reports events at or close to the time they happen, newspapers and magazines had to supplement their coverage and commentary in order to provide an additional dimension and thereby maintain a product that people would want to buy. Moreover, they had to find news by investigating activities that on the surface might not have appeared newsworthy.

The *Washington Post's* reporting of the Watergate scandals during 1972 and 1973 is a good example of the power and profitability of investigative journalism. The *Post* reported that White House aides had broken into the Democratic National Committee headquarters at the Watergate complex and that President Nixon had participated in a cover-up of the attempted burglary. Attacked by high-level officials

The war in Vietnam was the first one brought into the living rooms of most Americans. Media coverage of the war—especially the televised images of death, destruction, and incredible suffering—helped turn public opinion against United States involvement in Vietnam. This is one of the most famous photographs of any war, taken in 1972 and captioned "Terror of War." Children flee in panic from an air strike in which napalm bombs were dropped. The girl in the center runs naked, having ripped off her burning clothes.

including the president and the vice president, the *Post* did not abandon the story. Its revelations eventually prompted a congressional investigation, the hiring of a special prosecutor, and ultimately the resignation of President Nixon. *Post* reporters Bob Woodward and Carl Bernstein, who broke the Watergate story, helped usher in a new era of investigative reporting.

The Vietnam War and Watergate were turning points in the relationship between the press and the government. The press accused the government of withholding and falsifying information, and the Johnson and Nixon administrations accused the media of being unfair and biased in their coverage of events. Although the intense hostility of the late 1960s and early 1970s has subsided, the credibility gap between news media and government has continued. The news media no longer give public officials the benefit of the doubt: they assume that when those in power speak on the record, they are seeking primarily to enhance their stature and self-interest. Government officials in turn see the media as hostile and overly negative; they point to that negativism when justifying their own attempts to place a favorable "spin" on the news.

A major change for the public in the 1980s and 1990s has been the growth and accessibility of cable television. Although cable television began to operate in the early 1950s, largely to improve television reception in areas that had difficulty getting a clear picture, it took several decades for the country to become wired for it and for companies to offer a wide selection of programming on it. By the middle of the 1980s cable was available in most metropolitan areas and, increasingly, in rural areas as well. By the mid 1990s more than 59 million households were subscribing

TABLE 11-3

USE AND TRUSTWORTHINESS OF MEDIA, 1963–1996 (PERCENT)

	1963	1976	1978	1982	1986	1988	1990	1992	1994	1996
Source of most news[a]										
Television	55	64	67	64	66	65	69	69	83	88
Newspapers	53	49	49	44	36	42	43	43	51	61
Radio	29	19	20	18	14	14	15	16	15	25
Magazines	6	7	5	6	4	4	3	4	10	18
People/Other	4	5	5	4	4	5	7	6	6	2
Most believable[b]/Best job[c]										
Television	36	51	47	53	55	49	54	56	—	50*
Newspapers	24	22	23	22	21	26	22	22	—	14
Radio	12	7	9	6	6	7	7	7	—	8
Magazines	10	9	9	8	7	5	4	4	—	4
Don't know/no answer	18	11	12	11	12	13	13	12	—	4

[a]From 1963 to 1992 the question was: "First, I'd like to ask you where you usually get most of your news about what's going on in the world today—from the newspapers or radio or television or magazines or talking to people or where?" (More than one answer permitted.) Since 1994 the question has been, "How have you been getting most of your news about national and international issues—from television, from newspapers, from radio or from magazines?" (Accept two answers.) Interviewers were told to probe for additional responses if only one was given.

[b]Question: "If you got conflicting or different reports of the same news story from radio, television, the magazines, and the newspapers, which of the four versions would you be most inclined to believe—the one on the radio or television or magazines or newspapers?" (Only one answer permitted.)

[c]Question: In your opinion, who has been doing the best job of covering the news lately?

*An additional response to this question was local TV news, which 20 percent chose.

Source: "America's Watching: Public Attitudes Toward Television 1993" (New York: The Network Television Association and the National Association of Broadcasters, 1993), 29, 31. Reprinted from Harold W. Stanley and Richard G. Niemi, Vital Statistics on American Politics (Washington, D.C.: Congressional Quarterly, 1994), 74. Reprinted by permission of Congressional Quarterly, Inc. Updated by authors with data from The Pew Research Center For The People & The Press, January 1996, 29–30.

to a basic cable service, approximately 62.4 percent of the total households with televisions.[13] Cable's revenues now approach those of radio and television broadcasting.[14]

The development of cable has more closely paralleled that of contemporary radio than that of television. Instead of appealing to the broadest possible audience, cable stations engage in what political scientist Austin Ranney describes as "narrowcasting," that is, offering specialized programming designed for specialized audiences.[15] For those interested in politics and government, the all-news and public affairs stations provide a seemingly endless amount of coverage.

Cable News Network (CNN) was the first to provide a 24-hour news service. Its worldwide news bureaus, correspondents, and satellite hookups challenged the near-monopoly on national and international news coverage that ABC, CBS, and NBC had enjoyed. With its exclusive focus on news and its capacity to report it as it happens from almost anywhere in the world, CNN soon became the network upon which the public and government depended for information about fast-breaking developments. Today, other cable networks have gotten into the 24-hour news business.

For public affairs, the Cable Satellite Public Affairs Network (C-SPAN) regularly televises official proceedings of government, including important committee hearings and formal sessions of both the House and the Senate, as well as presidential news conferences, academic conferences, and speeches by public officials. Approximately 6 to 8 million people watch these activities on the C-SPAN channels.

Instantaneous news, worldwide, is now a reality. It provides alternate, often superior information to the government's, and it shortens the time for communication and action. (Left) CBS's Dan Rather reports from Haiti, where, beginning in 1994, the United States sent troops to support a restoration of civilian government. (Right) On-going C-SPAN coverage of the House of Representatives shows members addressing their constituents in speeches that may have little if any legislative impact: the camera does not pan the floor of the House and thus does not reveal members' absence or inattention.

In the 1990s the expansion of cable news coverage, the high cost of maintaining foreign news bureaus and foreign correspondents, and shrinking profits prompted ABC, CBS, and NBC to cut back their news operations and reduce the amount of time they devoted to public affairs programming. This change was evident in the limited prime-time coverage of the Democratic and Republican national conventions in 1992 and 1996 by the three broadcast networks. In contrast, CNN, C-SPAN, and public television provided more extensive coverage.

Other developments in the electronic media include the improvement of satellite technology, which is particularly important for extending broad coverage to rural areas. The commercialization of small, relatively inexpensive satellite dishes has made satellite television more accessible to sparsely populated parts of the country not wired for cable. In addition, low-powered stations that provide specialized programming to local audiences have expanded.[16]

Not only has the diversity of programs increased, but so has the capacity of viewers to shift quickly from one channel to another by using remote controls. These devices have had a profound effect on news coverage. To prevent their audiences from getting bored and switching to other channels, the networks have speeded up the action, shortened the statements they air by candidates and public officials, and emphasized argumentation and conflict in these individuals' on-the-air remarks. Moreover, interactive radio and television shows, in which live audiences as well as

HELEN THOMAS, CONNIE CHUNG, TABITHA SOREN: THREE GENERATIONS OF WOMEN IN JOURNALISM

As more and more female faces appear in the male-dominated circles of politics and government, women are making corresponding gains as political correspondents. The experiences of three journalists from three generations—Helen Thomas, Connie Chung, and Tabitha Soren—provide a glimpse of the saga of American newswomen in the second half of the twentieth century.

Helen Thomas, the chief of the White House bureau for United Press International (UPI), represents those women who came of age around the time of World War II and often had to fight their own battles to get into the newsroom or to stay there. By the mid 1990s Thomas had been covering the White House for more than thirty-five years, longer than any other correspondent. She is familiar to television viewers as the person who frequently asks the first or second question at presidential press conferences as well as closes them by saying "Thank you, Mr. President."

Thomas was born in 1920 to an immigrant couple who had arrived at Ellis Island from Lebanon in 1903. Although her parents could neither read nor write, all their nine children went to college. In 1942, after graduating from Wayne State University in Detroit, Thomas went to Washington, D.C. During World War II, when women reporters were needed to replace men who had been drafted into the armed services, she began work as a copy assistant for UPI, a service that furnishes material to newspapers nationwide. She has been with UPI ever since. Unlike many women reporters who were let go when male journalists returned after the war, Thomas stayed on the job. In 1956 she was asked to cover the Justice Department, and later other federal agencies.

Transferred to the White House in 1961, Thomas first was assigned to the "women's beat," including the first lady as well as the personal life of the first family. But she was soon poking her nose into all aspects of the news of the day, and in 1971 she was promoted to chief correspondent of UPI's White House bureau.

Hard-working and driven, Thomas is highly regarded not only by her peers but also by the subjects of her coverage—the presidents and their press secretaries. Among her numerous "firsts" and other honors, she was the first female chief correspondent at the White House and the first female member and officer of the National Press Club. In August 1995 she celebrated her 75th birthday at the White House, and President Clinton helped her to blow out the candles on the cake.

A representative of the wider opportunities that became available to ethnic minorities as well as women in the baby boom generation, **Connie Chung** became the second woman and the first Asian American to anchor a television network newscast. She was born in 1946 in Washington, D.C., to which her parents had moved from their native China earlier that year. After graduating from the University of Maryland, Chung went to work in 1969 at a local television station in Washington, starting as a copy editor and then moving up to become first a writer and then a reporter.

In 1971 Chung began reporting for CBS News, where she covered the presidential campaign of Senator George McGovern and helped report the Watergate cover-up. After five years she was hired as an anchor at the CBS affiliate in Los Angeles. Then, in 1983, she switched to NBC, where she anchored the Saturday edition of *NBC Nightly News* and co-anchored a prime-time newsmagazine. In 1989 Chung returned to CBS to anchor *CBS Evening News on Sunday* as well as her own prime-time newsmagazine show. Her distinguished performance led to her promotion to a regular co-anchor slot for the *CBS Evening News* beginning in 1993.

Today news correspondents themselves can become newsworthy, and in 1995 Chung twice made the news in ways she probably would have preferred to avoid. First, during an interview, she coaxed the mother of House Speaker Newt Gingrich to confide, "just between us," what her son had said about Hillary Rodham Clinton. Mrs. Gingrich's whispered answer—"She's a bitch"—was broadcast to a national audience, and Chung was widely criticized. Then she was let go by CBS when the network returned to a single-anchor format on the *Evening News*. Rather than take up other career opportunities, Chung decided for the

Like those of their male colleagues, the relationships of women political journalists to the people they cover can range from the cozy to the confrontational. After covering the White House for more than three decades, Helen Thomas is virtually a part of the first family; President Clinton helped her blow out the candles on her 75th birthday cake. Ingratiating herself with her subject paid off, at least in the short run, for Connie Chung in an interview with Newt Gingrich's mother. When Mrs. Gingrich expressed reluctance to reveal how her son assessed Hillary Rodham Clinton, Chung coaxed, "Just between us . . ."; the candid reply, "She's a bitch," was broadcast on national television. Tabitha Soren took a harder line with Bob Dole in her MTV interview, repeatedly pressing the Republican presidential candidate to clarify his stance on abortion.

time being to devote herself full-time to the baby son that she and her husband, talk show host Maury Povich, had adopted. But few expect her to remain off the air for good.

Tabitha Soren, a news anchor for MTV as well as a contributing correspondent at NBC, is considered by many in the mainstream news media to be an exemplary voice for her own post–baby boomer "Generation X." Indeed, she was identified by *Newsweek* as one of nineteen "Xers" who had made a distinctive impact on current American culture.

Born Tabitha Sornberger in 1967 in San Antonio, she is the daughter of an Air Force officer and spent her childhood on military bases in the Philippines, Germany, and Florida. She studied journalism at New York University and served as an intern with CNN, ABC, and MTV. After her graduation in 1989, she spent a year and a half working for the ABC affiliate in Burlington, Vermont. Then, having shortened her name from Sornberger, she returned to New York to work at MTV.

Soren etched her MTV imprint during the 1992 presidential election. Until 1991, MTV's news coverage had focused heavily on rock stars, their tours, and other news about the music industry and popular culture. In 1992, however, MTV introduced a campaign news program called *Choose or Lose*, which presented election coverage in a breezy, fast-moving format. Soren, the chief designer of this innovative program, wanted to get young people involved and voting.

During the 1992 campaign, Soren had the opportunity to interview presidential candidate Bill Clinton on four occasions, as well as vice presidential nominee Al Gore and other Democratic candidates. In late October, even President George Bush agreed to an interview. Since that time, many major political figures have appeared on MTV, including President Clinton, Vice President Gore, Attorney General Janet Reno, and Newt Gingrich. In 1996, *Choose or Lose* started its presidential election coverage with a Soren interview of Republican candidate Bob Dole, then the Senate majority leader.

listeners and viewers comment and question on-the-air personalities, have now become standard fare.

Technology in the newsroom has changed as well. In fact, the technology now exists to eliminate newspapers altogether. There are services that deliver the news through a fiber-optic cable directly to the home or office, allowing the user to read the news, editorials, and other features on a computer screen.

The communications revolution continues to advance at a rapid rate. The Clinton administration has begun the development of a communications "super-highway," a voice, video, and data network that can transmit information in a matter of seconds across the country, enabling users to access hundreds of stations and data banks. As we have pointed out throughout this text, it is now possible to use the Internet to obtain a wealth of information about politics and government.

On-line media   The Internet was created in 1969 by experts in the Department of Defense who feared that the military communications system could be sabotaged or disrupted by a nuclear attack. To reduce the system's vulnerability to hostile forces, they decentralized it, creating a network of communications between computers. This network broke information into pieces and sent these pieces to designated points in the system where they were reassembled to produce a message. If for any reason a route was blocked, the packet of information would seek an alternate route.

At first, the system connected just the Pentagon's computers. By the 1980s, it extended to researchers and scholars at universities and to officials in other government agencies. By the 1990s, it expanded into the private sector. Policy makers quickly saw the Internet as an effective means to inform and communicate with the public. Not surprisingly, politicians saw its potential as well.

New communication technologies have often been exploited by creative politicians in their efforts to circumvent the existing news media and reach out to the public directly. As discussed earlier, President Franklin D. Roosevelt promoted his New Deal policies by speaking directly to Americans in their homes on the radio. In 1961, President Kennedy, inspired by the assessments of his 1960 debates with Richard M. Nixon, introduced televised "live" news conferences from the White House. Sixty years after Roosevelt's "fireside chat" initiative, the Clinton administration became the first to open itself to computer communication via the Internet. On June 1, 1993, the White House began to interact with the public through an electronic mail (*e-mail*) system originally developed at Massachusetts Institute of Technology during the 1992 Clinton-Gore presidential campaign. Since the White House kickoff, the scale and sophistication of on-line service to all three branches of government has been upgraded so rapidly that each month sees new sites added on the terrain of the federal information network.

The original White House interface was elevated to a substantially more sophisticated level on October 20, 1994, when Vice President Gore announced that an interactive multimedia server had started to function. Called *Welcome to the White House: An Interactive Citizens' Handbook*, the new Internet server is operated by means of the *World Wide Web (WWW)*, which is based on hypertext technology and is exceptionally "user-friendly." One can access text, pictures, and audio and video files from the White House by simply clicking a computer mouse at the appropriate icons or the highlighted key words.

The *Handbook*, which is linked directly to the websites of all cabinet-level departments and the other federal executive agencies, offers the public direct, rapid, and easy-to-use access to an enormous amount of government information. While the White House was taking the lead in getting into "cyberspace," Capitol Hill was

TWO CENTURIES OF HIGH-TECH POLITICS

1803 Because British troops destroyed many of his papers when he was governor of Virginia during the Revolutionary War, Thomas Jefferson experiments with copying letters on pantographs and letter presses.

1829 Andrew Jackson, assailed by scandal-mongering in the press (he was called, among other things, a bigamist), makes the newspaper magnate Amos Kendall a member of his informal cabinet. Kendall directs a panoply of administration-controlled newspapers and later becomes postmaster general, supervising political patronage.

1863 Communicating with his generals by telegraph helps make Abraham Lincoln a stickler for taut prose, according to his biographer Garry Wills.

1866 Andrew Johnson installs the White House's first telegraph.

1879 Rutherford B. Hayes installs the first White House telephone. It is rarely used until the first administration of Grover Cleveland, starting in 1885; he often answers it himself.

1924 Calvin Coolidge makes the first presidential radio speech.

1933 Franklin D. Roosevelt inaugurates the "fireside chat" to speak intimately to people at home—and bypass a hostile press. Social Security and other New Deal programs benefit IBM, whose punchcard systems and, later, computers are necessary for administering the vast databases they require.

1939 Roosevelt takes delivery of the first White House television set and makes the first presidential television appearance at the New York World's Fair.

1952 On election eve a Univac computer predicts the Eisenhower landslide, but the television networks refuse to believe it.

1961 Buoyed by his performance in campaign debates, in which television viewers thought he had won and radio listeners thought Richard M. Nixon had won, John F. Kennedy initiates live, televised news conferences.

1965 To watch the network news programs simultaneously, Lyndon B. Johnson installs three television sets in a huge cabinet, the ugliest piece of Oval Office furniture ever.

1970 The Xerox machine, used to disseminate the Pentagon papers, enrages President Nixon, whose downfall is guaranteed by the Oval Office taping system.

1977 Jimmy Carter attempts to revive the "fireside chat" on television, pushing his energy program while wearing a cardigan sweater in front of a real fireplace. Perhaps proving Marshall McLuhan's dictum that radio is a hot medium (and thus suitable for firesides) while television is a cool one, the public reaction is tepid.

1981 Ronald Reagan pioneers retro media, returning to weekly radio addresses. The White House hooks up to an e-mail system, which Oliver North shows can be erased faster than paper can be shredded.

1991 George Bush becomes the first president with a computer terminal but shows no sign of using it.

1993 Bill Clinton's White House goes on the Internet. A federal appeals court judge, Charles Rickey, rules that White House e-mail has the status of official government documents and orders it preserved.

1994 White House develops a sophisticated interactive website, allowing computer users to access executive-branch documents and hear Socks, the Clinton family's cat, meow.

1995 House and Senate establish websites, allowing the public to access bills, committee reports, and the *Congressional Record*. National party organizations also create their own home pages.

1996 Presidential candidates create home pages to communicate with voters. White House launches Cyber Ed truck, a cyberclassroom on wheels, to provide hands-on educational technology for children across the country. House of Representatives creates a standardized e-mail system.

SOURCE: *New York Times*, November 28, 1993, C7; ©1993; updated by authors.

The White House home page gives users of the World Wide Web access to material about the daily life of the first family as well as more substantive policy information.

also moving in the same direction. House Speaker Newt Gingrich was as enthusiastic as Vice President Gore in promoting the "information superhighway," and on January 4, 1995, the House of Representatives established Thomas, a database system named after Thomas Jefferson. The Senate website became operational later in the year. The sites of both House and Senate are linked directly to the interface of the Library of Congress, which offers information on daily congressional activities, the full text of bills introduced in Congress since 1973, and information on the library's huge collection, among other things. The number of individual legislators who have ventured onto the Internet has grown very rapidly as well. Today most senators and representatives can be contacted by e-mail and have their own "home pages" on the Web.[17]

The judicial branch has lagged behind the other two branches, though the Administrative Office of U.S. Courts (on behalf of the U.S. Courts) has developed a website called *U.S. Federal Judiciary* and the Federal Judicial Center has also established a website. For more information on the courts and the Internet, see the Where on the Web? box in Chapter 15.

Like television in the 1950s, the Internet has become a mass medium in the 1990s. According to a survey on information technology and its uses by the public, the Times Mirror Center reported that 5 million people subscribed to an on-line service in 1994; six months later that number had mushroomed to 12 million, with an additional 2 million people connected to the Internet directly without a consumer service.[18] And the number continues to grow. A poll conducted by Nielsen Media Research in October 1995 for a group of companies specializing in computer communications estimated that 37 million people in the United States and Canada had access to the Internet, although this figure has been criticized as inflated by one of the researchers who worked on the project.[19] By the year 2000, 52 million users are likely, with the majority in the United States.[20]

A relatively small percentage of Internet users have signed onto the Web with their own home page, although there are over 16 million pages on the Web and that number is growing exponentially. In contrast, there is relatively heavy use of e-mail for work and, increasingly, for personal communications.

Who are the principal users? Initially, they have been the young and the well educated. According to the Nielsen study, more than half are between the ages of 16 and 34.[21] In addition to age and education, the Times Mirror study found gender and income differences, with men and those in the higher income brackets the biggest users.[22] (See Table 11-4.) Obviously, e-mail and the World Wide Web are the communications of the future, used comparatively more at this time by the generation that grew up with them.

Rock the Vote, an organization dedicated to increasing the involvement of younger people in the political process, has a website in which users can access voter registration forms, complete them, and send them to a clearinghouse that mails them to the users' states. Those who register in this manner will be reminded on the Internet about the vote a few days before the election.

There have also been a few political candidates who campaigned solely on the Internet, such as a candidate for the city council of Sunnyvale, California, in 1993, who was elected with 60 percent of the vote. All the major contenders for the Republican presidential nomination in 1996 and the major party candidates in the general election had pages on which information about their campaigns could be accessed. The major parties have also set up pages: the Democratic National Committee initiated access on the Web in June 1995, and its Republican counterpart followed three months later. Among others with pages are most state governments and many newspapers and magazines.

Since the White House went on line, public access to government information has been improved substantially. Abundant information on the federal government is currently available to the public at a computer user's fingertips. The major government Internet sites are listed in the appropriate chapters of this text. Almost all of them are linked directly, thereby facilitating "surfing" from one site to another.

As the information explosion changes the ways in which people obtain political and other information, the type and amount of information they receive, the ways in which they contact their government, and the time frame in which public officials respond, politics and government are bound to be affected. The next two sections examine some of that impact by describing contemporary news media coverage of elections and government and exploring how that coverage affects the events that are reported.

NEWS MEDIA AND POLITICS

News media coverage of politics and government is not neutral. No coverage can be. What do the news media choose to emphasize, and to whom are their stories directed? How do candidates for political office react, and how do they try to shape the news to their advantage? Finally, what impact does all this have on voters?

The News Slant

The key to news media coverage of political events (as well as other kinds of events) is their **newsworthiness**. This complex concept includes timeliness, importance, conflict, drama, and surprise. To be considered news, an event must have the potential to capture the attention of the public: readers, listeners, and viewers. From the news media's perspective, their job is to emphasize events that have this potential.

TABLE 11-4 — USE OF HOUSEHOLD INFORMATION TECHNOLOGIES (PERCENTAGES)

	AT HOME				
	USES COMPUTER	HAS CD-ROM	SUBSCRIBES TO ANY ON-LINE INFO. SERVICE	USES E-MAIL REGULARLY	USES WWW
Total	32	15	6	7	3
Male	38	18	9	9	4
Female	28	13	4	6	2
White	33	16	7	7	3
Black	20	8	3	5	1
Hispanic	29	12	8	8	1
Age 18–29	38	18	9	12	6
30–49	41	20	9	9	3
50–64	26	12	4	6	1
65+	9	4	1	—	—
Age 18–29					
Male	41	20	14	14	8
Female	36	16	5	8	4
Age 30–49					
Male	44	22	10	9	5
Female	38	18	7	7	2
Age 50+					
Male	25	10	5	5	2
Female	13	6	1	2	0
College graduate	57	28	15	16	8
Some college	44	19	8	9	3
High school graduate	23	10	3	4	1
Less than high school	11	6	2	1	—

What is reported as news is also influenced by factors such as access and convenience. With limited resources, the media have to decide what to cover and how much time to devote to it. Along with newsworthiness, the cost of coverage and the amount of time and trouble it will take figure in that decision.

How does the slant of the news color coverage of an event? Consider an electoral campaign. Above all else, in the view of the media, election news must be exciting. Thus campaigns are reported as if they were sporting contests, with correspondents stressing the competitive, gaming aspect. According to the polls, which of the candidates is winning and losing, who is doing better than expected, and who is doing worse? Not only is the game of politics emphasized, but it is stressed at the expense of substantive policy issues—particularly at the beginning of the electoral process, when "horse race" stories tend to dominate the coverage (see Figure 11-3). Once a front-runner emerges, builds a lead, and thus makes the race less interesting, the focus shifts to questions about the candidates' character and to conflicts between candidates, their advisers and staff, and even the news media in the campaign.

TABLE 11-4	USE OF HOUSEHOLD INFORMATION TECHNOLOGIES (PERCENTAGES) (*continued*)

| | AT HOME | | SUBSCRIBES TO ANY ON-LINE INFO. SERVICE | USES E-MAIL REGULARLY | USES WWW |
	USES COMPUTER	HAS CD-ROM			
Family income					
More than $50,000	57	29	14	13	5
$30,000–49,000	37	18	6	7	4
$20,000–29,000	23	9	4	5	2
Less than $20,000	12	4	1	2	1
Children in home	42	21	7	8	3
No children	26	12	6	7	3
Employed	38	18	9	10	4
Unemployed	19	10	2	2	1
In school	53	24	13	17	7
Work at home[a]	53	26	14	15	5
Home-based business	53	25	12	9	3
East	32	17	7	8	2
Midwest	28	15	5	6	2
South	28	12	6	7	3
West	42	19	9	9	5
City	32	16	7	8	4
Small town	26	12	5	5	1
Suburb	47	22	10	11	4
Rural	28	14	5	6	2

[a]Respondent worked at home at least one day last week.

Source: "Americans Going Online . . . Explosive Growth, Uncertain Destinations," Times Mirror Center for the People and the Press, *October 16, 1995, 8. Reprinted by permission.*

Stories about the private lives and personalities of the candidates and their staffs have now become a fixture of campaign coverage. They began during the 1980 presidential primaries when the news media focused attention on Senator Edward Kennedy's troubled marriage and his 1969 car accident at Chappaquiddick, Massachusetts, in which a young woman drowned. Similarly, in 1988 news reports about Senator Gary Hart's female guest at his townhouse in Washington raised questions about his marital fidelity, his credibility, and his judgment. In the 1992 primaries, Bill Clinton also faced a barrage of questions about his personal life after a supermarket tabloid published a report linking him romantically with a woman who had been a club singer and a local television personality in Little Rock. More than half the network news stories about Clinton between January 1 and April 15, 1992, dealt with "the character issue."[23] As president and during the 1996 campaign, he continued to be plagued by these and other personal questions (a failed real estate investment by him and his wife, Mrs. Clinton's successful speculation in the futures market, and a sexual harassment charge stemming from the period when he was governor of Arkansas).

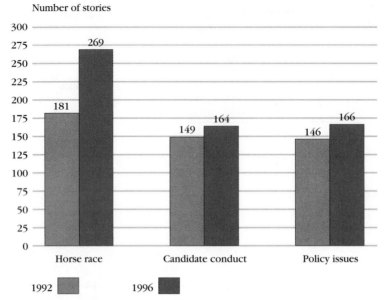

Note: A story may include more than one topic.

FIGURE 11-3

Focus of coverage of primaries on the evening news, January–March 1992 and 1996.

SOURCE: "The Bad News Campaign," *Media Monitor*, March/April 1996: 3.

In general, the issue of personality has received more attention in recent years than have issues of policy. The principal reason is that people find personality more interesting than complex, often abstract policy considerations. Another reason may have to do with the medium of television itself. The average length of a story on the evening news is 45 to 90 seconds, too short a time to provide in-depth analysis and barely long enough to let candidates discuss the issues.[24] In fact, policy issues accounted for less than one-third of all the campaign stories on the evening news programs broadcast by the three major networks in 1992 and during the 1996 Republican primaries and caucuses, compared with 40 percent in 1988.[25] (However, more attention was devoted to policy issues between the 1996 primaries and nominating conventions.[26])

In addition to the presumption about what is newsworthy in a campaign and how it should be presented, there is a larger framework into which that news is made to fit. According to political scientist Thomas E. Patterson, a dominant "story line" emerges in the media, and much of the campaign is explained in terms of it. In 1992, it was Pat Buchanan's surprising showing in the primaries against President Bush that was news, not Bush's easy wins against his Republican rival; in 1996, it was Buchanan's and Steve Forbes's early victories, not Robert Dole's organizational and reputational advantages.

In his analysis of the 1992 story line, Patterson writes:

> Bush's bad press was mainly a function of journalistic values. The news form itself affected both the content and the slant of most of his coverage. Bush's story was that of a reelection campaign in deep trouble—much like the story of a baseball team that was favored to win the pennant but stumbled early and never regained its stride.[27]

Media probing into the private lives of politicians has begun to extend to their staffs as well. During the 1996 Democratic National Convention, a tabloid newspaper reported that President Clinton's major adviser for his reelection campaign, Dick Morris, had been involved with a prostitute to whom he had disclosed detailed campaign information. Morris, the architect of the campaign's emphasis on "family values" and a former strategist for many top Republican as well as Democratic politicians, immediately resigned—but not without having lined up a lucrative book contract.

Patterson's point is that the press fits the news of the campaign into the accepted story rather than create new stories from the changing events of the campaign. Naturally, the story line that the news media present affects the electorate's perception of what is happening.

Not only is the news fit into a story line, but it is increasingly bad news. In an analysis of the evening news on the three major television networks during the 1992 presidential campaign, S. Robert Lichter and his associates found that 69 percent of the evaluations of President Bush were negative, as were 63 percent of the comments about Governor Clinton and 54 percent of those about Ross Perot after he got back into the race.[28] Similarly, during the 1996 primaries the four leading Republican candidates—Dole, Buchanan, Alexander, and Forbes—all received more negative than positive press. In fact, their speeches, their ads, and their interviews were less critical of their opponents than the media were of the candidates in general.[29] (See Figure 11-4.) Dole's negative press continued into the summer prior to the Republican convention. Clinton, however, received more favorable press during this period.[30]

What is the reason for all the negativism? Does it represent an ideological or political bias, as Dole charged in the 1996 general election campaign? Conservatives have alleged for years that the national news media are biased against conservative ideas and policy positions and the candidates who support them because most reporters are liberal. They point to a study, conducted at the end of the 1970s and the beginning of the 1980s by Lichter, Stanley Rothman, and Linda Lichter, that found the typical journalist much more likely to be liberal than conservative and Democratic than Republican. Liberals, however, point out that most media owners and editors are conservative and Republican. Nonetheless, determining that someone is liberal or conservative, Democratic or Republican, is not sufficient evidence to conclude that news coverage itself was and continues to be ideological and partisan. For that conclusion to be drawn, the content of the news must be analyzed, not the characteristics and attitudes of those who report, edit, or pay for it.

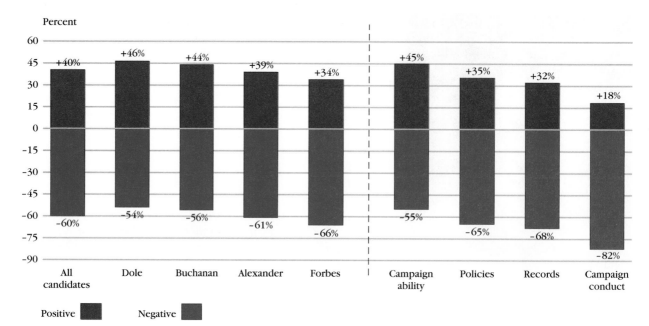

Percent

Note: Evaluations were made by reporters and nonpartisan sources
and refer to ABC, CBS, and NBC evening news election stories.

FIGURE 11-4

Mean evaluations of Republican primary candidates, January–March 1996.

SOURCE: "The Bad News Campaign," *Media Monitor*, March/April 1996: 3.

Although academic experts disagree on whether the news has an ideological bias, they do agree that it has a professional bias that contributes to negative coverage. That bias or orientation is dictated by the definition of what is news. A new face winning or an old face losing is news; an old one winning or a new one losing is not. Similarly, the first time a politician states a position, it may be news; the second time, it is not. Since candidates or public officials cannot provide new positions or new ideas every time they address a group—in fact, candidates normally give the same speech many times over—the correspondents who cover these events look for other things to report. Verbal slips, inconsistent statements, and other mistakes get more attention than would the news that a speech is well delivered or warmly received. Similarly, how the public reacts to what candidates say and do has become almost as newsworthy as the statement, event, or action itself.

Another aspect of contemporary news coverage that adversely affects a candidate's ability to appeal to voters is the increasing mediating role that correspondents play. News programs devote less time to the candidate's own words and more to the correspondents and others for their reaction. In 1968, the average length of a quotation from candidates on the evening television news was 42.3 seconds. In 1992 it was only 8.4 seconds; and during the January–March period in which the Republican nomination contest was decided in 1996, it was even less, averaging 7.2 seconds—with half of the "bites" 5 seconds or less (although it lengthened to 9.8 seconds after Dole had wrapped up the nomination and began articulating positions for the presidential election).[31] The candidates themselves accounted for only a small percentage of the airtime on campaign stories, with the reporters and others they interviewed accounting for most of the time. In short, the campaign is presented by television professionals who are oriented toward enhancing viewer interest, not by those who want to make their case. Under the circumstances, it is not surprising that politicians attempt to manipulate the news of their campaigns.

Manipulation of the News

Staging   People in the news, especially politicians, try to affect the coverage they receive. They do this by scheduling and staging events, by releasing information and granting access to reporters, and by preparing speeches and responses. To accommodate television's need for good visual images, newsmakers often pose in dramatic settings to create the image they wish to convey. Reagan's appearance on the shores of Normandy on the fortieth anniversary of the Allied invasion of Europe during World War II, Bush's Thanksgiving dinner with the troops on the Arabian desert during the 1990 buildup of United States forces for the Persian Gulf War, and Clinton's attendance at a memorial service in Oklahoma City following the 1995 bombing of the federal office building there are three illustrations of how recent presidents have used their position to advantage. Newt Gingrich's appearance with President Clinton at a senior citizens' event in New Hampshire and their handshake symbolizing an agreement to reform campaign finance is another.

Those who lack a presidential or even a House Speaker's podium have to use their imagination and creativity to generate a favorable and memorable image. In 1984, for example, when Senator Gary Hart was a candidate for the Democratic presidential nomination, he dressed as a lumberjack, threw an ax at a target, and hit it. This scene, shown on television repeatedly, reinforced Hart's image as vigorous, young, and unorthodox. In a debate during the 1988 Democratic primaries, Governor Bruce Babbitt suddenly stood up to dramatize his call for *higher* taxes. Although he asked the other candidates to do the same, none did. Television showed his gesture repeatedly because it was "good video"; Babbitt therefore succeeded in getting his message across. The problem in this case was the message; few people want to pay higher taxes.

Press secretaries control access to the candidates and to information released about them. In fact, because of the news media's constant need for new stories, reporters often turn for help to the subjects of their inquiry and to their staffs. An analysis of twenty newspapers found that during the 1968 campaign the candidates were the main source of more than half the election stories about themselves or their opponent.[32] In 1992, Republican officials provided the news media with information about H. Ross Perot's dealings with the government and his investigations of public officials—information that proved damaging to Perot.

Entertaining   One of the major changes in the relationship between politicians and the news media in the 1990s has been the use of the "soft news," or talk/entertainment, format by candidates and (to a lesser extent) public officials to present their views in their own words. Pioneered by Ross Perot on television and Jerry Brown on radio, this new format provides a user-friendly atmosphere in which to engage the public. In 1992 the presidential candidates and their running mates appeared on thirty-nine separate talk/entertainment programs. Both President Clinton and Speaker Gingrich also used this format after the 1994 election, Clinton on *Larry King Live* and Gingrich on MTV. In variations of the format such as town meetings and call-in shows, candidates and public officials can demonstrate their responsiveness, sincerity, and empathy by interacting with the audience. Clinton has been particularly effective in such settings.

In 1992, to reach larger, less politically involved audiences, presidential candidates began to appear on entertainment shows. Here Bill Clinton plays his saxophone for Arsenio Hall (left). This appearance, like one on MTV, contrasted the younger, "swinging" Clinton with the more aloof, stuffy George Bush—a contrast that helped Clinton capture the youth vote.

The talk/entertainment format has several other advantages for politicians, particularly candidates. For one thing, it distances them from the aggressive "gotcha" style of journalism in which national news correspondents frequently engage. They are treated better, more like celebrities than politicians. Their host tends to be more cordial and less adversarial than the national correspondents. Moreover, their audience is different. Those who watch the talk/entertainment shows tend to be less interested in politics and less partisan in their views, and thus may be more amenable to influence by those who appear on such programs.

Instead of being asked specific, often tricky, "hardball" questions that focus on personality, image, and controversy, politicians are asked "softer" questions that are more straightforward, issue oriented, and easier to answer; the questions may even have been screened in advance by program producers. And those being questioned can give longer answers that are broadcast in their entirety rather than in one or two sound bites. In fact, the programs themselves are often newsworthy, generating an even larger impact when excerpts from them are rebroadcast or summarized on the news. The larger audience, higher comfort level, and greater ability to project desired images and present seemingly spontaneous but often carefully crafted answers have made this format appealing for politicians who wish to supplement and, where possible, circumvent the national press coverage to reach the general public.

Political Advertising

Paid advertising can also be used to convey political messages. Associated primarily with election campaigns, it has been used as well to generate public support on a wide range of political issues. One of the most effective advertising campaigns in recent years was launched in 1994 by the Health Insurance Industry of America against President Clinton's health-care reform plan. The ads featured an average American couple named Harry and Louise, who voiced their fears that the Clinton plan would not allow them to choose their own doctors, would cost them more money, and would involve them in more government paperwork and red tape. Another very effective series of policy ads, aired in 1995 by the Democratic National Committee, in turn warned against the Republican plan to cut funding from the Medicare program.

The objectives of advertising are to gain recognition, to create images, and to educate people about the merits or liabilities of particular policies or candidates. Bill Clinton skillfully used advertising during his presidential campaigns to project an image of a New Democrat, a moderate, who could deal effectively with economic problems. He also used it to counter and preempt Republican criticism of himself and his administration.

Image making can be negative as well as positive. With the increasing emphasis placed on personal factors in politics, **negative advertising** has grown in importance in recent years, particularly during election campaigns. Researchers have estimated that at least half the advertising in the last three presidential campaigns was negative.[33]

One ad in 1988 evoked particularly strong emotions. Directed against Democratic candidate Michael Dukakis, the governor of Massachusetts, it featured a mug shot of Willie Horton, an African-American prisoner who had raped a white woman while on a weekend furlough from a Massachusetts jail. Aimed at those who were fearful of crime, of African Americans, and of liberals and their "do-good" social policies, the ad placed Dukakis squarely in the liberal, do-gooder camp. The commercial, sponsored by a political action committee supporting Bush, was supplemented by other PAC ads featuring relatives of the victims of Horton's crimes. The Bush campaign also produced ads of its own to reinforce the crime issue.

The cumulative impact of these negative ads left the impression that Dukakis released hardened criminals who then recommitted their heinous crimes against other innocent victims. By the end of the campaign, 25 percent of the electorate knew who Willie Horton was, what he did, and who had furloughed him; 49 percent thought Dukakis was soft on crime.[34]

Voters are becoming more leery of negative ads, however. Part of their skepticism has stemmed from the controversy generated by some of them, such as the one about Willie Horton. Part of it has also resulted from more critical evaluation and analysis of the ads by major news organizations.[35]

In recent years one of the most interesting advertising innovations has been the "infomercial" created by Ross Perot for his 1992 presidential campaign and used again in 1996. This type of ad featured the candidate himself seated at a desk with a pointer and computer-generated graphics, talking in a no-nonsense manner about economic and political problems. It was designed to reinforce Perot's homespun image as a straight-talking businessman who had none of the veneer and polish of slick politicians and Washington insiders.

The Impact of the Media on Electoral Politics

With all the effort and energy put into news coverage and the candidates' use of the media, one would think that the news media have a significant impact on the outcome of elections. Yet that impact is difficult to measure.

Research has found that the media (including hard news, soft news, and advertising) affect voters' awareness and impressions of candidates more than they influence their political attitudes or cause them to change their opinions on major issues. The media do, however, elevate the importance of certain issues through the attention they devote to them. In this way, the media are able to influence the criteria that voters use to evaluate candidates and decide for whom to vote.

The news media are usually more influential at the beginning of the electoral process, when people have relatively little knowledge about the candidates and their positions, than at the end. Especially in presidential elections, the disproportionate coverage given to the candidates in the first primaries and caucuses can be crucial to their success in winning the nomination. In 1988 two states, Iowa and New Hampshire, with just 3 percent of the United States population, received 34 percent of all the prenomination campaign coverage on the networks' evening news.[36] In 1992 and 1996 the pattern was the same, with the bulk of press attention devoted to these early contests.[37]

News media coverage affects voter turnout. By emphasizing certain issues and personal characteristics, the press sets the campaign agenda and frames discussion. By evaluating the candidates and their campaigns, by reporting public sentiment, and by forecasting the likely outcome, they may influence that outcome. Thus they become participant observers.

The news media have also affected the political parties by becoming today the principal vehicle through which campaigns are communicated. Voters no longer need to turn to the parties for information about candidates. Conversely, candidates gain independence from party organizations by mounting direct media-based appeals.

Not only may the media influence which candidates are elected; they also influence what those candidates do after being elected. Clinton's adherence to his economic stimulus program at the beginning of his presidency in spite of economic recovery, and Gingrich's promise to vote on all the proposals contained in the Republicans' Contract with America within the first 100 days of the 104th Congress, indicate how much the publicity given to campaign promises shapes the policy agenda after an election. Bush's reversal on his "Read my lips, no new taxes" pledge and his subsequent election defeat reveal the costs of breaking a major promise to the American voters.

Finally, the news media shape the environment for governing. Candidates who emphasize their leadership capabilities, and media that focus on these qualities, create expectations that may be difficult to achieve or ignore. Telegenic candidates (those who look good on television) are expected to be telegenic leaders, to use the style of campaigning that got them into office to stay in office. Moreover, they are expected to perform their official duties in full public view. Behind-the-scenes negotiation, quiet diplomacy, confidential communications—all necessary for effective decision making—are more difficult in an age when the news media see it as their right and responsibility to report on the politics and process of policy making as well as the policy itself.

NEWS MEDIA AND GOVERNMENT

Coverage of public officials and policies does not end with the election. Often the news is an important factor in shaping debates over the issues and the evaluation of political leaders.

Certain journalistic conventions shape the reporting and presentation of national news. The focus on government activities centers on people rather than on institutions or policy, partly because most issues and operations of government are so complex that they are difficult to explain in a news story. Little background or contextual information is provided, particularly by the electronic media. Instead, the personal dimensions of the story are emphasized. For example, the personalities and actions of those who were involved in the Iran-contra affair were more interesting to the American public than were details about the confusing arms sales and ways in which funds were diverted; similarly, it was the Clintons' role in Whitewater that captivated public attention, not the complex financial transaction.

In addition, news coverage often stresses the style and strategy employed by government officials to pass or defeat a particular piece of legislation, rather than the effect the policy might have on the country. This is a variation of the "horse race" journalism that commonly appears in election coverage. Policy issues are presented as two-sided arguments. Congressional votes are portrayed as either wins or losses for the president or congressional leadership; conflicts within agencies or committees are seen as pluses or minuses for one individual or group against another. In the mid 1990s, the news media variously described the debate and division over how to balance the budget in seven years as a tug of war between the administration and Congress; between Clinton, Dole, and Gingrich; between Democrats and Republicans; and between liberals and conservatives.

In their watchdog role the news media tend to emphasize failures rather than successes, what does not work rather than what does. Bad news is almost always reported; good news may not be.

Coverage of the President

In their coverage of the national government, the news media focus on the presidency. One media watcher found that President Clinton was featured in one out of every eight network stories on the evening news in 1994.[38] Congress traditionally gets much less attention than the president, although following the 1994 midterm elections, coverage of Congress exceeded that of the president by a margin of about 2 to 1.[39]

The reason that the presidency receives so much attention is that the president is seen as the principal initiator and prime mover of the political system, the head of the government and head of state, a chieftain with multiple roles, all deserving attention. Moreover, the presidency provides a "handle" for evaluating the many facets of government. The president personifies the government, at least in the view of the news media.

The amount of coverage devoted to the rest of the executive branch varies. Certain cabinet secretaries and departments (State, Defense, Justice, Treasury) usually get more than others because the problems they deal with and the policies they implement have more important or visible consequences. The bureaucracy that actually implements policies is given even less attention, except for instances of fraud, waste, and abuse. However, specialized media, such as trade journals and newsletters, concentrate on specific areas of policy and on the congressional committees and executive agencies that deal with them. Directed toward (and frequently published by) concerned interest groups, these publications provide in-depth coverage for those who are most affected by the policies.

The news media's focus on the president naturally produces incentives for an administration to try to shape the coverage it receives. Presidents want to place their administration in a favorable light and build support for their policies. They may also want to use the media to communicate with Congress and with foreign leaders without having to go through formal channels such as submitting a presidential message to Congress or calling in the ambassador of another country to deliver an official letter about the United States position on an issue of mutual concern.

The president has many tools for "managing" the news. For example, the release of news may be timed to make the administration look good. If good news is released, it is likely to be the only information made available by the administration at that time. If bad news must be released, other announcements may also be made in an attempt to obscure it; and if possible, it is made public over the weekend, when less attention will be paid to it. The general rule is that good news is announced by the president and bad news by others, often the White House press secretary or a cabinet official.

Presidents may use other tactics to avoid commenting on unpleasant topics. Whenever Ronald Reagan left for trips that were covered by the media, the helicopter that took him to his plane would remain running while the president walked to and from it. Reporters would shout questions, and if the president did not wish to answer them, he would point to the helicopter and indicate that he could not hear what was being said. Facilities for press conferences were also arranged so that the president would not have to go past reporters after the conference was over; he simply turned around and walked out of the room, thereby avoiding further questioning.

The White House can also take more direct steps to affect what the media report.

President Reagan points to his ear and indicates that he cannot hear the questions shouted by reporters as he walks to his helicopter. Reagan avoided questions that he did not wish to answer, which gave his administration considerable control over its media agenda.

With limited resources to discover presidential news and limited time to air it, reporters tend to rely on the pictures and stories made available to them by White House sources. Among the services provided to the White House press corps that may help shape the news are briefings, interviews, off-the-record background sessions, photo opportunities, travel arrangements, and handouts and other press releases. The Clinton administration held as many as three press briefings a day not only to present the president's perspective but to give reporters stories, keeping them busy and thereby limiting their time to pursue other leads. The news media depend heavily on these services, especially when the president is away from Washington and their access to other decision makers is extremely limited. One of the reasons that presidents choose to meet foreign leaders abroad is that reporters' access can be more limited than in the United States.

The dependence of the press on government became a subject of some controversy during and after the military actions in Grenada (1983), Panama (1989–1990), and the Persian Gulf (1991). In all three campaigns, the military operations were kept secret and reporters were barred from combat areas. Some of them were given limited access to the staging areas, but only under military supervision. As a result, reporters had to rely on government briefings and films, some of which turned out to be incorrect or misleading. Once the news media could obtain greater access and more information, various foul-ups came to light, particularly the poor logistical coordination of the Grenada invasion and the overblown success attributed to the Patriot missile defense system during the Persian Gulf War.

In addition to the comprehensive coverage of presidential activities, the president can usually obtain airtime for major speeches and press conferences in times of crisis or, occasionally, when making a major policy announcement. If the news media perceive that partisan politics is a primary motivation for such a request, however, they are less apt to provide that free time. When President Clinton announced in the spring of 1995 that he wished to hold a prime-time press conference after the House

In recent administrations presidential press conferences have become more formal, made-for-television productions. Here President Clinton meets the press in the East Room of the White House.

of Representatives had voted on all the items in the Contract with America, only one major network chose to cover the event in addition to CNN and public television.[40] Moreover, presidents have to be careful to avoid overexposure. A presidential media event should be a special occasion, not a commonplace occurrence. During his first two years in office, Clinton was accused of making too many public appearances in too many ordinary settings, and thereby diminishing the dignity of his office.

Despite the many ways in which the White House can curry favor with reporters, stage events, control access to information, and direct public attention, presidential news is often unfavorable. In an analysis of evening news coverage of the first twenty-eight months of the Clinton administration, Lichter and his associates found that the president was the object of 3,500 negative comments. His ratio of bad news to good news was 5 to 3 (63 percent bad compared with 37 percent good).[41] Figure 11-5 traces both Clinton's television news coverage and his public-opinion approval ratings during this period.

Coverage of Congress

Congress is less newsworthy than the president most of the time. The commercial television networks and CNN occasionally offer live coverage of events such as major speeches, committee hearings, and floor debates. In recent years, these have included the Senate hearings on the confirmation of Clarence Thomas as a Supreme Court justice in 1991 and of Dr. Henry Foster as surgeon general in 1995 and the

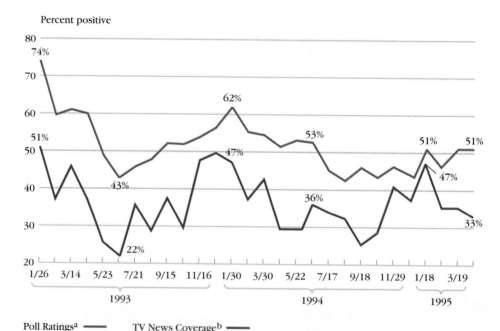

Poll Ratings[a] ———   TV News Coverage[b] ———

[a]Poll Ratings based on Gallup/*USA Today*/CNN polls. Excludes "don't know" responses; therefore ratings may appear higher than reported elsewhere.

[b]TV News Coverage based on CMPA content analysis of sound bites on the ABC, CBS, and NBC evening news programs.

FIGURE 11-5

President Clinton's evaluations on television and by the public, 1993–1995.

SOURCE: "The Invisible Man, TV News Coverage of President Bill Clinton, 1993–1995," *Media Monitor*, May/June 1995: 5. Reprinted by permission.

floor debate in the Senate over the authorization of military force against Iraq in 1991. Other famous congressional hearings that have received live coverage include the investigations of the Iran-contra affair during the Reagan administration and of Watergate and related scandals during the Nixon administration, as well as Senator Joseph McCarthy's hunt for communists in the government during the Eisenhower administration.

Most of the coverage on the major broadcast networks is not live, however. Rather, they report snippets of what Congress does or does not do and how representatives and senators behave. The major live coverage is on C-SPAN, which records the official proceedings on the House and Senate floors and, along with CNN, covers selected committee hearings.

With 535 members of Congress, most eager for public attention, there is no shortage of people willing to be interviewed. The open environment encourages the news media to assign a host of reporters and correspondents to the Capitol Hill "beat."

The focus of congressional coverage tends to be on the final stages of the law-making process and frequently on the final vote that will determine a bill's fate. The formative processes of legislation—the introduction of a bill, subcommittee and committee hearings—are largely ignored, except for controversies over presidential initiatives and investigations by key committees. Moreover, the major media give little emphasis to the substance of policy and its consequences for society. When substantive policy is discussed, it is frequently presented in simplified form and as a divisive political issue. Newspapers and news magazines provide more in-depth coverage of policy issues than do the electronic media, but the most in-depth coverage comes from the specialty press—journals that focus on Congress, such as *Congressional Quarterly*, *Roll Call*, *The Hill*, and the newsletters of interest groups.

Instead of policy, the major media tend to stress the divisions within Congress, the difficulties its members have in reaching agreement, and the obstacles to the president's legislative leadership. Because the internal policy-making processes of Congress are complex, slow-moving, undramatic, and often unpredictable, the media describe Congress as constantly involved in struggles against itself or against the president. Even during the early days of the 104th, Republican-controlled Congress, Lichter and his associates found negative comments exceeding positive ones on every issue the Republicans advocated except for Congress reforming itself.[42] Is it any wonder that the public continues to have such negative perceptions of Congress and the job it is doing?

Even when Congress is inquiring into allegations of abuse and misconduct by public officials, it may be pictured in an unfavorable light. The appearance of Colonel Oliver North before the joint congressional committee investigating the Iran-contra affair produced such an effect, as North's commanding presence, well-articulated convictions, and persuasiveness in explaining his actions captured the attention and evoked the sympathies of many viewers. Similarly, Attorney General Janet Reno's testimony in 1993 before the congressional committee investigating the tragedy that occurred when federal agents stormed the compound of the Branch Davidian religious sect near Waco, Texas, generated more public approbation for her than for her congressional critics. So did her appearance two years later before another committee reinvestigating the government's action.

In addition to being harsh on Congress as an institution, the media are tough on its members—when they get any coverage at all. The personal foibles and questionable behaviors of members of Congress—their abuse of banking and postal privileges, periodic charges of sexual harassment, and investigations into the fraudulent use of public funds—all command attention. The public service, policy positions,

Media coverage of Congress often emphasizes the personalities of public officials, with most of the attention going to investigations and hearings, presidential involvement in legislation, and major policy conflicts. (Left) Attorney General Janet Reno pounds her fist during testimony before the committee investigating the ill-fated government raid on the Branch Davidian compound at Waco, Texas, in 1993. Her somber but self-confident defense turned public opinion against her congressional critics. (Right) Republican senators Alan Simpson and Orrin Hatch confer during hearings on the confirmation of Clarence Thomas for the Supreme Court. In defending Thomas against charges of sexual harassment brought by Anita Hill, the senators used the hearings to voice and build support for the nominee and for their own conservative judicial philosophy.

and legislative work of most members do not. Only the policy positions of the leaders of the House and Senate and their role on controversial issues receive coverage in the national media, and much of it is not flattering. During the first four months of 1995, House Speaker Gingrich received 4.2 hours of airtime (138 stories) on the evening news programs of the three major television networks, compared with 22 minutes for his predecessor during all of 1994. Senator Robert Dole was on the air for a total of one hour (43 stories) during the same period. The "spin" on Gingrich was highly negative.[43]

How the news media report on Congress and what they report affects the behavior of representatives and senators in several fundamental ways. Members of Congress consciously position themselves to be newsmakers, granting interviews to reporters, attending and participating in committee hearings that the news media are likely to cover, using their staffs to issue press releases about their positions and legislative initiatives, and keeping the press (particularly the local media in their home states and districts) informed about their activities. Most of them take advantage of radio and television studios in Congress to record programs for the folks back home. This media-oriented behavior has led one student of Congress to conclude that "making news has become a crucial component of making laws."[44]

In contrast to the mostly negative coverage by the national media, the local news media present a different picture. They report less on Congress as a whole and more on local representatives, particularly when they are back home in their districts.

Local coverage tends to be of the "soft," human interest variety—a speech to the chamber of commerce, a tour of the state fair, a ceremony at a high school graduation, a ribbon cutting at a senior center financed by federal funds that the member helped obtain. Most of this coverage conveys a favorable image of the member, in sharp contrast to the generally harsh evaluation of Congress as an institution. Local coverage is important to the members because it conveys to constituents the message that they are being well represented.

Coverage of the Judiciary

The third branch of government, the judiciary, is often a stranger to the national media, except during major trials or controversial hearings such as the confirmation hearings for Clarence Thomas. The Supreme Court receives only a fraction of the attention received by the president and Congress, and only a few news organizations assign reporters to it on a full-time basis.

There are several reasons for the dearth of coverage of the judiciary. The Supreme Court does not welcome attention: justices rarely give interviews or discuss the decision-making process in which they are involved. In addition to the problem of access, many judicial decisions are complex. To understand them, one must give them careful consideration, often applying specialized legal knowledge. Only a few major newspapers, networks, and magazines can afford to hire journalists who have this knowledge. Therefore, the initial reports of Supreme Court decisions are often brief descriptions of the majority and minority opinions, the justices who voted on each side, and the implications of the decision. This information is frequently presented in the context of whose interests were benefited or hurt by the judgment.

Reporters who cover the lower courts tend not to be lawyers or students of the law. Their focus is often on sensational cases rather than on far-reaching legal issues and trends. Trials for murder, rape, child molestation, and embezzlement make front-page news in Washington and other parts of the country, but speeches by Supreme Court justices on legal trends and constitutional interpretation rarely do.

At the state level, coverage of the judiciary is more common because many judges are elected rather than appointed. And some state courts now permit radio and television coverage of trials, some of which appear on the cable court channel. Moreover, highly publicized events involving alleged criminal activity, such as the O. J. Simpson and Susan Smith murder trials and the beating of Rodney King by several Los Angeles policemen, gain coverage by virtue of the actions or the people involved.[45]

THE IMPACT OF THE NEWS MEDIA ON PUBLIC POLICY

News media coverage of institutions of government naturally has an impact on the public's evaluation of those institutions. According to S. Robert Lichter, the president's public opinion ratings follow news coverage. Lichter found that monthly variations in President Clinton's good press/bad press ratio were reflected in each subsequent Gallup poll.[46] (See Figure 11-4 on page 398.) Moreover, the more attention the president received, the stronger the relationship.

Similarly with respect to Congress, public approval followed media coverage. At the beginning of the 104th Congress, hopes were high, coverage favorable, and the public more approving than during the same period of the previous Congress. However, as the news media increased the amount of congressional news, emphasizing internal divisions between the Republicans in the House and the Senate and their failure to reach agreement on a broad range of policy issues (including the principal priorities in the Contract with America), the evaluation of Congress declined sharply.

A similar explanation can be made for the judicial system, whose favorable evaluation declined from 43 percent in January 1994 to 35 percent two years later. One explanation for the decline advanced by the Pew Research Center in its survey of public opinion was the unfavorable reaction to the length, legal maneuverings, and verdict of the O. J. Simpson murder trial, which was watched by millions of Americans.[47]

In addition to affecting the public's assessment of how government is working, news coverage impacts the content of policy as well as the behavior of public officials. It does so in three ways: it shapes priorities; it shortens time frames; and it limits options.

The news media help set the agenda for government. For example, in 1979–1980, through their extensive daily coverage of the Iranian hostage crisis, when diplomats at the American embassy in Tehran were taken hostage by paramilitary guards loyal to the Iranian government, the news media kept the problem before the public and thereby heightened the demand for a satisfactory solution. Coverage of the hostage crisis also raised expectations for a quick solution, effectively shortening the response time available to the Carter administration. The daily television coverage began by noting the number of days the hostages had been in captivity and thus reminded the public not only of the problem but also of the administration's inability to deal with it.[48]

How the press covers an event or policy issue and how the public reacts to that coverage may also limit the options available to public officials. At the beginning of the Clinton administration, for example, administration officials "floated" various ideas for reducing the federal budget deficit. One involved a delay in the cost-of-living adjustment for Social Security. Negative public reaction to this report doomed the proposal and even led the president to deny that his administration was seriously considering it.

Although the publicizing of proposed decisions and actions may generate a hostile response, it may also produce public support. In either situation the news media perform a necessary role in a democratic society, linking the public to their government. This linkage enables citizens to be informed about public issues and to make judgments about how public policy affects society. These judgments in turn provide public officials with broad policy guidelines and a time frame in which to respond, both of which are essential to the effective functioning of a representative government.

SUMMARY

The news media form a critical link between the public and their government. This link functions as a conduit through which communications flow and by which those communications affect elections, government, and public policy. The politics of American government is shaped by the type of information the media convey, the manner in which they convey it, and the impact that it has on public opinion and public participation in the political process on one hand and on the government's decisions, actions, and public policy on the other. Whatever that impact, it embroils the news media in these politics as the fourth branch of government.

Few would deny that a free press is essential for a

democratic society. To be free, however, the press must have the right to investigate and report about people and events. The First Amendment guarantees that right, but the Supreme Court has also ruled that it must be balanced by the rights of others to privacy, truthfulness, and fairness and by the need of the country to protect its national security. It is up to the judiciary to determine the boundaries between freedom of the press and individual and societal rights.

Limits placed on print journalism are less extensive than those on the electronic media. Because broadcasters use the public airwaves, they are required to operate in the public interest and have been subject to rules designed to ensure *fairness* in the discussion of important issues, *equal time* for candidates to present their views to the electorate, and the *right of rebuttal* for those attacked on the air. The result of these rules, however, has been to discourage the electronic media from becoming a forum for debate because of the requirement to provide free and equal time for opposing points of view.

Free time costs money, and the American media are predominantly private and profit-oriented. Being profit-oriented forces them to entertain as they inform in order to capture and hold the attention of as large an audience as possible. Thus they emphasize competition, conflict, and human interest and deemphasize detailed discussion of policy issues.

The history of the news media in the United States illustrates the tension between the democratic goals of informing the public and the economic interests of maintaining as large an audience as possible. Mass journalism developed during the nineteenth century, spurred by the invention of the telegraph and later by sensational *yellow journalism*. During the twentieth century, first radio and then television became the most important medium for reporting fast-breaking news stories and foreign news.

In the past two decades communication satellites, fiber optics, and new on-line technologies have opened up additional channels for communicating news quickly. For television, the major change has been the growth of cable and satellite networks. The Cable News Network can report news as it happens almost anywhere in the world, and public service cable channels provide in-depth coverage of some of the official proceedings of government as well as discussion of public issues. Furthermore, the use of the Internet as an interactive link between the people, politicians, and government officials is fast developing as a major vehicle by which information is conveyed and public opinion expressed.

The mass media have had a major impact on politics and government. Their coverage is slanted toward material that has *newsworthiness*, and that material is placed within the context of a dominant story line.

The decline in partisanship, the emphasis on personality, and the importance of visual imagery have increased the impact of the mass media on candidates and elections, particularly during the early phases of campaigns, when less is known about the candidates. Over the long haul, the news media influence the issues of the campaign and affect the public's perception of the candidates and their suitability for office.

The game format, which is used to describe campaigning, also extends to the coverage of government. Issues are portrayed as arguments between two sides, congressional votes as victories or defeats for the president or the Congress, the Democrats or the Republicans. The news media also tend to emphasize issues and events that create criticism of government and those who serve in it; the media justify this emphasis in terms of their watchdog role.

Coverage of the national government usually focuses on the president and the administration's policy agenda. Although Congress usually gets less coverage, the 1994 election of the first Republican Congress in forty years made the new Congress more newsworthy than its predecessor. As a consequence, it received more coverage but not necessarily more favorable coverage. In general, the national press are often harsh critics. Local news media, however, report more favorably on their own representatives, especially when they are back in their home districts. In contrast to the critical scrutiny of Congress and the president, the judiciary receives little media coverage except during controversial hearings or major trials.

The news media affect public policy through the issues they choose to cover and the information they choose to disclose. Those choices affect the government's agenda and priorities, shorten time frames for policy decisions, and limit the options of government officials. They also shape public and government evaluations, analyses, and recommendations. The news media's increasingly critical evaluations of politics and government have contributed to lower public esteem for the political system and how it works.

shield laws
prior restraint
fairness doctrine

equal time rule
right of rebuttal
yellow journalism

newsworthiness
negative advertising

SCHOLARLY STUDIES

Abramson, Jeffrey B., F. Christopher Arterton, and Gary R. Orren. *The Electronic Commonwealth: The Impact of New Media Technologies on Democratic Politics.* New York: Basic Books, 1990. An insightful analysis of how contemporary changes in the media have affected and may continue to affect democratic politics.

Adatto, Kiku. *Picture Perfect: The Art and Artifice of Public Image Making.* New York: Basic Books, 1994. A well-researched book discussing how and why news media coverage of presidential elections has become increasingly superficial.

Ansolabehere, Stephen, and Shanto Iyengar. *Going Negative: How Political Advertisements Shrink and Polarize the Electorate.* New York: Free Press, 1995. Based on a research project in which the authors conducted experiments to measure the influence of negative advertising on voting behavior, this book shows how such ads depress turnout and lower trust in government.

Fallows, James M. *Breaking the News: How the Media Undermine American Democracy.* New York: Pantheon, 1996. A very critical study of the news media and their impact on politics and government.

Graber, Doris A. *Mass Media and American Politics.* 4th ed. Washington, D.C.: Congressional Quarterly, 1993. A comprehensive discussion of media and government, from ownership patterns to press freedom to characteristics of coverage and its effects.

Iyengar, Shanto, and Donald R. Kinder. *News That Matters.* Chicago: University of Chicago Press, 1989. A study that clearly shows the ability of television news to set the agenda for the public.

McCubbins, Mathew D., with John H. Aldrich, F. Christopher Arterton, Samuel L. Popkin, and Larry J. Sabato. *Under the Watchful Eye.* Washington, D.C.: Congressional Quarterly, 1992. A brief but insightful series of essays on presidential campaigning.

"Media and Politics." *PS* 29 (March 1996): 10–36. A symposium in which political scientists discuss various ways in which their discipline looks at this topic.

Owen, Diana. *Media Messages in American Presidential Elections.* Westport, Conn.: Greenwood Press, 1991. A scholarly analysis of the influence of special types of media messages on how people learn about the candidates and issues during recent presidential campaigns.

Patterson, Thomas E. *Out of Order.* New York: Knopf, 1993. A creative, hard-hitting analysis of the news media's coverage of presidential elections, focusing on 1992. The author suggests reforms for the presidential selection process.

Spitzer, Robert J., ed. *Media and Public Policy.* Westport, Conn.: Praeger, 1993. Based on papers delivered at recent conferences, the book presents contributions from fifteen scholars that address the link between the news media and public policy.

West, Darrel M. *Air Wars: Television Advertising in Election Campaigns, 1952–1992.* Washington, D.C.: Congressional Quarterly, 1993. A study by a political scientist about the influence of television and radio commercials on American voters.

LEISURE READING

Bernstein, Carl, and Bob Woodward. *All the President's Men.* New York: Simon and Schuster, 1987. A gripping account by the two *Washington Post* reporters who uncovered the truth behind the Watergate break-in.

Halberstam, David. *The Powers That Be.* New York: Knopf, 1979. A lengthy but highly readable account of the development, organization, and operation of media giants CBS, the *New York Times*, Time Inc., the *Los Angeles Times*, and the *Washington Post*.

Hertsgaard, Mark. *On Bended Knee: The Press and the Reagan Presidency.* New York: Farrar, Straus and Giroux, 1988. A journalist's description of how the Reagan administration successfully manipulated the media.

Powell, Jody. *The Other Side of the Story*. New York: Morrow, 1984. The target of media coverage as White House press secretary under President Carter, Powell discusses the trials and tribulations of bad press coverage.

Rosenstiel, Tom. *Strange Bedfellows: How Television and Presidential Candidates Changed American Politics*. New York: Hyperion, 1992. The author, a media and political reporter on the staff of the *Los Angeles Times*, singles out ABC News to investigate the role of network news and its influence in the 1992 presidential election.

PRIMARY SOURCES

The New York Times Index. New York: New York Times Company, semimonthly with quarterly compilations. A subject index of articles appearing in the *New York Times* since it was founded in 1851. A "How to Use" section appears at the end of each volume.

Public Affairs Video Archives. West Lafayette, Ind.: Purdue University, annual. A chronological index of public affairs events and programs telecast by C-SPAN each year. Volumes began in 1987.

The Washington Post. Ann Arbor: University Microfilms, annual. A subject index of the articles appearing in the *Washington Post*.

ORGANIZATIONS

Accuracy in Media, 4455 Connecticut Ave., N.W., Washington, DC 20008; phone (202) 364-4401, fax (202) 364-4098, Internet http://www.aim.org An organization with a conservative orientation that researches what it sees as examples of liberal bias in the media.

Center for Media and Public Affairs, 2100 L Street, N.W., Suite 303, Washington, DC 20037; phone (202) 223-2942, fax (202) 872-4014 Internet http://www.proxima.com:8080/cmpa/ An organization that conducts scientific studies of how television news treats contemporary social and political issues.

Corporation for Public Broadcasting, 901 E Street, N.W., Washington, DC 20004; phone (202) 879-9600, fax (202) 783-1019, e-mail comments@cpb.org Internet http://www.cpb.org A government corporation that funds public broadcasting.

Federal Communications Commission, 1919 M Street, N.W., Washington, DC 20554; phone (202) 418-0126, fax (202) 418-2840, Internet http.//www.fcc.gov/ The government agency that regulates the use of the airwaves in the United States.

The Pew Research Center for the People & the Press, 1875 Eye Street, N.W., Suite 1110, Washington, DC 20006; phone (202) 293-3126, fax (202) 293-2569 Internet http://www.people-press.org/ Does national surveys on public opinion, especially about the news media and current issues.

Reporters Committee for Freedom of the Press, 1101 Wilson Blvd., Suite 1910, Arlington, VA 22209; phone (703) 807-2100, fax (703) 807-2109, Internet http://www.rcfp.org/rcfp/ A group that examines First Amendment issues pertaining to freedom of the press.

Congress

T he faxes came spinning out of National Rifle Association headquarters as soon as the vote was over:

On March 22, the U.S. House of Representatives voted to REPEAL the 1994 Clinton gun and magazine ban! On a bi-partisan 239 to 173 vote, lawmakers put the interests of law-abiding gun owners ahead of the political posturing of Bill Clinton and his anti-gun allies in the House. This historic vote marks the first time in a decade that Congress has reaffirmed the rights of gun owners and the value of the Second Amendment. . . . many thanks to you—our volunteers and members across the country—whose hard work and efforts made this victory possible.

It looked like a great victory. And in a sense it was, at least in the ways of contemporary Washington politics. Sometimes merely looking victorious is good enough.

But no public policy was changed when the House voted in 1996 to repeal the ban Congress had placed in 1994 on the sale of assault weapons. Nor did anyone in Washington expect a change. Bob Dole, the Senate majority leader and soon to be his party's nominee for president, had no intention even of bringing the repeal to a vote in the Senate, where he knew it could not survive a filibuster. And President Clinton had promised to veto the repeal if it ever came to his desk. The House vote was about politics, not policy; about an election just past and an election just ahead, about the role that interest groups have come to play in congressional behavior, and about a new political age in which symbolism is often as important as substance.

In 1994, Republicans had regained control of the House of Representatives for the first time in forty years. Many Republican candidates had received significant financial support from the Political Victory Fund, the political action committee of the National Rifle Association (NRA). With more than 3 million members dedicated to preventing interference with the right of citizens to own guns, the NRA had been remarkably successful in 1994 in targeting Democrats who voted for the assault weapons ban. Of the 34 Democratic incumbents defeated that year, 29 had voted for the ban.

To ensure the protection of its new supporters, the NRA had already begun to aid the reelection campaigns of many of the Republicans first elected in 1994. Of the $229,993 the NRA's Political Victory Fund contributed to freshmen during 1995, almost 96 percent had gone to Republicans.

But such support rarely comes without strings, or at least strong expectations. Republican leaders had promised the NRA that there would be a vote to repeal the assault weapons ban. Even when it seemed impossible to win such a vote, the leadership felt compelled to fulfill its promise. "We told members for over a year we'd have this vote, and we're having this vote," said Representative John Boehner of Ohio, the chairman of the Republican Conference. Democratic representative Charles Schumer of New York, the House sponsor of the ban, saw it differently: "Newt Gingrich bent his knee and is kissing the ring of the NRA."

When the time came, 66 of the 74 Republican freshmen voted to repeal the ban on assault weapons. They hadn't changed the law, but they had begun the position-taking—and the fundraising—for reelection in 1996.[1]

A s the attention to the assault weapons ban clearly demonstrates, politics is the most persistent and most important element in the legislative process. Indeed, politics dominates day-to-day life in Congress. Members of Congress struggle constantly to build political coalitions for or against particular bills. They fight to change the institution's procedures and organization to gain leverage over legislative decisions. They do constant battle with other political institutions, especially the president and the bureaucracy, to assert their institutional prerogatives and to influence the shape of public policy. And as in the case of the assault weapons ban, they sometimes must go through major legislative maneuvers largely for political reasons.

This chapter examines the central role of Congress in the American government. It views Congress first from a broad perspective: What sort of institution is Congress? Who are its members? What kind of environment do they work in? Next the chapter examines the organization and principal functions of Congress, especially its responsibilities for constituency representation, legislation, and administrative oversight. It explores the role of political parties and legislative committees in organizing and accomplishing the work of Congress, and the increasingly significant role that interest groups and political action committees play in the legislative process. Each of these topics reveals something about how politics determines what Congress does.

THE INSTITUTION OF CONGRESS

The United States Congress is a **bicameral legislature**—that is, it is composed of two legislative bodies. The larger is the House of Representatives, which has 435 voting members plus 5 other delegates who represent the District of Columbia and the United States territories and possessions; these delegates have a vote on committees and subcommittees but do not vote on passage of bills in the full House. Each member of the House represents a congressional district with a population of about 600,000 (in accordance with the principle of *one person, one vote*). The districts are distributed among the states according to population, with each state having at least one and California having the largest number (52). All House members serve terms of two years.

The smaller legislative chamber is the Senate. It has 100 members, two from each state. Senators serve six-year terms, but the terms are staggered so that every two years approximately one-third of the seats in the Senate are up for election.

Elections to Congress occur in November in even-numbered years. The new Congress convenes in the following January. Each Congress lasts two years and is numbered; thus the First Congress convened in 1789, and the 104th convened in 1995. The first year of a Congress is called the first session, and the second year is called the second session. The first session of the 104th Congress met in 1995, and the second session in 1996.

The Members of Congress

The Constitution establishes minimum requirements for service in Congress. To serve in the House, one must have reached the age of 25, have been a United States citizen for seven years, and be a resident of the state (but not necessarily the district) from which one is elected. Senators must also be residents of the states from which they are elected, and they must be at least 30 years old and have been United States citizens for nine years at the time they begin their service.

Although all members of Congress have those simple qualifications in common, they differ widely in other ways.[2] In their speech, ideas, and values they mirror the regional and religious diversity of the American people. Table 12-1 provides some indication of how diverse Congress is in terms of age, gender, ethnicity, occupation, and religion.

TABLE 12-1 MEMBERS OF THE 104TH CONGRESS

	HOUSE	SENATE
Average age	58.4	50.9
Women	49	8
African Americans	39	1
Hispanics	18	0
Asians/Pacific Islanders	6	2
Native Americans	0	1
Principal occupations[a]		
Law	170	54
Business or banking	163	24
Politics/public service	102	12
Education	76	10
Real estate	28	3
Journalism	15	8
Agriculture	19	9
Engineering	6	0
Medicine	10	1
Homemaker	1	0
Clergy	2	0
Religious affiliations		
Mainline Protestant	153	47
Evangelical Protestant	72	10
Unspecified Protestant	38	3
Mormon	10	3
Roman Catholic	125	20
Jewish	24	9

[a]Some members specified more than one principal occupation.

Source: CQ Weekly Report, *November 12, 1994, 9-12.*

MANDATORY TERM LIMITS

In the early 1990s the combination of public dissatisfaction with the performance of Congress and remarkably high reelection rates for its members led to calls for the imposition of mandatory limits on the number of terms a member could serve. The framers of the Constitution had debated this matter at some length, concluding that the decision was best left to the voters in individual states and districts. No term limits were included in the language of the Constitution.

In 1988 and 1992, however, the national Republican party campaign platform called for mandatory term limits for members of Congress. The party's nominees for president and vice president, George Bush and Dan Quayle, strongly endorsed the proposal. In 1990 voters in California, Colorado, and Oklahoma imposed term limits on members of their state legislatures, and citizens in the state of Washington narrowly defeated a proposal to impose limits on the terms of their representatives in Congress. In 1992 and 1994, a number of other states followed suit by approving term-limitation measures. Public opinion polls suggested that term limits was an idea whose time had come.

Most of the proposals called for limits of twelve consecutive years on House or Senate service. Senators would be forced to retire after two six-year terms, House members after six two-year terms. Proponents of term limits argued that they were the only effective way of ensuring significant turnover in Congress. As Republican Ernest Jim Istook argued in a House speech:

our country has grown large and Government has grown even larger. It has created a system whereby too many people in politics know no other way to make a living. And too often they are isolated and unfamiliar with normal and everyday life. This is not healthy for America. It is especially fascinating to read studies which show the longer somebody serves in Congress, the more they tend to vote for big government, and bigger taxes, and to oppose cutting spending and cutting the size of government. The system has become a narcotic for too many people.[1]

Opponents of term limits argued that they are too blunt an instrument for solving the problems of Congress. They would force the retirement of good legislators as well as bad ones and deny voters the right to choose whomever they wanted to represent them. And, by removing from Congress its most experienced and powerful members, the imposition of term limits would inevitably enhance the influence of nonelected congressional staff and executive-branch bureaucrats.

In March 1995, a constitutional amendment to limit congressional terms came to the floor of the House for a vote. The proposal fell significantly short of the necessary two-thirds majority, getting just 227 votes instead of the 290 it would have needed if every House member had voted. Representative Henry Hyde (R-Illinois), serving his eleventh

Despite their varied backgrounds, members cannot be accurately described as a cross-section of the American people. As a group they rank relatively high in socioeconomic status. Few blue-collar workers serve in Congress, and not one of its members is poor. The percentages of women and of members of ethnic minorities are also much smaller than their proportions in the population as a whole. Also notable is the preponderance of lawyers and the dearth of members with scientific backgrounds. Lawyers have long been the dominant occupational group in Congress—not a surprising statistic, given the importance of lawmaking as a legislative responsibility. The small number of members with scientific training is more problematic, however, because the agenda facing Congress includes many issues of technical complexity (such as space exploration, the survival of endangered species, and the establishment of standards for high-definition television). Members of Congress must often rely on the expertise of others—the executive branch, their own staffs, and

"I'd like to propose a bill to the effect that we can remain freshmen indefinitely."

they are going to have the incision and he approaches with the electric saw, ask him one question: Are you a careerist?

Is running a modern complex society of 250 million people and a $6 trillion economy all that easy? To do your job . . . you have to know something about the environment, health care, banking and finance and tax policy, farm problems, weapons systems, Bosnia and Herzegovina and North Korea, not to mention Nagorno-Karabakh, foreign policy, the administration of justice, crime and punishment, education and welfare, budgeting in the trillions of dollars, and immigration. And I have not scratched the surface. We need our best people to deal with these issues. We in Congress deal with ultimate issues: life and death, war and peace, drawing the line between liberty and order. And do you ever really doubt that America will never again have a real crisis? With a revolving-door Congress, where will we get our Everett Dirksens, our Scoop Jacksons, our Arthur Vandenbergs, our Hubert Humphreys, our Barry Goldwaters, our Sam Ervins? You do not get them out of the phone book. Where did Shimon Peres and Yitzhak Rabin get the self-confidence to negotiate peace for their people with the PLO? I will tell you where: experience, bloody, bloody experience.[2]

Despite the defeat of the constitutional amendment, popular support for term limits in America in the 1990s remains strong. The issue will no doubt return again for future congressional votes. How would you vote?

term, gave the most impassioned speech against the amendment:

I just cannot be an accessory to the dumbing down of democracy. . . . Have you ever been in a storm at sea? I have, and I knew real terror until I looked up on the bridge and the old Norwegian skipper, who had been to sea for 45 years, was up there sucking on his pipe. And I can tell you that was reassuring. When that dentist bends over with the drill whirring, do you not hope he has done that work for a few years? And when the neurosurgeon has shaved your head and they have made the pencil mark on your skull where

[1]*Congressional Record*, March 29, 1995, H3917.
[2]*Congressional Record*, March 29, 1995, H3917.

special interest groups—to guide their decision making on issues that involve complex technology and groundbreaking science.

The Work Environment

In recent decades, service in Congress has become difficult and demanding. The demands on a member's time are enormous and constant. Hundreds of thousands of people view the member as their personal representative in the federal government. When they have problems such as a lost Social Security check or when they need help in getting a small-business loan or a passport, they expect their representative to assist them. They also expect their representative to be a source of information about what is going on in Washington and around the world.

Members are also legislators. Each year they must vote on hundreds of issues,

A special election in Chicago in 1995 sent Jesse Jackson Jr. (center) to Congress. Here, after reenacting his taking of the oath of office, he shares a joke with his wife, Sandi; his father (right); and House Speaker Newt Gingrich (left). Despite gains in recent years, racial and ethnic minorities are still underrepresented in Congress relative to their proportion in the population.

many of which are too complex to be grasped in the short time available before the vote. Each member also serves on several congressional committees and subcommittees, where members are expected to involve themselves deeply in the development of new legislation and in reviewing the implementation of legislation passed by previous Congresses. Furthermore, they must attend meetings of party caucuses and other specialized groups that members form to help advance their legislative priorities.

In addition, most members of Congress are candidates for reelection. The election campaign requires frequent meetings with the leaders of various interest groups in the home state or district, regular travel to meet with constituents, and contact with political action committees and other funding sources to ensure the availability of campaign funds.

Missing from this catalog of activities is adequate time for serious reading, reflection, and creative thought. Members of Congress spend so much time trying to get through their daily schedules that they have little or no free time to think about policy objectives and legislative priorities. In fact, one study in the 1970s found that in an average day a member of the House had only eleven minutes for uninterrupted reflection.[3] Most members lament this situation, but few have found a way to avoid it.

Staff and Support Services

To help them deal with their workloads, senators and representatives are surrounded by thousands of congressional employees whose principal responsibility is to provide various kinds of support. One form of support is provided by personal

Inside the typically crowded, busy office of a member of the House of Representatives, staff members endure overcrowding, long hours, and shared facilities. The growth of congressional staffs has been spurred both by workloads and by the desire to be reelected.

staffs. Each member has the authority to hire staff employees to work for him or her alone. In the House, staff allowances are the same for all members; in the Senate, they are based on the population of the state that a senator represents. In recent years House members have typically had about twenty people on their personal staffs. Senators have larger staffs; those from the largest states employ as many as sixty people. The personal staff is divided between the member's Washington office and the offices that most members maintain in their home districts or states.

Personal staff aides perform a variety of functions. They do routine clerical chores: word processing, greeting visitors, answering the mail, photocopying. They write speeches and help the member develop policy initiatives. They meet with lobbyists and constituents. They handle **casework**, that is, the individual problems that constituents bring to the member's attention for assistance or solution.[4] They work closely on issues that come up in the committees on which their employers serve, and they monitor issues as they develop in other committees, especially legislation that may be of concern to constituents.

Another important group of congressional employees are committee staff members. Congress has hundreds of committees and subcommittees, and each has its own staff, which assists committee members in setting an agenda, scheduling hearings, developing legislation, and overseeing the work of the executive agencies that fall within its area of interest. The way that committee staff employees are hired differs between the House and the Senate and even from one committee to another. Most commonly, however, a committee or subcommittee hires one group of staff employees to serve the members from the majority party and another group to serve the members from the minority party. (The majority party outnumbers the minority in membership and staff size on all but a few committees.) The majority staff is usually hired by the committee chair (who is always a member of the majority party); the minority staff is usually hired by the highest-ranking minority member of the committee.

Politics plays a large role in committee staffing. Staff members who work for the majority party are expected to share that party's views on relevant policy matters; the minority party imposes the same expectations. When control of the House or

Senate changes from one party to the other, as occurred after the 1994 elections, some of the (former) majority staff members lose their jobs and are replaced by staff chosen by the other party.

A third important group of congressional employees includes those who work for the three specialized support agencies in the legislative branch:

1. The Congressional Research Service is part of the Library of Congress; its professional staff conducts studies on a wide range of topics at the request of members and subcommittees.
2. The Congressional Budget Office, established in 1974, provides Congress with its own source of economic information and analysis.
3. The General Accounting Office determines whether government programs have been cost-effective (it is described in detail later in this chapter).

Table 12-2 indicates the number of people employed in congressional staff and support functions, a number that has risen sharply over the last few decades. This rapid expansion has resulted partly from a series of important changes in Congress itself and in the federal government as a whole. The federal budget increased tenfold from the mid 1970s to the mid 1990s and hundreds of new government programs have been initiated. Moreover, public dissatisfaction with the presidencies of Lyndon Johnson and Richard Nixon created a demand for greater congressional effectiveness and more vigilant oversight of executive actions. All these changes provided incentives for increases in congressional capabilities and led directly to staff expansion. When federal intelligence agencies committed serious abuses of authority

TABLE 12-2 **CONGRESSIONAL STAFF, 1993**

	NUMBER OF EMPLOYEES
House of Representatives	
Committee staff	2,147
Personal staff	7,400
Leadership staff[a]	137
Officers of the House staff[b]	1,194
Senate	
Committee staff	994
Personal staff	4,138
Leadership staff[a]	100
Officers of the Senate staff[b]	1,165
Joint committee staffs	145
Support agencies	
General Accounting Office	4,958
Congressional Research Service	814
Congressional Budget Office	230

[a]Staff who work directly for the party leaders in each house on leadership matters.
[b]Includes doorkeepers, parliamentarians, sergeants-at-arms, clerk of the House, Senate majority and minority secretaries, and postmasters.

Source: Norman J. Ornstein et al., Vital Statistics on Congress, 1995-1996 (Washington, D.C.: Congressional Quarterly, 1996), 131.

in the 1970s, for example, two new congressional committees were created to oversee those agencies. In 1990 those committees employed almost one hundred staff members.

Another, equally important reason that congressional staffs have continued to grow has been the widespread perception among members of Congress that staff aides help members do things that contribute directly to reelection. The more legislation members can be involved in, the more publicity their offices can generate; and the more efficiently and successfully they can respond to constituents' requests for help, the more likely they are to succeed at election time. To the intensely political people who serve in Congress, the prospect of reelection has been a powerful motive for the steady enlargement of congressional staff and support agencies— yet another way in which politics helps to determine the shape of American government.

After they took control of Congress in 1995, however, Republicans sought to reduce congressional staffs as part of a broader set of election promises to reduce the size of the federal government. In the House, the Republican majority eliminated 3 full committees, cut funding for 28 legislative service organizations, reduced committee staff by one-third, and cut overall spending for operations of the House by $155 million.

THE ORGANIZATION OF CONGRESS

How does Congress set its agenda and organize the flow of its business? In a sense, these are technical questions because they involve the mechanics of congressional operation. But they are much more than that. The way Congress organizes itself reveals a great deal about the allocation of legislative power, and that allocation of power tells us much about the politics of public policy making.

The internal structure of Congress has changed and grown over time, as each generation of legislators has shaped Congress to fit its needs. Early in the nation's history, parties emerged to organize the business of the initial Congresses, and party caucuses hammered out important policy decisions. For a few decades after the Civil War, committees began to play a more dominant role in lawmaking. By the last decade of the nineteenth century, however, party leaders in Congress, particularly the Speaker of the House and the majority leader of the Senate, had become the principal powers.

But the party leaders of the time, notably Speaker Joseph G. Cannon (R-Illinois) and Speaker Thomas Brackett Reed (R-Maine), became so dominant that the rank and file staged a revolt at the end of the first decade of the twentieth century. The authority of the party leaders was reduced, and for most of the next seventy years committees were again the power centers in Congress. A **seniority system** ensured that the member of the majority party with the longest consecutive service on each committee would automatically chair the committee for as long as he or she remained in Congress. Seniority permitted the committee chairs, many of whom were elderly men, to assume powerful roles in the legislative process. But another revolt (described on page 453), this time against the dominance of the committee chairs, unfolded in the 1970s and produced another restructuring of congressional power.[5]

Throughout these decades of change, two principles have remained at the core of congressional organization: (1) control of the legislative agenda and the legislative machinery ought to be in the hands of the majority party; and (2) for purposes of efficiency and enhanced expertise, most day-to-day details of legislative work ought to be handled by small groups of legislators meeting as committees. Indeed, since the early decades of the nineteenth century the party system and the committee system have been the dominant elements in every scheme of congressional organization.

Congressional Parties

The single most distinctive feature of political parties in Congress is their limited control over their own members, particularly over the way their members vote. In legislatures in other countries, **party discipline** is normal. Party leaders in the legislatures of Britain and France, for example, can count on the members of their party to support them on virtually every vote, and if they do not, the party can impose penalties on them. Not so in the United States. When the two parties take opposing positions on an issue, typically some—and sometimes many—members of each party will defect to the opposition.

The absence of party discipline reflects, more than anything else, the limited authority of party leaders in Congress. In both the House and the Senate, leaders have very little direct control over the members of their own party and therefore have few ways either to force them to vote for the party's position on a bill or to punish them if they do not. They cannot prevent party members from running for reelection; they have little influence on the outcome of elections; and, without the support of the majority of their party, they cannot even affect committee assignments. To understand better the relationship between party leaders and rank-and-file party members, it is useful to look separately at party organization in the House and the Senate.

Parties in the House   Because the House is larger than the Senate, parties play a more important role there in organizing the legislative agenda and building legislative majorities. The majority party has the principal responsibility for both tasks. It controls the selection of the Speaker of the House, and its members compose a majority on each committee and subcommittee.

The **Speaker** is almost always the most important figure in the House. Technically, the Speaker is the presiding officer, although little of the Speaker's time is actually spent in the chair. Political leadership of the majority party is the Speaker's dominant concern. Working with other party leaders—especially those designated as **whips** — the Speaker helps determine the issues that will be given top priority in the House.[6] Among the Speaker's other duties are participating in scheduling debates; mediating among members of the majority party who disagree on important legislation; working with the White House to coordinate measures that are important to the president; and assisting members of the majority party in such matters as getting the committee assignments they want and retaining their seats at election time.[7]

Although the Speaker's leadership is based more on persuasion and political skill than on any real authority over individual House members, an astute Speaker has a substantial impact on the kinds of policy issues that come before the House and the way they are decided. A successful Speaker commands the respect of other party members and is able to convince them to support his or her position on critical policy issues. Strong Speakers make full use of the tools of authority available to them: parliamentary direction of floor debate and assignment of bills to committee, control over the flow of information within the House, scheduling of legislative action, appointment powers, and personal prestige and influence with other political actors in Washington. For example, a member who consistently supports the Speaker can expect assignment to preferred committees, assistance in securing campaign funds

NEWT GINGRICH: OUTSPOKEN SPEAKER

His Democratic targets likened him to a pit bull, and even many of his Republican colleagues saw his take-no-prisoners strategies and language as damaging to their cause. But Representative Newt Gingrich (R-Georgia) brushed off his critics, and after sixteen years in the House his tenacity paid off. In 1995, riding a wave of popular support for the Republican Contract with America, a legislative agenda engineered mainly by him and signed onto by Republican congressional candidates nationwide, he became the first Republican Speaker of the House in four decades.

After two narrow losses, Gingrich was first elected to the House in 1978. A university professor of history, he became known for his unique political vision, combining staunch free-market conservatism with a fascination with technology and patterns of social change. In a party that traditionally eschews intellectualism, Gingrich was of a new breed. Even more than his ideas and his charismatic articulation of them, however, he gained attention for his love of confrontation. Frustrated by the Democrats' stranglehold on the House, Gingrich made it his goal above all else to topple their nearly 2-to-1 majority.

Speaker Gingrich (left) *confers with House Majority Leader Dick Armey during a Republican meeting in 1995.*

As his career in the House progressed, he began to ruffle feathers on both sides of the aisle. More traditional conservatives such as Senate Republican leader Bob Dole saw him as a hothead whose uncompromising ambitions disrupted a smooth legislative process. House Democrats, for their part, resented his unrelenting attacks on individual members of Congress. Only weeks after assuming office, he began to call for Charles C. Diggs Jr., a Michigan Democrat, to be expelled on kickback charges. Several years later he did the same to Massachusetts Democrat Gerry Studds for having had sex with a congressional page. Neither was expelled, but both were censured. Gingrich scored more points in 1984, when Speaker Thomas P. O'Neill's rejoinder to one of Gingrich's accusations against House Democrats was so indignant that it was stricken from the record, an almost unheard-of humiliation for a House Speaker.

Until the 1994 elections Gingrich's most resounding coup had come in 1989, when his call for an investigation into shady financial dealings by Speaker Jim Wright ultimately brought about Wright's resignation. An astonishing act of political *chutzpah*, this immediately won Gingrich the position of House minority

whip, responsible for building consensus among Republicans. Gingrich's further use of guerrillalike tactics to fulfill that task ultimately led to the 1994 Contract with America, which focused on themes not only that the public supported but that nearly all conservatives agreed with, including lower taxes, spending cuts, reductions in federal bureaucracy and regulation, and the transfer of power to the states. This show of unity caused a mini-renaissance among the Republicans, who gained control of both houses and elevated Gingrich to the position of Speaker.

After his tenure as Speaker began, Gingrich found the tables to be turned in some respects. He drew criticism for accepting a $4.5 million advance for his book of political thought, *To Renew America* (criticism that convinced him to save face by rejecting the money), and the House launched an ethics investigation into fundraising for him and for political organizations he created. Moreover, his legislative agenda met with mixed success in the face of determined Democratic opposition, and many Democrats—noting his high "unfavorable" ratings in public opinion polls—tried to associate their Republican opponents with him in the 1996 congressional elections.

from political action committees, and help from the leadership in gaining passage of legislation introduced by that member.[8]

When Newt Gingrich was elected Speaker by the new House Republican majority in the 104th Congress, he quickly asserted himself as one of the most potent legislative leaders of his time. He dominated the House agenda, selected all of the committee and some of the subcommittee chairs, and became the leading public spokesman for Republican policies. Whether Gingrich's power will endure remains to be seen. But in the first year of the 104th Congress, Gingrich assumed and exercised congressional leadership power that was unprecedented in the second half of the twentieth century.

The Speaker does not act alone in attempting to guide the operations of the House. Figure 12-1 shows the elaborate structure of majority party organization in the 104th Congress. The Speaker is supported by, and works through, a variety of committees and networks that enhance internal communication in the party, aid in the formation of party positions on policy issues, and help improve the chances of the party's candidates for seats in the House.

The size and complexity of the majority party leadership in the House reflect the difficulty of maintaining unity and building legislative majorities among a group with several hundred members whose leaders lack the authority to demand support. A less complex leadership structure would be sufficient if the majority party leaders had more authority.

The minority party in the House has its own elected leaders and a structure that mirrors, on a reduced scale, the organization of the majority party. There are, of course, fewer members to organize in the minority party, and the minority party has less responsibility for managing the House agenda. The leader of the minority party is the minority leader, who is assisted by the minority whip. Both are elected by the minority party caucus, made up of all the minority party members.

Parties in the Senate   Because the Senate is smaller and individual senators are able to deal with each other directly on most matters, parties play a much less important role there than in the House. Most leadership functions in the Senate are concentrated in the hands of the elected party leaders. The majority party elects a majority leader and a majority whip; the minority party elects a minority leader and a minority whip. Each party also has a structure of leadership committees, but these have less influence on party operations than do their counterparts in the House.[9]

The primary job of the party leaders, especially the majority leader, is to organize

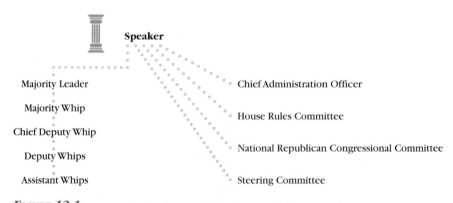

FIGURE 12-1

Majority party organization in the House of Representatives, 104th Congress.

the business of the Senate: to nudge legislation along through the legislative process, to schedule debate, and to oversee most aspects of day-to-day administration. Party leaders also help the proponents of legislation round up the votes necessary to make a majority, meet regularly with the president to discuss policy and legislative strategy, and serve as public spokespersons for their party on important policy matters. The spokesperson role is especially prominent for the leaders of the party of which the president is not a member. During the Republican administration of George Bush, for example, Senator George Mitchell (D-Maine), the majority leader, was an important spokesperson for the Democrats. When Bush was replaced by Bill Clinton, a Democrat, Senator Robert Dole (R-Kansas) became a leading articulator of the views of his party, particularly when those views clashed with the president's.

Despite the extent of their duties and their public visibility, party leaders in the Senate are severely constrained in their ability to influence the outcome of policy debates. Their control over the votes and activities of other members of their party is even weaker than that of their House counterparts. In the Senate, therefore, leadership is even more dependent on persuasion and political sensitivities than it is in the House. Senator Mike Mansfield (D-Montana), who served as majority leader in the Senate longer than anyone else in this century, once said:

> What power do the leaders have to force these committees, to twist their arms, to wheel and deal, and so forth and so on, to get them to rush things up or to speed their procedure? The leaders in the Senate, at least, have no power delegated to them except on the basis of courtesy, accommodation, and a sense of responsibility.[10]

Leadership styles in the Senate are constantly changing. When Lyndon Johnson (D-Texas) was majority leader in the 1950s, he used his position to dominate his party and its policy agenda. In contrast, recent Senate majority leaders—Mike Mansfield (1961-1976), Robert Byrd (1977-1980, 1987-1988), Howard Baker (1981-1984), Robert Dole (1985-1986, 1995-1996), George Mitchell (1989-1994), and Trent Lott (1996-   )—have defined their roles more in administrative than in policy terms. They have concentrated on organizing the business of the Senate to fit the needs of individual members and have spent less time trying to define positions on issues. Since 1961, when Johnson left the Senate to become vice president, the party system in the Senate has ceased to play a major role in the development of public policy. Most of its former activities in that regard have been absorbed by Senate committees and by individual senators.

Party politics in Congress   The proponents of each bill introduced in Congress must form a coalition in support of that bill. These coalitions, which may include members of the opposition party, vanish as quickly as they appear; their composition changes from bill to bill and from day to day. Politics in Congress focuses on the task of building these shifting alliances. Bargaining and negotiation among individual members, rather than edicts from party leaders, are the principal techniques used in the formation of coalitions. Party leaders often play an important role, but the role is that of lead negotiator, not commanding officer.[11]

In recent years some individual legislators, known as **issue entrepreneurs**, have tended to specialize in particular substantive matters and to seek support among their colleagues for policies dealing with those matters. In the House, issue entrepreneurs are often subcommittee chairs; in the Senate, entrepreneurship is widely dispersed and bears little relation to formal institutional roles. For six years in the 1980s, for example, Representative Romano Mazzoli (D-Kentucky) worked to build

Senator Trent Lott (second from left) *smiles with Republican colleagues at a news conference after his election as Senate majority leader in 1996. Lott defeated fellow Mississippian Thad Cochran* (left) *in the contest to succeed Bob Dole, who resigned as majority leader to campaign full-time for the presidency.*

congressional support for a major new immigration law. This legislation held little interest for most of Mazzoli's constituents in Louisville but was part of his sphere of influence as chair of the House Judiciary Committee's subcommittee on immigration. In the Senate, Barbara Mikulski (D-Maryland) was a major architect of the coalition that passed the Child Abuse Act in 1984. Her interest in this issue bore no direct relationship to any of her committee assignments; instead, it stemmed from her experience as a social worker and her leadership in the movement for women's rights. In the debate on tax policy at the beginning of the Clinton administration, Senator Bill Bradley (D-New Jersey) played an influential role, as he had on earlier tax policy debates in the 1980s. From the outset of his Senate career, Bradley had worked hard to educate himself on tax issues, and his knowledge commanded considerable respect among his colleagues.

Leadership is always necessary in the bargaining and negotiation that constitute legislative politics (see the profile on page 425). It often takes years to get a bill enacted, and someone has to persist in seeking the support that ultimately adds up to a legislative majority. But in the United States Congress that role is not the sole province of the party leaders. Because party discipline is weak, legislative leadership is decentralized and the construction of coalitions is a painstaking and time-consuming process of give-and-take among individual members.

The Committee System

Most of the work of Congress is done in committees, which serve a number of important functions. Committees prepare legislation for consideration on the floors of the House and Senate, but they also delete from the legislative agenda matters that

Senate Minority Leader Thomas Daschle and a group of Democratic colleagues at a news conference in early 1995. After the Republican victory in the 1994 elections, Democrats in both the Senate and the House had to adjust to the unfamiliar role of underdogs.

are not important, urgent, or politically viable. In fact, only a small percentage of the bills that are referred to a committee survive its scrutiny.

Committees also hold public hearings at which experts, leaders of interest groups, and other supporters and opponents of bills are permitted to express their views. In addition, they initiate studies, conduct investigations, and publish information. Each year, for example, the State Department is required by law to submit a report to Congress on the human rights policies of all the world's countries. The House Foreign Affairs Committee's subcommittee on human rights and international organizations holds hearings at which it reviews that report and receives comments on it from government officials, interest groups, and private citizens. The subcommittee publishes those hearings, which are used by other committees in their annual decisions on American foreign aid.

Another important function of committees is **administrative oversight**. Committees monitor the work of the executive agencies in their areas of jurisdiction, review budget requests, and pass judgment on the qualifications of presidential appointees. In fact, they are the principal contact points between the executive and legislative branches. (The oversight function is discussed in detail on pages 448–453.)

Most important, however, committees are the primary source of creativity and policy leadership in Congress. The most knowledgeable military specialists in Congress are members of the House and Senate Armed Services Committees. Those who are most familiar with farm issues are on the Agriculture Committees. Because the senior members of most congressional committees have been dealing for several decades with the policy issues that fall within their committee's area of jurisdiction, they are as well informed about those issues as anyone in the federal government. And they have the support of specialists on the committee staffs. It is not surprising,

CONGRESSIONAL LEADERSHIP

The character of congressional party leadership has evolved considerably during this century. In the first decade, Joseph G. Cannon (R-Illinois) in the House and Nelson W. Aldrich (R-Rhode Island) in the Senate dominated the legislative process. In the decades that followed, the seniority system became more rigid and the chairs of the standing committees came to share legislative power with the party leaders. Since 1960 legislative power has decentralized even further, placing new demands and constraints on party leaders. In the statements that follow, some recent party leaders describe their work.

Thomas P. O'Neill Jr. (D-Massachusetts),
House Speaker (1977–1986)

[At a meeting with a handful of legislative leaders in 1942, President Franklin Roosevelt introduced Albert Einstein.] Einstein explained the theory of the atomic bomb, and told the group that Hitler also had scientists working on it, and that the first nation to get the bomb would win the war and control the world.

Einstein estimated that the project would cost two billion dollars. Not surprisingly, the president was concerned about how to allocate that kind of money without alerting the public or the press.

"Leave it to me," said Sam Rayburn [then Speaker of the House]. The next day Sam called all the committee and subcommittee chairmen and told them to put an extra hundred million dollars into their budgets.

"Yes, Mr. Rayburn," they all said. There were no questions asked and no meetings held. The Manhattan Project was one of the best-kept secrets in history. The money was allocated and nobody on the committees ever questioned why a chairman was setting aside a certain amount for reasons he didn't even know about.

But that's the way things worked in Sam's time. Today, of course, you'd have ninety-two guys wanting to know what was happening and where the money was going.[1]

John McCormack (D-Massachusetts),
House Speaker (1962–1970)

I have never asked a member to vote against his conscience. If he mentions his conscience—that's all. I don't press him any further.[2]

Charles Halleck (R-Illinois),
House Minority Leader (1959–1964)

You get pressure from guys who have come along with you on a tough vote about the fellows who went off the reservation. Some of them want to read these guys out of the party. But, hell, there may be a vote next week when you need a fellow who has strayed real bad and you can catch him on the rebound.[3]

Carl Albert (D-Oklahoma),
House Speaker (1971–1976)

If you can't win them by persuasion, you can't win them at all. If you whip them into line every time, by the time you reach the third vote you're through.[4]

Mike Mansfield (D-Montana),
Senate Majority Leader (1961–1976)

It's pretty hard to hold the leadership accountable, because we can't dictate to our associates how they should vote. I think that these people who are representing the various states have been sent here to exercise their own judgment, that they should not be pressured because that's a counterproductive tactic.

I watched Lyndon Johnson while I was assistant majority leader for four years, and our styles are diametrically different. He was a man who liked to keep power in his own hands. He would like to collect IOU's. . . . I don't collect any IOU's. I don't do any special favors. I try to treat all Senators alike, and I think that's the best way to operate in the long run, because that way you maintain their respect and confidence. And that's what the ball game is all about.[5]

[1] Thomas P. O'Neill Jr. and William Novak, *Man of the House* (New York: Random House, 1987), 129.
[2] Quoted in Donald G. Tacheron and Morris K. Udall, *The Job of the Congressman*, 2d ed. (Indianapolis: Bobbs-Merrill, 1970), 18.
[3] Ibid., 19.
[4] Ibid.
[5] Quoted in Daniel Rapoport, "It's Not a Happy Time for House, Senate Leadership," *National Journal*, February 7, 1976, 173.

therefore, that committees initiate much of the legislation that makes its way to the floors of the House and Senate.[12]

Of the several kinds of committees that Congress uses, the most common and most important are **standing committees**, permanent committees that have full authority to recommend legislation. A few of them, like the Rules Committee in the House, are responsible for organizing and regulating the operations of Congress. Most standing committees have jurisdictions defined along substantive policy lines: energy, agriculture, foreign relations, and so on.

Most of the standing committees are divided into subcommittees, which hold most of the hearings and conduct the initial review of most legislation. Full committees rarely convene to consider a piece of legislation until after it has been carefully reviewed by the appropriate subcommittee. As the legislative workload has grown in size and complexity, experience and specialized knowledge have made the subcommittees increasingly important.

The committee system also includes a variety of **select**, or **special**, **committees**. These are temporary committees created to deal with specific issues; they disband when they have completed their work. Many select committees have clearly limited functions and authority. Most, for instance, are not authorized to recommend legislation. Among the best-known recent temporary committees were the Senate Select Committee on Presidential Campaign Activities, which uncovered much of the Watergate scandal in the 1970s, and the House Select Committee to Investigate Covert Arms Transactions with Iran, which joined its Senate counterpart in exploring the Iran-contra affair in the 1980s. The standing and select committees of the 104th Congress are listed in Table 12-3 on page 432.

Joint committees are composed of members of both houses of Congress. Some of them, called standing joint committees, are permanent groups with no authority to initiate legislation; the most important of these is the Joint Committee on the Economy, which receives and reviews the president's annual Economic Report and conducts studies of the national economy. In addition to the standing joint committees, hundreds of temporary joint committees known as **joint conference committees** are formed during each Congress. Their principal function is to resolve the differences that occur when the House and Senate pass varying forms of the same bill. At the end of the 101st Congress, for example, House and Senate conferees wrangled over different versions of the Clean Air Act. The House bill had included tougher controls than the Senate bill on emissions from steel plants, and a compromise in the conference committee retained the House standards but gave steelmakers more time to comply with them. Conference committee deliberations frequently produce compromise outcomes of this sort.

Some committees and subcommittees have especially powerful or effective chairs who are able to dominate the group's internal politics. Representative Jamie Whitten (D-Mississippi), for example, was long a potent force on the House Appropriations Committee, which he chaired throughout the 1980s and into the 1990s. But his influence was particularly strong in the Committee's subcommittee on agriculture, which he also chaired during that period. Whitten dominated the staff, cultivated close and supportive relationships with agricultural interest groups, nurtured long-standing friendships with key bureaucrats in the Agriculture Department, and drew strategically and effectively on his deep store of personal knowledge of agriculture programs. All these resources gave him peerless influence in shaping and guiding agriculture policy over several decades. Indeed, so profound was his impact on agriculture policy that he was often called the "permanent secretary of agriculture."

TABLE 12-3 **COMMITTEES OF THE 104TH CONGRESS, 1995**

House Committees	Number of Subcommittees	Senate Committees	Number of Subcommittees
Agriculture	5	Agriculture, Nutrition, and Forestry	4
Appropriations	13	Appropriations	13
Banking and Financial Services	5	Armed Services	6
Budget	0	Banking, Housing, and Urban Affairs	5
Commerce	5	Budget	0
Economic and Educational Opportunities	5	Commerce, Science, Transportation	6
Government Reform and Oversight	7	Energy and Natural Resources	5
House Oversight	0	Environment and Public Works	4
International Relations	5	Finance	6
Judiciary	5	Foreign Relations	7
National Security	5	Governmental Affairs	3
Resources	5	Indian Affairs	0
Rules	2	Judiciary	6
Science	4	Labor and Human Resources	4
Select Intelligence	2	Rules and Administration	0
Small Business	4	Select Ethics	0
Standards of Official Conduct	0	Select Intelligence	0
Transportation and Infrastructure	6	Small Business	0
Veterans' Affairs	3	Special Aging	0
Ways and Means	5	Veterans' Affairs	0
Total 20	**86**	**Total 20**	**69**

Source: Congressional Quarterly, Players, Politics and Turf of the 104th Congress *(Washington, D. C.: Congressional Quarterly 1996).*

In other House committees and especially in the Senate, committee chairs are not so dominant. Like party leaders, they have to engage in constant negotiation with the members of their committee or subcommittee to build support for legislation they favor. Their legislative success thus rests heavily on their political skills.

THE FUNCTIONS OF CONGRESS

Because the framers of the Constitution viewed the legislative branch as the safest and most reliable arbiter of the disagreements that are likely to arise among a democratic people, they gave Congress a number of important functions. Those functions have expanded in number and complexity as the scope of the federal government's responsibilities has grown. Historically, the two most significant congressional functions were legislation and representation. In this century, the expansion of presidential power and the growth of a large federal bureaucracy have added a third major function—administrative oversight—to the legislature's responsibilities.

People who are not very familiar with Congress tend to regard it as a kind of factory where laws are made. In reality, Congress makes very few public laws, a couple of hundred at most, even in its most productive years; and many of those laws are of very minor consequence—for example, the laws passed in the 103rd Congress to proclaim October 16–24 as National Character Counts Week (PL 103-301) or to redesignate the Post Office building at 13th and Rockland Streets in Reading, Pennsylvania, as the Gus Yatron Postal Facility (PL 103-315).

Legislation, or lawmaking, is accomplished through deliberation and partisan adjustment, a process that involves information gathering, prolonged discussion, complex and often tedious negotiation, bargaining, and compromise. Most of the time the result of this process is nothing. In fact, 90 percent of the bills introduced in a typical Congress never become law, and enactment of the few that survive may require years, even decades. A long gestation period is common for significant legislation. For example, Congress debated tax reform for more than five years before it passed the Tax Reform Act of 1986. Federally funded health care for the elderly, a proposal first introduced during the Truman administration, was not enacted (as Medicare) until 1965. The line-item veto bill passed by both houses of the 104th Congress had been debated repeatedly over the entire history of the United States.

In recent decades the impediments to legislation have been greatly increased by the proliferation and growing sophistication of political interest groups (see Chapter 8), which affect lawmaking at every stage. They propose and help draft legislation. They testify at hearings. They lobby members in committee and during floor debate. They try to pressure the president to veto bills that they oppose. Moreover, the influence of political interest groups has been magnified by the rapid growth in the campaign contributions made by political action committees. Many members of Congress feel indebted to groups that support their campaigns, or at least feel obligated to listen when representatives of those groups present their positions on legislation.[13]

The pervasiveness of political maneuvering and bargaining among groups means that most legislative decisions are compromises, and compromise usually weakens the impact of legislation. Yet the openness of congressional lawmaking to politics can also be viewed as one of its strengths. Politics flourishes in Congress, that is, because the setting provides a forum for a broad spectrum of voices and opinions, and because the legislative process provides many opportunities for individuals and groups to express the content and the intensity of their concerns. This feature of the lawmaking process also has the advantage of legitimating public policy decisions, or making them seem fair and acceptable even to those who disagree with them. Everyone has opportunities to speak out about legislation and to try to influence its ultimate shape. Few laws are totally abhorrent to any group, because all groups are able to achieve at least some protection for the interests they value most. And groups can always try to enact new laws to undo the harm they perceive in existing ones.

In 1989, for example, Congress completely reversed itself in response to intense public pressure. In 1988 both houses had strongly supported a bill to improve health insurance coverage for elderly people suffering a catastrophic illness. In passing this legislation, Congress believed that it was responding to genuine concerns of the elderly, and indeed, it was. But no one foresaw the anger that soon arose over the new tax, amounting to as much as $800 a year for some senior citizens, that was created to fund this insurance coverage. Tens of thousands of elderly citizens and their

COUNTERPARTS OF CONGRESS:
THE BRITISH AND FRENCH PARLIAMENTS

A member of the British or French parliament watching the American Congress for the first time might have the same reaction as a European watching American football: impressed by the spectacle, but mystified by the logic. Although the national legislatures of the United States, Britain, and France appear superficially similar, the British and French parliaments differ from the American Congress in fundamental and important ways.

Like Congress, the British Parliament is bicameral; but its two houses, the House of Commons and the House of Lords, are not coequal. Commons is the dominant house, having the power to override Lords if the two houses disagree. Commons is composed of 650 members (usually called MPs) who represent geographical constituencies. MPs need not reside in or have any prior relationship with their constituency, though many do; to guarantee their election, some are assigned by their parties to run in certain districts where the party is strong. Unlike their American counterparts, MPs have small offices and usually share secretaries and telephones with their colleagues. They frequently resort to meeting constituents on benches in hallways because no other private space is available.

It is often said about the United States Congress that "all politics is local." Quite the opposite is true in the British Parliament. Although MPs perform some services for their constituents, their principal focus is on national policies formulated by party leaders. British politics is dominated by parties, and legislative party discipline is rarely violated—and never on matters of high importance. The American tradition in which members of Congress vote with their district against their party leaders has no counterpart in Britain, and any MP who tried it would soon be removed from his or her seat.

The separation of powers characteristic of American government is also not a significant element of the British political tradition, and the British "government" is drawn from the Parliament. After an election, the leader of the party that gains a majority of seats in Commons is invited by the monarch to form a government. The party leader serves as prime minister, or head of government, and other leaders of the majority party fill the important cabinet ministries.

In contrast to the president of the United States, who initiates bills with no guarantee that they will even receive a hearing, much less remain in their original form or be passed, the British government knows that the legislation it submits to Parliament will usually be approved by a straight party-line vote. There are committees in Parliament, as there are in Congress, but they do not have permanent jurisdictions or staffs or any significant influence on the outcome of votes. The agenda and legislative output of Parliament are dominated by the majority party.

Ample political debate goes on in Britain, as in the United States, but it tends to unfold in different places. British election campaigns, though much shorter than those in America, generally offer the voters clear choices between competing philosophies and ideologies. In an important sense, the votes cast by the British people set a direction for government in the years that follow, and the winning party then implements a set of policies laid out in its platform, or "programme." Until the next election, political debate occurs most frequently within the majority party, and especially within the cabinet.

The national legislature in France plays a role somewhere between the extremes represented by its American and British counterparts. Its nature is determined by the constitution of the Fifth French Republic, enacted in 1958, which was a response to the perception that the French Parliament had become too powerful and too unstable. The new constitution created a mixture of presidential and parliamentary systems, significantly strengthening executive authority by creating an independently elected president with a seven-year term. The bicameral legislature consists of a National Assembly, whose members are popularly elected for five-year terms, and a Senate, whose members are indirectly elected for nine-year terms by an Electoral College composed of local officials. The prime minister and a council of ministers, collectively known as the government, are appointed and may be dismissed by the president.

Unlike their counterparts in the American Congress, members of opposing parties in the British House of Commons sit directly facing each other—and do not hesitate to jeer speakers with whom they disagree.

The prime minister can also be ousted by a vote of censure in the National Assembly. There is no requirement that the prime minister or the other ministers be members of the legislature, and typically about one-third of the ministers are former bureaucrats rather than legislators.

Members of the National Assembly, of whom there are almost six hundred, represent single-member geographic constituencies. Commonly, however, they are not residents of the areas they represent, having instead been "parachuted in" by their party to run for office. Members do perform some services for the people they represent, but their principal responsibility is to support party leaders on legislative votes.

Committees exist in both the National Assembly and the Senate, but their role is limited. Like parliamentary committees in Britain, committees in France have very small staffs and do not have permanent jurisdictions. They help to work out the details of leg-islation after the important decisions have been made by the government or the Parliament itself.

The government of France controls the parliamentary agenda and can insist that the Parliament vote on its proposals without amendment. Because of tight party discipline, the government can usually count on loyal support from the delegates in the majority party or coalition. In formulating legislation, the National Assembly is the more important of the two houses of Parliament. If the two houses disagree on legislation, the prime minister can designate a joint committee to work out the differences. If that fails, the government can ask the National Assembly to decide the issue on its own, without the participation of the Senate. By not convening a joint committee, the government may occasionally let the Senate block a piece of undesired legislation passed in the National Assembly. But in all instances, the government is in the driver's seat as long as the majority coalition in Parliament hangs together.

interest groups pressured Congress to repeal the tax. As a result, the program was terminated before it ever went into effect.

The lawmaking process It is no simple matter to enact a law in the United States. A bill becomes a law only after it has successfully passed a number of hurdles, traps, and pitfalls. It can die in subcommittee, in full committee, on the floor of either house, in conference committee, or by presidential veto. It must pass all these obstacles to become law; defeat at any one of them will likely be a death knell. Figure 12-2 indicates the complexity of the congressional lawmaking process.

The process begins when an individual member of the House or Senate introduces a bill. A **bill** is a proposal, drafted in the form of a law, that a member would like his or her colleagues to consider. A bill may be introduced in either house of Congress by any member of that house. Often, to give the appearance of broad political support, members solicit their colleagues to cosponsor a bill. When a bill is introduced, it is assigned a number by the clerk and referred to a committee by the presiding officer. Many bills go no farther; they die because the committee lacks the time or interest to deal with them.

For bills that do not die, the next step is examination by the committee.[14] Most congressional committees have subcommittees that conduct the initial examination of legislative proposals. Subcommittees hold hearings at which they gather written and oral testimony from witnesses who have knowledge of, or interest in, the bill. Typically the list of witnesses includes the congressional proponents of the bill, officials from agencies with a direct interest in it, the leaders of concerned interest groups, state and local officials who may be affected if the bill becomes law, and individuals who are directly concerned because the bill will affect their taxes or benefits. At hearings in the early 1990s on the regulation of cable television, for example, members of Congress heard testimony from local cable company owners and from the National Cable Television Association in opposition to federal control. They also heard from local mayors, the National League of Cities, and the Consumer Federation of America about the need for more consistent and effective federal regulation.

At the conclusion of the hearings, the subcommittee votes on the bill. Usually the voting occurs after a **mark-up session** in which all the members of the subcommittee participate in revising the bill to put it into a form that is acceptable to a majority of them. If the subcommittee supports the bill it is returned to the full committee, where another mark-up may take place, followed by a vote of the full committee.

Mark-up sessions are a key battleground for all the political forces that seek to shape the text—and thus the impact—of a bill. In 1986, for example, Congress passed the most significant reform of federal tax policies in decades. The mark-up in the Senate Finance Committee occurred in a room full of tax lobbyists who communicated with senators and staff throughout the process, often haggling over the tiniest details. In a tax bill, of course, a tiny detail can be worth hundreds of thousands of dollars to individual taxpayers.

If a majority of the full committee supports the bill, it is reported to the full House or Senate. The committee normally issues a written report in which it explains the contents of the bill, justifies committee support for it, and explains the arguments of dissenting committee members.

The House's procedure at this point differs from the Senate's. Bills reported out of committee in the Senate go directly to the floor, where debate is scheduled by the party leaders. The House, because of its larger size, has a Rules Committee that

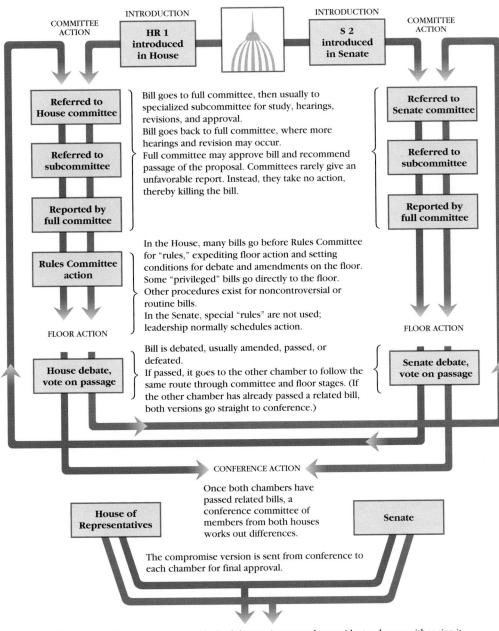

COMMITTEE ACTION

INTRODUCTION
HR 1 introduced in House

INTRODUCTION
S 2 introduced in Senate

COMMITTEE ACTION

Referred to House committee

Referred to subcommittee

Reported by full committee

Bill goes to full committee, then usually to specialized subcommittee for study, hearings, revisions, and approval.
Bill goes back to full committee, where more hearings and revision may occur.
Full committee may approve bill and recommend passage of the proposal. Committees rarely give an unfavorable report. Instead, they take no action, thereby killing the bill.

Referred to Senate committee

Referred to subcommittee

Reported by full committee

Rules Committee action

In the House, many bills go before Rules Committee for "rules," expediting floor action and setting conditions for debate and amendments on the floor. Some "privileged" bills go directly to the floor. Other procedures exist for noncontroversial or routine bills.
In the Senate, special "rules" are not used; leadership normally schedules action.

FLOOR ACTION

FLOOR ACTION

House debate, vote on passage

Bill is debated, usually amended, passed, or defeated.
If passed, it goes to the other chamber to follow the same route through committee and floor stages. (If the other chamber has already passed a related bill, both versions go straight to conference.)

Senate debate, vote on passage

CONFERENCE ACTION

House of Representatives

Once both chambers have passed related bills, a conference committee of members from both houses works out differences.

Senate

The compromise version is sent from conference to each chamber for final approval.

The compromise version approved by both houses is sent to the president, who can either sign it into law or veto it (or in some cases parts of it) and return it to Congress.
Congress may override a regular veto by a two-thirds majority vote in both houses. When this happens, the bill then becomes law without the president's signature.

HR 1 VETO

S 2 Signed

FIGURE 12-2
How a bill becomes a law.

SOURCE: *Guide to Congress* (Washington, D.C.: Congressional Quarterly, 1976), 345; updated by the authors. Reprinted by permission of Congressional Quarterly, Inc.

determines when a bill will be debated, how long the debate will last, and what kinds of amendments (if any) may be introduced during debate. Because the rule that governs a bill's consideration on the floor often has a significant impact on its final shape, the Rules Committee sometimes wields significant power in the House legislative process. For example, the committee that reports a bill often wants it to go to the House floor with few or no amendments permitted, whereas opponents of the bill want free rein to amend so that they can cripple it or water it down. The Rules Committee must referee these disputes.

Once a bill has been reported to the floor, it is placed on a legislative calendar. In the House, debate is usually limited to a few hours or less, depending on how important or controversial a bill is. Senate floor rules are less rigid, and debate there may last for several hours or days or, in some cases, weeks. In each house, debate is usually controlled by members who are designated as floor managers for the bill. The floor manager for the proponents (typically a committee or subcommittee chair who has worked on the bill) and the floor manager for the opposition (usually, but not always, a member of the minority party) organize the debate and allot time to other members who share their views on the bill.[15]

During the debate individual members may introduce amendments that change the substance of the bill in some way. The House has much more rigid rules about amendments than the Senate. Unless the rule on the bill specifically permits otherwise, amendments offered in the House must be directly related, or germane, to the substance of the bill. In the Senate there are few restrictions on amendments, and senators are more prone to attaching nongermane amendments to any bill that happens to be under consideration. A common political tactic in the Senate, for example, is to attach a controversial unrelated provision to an essential or popular piece of legislation. Such additions are called **riders** because they "ride" through the legislative process on the backs of other bills when they might not have survived on their own. In 1990, for example, proponents attached to a widely supported bill creating new federal judgeships a proposal that would permit the copyrighting of architectural designs of buildings. The amendment bore no relation to the content of the judgeship bill; the bill was simply a convenient vehicle for the amendment to "ride."

Amendments are voted on as they are introduced. Those that receive the support of a majority are integrated into the bill. When debate is completed and all amendments have been considered, a final vote on the bill occurs. Today this is almost always a recorded vote—that is, the position of each member is noted and recorded in the *Congressional Record,* the official journal of House and Senate proceedings. Senators vote orally when their names are called by the clerk. In the House, voting is done electronically. Members insert a plastic card in one of the teller machines on the House floor and push a button to indicate a vote of yea, nay, or present. Each member's vote is then indicated on a large tote board on the wall at the front of the chamber.

How do members decide their position on a bill or an amendment? For most members, the answer involves a complex personal calculus. Although the position taken by the party leaders often has a significant impact, Congress does not have the kind of party discipline that requires members to vote the party line on every issue. Some issues are highly relevant to particular members' constituents, and on such votes these members are strongly inclined to take a position that best serves the interests of the people they represent. On other issues, members' personal views may determine how they vote. Some votes come in response to heavy lobbying by the president or by interest groups.[16] On a great many legislative votes most or all of these pressures are at work, often tugging members in different directions. Most

Marjorie Margolies Mezvinsky, a first-term Democratic representative from Pennsylvania, cast the deciding vote approving President Clinton's 1993 budget proposal. The vote proved fatal to her chances for reelection from her historically Republican district.

studies suggest that in such situations constituency interests and party loyalty weigh most heavily. But there is no simple, consistent explanation of individual voting behavior.

Even if a majority of the members present vote in favor of a bill, to become law it also requires approval by the other house, which must go through the same process. It often happens that when a bill passes in the second house, it differs from the version passed in the first house. To resolve the differences, a joint conference committee is created. Its sole purpose is to construct from the differing versions a single bill that can win the approval of both houses. When the conference committee has completed its work (usually by forging a compromise), it reports back to each house, and another floor vote is taken in each house. If both houses agree to the conference committee's version of the bill, it is sent to the president for signature.

The president has several options. One is to sign the bill, at which point it becomes law. Another is to allow the bill to become law without a signature; this will occur ten working days after the bill is received, if Congress is still in session. The president may also veto the bill by declining to sign it and returning it within ten days to the house where it originated, accompanied by a message stating the reasons for the veto. Congress then has an opportunity to override the president's veto. An override, however, requires a two-thirds majority in each house and, as Table 12-4 (see page 440) indicates, rarely happens.

If the annual session of Congress ends within ten days of the passage of a bill, the president may exercise another option, the **pocket veto**, simply by declining to sign

TABLE 12-4   PRESIDENTIAL VETOES OF CONGRESSIONAL BILLS, 1933–1996

PERIOD	PRESIDENT	REGULAR VETOES	POCKET VETOES	TOTAL VETOES	VETOES OVERRIDDEN
1933–1945	Roosevelt	372	263	635	9
1945–1953	Truman	180	70	250	12
1953–1961	Eisenhower	73	108	181	2
1961–1963	Kennedy	12	9	21	0
1963–1969	Johnson	16	14	30	0
1969–1974	Nixon	24	18	42	6
1974–1977	Ford	53	19	72	12
1977–1981	Carter	13	18	31	2
1981–1989	Reagan	39	39	78	9
1989–1993	Bush	31[a]	15	46	1
1993–1996	Clinton	11	0	11	1

[a]President Bush contended that four of his regular vetoes were pocket vetoes. Some members of Congress disagreed, noting that the president can exercise a pocket veto only after Congress has adjourned for the year, not during a recess. The dispute over terminology was not resolved, and all of those vetoes are listed here as regular vetoes.

Source: Data from Congressional Quarterly Weekly Report, December 19, 1992, 3925–3926. Post-1992 data compiled from Congressional Quarterly Weekly Reports.

the bill. Because Congress is not in session, the president does not return the bill, nor is there any possibility of a congressional override. Because many bills are passed in the legislative rush that comes at the end of a congressional session, opportunities for pocket vetoes occur with some frequency.

In 1996, presidents were given still another option in some cases when President Clinton signed a bill creating a **line-item veto**. This permits the president to veto portions—or line items—of certain kinds of legislation while allowing the remainder of the bill to become law. Traditionally, presidents could kill objectionable portions of a bill only by vetoing the entire bill.

The line-item veto was scheduled to go into effect on January 1, 1997. Under its provisions, Congress may replace a line item that a president has vetoed only by passing another law for that purpose. The president may veto this new law, however, which could then be overridden by Congress only with the traditional two-thirds majorities in each house.

There was some uncertainty about the constitutionality of this new authority at the time it was created, with some critics alleging that the creation amounted to a significant amendment of the Constitution without going through the amendment process. Lawsuits testing this contention were expected.

The veto power is an important source of political leverage in the struggle between the president and Congress over the shape of legislation. For example, after the Chinese government's crackdown on dissident students in 1989, Congress passed a bill that would have allowed Chinese students to stay in the United States longer than their original visas permitted. This measure was intended to protect the students from prosecution when they returned to China. President Bush vetoed the bill. He was concerned with the effect it would have on his efforts to reestablish relations with China, and he believed that protection of the Chinese students could be accomplished by other means. Bush's veto angered many members of Congress, where the bill had passed overwhelmingly. The House overrode the veto by a vote of 390 to 25. But Bush lobbied heavily in the Senate to retain support for his authority to lead the country in foreign affairs. The Senate voted 62 to 37 to override, a few votes short of the two-thirds majority needed. The veto stood.

Rules, procedures, and precedents   The lawmaking process is governed by a highly developed set of rules and precedents. The first rules, written by Thomas Jefferson, still exist, although they have been altered considerably since Jefferson's time. Rules and precedents control such matters as parliamentary procedures in debate, the assignment of bills to committees, the operations of committees, and legislative recordkeeping. Because the rules shape political conflicts in Congress and play a large role in determining the strategies of political adversaries, some of their general effects on the operations and decisions of Congress are worth noting.[17]

First, the rules enforce a decentralization of legislative power in both houses of Congress. They require that legislation be considered and acted on at a number of points (committee, subcommittee, floor, and joint conference) before final passage. In effect, each of these stages is a veto point, for defeat at any one of them usually kills a bill. There are procedures in the House and Senate rules for bypassing some of these steps, but they are unwieldy and rarely employed. Hence, members who control the veto points in the legislative process—an especially strong and obdurate committee chair, for instance—have significant power in determining what will or will not become law.

Second, the rules favor the status quo by, in effect, biasing the legislative process against change. The proponents of a new piece of legislation must succeed at every stage in the process: their bill must win majorities in subcommittee, in full committee, on the floor, and so on. Opponents must win at only one of these stages: they can defeat the bill in subcommittee, in full committee, or wherever they can construct a majority in opposition to the bill. The cards thus are stacked against new legislation. In recent Congresses only about 5 percent of all bills and joint resolutions introduced have been enacted.

Third, the rules work to slow the pace of legislative consideration. Congress has occasionally shown an ability to legislate quickly, particularly when confronted with a national security crisis. In September 1983, for instance, Congress was able in just a few days to work out a compromise with President Reagan permitting American peacekeeping forces to remain in Lebanon. In 1964, responding to reports of North Vietnamese attacks on American naval vessels, Congress passed in one day a resolution authorizing President Johnson to respond to the attacks. But quick action by Congress is the exception, not the norm. Most of the time the legislative process grinds away slowly because so many participants at so many stages have to study and deliberate.

Fourth, the rules provide several mechanisms by which determined minorities can thwart the will of congressional majorities. In the Senate, for instance, much is accomplished through a procedure called **unanimous consent**. Action can be taken without debate when all members consent to that procedure, but only one dissenting senator can prevent action under unanimous consent and thus slow the progress of the Senate. Senator Jesse Helms (R-North Carolina) has sometimes used this tactic to force the Senate to pay attention to issues that are important to him personally. His objections to unanimous consent resolutions have earned him the title "Senator No."

Also in the Senate, which has a long tradition of unlimited debate, a small group of senators may delay or even prevent a vote on a bill by carrying out a **filibuster**. They do this by gaining recognition to speak in debate and then not relinquishing the floor. Some senators have held the floor for more than twenty-four consecutive

MILITARY BASE CLOSINGS

Across the mouth of the James River from Norfolk, Virginia, sits Fort Monroe, constructed during the War of 1812. Though a relic of the early-nineteenth century, Fort Monroe continued to be an active military base into the last decade of the twentieth. The Department of Defense had sought for years to close the fort, arguing that it was costly to operate and no longer served any needed military purpose. But the base remained open because Virginia's representatives in Congress consistently and effectively fought its closing. Determining which bases the armed forces should operate may seem a technical question, a matter of efficient and effective government. It is also a highly combustible political issue.

For members of Congress, few issues more fully provoke the conflict between national and constituent interests than does the closing of military bases. There are hundreds of military installations scattered all over the United States. By bringing federal personnel and federal dollars into the state and congressional district where it is located, each of them helps to support the local economy. But as military strategies change, some bases become obsolete or unnecessary; and to reduce costs, the Department of Defense seeks to close them. That's when the conflict sets in.

Most members of Congress believe in tight budgets and the avoidance of wasteful spending. All other things being equal, they would willingly vote to close military bases that no longer serve any important purpose. A member's perceptions often change, however, when one of the bases recommended for closing is in his or her own state or district. In such cases, members almost always oppose the closing in order to protect the local economy. But they also do so for personal reasons. A base closing is often viewed as

evidence that a member lacks clout in Washington, and a future opponent will fix on it as evidence of poor representation, in the same way that an incumbent will focus on the prevention of a base closing as evidence of effective representation.

Historically, members have helped each other in the effort to forestall base closings. Few members could single-handedly prevent a closing, but all the members from districts with proposed closings have had enough collective clout to thwart many closings. Often reaching across party and ideological lines, these political coalitions have made it extremely difficult for the Defense Department to close any bases. In 1976 Congress passed a bill requiring congressional approval of all base closings. President Gerald Ford vetoed the bill, but Congress later passed another measure requiring hazardous-waste studies to be conducted on any base that was proposed for closing. In the fourteen years after this time-consuming requirement went into effect, not a single base was closed.

To undercut the political coalitions that had so often prevented closings, in 1988 some members of Congress proposed a new approach. Under this procedure, (1) the Defense Department makes its recommendations, (2) which are then reviewed by an independent base closure commission, (3) which makes its own recommendations to the president, (4) who reviews the commission's recommendations and forwards his own proposal to Congress. Congress has final authority, but in voting on the president's recommendations it can only accept or reject the entire list. No amendments are permitted.

Between 1988 and 1995, there were four rounds of closings involving hundreds of military installations. In each case, the president accepted and forwarded the independent commission's recommendations

hours, and a group of senators working together can hold the floor indefinitely. It now takes a vote by three-fifths of the entire Senate (sixty senators) to invoke **cloture** and thereby end a filibuster. This means that if 41 percent or more of the senators are intensely opposed to a bill that has majority support, final action on the bill can be slowed or prevented. Even after cloture, loopholes in the Senate rules permit a single senator to prolong debate.

Residents of Atwater, California, wave good-bye in early 1995 to the last plane at Castle Air Force Base. At the height of the cold war 5,000 people worked at the base, which served as a station for B-52 bombers. Because a base closing can devastate a local economy, members of Congress fight hard to keep bases open in their districts.

without alteration. In each case as well, despite howls of opposition from members representing districts with bases on the closure list, Congress approved the recommendation. But none of the lists included Fort Monroe—perhaps an indication of the indirect influence exerted on the decision makers by Virginia's Senator John Warner, one of the most powerful Republican members of Congress on military affairs.

Discussion Questions

1. How does the new procedure for closing bases alter the politics of congressional decision making on this matter? With what effect?
2. Are members of Congress being irresponsible when they oppose the closing of an obsolete military base in their district? Why or why not?
3. How might the base-closing process be improved?

In 1995, President Clinton's nomination of Dr. Henry W. Foster Jr. to be surgeon general of the United States was defeated when opponents undertook a filibuster. Although Foster had earned a reputation as a national leader in efforts to reduce teenage pregnancy, the revelation that he had occasionally performed abortions as part of his obstetrics practice doomed his chances. Contributing to the opposition were the desire of the new Republican congressional leadership to assert itself against Clinton and the desire of several Republican senators—Robert Dole, Phil Gramm, and Richard Lugar—to strengthen their pro-life credentials for the 1996 race for the Republican presidential nomination. (Gramm led the filibuster effort.) When after several attempts Foster's supporters could persuade only fifty-seven senators to vote for cloture, they gave up. The nomination was withdrawn from the calendar and effectively killed. (The successful Republican effort to kill President Clinton's economic stimulus proposal in the spring of 1993 is another example of the filibuster at work.)

Finally, a bill can die when a majority of the members of a committee or a subcommittee opposes it, even though a majority of the members of the house in which it was introduced favors it. In these and other ways, the rules permit the will of a determined minority to supersede that of a majority.

The legislative process is decentralized, slow, and tedious, and it crushes most bills. For members of Congress who have legislative goals, it is a demanding consumer of time and effort and an unrelenting source of frustration. But it does ensure that in most cases new laws are carefully considered and solidly supported before they are enacted.

Representation

In the United States, participation in the national government occurs through the process of **representation**. The framers of the Constitution were most concerned about the quality of representation. To help ensure that members of Congress would be sensitive to the interests of the people they represent, the Constitution requires that they reside in the state from which they are elected. This requirement does not exist in most other countries. To ensure that the people know what the government is doing, the Constitution requires both houses of Congress to keep and publish a journal of their activities in which the yea and nay votes are recorded so that individual members can be held accountable. And to ensure that members of Congress keep faith with their constituents, the Constitution provides for regular and frequent elections.

Every member of Congress represents two groups of citizens. In that every member has some responsibility to the national interest, he or she represents the nation as a whole. The member also represents a **constituency**, the state or congressional district that elects her or him to Congress.

The interests of these two groups may be in conflict. Sometimes what is best for the district may not be best for the nation. Higher farm prices benefit individual farmers but not the nation's consumers. Federal subsidies for the construction of a dam in a particular district will have local benefits but will cause an increase in everyone's taxes (a similar problem—the closing of military bases—is discussed in the Case Study box on pages 442–443). Members also confront conflicts between their own views and the views of their constituents. Some policies that a representative believes to be best for the nation may have little support in his or her own district.

Constituent relations   How do members of Congress keep in touch with their constituents? How do they know their constituents' opinions? How do they deal with disagreements within their constituency? Each member develops his or her own ways of doing these things.

Constituencies are not monolithic, single-minded groups of voters. They tend instead to be composed of people with varying attitudes, levels of information, inter-

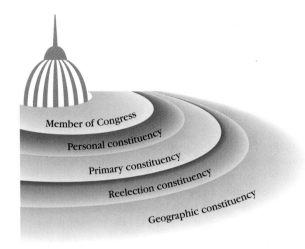

Member of Congress

Personal constituency

Primary constituency

Reelection constituency

Geographic constituency

FIGURE 12-3
House members' perception
of their constituencies.

SOURCE: Adapted from Richard F.
Fenno Jr., *Homestyle: House
Members in Their Districts*
(Boston: Little, Brown, 1978),
1–27.

ests, and partisan preferences. Richard Fenno, a political scientist who has studied relationships between members of Congress and their constituents, has indicated that most members view their constituencies in several different ways, or as what he calls a "nest of concentric circles"[18] (see Figure 12-3). The outer and largest of these circles is the "geographic constituency," the whole district viewed from the standpoint of location and demographic characteristics. Is it a farm district or an inner-city district? What are its principal commercial products? What is the religious and ethnic composition of the people who live there? The largest circle represents the district in the broadest sense.

The next circle is the "reelection constituency," the people who vote for the member in the general election. The reelection constituency is more important than the geographic constituency in determining the member's positions on policy issues. Indeed, members often perceive communities and special interests in their districts in terms of the political support they provide, saying things like "I never get many votes over on the west side" or "I can always count on the support of the Chamber of Commerce crowd." It is a fact of political life that members of Congress are more responsive to those who vote for them than to those who do not.

Members of Congress are even more responsive to people in the inner circle, the "primary constituency." These are the people who provide loyal support in primary elections, who not only vote for members but also work and spend for them. They form the core of the member's political support.

The fourth circle is the "personal constituency," people with whom the member has close personal ties. Although some may be active in politics and others not, this group includes the people who are most likely to advise the member on political and policy matters and whose advice the member is most likely to trust and follow. Like the primary constituency, they provide funds and help during campaigns.

Fenno's explanation of congressional constituencies sheds light on the politics of representation. Constituencies are quite complex, with overlapping and often conflicting interests. As a consequence, members must constantly interact with the "folks back home" to discern the direction and intensity of their constituents' opinions.

The representative at work   Although many people think that representation is a one-way process, that representatives are given "instructions" by their constituents

CONTACTING YOUR REPRESENTATIVES IN WASHINGTON

The United States Congress is one of the most accessible legislatures in the world. Debates and votes are open to the public and are reported in full. Anyone can phone, write, or visit the office of a member of Congress.

A good source of background information about members of Congress is *The Almanac of American Politics*, published biennially. To find out exactly what a member has said on the floor of Congress and how he or she has voted on a bill, check the *Congressional Record*, the official journal of congressional proceedings. It is published every day that Congress is in session. To learn a member's position on any issue, start with the *Congressional Quarterly Weekly Report*, a magazine known as *CQ*. At the end of each week's *CQ* is a list of each member's vote on every bill on which there is a recorded vote.

When writing to a member of Congress, address the letter as follows:

Honorable John A. Cruz
United States Senate
Washington, DC 20510

Honorable Sally S. Goodman
United States House of Representatives
Washington, DC 20515

Normally, the member's office will respond by mail within two or three weeks on a policy issue. A response may take longer if you write about a personal problem involving an agency of the government.

To contact a member's local office, look for the address and phone number in the government pages (blue pages) of the local phone book. A call to the local office will often provide the quickest solution to a problem or the most efficient (and least expensive) way to register your views on a policy issue. To phone your representative's Washington office, call the Capitol switchboard: (202) 224-3121.

Most members of Congress also have e-mail addresses. These can be located in many ways, but one of the most efficient is to look them up in the "Congressional E-mail Addresses" page on the World Wide Web portion of the Internet. The Internet address is:

http://akebono.stanford.edu/yahoo/ Government/Legislative Branch/ Congressional E-mail Addresses/

If you wish to visit your representative's office to get help with a problem or to express your views while you are in Washington, D.C., call ahead. Members of Congress are always happy to see their constituents. Remember, though, that their schedules are hectic, and they are rarely available for unscheduled visits.

and simply react to those instructions, this is a misperception. Members rarely receive anything resembling instructions from home. They do tend to hear a good deal from the people they represent, but studies of congressional mail suggest that this type of communication has a number of limitations.

First, although members may receive thousands of letters, faxes, and e-mail communications each week, most of their constituents never write or call. A flood of communications about some particular issue is likely to indicate a campaign "stimulated" by one or more interest groups. The communications that members receive on such occasions often look or sound exactly the same, and this somewhat diminishes their impact. Public opinion polls indicate that only about 15 percent of all adults have ever communicated with their representatives in Congress.[19]

Second, many of the communications that members receive have little to do with legislative issues. They are requests for help with specific problems such as expediting a passport, assisting with a grant application, or getting a disabled veteran into a veterans' hospital.

CONGRESS

Do you need to know the status of an item in this year's federal budget? Perhaps you want to contact your representative in Congress or find out which committees will be holding hearings on a bill that concerns you. Or maybe you need to do research for a term paper on the congressional leadership. For information about Congress, the following Internet locations are good starting points.

HOW A BILL BECOMES A LAW

A full description of all the steps in the lawmaking process is available at **http://www.vote smart.org/reference/primer/billlaw.html**

THOMAS: CONGRESS'S GATEWAY

Named after Thomas Jefferson, this site, **http://thomas.loc.gov/** was created early in 1995 to be the central repository of information about Congress. Here one can find the full text of the *Congressional Record* and all bills introduced in Congress, information about each member's vote on every bill, and a wide variety of other information. All the databases at this site are searchable by key words, name, or bill number.

GPO ACCESS ON THE WEB

This site at **http://thorplus.lib.purdue.edu:80/gpo/** provides several valuable databases, most of which start with information from the 103rd Congress in 1993. Congressional bills, the *Congressional Record Index* and the full text of the *Congressional Record*, the *History of Bills*, the full text of public laws, the *Congressional Directory*, House and Senate

calendars, and a wide range of other legislative documents are available.

CONGRESSIONAL DIRECTORIES

Check out **gopher://marvel.loc.gov/11/congress/directory/** for addresses and committee assignments of members of Congress, or try **http://www.house.gov/MemberWWW.html** for a link to e-mail addresses and home pages of members of the House of Representatives. The main entry page for information on the Senate and individual senators is **http://www.senate.gov**, which includes e-mail addresses for senators but is not as complete or well developed as the House home pages.

CONGRESSIONAL QUARTERLY

The address **http://voter96.cqalert.com** is an entry page for information and resources from the *Congressional Quarterly* service. The site includes lead stories from the *Congressional Quarterly Weekly Report*, analysis of major issues, members' votes on individual issues, and congressional election results.

VOTING, CAMPAIGN FINANCE, ISSUE POSITIONS OF MEMBERS

The address **http://www.vote-smart.org/congress/index.html** will link you to a variety of information about members, voting patterns, sources of campaign funds, and issues before Congress.

CONGRESSIONAL LEADERSHIP

The site at **http://www.vote-smart.org/reference/primer/clead.html** provides special information about and by the congressional leadership.

Third, many of the communications that a member receives contradict each other. Some constituents may recommend a vote for a bill, others a vote against it. On clean-air legislation, for instance, environmentalists may want the member to vote for stringent regulations, but factory owners may want weaker regulations. Members hear a lot from constituents—veterans, farmers, schools, hospitals, and others—who want increases in the benefits they receive from the government. But they also hear frequently from people who want budget cuts and lower taxes.

Fourth, members hear nothing or next to nothing from their constituents about many issues, especially issues that have little direct bearing on the district. Members from inner-city districts hear little from their constituents about agricultural subsidies, for example; representatives from New England hear little from the folks at home about coal mine safety.

To overcome deficiencies in the communications received from constituents, many members of Congress work hard to interact with the people they represent. They try to improve their understanding of constituent opinion, especially on complex issues that are important to the district. But they also want to build constituent support for their own views. For many issues on which the members' personal opinions are clearly formulated, constituents' opinions are ambiguous or contradictory. In these cases members have genuine opportunities to become opinion leaders in their districts. Leadership of constituent opinion is an important, but often overlooked, component of the representative relationship.

Members of Congress have developed a number of successful techniques for reaching out to their districts. A generous **franking privilege** enables them to mail newsletters and questionnaires to every postal box in their states or districts, free of charge, and the congressional recording studios enable them to send video or audio tapes to television and radio stations back home. Members also receive ample funds for travel between Washington and their districts. Most spend at least part of every month back home, aided by the typical monthly schedule of Congress: three weeks in session and one week for "district work periods." Many of those who live east of the Mississippi River try to get home every week. In addition to their Washington offices, all members have one or more offices in their districts with full-time staffs. Members also keep in touch by reading local newspapers, telephoning district leaders, and meeting with visitors from the district when they come to Washington.

But the relationship between members and their constituents is based on more than just the frequency and technology of communication. Most members have grown up in their districts. Their political socialization took place there; they entered politics and achieved their first political successes there. As a result, they tend to share the economic and social values of the people they represent, not simply because it is politically expedient to do so but because those are their personal values as well. In reality, much of the relationship between members and their districts is felt rather than communicated.

Chapter 10 noted the extraordinary success rate of members of Congress who run for reelection. Here is an important part of the reason. In their voting behavior Americans seem to be expressing considerable satisfaction with the way they are represented by their own member of Congress. Far from being easy or automatic, this satisfaction reflects the substantial effort that contemporary members of Congress apply to their responsibilities as representatives and the abundant array of resources available to them in carrying out those responsibilities. Recent studies of the House of Representatives, for example, show that on average House members now have more than a quarter of their allotted staff working on specific constituent problems. For members of Congress, the clear electoral reward for responsive representation[20] gives them a powerful incentive to concentrate a substantial portion of their energies on this aspect of their job.

Administrative Oversight

Administrative oversight is another essential congressional function. Because Congress is ill equipped to make every important public policy decision, in many areas it delegates responsibility to bureaucratic agencies, charging them with mak-

Freshman Republican representative David McIntosh greets citizens in his Indiana district. Public expectations require all members of Congress to stay in close touch with the people they represent.

ing expert decisions but subjecting those decisions to legislative review. When this process works as intended, it combines bureaucratic expertise and popular control. The policy experts in the executive branch of government make the day-to-day decisions of public policy, and the people's representatives in the legislative branch review them and, when necessary, attempt to alter them.

The importance of administrative oversight derives from the view, widely held among the framers of the Constitution, that the American people should be not only served by their government but protected from it as well. As public policy grows more complex, the opportunities for administrative error and abuse increase. Pentagon procurement scandals, flaws in the 1990 census count, and the *Challenger* shuttle disaster are examples of such errors. Vigilant oversight has become increasingly important.

Techniques   Congress performs its oversight function in a great many ways.[21] Most of the standing committees of Congress conduct **oversight hearings** as a regular part of their responsibilities. (Some have subcommittees to which they assign those hearings.) During an oversight hearing the activities of an executive agency or the management of a specific program are reviewed in depth. Often held when the authorized tenure of an agency or a program is nearing an end, the hearing is usually preceded by an investigation by the committee staff. At the hearing itself, executive-branch officials are called on to explain their activities and to answer the committee's questions. The report produced by an oversight hearing may suggest changes in administrative procedures, reauthorization of the agency or program, or legislation to remedy its perceived defects.

Political conflict over institutional powers often emerges in oversight hearings. In 1989, for example, the House Intelligence Committee sought at several such hearings to obtain copies of internal reports issued by the inspector general of the Central Intelligence Agency (CIA) that examined the agency's activities and administration. William Webster, the director of the CIA, refused to release the reports. After months of wrangling, the committee finally voted to include in the 1990 authorization legislation for the CIA a provision that would broaden congressional access to the reports. In other words, having failed to obtain the reports through the oversight process, the committee turned to the legislative process, where its authority was more formal—and ultimately more effective.

In addition to oversight hearings, Congress conducts **special investigations**. Some of these investigations are virtually indistinguishable from oversight hearings. They are conducted by permanent committees and subcommittees with no special appropriations of funds or additions to committee staffs. More commonly, however, investigations differ from routine oversight hearings in the depth of their examinations, the vigor with which they are conducted, and the amount of funds and staff resources committed to them.

Congress often establishes temporary committees to conduct major investigations. Each committee has its own staff (frequently headed by an attorney with a national reputation) and its own, often very ample, budget. For example, to conduct the investigation of 1972 presidential campaign activities, which came to be known as the Watergate investigation, a separate committee headed by Senator Sam Ervin (D-North Carolina) was established. It lasted for a year and a half and had a budget of almost $2 million and a staff of more than sixty people. Similar investigations have been conducted in the past four decades on such matters as the assassination of President John F. Kennedy, the fate of soldiers missing in action in Vietnam, and the diversion of funds by Reagan administration officials from Iranian arms sales to the contras in Nicaragua.

Special investigations often raise tension between Congress and presidents, who claim that such investigations are inspired by the opposition party to embarrass or weaken the administration. In the late 1940s, President Harry Truman, a Democrat, made the claim of partisanship against a young Republican representative named Richard Nixon for his role in the aggressive investigation of communist influence in Truman's administration. A quarter of a century later, Nixon, then the Republican president, made the same claim against the Democrats who led the Watergate investigations.

Employees of the executive branch also fall under congressional oversight through **personnel controls**. Those who serve at the top levels—cabinet secretaries, agency heads, regulatory commissioners—are presidential appointees whose appointments are subject to Senate confirmation. When the president nominates a candidate to fill one of these positions, the nomination must be reviewed and approved by majority vote in the Senate before it takes effect. The Senate can, and occasionally does, reject candidates proposed by the president, as it did in the case of Henry Foster.

In addition, Congress has control over the salaries and employment conditions of all federal employees, both career civil servants and presidential appointees. It sets pay scales; establishes "personnel ceilings" that limit the number of people who can work in a specified agency or office; creates general hiring qualifications; and approves routine personnel policies regarding annual leave, sick pay, dismissals,

Chairman Sam Ervin (D-North Carolina) with members and counsel of the Senate Select Committee on Presidential Campaign Activities—better known as the Watergate committee. Their televised hearings into the Nixon administration's corruption held Americans spellbound in 1973.

retirements, and pensions. This range of control gives Congress some discretion in determining who will work where in the executive branch and under what conditions. Congress sought to enlarge its political control over the activities of the inspector general of the CIA, for example, by enacting legislation making that position a presidential appointment subject to Senate confirmation.

Financial control—the power of the purse—is the most important and effective of Congress's techniques for overseeing the work of the executive branch. The Constitution (Article I, Section 9) is quite specific on this point: "No money shall be drawn from the treasury, but in consequence of appropriations made by law." Before Congress appropriates funds to an agency or program, it assesses the manner in which previous appropriations have been used, and it examines the stated plans for the use of the funds being requested. This work is usually conducted by the House and Senate Appropriations Committees, which hold annual hearings for virtually every program and agency in the government. At the hearings executive-branch officials must explain their past activities and defend their budget requests for the coming year.[22]

In a great many cases Congress appropriates less money than executive agencies request.[23] By shifting funds from one program to another, it may also change the priorities reflected in executive budget requests. In 1995, for example, the House slashed President Clinton's request for antimissile defenses from $3 billion to $763 million, and instead appropriated $553 million to resume production of the B-2 bomber, which neither the president nor Pentagon leaders wanted.

Another tool of congressional oversight is the General Accounting Office (GAO), the federal government's accounting arm. Located in the legislative branch, the GAO conducts audits of government programs to determine whether they have been well managed and whether their benefits justify their costs. GAO audit reports are submitted to Congress, which sometimes uses them to target inefficiency or malfeasance in the management of federal programs or in the use of federal funds. Much of the information that led to intense congressional review of mismanagement in the Department of Housing and Urban Development (HUD) during the Reagan administration came from GAO audits.

Finally, should other means of oversight prove insufficient, **impeachment** constitutes the legislature's weapon of last resort. It is the power to remove from office the president, the vice president, or any other civil officer of the United States who has been found guilty of (in the words of Article II, Section 4, of the Constitution) "treason, bribery, or other high crimes and misdemeanors."

The impeachment process begins with the introduction of a bill of impeachment in the House of Representatives. This bill is referred to the Judiciary Committee, which may do nothing or may debate the bill and report it to the full House. In the latter case, the House debates the charges and then votes. If a majority opposes the bill, the charges are dropped; if a majority supports the bill, the person is impeached. The process then moves to the Senate for trial, with the members of the Senate serving, in effect, as the jury. When the impeached officer is the president, and only then, the Chief Justice of the United States presides over the Senate trial. Conviction by the Senate requires the assent of two-thirds of the senators present and voting.

As this description suggests, the framers of the Constitution devised an impeachment procedure that is unwieldy and difficult to use.[24] They did not intend impeachment to be routinely used, and it has not been. Over the course of American history, impeachment proceedings have been initiated in the House more than sixty times, but as of the end of 1995 only fifteen federal officials had ever been impeached and only seven had been convicted. Most of them were federal judges, including three who were impeached and removed from office in the 1980s.

Only one president, Andrew Johnson, has been impeached, on the grounds not of corruption but of personnel actions that offended his opponents in Congress. He was acquitted in 1868 and remained in office until the expiration of his term. Richard Nixon's timely resignation in 1974—he decided to resign when support from members of his own party in Congress collapsed—prevented his near-certain impeachment and conviction.

Performance Congress has often been criticized for inconsistency in the performance of its oversight function and for failing to uncover or remedy inefficiencies in the management of executive agencies. Given the ample opportunities available for effective oversight, what accounts for these shortfalls?

The best way to answer this question is to look at oversight from the perspective of individual members of Congress. As former representative Norman Y. Mineta (D-California) once said, "Oversight is very tough. It's time-consuming, painstaking investigative work. And there's no political appeal in it. There's much more appeal in getting a bill passed and saying, 'Here's what my bill will do for senior citizens.'"[25]

Mineta's remarks neatly summarize the numerous disincentives to effective administrative oversight. Oversight provides fewer rewards to individual members than other congressional activities provide. Except in a highly publicized episode like the Watergate investigation, it rarely wins acclaim or publicity for a member. It fuels institutional rivalry, often angering the target agency and the political interest groups that benefit from that agency's programs. Finally, oversight takes away from time that might be spent more profitably on legislation or constituent relations. For these reasons the incentive systems that govern the behavior of most individual members may not inspire the arduous and often unrewarding effort required for successful oversight.

CONGRESSIONAL REFORM AND ITS IMPACT

After 1968, Congress changed its rules and procedures in dramatic ways. To understand those changes, put yourself in the position of a new member who is trying to establish a legislative career. To establish a career, you need to accomplish two things: (1) get yourself reelected every time your term is over, and (2) make your influence felt in legislative policy making. The former is essential to any legislative career at all; the latter is essential to achieving a measure of satisfaction and success.

During the 1950s and early 1960s, however, a new legislator could not easily accomplish either goal. The electoral process was dominated by party leaders outside Congress to whom members were often beholden. The internal operations of Congress were dominated by the chairs of the powerful committees and by the party leaders, such as Senate Majority Leader Lyndon Johnson and House Speaker Sam Rayburn, who worked with them. Junior members had small staffs, meager allowances, little access to committee and subcommittee influence, and minimal impact on the policy agenda.

That situation began to change in the late 1960s under the impetus of an organization called the Democratic Study Group (DSG), formed by Democrats recently elected to the House. The DSG sought to alter House rules so that members who lacked seniority could play a more significant role in legislative policy making. Beginning in 1968, its efforts succeeded. The turning point came in 1974, when the seventy-five Democrats newly elected to the House banded together to accelerate the reform movement.

These new members were different in important ways from members elected earlier in the twentieth century.[26] Many were younger and less politically experienced; fewer had served in state legislatures before coming to Congress; and as a group they were far less likely to possess long-standing connections to state or local political party organizations. Furthermore, on the whole they were more independent and more ideological and issue oriented than most of their predecessors. As a result, they were far less tolerant of the traditions and procedures of Congress that denied new members access to legislative power. The "Class of '74" stimulated revisions in House rules and Democratic party procedures to permit broader participation in decision making and more equitable access to resources and to positions of influence.

The first target of reform was the seniority system. For most of the twentieth century, committee chairs had automatically gone to the member of the majority party with the longest consecutive service on the committee. No meaningful provision existed for altering that selection process or for removing committee chairs who were unresponsive to their party leaders or colleagues. Safe from the threat of removal, some chairs acted arbitrarily: putting on the committee agenda only the bills that they personally supported, granting subcommittee chairs to their friends and not to their adversaries, tightly controlling staff and other committee resources.

IMMIGRATION: THE NATIVES GET RESTLESS

Immigration. For most of American history, this has been a word that inspired warm feelings and rich memories. "A nation of immigrants," Americans were called. "Give me your tired, your poor, / Your huddled masses yearning to breathe free," American schoolchildren recited from Emma Lazarus's poem about the Statue of Liberty. Americans looked with pride on their immigrant heroes and retold stories of the struggle and determination of their own ancestors to make a better life in a new country.

But today immigration often strikes a different chord in the American psyche and evokes less sentimental images. To some, it has come to mean illegal entry and increased taxes, criminal gangs and more competition for work. In the 1990s many Americans wanted to put the brakes on immigration, and they found responsive politicians to lead the effort.

Why now? The answer lies in a very powerful demographic reality: the United States population has never been more diverse than it is in the late 1990s, and one reason is a recent acceleration in immigration. Net immigration (the number of people arriving minus the number leaving) has been steadily rising since World War II. But the rush of new immigrants in the 1980s accounted for more than 30 percent of all population growth, the largest proportion since the first decade of the twentieth century.

Equally important in stimulating a political backlash has been the concentration of these new immigrants in a few areas where their swelling numbers have made them a significant economic and cultural presence. Among foreign-born Americans counted in the 1990 census, who did not include most of the millions of illegal aliens, 25 percent were from Central America and another 25 percent from Asia. These populations were highly concentrated in a few states and within certain parts of those states: Hispanics, for example, now outnumber all other ethnic and racial groups combined in dozens of counties in New Mexico, Texas, Arizona, Colorado, and California.

More than any other state, California has been dramatically affected by recent immigration patterns. By 1990, 10 percent of California's population was Asian and 25 percent Hispanic; the portion that was non-Hispanic white had dropped to 57 percent from 76 percent in 1980. In 1994 a group of citizens placed a referendum question on the state's ballot, Proposition 187, to make illegal aliens ineligible for public school, public health care, and other public social services. Proponents argued that this was one way to curb the flood of illegal immigrants and to reduce the tax burden they imposed by using public services. Opponents, on the other hand, warned that denying benefits to illegal immigrants would only force them into socially undesirable behavior like crime and gang membership.

The citizens of California voted overwhelmingly in favor of Proposition 187 (59 percent to 41 percent) and sent a loud message booming across the political landscape. When the 104th Congress convened in 1995, immigration reform became one of the highest priorities of the new Republican majority. As part of the welfare reform bill enacted in 1996, noncitizens became ineligible for most welfare benefits, such as food stamps, Medicaid, and Supplemental Security payments. The legislation was notable in that it imposed these cutbacks not only on illegal but also on legal immigrants, who critics say often abuse immigration laws by using loopholes to bring large extended families to the United States. Another bill enacted in 1996 sought to clamp down on illegal immigration by increasing penalties for document fraud and by funding 1,200 additional Immigration and Naturalization Service agents, 5,000 more border guards, and construction of a fence along portions of the California-Mexico border.

The debate over immigration reflects some new realities of American self-perception. In times past, immigration was usually seen as desirable: a source of people to settle the frontier; to do the hard, dirty work of an industrializing economy; to provide consumers for the products of that economy. Periodically, there have been exceptions to this pattern. The Know-Nothing and Free Soil parties campaigned (with little success) against the influx of Irish Catholics and Germans that began in the 1840s. From 1924 to 1965, Congress imposed quotas that sharply cut back total immigration, favored immigrants from northern and western Europe, and prohibited all immigration from Asia. In general, however, Americans have welcomed immigrants and made it easy for them to attain citizenship.

Federal legislation in 1996 to withhold government benefits from legal immigrants who are not American citizens led to a wave of applications for citizenship. (Left) *New citizens take the oath of allegiance. Another measure was aimed at illegal aliens, like those shown* (right) *running away from federal agents in Laredo, Texas.*

Now, however, many Americans see a crowded country with little room for new settlers and little ability to absorb their environmental effects. They see (and hear) a culture in which the position of English as the common language is challenged. They see a government that pours out costly benefits to provide for the education, health, and welfare of all residents, whether citizens or not. And, they see an economy with stagnating wages for most workers, a growing income gap between rich and poor, and a connection between these conditions and a continuing influx of workers from abroad who are willing to work more cheaply than native-born Americans.

As the perceptual distance and the political barriers between countries continue to diminish in the twenty-first century, immigration pressures will grow. Those pressures will raise the stakes of the immigration debate. And that, no doubt, will turn up the heat generated by the debaters in Congress.

To get more information about this issue or to become involved in the debate, contact one of the following groups:

Supporting efforts to curtail legal immigration:

Federation for American Immigration Reform
1666 Connecticut Ave., N.W., Suite 400,
Washington, DC 20009
1-800-395-0890
e-mail: fair@fairus.org

Opposing most efforts to curtail legal immigration:

The National Network for Immigrant and Refugee Rights
310 8th Street, Suite 307
Oakland, CA 94607
(510) 465-1984
(510) 465-7548 (fax)
e-mail: nnirr@igc.apc.org

In the heyday of the seniority system, Congress operated very much like an oligarchy in which a score or so of committee chairs dominated.

In the 1970s the newer members of the House succeeded in loosening the hold of the seniority system. Although most committees continue to be chaired by the senior majority party member of the committee, the majority party caucus now elects committee chairs at the beginning of each Congress. Some senior members have been removed by this procedure, and those removals have had a chastening effect on the others. In addition, committee chairs have lost much of the control they once had over subcommittees and committee resources. Though still powerful figures in Congress, committee chairs are no longer an unassailable oligarchy.

During the 1970s junior members also started to get seats on the most prestigious committees. The number of subcommittees grew to the extent that virtually every member of the majority party could expect to chair a subcommittee after just a few years in Congress, and the enlargement of subcommittee and personal staffs and the growth in support agencies like the Congressional Research Service made individual members less reliant on congressional leaders for information. All these changes enhanced the ability of new members to develop legislation and conduct their own inquiries. As a result, legislative initiatives succeeded that might previously have been quashed at the whim of a party leader or committee chair.

The most far-reaching reform took place in the House, but similar efforts were under way in the Senate. In both houses individual members achieved greater and more effective involvement in the legislative process, and they acquired more autonomy than their counterparts had at any time in this century.

For the performance of Congress as an institution, this change had both advantages and disadvantages.[27] Although the openness and representative quality of the legislative process expanded, Congress's capacity for coordination was weakened because the autonomy of members came at the expense of the authority of leaders. No individual or ruling elite could provide a clear sense of direction, set priorities, or coordinate legislative activities.

In the early 1980s a reaction set in to this powerful wave of congressional reform, leading to what some scholars have referred to as the "postreform Congress."[28] It is characterized principally by a resurgence in partisanship. Party leaders, especially in the House, have regained a significant portion of the influence they lost during the previous two decades. In part, their success has resulted from internal efforts to reinvigorate and institutionalize the party caucuses. Party leadership committees like the Republican Policy Committees in the House and Senate have become important forums for the development of substantive party positions. The whip system in the House, an essential element of the party leadership structure, has grown so that now nearly a quarter of House Republicans have whip responsibilities.

Two other changes in the 1980s abetted the revitalization of congressional partisanship. One was the growing ideological homogeneity of the legislative parties. As politics in the South was changing, the southern Democrats in Congress came to resemble their northern colleagues more closely than at any time since World War II. At the same time, the liberal, or moderate, wing of the Republican party was shrinking almost to the vanishing point. Beginning in the late 1970s, therefore, party unity in floor voting began to grow. Although the congressional Democrats and Republicans can hardly be compared to the tightly disciplined parliamentary parties of western Europe, they did reach important new levels of internal unity and consistency in the postreform period. This trend is shown in Figure 12-4, which charts the extent to which members vote with their own party on issues where a majority of one party opposes a majority of the other.

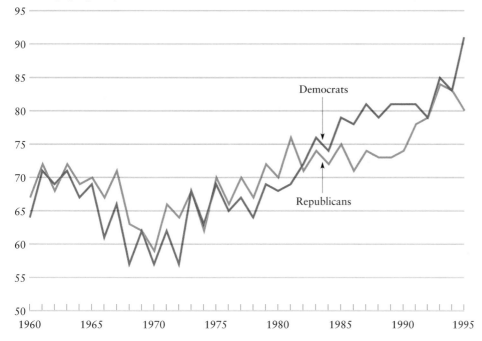

Average party unity scores

Democrats

Republicans

FIGURE 12-4

Party unity scores in House and Senate combined, 1960–1995.

SOURCE: Calculated by the author from data in several issues of *Congressional Quarterly Weekly Report*.

The momentum of party revitalization in Congress was accelerated by a period of divided government that lasted from 1981 through 1992. With Republicans firmly in control of the White House and Democrats equally firmly in control of the House of Representatives, partisan disagreements between the executive and legislative branches reinforced party unity in Congress. Realizing that they had little chance for presidential support of their policy initiatives, Democrats in Congress turned increasingly to their own party leaders, to whom they began to grant the instruments of power and the deference they needed to construct and pursue a party program. Emboldened, successive Speakers of the House responded with increasingly vigorous leadership efforts.

When the Republicans took control of both houses of Congress after the 1994 elections, they wasted no time in taking policy initiatives in a number of areas. In the House especially, the new Speaker, Newt Gingrich, asserted firmer leadership over his party than had any Speaker in decades. He was highly successful in maintaining Republican cohesion in support of a lengthy agenda of legislative proposals.

The contemporary Congress thus is a product of two recent trends. One was driven by the needs of individual members for electoral security and internal influence, the other by institutional needs for centralized leadership. In an era marked by large budget deficits and critical shortages of funds for new programs, Congress often struggles to resolve conflicts between competing groups making demands on the same limited resources. Coping with policy issues that require painstaking compromises that impose sacrifices on specific segments of the population has always been difficult for Congress. Those, however, are precisely the kinds of issues that occupy the most prominent positions on the current legislative agenda. And because of recent reforms, compromise is more difficult to accomplish. President Clinton's initial proposals for deficit reduction in 1993, for example, quickly ran into opposition from a variety of interests: western ranchers who did not want to pay fees for the right to graze their cattle on public lands, oil producers who did not want their products burdened with new taxes, the elderly who held out against any decrease in annual cost-of-living adjustments to Social Security benefits. Everyone, it seemed, was for deficit reduction, but no one wanted to bear the cost.

Over the course of American history, the internal organization of Congress has swung back and forth between the desire for a legislative process that is truly democratic and participatory and the desire for legislative efficiency. These are contradictory goals. Efficiency requires centralization of authority; broad participation does not easily tolerate centralized authority. Unable to accomplish both objectives simultaneously, Congress periodically reforms itself to adjust the balance between them. The legislative upheaval of the 1960s and 1970s maximized procedural democracy and broad participation in decision making at the expense of legislative efficiency. The efforts of the recent postreform period swung the balance in the other direction by empowering central leadership mechanisms. If history is a reliable guide, neither change will be permanent.

SUMMARY

Congress is a *bicameral legislature* composed of two legislative bodies: the House of Representatives and the Senate. Each member of the House represents a district with a population of about 600,000 and serves for a two-year term. Senators serve six-year terms; there are two senators from each state.

Members of Congress typically have large staffs of aides who do clerical chores, write speeches, meet with lobbyists, and handle *casework*—the individual problems of constituents. Congressional committees also have staffs, which assist them in setting an agenda, scheduling hearings, developing legislation, and overseeing the work of executive agencies. A third group of congressional employees includes those who work for specialized support agencies: the Congressional Research Service, the Congressional Budget Office, and the General Accounting Office. The number of congressional employees has grown rapidly in recent years.

In the initial Congresses, party caucuses hammered out important policy decisions. Committees began to play a more dominant role after the Civil War, but by the end of the nineteenth century party leaders in Congress had become the principal powers. Within a decade they had become so powerful that a revolt occurred and the committees again became the power centers. The *seniority system* ensured that the member of the majority party with the longest consecutive service on a committee would automatically be its chair.

Whereas tight *party discipline* is normal in legislatures in Britain and France, political parties in Congress have limited control over their own members. In the House, the majority party controls the selection of the *Speaker of the House.* Working with other party leaders, especially *whips*, the Speaker helps determine the issues that will be given top priority. The Speaker's leadership is based less on real power than on persuasion and political skill. In the Senate, the primary job of the party leaders is to organize the business of the Senate.

The proponents of each bill introduced in Congress must form a coalition in support of that bill. Politics in Congress focuses on the task of building these shifting alliances. In recent years individual legislators known as *issue entrepreneurs* have tended to specialize in particular substantive matters and to seek support among their colleagues for policies dealing with those matters.

Most of the work of Congress is done in committees. Committees hold public hearings at which supporters and opponents of bills may express their views. They also engage in *administrative oversight*— monitoring the work of the executive agencies in their areas of jurisdiction, reviewing budget requests, and passing judgment on the qualifications of presidential appointees. *Standing committees* are permanent committees that have full authority to recommend legislation; most are divided into subcommittees. *Select (special) committees* are created to deal with a specific set of issues and have limited functions and authority. *Joint committees* are composed of members of both houses of Congress; *joint conference committees* are formed to resolve the differences that occur when the two houses pass varying forms of the same bill.

Legislation is accomplished through deliberation and partisan adjustment. A long gestation period is common for significant legislation, and 90 percent of the bills introduced in a typical Congress never become law.

The lawmaking process begins when a member of the House or Senate introduces a *bill*, or proposal, for consideration. The bill is assigned to a committee, which may decide not to consider it. If the bill is considered, it is initially examined by a subcommittee, which may hold hearings on the subject of the bill. At the conclusion of the hearings, the subcommittee holds a *mark-up session*, in which the bill is revised and then voted on. If the subcommittee supports the bill it is returned to the full committee, where another mark-up and vote take place.

If a majority of the full committee supports the bill, it is reported to the full House or Senate. It is then placed on a legislative calendar and sent to the floor for debate. During the debate individual members may introduce amendments. In the Senate, controversial provisions called *riders* are often attached to popular bills. When voting on a bill, senators vote orally in a roll-call vote; representatives vote electronically. If a majority of the members present vote in favor of the bill, it is sent to the other house, where the process is repeated. If the two houses pass different versions of the bill, it is sent to a conference committee. If both houses agree to the conference committee's version, the bill is sent to the president for signature.

The president may sign the bill or allow it to become law without a signature. He may also veto the bill by declining to sign it and returning it to Congress within ten days. Congress may override a veto, but an override requires a two-thirds majority in each house and hence is rare. If the annual session of Congress ends within ten days of the passage of a bill, the president may exercise a *pocket veto* by simply declining to sign the bill. If legislation enacted in 1996 survives constitutional review, he may use a *line-item veto* to kill portions of certain kinds of legislation.

Congressional rules and procedures require that legislation be considered and acted on at a number of points; defeat at any of those points usually kills the bill. The rules thus favor proponents of the status quo, work to slow the pace of legislation, and enable determined minorities to thwart the will of majorities. In the Senate, a single senator can delay or prevent action by objecting to the procedure known as *unanimous consent.* Or a small group of senators may prevent a vote on a bill through a *filibuster,* in which they gain recognition to speak and then do not relinquish the floor. A vote by three-fifths of the entire Senate is required to invoke *cloture* and end a filibuster.

Many members of Congress work hard to interact with the people they represent. Their *franking privilege* enables them to mail newsletters and questionnaires to their constituents free of charge. They travel frequently between Washington and their home state or district, where they also maintain offices with full-time staffs.

Most of the permanent committees of Congress conduct *oversight hearings,* in which the activities of an executive agency or the management of a specific program are reviewed in depth. In addition, Congress often establishes a temporary committee to conduct *special investigations.* Employees and agencies of the executive branch fall under congressional oversight through *personnel controls* and *financial control.* The legislature also has the power to remove a public official by means of *impeachment.*

During the 1970s a number of reforms were made in congressional rules and procedures. In the House, the majority party now elects committee chairs at the beginning of each Congress. Junior members may get seats on prestigious committees and may chair subcommittees. In both houses of Congress, individual members have more effective involvement in the legislative process and more autonomy than their counterparts of earlier decades had.

bicameral legislature
casework
seniority system
party discipline
Speaker of the House
whip
issue entrepreneur
administrative oversight
standing committee
select (special) committee

joint committee
joint conference committee
legislation
bill
mark-up session
rider
pocket veto
line-item veto
unanimous consent
filibuster

cloture
representation
constituency
franking privilege
oversight hearings
special investigation
personnel controls
financial control
impeachment

RESOURCES

SCHOLARLY STUDIES

Davidson, Roger H. *The Postreform Congress.* New York: St. Martin's Press, 1992. A collection of readings exploring the readjustments that occurred in both houses of Congress after the dynamic reforms of the 1970s.

Fenno, Richard F., Jr. *Homestyle: House Members in Their Districts.* New York: HarperCollins, 1987. An examination of the relationship between members of Congress and their constituents. Identifies different ways in which members conceptualize the people and regions they represent.

Hibbing, John R. *Congressional Careers: Contours of Life in the U.S. House of Representatives.* Chapel Hill: University of North Carolina Press, 1991. An exploration of the career patterns and professional lifestyles of members of the House of Representatives.

Jones, Charles O. *Separate But Equal Branches: Congress and the Presidency.* Chatham, N.J.: Chatham House, 1995. A new and insightful analysis of the roles of Congress in the late twentieth century.

Light, Paul C. *Forging Legislation.* New York: Norton, 1991. A revealing case study of the legislative process; the author follows from inception to enactment a bill to create the Department of Veterans Affairs.

Rohde, David W. *Parties and Leaders in the Postreform House.* Chicago: University of Chicago Press, 1991. An empirical analysis of revitalized partisanship in the House of Representatives after 1980.

LEISURE READING

Drew, Elizabeth. *Showdown: The Struggle Between the Gingrich Congress and the Clinton White House.* New York: Simon and Schuster, 1996. A leading journalist draws a rich and revealing portrait of the tensions of divided government.

Drury, Allen. *Advise and Consent.* New York: Doubleday, 1959. A Pulitzer Prize–winning novel about the political intrigue over Senate confirmation of a presidential appointment.

O'Neill, Thomas P., Jr., and William Novak. *Man of the House.* New York: Random House, 1987. Reminiscences by former Speaker of the House "Tip" O'Neill, with word portraits of many postwar American political leaders.

Rudman, Warren. *Combat: Twelve Years in the U.S. Senate.* New York: Random House, 1996. A candid former senator explains how the system works—and doesn't work—in the contemporary Congress.

PRIMARY SOURCES

Congressional Directory. Washington, D.C.: Government Printing Office, annual. An official compendium of information about congressional organizations and operations.

Congressional Quarterly. *Congress and the Nation.* Vols 1–8. Washington, D.C.: Congressional Quarterly, quadrennial. Extensive reviews of politics and policy for the previous four years. Published at the end of each presidential term.

Congressional Quarterly. *Guide to Congress.* 4th ed.

Washington, D.C.: Congressional Quarterly, 1991. A comprehensive history and analysis of all phases of congressional operations.

Congressional Quarterly. *Politics in America.* Washington, D.C.: Congressional Quarterly, biennial. Backgrounds and voting records of all members of Congress and descriptions of each state and congressional district. Updated after each congressional election.

ORGANIZATIONS

Center for Democracy, 1101 15th Street, N.W., Washington, DC 20005; phone (202) 429-9141, fax (202) 293-1768. Nonpartisan organization that works to strengthen democratic institutions. Monitors elections and provides democratizing governments with technical and informational assistance.

Center for Responsive Politics, 1320 19th Street, N.W., Washington, DC 20036; phone (202) 857-0044, fax (202) 857-7809, Internet http://www.votesmart.org/congress/finance/crp.html Conducts research on Congress and related issues with particular interest in campaign finance and congressional operations.

U.S. Capitol Historical Society, 200 Maryland Avenue, N.E., Washington, DC 20002; phone (202) 543-8919, fax (202) 544-8244. Conducts historical research and maintains information centers in the Capitol.

13

The Presidency

Bill Clinton faced major economic and budgetary problems when he entered the presidency. But they came as no surprise. He had talked about them during his campaign. He held a public seminar to discuss them as president-elect. He spoke about them during his first address to Congress and throughout his first six months in office. But he didn't realize how difficult they would be to solve.

The basic issue was simple enough to articulate but hard to resolve. The economy was in recession in 1992, and Clinton had promised to

stimulate it. The federal budget was out of balance, and Clinton had promised to reduce that imbalance substantially. How could he do both simultaneously?

The policy solution was complicated by promises Clinton had made during his presidential campaign. One promise that he had often repeated in an effort to gain votes was to cut income taxes on the hard-pressed middle class. In addition, he had promised legislation to encourage savings and investment, providing tax incentives to individuals and businesses. However, both of these measures would reduce revenues for government, at least in the short run, and therefore would increase rather than decrease the budget deficit. Moreover, the president was under pressure from his Democratic constituency and some members of Congress to increase spending for a variety of domestic programs that had not fared well financially during the administrations of his predecessors, presidents Reagan and Bush.

Several groups vied for the president's attention. Clinton's political advisers urged him to pursue a populist policy in which economic stimulation would be the primary objective and a middle-class tax cut a principal stimulator. They also recommended that the president create jobs programs and extend the maximum period for which laid-off workers could receive unemployment benefits. To pay for these programs, they argued for higher taxes on the rich and a reduction of government subsidies to business.

The president's economic advisers, on the other hand, cautioned against decreased taxes, increased spending, and any programs that would increase burdens on business. They saw the deficit as the primary issue and believed that only through substantial cuts in government expenditures plus some increase in revenue could this issue be satisfactorily addressed.

Whatever policy Clinton chose, Congress would have to be involved. Congressional sentiment was divided, largely along partisan lines. The Republican minority in 1993 were dead set against any increase in taxes; they wanted deficit reduction to be achieved through massive government spending cuts. As the party out of power, they would not have to take the heat for such cuts from those who would be adversely affected by them. Nor did Republicans see the need for a stimulus bill, as the economy was gradually improving.

Congressional Democrats were much less united, with liberal members, particularly those from urban areas, wanting the president to create more jobs. Not only did they support increased government spending, but they opposed reductions to programs that benefited their traditional political constituencies. Moderate and conservative Democrats, primarily those from the South, were more sympathetic to spending cuts and opposed new taxes.

Over the first four months of his administration, Clinton vacillated among the positions of his various advisers and congressional allies. A politician who desired to please, he struggled to find a consensus, one that would meet with some approval from each of these groups. In doing so, he made decisions and then was forced to reverse some of them when new information became available. Moreover, his decision making was affected by leaks of potential policy options to the news media. These leaks embarrassed the president and limited his discretion, forcing him to back off from proposals that had produced a strongly negative public reaction. The leaks also contributed to the impression of mixed messages that emanated from the White House.

As delay and indecision continued, the media depicted a presidency in disarray with little leadership from the top. All these factors lowered public confidence in Clinton and weakened his already weak political position (he had received only 43 percent of the vote). In the end he proposed a $16 billion economic stimulus package as his number one priority. It was enacted by the House of Representatives but defeated in the Senate by a Republican-led filibuster. His second priority, a deficit-reduction bill, was substantially modified by Congress before it was enacted by the barest of margins in August 1993. In the process the president was forced to make a number of highly publicized compromises. He had finally achieved a major goal, but his reputation as a decision maker, legislative leader, and communicator-in-chief all suffered in the process. His political capital had been depleted.

Clinton's first six months in office had been rough, but his difficulties are characteristic of the modern presidency. Moreover, the manner of his defeat and victory, and the methods he used to pursue his objectives, were not unique. All presidents face a multitude of problems when taking office. Part of their challenge is to establish priorities to deal with them. Presidents also face a multitude of choices with differing payoffs. Part of their challenge is to evaluate these payoffs and select the options that are both optimal and feasible. Finally, presidents are subject to a multitude of pressures. Some are generated by their political campaign and the promises they and their party have made to get elected. Some are the result of the institutional divisions and political composition of government and the forces that naturally impact on the policy process. Some are situational, varying with the time, issues, and events. Whatever these pressures, presidents have to deal with them; and they have to do so in a manner that is consistent with the dignity of their office, the goals of their policy, and the political environment in which they find themselves. In other words, they have to be political leaders if they are to be successful.

Politics pervades the presidency. It affects how presidents get into office, what they do while there, and when and how they do it. Whereas politics inflates expectations of presidential performance, it also undercuts the achievement of those expectations over time. And it does this in all aspects of the policy-making process, from agenda setting to consensus building to the implementation of legislation.

But presidents have no choice. Their presidency has to function as a political institution. And only effective political leadership can overcome the constitutional constraints, generated by separate institutions sharing powers and responsibilities, to initiate national policy; only effective political leadership can unite a diverse nation and build a policy consensus behind that policy; only effective political leadership can coordinate the various officials who will oversee the implementation of that policy and are held accountable for its success or failure. Thus politics creates the dilemma of the modern presidency, but it also provides presidents with their only solution to that dilemma in normal times: strong political leadership.

Clinton's predicament is one that his successors will continue to face. Presidents often face a "damned if they do, damned if they don't" dilemma. They are expected to act in accordance with their previously stated goals and positions even though circumstances may have changed. They are expected to be sensitive to public interests and pressures even though those interests and pressures may be ambiguous, contradictory, and fluid. They are expected to respond quickly and decisively to policy problems, to initiate and propose solutions, and to build support for them even though their information may be incomplete, their advisers may be divided, and the environment within which they operate may be hostile. And they are expected to solve the problems even though they do not control all or even most of the factors that generated them. Moreover, if the problems persist, they will probably be blamed and their capacity to lead in the future may be impaired.

THE LEADERSHIP DILEMMA

Presidents have a persistent leadership problem, whose roots lie in the American system of government.[1] To achieve their goals, presidents need the cooperation of many individuals over whom they may have little or no influence. Yet the Constitution divides authority, institutions share power, and political parties often lack cohesion and have difficulty maintaining long-term policy positions.

The pluralistic nature of American society is another source of the difficulty. Presidents are required to do what is best for the country. Yet assessments of their actions usually depend on how those actions affect individuals and groups, not society as a whole. The leadership problem has been aggravated in the last two decades by the proliferation of constituencies, each represented by a variety of single-issue groups, and by the negativism of the news media. The range of groups with an interest in most public policy issues has forced contemporary presidents to devote increasing amounts of time and energy to dealing with these groups to mobilize support for their policies.

How can presidents overcome their leadership problem? The key to presidential success is the skillful use of legal, institutional, and political powers:

1. *Legal powers.* Presidents can utilize the formal authority that is vested in the presidency. Here they command by virtue of constitutional and statutory powers as well as by precedent.

2. *Institutional powers.* Presidents can utilize subordinates in the executive branch. Here they delegate to others the job of collecting information and assessing options while reserving the critical decisions for themselves.
3. *Political powers.* Presidents can utilize the informal powers of the presidency. Here they persuade on the basis of their elected position, political reputation, and public approval.

This chapter focuses on those powers and the environment in which they are exercised. It begins by exploring the legal basis of presidential authority, the creation of the executive at the Constitutional Convention, and the evolution of presidential powers through statute and precedent. Next it looks at presidential leadership and the institutional and personal resources necessary to achieve it. The chapter concludes by examining how presidents use their political powers to try to get things done—how they attempt to make, sell, and implement public policy. In each of these areas it explores the politics of the contemporary presidency.

THE AUTHORITY OF THE PRESIDENCY

Empowering the Institution

The formal powers of the presidency are stated in Article II of the Constitution. Today, as in the past, they arouse controversy. When the institution of the presidency was created at the Constitutional Convention, there was a consensus on having a strong executive, but disagreement over how strong it should be. The structure of the institution, the authority vested in it, and the nature and operation of the selection process were all contentious issues. The framers had to decide whether the executive branch should be headed by a single person or by several people, whether the chief executive should be chosen by those in government or by those outside of it, and whether the traditional powers of the chief executive should be subject to additional checks or be left alone.

In resolving the first of these issues, the delegates to the Constitutional Convention created a single executive, but one that would not be so strong as to threaten the other institutions of the national government.[2] Determining how the president was to be chosen was the second contentious issue they had to consider, and it was harder to resolve. The delegates debated several options for election: by the people, by Congress, or by a group of specially chosen electors. Direct election by the people was rejected as undesirable and infeasible. The framers believed that the general electorate would not make an informed, dispassionate, rational judgment; moreover, they thought the country too large, its communications too primitive, and its sectional rivalries too great to permit an honest national election.

Selection by Congress would solve those problems but would create others. How could a president who was dependent on Congress for election and reelection exercise power independently? One possible solution—a single, long term of office (seven years)—created another potential hazard: Who or what body would ensure that the president acted responsibly? When this question was raised at the Constitutional Convention, the delegates voted against a single term, thereby making the option of election by the legislature much less desirable.

The third alternative, to have electors choose the president, was proposed toward the end of the convention. Known as the Electoral College compromise, it was designed to meet the objections of two groups: those who feared legislative selection but saw the benefits of having a small group make the decision, and those who desired to give the people a voice in the election but feared their judgment.

Empowering the executive proved to be a less controversial issue than presidential selection. Because of their initial consensus on the nature of executive authority, the delegates focused on the issue of how to prevent that authority from being abused. Their resolution of this problem was to create a system of checks and balances that required the concurrence of one or both houses of Congress for the exercise of those executive powers that had been most abused during the colonial period: the power to make appointments, to enter into treaties, and to veto legislation. Congress was also given the right to declare war and to impeach an executive who violated the public trust by committing treason, bribery, or other "high crimes and misdemeanors."

Much remained for later generations to interpret, however. The president's authority was not defined with nearly the same precision in Article II as the authority of Congress had been in Article I. Having left executive authority vague, the framers ensured it would be flexible enough to adjust to changing circumstances. They also ensured that controversy about it would persist (see the Constitutional Conflict box on page 468).

The Evolution of Presidential Authority

Over the years Congress and the president have clashed repeatedly over the exercise of their respective powers. If the framers were alive today, they would not be surprised. The constitutional structure they established was based on the assumption that institutional rivalry would limit the excesses and abuses of power. This has indeed been the case for most of American history, but the rivalry between the two branches has also made governing difficult, and the demands placed on government have increased substantially since the Constitution was written.

What powers were initially given to the president, and how have those powers evolved over the years? Charged with faithfully executing the law, the president was given a broad grant of executive authority as well as more narrowly defined legislative and judicial powers.

The power to execute   According to the Constitution, the president was to have primary responsibility for overseeing the execution of the law. The framers, however, did not believe that the president would perform this function alone. Others would assist. The issue was how to select the most qualified assistants and ensure that they would act in the country's interest, not their own self-interest. To resolve this dilemma, the president was given the power to nominate assistants, subject to the advice and consent of the Senate. Moreover, as part of the system of checks and balances, Congress was to be responsible for the creation of the executive departments and agencies. Thus the president was placed in the unenviable position of directing a branch of government without being able to exercise total control over its personnel and structure.

Almost immediately members of the legislature challenged the president's discretion to choose people to work in the executive branch. In 1789, Georgia's two senators opposed George Washington's nomination of Benjamin Fishbourn to be naval officer of the port of Savannah and persuaded their colleagues to reject the nomination. To minimize the likelihood of other rejections, Washington began to consult with the senators from the same state as the prospective nominee *before* placing a

THE LINE-ITEM VETO

Can presidents veto part of a law enacted by Congress, or must they negate the entire bill? Article I, Section 7, of the Constitution says:

Every bill which shall have passed the House of Representatives and the Senate, shall, before it become a law, be presented to the President of the United States; if he approve he shall sign it, but if not he shall return it with his objections to that house in which it originated, who shall enter the objections at large on their journal, and proceed to reconsider it.

Those who argue that presidents have the authority to veto part of a bill point to the oath presidents take to defend the Constitution as justification for their refusal to execute any provision of any law that they believe conflicts with the Constitution. President Bush agreed with this interpretation in 1989 when he announced that he had signed legislation containing an unconstitutional and therefore unenforceable provision. One year later Bush identified thirty-one such provisions in nine bills; he approved each of the bills but declared the provisions he believed to be unconstitutional to be without legal force.

However, Bush's interpretation has been disputed by many constitutional experts, including his own attorney general, William Barr, who contend that the constitutional language is quite clear: it says "bill," not "part of a bill." And the accepted practice has been that only entire bills have been vetoed.

Nonetheless, there has been a continuing debate over the desirability of giving the president formal authority to exercise a so-called line-item veto. Forty-three state governors now have this authority, and Presidents Reagan, Bush, and Clinton all requested it. In 1996, in light of the growing federal budget deficit and the difficulty that Congress and the president have had in reducing it, Congress enacted legislation creating a line-item veto for appropriations bills. The legislation, to take effect on January 1, 1997, is to remain in effect for eight years. Here's how it works:

1. After Congress enacts a bill that appropriates money, the president has five days to veto any individual appropriation in it or any tax benefit that affects 100 or fewer people. Although current entitlement benefits such as Social Security and Medicare payments are exempt from the line-item veto, new entitlements that Congress enacts would be subject to it. Only dollar amounts may be vetoed. Presidents cannot reduce or add to spending items, nor can they change the language in the legislation.
2. If the president uses the line-item veto to cancel spending, Congress can enact legislation to restore it. However, this legislation is subject to a regular veto. To override such a veto, the usual two-thirds vote in each house is required.

The line-item veto is intended to save money by allowing the president to cut unwise expenditures. It shifts considerable political power from Congress to the president, since a relatively small percentage of presidential vetoes (only about 4 percent) have been overridden. On the other hand, it also lets Congress off the hook if members propose appropriations to please their constituents, since the president would have the responsibility to delete these appropriations and would take the political heat for doing so or not doing so. However, if Congress really wants specific appropriations and believes the president may veto them, it could offer the administration a deal for not exercising the line-item veto. Such a deal might actually increase appropriations. Only time will tell whether significant savings can be obtained by the exercise of this new presidential power.

As soon as the new legislation was enacted, its constitutionality was challenged. The legal issue, which the federal judiciary will determine, is whether Congress has the power, short of a constitutional amendment, to allow the president to negate part of a bill.

name in nomination. Presidents still follow this practice, which is known as **senatorial courtesy**.

Today the prerogatives of senators have expanded. Any senator can delay or in some cases even prevent a presidential nomination by simply stating his or her opposition to it. If other senators back up their colleague, the president may be forced to withdraw the nomination. In 1995, President Clinton had to withdraw the nomination of Robert Pastor to be ambassador to Panama after Senator Jesse Helms, who had held up the nomination in 1994, threatened to kill it a year later when he became chairman of the Senate Foreign Relations Committee. Clinton had no choice.[3] Although senatorial courtesy limits the president's ability to choose subordinates, it also enhances the prospects of confirmation when the relevant senators support or at least do not oppose the nomination.

The Constitution specifically divides the responsibility for appointments, but it is far less clear about removal from office. Those who abuse their authority by committing treason, high crimes, or misdemeanors are subject to impeachment, but what about those who do not commit a crime yet are undesirable because of incompetence, insubordination, or incompatibility with their superiors? The First Congress dealt with this issue in 1789 when it established the executive departments. Four methods for removing department officials were debated: by the president alone, by the president with the advice and consent of the Senate, by the statute that created the position, and by impeachment. In the end, a closely divided Congress vested removal power in the president alone. By virtue of this decision, all political appointees who serve in executive positions do so at the pleasure of the president. A 1926 Supreme Court decision, *Myer v. United States* (written by Chief Justice and former president William Howard Taft), upheld this broad interpretation of executive authority.

Subsequent Court decisions, however, have narrowed the president's discretion to remove executive branch officials who serve on independent regulatory agencies, such as the Federal Trade Commission, the Federal Election Commission, or the Federal Reserve Board. Most civil servants are also exempt from the president's removal power. Thus President Clinton could and did request the resignation of the ninety-three U.S. attorneys, the chief prosecutors in each of the federal judicial dis-

President Clinton's first secretary of agriculture, Mike Espy, at the 1994 news conference where he announced his resignation. He had been accused of using the perquisites of his office for personal gain. Earlier, Clinton had asked Defense Secretary Les Aspin to step down because of ineffective management of his department. Removing political appointees is always embarrassing for presidents because it calls their original judgment into question.

tricts in the United States, all of whom were appointed by his Republican predecessors. But he could not demand that the judges whom these presidents had appointed resign, since they hold office during good behavior for life. Nor could Clinton require Reagan or Bush appointees to federal regulatory agencies, such as the Federal Election Commission, to resign before their terms expired.

Moreover, even though the president can remove many appointees, doing so may be politically harmful. Forcing people out calls attention to a problem and to the president's failure to deal with it effectively. Nevertheless, Richard Nixon, Jimmy Carter, Ronald Reagan, George Bush, and Bill Clinton all had to ask for the resignations of at least one of their cabinet secretaries.[4] Sometimes requested resignations are not forthcoming. When FBI director William Sessions refused to step down in 1993, President Clinton had to fire him.

The power to hire and fire can foster but not guarantee cooperation and the effective execution of the laws. Executive officials exercise considerable discretion in their jobs, and the president's ability to oversee them is limited. Furthermore, Congress exercises its own oversight over the departments and agencies by defining their jurisdictions, authorizing their programs, appropriating their funds, and investigating their activities. Presidents do have some control over the direction and budgets they provide their subordinates, but as chief executives they are able to exercise relatively little influence over day-to-day activities in the departments and agencies.

One way that presidents can try to exert such influence is to issue an **executive memorandum** or a formal **executive order** requiring executive branch officials to implement policy in a particular way. These memoranda and orders are usually very specific: they apply to a particular agency and require its officials to perform a task in a particular way. But they can also have broad policy implications. This was the case, for example, with Kennedy's order declaring segregated housing off-limits to military personnel, Reagan's order requiring all executive departments and agencies to assess the costs of any new regulation before promulgating it, and Clinton's memorandum eliminating the "gag rule" that had prevented federally funded family-planning clinics from discussing abortion with their clients (see the box on page 471).

Although presidents have the authority to issue memoranda and orders to their subordinates, they lack the time and expertise to do so on a regular basis, especially when technical information is involved. Thus it is difficult for a president to oversee the executive branch by executive order alone. Moreover, Congress can countermand an executive order through legislation, although that legislation is subject to presidential veto.

For all these reasons, presidents have tended to leave the business of implementation to those in charge of the departments and agencies, occasionally with disastrous results. President Reagan is a case in point. Having little interest in administrative matters, he did not exercise close oversight over department heads and others within his administration. Had he done so, problems involving conflicts of interest among political appointees in the Department of Justice, political favoritism in the awarding of contracts in the Department of Housing and Urban Development, and irregularities in contracting in the Department of Defense might have been avoided. The Iran-contra affair is another situation in which Reagan's hands-off management style came back to haunt him. (See the Case Study box on page 472).

The power to legislate   Although shared responsibilities and dispersed powers have limited the president's ability and incentive to oversee the law, they have not precluded presidents from assuming greater responsibility in the lawmaking process.

A PRESIDENTIAL MEMORANDUM

Memorandum on the Title X "Gag Rule"
January 22, 1993
Memorandum for the Secretary of Health and Human Services
Subject: The Title X "Gag Rule"

Title X of the Public Health Services Act provides Federal funding for family planning clinics to provide services for low-income patients. The Act specifies that Title X funds may not be used for the performance of abortions, but places no restrictions on the ability of clinics that receive Title X funds to provide abortion counseling and referrals or to perform abortions using non–Title X funds. During the first 18 years of the program, medical professionals at Title X clinics provided complete, uncensored information, including nondirective abortion counseling. In February 1988, the Department of Health and Human Services adopted regulations, which have become known as the "Gag Rule," prohibiting Title X recipients from providing their patients with information, counseling, or referrals concerning abortion. Subsequent attempts by the Bush Administration to modify the Gag Rule and ensuing litigation have created confusion and uncertainty about the current legal status of the regulations.

The Gag Rule endangers women's lives and health by preventing them from receiving complete and accurate medical information and interferes with the doctor-patient relationship by prohibiting information that medical professionals are otherwise ethically and legally required to provide to their patients. Furthermore, the Gag Rule contravenes the clear intent of a majority of the members of both the United States Senate and House of Representatives, which twice passed legislation to block the Gag Rule's enforcement but failed to override Presidential vetoes.

For these reasons, you have informed me that you will suspend the Gag Rule pending the promulgation of new regulations in accordance with the "notice and comment" procedures of the Administrative Procedure Act. I hereby direct you to take that action as soon as possible. I further direct that, within 30 days, you publish in the *Federal Register* new proposed regulations for public comment.

You are hereby authorized and directed to publish this memorandum in the *Federal Register*.

William J. Clinton

SOURCE: *Weekly Compilation of Presidential Documents,* January 25, 1993, 87–88.

The exercise of presidential power sometimes affects ordinary Americans in very direct ways. Because of President Clinton's executive order revoking the "gag rule" imposed under the Reagan and Bush administrations, doctors at federally funded family planning clinics, like this one in New York City, may provide clients with information, counseling, and referrals concerning abortion.

THE IRAN-CONTRA AFFAIR

Congress and the presidency are engaged in a perpetual struggle. They differ over the scope of each other's powers, the wisdom of each other's policies, and the ways in which policies should be implemented if they become law. The Iran-contra affair illustrates all these areas of conflict.

The Boland Amendment, a provision attached to appropriations bills from 1982 to 1986, prohibited executive agencies involved in intelligence activities from spending federal funds, either directly or indirectly, on military operations in Nicaragua. Despite this restriction, Lt. Col. Oliver North and other officials on the National Security Council (NSC) staff diverted money from the secret sale of arms to Iran to guerrillas, known as the contras, who were fighting to overthrow Nicaragua's Marxist government. The officials believed that they were pursuing presidential policy that supported the armed insurgents in Nicaragua, and were therefore not bound by the Boland Amendment. Colonel North kept his actions secret even from Congress. For over nine months Congress was not informed about either the arms sales or the diversion of funds, in spite of a law that requires the president to fully inform the intelligence committees of Congress about such activities in a timely fashion. When the diversion became public,

the president claimed that he was unaware of it. Subsequently two commissions, one appointed by Reagan and the other by Congress, criticized the actions of several national security aides, and blamed the president for his failure to supervise them properly.

In addition to the problems of Reagan's management style, there was another, perhaps more serious issue. Did the president violate the law by not telling Congress about these covert activities? Did the sale of arms to Iran and the diversion of profits to the contras fall within the purview of Congress's authority to make the law or the president's authority to conduct foreign policy? Despite the findings of the investigative committees, these issues remain the subject of considerable debate.

Discussion Questions

1. Is the United States Constitution outdated in terms of the making and executing of foreign policy?
2. Should Congress or the president exercise the power to make foreign policy, or should that power be shared?
3. How can institutional conflicts like the Iran-contra affair be avoided in the future?

The framers of the Constitution anticipated only a modest policy-making role for the president, primarily in foreign affairs, but today presidents are expected to be active legislators even though their formal authority is quite limited. They are to be both chief of state *and* head of government. It is the latter role that gives them the most difficulty.

Article II of the Constitution spells out only four legislative duties and responsibilities for the president:

1. to inform Congress from time to time about the state of the union;
2. to recommend necessary and expedient legislation;
3. to summon Congress into special session and adjourn it if the two houses cannot agree on adjournment; and
4. to negate an act of Congress by vetoing it.

With the exception of the veto (which Congress can override by a two-thirds vote of both houses), these legislative responsibilities were designed to facilitate government in emergencies. Over the years, however, presidents have used their legislative duties and powers to enhance their policy-making roles in foreign and domestic affairs and to extend their influence in Congress. In the international arena they have established and curtailed relations with other countries, as Jimmy Carter did when he recognized the People's Republic as the legitimate government of China and terminated official relations with the Chinese Nationalists on the island of Taiwan. Presidents have entered into **executive agreements**, agreements with other heads of governments, as George Bush did when he renegotiated the rental agreements on American military bases in Spain.[5] Finally, presidents have used diplomacy and armed forces to protect American interests, as Clinton did in 1995 when he ordered the United States military to aid in peacekeeping operations in Bosnia and in 1996 when he ordered air strikes against Iraq for moving troops and firing on American military planes in defiance of international restrictions.

Although Congress has generally accepted presidential leadership in foreign and military affairs, it has not always approved what presidents have done. In some cases Congress has criticized and formally condemned presidents, as it did after James K. Polk sent troops into territory claimed by Mexico in 1846. In other instances it has used its appropriations power to thwart presidential policy, as when Nixon was denied funding for bombing operations in Cambodia in the early 1970s and Clinton was forced to use his discretionary authority to help Mexico stabilize its currency when Congress refused to do so in 1995.

Congress has also tried to limit the president's power to involve American troops in hostile or potentially hostile situations. In 1973, the War Powers Resolution was enacted over President Nixon's veto. This statute requires the president to consult with Congress and gain its approval when ordering armed forces into hostile situations without a declaration of war. In 1991, Congress debated but eventually enacted resolutions authorizing President Bush to use force in the Persian Gulf. A similar debate was initiated in 1994 over the projected use of U.S. forces to depose a military dictatorship in Haiti; before Congress concluded its debate, however, former president Carter, acting on behalf of the Clinton administration, worked out a peaceful resolution of the problem. In 1995, Congress enacted a resolution to support American troops in Bosnia but not the Clinton administration's policy that sent them there.

Congressional involvement in foreign policy decision making has been most evident in recent years. The absence of a public consensus on many foreign policy matters, the growth of political interest groups concerned with international affairs and their domestic impact, and the increasing interdependence of the American economy with the economies of other countries have encouraged that involvement, as has public dissatisfaction with specific presidential actions and initiatives. In short, presidential leadership in foreign affairs is still expected, but congressional approval can no longer be taken for granted.

The president's role as domestic policy maker and chief legislator is a more recent development. Throughout most of the nineteenth century, Congress was seen as the principal architect of domestic policy. Not until the beginning of the twentieth century did presidents become more actively engaged in proposing legislation, and not until the end of Franklin Roosevelt's administration did formulating new domestic policy become an important presidential activity.

Today presidents are expected to set the domestic policy agenda after their election, to present an annual legislative program to Congress, to lobby for that program, and to oversee its implementation. However, they frequently lack the political clout to achieve their policy goals, particularly in Congress. Unlike the British and German prime ministers, for example, who can count on partisan support to gain their programmatic objectives, the president of the United States cannot. Clinton's failure to obtain the approval of a Democratic Congress for his economic stimulus and health-care plans are among the most recent examples of this presidential problem.

The power to judge   Derived from the traditional status of the king as the court of last resort, the president's judicial powers include issuing pardons, granting clemency, and proclaiming amnesty. Although the scope of these powers has not been subject to much controversy, their exercise has been. President Gerald Ford's pardon of his predecessor, Richard Nixon, in 1974 is a case in point. Issued before any judicial proceedings could determine Nixon's innocence or guilt in the Watergate affair, the pardon, which subverted the legal process, was criticized as ill timed and politically inspired. Ford's power to issue it, however, was not in dispute. Similarly, President Carter's proclamation of amnesty for Vietnam War-era draft resisters in 1977 was criticized by veterans' groups and members of Congress, yet there was little these critics could do to prevent those actions from taking effect.

Presidents can exercise judicial power in other ways. They can influence the composition of the federal judiciary through their nominations of judges—subject, of course, to Senate approval (for an extended discussion of judicial appointments, see Chapter 15). In addition, they and their political appointees in the Justice Department can determine the government's position on controversial legal matters, deciding which cases the department will prosecute and whether to appeal adverse decisions to a higher court. Similarly, in cases in which the government is not

One month into office in 1974, President Gerald Ford signs the document that pardoned his predecessor, Richard Nixon, for all federal crimes he "committed or may have committed or taken part in." Both men vehemently denied charges that a deal had been struck, with Nixon agreeing to resign if his vice president would grant the pardon upon taking office.

directly involved but has an interest, the Justice Department can try to influence judges' thinking by filing an *amicus curiae* brief setting forth the administration's position. There is little that presidents can do, however, if the final judgment of the court goes against their position.

The independence of the judiciary in deciding matters of law limits the extent to which presidents can directly influence judicial decisions. Clinton discovered this in 1996 when Judge Harold Baer Jr., whom he had appointed to a United States district court in New York City, initially decided that 80 pounds of cocaine and heroin was inadmissible as evidence of drug dealing because the police had lacked "probable cause" for the search in which it was found. After a huge public outcry against the ruling, Republican members of Congress called for Baer's impeachment and criticized what they said were Clinton's liberal judicial appointments. The president indicated that he thought the judge should reverse the ruling or resign, but he had no way to compel either action. In the midst of the controversy, Chief Justice William Rehnquist made a speech defending judicial independence from the other branches of government. Shortly thereafter the immediate issue was rendered moot when Baer, after hearing new evidence against the defendants, did reverse himself and allow the drugs as evidence. Despite occasional incidents like the Baer affair, in general the relationship between the president and the federal judiciary tends to be more distant, less visible, and less conflicted than the relationship between the president and Congress.

PRESIDENTIAL LEADERSHIP

The roles and responsibilities of presidents have expanded, but the formal authority of the president has not kept pace. Thus presidents need to exercise political leadership to close the gap between expectations and performance. They must try to persuade others to follow their lead by bargaining behind closed doors and making a public appeal.

Bargaining

In his classic study, *Presidential Power*, Richard E. Neustadt points out that presidents must be persuasive; they must be able to convince others that it is in *their* interest to do what the president wants.[6] Being persuasive often involves bargaining behind closed doors.

In the give-and-take of bargaining, presidents enjoy certain advantages. Their office is respected. Others look to them for guidance and leadership. Moreover, they control some valued commodities such as publicity, nominations, even social invitations, and they can use their discretion to propose and implement programs that benefit particular groups and constituencies. They can also impose a variety of sanctions, usually as a last resort. Sanctions range from not doing favors, not raising money, or not offering jobs to certain people to campaigning against those who oppose presidential policies.

Consider the case of Richard Shelby, who as a Democratic senator from Alabama embarrassed the Clinton administration by publicly criticizing the new taxes President Clinton advocated to reduce the federal budget deficit. To punish the senator and encourage other Democrats to toe the line, the director of the president's Office of Management and Budget suggested that NASA might transfer jobs from a facility in Shelby's state to one in Texas. To reinforce the point, the administration gave Shelby only one ticket to attend the president's reception for the University of

Alabama football team at the White House, whereas fellow Alabama senator Howell Heflin received eleven. (Shelby subsequently got even. After the 1994 elections, he switched parties and became a Republican.)

In addition to wielding rewards and sanctions, however, presidents need to be able to persuade by their personal impact. Neustadt identifies two strategic imperatives that contribute to a president's persuasive ability: reputation in Washington, and prestige with the general public. Reputation affects what presidents can do. Presidents who say what they mean and do what they say are likely to gain more support than those whose priorities are unclear and whose positions are subject to continual change.[7] Reputation in turn helps shape the public's perceptions, which are closely linked to the president's prestige. In general, presidents who enjoy the broadest public support are likely to be most persuasive with Congress, executive officials, foreign leaders, and others.

Political scientists have found empirical evidence to support the proposition that presidents' legislative influence increases as their popularity, measured in terms of public approval, increases. Political scientist George C. Edwards III, who has analyzed the results of Gallup polls and congressional voting patterns over several decades, found that the more popular presidents were, the more congressional support they received regardless of their partisan affiliation.[8]

For public approval to be converted into congressional votes, however, there must be a relationship between the basis of the president's popularity and the issue before Congress. George Bush found this out the hard way during the budget deficit debate of 1990. His plea to the American people and to Republican members of Congress to support the compromise that his administration had negotiated with the Democratic leadership fell on deaf ears despite his high standing in the polls. In 1990, Americans approved of Bush's performance as president in foreign affairs, but

Like the Wizard of Oz, presidents seem much more powerful than they actually are. Early in his presidency, Bill Clinton learned this lesson the hard way. His proposals to end discrimination against homosexuals in the military, to stimulate the economy, and to reduce the deficit were substantially modified or defeated—and in Clinton's second year his major priority, health care reform, died in Congress.

many did not support his budget policy. Similarly, despite Bush's popularity after the Persian Gulf War in 1991, Congress did not rush to support his domestic legislative initiatives.

Going Public

Appealing to the public by giving major addresses, holding press conferences and town meetings, and participating in other citizen-oriented events augments presidential power in two fundamental ways.[9] First, it legitimizes the position of the president in the eyes of others. Public support enables presidents to withstand criticism better, and it decreases the amount of criticism they are likely to receive. People are less likely to oppose a popular president than an unpopular one.

Going public also enables the president to apply pressure more effectively. Elected officials are usually very responsive to the beliefs and desires of organized groups and coalitions that may support or oppose them the next time they seek office. Political appointees and even civil servants are also sensitive to the needs of the groups affected by their decisions and policies.

On the other hand, there are dangers to relying too heavily on the public. Its opinion tends to be volatile and inconsistent. Moreover, public approval is usually tied to visible results. For policies that take time to work, such as changes in tax law designed to stimulate the economy or encourage savings, the tide of opinion can turn against the president before the program has been completed or the intended effect has occurred. Thus during the 1981–1982 recession President Reagan had to plead with Congress and the public to give his economic program more time to work.

Presidents face another problem when they go public: they raise expectations, sometimes to unrealistic heights. Failure to meet these expectations results in disappointment and damages a president's reputation, making it difficult to generate support for other proposals down the line. The high priority that President Clinton gave to health-care reform early in his administration is a classic example. By emphasizing this issue and his plans for dealing with it, Clinton heightened public awareness of the problem and created expectations. When his plan failed to win the support of Congress, the president's prestige fell.

The electoral process also tends to inflate public hopes. In his quest for the presidency, Jimmy Carter talked in unequivocal terms about the strong, honest, purposeful leadership he would provide as president. His inability to project that type of leadership or to make good on all of the 125 promises he had made during the campaign and reiterated after he took office contributed to the sharp decline in his popularity during his four years in office. All presidents are judged to some extent by the promises they make, duly recorded by the news media.

These examples illustrate the necessity and hazards of going public. Although public approval may contribute to power in the short run, it also raises the stakes and may ultimately hurt a president's image and reduce the ability to lead in the long run. In an age dominated by television, however, presidents often have little alternative but to take the public route to build and maintain popular support.

INSTITUTIONAL AND PERSONNEL RESOURCES

Presidents need help. Their job is too big, their tasks are too diverse, and their expectations are too great for them to operate alone. The Constitution anticipated that the president would have advisers, but it did not establish an advisory structure.

Beyond the role of the Senate in providing advice and consent to appointments and treaties, presidents were left to their own devices.

The Cabinet

In 1792, President Washington began to meet frequently with the heads of the three executive departments in existence at that time—State, War, and Treasury—plus the attorney general, who initially had no department. These meetings became more frequent and eventually evolved into an informal advisory system. Known as the **cabinet**, it assumed a partisan character in 1794 after Thomas Jefferson resigned as secretary of state to protest the administration's economic and foreign policies.

For more than 160 years the cabinet, composed of the heads of the various executive departments plus the vice president, functioned as the president's principal advisory body. (Figure 13-1 depicts the growth of the cabinet over the years.) Administration positions on controversial proposals were often thrashed out at cabinet meetings. Department secretaries also lent their prestige to the president, helping the administration maintain its political support in the party, Congress, and the country.

Members of the Clinton cabinet applaud loyally at the president's 1996 State of the Union address. With the decline of the cabinet's role as an advisory body, such group appearances by its members have become increasingly rare.

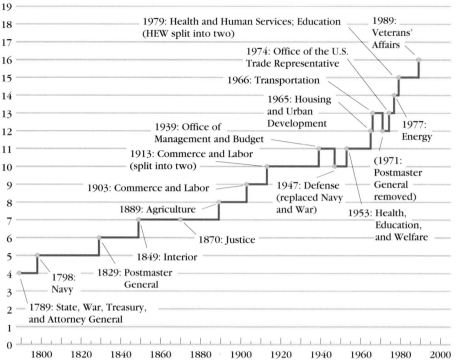

Number of agencies and positions

1979: Health and Human Services; Education (HEW split into two)

1989: Veterans' Affairs

1974: Office of the U.S. Trade Representative

1966: Transportation

1965: Housing and Urban Development

1939: Office of Management and Budget

1977: Energy

1913: Commerce and Labor (split into two)

1903: Commerce and Labor

1947: Defense (replaced Navy and War)

(1971: Postmaster General removed)

1889: Agriculture

1953: Health, Education, and Welfare

1870: Justice

1849: Interior

1829: Postmaster General

1798: Navy

1789: State, War, Treasury, and Attorney General

FIGURE 13-1

The development of the president's cabinet.

SOURCE: *Washington Post*, February 9, 1993, A15. © 1993 The Washington Post. Reprinted with permission.

In the 1960s, the relationship between the president and the cabinet began to change. As presidents began to shape public opinion and exercise more legislative leadership on their own, their reliance on the cabinet declined. President Eisenhower was the last to use his cabinet as a policy-making body.

Although presidents have continued to consult with department heads individually or in small groups, they have turned increasingly to smaller, more cohesive bodies for policy advice and coordination. Presidents Reagan and Bush created cabinet councils, organized on the basis of broad policy areas, to debate policy, develop recommendations, and help in the implementation of key presidential priorities. President Clinton has used a variation of this approach, with three policy councils operating in the economic, domestic, and national security spheres, respectively.

Thus the United States cabinet today is not nearly as important a policy-making body as its counterparts are in other democratic governments. In Switzerland, a Federal Council operates as a collective executive; in Israel, the cabinet, composed of leaders of the parties that comprise the governing coalition, must approve major government initiatives or they will likely fail to gain majority support in the legislature. In Great Britain, rifts in the cabinet can lead to a parliamentary vote of no confidence in the government, whereas in the United States rifts lead to the resignation of those who disagree with the administration's policy.

The Executive Office of the President

With the cabinet declining in importance, presidents have turned increasingly to their own staffs for advice, coordination, and public relations. Before 1939, presidential staffs were very small. In fact, not until 1857 did Congress authorize the president to hire a secretary. What help presidents had before that year, they paid for themselves.

Small staffs forced chief executives to do much of the administrative work themselves. George Washington maintained custody of the public papers; Abraham Lincoln wrote his own speeches; Grover Cleveland often answered the White House phone; Woodrow Wilson typed the final drafts of his principal addresses.

The inadequacy of presidential staffing became evident during the first term of Franklin Roosevelt's administration. In 1936, responding to criticism that his presidency was not being run efficiently, Roosevelt appointed a committee to study the problem. The committee proposed the establishment of an official presidential office, and in 1939 Congress gave the president the authority to do so.

The first **Executive Office of the President** (EOP) consisted of five separate units: three wartime agencies, the Bureau of the Budget, and a White House Office. Over the years the EOP has grown in size, responsibility, and power. Today it consists of twelve offices (including the president's) and two executive residences and has over 1,700 employees and a budget of $214 million (see Figure 13-2). The largest and most powerful units are the Office of Management and Budget and the White House Office.

The Office of Management and Budget   The Budget and Accounting Act of 1921 created a Bureau of the Budget to help the president prepare an annual budget to be submitted to Congress. Initially housed in the Department of the Treasury, the bureau was moved into the newly created EOP in 1939. This move converted the Budget Bureau into an important presidential agency, extending the president's reach and influence to the ongoing budgetary process.

As the substantive policy-making responsibilities of the presidency increased, the bureau was given an additional role—to coordinate legislative policy for the president. During the 1950s and 1960s, senior officials in the Budget Bureau also served as an institutional memory for the White House, providing it with information and expertise about how to get things done within the government. This source of knowledge by experienced and trustworthy civil servants facilitated the operation of government, particularly during presidential transitions.

The increasing importance of the budget office led President Nixon to rename and restructure it in 1970.[10] Now called the **Office of Management and Budget** (OMB), it assumed management advisory responsibilities in addition to its budgetary review and legislative policy functions. Nixon also increased the number of political appointees in the OMB, reducing the role of senior civil servants during transitions and downgrading their influence in the budgetary and policy-making processes. This practice has continued in subsequent administrations. Today there are approximately two dozen political appointees in the OMB.

To the extent that presidents require executive departments to consult with the OMB and allow it to have the last word, it has become both feared and powerful. It has gained a reputation as the institution that says no. In the process it has generated considerable controversy, much of it stemming from the OMB's budgetary orientation and presidential perspective in contrast to the service orientation and more parochial views of the departments and agencies.

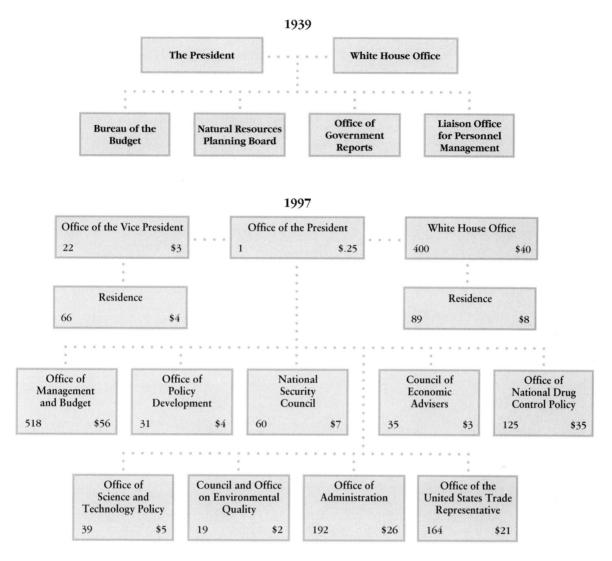

1939

The President ········· White House Office

Bureau of the Budget | Natural Resources Planning Board | Office of Government Reports | Liaison Office for Personnel Management

1997

| Office of the Vice President | Office of the President | White House Office |
| 22 | $3 | 1 | $.25 | 400 | $40 |

| Residence | Residence |
| 66 | $4 | 89 | $8 |

| Office of Management and Budget | Office of Policy Development | National Security Council | Council of Economic Advisers | Office of National Drug Control Policy |
| 518 | $56 | 31 | $4 | 60 | $7 | 35 | $3 | 125 | $35 |

| Office of Science and Technology Policy | Council and Office on Environmental Quality | Office of Administration | Office of the United States Trade Representative |
| 39 | $5 | 19 | $2 | 192 | $26 | 164 | $21 |

Numbers on left indicate full-time personnel. Dollar amounts in millions
indicate proposed budget authority for the 1997 fiscal year.

FIGURE 13-2

The Executive Office of the President—at its inception and in 1997.

SOURCE: Budget of the United States Government, Fiscal Year 1997. Washington, D.C.: Government Printing Office, 1996.

In its policy recommendations, the OMB traditionally tries to save money by limiting spending, thereby pitting departments and agencies against one another and against the OMB in the battle for funds. The OMB is also concerned with setting precedents, in contrast to the departments, which are more sensitive to protecting their interests and those of their clientele. Thus the OMB would be inclined to oppose a program likely to result in a large increase in expenditures, but a department whose clientele benefited from the program would probably support it. The conflict resulting from the politics of budgeting is continuous.

In addition to its budgetary and management functions, the OMB performs another critical role for the president. It acts as a central clearinghouse, monitoring what the executive departments and agencies want to do and how they want to do it. All proposals for new legislation, positions on existing legislation, and testimony before congressional committees must be cleared in advance by the OMB to make certain that they are in accord with the president's objectives. This is known as the **central clearance process**. At the end of the legislative process, the OMB also coordinates executive branch recommendations to the president to approve or disapprove legislation enacted by Congress. This is known as the **enrolled bill process**. These two processes are illustrated in Figure 13-3.

The OMB performs still another clearance operation for pending regulations to be issued by the departments and agencies. In exercising this **regulatory review**, the OMB must determine if a regulation is necessary, consistent with administration policy and legislative intent, and cost effective.

In short, since its inception the OMB has been a potent instrument of presidential power. Nixon and Ford turned to it to improve the management of government. Carter used it to reorganize parts of the executive branch, including his own office. Reagan, Bush, and Clinton relied on it to achieve significant budget cuts as well as to help them maintain oversight over the executive branch.

The White House Office   Like the OMB, the **White House Office** has evolved into a large and potent presidential staff. From its inception in 1939 until the mid 1960s, the office was relatively small and informal. A handful of administrative aides

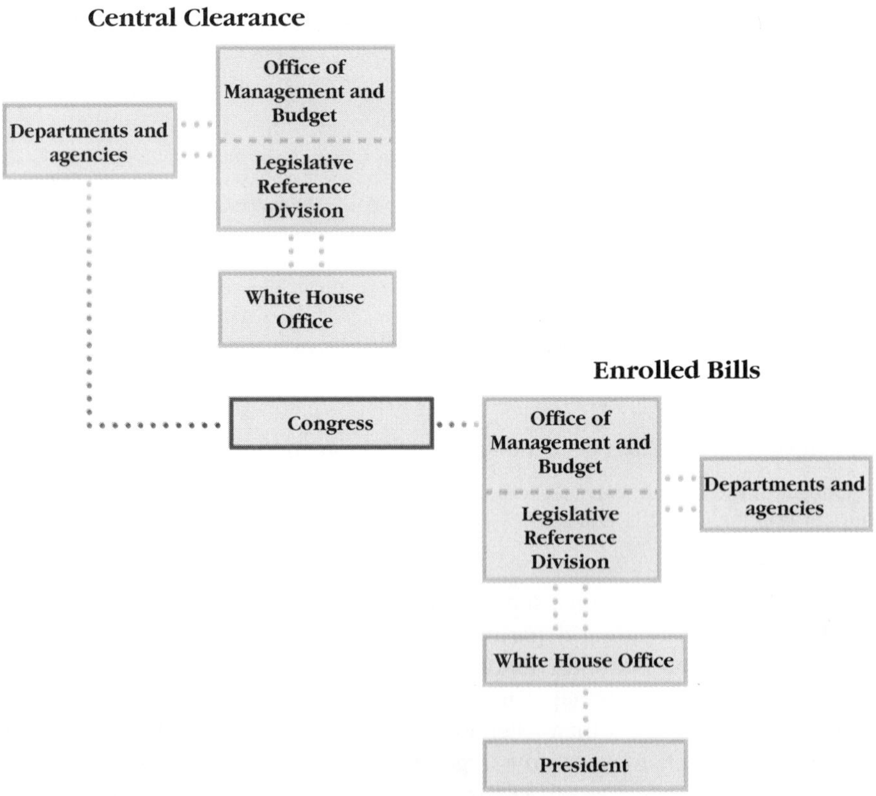

FIGURE 13-3
The central clearance and enrolled bill processes.

performed assignments dictated by specific presidential needs, such as writing a speech, planning a trip, or getting sufficient information for the president to make a decision. The president's assistants did not exercise exclusive domain over a policy or functional area; they did not rival cabinet secretaries for status and influence. Rather, they acted as personal assistants, enhancing the information available to the president, extending the influence of the presidency, and coordinating presidential activities with those of the rest of the government.

Gradually the staff began to expand. During the 1950s, an official liaison with Congress was established. During the 1960s, a policy-making capacity in national security and domestic affairs was created. During the 1970s and 1980s, regular links with the president's principal constituencies—interest groups, state and local governments, and the political parties—were set up. By the 1990s, an economic policy council was added.

As presidential responsibilities have grown, so has the White House Office staff. In 1950, it numbered about 300 people; by 1960, it exceeded 400; by 1970, it was close to 500. After the Watergate scandal, in which a number of presidential aides were implicated, the size of the White House payroll declined. Today the White House Office has an official staff size of approximately 400, plus another 100 people from the executive departments and agencies who are detailed to the White House for special assignments. Its budget is $40 million.[11]

In theory most White House Offices in recent decades have had similar structures and decision-making processes. There is a formalized structure with a chief of staff, policy assistants, a large public relations operation, and the traditional units that help the president meet his day-to-day responsibilities and link him to his principal constituencies (see Figure 13-4). In practice, however, recent Republican staffs have tended to be more hierarchical in organization, more clearcut in areas of responsibility, and more formal in decision-making processes than have their Democratic counterparts. Also, recent Republican presidents have distanced themselves more from day-to-day operations and middle-level policy-making issues than have recent Democratic presidents, who have tended to place themselves in the midst of their administrations' political, policy, and personnel decisions.

The bureaucratized White House has presented presidents with their own internal management problems: how to supervise the operation of a sizable, diverse, and increasingly specialized staff. Presidents Ford and Carter tried unsuccessfully to do this supervision themselves. Inundated with decisions that could have been settled by others, both presidents eventually turned to a chief of staff to oversee these and other administrative tasks. Their successors have also depended on a chief of staff to run the White House.

The president's chief of staff has three important responsibilities: (1) to act as an honest broker, ensuring that the president has a wide range of information and advice; (2) to offer recommendations to the president about decisions that need to be made and actions that need to be taken; and (3) to serve as a lightning rod for criticism directed at the president. The general rule of thumb in the White House is that the president should be credited with all good news and favorable actions and the staff should be blamed for the major foul-ups and problems. Thus when President Clinton found himself in difficulty after only four months in office, he appointed as counselor a man who had served in two previous Republican White Houses, David Gergen, and moved other senior aides to new positions. When President Bush's popularity began to tumble at the end of his third year in office, he replaced top White House personnel, including his chief of staff, and added a new domestic policy counselor.[12] And when President Reagan was criticized for

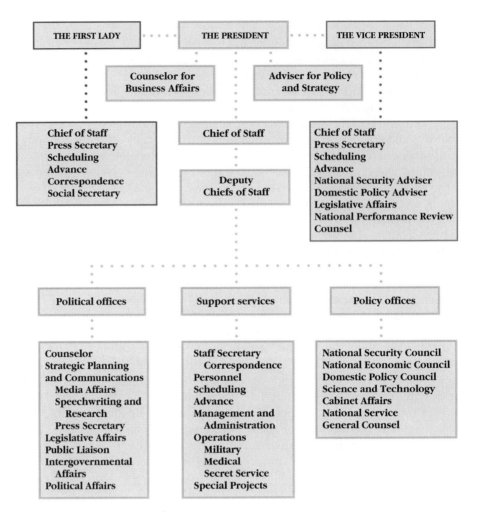

FIGURE 13-4
The contemporary White House Office.

the excesses of his national security staff during the Iran-contra affair, he fired his national security adviser, John Poindexter, accepted the resignation of staff aide Oliver North, and replaced his chief of staff, Donald Regan.

As the White House Office has expanded in functions and responsibilities, power has shifted to it from the departments and agencies. This shift has enhanced the status, visibility, and influence of the president's principal aides and decreased those of many cabinet secretaries. Proximity to the president's Oval Office, illustrated in Figure 13–5, growing policy-making responsibilities, and large support staffs have placed White House aides in a better position than other executive branch officials to shape administration goals and coordinate strategies to achieve them.

By providing a cadre of politically loyal strategists and technicians, the larger, more powerful White House Office has increased presidential discretion and influence. No longer must the president depend solely or primarily on officials in the executive departments and agencies. The White House now provides a supportive environment, one tuned to the president's philosophy, policy objectives, and time frame.

But these changes have also created tensions between the officials in the White

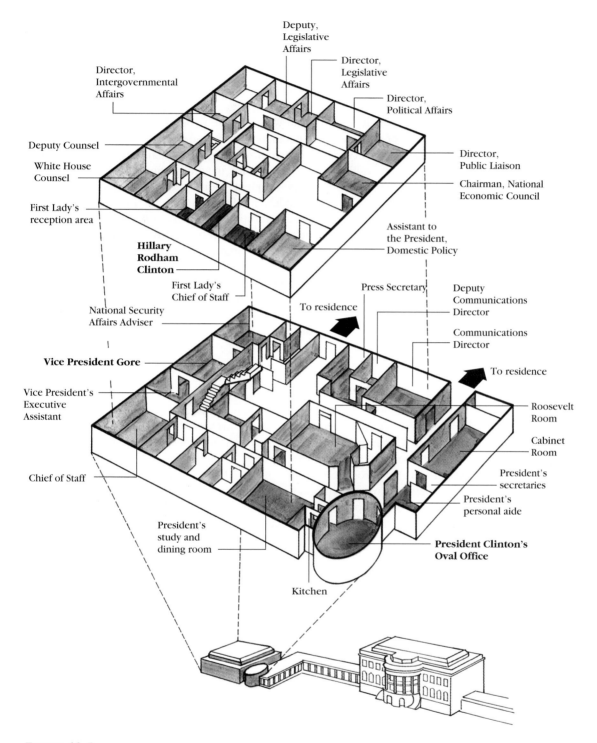

FIGURE 13-5

An exploded view of the west wing of the White House at the start of the Clinton administration.

SOURCE: *Washington Post*, February 5, 1993, A23. © 1993 The Washington Post. Reprinted with permission.

House and those in the departments and agencies. Complaints have been heard from cabinet officials that the White House is formulating more and more major policies, that presidents and their staffs are getting more directly involved in the implementation of policy, and that the access of department secretaries and their deputies to top White House policy makers is being impaired. Tension has also increased between political appointees and civil servants.

Internal staff conflicts within the White House Office have also become evident and the subject of considerable speculation in the news media. Turf battles, policy disputes, and personality clashes have now become standard fare. These conflicts, which often become public, make it harder for an administration to speak with a single voice. Leaks have become more frequent, along with "kiss-and-tell" books and articles by departing presidential aides. In short, the White House has become a battleground in which personal and institutional politics *within* the administration influence decisions almost as much as political pressures from outside it.

President Clinton had particular difficulty in finding the right people for his White House. Several embarrassing incidents during the early years of his administration forced him to shift senior aides and revise White House operations. In his first three years Clinton had two chiefs of staff, five deputy chiefs of staff, four counsels, three legislative liaison heads, three communication directors, two press secretaries, and many other changes in White House personnel.

The President's Spouse

The role of the president's spouse has expanded to include more than simply ceremonial and social responsibilities. A president's spouse is expected to campaign, to make speeches, and to attend events in the president's absence and on the president's behalf. Communicating public reactions and perspectives to the president is another important task, one that Eleanor Roosevelt pioneered as first lady. Mrs. Roosevelt traveled across the country for her husband, monitoring public opinion and reporting the country's mood to him, and writing a newspaper column entitled "My Day" (see the People in Politics box on pages 488–489).

All too often, personal aides are reluctant to tell a president bad news. A presidential spouse may be in a better position to do so. For example, Nancy Reagan was instrumental in conveying to her husband which of his top aides and department secretaries were not serving him well. Her efforts culminated in the resignation of two senior administration officials in the president's second term, his chief of staff and his attorney general.

Presidential spouses have also involved themselves on issues of public policy. Betty Ford and Rosalynn Carter spoke out on health-care issues, and Mrs. Carter was the first spouse to attend cabinet meetings regularly. Nancy Reagan promoted the Reagan administration's campaign against illegal drugs.

Hillary Rodham Clinton has been the most active spouse thus far in the formulation and coordination of policy. The first to be given an office in the west wing of the White House with the rest of the president's principal policy advisers, Mrs. Clinton coordinated and tried to gain support for the administration's health-care initiatives. She also began writing a newspaper column.

Mrs. Clinton's role was not without controversy, however. Critics complained that her unique relationship to the president made her less subject to the usual constraints on presidential advisers—she could not be fired—and placed her in a position to impose her own views on the president and those around him and to prevent others from reaching him. Mrs. Clinton's support of a comprehensive health care plan that provided universal care for all Americans is a good example of an issue in which the first lady's strongly held views carried the day with the president despite concerns that the plan was too costly, too complex, and too bureaucratic.

A reluctance to be disrespectful to the first lady may also act to inhibit critical discussion in her presence, particularly on issues in which her position is well known. This reluctance makes her less vulnerable to criticism than are others in a position to influence public policy. Moreover, the first lady's involvement in an issue heightens public awareness, focuses media attention, and indicates the importance the administration attaches to a proposal. Thus when the proposal is defeated, as was the case with health care, the loss has larger political implications for the president than it otherwise would. Following the 1994 midterm elections, Mrs. Clinton played a less visible policy-making role in the Clinton administration.

Mrs. Clinton's political and policy roles could only be advisory. By law, members of the president's immediate family may not hold a paid appointed position with the federal government, although they may hold a private sector job. Elizabeth Dole, wife of 1996 Republican presidential candidate Robert Dole, announced her intention to continue as president of the American Red Cross if her husband was elected president.

After the health-care reform plan she had put together died in Congress, Hillary Rodham Clinton refocused her public activities on areas that were less controversial, at least among Americans. She took a particular interest in the welfare of women and children. Speaking to a conference on women's issues in China in 1995, she urged concern for the rights of all people regardless of their gender, nationality, or ethnicity. In this context, her remarks provided oblique criticism of the traditional devaluing of women and girls within Chinese society as well as of the Chinese government's record on human rights.

ELEANOR ROOSEVELT AND HILLARY RODHAM CLINTON: POWERFUL BUT POLARIZING

When Bill Clinton ran for president in 1992, he indicated that his wife would play an important role in his administration. "Elect one and you get two," he said. Following through on his promise, the president gave Hillary Rodham Clinton an office in the west wing of the White House and subsequently appointed her to oversee a major priority of his administration, its health-care reform program. The appointment engendered considerable controversy. Should a presidential spouse be engaged in matters of public policy, or should she limit herself to the more traditional ceremonial and social responsibilities?

It was not the first time that such a controversy had arisen. In particular, Eleanor Roosevelt's role in Franklin Delano Roosevelt's administration sparked similar debate. When Franklin Roosevelt was stricken with polio in 1921, which left his legs paralyzed and for a while made him unable to participate in public affairs, his wife became his stand-in, partly to keep his name in the forefront of Democratic party politics and partly to fulfill her own interests. Thus by the time Roosevelt became president in 1933, Mrs. Roosevelt was an accomplished politician and a respected leader in her own right. Throughout his twelve years in the White House, her influence on the president, and thus on the nation, was profound.

She was particularly active in social issues, as her early civil rights efforts attest. In 1936 Marian Anderson sang at the White House, but three years later the Daughters of the American Revolution (DAR) refused to let her rent their Washington auditorium, Constitution Hall, for a concert because she was an African American. Outraged, Eleanor Roosevelt promptly resigned her membership in the DAR and helped arrange for Anderson to perform at an open-air concert at the Lincoln Memorial that was attended by seventy-five thousand people. Later that year, Mrs. Roosevelt joined the NAACP (the National Association for the Advancement of Colored People).

The issue of racial discrimination in the military and defense industries became increasingly urgent to African Americans as the likelihood of United States participation in World War II grew in 1940. Working with the leaders of the NAACP, Mrs. Roosevelt pressed her husband to use his executive authority to order the removal of racial barriers. Finally her influence, and the NAACP's threat of a march on Washington, led the president to sign an executive order that mandated nondiscrimination in defense industries and set up a Fair Employment Practices Committee to enforce the order.

Like Mrs. Roosevelt, Mrs. Clinton has been active and outspoken—and has become a lightning rod for critics of her husband's administration. In many respects, Mrs. Roosevelt has been her role model as first lady. Indeed, journalist Bob Woodward reported in his 1996 book *The Choice* that Mrs. Clinton had engaged in several imaginary conversations with Mrs. Roosevelt in an effort to understand and overcome the public criticism that she was encountering. A lawyer who had practiced with a prestigious Arkansas firm during the time her husband was governor, Mrs. Clinton had been associated with a variety of liberal causes that she continued to advocate after he became president. Charged with overseeing the development, coordination, and presentation of the administration's health-care reform program during the 1993–1994 period, she was instrumental in shaping the final proposal, which called for universal health coverage and managed care. She also took the lead in lobbying for the plan in Congress and before various interest groups, and in building support for it among the general public.

When the Democratic-controlled 103rd Congress failed to enact the proposal, Mrs. Clinton became the target of considerable criticism. Her alleged involvement in the firing of personnel in the White House Travel Office, her involvement in the failed Whitewater real estate development in Arkansas while her husband was governor, the removal of papers pertaining to the Whitewater investigation from the office of a senior White House aide who committed suicide, and questions about her commodities trading in Arkansas contributed to her image problem. Public opinion polls indicated that Mrs. Clinton had become

Like her husband, Eleanor Roosevelt became a master of the mass media, notably radio. She also wrote a daily newspaper column called "My Day." Hillary Rodham Clinton, shown testifying before Congress about health-care reform, took an even more prominent public role in her husband's administration—and came in for even more criticism than Mrs. Roosevelt had received.

a partisan first lady; Democrats approved of her, but Republicans did not.

With the Democrats' defeat in the 1994 midterm elections and the decline in Mrs. Clinton's popularity—she was the first president's wife to be less popular than her husband—she assumed a less visible policy and political role. Although she was still active behind the scenes, her public appearances tended to be more ceremonial and her pronouncements pertained primarily to "women's issues" such as educational and economic opportunities for women and health and human rights for everyone. She attended women's conferences in China and Latin America and published a best-selling book about children but refrained from getting involved in contentious domestic issues. Nevertheless, she remained a divisive figure

politically. Her book even became a target for ridicule by Republican presidential candidate Robert Dole in his speech at the party's 1996 convention. Two weeks later Mrs. Clinton herself addressed the Democratic convention, defending her stance that children's welfare depends not just on their own families but on a network of community and government support.

Eleanor Roosevelt and Hillary Rodham Clinton certainly won't be the last presidential spouses to have a discernible policy influence and public impact, and their activity and experience raise important issues about the role of presidential spouses. Should they be given official responsibilities? Should they be entrusted with a policy-making and advocacy role? Should they act as personal representative of the president or the country? What do you think?

The Vice Presidency

Like the roles of the OMB and the White House Office, that of the vice presidency has been enlarged, and the stature of the office enhanced. Today the vice presidency is considered prestigious in its own right. That was not always the case.

Throughout much of American history, in fact, the position was not well regarded even by those who served in it. The nation's first vice president, John Adams, complained, "My country has in its wisdom contrived for me the most insignificant office that ever the invention of man contrived or his imagination conceived."[13] Thomas Jefferson, the second person to hold the office, was not quite as critical. Describing his job as "honorable and easy," he added, "I am unable to decide whether I would rather have it or not have it."[14]

Why was such a position created in the first place? The framers did not discuss a vice presidency until the end of the Constitutional Convention. Although they wanted to ensure an orderly succession if the presidency became vacant, there were other ways to do so. The manner in which the vice president was to be selected, however, offers a clue as to why the framers established this position. Originally, the candidate with the second-highest number of Electoral College votes was to become the vice president. This placed the second-most-qualified person (in the judgment of the electors) in a position to take over if something happened to the president.

In 1800, however, the presidential election ended in a tie in the Electoral College. Since the electors could not designate which position, president or vice president, they wished Jefferson and Burr to have, both Democratic-Republican candidates received the same number of votes and the House of Representatives had to determine the winner. To prevent this situation from happening again, Congress proposed and the states ratified the Twelfth Amendment to the Constitution, which requires separate Electoral College ballots for president and vice president. This modification in voting upset the logic of the framers' reasoning, because the political parties began to choose their vice presidential nominees for reasons of partisanship rather than merit. It is probably no coincidence that the office declined in importance following the enactment of this amendment. (See the box on page 492.)

Until the middle of the twentieth century, vice presidents performed very limited functions. But after Franklin Roosevelt's sudden death in 1945, Eisenhower's illnesses in the 1950s, and Kennedy's assassination in 1963, the position of vice president became a subject of public concern and congressional action, namely the Twenty-Fifth Amendment. Ratified by the states in 1967, this amendment permits the president to appoint a vice president if that position becomes vacant, subject to the approval of a majority in both houses of Congress.

Since the end of World War II, presidents have also done more to prepare their vice presidents for the job that they might have to assume eventually. Eisenhower invited Vice President Richard Nixon to attend cabinet, National Security Council, and legislative strategy meetings and to preside over these sessions during Eisenhower's absences. Nixon also represented the president on a number of well-publicized trips abroad. Lyndon Johnson, John Kennedy's vice president, also participated in a variety of administrative activities, from coordinating efforts to eliminate racial discrimination to promoting the exploration of outer space and lobbying Congress.

Despite their own "enhanced" experiences, neither President Johnson nor President Nixon gave major new responsibilities to their own vice presidents. But Presidents Ford and Carter did. Vice presidents Nelson Rockefeller and Walter Mondale regularly advised Ford and Carter, respectively, on policy issues, particularly in the domestic sphere, and acted as their liaison with Congress, interest groups, and the president's political party. Symbolically, Jimmy Carter gave Walter Mondale an office in the west wing of the White House, close to the Oval Office, thereby indicating to others how he regarded his vice president. Although vice presidents George Bush and Dan Quayle did not exert as much clout in their respective administrations as Mondale did in his, they too participated in major policy discussions, headed committees to examine interagency problems, and represented their president on trips abroad.

Vice President Al Gore has been an important Clinton adviser with regular input into major decisions about policy and strategy. He has a weekly lunch with the president and is a regular participant in political strategy meetings. Heading the administration's National Performance Review, its effort to "reinvent government," Gore has also been charged with overseeing the coordination of regulatory priorities and agendas. A key legislative lobbyist, he cast the tie-breaking vote in the Senate on the 1993 deficit reduction proposal. Additionally, he has performed the traditional vice presidential roles of political fundraising and public outreach. Increasingly, he also became involved in foreign policy issues as an adviser, spokesman, and personal emissary for the president.

In the twentieth century, six vice presidents have succeeded to the presidency; and one former vice president, Richard Nixon, was elected to it after having been out of office for eight years. The changes in the contemporary vice presidency have made the office more attractive, to the point where it is now regarded as a stepping-stone to the presidency. Increased visibility and political influence have made vice presidents front-runners in their party's nomination process. This, in turn, has increased the chances for a vice president to be elected president, as George Bush was in 1988.

Sharing the same regional and generational background, Al Gore and Bill Clinton enjoy a close personal and professional relationship.

VICE PRESIDENTIAL VICES

Not only have some vice presidents not had the most distinguished qualifications for office, but their behavior in office has been occasionally indiscreet or of dubious morality and legality. In the early nineteenth century the vice presidency was a hotbed of controversy. Aaron Burr, the nation's third vice president, killed Alexander Hamilton in a duel and was indicted for murder while serving in office. (A few years later he was tried and acquitted of treason charges relating to another matter.) Richard M. Johnson, who served as vice president under Martin Van Buren, kept a series of slave mistresses and spent one summer during his tenure managing a tavern. In the 1870s both of Ulysses Grant's vice presidents, Schuyler Colfax and Henry Wilson, were implicated in a stock scandal.

By the turn of the century, scandals involving the vice presidency had become less frequent, but for several decades thereafter vice presidents suffered from a well-deserved reputation for mediocrity. Controversies resurfaced after World War II. While campaigning with Dwight Eisenhower in 1952, Richard Nixon was accused of maintaining a secret slush fund of campaign contributions. He defended himself in a nationally televised address that ended the controversy but failed to change his reputation as a cutthroat politician out to further his own interests. Twenty years later Nixon's vice president, Spiro Agnew, was forced to resign for accepting kickbacks during his tenure as vice president.

Agnew was the second vice president to resign from office (the first was John C. Calhoun, who resigned in 1832 as Andrew Jackson's vice president over the issue of states' rights). Since Agnew's resignation in 1973, no public scandals have marred the office, although questions about Dan Quayle's qualifications resurfaced throughout his vice presidency during George Bush's administration.

SOURCE: Marie D. Natoli, *American Prince, American Pauper: The Contemporary Vice Presidency in Perspective* (Westport, Conn.: Greenwood Press, 1985); and Michael Dorman, *The Second Man* (New York: Delacorte Press, 1968).

Spiro Agnew (left) *leaves federal court in 1973. He pleaded "no contest" to one charge of tax evasion rather than face criminal charges of taking kickbacks. "It is in the best interests of the Nation that I relinquish the Vice Presidency," he wrote to President Nixon.*

THE PRESIDENCY

The White House went on the Internet in June 1993. Today you can obtain a variety of information about the presidency, such as speeches, reports, press briefings, even letters—all updated daily from the White House home page. You can also access from it all cabinet-level websites as well as sites sponsored by several independent agencies and commissions. Moreover, you can send communications via e-mail to the president, vice president, and other executive officials. Here's how to do so.

The White House home page can be accessed at **http://www.whitehouse.gov** and direct e-mail can be sent to the following addresses: **president@whitehouse.gov** and **vice.president@whitehouse.gov**

Try the following addresses on Usenet/Netnews if you would like to sign up for more electronic publications from the White House: (1) **alt.politics.clinton** (2) **alt.politics.reform** (3) **alt.news-media** or (4) **alt.activism** Also, take a look at **GO WHITEHOUSE** (Compuserve),

VIEW WHITEHOUSE (MCI), or **pol.govinfo.usa** (on Peacenet or Econet). Or, to receive publications on specific subjects, send an e-mail message to: **Publications@Research.ai.mit.edu** and at the "subject" box, type one of the following commands:

Receive All
Receive Economy
Receive Education
Receive Environment
Receive Executive Acts
Receive Foreign
Receive Government
Receive Healthcare
Receive International Security
Receive Legislation
Receive Party
Receive Personnel
Receive Technology
Receive Social

Unlike the relationship between the president and the cabinet or between presidential staff and executive departments and agencies, the relationship between the vice president and the president cannot tolerate tension. They are elected on the same ticket and are expected to work together, with the president calling the shots. A vice president who hopes to have any influence in the administration, to be chosen as a running mate for a second term, or to gain the president's support for a future presidential campaign cannot disagree publicly with the "boss," take attention away from him, or appear eager to have the number one job. Thus after President Reagan was shot in 1981, Vice President Bush, who was in Texas at the time of the assassination attempt, had his helicopter land at the vice president's residence in Washington, D.C., rather than at the White House, to avoid any appearance that he was eager to take over as president.

THE PERSONAL DIMENSION

Presidents need advice, but they also have discretion in making decisions and conditioning their relationships with others. How skilled and smart they are, what they believe, how quickly they absorb information and take action, how they view their roles and tasks, how they feel on a particular day, and how they feel about themselves in general all affect their perceptions, their evaluations, and ultimately their words, decisions, and behavior.

KEEPING UP WITH THE PRESIDENT

In addition to the Internet, there are other ways of finding out what the president is saying and doing.

Everything the president officially says is a matter of public record. All the president's public speeches, remarks, proclamations, executive orders, letters, and so on are preserved and published by the National Archives and Records Administration. These documents are found in all federal depository libraries and in many other research libraries.

The *Federal Register* publishes a daily record of the president's words and official actions. A weekly record, along with a digest of the president's activities that week, is found in the *Weekly Compilation of Presidential Documents*. A complete record of the president's speeches appears annually in the *Public*

Papers of the Presidents. In fact, *Codification of Presidential Proclamations and Executive Orders* contains these documents from 1945 to 1989 in one convenient, indexed volume. More recent executive orders and memoranda can be found in the *Federal Register* and in the *Weekly Compilation of Presidential Documents*.

The *New York Times* usually runs the full text of major presidential speeches and transcripts of most presidential press conferences on the day after they occur.

A recorded message for the press listing the president's schedule for the day can be heard by calling (202) 456-2343. A similar message for the first lady can be heard at (202) 456-6269.

Physical Health

Despite the importance of health, public information about the diagnosis and treatment of presidential illnesses is usually vague and incomplete, particularly at the onset of a problem. In an effort to prevent precipitous reactions and maintain continuity, White House spokespersons have tended to downplay the president's medical problems and not fully inform the public about them. Thus it was not until weeks after Ronald Reagan left the hospital following the 1981 attempt on his life that the public learned how close to death he actually had come. Similarly, Grover Cleveland's two cancer operations in 1893, Woodrow Wilson's incapacity after a stroke in 1919–1920, Franklin Roosevelt's worsening health during the mid 1940s, and John F. Kennedy's affliction with Addison's disease were not publicized during their tenure in office.

In the second half of the twentieth century, presidents seem to have had more than their share of illnesses.[15] Dwight Eisenhower had three major illnesses: coronary thrombosis in 1955, acute ileitis in 1956, and a minor stroke in 1957. In addition to Addison's disease, Kennedy had a back problem that was treated with special braces, exercises, and a chair designed to alleviate pressure. Lyndon Johnson had gall bladder and hernia operations during his presidency and caught pneumonia on at least one occasion; moreover, the burdens of the Vietnam War put both him and his successor, Richard Nixon, under severe psychological strain. (Nixon also was stressed by the Watergate scandal.) Reagan had malignant growths removed from his colon and face and may have been subject to the onset of Alzheimer's disease during the later years of his presidency. George Bush was treated for an overactive thyroid (Graves' disease) and had precancerous skin growths removed. Bill Clinton regularly gets shots for allergies and his characteristic hoarseness.

The effects of illness, injury, and mental stress on presidential performance vary. Some presidents are better able than others to cope with them. In general, the more

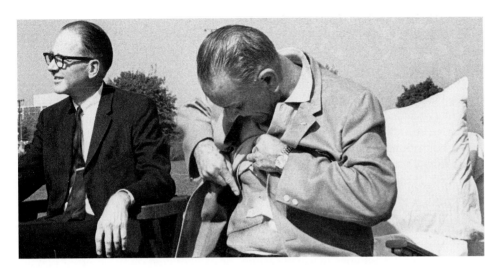

Lyndon Johnson was hospitalized several times during his presidency. Leaving the hospital in 1965, he points to the spot where the doctors "messed around" in removing his gall bladder. The public got quite a few chances to see the incision. The shape of the scar resembled that of Vietnam, and Johnson often displayed it as a symbol of how the Vietnam War had wounded him.

serious the medical problem and the longer the recovery period, the more removed presidents have become from the day-to-day functioning of their office, with critical decisions delayed or delegated to others.

What is more difficult to discern is how decision making is affected when presidents are not feeling up to par or when their judgment is affected by medication or pain. Consider, for example, the incredible amount of activity that President Bush engaged in at the beginning of the Persian Gulf crisis. Determined not to become a prisoner of the White House as Jimmy Carter had been during the early months of the Iranian hostage crisis in 1979, Bush frantically vacationed in Maine with what a journalist described as "nonstop golf and horseshoes, iron-man jogs, marathon sets of tennis, relentless trolls for bluefish aboard his speedboat, *Fidelity*."[16] Was this activity a consequence of his overactive thyroid, frustration over his inability to prevent or thwart the Iraqi invasion of Kuwait, or simply business-as-usual for George Bush?

Character

Common sense suggests that personality also affects behavior, but the impact of personality is very hard to discern even by those who are trained to do so. It must be inferred from rhetoric and behavior. How much did George Bush's reaction to press stories that he was weak and indecisive in the failed Panamanian coup attempt in 1989 influence his later decision to use overwhelming military force to invade Panama and remove dictator Manuel Noriega from power? How much has Bill Clinton's penchant for compromise been a consequence of his need to play the kind of mediating, healing role that he did between his mother and alcoholic stepfather? Although these questions are difficult to answer with any degree of certainty, the assumption that underlies them still seems valid: that self-esteem, confidence, and feelings of being appreciated, attractive, approved, and in control affect how presidents organize their White House, make decisions, and interact with their aides.

Political scientist James David Barber has advanced a psychological model for explaining presidential behavior (see the box on page 497). His model describes how presidents approach their job in terms of their level of activity (active or passive) and their ability to relate to others and enjoy their work (positive or negative).[17]

Of the four character types in this schema, Barber considers the *active-positive* to be best suited to the presidency. Such a person brings to the office the high level of activity needed to sustain the multiple roles a president must assume. Moreover, a positive attitude toward work generates its own psychological and physical benefits. It contributes to a heightened energy level; it eases the inevitable conflicts that result from competing perspectives, interests, goals, and ambitions; and it increases tolerance. Presidents who enjoy their work tend to be more eager and better able to take on new and difficult challenges than those who do not. *Active-negative* presidents, on the other hand, tend to be dangerous because they become rigid and unyielding when their decisions are challenged. They take those challenges personally.

Barber's model assumes that typecasting, or categorizing on the basis of certain dominant traits, can provide valuable clues to the problems that might develop during a presidency. Although the model cannot predict with certainty or anticipate particular reactions to particular events, it can indicate general tendencies and reactions to which certain personality types are prone.

However, there is a problem with this kind of analysis. Presidents who have been characterized as psychologically most qualified have not always turned out to be the most effective in office, and those who have been considered to be the most successful have not always had the most desirable psychological qualities. Franklin Roosevelt is an example of an active-positive type who is generally regarded as a great president. James Polk and Woodrow Wilson, also well regarded by some presidential scholars, are examples of active-negative types. Dwight Eisenhower and Ronald Reagan, both extremely popular presidents, are considered passive types— passive-negative in Eisenhower's case. Gerald Ford and Jimmy Carter, who were much less popular and, many would argue, less successful than Eisenhower and Reagan, are both active-positive types according to Barber. Abraham Lincoln, categorized as active-negative by political scientist Jeffrey Tulis, is generally considered one of the nation's greatest presidents.[18]

Barber's model has been criticized on a number of grounds: (1) his categories are too simplistic and too broad; (2) personalities do not fit neatly or easily into them; and (3) the expectations that flow from them are too general to be useful as explanations for individual behavior, much less as predictions of future actions. Despite these criticisms, Barber's model continues to frame much of the debate on personality and the presidency. Although he has not succeeded in providing a comprehensive theory or an airtight explanation of why presidents behave as they do, Barber has focused attention on the importance of personality and has identified certain facets of it that must be considered in discussions of presidential leadership.

Managerial Style

Presidents interact with their subordinates and make decisions in a variety of ways. Some presidents feel that they must dominate. For example, Lyndon Johnson monopolized discussions with his staff and was unable to accept criticism. Kennedy and Bush treated their assistants more as equals.

Some presidents need to operate in a protective environment. Nixon saw only a

PRESIDENTIAL CHARACTER TYPES

ACTIVE-POSITIVE

An energetic president who enjoys the work and tends to be productive and capable of adjusting to new situations. Such a person generally feels confident and self-assured.

ACTIVE-NEGATIVE

A president who works hard but does not gain much pleasure from the work and tends to be intense, compulsive, and aggressive. Such a person may pursue public actions in a self-interested manner and generally feels insecure, using the position of the presidency to overcome feelings of inadequacy and even impotence.

PASSIVE-POSITIVE

A relatively receptive, laid-back president who wants to gain agreement and to mute dissent at all costs. Such a person is likely to feel pessimistic and unloved on a deep psychological level. As president, the passive-positive individual attempts to compensate for these feelings by being overly optimistic and by continually trying to elicit agreement and support from others.

PASSIVE-NEGATIVE

A president who abhors politics and withdraws from interpersonal relationships. Such an individual is ill suited for political office, much less for the nation's highest one. Suffering from low self-esteem and a sense of uselessness, a passive-negative president is likely to take refuge in generalized principles and standard procedures.

THE CHARACTER TYPES OF SELECTED PRESIDENTS

Active-Positive	*Active-Negative*
Franklin D. Roosevelt	James Polk
Harry S Truman	Abraham Lincoln
John F. Kennedy	Woodrow Wilson
Gerald Ford	Herbert Hoover
Jimmy Carter	Lyndon B. Johnson
George Bush	Richard M. Nixon

Passive-Positive	*Passive-Negative*
William Howard Taft	Calvin Coolidge
Warren G. Harding	Dwight Eisenhower
Ronald Reagan	

SOURCES: Description of character types adapted from James David Barber, *The Presidential Character*, 4th ed. (Englewood Cliffs, N.J.: Prentice-Hall, 1992), 9–10. Reprinted by permission of the author. Classification of selected presidents from Barber, *The Presidential Character*, 4th ed.; and Jeffrey Tulis, "On Presidential Character," in *The Presidency in the Constitutional Order*, ed. Joseph M. Bessette and Jeffrey Tulis (Baton Rouge: Louisiana State University Press, 1981), 293–301.

few trusted aides and wanted all recommendations and advice to be presented to him in writing. Ford, Eisenhower, and Reagan were more open, saw more people, and were willing to make decisions on the basis of oral presentations.

Some presidents need to be involved in everything. Johnson, Carter, Bush, and Clinton have taken a hands-on approach to decision making. In contrast, Eisenhower and Reagan delegated considerable authority to others, waiting for issues to be brought to them rather than reaching out for them.

A president's managerial style affects the way the White House works. Nixon's standoffish manner, his unwillingness to interact with many aides, and his all-business approach created an atmosphere in which aides had to prove how tough they were, how long they toiled, and how many sacrifices they made. His successors, Ford and Carter, were more tolerant, more open, and less imposing. In their administrations there were fewer penalties for poor performance, and presidential assistants who did not produce good work were circumvented rather than being asked to leave.

Presidents need all the help they can get. Here two of the Clinton administration's top officials—General John Shalikashvili, chairman of the Joint Chiefs of Staff, and Leon Panetta, White House chief of staff—appear on NBC's Meet the Press *to discuss the United States intervention in Haiti in 1994. Acting as administration spokesmen is an important part of their jobs.*

Ronald Reagan was perceived as benevolent but distant by his aides. A passive administrator, he delegated operational responsibility for the White House Office to his senior aides. In theory presidential assistants reported to Reagan, but in practice they answered to his chief of staff. Presidents Bush and Clinton were more active managers, although each delegated the day-to-day responsibility of running the White House Office to others.

Belief System

Belief systems are shaped by the way in which individuals view themselves and others. Beliefs about how the world works provide a frame of reference for presidents, who must filter information, evaluate options, and choose a course of action that is consistent with their policy goals.[19]

At the outset of the Cuban missile crisis, for example, President Kennedy ruled out diplomatic and other nonmilitary responses and considered a fairly narrow range of military options. He believed that the presence of Soviet missiles in Cuba posed a major threat to national security and that the Soviet Union would remove the missiles only if forced to do so by the threat of American military sanctions. His decision to institute a blockade of Cuba rather than employ diplomatic means followed naturally from these premises. Similarly, President Reagan believed that the Soviet Union would negotiate an arms treaty only if it were convinced that the United States had a superior military force. His policy was to build up that force and to use the build-up as a negotiating chip.

The president's world view is especially likely to limit consideration of alternatives in a crisis. The North Korean invasion of South Korea in 1950, the domestic strife in Nicaragua in the mid 1980s, and the Iraqi invasion of Kuwait in 1990 were seen by presidents Truman, Reagan, and Bush, respectively, as threats to the United States and its interests, and they decided that American armed forces needed to be employed. In contrast, President Carter did not view the hostage crisis in Iran as a grave threat to American national security. Preoccupied with safeguarding the lives of those who had been taken prisoner, he spent a year trying to find an acceptable, diplomatic solution to the crisis.

In some situations, presidents do not have strongly held opinions that dictate a particular response. Under such circumstances they will follow opinion—their advisers', the public's, or both—rather than lead it.

THE POLITICS OF PRESIDENTIAL POLICY MAKING

The increasing number of presidential decisions that have major national and international consequences has inflated the importance of the president's character, managerial style, and beliefs. It has also directed attention to the president's changing policy role. The framers of the Constitution intended for presidents to have an impact on public policy, but they did not expect them to dominate the policy process. Yet that is precisely what happens much of the time. As we noted at the beginning of this chapter, the president's problem is that public expectations of presidential policy leadership, particularly in the domestic area, frequently exceed the president's ability to meet those expectations. Disappointment in presidential performance is often the result.

Although presidents have considerable personnel resources at their disposal— policy experts, political strategists, and support staff in the executive branch and the Executive Office—these advisers frequently disagree about what to do and how to do it. Nor does a public consensus exist on how most issues should be resolved. Moreover, the president's constitutional authority is extremely limited. These constraints make the formulation and management of public policy a time-consuming and difficult process. Presidents use diverse strategies and techniques to overcome these constraints to setting an agenda, influencing Congress, building public support, and implementing priorities.

Setting the Agenda

Presidential agendas used to be laundry lists of proposals designed to appeal to as broad a segment of electoral supporters as possible. Franklin Roosevelt's New Deal, Truman's Fair Deal, Kennedy's New Frontier, Johnson's Great Society, and Nixon's New Federalism programs fit this description. Beginning in the 1980s and continuing into the 1990s, however, policy agendas have been of necessity more limited, as scarce resources and continuing budget deficits have forced presidents to reduce the number and costs of their programs.

By limiting their proposals and establishing clear priorities, presidents try to set the pace and tone of public debate and hope to give the impression that they are in charge. Limiting priorities has several advantages for presidents. Not only does it enable them to concentrate their administrations' resources on the issues that are most important to them, but it also gives them leverage over the news media's agenda.

The disadvantage of focusing on a few policy proposals, on the other hand, is that issues that a sizable portion of the public believe are important may be ignored. And if the few designated priorities are not converted into public policy, as occurred during Clinton's first two years in office, the president's reputation may be damaged more than it would otherwise have been with a mixed record of successes and failures.

A policy agenda is not determined solely by the president. Congress contributes to it, as do individuals and groups outside the government. Moreover, it often takes several years for an idea to germinate, for policy to crystallize into a concrete proposal, and for sufficient support to be mobilized for it. Many of the ideas for Johnson's Great Society program originated during the Kennedy administration. Much of Reagan's legislative agenda was created during his 1976 and 1980 campaigns for the presidency.[20] Major policy proposals enacted during the Clinton administration (such as deficit reduction, gun control, multilateral trade agreements, even the motor-voter bill) had been considered by previous Republican administrations and Democratic Congresses.

Timing is another strategic concern of presidents intent on achieving their legislative policy goals. Presidential influence tends to decrease over time. As members of Congress position themselves for the next election, as bureaucrats begin to press their claims on political appointees, and as the opposition party begins to coalesce against the incumbent, achieving domestic policy goals may become more difficult for the president. This problem may become acute following a midterm election, as it did for Clinton in 1994. Presidents tend to be least influential at the end of their term, and particularly if it is their second term. During this period the phrase **lame duck** is often used to describe the incumbent. Like a duck that cannot fly because its wings have been clipped, presidents lose momentum and power as their administration draws to a close.

Presidents' reputations are built early and tend to outlast their ability to achieve policy successes. Thus presidents need to take advantage of their initial position of strength and move as quickly as possible after inauguration to achieve their most important programmatic goals. Jimmy Carter and Bill Clinton found this out the hard way. They used the early months of their administrations to develop their principal priorities. By the time those priorities had been converted into legislative proposals, Carter and Clinton had lost much of the momentum that presidents have at the beginning of their term, when public expectations are high and media criticism is low. In contrast, Ronald Reagan moved more quickly to achieve key components of his legislative agenda.

Influencing the Legislature

Presidents have to work hard at influencing Congress. Differing interests, constituencies, and even parties affect presidential and congressional perspectives and policy decisions. Key to success is a president's ability to focus and orchestrate the administration's major efforts, a task that requires the mobilization of cabinet heads, other executive officials, party leaders, and representatives of sympathetic interest groups behind presidential priorities. During the Reagan administration the White House Office assembled a legislative strategy group to accomplish this task. The Bush and Clinton administrations operated in a more ad hoc manner initially when dealing with Congress, although the Clinton administration improved its legislative coordination after Leon Panetta, a former member of Congress, took over as White House chief of staff.

The congressional leadership must also be involved in the development of legislative proposals. The nature of that involvement depends on the policy in question as well as on the political composition of Congress. Carter and Reagan relied on their own party's congressional leaders, bringing in the opposition leaders when necessary. Facing Democratic majorities in both houses of Congress, Bush adopted a bipartisan approach and dealt directly and regularly with the Democratic leadership. Clinton, when he inherited these majorities, initially adopted a partisan legislative strategy. Although this approach worked well in 1993, in the House of Representatives, where a cohesive majority can dominate, in the Senate the president's failure to consult with Republicans resulted in filibusters that killed or modified House-enacted legislation supported by the administration. Such setbacks combined with the results of the 1994 midterm election forced the president to alter his strategy, take centrist policy positions that were consistent with public opinion, and deal with the Republican leadership.

Regardless of their strategic approach, presidents must be personally involved in lobbying for their legislative goals. The extent of this involvement is often taken as a sign of how much importance is attached to a particular issue. There are a variety of ways for getting involved, ranging from requesting support to twisting arms to making deals. Lyndon Johnson was legendary for effective lobbying. He communicated constantly with members of Congress, attempting to persuade them of the merits of his proposals. Sometimes he accompanied his case with implicit promises or veiled threats. Clark Clifford, a cabinet secretary and personal adviser to Johnson, described the president's persuasive style in the following way:

> President Johnson calls in a senator and he says, "Joe . . . Does that law partner of yours still want to be a federal judge?"
>
> "Oh," he says, "he certainly does."
>
> "Well," he says, "you know I've been thinking about that lately and we're going to talk about that. But in the process of talking about that, I want to talk with you about the fact that I think we've got to increase our Social Security program."
>
> "Well, Mr. President, I've spoken against that."
>
> "Well, I know, Joe. But times have changed. And you think about it awhile. . . . Let a week go by, you call me."
>
> Joe calls him in a week and says, "Mr. President, I've been thinking about that and I think there's a lot of merit to your position. And I believe I can change on . . . Social Security. I want to come over and talk to you. And, incidentally, I talked to my partner, and he is just tickled to death."[21]

Despite such tactics, presidential arm-twisting may still be only marginally effective. Most presidents cannot dictate to Congress, nor can they easily reverse overwhelming sentiment on an issue. In fact, congruity between what Congress and presidents desire is often critical in determining the outcome of an issue. According to Charles O. Jones, congruity is likely to be most influenced by the election results (such as those of 1964 and 1980, when the president's party did relatively well in the congressional elections) or by significant events (such as the Kennedy assassination or the Watergate affair). Thus Johnson after the 1964 election and Reagan after 1980 benefited from a Congress that was responsive to their agendas, but Ford, Bush, and Clinton following the 1994 midterm election suffered at the hands of a Congress that had a different political agenda.

In recent times the Johnson and Reagan experiences have been the exception, not the rule. Since 1968, divided government, with different parties controlling Congress and the White House, or divisions within the majority party in one or both houses, has been the norm. These partisan divisions have reduced the president's effectiveness in dealing with Congress, although they have not eliminated it entirely.

Dealing with Congress is often difficult for the president, particularly when it is controlled by the other party. Here House Speaker Newt Gingrich and President Clinton seem jovial during their 1995–1996 budget talks. But the negotiations failed, and much of the government had to shut down for the second time in a month.

How effective can presidents be? According to political scientist George Edwards, presidents can influence Congress only at the margins.[22] In a closely divided legislature, however, affecting the votes of a few members of Congress can be crucial. One measure of how influential presidents actually are is the proportion of legislation on which members of Congress vote in accordance with the stated position of the president. Figure 13-6 graphs the support scores of presidents since 1953.

Presidential support increases when the president's party controls both houses of Congress. But partisan control is not the guarantee of legislative success that it is in parliamentary systems such as those of Great Britain and Israel, in which straight party voting is expected and prime ministers are selected because they control a partisan legislative majority. In the United States, presidents have to work to build and maintain majorities even within their own party. On the other hand, they may have more success in attracting opposition support than do executives in a parliamentary system. Clinton received more support from Republicans than Democrats in the votes on two free trade initiatives, the North American Free Trade Agreement (NAFTA) and the General Agreement on Tariffs and Trade (GATT), in 1993 and 1994, respectively.

Although presidential influence varies with the issue, presidents generally have had more success on foreign policy issues than on domestic ones. This success, which was particularly evident in the period from the end of World War II to the Vietnam War, led some political scientists to conclude that there were actually two presidencies: one in foreign affairs and one in domestic policy.[23] Today the distinction between foreign and domestic policies is less clearcut. Foreign policy issues have a greater impact on domestic policy than they did in earlier decades, and there-

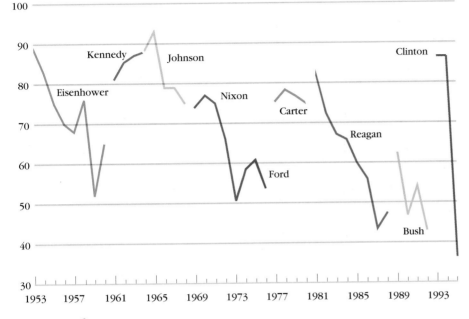

Percent

FIGURE 13-6
Presidential success in Congress.

SOURCE: *Congressional Quarterly Weekly Report*, January 27, 1996, 239.

fore, Congress has become more interested and involved in foreign policy matters. As a consequence, presidents can no longer be assured that their foreign policy initiatives will always prevail. They must mobilize support for them much as they do in the domestic arena.

Although in normal times presidents cannot impose legislation on Congress, by exercising a veto they usually can prevent legislation that they do not like from becoming law. The veto is not absolute, but it is a potent weapon. A very low percentage of all presidential vetoes have been overridden (see Table 12-4 on page 440). Additionally, Congress has now granted the president a line-item veto for appropriations bills. This legislation, if upheld by the courts, would allow the president to veto individual items in spending bills. The items could be restored by Congress but would then be subject to a regular veto and the regular override requirement of a two-thirds vote in both houses. (See the Constitutional Conflict box on page 468.)

The threat of exercising the veto power is frequently used to try to get Congress to modify a proposal. To make a veto threat stick, however, the president must be prepared to exercise it and must have reason to believe that it will be sustained. George Bush and Bill Clinton have both used the veto effectively as a tactic for dealing with congressional majorities of the opposite party. They indicated how far they were willing to go on legislative proposals, suggested what they were prepared to veto, and sustained their threat by doing so. Both however, suffered veto overrides.

Clinton's most effective use of the veto occurred during his budget battle with the Republican Congress in 1995–1996. First he vetoed a comprehensive budget reconciliation bill in which the Republicans wished to impose greater spending and tax cuts than the president wanted. He then vetoed several appropriations bills that contained what he considered insufficient funding for particular departments and

THE WHITE HOUSE E-MAIL CONTROVERSY

During the Watergate scandal in the early 1970s, the most incriminating evidence implicating President Nixon in a coverup of the crime came from the tapes of Oval Office conversations that he had secretly made. Nixon released the tapes only after a legal battle in which the Supreme Court ordered him to do so. Two decades later, with advances in technology, electronic records of White House communications again became the subject of legal controversy over a president's (and others') right of privacy.

During the Reagan administration, the new White House e-mail system became the principal means by which national security staffer Lt. Col. Oliver North communicated with his superior, Adm. John Poindexter, during the period when United States funds obtained from the sale of arms to Iran were being diverted to the contra rebels in Nicaragua. When the sale and diversion became public, North and Poindexter deleted most of their e-mail correspondence to each other. However, their messages were subsequently retrieved from a back-up system. Both the independent counsel and the congressional commission that investigated the Iran-contra affair cited these messages as evidence of the complicity of presidential staff in the illegal transaction.

As the Reagan presidency was drawing to a close, the administration sought to destroy all its e-mail tapes and hard drives that were not required for the trials of the individuals who were allegedly involved in the Iran-contra affair. However, an organization called the National Security Archive filed a Freedom of Information Act request for the tapes and drives and then went to court to prevent their destruction.

In defending its attempt to destroy the tapes and drives, the Reagan administration argued that clearing the files was part of the normal transition process in which all official records were sent to the National Archives to become part of the outgoing president's official library and nonofficial files and papers were thrown out so that the new president could start with a clean slate. Not only did the administration want to protect the privacy of its own internal communications, some of which if revealed might be embarrassing for those who sent them, but it wanted to protect the ability of future White House officials to communicate honestly and candidly with one another. It argued that e-mail was more like telephone and direct person-to-person conversations, which were not generally recorded and preserved.

The court issued a temporary restraining order, preventing the Reagan White House from destroying its e-mail prior to a full judicial consideration of the issue. No decision was rendered during the Bush administration, however, so when it left office the same scenario repeated itself. The National Security Archive again went to court to request that Bush's e-mail be included in the case. Although Judge Charles Richey of the U.S. District Court concurred, the Bush administration still ordered the National Archives to remove but not destroy all computer tapes prior to the beginning of the Clinton administration. In fact, the administration worked out a deal with the chief archivist, Don W. Wilson, that gave Bush custody over the tapes. Judge Richey subsequently ruled that this agreement was invalid and that e-mail was indeed part of the official White House records.

The Clinton administration, taking the Reagan-Bush position on the issue, appealed the decision. However, a unanimous court of appeals, chaired by Judge Abner Mikva, upheld the lower court's ruling, thereby resolving the judicial issue.

Critics of the decision see it as impeding candid communications, even distorting the historical record by discouraging all forms of written communication; moreover, they argue that it is potentially harmful to national security. Proponents, on the other hand, believe these fears are overblown. They contend that sufficient safeguards already exist to protect privacy, classified information, and predecisional deliberative records and that considering e-mail part of the public record will help to hold public officials accountable as in the Iran-contra affair.[1]

[1]Current law prevents classified information from becoming public for twelve years after an administration leaves office; other predecisional deliberative records are protected for five years.

SOURCE: Tom Blanton, ed., *White House E-Mail* (New York: New Press, 1995).

agencies. Because of the failure of Congress and the president to agree on these appropriations, much of the government was forced to shut down twice, suspending many services in the process. The public blamed the Republicans more than Clinton for the shutdowns, creating pressure on them to compromise with the president.

Building Public Support

Because public backing contributes to the president's success in Congress, presidents devote much time and effort to shaping public opinion. The White House Office works hard to promote a favorable image and public response by influencing the form, content, and timing of information that flows from the government. It provides a host of services for the media, from information packets to daily briefings to interviews and photo opportunities. These efforts to shape news coverage of the president can succeed if the media are primarily dependent on material supplied by the White House.

The pomp and ceremony of the presidency also help the president. The public aspects of the institution receive extensive coverage and enhance the stature of the person who occupies the Oval Office. Recognizing this effect, presidents go public more now than in the past.

When the peace agreement between Israel and the Palestine Liberation Organization seemed threatened by violent clashes in the fall of 1996, President Clinton persuaded PLO leader Yassir Arafat (left) *and Israeli prime minister Benjamin Netanyahu* (right) *to come to Washington to try to defuse the crisis. Such images of the president as international peacemaker often boost public support for his administration. In fact, Clinton's Republican opponent in the 1996 presidential election, Robert Dole, charged that this "photo-op" was the primary motive behind the invitation—an accusation indignantly denied by the White House.*

Jimmy Carter is a good example of a president who used symbolism to boost his popularity. In the aftermath of Watergate, he played down the grandeur of office: he walked down Pennsylvania Avenue following his inauguration, wore a sweater when he delivered his first address to the nation, and dispensed with the playing of "Hail to the Chief" at public ceremonies. But when his popularity declined, he began dressing more formally and reinstated "Hail to the Chief." Other examples of presidents using ceremony to enhance their public image include Reagan's speech at the site of the D-Day invasion that was the turning point of World War II, Bush's Thanksgiving dinner with the troops in Saudi Arabia during the buildup to the Persian Gulf War in 1990, Clinton's presiding over the signing of the agreements between Israel and the Palestine Liberation Organization in 1993 and 1995, his involvement in the Bosnian peace accord in 1995, and his public extensions of empathy to victims of terrorism and natural disasters.

Presidents can also be their own best boosters. By virtue of their position, they command attention, and thus they have often resorted to national addresses to enhance their public support. Franklin D. Roosevelt and Reagan were extremely successful at building and maintaining loyal followings through direct public appeals. Roosevelt's "fireside chats" calmed a jittery nation during the Great Depression and World War II; similarly, Reagan's White House addresses, particularly during his first term in office, buoyed the spirits of a people upset by a stagnant and inflated economy.

Roosevelt's and Reagan's successes stemmed from their communication skills. Roosevelt had a reassuring tone that was well suited to radio, and Reagan, an experienced actor, talked in a soft but earnest voice to his television audience. In a different way, John F. Kennedy's quick wit and pleasant appearance also projected a favorable image. In contrast, Jimmy Carter's low, monotonous singsong, Gerald Ford's and George Bush's inarticulateness, and Lyndon Johnson's and Richard Nixon's unease, particularly before a television camera, adversely affected their ability to persuade the public. Clinton's knowledge of the issues, his interactive skills, and his crowd-pleasing talents have been an asset to his presidency. But he also has tended to talk too frequently, for too long, and in too much detail—to think out loud—all of which have reduced the "presidential" impact of his remarks.

One device that some presidents have used successfully to demonstrate their mastery of the issues and to build support for their programs is the press conference. Roosevelt, Kennedy, Carter, Bush, and Clinton have done well in these forums, where their extensive knowledge about policy and personnel have stood them in good stead with the White House reporters. Ronald Reagan fared less well. Lacking detailed information, he was unable to answer questions as accurately and fully as the press demanded. The need for extensive preparation and the fear of making embarrassing mistakes discouraged him from holding many press conferences. Even though Clinton's performances at press conferences have been favorably evaluated, he also has not held many prime-time press conferences, preferring the more congenial public format of a town meeting with average citizens to the more adversarial confrontation with the Washington press corps.

The extensive efforts by the White House to secure favorable media coverage are a direct response to the situation in which presidents often find themselves. The general public is often divided, uninterested, and uninvolved; but organized groups, political parties, and public officials are not shy about taking stands and promoting their positions. Thus the president has to take his communicator-in-chief role seriously and try to build consensus both inside and outside the government.

Every president has a different style, which may reflect political priorities as well as personal preferences. Emphasizing a down-to-earth manner in contrast to the regal style of Presidents Johnson and Nixon, Jimmy Carter and his wife, Rosalynn, walked hand in hand down Pennsylvania Avenue following his inauguration in 1977. In leather and Stetsons, Ronald Reagan and his wife, Nancy, embodied the mythic West in their horseback rides on their California ranch. George Bush, determined to show he would not be held prisoner in the White House during the Persian Gulf crisis as Carter had been during the Iranian hostage crisis, enjoyed some typically hectic leisure in 1990 on his motorboat off the Maine coast. And Bill Clinton distanced himself from the privileged background and preppy tastes of Bush by stopping in at McDonald's on his morning jogs—often leaving with both hands full.

Implementing Priorities in the Executive Branch

Implementation is the final stage in the policy process. Here the president must deal primarily with officials in the executive branch. Traditionally presidents have not gotten deeply involved in the details of implementation because of the size of the bureaucracy, time constraints, and their limited resources for affecting executive-branch decisions. However, with the increased attention given to management issues such as bureaucratic red tape, federal contracting, nonperformance of services, and allegations of mismanagement, the efficient operation of government has become a salient concern for every administration.

The easiest and most direct way for presidents to exercise control over policy implementation is to have White House aides communicate their wishes to those in the departments and agencies who are responsible for implementing them. In most cases a telephone call or White House meeting will suffice. Occasionally an executive order may be necessary.

The president can also oversee the regulations that departments and agencies issue to implement legislation. President Carter standardized procedures for issuing these regulations, and President Reagan created the division in the Office of Management and Budget that reviews them. President Clinton has modified that review process.

Presidents also have indirect means of affecting executive-branch decision making. They have some discretion to reorganize the executive branch, subject to congressional approval, and can use the annual budget process as a means of establishing new priorities, reaffirming existing ones, and rewarding or penalizing particular departments and agencies. However, the contrast in this regard between the American president and the heads of other governments is dramatic. The British prime minister and the French president, for example, have complete discretion in filling executive appointments and making structural changes. To a lesser extent, the Italian and Japanese prime ministers exercise this power as well.

A significant part of the president's management problem is rooted in the sharing of powers, which creates multiple allegiances for executive branch agencies; they must be sensitive both to the interests of Congress and to those of the presidency. Part of the difficulty also stems from a civil service system based on merit and not partisanship. Finally, the development of an outside clientele for the departments and agencies has also eroded the president's influence. Even political appointees must be sensitive to the interests and needs of their department's constituency. When those interests and needs are at odds with the president's, political appointees face a dilemma. If they are to maintain credibility with the clients they serve, they must be advocates for them; but over time this advocacy may strain their relationship with the president.

Exercising Leadership

The problems that presidents encounter in their efforts to make and implement public policy are the consequences of multiple pressures that affect all aspects of presidential decision making. In a pluralistic society in which political actors and institutions are responsive to their clienteles, politics is likely to occur within and between institutions of government, making it hard for any one of them to dominate the policy-making process.

This situation is precisely what the framers desired and the Constitution intended. It places the burden on the advocates of change: it is they who must form coalitions and gain the support of those who share power. This burden of consensus building often falls on the president's shoulders, and it is a heavy one. Reflecting on his first two years in office, Clinton commented: "I was a prime minister, not a president. I got caught up in the parliamentary aspect of the presidency and missed the leadership, the bully pulpit function which is so critical."[24]

The dilemma, as we explained at the beginning of this chapter, is the gap that often exists between public expectations and presidential performance. Sometimes the gap can be bridged by the exercise of strong political leadership. But even if the president does try to exercise that leadership, even if the president is sensitive to the politics of the presidency, success is not guaranteed. Presidents still must contend with factors beyond their personal and institutional control; they are still hostage to events. In the end, their reaction to events, what they say and do when conditions are not favorable, is the true test of their leadership skills. In good times it is harder to exercise these skills; presidents tend to merely preside over the government. In bad times power flows to them; they may prevail.

SUMMARY

The presidency is a political institution. It operates within a political environment that requires the skillful exercise of presidential power. Politics generates the demands and pressures on the president, the issues and conflicts that need to be resolved, and the resources that can be utilized in that resolution. In this sense, the politics of the presidency creates both challenges and opportunities; how presidents handle them becomes in large measure the criterion by which their performance in office and place in history are evaluated.

Political struggles have beset the presidency since its creation. In establishing the nature of the office, the mode of selection, and the extent and limits of its powers, the framers juxtaposed in Article II the need for energy with the desire for safety, the need for flexibility with the desire for accountability, and the need for dispatch with the desire for consensus.

In empowering the president with executive responsibilities the framers gave the institution a broad grant of authority, to be checked by the requirement for joint institutional involvement in the exercise of most of those powers. Thus the president could nominate subject to the advice and consent of the Senate; subsequently the president was given the right to remove political appointees in the executive branch. As chief executive the president could direct subordinates through *executive orders* and *executive memoranda*, but Congress retained the authority to structure the executive branch as well as authorize its programs and appropriate funds for them. The president was also given some legislative duties and responsibilities, including the right to recommend and the power to veto. But Congress has the last word. The president can also affect the judiciary through the nomination of judges, litigation by the government, and the issuance of pardons, clemency, and amnesty for those convicted or accused of federal crimes.

The president's limited constitutional authority but growing roles and responsibilities have forced those who have occupied the Oval Office to utilize their political skills to compensate for their lack of formal powers. In doing so, they have had to bargain and cajole with others in the government and build support outside of it by *going public*. How they perform these tasks affects their reputation and prestige, which impact on their ability to achieve their policy goals.

The institutional resources of the presidency contribute to its exercise of power. These resources include the *cabinet* and the *Executive Office of the President*, which together function to maximize presidential information, liaison, and influence. Of these units those closest to the president, the *White House Office* and the *Office of Management and Budget*, tend to be most critical to the president's successful exercise of power.

The vice presidency has also increased in esteem and influence in the contemporary period. Not only have some vice presidents been important presidential advisers, but they have also performed a variety of political, diplomatic, and administrative functions for the administration—with, of course, the encouragement of the president. The role of the president's spouse has also been enhanced, but not without controversy. Much of this controversy grows out of the fact that whereas the vice president is elected, the spouse is not.

How presidents interact with others, how they approach their job, and how flexible they are all depend to a large extent on their personality. In examining the impact of personality on performance in office, James David Barber has advanced a psychological model in which he describes job performance in terms of level of activity (active or passive) and ability to relate to others (positive or negative). Barber considers the active-positive type best suited to the presidency. Critics claim that Barber's categories are simplistic and too general to be useful. Nevertheless, Barber has focused attention on the importance of presidential personality.

Presidents have two basic roles: head of government and head of state. Most attention is focused on the role of head of government. Key to presidents' success in this role is their ability to set and promote a domestic policy agenda, mobilize support for it, and oversee its implementation. These are not easy tasks, because the problems are complex, the time frames for fixing them are usually short, and the resources at the president's disposal are limited. But the real difficulty for presidents is getting others with different goals, different perspectives, different time frames, and different constituencies to follow their lead. This requires great skill in defining the issue, shaping the political environment, selling a course of action to the American people, and bargaining with other public officials.

Leading the country in the international arena involves many of the same skills. However, there is a greater tendency to defer to the president's lead in foreign affairs, especially in times of crisis. The presidency was designed for quick and decisive action in emergencies, but not in situations in which policy making can be slower and more deliberative.

KEY TERMS

senatorial courtesy
executive memorandum
executive order
executive agreement
going public

cabinet
Executive Office of the President
Office of Management and Budget
central clearance process
enrolled bill process

regulatory review
White House Office
lame duck

RESOURCES

SCHOLARLY STUDIES

Barber, James David. *The Presidential Character.* 5th ed. Englewood Cliffs, N.J.: Prentice-Hall, 1996. A pioneering but controversial study of the impact of personality on performance in office. Short, psychologically oriented chapters on individual presidents make for interesting reading and speculative interpretations.

Campbell, Colin, and Bert A. Rockman, eds. *The Clinton Presidency: First Appraisals.* Chatham, N.J.: Chatham House, 1996. A critical midterm evaluation of Clinton's first term by a group of prominent presidency watchers.

Edwards, George C., III. *At the Margins: Presidential Leadership of Congress.* New Haven: Yale University Press, 1990. A quantitative analysis of congressional roll call votes aimed at measuring presidential influence in Congress.

Edwards, George C., III, and Stephen J. Wayne. *Presidential Leadership.* 4th ed. New York: St. Martin's Press, 1997. A comprehensive text that synthesizes the principal political science literature on and knowledge about the presidency.

Jones, Charles O. *The Presidency in a Separated System.* Washington, D.C.: Brookings Institution, 1994. Assesses the presidency within the framework of the constitutional system of separate institutions competing for shared powers.

Kernell, Samuel. *Going Public.* 2d ed. Washington, D.C.: Congressional Quarterly, 1993. Argues effectively that presidents need to adopt a public strategy to achieve their policy objectives.

Nelson, Michael. *The Presidency and the Political*

System. 4th ed. Washington, D.C.: Congressional Quarterly, 1994. An excellent collection of readings on multiple aspects of the contemporary presidency.

Neustadt, Richard E. *Presidential Power and the Modern President.* New York: Free Press, 1990. The classic study, originally published in 1960, of the president's basic leadership dilemma: how to exert influence within a highly decentralized political system in normal times. To this work, Neustadt has added his reflections in chapters dealing with presidents Kennedy through Carter.

Skowronek, Stephen. *The Politics Presidents Make.* Cambridge, Mass.: Belknap Press, 1993. An intellectually sophisticated study of leadership patterns in the presidency from John Adams to George Bush.

LEISURE READING

Birnbaum, Jeffrey. *The Madhouse.* New York: Times Books, 1996. A discussion of the trials and tribulations of White House staffers in the Clinton administration.

Drew, Elizabeth. *On the Edge: The Clinton Presidency.* New York: Simon and Schuster, 1994. A journalist's view of the operation of the Clinton administration during its first year in office.

Drew, Elizabeth. *Showdown: The Struggle Between the Gingrich Congress and the Clinton White House.* New York: Simon and Schuster, 1996. Chronicles the confrontation between Congress and the presidency in 1995–1996 when the Republicans tried to impose major spending and tax cuts and Clinton opposed them.

Goodwin, Doris K. *Lyndon Johnson and the American Dream.* New York: St. Martin's Press, 1991. A psychologically oriented biography by a person who was very close to President Johnson during his last year in office.

Reedy, George. *The Twilight of the Presidency.* New York: New American Library, 1987. A discussion of the dangers that presidents should avoid: a swelled head, overzealous loyal assistants, and a rarefied and unreal atmosphere for decision making.

Woodward, Bob. *The Agenda: Inside the Clinton White House.* New York: Simon and Schuster, 1994. An inside account of the political pressures on the formation of economic policy in the first six months of the Clinton administration.

Woodward, Bob, and Carl Bernstein. *The Final Days.* New York: Simon and Schuster, 1989. A gripping account of a damaged presidency—Richard Nixon's last days in office.

PRIMARY SOURCES

Levy, Leonard W., and Louis Fisher, eds. *Encyclopedia of the American Presidency.* New York: Simon and Schuster, 1994. An encyclopedia of short articles about the presidency, written by leading scholars.

Nelson, Michael, ed. *Guide to the Presidency.* Washington, D.C.: Congressional Quarterly, 1989. A collection of brief biographies and institutional histories, as well as descriptions of many facets of the contemporary presidency.

Office of Management and Budget, Executive Office of the President, Washington, DC 20501; phone (202) 395-3000, fax (202) 395-3888, e-mail http://www.whitehouse.gov/whitehouse/eop/html/other/omb.html Distributes an annual budget for the United States government and other documents of interest to students of the presidency.

Weekly Compilation of Presidential Documents. Washington, D.C.: U.S. Government Printing Office. A selective compilation of the official presidency: schedules, speeches, news conferences, executive orders, presidential proclamations, nominations, appointments, and communiqués to foreign heads of state.

The White House, 1600 Pennsylvania Avenue, N.W., Washington, DC 20500; phone (202) 456-1414, fax (202) 456-2461, e-mail president @ whitehouse. gov:http:/www.whitehouse.gov Provides information and press releases about the president and his programs.

ORGANIZATIONS

Center for the Study of the Presidency, 208 East 75th Street, New York, NY 10021; phone (212) 249-1200, fax (212) 628-9503. Publishes the journal *Presidential Studies Quarterly* and occasional books; organizes annual conferences on the presidency.

White Burkett Miller Center of Public Affairs, University of Virginia, Charlottesville, VA 22905; phone (804) 924-7236, fax (804) 982-2739, e-mail: kwt8b@virginia.edu Holds seminars and publishes monographs and articles on the contemporary presidency.

The Executive Bureaucracy

O n April 19, 1995, Americans were horrified by sights of devastation from the terrorist bombing of the Alfred P. Murrah Federal Building in Oklahoma City. But not many thought of this awful attack as having much to do with politics. In fact, it did—in many ways.

After weeks of dangerous digging, it was determined that 167 people had died in the rubble. Some of these were children in a day-care center. Many were citizens tending to their business with the Social Security Administration, the Department of Transportation, or one of the twelve other federal agencies and departments that had offices in the building. Many more were employees in these offices—bureaucrats—doing their jobs.

One of those employees was Julie Welch. Twenty-three years old and a recent graduate of Marquette University, Welch was starting her career as an interpreter for the Social Security Administration, helping Spanish-speaking citizens in their dealings with the federal government. At her funeral the following week, her friends noted her compassion for people less fortunate than she was and her pleasure at having found a job that allowed her to help them.[1]

Over the next few months, investigators began trying to put together the story behind the bombing. According to federal indictments, it was the work of several men upset with the actions of the Federal Bureau of Investigation (FBI) and the Bureau of Alcohol, Tobacco, and Firearms (ATF). The indictments alleged that the perpetrators particularly resented the bureaus' 1993 raid on the Texas compound of the Branch Davidian religious sect, which resulted in dozens of deaths, and the 1992 attack on the Idaho home of white separatist Randy Weaver, in which ATF agents shot and killed Weaver's wife.

Whether or not it was the target of the Oklahoma City bombing, the ATF has long been a controversial federal agency. Its mission is to regulate traffic in three commodities—alcohol, tobacco, and guns—that are widely possessed in America, sometimes legally, sometimes not. Often, ATF agents must track and arrest citizens who are breaking laws that many Americans dislike or routinely disobey. Moreover, these citizens are often violent and heavily armed criminals who would rather shoot than surrender.

So ATF agents are often in the spotlight and often criticized for heavy-handedness and overreaction. In fact, in the months that followed the Oklahoma City bombing, several congressional committees conducted investigations of the ATF and FBI to determine whether their actions in the Texas and Idaho incidents had violated the law or appropriate administrative procedure.

In a complex government like America's, there is a constant tension between the need to delegate authority to executive agencies to implement the law and the need to hold those agencies accountable for their exercise of that authority. Americans often disagree about whether administrative agencies perform well or badly. Some want to give agencies more latitude to do their jobs; others want tighter restraints to prevent them from exceeding their proper authority. Sometimes those debates occur in elections where some candidates call for more active federal regulation and others call for less regulation altogether. Often the debates take place in Congress, in the legislative and oversight processes. And sometimes, as perhaps in Oklahoma City, there is no debate at all—only wanton acts of violence seeking to make a political point. Politics, the mundane politics of bureaucracy, comes in many forms: some elevated and eloquent, some secretive and cruel.

The federal bureaucracy is the part of government that implements decisions made by the president, Congress, and the federal courts. Many people believe that bureaucracies are complex, apolitical, and controlled by stringent rules and procedures. That is only partially true. The federal bureaucracy is certainly complex, and its activities are guided by a mystifying array of rules, but it is anything but apolitical.

The administrative offices and the people who staff them are important political actors. Having their own policy preferences and prejudices, they fight to protect and expand their own vision of what is best for the country. They are not merely neutral implementers of decisions made elsewhere in the political process; they are at the center of that process, involved in the struggles among individuals, interest groups, and government institutions to affect decisions. One cannot understand the administration of public policy without acknowledging its fundamental political character. Politics is as common an occurrence and as profound a force in the halls and offices of federal agencies as it is anywhere else in government.

When you hear the word "bureaucrat," what images come to mind? An overweight middle-aged man sitting at a desk shuffling papers from one pile to another, or an air traffic controller bringing planes in through an ice storm? A curt woman peering out through a barred window to announce that the deadline for your application was yesterday, or a young microbiologist doing AIDS research? An anonymous person with an ink pad and stamp who sends you the wrong tax forms, or a diplomat held hostage in a small African nation?

The word "bureaucrat" is loosely used to describe career government employees. It often brings to mind a bored and rigid person interested only in collecting a paycheck and putting in the time to get a lucrative pension. But among the millions of career government employees, many have demanding, important, and interesting jobs, and most enjoy their work and do it skillfully (see the profile of Robert Frasure on page 523).

This chapter looks at American public servants, the work they do, and the political environment they do it in. The discussion begins with the size and shape of the contemporary executive branch, how it is structured and staffed. Then the chapter examines the roles that bureaucratic agencies play in the policy-making process. It concludes by probing the issue of bureaucratic accountability.

THE ORGANIZATION OF THE FEDERAL BUREAUCRACY

Bureaucracy is a system for carrying on the business of an organization by means of a clear hierarchy of authority and an emphasis on fixed routines. Bureaucracies have jurisdictions established by law or administrative rules, and their employees are specialists who are trained to perform the specific tasks assigned to them and who maintain written records of their decisions and activities. The point of bureaucracies is to achieve objectivity, precision, efficiency, continuity, consistency, and fairness.

Bureaucracies have been around for most of the history of human civilization. The early Catholic Church, ancient China, and the Roman Empire all relied on bureaucratic principles of organization. Not until the nineteenth century, however, as industrialization occurred and governments became more active in social and economic affairs, did bureaucracy become a prominent organizational system.

Except for the Post Office Department, the administrative agencies of the United States government were few in number and small in size until the second half of the nineteenth century. (See the box on pages 518–519.) Their growth began to accelerate after the Civil War as the population and the range of federal activities expanded. Nevertheless, the federal bureaucracy remained a relatively small enterprise until the onset of the Great Depression and World War II. Today the executive branch is the largest component of the federal government. Its civilian employees number 3 million; its military employees, 1.4 million; and there are more than a hundred separate organizational units. Federal employees include not only clerks, soldiers, and letter carriers but also physicians, attorneys, physicists, historians, economists, accountants, and pharmacists. In size and complexity the federal executive branch is an entity without peer in American society.

Types of Organizational Structures

The federal bureaucracy is composed of many kinds of organizations. Because the labels attached to particular units do not always precisely define their functions or levels of authority, its structure is a little difficult to comprehend at first. Sometimes an "agency," a "bureau," and an "office" are indistinguishable from one another. Some agencies are subunits of cabinet departments, and others are independent from those departments. A bureau may be a small, barely visible unit like the Bureau of Quality Control in the Health Care Financing Administration, or it may be relatively large and highly visible, like the FBI.

Politics is responsible for this apparent confusion, because the creation of bureaucratic organizations is itself a political process. What a unit is called, where it is placed in the executive branch, the degree of authority it is granted, and the qualifications established for its leaders are all political decisions. They reflect the balance of political forces existing at the time the unit was created. Because the balance of political forces changes over time, units created in one period often differ from units created in another.

Figure 14-1 shows the organizational structure of the entire federal government. Figure 14-2 shows the structure of a single cabinet department, the Department of Agriculture.

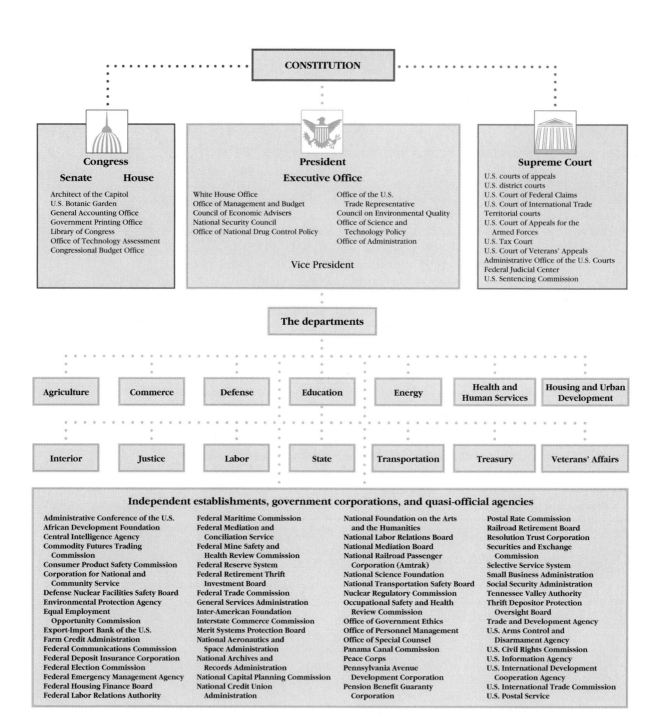

FIGURE 14-1

The government of the United States.

SOURCE: *United States Government Manual, 1995/96* (Washington, D.C.: Government Printing Office, 1995), 22.

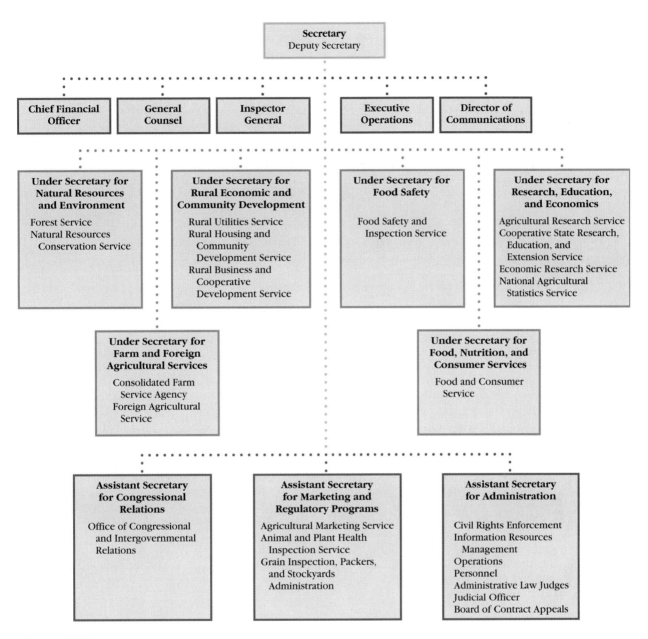

FIGURE 14-2
The Department of Agriculture.

SOURCE: *United States Government Manual, 1995/96* (Washington, D.C.: Government Printing Office, 1995), 113.

Departments   The major operating units of the federal government are **depart-ments**. There are fourteen of them, each an aggregate of many related functions. The head of a department—the secretary or, in the case of the Justice Department, the attorney general—is a member of the president's cabinet. The number of depart-ments is not fixed. In the late 1970s two new ones were added: the Department of Education and the Department of Energy. In 1988 the Veterans Administration, an independent agency, was replaced with the Department of Veterans' Affairs.

BUREAUCRACY'S BEGINNINGS: SMALL AND SWAMPY

The framers of the United States Constitution spent little of their time debating, or even thinking about, the organization and operation of the executive branch. Though Alexander Hamilton later wrote in *The Federalist* papers that "the true test of a good government is its aptitude and tendency to produce a good administration," he and his colleagues approved a Constitution that made no mention of any cabinet departments or government agencies. Nor did it provide for a civil service or envision the need for economic regulation or administrative rule making. Virtually all the details of administration were left to the creation of future presidents and Congresses.

By 1802, thirteen years after George Washington's first inauguration and two years after the federal government moved permanently to the new capital in the District of Columbia, an infant bureaucracy had begun to take shape. Only three public buildings then stood in the District, each still in some stage of construction: the executive mansion (later to be called the White House), the Treasury Department, and the Capitol. Total employment of the federal government was less than 10,000, of whom almost 6,500 were uniformed members of the Army, Navy, and Marine Corps.

The 2,900 civilian employees of the government were concentrated in the Treasury and the Post Office. Twelve hundred of them were collectors of revenue. Since customs duties were then the principal source of federal revenues, most of the collectors were located in port cities along the Atlantic coast. Almost a thousand deputy postmasters were likewise scattered among the population operating local post offices.

In Washington itself, the bureaucratic presence was tiny. The Treasury employed 89 people in the capital, the State Department 9, and the Attorney General (there was not yet a Justice Department) less than two dozen. A total of 30 people worked in Washington for the War and Navy Departments (separate then, nearly

a century and a half before the creation of the modern Department of Defense). At the United States Mint, where all the money for the new government was manufactured, 13 people were employed. And the Commissioner of Patents toiled alone.

On Capitol Hill there were 152 people on the federal payroll, a figure that included all the senators and representatives and the vice president as well as their clerks and ancillary personnel. The Supreme Court had 7 employees: the 6 justices and the 1 clerk they shared during the two months out of each year that the court was in session. As for the presidency, it was little more than the president himself. President Jefferson maintained one personal secretary, whom he paid from the appropriation for the maintenance of the executive mansion.

The infant bureaucracy was so small because the functions of the federal government were so limited. More than 90 percent of federal personnel were employed in two functions: collecting revenues and providing for the national defense. Significantly more people were engaged in making law than in enforcing it, very much the opposite of current ratios.

Except for delivering the mail, the federal government at the beginning of the nineteenth century provided few services for the people it served. Americans today count on their national government to manage a national pension system, support the poor and disabled, regulate businesses, fund education, build roads and airports, conduct scientific research, supervise public health, send rockets into space, and perform hundreds of other functions that could not even have been imagined when a tiny band of public servants moved their headquarters to a swampy site at the junction of the Anacostia and Potomac rivers nearly two centuries ago.

SOURCE: James Sterling Young, *The Washington Community, 1800–1828* (New York: Columbia University Press, 1966). Reprinted with permission of the publisher.

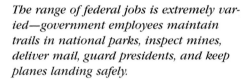

The range of federal jobs is extremely varied—government employees maintain trails in national parks, inspect mines, deliver mail, guard presidents, and keep planes landing safely.

Agencies   In general, an **agency** is responsible for a narrower set of functions than a department. Some agencies exist within departments, and some are independent. The Social Security Administration, a very large agency, is part of the Department of Health and Human Services. The Coast Guard, another agency, is located in the Department of Transportation in peacetime and in the Department of Defense in wartime. (Notice that agencies do not necessarily have the word "agency" in their name.) The General Services Administration and the United States Information Agency are independent agencies; they are not components of any of the departments.

Although an agency's jurisdiction is likely to be narrower than a department's, some agencies spend more money and employ more people than some departments do. For example, the National Aeronautics and Space Administration is an independent agency that had an annual budget of more than $14 billion for fiscal year 1996. The State Department had an annual budget of $5 billion in the same year.

Bureaus, offices, administrations, services The subunits of agencies and departments have a variety of names, none denoting a set of consistent, distinguishable characteristics. In the Department of Agriculture, for instance, the Food and Nutrition Service, the Packers and Stockyards Administration, and the World Agricultural Outlook Board are all located at roughly the same level in the hierarchy. The differences in their titles do not indicate significant differences in their authority or functions.

Bureaus and other subunits are the specialized operating units of the government. Their jurisdictions are defined by the programs Congress has assigned to them and tend to be quite specific. Although many of these units may exist within the same department, they do not necessarily work closely together. Often, in fact, they engage in intense political competition for larger budgets and for a dominant role in determining policies that affect the groups they serve. The Army and the Marine Corps, for example, have often been at odds over which of them ought to have jurisdiction over land warfare, each wanting a larger share of responsibility—and of resources.

Independent regulatory commissions Each **independent regulatory commission** is independent of any department and to some extent is independent of presidential control. Each is run by a group of commissioners and has both quasi-legislative and quasi-judicial authority—that is, it can issue rules and regulations and can adjudicate disputes and issue rulings. The principal purpose of the regulatory commissions is to regulate commerce and trade in an assigned area of jurisdiction. For example, the Securities and Exchange Commission (SEC) regulates the stock markets, and the Federal Communications Commission (FCC) regulates telephones and the use of the public airwaves for radio and television broadcasting.

Currently there are about a dozen independent regulatory commissions. Each has at least five commissioners, who serve for fixed but staggered terms. The president is permitted to make appointments only as vacancies occur and thus does not have the same degree of control over personnel in these units as over employees in the agencies and departments.

Government corporations The federal government owns, in whole or in part, a variety of economic enterprises. Most of these are operated as **government corporations**,[2] a form of ownership that is supposed to protect the enterprises against political meddling and encourage them to use businesslike and efficient methods of operation. Most of the government corporations have a board of directors whose members are appointed by the president, usually for long and staggered terms that make it difficult for any single president to radically change the board's composition. Nevertheless, politics sometimes influences the selection of directors of government corporations, as well as the corporations' decisions and activities. For example, President Reagan appointed several people with strong conservative views to the board of the Corporation for Public Broadcasting.

Most of the corporations can operate their own personnel systems, borrow money, sell stock, even operate at a profit. Some, like the Federal Deposit Insurance Corporation (FDIC) and the Tennessee Valley Authority (TVA), are totally independent. Others fall within a department's jurisdiction, like the Commodity Credit Corporation in the Department of Agriculture.

Boards, committees, commissions, advisory committees In addition to the major structural entities already identified, the federal government contains a great many units of lesser significance. Some, like the Committee for the Implementation of Textile Agreements, have very narrow functions; others, like the Federal Financing Bank Advisory Council, provide advice to other agencies. Few of these advisory committees have any significant impact on public policy. Rather, many of them serve primarily as places where presidents can make appointments to reward individuals for their political support. Hundreds of advisory committees are located throughout the federal government. Most of the people who serve on them work for the federal government for only a few days each year and regard their appointments as honorific.[3]

Staffing the Bureaucracy

Despite the variations in the organizational units that make up the executive bureaucracy, and the efforts that have been made to limit political influence in some of them, no bureaucratic structure can be immune from or insensitive to the strong political forces at work in its environment. Administrative decisions have political consequences and hence are subject to political pressures and cross-pressures. The nature of democracy requires that government officials be responsive to the publics they serve. However, the extent to which that responsiveness is partisan in character has long been the subject of controversy, especially in the selection of personnel to serve in the executive branch.

Before 1883, nonelective positions in the federal bureaucracy were filled by means of **patronage**—the distribution of jobs by winning candidates to those who had worked for their political campaign and supported their party. "To the victor go the spoils" was the rallying cry of the day, and the spoils of election victory were usually jobs in government. This use of patronage in federal employment was known as the **spoils system**.[4]

By the latter part of the nineteenth century the spoils system had fallen into disrepute: administration was often in the hands of political hacks, corruption was common, and fending off job seekers was a major burden for successful politicians. In 1881 a disappointed applicant for a federal job shot and killed President James A. Garfield, an event that strengthened cries for reform of the federal personnel system. In 1883 Congress responded by passing the Pendleton Act, which established the **civil service system**.

The civil service system requires that two important criteria be met in hiring people for government jobs. First, jobs must be open to any citizen regardless of his or her political preference; everyone must have an opportunity to compete. Second, civil servants must be chosen on the basis of some objective measure of their abilities—that is, on their merits. Historically the second criterion has meant qualification based on open, competitive examinations.

The civil service system At first the civil service system covered only a small percentage of federal employees. Gradually its coverage grew, until today it includes more than 90 percent of all federal employees. About two-thirds of the civil service employees are in what is known as the regular **civil service**, a group that includes most of the career employees of the departments and the major agencies. Regardless of where they work, their salaries and fringe benefits are determined by Congress and implemented by the Office of Personnel Management, an independent agency in the executive branch. All civil service positions are graded according to the character of the work to be done, and a pay range is assigned to each grade level (see Table 14-1).

TABLE 14-1	SALARY SCHEDULE OF THE REGULAR CIVIL SERVICE (EFFECTIVE JANUARY 1996)
JOB CHARACTERISTICS AND GRADE	PAY RANGE
Menial, clerical	
GS-1[a]	$13,132–16,425
GS-2	14,764–18,577
GS-3	16,111–20,940
GS-4	18,085–23,515
Management entry; low-level supervisory	
GS-5	20,233–26,303
GS-6	22,554–29,320
GS-7	25,061–32,582
GS-8	27,756–36,088
Technical; mid-level supervisory	
GS-9	30,658–39,858
GS-10	33,762–43,888
GS-11	37,094–48,222
GS-12	44,458–57,800
Highly technical; middle management	
GS-13	52,867–68,729
GS-14	62,473–81,217
GS-15	73,486–95,531

[a]GS stands for "general schedule."

Source: U.S. Office of Personnel Management and Washington Post, *October 8, 1995, 53.*

In 1979 the **Senior Executive Service (SES)** was created to provide departments and agencies with greater flexibility in deploying, compensating, and (if necessary) removing senior managers and technical specialists. There are now about eight thousand SES members, of whom at least 90 percent must always be career federal employees. Although they are entitled, and sometimes encouraged, to move from one agency to another where their skills and experience are needed, most spend their entire careers in a single agency. SES members have their own pay grades (see Table 14-2), and they are eligible each year for merit pay raises and special performance and incentive bonuses.

About one-third of the federal government's civilian career employees work in agencies that have their own merit systems, distinct from the regular civil service.

TABLE 14-2	SALARY SCHEDULE OF THE SENIOR EXECUTIVE SERVICE (EFFECTIVE JANUARY 1996)	
	LEVEL	SALARY
	ES-1[a]	$ 94,800
	ES-2	99,300
	ES-3	103,800
	ES-4	109,400
	ES-5	114,000
	ES-6	115,700

[a]ES stands for "executive schedule." Figures are base salaries; supplements are paid in areas with higher living costs.

Source: U.S. Office of Personnel Management.

ROBERT FRASURE: PUBLIC SERVANT

Before the accident, Robert Frasure, like most career civil servants, had spent most of his adult life practicing the arts of government with little public notice. Frasure was an American diplomat, a career foreign service officer. A graduate of West Virginia University, he had earned a Ph.D. from Duke University and had been a college professor for a short time before entering the foreign service in the 1970s. His career then followed a typical route for talented foreign service officers, with service at American embassies throughout Europe and Africa. In 1990 and 1991 he served on the staff of President Bush's National Security Council, and in 1991 he received the Presidential Medal for Exceptional Service for his work in alleviating starvation in Ethiopia. He served as American ambassador to the former Soviet republic of Estonia before becoming deputy assistant secretary of state in 1994.

In this post, Frasure served as America's principal representative in a five-nation group of diplomats working to secure a lasting peace in Bosnia. For months he participated in painstaking and often fruitless negotiations between the warring parties. Frasure was a realist. He knew that any peace in Bosnia would be hard to achieve. But he also believed in the value of diplomacy and he practiced that craft with great skill. Secretary of State Warren Christopher called him "one of the most dedicated and courageous public servants with whom I have ever had the privilege of working."

On August 19, 1995, Frasure was traveling with two other American members of the diplomatic team, searching for peace in Bosnia, Joseph Kruzel and Colonel Nelson Drew. They were on their way to yet another negotiating session, carrying with them a new plan for a Bosnian peace. Because of the constant danger of the war zone in which they worked, they rode in an armored personnel carrier. Traveling along mountainous roads after a heavy rain, their vehicle plunged into a ravine and all three men died.

Robert Frasure was not the first foreign service officer to die at his work, nor will he be the last. At his funeral in Arlington National Cemetery, President Clinton called him a "quiet American hero." Across the world in Estonia, where Frasure had been the

Robert Frasure, a distinguished U.S. foreign service officer, was killed in the midst of a peace mission to Bosnia on August 19, 1995.

first American ambassador since World War II, President Lennart Meri spoke for his own saddened nation: "His dedication to what is good and right in this world, and the skill with which he pursued those goals, was most evident in his work on the negotiating process for the withdrawal of Russian troops from Estonia. Without the support of the United States during those negotiations, and without Bob's drive to push the process along, I wonder whether we would have accomplished our goal with some time to spare. In this way, Bob-Frasure-as-diplomat played a great personal role in guaranteeing the true independence of Estonia."

For many government employees, public service is a thankless job. The brunt of comedians' jokes and politicians' jibes, they endure in silence the scorn of the people they serve—until their funerals, that is, when we take stock of what the world would be like if Americans and Estonians and Bosnians couldn't rely on people like Robert Frasure.

SOURCE: State Department documents.

These agencies include the TVA, the FBI, the Public Health Service, the Foreign Service, and the Postal Service. In addition, members of the uniformed armed services are part of an entirely separate career system with its own ranks and rules. In most cases, the reasons for the existence of the separate merit systems have to do with politics and tradition. The agency merit systems work in much the same way as the regular civil service, but they have different terminology and are run by the agencies themselves, not by the Office of Personnel Management.

Once federal employees are installed in one of the government's career personnel systems, they are relatively secure in their jobs. This security is intended to protect them from inappropriate political pressures and from removal when there is a change of administration. Career employees are seldom removed unless there is a reduction in federal employment—a **reduction in force**—a tactic used aggressively at the beginning of the Reagan presidency but used rarely by Reagan's predecessors. Although career employees can also be removed for inadequate performance, proving that performance is inadequate is very difficult for managers to do. Because of an elaborate appeals procedure, firing a civil servant may take two years or more; as a consequence, it rarely happens.

Among the 10 percent of federal employees who are not part of the career merit system are a variety of people whose jobs are incompatible with systematic personnel procedures or competitive selection techniques. These include presidential appointees to the top positions in the government, some attorneys, faculty members at the military service academies, undercover drug enforcement agents, foreign nationals who work at United States installations overseas, and employees who hold short-term or summer jobs.

Political appointees   Nearly all the top-level positions in the executive branch are held by political appointees. Typically, they are individuals from the private sector who serve in the government for only a short time (about two years on average). Included in this group are cabinet secretaries and the senior officers in each of the cabinet departments, heads of the independent agencies, and members of the federal regulatory commissions, all of whom are appointed by the president and confirmed by the Senate.

Some appointees, like regulatory commissioners, have fixed terms of service. Most, however, serve at the pleasure of the president: they can be removed by a president who is unhappy with their performance or loyalty. In 1970, for example, Richard Nixon fired Secretary of the Interior Walter Hickel after Hickel released to the press a letter criticizing the invasion of Cambodia by American forces. Jimmy Carter sought the resignations of several of his cabinet members—Joseph Califano (Health and Human Services), Michael Blumenthal (Treasury), and Brock Adams (Transportation)—after a review of their performance in 1979. In December 1994, Bill Clinton fired Joycelyn Elders, the surgeon general he had appointed, after she made remarks that were politically embarrassing to him.

The system of drawing the highest-ranking executive-branch officials from the private sector is uniquely American. No other country relies so heavily on leaders who are not career government employees. The American approach has several advantages. It ensures a constant infusion of new creative energy and fosters responsiveness to the popular will. Moreover, the dual tests of presidential nomination and Senate confirmation promote care and judiciousness in the choice of people to fill important government offices.[5]

But there are disadvantages as well. For one thing, leaders often lack experience or technical competence in the complex policy areas over which they have jurisdic-

For President Clinton, appointments to the post of surgeon general of the United States proved especially difficult politically. His first appointee, Joycelyn Elders, candidly and publicly discussed sensitive issues about young people's sexuality; Clinton finally decided he could no longer politically afford her outspoken nature and fired her. To replace her, he proposed Henry Foster, whose nomination was filibustered to death after he acknowledged that as an obstetrician/gynecologist he had performed abortions.

tion. Many members of regulatory commissions, for example, receive their appointments as rewards for previous support of the president. In addition, the short tenure of most appointees leads to inconsistency in administration and policy direction and creates a greater potential for ethical violations, since appointees tend to be less aware of and less influenced by ethical codes for government employees than are career civil servants. Many appointees are more concerned with making an impact in a brief time than with management or program initiatives that may take a while to bear fruit.

The Executive Bureaucracy in Perspective

The personnel structure of the executive bureaucracy, like its organizational structure, is complex and confusing, following few logical principles or sets of decision-making rules. The bureaucracy has been developing over two centuries of practice and experimentation; it is not the product of a single blueprint. Although administrative units have been added and eliminated, merged and subdivided, the structure and location of those that currently exist reflect the political battles surrounding their origins rather than any consistent administrative theory. The personnel system shows the same inconsistencies. The head of one bureau is a career civil servant; the head of another is a presidential appointee. One must look to the political history of each bureau to explain such inconsistencies, since the process of constructing a government is no less political than the process of operating one.

In 1979, for example, Congress created a new cabinet department, the Depart-

FASHIONED IN PARIS:
THE FRENCH BUREAUCRACY

At first glance, the administration of public affairs in France appears poles apart from the way in which bureaucracy operates in the United States. Closer inspection, however, suggests some important similarities.

Government in the United States is deeply rooted in an emphasis on local rights and responsibilities, with divisions of power and authority throughout the political system. In France, the system is based on a unified, integrated, and centralized structure of government. French administration is organized as a pyramid. Arranged from the bottom to the top of the pyramid are the more than 36,000 local communes, the 96 departments, the 21 regions, and finally the central national bureaucracy in Paris.

Although some decision making is decentralized to the regional and local level, virtually all important administrative decisions are made in Paris at the senior levels of the bureaucracy. The substantive business of French government is divided among a varying number of ministries (generally fifteen to twenty), comparable to cabinet departments in the United States. These include the ministries of Justice, Interior, Foreign Affairs, Defense, Solidarity (health and human services), and Education.

The Ministry of the Interior, for example, is responsible for all police work throughout the country, including local traffic administration. All police officers in France (the *gendarmerie*) are technically employees of the Ministry of the Interior. In the United States, by contrast, local police forces are operated by local governments, which hire their own officers and make their own policies. Nearly all important American law enforcement decisions are made locally. In France, all the important law enforcement decisions are made in the central Ministry of the Interior. Little discretion in interpreting the law is left to local communities or individual police officers.

The French ministries are headed by ministers and junior ministers (called secretaries of state). The ministers are chosen by the prime minister (the head of the French government), but many—usually about one-third—are career civil servants. This, too, is different from the practice in the United States, where none of the top officials in the cabinet departments and independent agencies are career civil servants. Appointed by the president, these officials are often called "in-and-outers" because they enter government for short periods of service and then return to the private sector. There is no analog to this practice in France, where all but the very top government officials must prepare for their responsibilities through formal training and a career in public administration. In the United States, newly elected presidents fill thousands of administrative positions. When French elections bring new presidents or prime ministers to power, there is substantially less turnover in the senior positions in the government.

The top levels of the French civil service—the so-called *grands corps*—are filled with people who have all received their professional education at the École

ment of Education. Among the principal proponents of this change in the structure of government was the National Education Association (NEA), a powerful organization of elementary and secondary school teachers. Opponents of the new department included another teachers' organization, the American Federation of Teachers (AFT). Whereas the NEA sought to increase its political advantage by reshaping the administration of education programs, the AFT sought to retain relationships it had already developed within the existing educational bureaucracy. After Congress had approved the creation of the new department, both organizations lobbied President Carter to appoint a secretary who would be responsive to their individual interests.

National d'Administration (ENA) or at other prestigious institutions of higher education whose sole purpose is the training of future civil servants. Graduation from one of these schools is literally the only route of entry to the higher civil service in France. In the United States, the 9,700 members of the Senior Executive Service are usually career civil servants (10 percent are not), but their educational backgrounds vary widely. Most of them entered the civil service at relatively low levels and worked their way to the top.

Although most observers would describe administration in France as more legalistic and certainly more centralized than American administration, the bureaucracy in both countries is riven with politics. In France, as in the United States, new ministries are created and old ones reorganized to satisfy external political pressures. Conflicts between bureaucratic organizations sharing jurisdiction over policy areas such as energy or the environment are as common in France as in the United States. French agencies fight with the Court of Accounts and the Inspectorate of Finances just as American agencies fight with the Office of Management and Budget. And within French agencies, as within their American counterparts, the technical specialists are often at odds with the administrative generalists.

It is no surprise, then, that most public administration scholars conclude that no matter how the organizational boxes are arranged or the bureaucrats selected, politics is a fact of bureaucratic life.

Unlike most police officers in the United States, all of those in France, including these two gendarmes directing traffic in Paris, come under the control of the national government. But even though the French bureaucracy is far more centralized than its American counterpart, it is no less subject to political pressures.

To prevent the appearance of favoring one group or one educational interest over another, Carter decided to appoint Shirley Hufstedler, a federal judge with no direct experience in educational matters.

When legislators create a new agency, their decisions about where to locate it, what to call it, and what to include in it are strongly influenced by the search for political advantage. When presidents appoint the leaders of such an agency, they too are deeply affected by the political situation of the moment. Legislators and presidents are politicians, and they are much less concerned with symmetry and consistency than with policy outcomes. As Harold Seidman has noted, "Economy and efficiency are demonstrably not the prime purposes of public administration. The basic issues of federal organization and administration relate to power: Who shall control it and to what ends?"[6]

FUNCTIONS OF THE EXECUTIVE BUREAUCRACY

Many people assume that the executive bureaucracy merely executes policy decisions made by Congress and the president. In fact, the administrative agencies of the federal government are themselves important participants in policy making. Almost every public policy is shaped in some ways by the characteristics and the actions of the agencies that oversee its implementation.

Implementation

The primary task of federal agencies is to interpret and implement the public policies that emerge from the legislative process. For example, if a statute declares that the average fuel efficiency of automobiles sold in the United States must be 23 miles per gallon, an agency has to determine when and how to measure fuel efficiency, how to certify satisfaction of the standard, and how to bring companies that fail to meet the standard into compliance. Authority to perform these functions is delegated to the agency by Congress. In exercising such authority, however, the agency normally has a great deal of discretion.[7] That discretion is a powerful invitation to political pressure. Indeed, political interests that fail to accomplish their goals in the legislative process often redouble their efforts to obtain satisfaction in the administrative process, and their opponents must assert themselves there as well. Battles lost in the legislative branch are routinely refought in the executive branch.

The principal responsibility of most public agencies is action. They are the delivery end of the policy-making process, the government's agents in dealing directly with the people (hence the name "agency"). Their task is to translate the policy objectives determined in the legislative process into goods and services that will help accomplish those objectives. They do this in a number of ways, including regulation, rule making, adjudication, compliance enforcement, and allocation of funds.

Regulation   In regulating economic and social activity, agencies are guided by two primary objectives: (1) to maintain the stability of the free-market system and its openness to competition, and (2) to protect the health, safety, and welfare of the American people. The first agency designed solely to perform regulatory activities was the Interstate Commerce Commission, established in 1887. Many others have been added since. There are now few economic functions that do not fall under the regulatory jurisdiction of one or more federal agencies in what has become a heavily regulated American economy.[8]

Contemporary regulation takes two broad forms: economic regulation and social regulation. **Economic regulation** aims to control prices, market entry, and conditions of service in specific industries. The principal objective of economic regulation is to promote competition within a single industry while at the same time protecting the competitive position of individual companies. Economic regulation expanded significantly from 1887 into the 1960s, and such industries as computer software development and telecommunications are still heavily influenced by it.

Since the late 1960s, however, there has been a significant movement toward **deregulation**—freeing some industries from the broad government control of ear-

THE FEDERAL BUREAUCRACY

Would you like to apply for a federal job? Have you ever wondered whether a bill you've heard about has become a law? Would you like to visit an Internet site that links you to any agency or department in the federal government? The following Internet sites can help you navigate the complicated bureaucracy that makes up the federal government.

FEDWORLD
HTTP://WWW.FEDWORLD.GOV/

A gateway site to most federal agencies and sources of federal government information. FedWorld is a good starting point for any search for information about the federal government.

FEDERAL REGISTER
HTTP://WWW.GPO.UCOP.EDU/SEARCH/FEDFLD.HTML

The *Federal Register* is the official publication for presidential documents and executive orders as well as notices, rules, and proposed rules from federal agencies and organizations. The *Federal Register* is published Monday through Friday, except federal holidays.

GOVERNMENT MANUAL
HTTP://WWW.GPO.UCOP.EDU/CATALOG/GOVMAN.HTML

The Government Manual is prepared by the Office of the Federal Register, National Archives. It contains a description of the functions, organization, and leading officials of every federal department and agency, as well as organizational charts of most agencies.

UNITED STATES CODE
HTTP://WWW.GPO.UCOP.EDU/SEARCH/USCODE.HTML

The United States Code is prepared and published by the Office of the Law Revision Counsel, U.S. House of Representatives, and contains the general and permanent laws of the United States in effect as of January 1994 or January 1995, depending on the title.

APPLYING FOR A FEDERAL JOB
HTTP://HELIX.NIH.GOV:8001/JOBS/OF510.HTML

Complete information on how to apply for federal jobs provided by the U.S. Office of Personnel Management.

---

lier years.[9] The effects of deregulation on commercial air travel are generally well known. For more than four decades the Civil Aeronautics Board (CAB) regulated domestic air travel. During that time no major new national air carriers entered the marketplace, and CAB decisions tightly controlled airline fares and routes. In the 1970s the president and Congress moved to deregulate the airline industry in order to stimulate competition. The CAB went out of existence, price competition intensified, new airlines sprouted up, and several mergers occurred. All this was a mixed blessing for consumers. Air travel opportunities improved for those in population centers where airline competition was strongest, but it became more difficult, more expensive, and less reliable for those in less populated areas served by fewer carriers. In the years that followed, many airlines experienced financial problems, the cost of some air travel escalated, concern about safety grew, and some people called for reregulation of the industry by the federal government.

Social regulation, the second form of regulatory policy, aims to control the social and physical impact of a wide range of economic activities. Government action in this area has increased greatly since the 1960s, when a series of books, articles, and television programs generated publicity about the threats to health and safety posed by everyday consumer goods. Public interest groups, spearheaded by the efforts of consumer activist Ralph Nader, put political pressure on Congress and the administrative agencies for greater protection of consumer welfare in such areas as automobile safety, truth in advertising, and truth in lending. (See the box about

Nader on page 239.) At the same time, increasingly prominent civil rights groups demanded federal action to prevent discrimination against women and members of minority groups. Shortly thereafter, protection of the natural environment became a central issue on the policy agenda. Each of these initiatives found important support among the American people and yielded a stream of new regulatory legislation.

To implement this legislation, new regulatory commissions such as the Equal Employment Opportunity Commission and the Consumer Product Safety Commission were created, most of them under the jurisdiction of executive-branch agencies. New policies required manufacturers to be truthful on product labels and in advertising, to provide safe and healthy working conditions, and to ensure equal employment opportunities for women, minorities, the elderly, and the disabled. Expensive programs for the inspection and testing of food, drugs, and consumer products were established, and greater authority was delegated to federal agencies to ban the sale of products they found to be unsafe. (For example, the Consumer Product Safety Commission required manufacturers of cribs to reduce the space between the slats to prevent injuries to infants.) Broad policies were created to protect the natural environment and prevent air, water, and noise pollution.

The new emphasis on social regulation greatly expanded the scope of federal regulatory activity. By 1975 it was hard to find a business enterprise anywhere in the United States that was not subject to at least one regulatory program, and owners and managers were beginning to complain about the regulatory burden. Their objectives focused not only on the costs they incurred in complying but also on the uncertainty that resulted from constant changes in requirements, which made long-range planning both risky and difficult. In addition, they were unhappy about having to deal with powerful executive agencies that, in their view, were overly committed to the concerns of consumers and insufficiently sensitive to the needs of producers. By the mid 1970s opponents of social regulation were mustering their own political forces to influence the federal government to lessen the regulatory burden. Subsequent efforts to extend social regulation have generated intense political conflict.[10]

Rule making   Most agencies, operating within the jurisdiction granted them by Congress, have the authority to issue rules. Rules are best described as elaborations of the law. If the law says that you cannot fly an airplane without a pilot's license, rules will describe in detail the steps that you must take to get a license and the penalties you will incur if you fly without one. Rules have the force of law.

In making rules, agencies must follow procedures laid down in the Administrative Procedures Act of 1946 and its amendments. A number of steps must be completed before a new rule can take effect.[11] For example, the draft of a new rule must be published in the *Federal Register* at least thirty days before the rule is to go into effect. When the draft of the rule is published, the agency must invite public comment on it. After the comments have been reviewed (a task that may take months or even years) and any changes are made, the rule is issued officially when it is published in final form in the *Federal Register* and codified in a volume called the *Code of Federal Regulations*.

As the scope of government activity has expanded in the twentieth century, so too has the number of administrative rules. In 1960 there were 14,479 pages in the *Federal Register*; by 1979 the number was up to 71,191.[12] As a result of deregulation during the Reagan administration, the number of *Federal Register* pages declined to 50,997 in 1984, but by the mid 1990s it had crept back up to the range of 68,000.

Rule making has become a very important part of policy making, since the "law"

USING THE *FEDERAL REGISTER*

The *Federal Register* publishes government regulations and legal notices as they are issued by federal agencies. These include presidential proclamations and executive orders, federal agency documents having general applicability and legal effect, documents required to be published by act of Congress, and other federal agency documents of public interest.

Using the *Federal Register* can be a challenge. The documents it contains are organized by type—notices, proposed rules and regulations, final rules and regulations, and presidential documents. In the notices section are found notices of hearings and investigations, committee meetings, agency decisions and rulings, and other administrative matters. The proposed and final rules and regulations sections contain regulatory documents having general applicability and legal effect. Presidential documents include executive orders, proclamations, and other documents from the president.

Within each type, the documents are organized alphabetically by agency. Each document is filed with the *Federal Register* by the agency; it is then assigned a *Federal Register* document number. For example, the Appalachian States Low-Level Radioactive Waste Commission notice of an open meeting, filed on May 15, 1992, was assigned the number FR Doc 92-11362. The 92 in the number indicates the year the document was filed; the rest of the number indicates that it was the 11,362nd document filed with the *Federal Register* that year. The notice appears on page 21057 of volume 57, number 96, dated May 18, 1992.

A specific document is relatively easy to find if you know its *Federal Register* document number. This number immediately narrows the search to a particular year and quickly narrows it to a specific week. If you do not know the document number, you must search through the quarterly or cumulative indexes to find the document. The index entries are arranged first under the name of the agency that issued the document, then by the type of document (rule, notice, and so on). The number that appears at the end of each index entry identifies the page in the *Federal Register* on which the document begins.

Determining which agency might have issued a document is often the most difficult part of finding it. A helpful tool is the *United States Government Manual*. This volume, found in most libraries, lists and describes all the branches and departments of the government. Deciding into what category the document falls is a simpler step. Generally, if an issue is still in the decision-making process, documents relating to it (notices of hearings, for example) will be found in the notices section. Once a decision has been made, look in the rules and regulations section to see how it is being implemented. To find presidential documents, two other publications from the *Federal Register* are also useful: *Codification of Presidential Proclamations and Executive Orders* and *Weekly Compilation of Presidential Documents*.

Even experienced researchers sometimes have trouble finding documents in the *Federal Register*. Fortunately, helpful staff members in the Finding Aids Unit of the National Archives are readily available by telephone at (202) 523-5227. The *Federal Register* is published daily, Monday through Friday, by the Office of the Federal Register, National Archives and Records Administration. Copies are found in most large libraries and in all federal depository libraries. In addition, access to the *Federal Register* is increasingly available through the Internet. The Government Printing Office maintains a site (**http://thorplus.lib.purdue.edu.80/gpo/**) that provides text from the *Federal Register* for 1994 to the present.

made by executive agencies often does as much to determine the shape of public policies as does the law made by Congress. Recognizing this, the Reagan administration made a determined attempt to gain full control over administrative rules. Beginning in 1981, it required that all major proposed rules be reviewed and approved by the Office of Management and Budget before publication. In 1990, however, the Supreme Court limited the scope of the OMB's power to review administrative rules.

Adjudication No matter how diligently executive agencies strive to remove ambiguity from the rules they issue, they are never completely successful. There are always some areas of uncertainty about the application of a specific law or rule to a particular circumstance. An agency may interpret a rule to mean one thing; a corporation may interpret it to mean another. When such differences of opinion occur, the agency is often asked to hold a hearing at which the affected party appeals what it perceives as an inappropriate or unfair interpretation.

Each year, for example, the National Highway Traffic Safety Administration (NHTSA) inspects automobiles for safety defects. If it finds a defect, the NHTSA informs the manufacturer and holds a hearing to determine whether to order the automaker to recall all the affected vehicles and repair the defect. To avoid embarrassment and potential financial loss, manufacturers usually voluntarily recall vehicles before the NHTSA requires them to. But not always. In 1984, for example, the NHTSA required General Motors to recall more than a million vehicles that proved to have defective braking systems.

The hearings are often run like legal proceedings. Attorneys are usually present for both sides. Sometimes a hearing is presided over by an **administrative law judge**, an independent third party whose rulings are binding on both the agency and the complainant, although either side may appeal a ruling in the federal courts. Many of the rulings are published in the *Federal Register* so that other interested parties can get a clearer picture of the application of rules and laws to specific cases.[13]

Compliance enforcement Ensuring that laws and rules are obeyed is one of the important tasks of executive agencies. For some—the FBI and the Bureau of Alcohol, Tobacco, and Firearms, for instance—it is the dominant concern, but virtually all agencies spend some of their efforts on compliance enforcement.

Many government agencies intersect with the daily lives of ordinary citizens. To ensure quality, USDA graders inspect and approve the beef we consume; the IRS manages massive bureaucratic routines to collect our taxes.

Some agencies conduct regular, scheduled inspections to ensure that agency guidelines are followed. For example, the Department of Agriculture routinely inspects food-processing facilities; the tag "USDA inspected" on food products indicates that they were processed under conditions that satisfied federal government standards. Other agencies prefer to make unscheduled inspections. The Coast Guard, for instance, follows the practice of stopping private boats without prior notice to inspect their life-saving equipment. In addition, many government agencies employ accountants to examine the financial records of individuals, corporations, or groups to ensure that they are complying with applicable laws and rules. The Internal Revenue Service audits individual and corporate tax returns for this purpose, and the Comptroller of the Currency audits the financial records of national banks.

The imposition of reporting requirements is another way in which compliance enforcement is carried out. Institutions and corporations are required to file periodic reports on their activities. Employers, for instance, must file regular reports on the number of workers they employ, the amounts they have withheld from paychecks for taxes, and other matters relevant to specific businesses. Federal contractors must file reports indicating that their employment practices are nondiscriminatory. When businesspeople complain about the red tape they have to endure as a result of government regulation, they often identify these reports as the principal culprits.

One other important way in which agencies oversee compliance with laws and rules is by responding to complaints. Noncompliance often harms someone, and the harmed party may bring a complaint to the government agency that has jurisdiction. If a factory is dumping more pollutants into a stream than the law permits, people who enjoy fishing in that stream may bring a complaint to the Environmental Protection Agency. If the EPA finds that the factory is indeed violating the law, it can take steps to bring the factory into compliance.

Allocation of funds   In one way or another, almost all government agencies allocate funds to purchase the goods and services necessary to implement federal programs. The awarding of contracts is one of the principal ways they do this.[14] Federal contractors include construction companies that build veterans' hospitals, corporations that supply ships for the Navy, organizations that do economic research for the Treasury Department, museums that mount exhibits sponsored by the National Endowment for the Arts, and a wide variety of other individuals and organizations.

Policy Making

That agencies play an important role in making public policy is not surprising if you think about it, for agency employees are usually experts in a particular policy area. Because their day-to-day activities provide a unique vantage point for observing the strengths and weaknesses of particular programs, it is only natural for them to suggest policy changes. Soldiers who find that their rifles jam in wet weather may suggest changes in weapon design. Tax auditors who see that much revenue is being lost because of a loophole in the tax laws may recommend changes to close the loophole.

More important, agency employees have ideas of their own. Their training, their experience, and the values that prevail in their work environment shape their perceptions of the form policies should take. Agency staffs may care deeply about the policies for which they are responsible, and they play a very active role in trying to define and perfect them. Often they become vigorous advocates of their own views, negotiating with their superiors in the bureaucracy, with members and staff in Congress, and with their political constituencies to try to bring policies into line with their ideas.[15]

Admiral Hyman Rickover of the United States Navy illustrates the significant influence that members of the bureaucracy can sometimes have on public policy. For three decades, beginning in the 1950s and lasting into the 1980s, Rickover was the federal government's leading expert on nuclear-powered ships and the leading advocate of expanding the role of nuclear-powered vessels in American military strategy. He was also a formidable player in the political process, spending large amounts of time cultivating the congressional committees that reviewed naval policy and budgets and building support for his views in the White House and among powerful outside interests. Rickover's success in influencing policy resulted from a combination of expertise, reputation, and substantial political skills.[16]

Bureaucratic agencies share some of the characteristics of other institutions that participate in policy making. Despite efforts to isolate them from partisan politics, bureaucracies are intensely political organizations. They are concerned about their own interests; they seek to enlarge their resources and protect their turf; they develop mutually beneficial long-term relationships with other political actors; and they engage in bargaining and negotiation to accomplish their objectives. The political character of the American policy-making process shapes the bureaucracy as thoroughly as it shapes Congress, the courts, the presidency, and interest group activity. But bureaucratic agencies are also distinct from other kinds of government decision makers in some important ways: their hierarchical organization, their character and culture, their professionalization, and their organizational pathologies.

Hierarchy   Most bureaucratic decision making is hierarchical. Policy proposals typically emerge first at the lowest organizational levels, in the offices and bureaus that are most directly exposed to specific policy environments. Officials there make recommendations to their superiors, who in turn make recommendations to their superiors, and so on up the levels of hierarchy.

Along the way, two important things happen. One is filtering, a process by which some proposals are eliminated as unnecessary, too costly, or untimely. Part of the responsibility of managers in the bureaucratic hierarchy is to filter out policy proposals that should not be recommended for further consideration higher up. Many proposals die this way, in the internal review process of the agencies in which they originate. Often they are rejected after political struggles that may involve people and interests from outside the agency.

The secretary of defense, for example, may receive a proposal from the Navy for a new carrier-based fighter airplane. Although the Navy may be enthusiastic about the plane, the secretary may reject the proposal after determining that the plane is not a significant enough improvement over current fighters to justify the cost of a new weapons system. This is a filtering decision. The secretary's decision will be complicated by heavy pressure from the Navy, the manufacturer of the new plane, and the members of Congress from the districts in which the planes would be built.

Another important activity of bureaucratic agencies is enforcing coordination. Every agency has many subunits that propose new policies and new expenditures of funds. Because the sum of these proposed expenditures always exceeds available resources, managers must set priorities: Which requests should be approved as recommended, which should be modified, and which should be rejected? Priority setting occurs at every level in the hierarchy, so programs that survive initial review at the lowest levels may die at higher levels when they come into conflict with other proposals. A recommendation to improve dairy price supports may appear perfectly sensible when compared with a proposal to increase cotton price supports. But it may not fare so well when it is compared with a proposal for developing new soil conservation projects. The first comparison, between price supports for various agricultural commodities, is made at a low level in the hierarchy. The second comparison, involving two different kinds of policies, is made at a much higher level.

Character and culture   Bureaucratic agencies are not empty vessels into which new programs are poured for implementation. Every agency has its own character and culture, and over time it acquires certain biases. Initially these come from the kinds of programs an agency is asked to administer, but they are reinforced by the agency's contacts with the interest groups it serves, by the ways in which it recruits new employees, and by the operating procedures it employs.

The Labor Department is a case in point. Initially created to protect the health and safety of American workers, it quickly came to be perceived as an advocate for workers in the policy-making process. Its relationship with labor unions was symbiotic: organized labor and the Labor Department supported each other. Thus people opposed to the labor movement found a hostile reception at the Labor Department and either did not seek or were not offered employment there. When the Reagan administration sought to sever the traditional relationship by appointing officials hostile to unions to senior positions in the department, it drew heavy criticism from union leaders and their friends in Congress.

One of the important ways in which agencies institutionalize their biases is by routinizing their work. They develop **standard operating procedures (SOPs)**— predetermined ways of responding to a particular problem or set of circumstances. For example, the State Department has SOPs for dealing with foreign citizens who

An agency often reflects the philosophy and interests of its leader. James Watt (left), *President Reagan's Secretary of the Interior from 1981 to 1983, had little patience with conservationists and let it be known. One of his successors, Bruce Babbitt* (right), *showed a flair for listening and making compromises, as when he discussed President Clinton's forest plan with workers at a mill in 1993.*

enter American embassies seeking political asylum. The Navy has SOPs for responding to contacts with foreign vessels in international waters. The IRS has SOPs for determining whether a tax return will be audited. Although SOPs simplify bureaucratic decisions and contribute to their consistency, they also channel bureaucratic activity into rigid patterns and thus make agencies less adaptable to change, especially change that is imposed from outside—by Congress or the president. (Presidents' expressions of frustration in dealing with the federal bureaucracy are quoted in the box on page 537.)

During the Cuban missile crisis in 1962, for example, Secretary of Defense Robert McNamara was worried about the way in which the Navy intended to carry out President John Kennedy's orders to blockade all shipping to and from Cuba. He posed a series of hard questions to Admiral George Anderson, the chief of naval operations, about procedures for managing a blockade at sea. Anderson waved the *Manual of Naval Regulations* in McNamara's face and said, "It's all in there." McNamara replied, "I don't give a damn what John Paul Jones would have done. I want to know what you are going to do now." Anderson ended the exchange by saying, "Mr. Secretary, if you and your Deputy will go back to your offices, the Navy will run the blockade."[17]

Professionalization In recent years decision making by the executive bureaucracy has become increasingly professionalized because of the technical complexity of modern public policy. To deal with this complexity, agencies hire experts. For example, in recent years the federal government employed 150,000 architects and engineers, 10,000 physicians, 14,000 scientists, and more than 30,000 attorneys.[18] Because of their command of specific and detailed information, such experts have steadily enlarged their role in bureaucratic policy making. What experts add to this process is a reliance on professional as well as political criteria. As Francis E. Rourke has noted:

> The framing of public policy in a bureaucratic setting can be seen to involve a constant interplay between two quite different sets of factors. It becomes in effect a mixed system of politics and professionalism. Clearly political considerations have to be taken into account in bureaucratic policy making in terms of the impact of decisions upon the outside community. At the same time, however, policy decisions certainly cannot fly in the face of professional advice when there is agreement among the experts as to the technically sound course of action.[19]

Striking a balance between professional advice and political realities is a constant struggle for executive-branch officials. When health policy officials in the Reagan administration planned a national survey of Americans' sexual habits to assist in planning a program to combat the spread of AIDS, OMB leaders quashed the survey because they found some of its questions inappropriate. Those who intervened were responding to the moral qualms of congressional conservatives on whom the administration relied heavily for support.

Bureaucratic pathologies The natural characteristics of bureaucratic agencies often produce certain pathologies, unhealthy conditions that adversely affect the way they approach policy decisions. These reduce the efficiency and effectiveness of some agencies and are a principal source of the criticism directed at the federal bureaucracy.

PRESIDENTS ON THE BUREAUCRACY

Every modern president has experienced some frustration in dealing with the federal bureaucracy. Clearly, what is called the executive branch is not always the executive's branch.

Franklin D. Roosevelt

The Treasury is so large and far-flung and ingrained in its practices that I find it almost impossible to get the actions and results I want. But the Treasury is not to be compared with the State Department. You should go through the experience of trying to get any changes in the thinking, policy, and action of the career diplomats and then you'd know what a real problem was. But the Treasury and State departments put together are nothing compared with the Navy. To change anything in the Navy is like punching a feather bed. You punch it with your right and you punch it with your left until you are finally exhausted, and then you find the damn bed just as it was before you started punching.

Harry S Truman

I thought I was President, but when it comes to these bureaucracies, I can't make them do a damn thing.

[After General Dwight Eisenhower takes office as president, he] will sit here and he'll say, 'Do this! Do that!' And nothing will happen. Poor Ike—it won't be a bit like the Army. He'll find it very frustrating.

John F. Kennedy

[National Security Adviser McGeorge] Bundy and I get more done in one day than they do in six months at State. The State Department is a bowl full of jelly.

Richard M. Nixon

We have no discipline in this bureaucracy. We never fire anybody. We never reprimand anybody. We never demote anybody. We always promote the sons-of-bitches that kick us in the ass.

Jimmy Carter

Before I became president, I realized and I was warned that dealing with the federal bureaucracy would be one of the worst problems I would have to face. It has been even worse than I had anticipated.

Ronald Reagan

Once a program gets started, it's virtually impossible to reduce or stop it. Every one of these programs . . . develops a powerful constituency in Congress, and a bureaucracy that is dedicated to preserving it. . . . The tendency of government and its programs to grow are about the nearest thing to eternal life we'll ever see on this earth.

Persistence is a bureaucratic pathology. Agencies often endure long after their reason for existence has passed. Once created, they are hard to abolish. The National Screw Thread Commission, for instance, was established during World War I to standardize screw threads for military equipment. It had little to do after the war ended in 1918 and did not hold a meeting or issue a report for a decade. Yet it continued to occupy a suite of offices and employ a staff until 1934.

Conservatism is a bureaucratic pathology. As noted earlier, agencies become set in their ways and tend to resist new ideas or new techniques that threaten to disrupt business as usual. For example, when General Billy Mitchell pushed for the creation of a permanent air force after World War I, he was resisted by the military establishment, which viewed airplanes as little more than glamorous gimmicks. Mitchell took his case to the public, arguing that air power would be critical in future wars. Demoted, transferred, and ultimately court-martialed for his efforts, he died a frustrated man in 1936, just five years before the Japanese attack on the United States naval base at Pearl Harbor demonstrated convincingly how right he had been.[20]

Expansionism is a bureaucratic pathology. The one change that nearly all agencies seem to welcome, growth creates new opportunities for promotion, prestige, power, and policy impact—all matters of importance to bureaucrats. The desire to grow is based in large part on the perception that growth will make life in the agency more pleasant and meaningful. History provides few examples of agencies requesting smaller budgets, cutbacks in personnel, or reductions in the scope of their programs. But agency growth is often driven by self-interest rather than public need. Even in agencies whose programs are outmoded or whose benefits are difficult to demonstrate, expansionism is a strong and common tendency. Only the vigilance of executives and legislators can keep it in check.

Capture, the tendency of an agency to develop a symbiotic relationship with the special interests that it oversees and thus to protect rather than regulate those interests, is a bureaucratic pathology. The relationship between the Labor Department and labor unions has already been mentioned, but the capture of an agency by its clients is a special problem for regulatory commissions. The Civil Aeronautics Board, for example, during much of its existence protected commercial air carriers from the rigors of competition by refusing to certify new airlines. Similarly, at certain periods the Interstate Commerce Commission and the Federal Communications Commission were composed of commissioners who were very supportive of the industries regulated by those commissions. Many of the commissioners, in fact, were former employees of the regulated industries. Interest groups put constant political pressure on presidents to nominate and on senators to confirm regulators who are sympathetic to the industries they will be regulating.[21]

The **territorial imperative**, the irresistible urge of an agency to jealously guard its own territory or turf, is a bureaucratic pathology. Indeed, the most furious conflicts that agencies wage are those with other agencies that seem to be encroaching on their area of jurisdiction. Most turf battles center on control over programs. For decades, for instance, the Department of Agriculture has battled successfully to keep the Forest Service under its jurisdiction, despite the reasonable claim that the Forest Service's function (managing the national forests) more closely fits the mission of the Interior Department (which oversees the national parks). The relevant congressional committees and affected interest groups have been in the middle of this political struggle. In this case, as in all others, the interest groups look to Congress to help them with the bureaucracy, and they look to the bureaucracy to help them with Congress.

Every agency suffers, at least occasionally, from some of these pathologies. They are a common part of administrative life. They add new dimensions to the political struggles within the executive branch and between executive agencies and other political actors. And they help account not only for the difficulties in imposing a rational pattern of organization on the federal executive branch but also for the problems that presidents encounter in their efforts to use the executive branch for their own purposes.

Determinants of Bureaucratic Influence

Agencies vary in their ability to affect public policy. Some, like the Marine Corps, are potent and respected. Others, like the Occupational Safety and Health Administration, are weak and maligned. Still others, like the Energy Department, are influential in some periods and less influential in others.

Many scholars have tried to identify factors that help certain agencies play a substantial role in shaping public policy. Francis E. Rourke has identified four such factors: expertise, political support, organizational vitality, and leadership.[22] To a significant extent, the ways in which these variables combine determine an agency's impact. They are not all easily controlled, however. Sometimes agencies are under presidential orders to pursue policies that are unpopular with their political constituencies. Leadership selection is an imperfect art, and old agencies are hard to shake out of their familiar habits. Thus it is not surprising that agencies differ—often widely—in their ability to shape public policy.

Expertise   Specialized knowledge has long been regarded as bureaucracy's principal contribution to the process of government. But some kinds of expertise are more valuable than others. The more technical and specialized an agency's expertise is, the greater will be the agency's opportunity to dominate policy making in its area of concern. If an agency has technical capabilities that few people possess or understand, challenges to its judgment will be rare. For many years the space program was in this position. Because most of the country's experts on space and rocketry worked for the government, there was little opportunity for serious technical criticism of the federal space program. Once the political decision to explore space was made, policy decisions on how to go about it were left largely to the National Aeronautics and Space Administration.

Conversely, the more widely expertise is available outside an agency, the less valuable it is likely to be as a source of agency influence on public policy. The federal agencies that specialize in economic policy, for instance, have no corner on the market of economic expertise. Their recommendations are routinely challenged by other experts, both in and out of the government.

Political support   The more widespread and intense an agency's support is in Congress, in the White House, among interest groups, and in the public mind, the greater its ability to affect policy making in its area of jurisdiction. Agencies therefore work hard to cultivate external support. For example, they cooperate closely with the congressional committees that oversee their programs and their budgets, doing everything in their power to curry the favor of committee members. They also try to develop strongly supportive clienteles among the groups that benefit from their pro-

J. Edgar Hoover (left), *going to the fights in 1936 with friend Clyde Tolson. Hoover led the FBI for nearly five decades, and from the 1930s through the 1950s his handling of public relations gained strong support for the bureau. But Hoover sometimes used his authority and the FBI's resources to weaken or blackmail his enemies and those whose political views he disliked.*

grams, hoping that those clienteles will generate political pressure for the continuation and growth of those programs.

During the forty-eight years that J. Edgar Hoover was FBI director, the FBI was remarkably successful in cultivating external support. It assisted in the production of radio programs and films that glorified its accomplishments, and it created the "Ten Most Wanted" list to dramatize its crime-busting efforts. Hoover himself devoted considerable attention to relations with his congressional overseers. As a result, FBI budget requests were rarely cut and FBI recommendations regarding crime policies were usually heeded.

The close relationships that often develop among executive agencies, special interest groups, and congressional subcommittees are called **iron triangles** or **subgovernments**. All across the government, in almost every policy area, these mutually supportive relationships exist. Some of the most powerful participants in each triangle endure year after year: the subcommittee's ranking members and staff, the agency bureaucrats, and the leaders of the special interest groups (see Figure 14-3). They come to know each other well, and over time they develop understandings and procedures that allow all three points on the triangle to serve the interests of the affected constituents.

Recent changes in American political life have caused some analysts to suggest a revision of the iron-triangle metaphor. Noting the growing prominence of experts in health, transportation, welfare, and many other areas of public policy, they argue that political power increasingly resides in issue networks. An **issue network** consists of specialists in a particular subject working in bureaucratic agencies at all levels of government, along with experts employed by legislative committee staffs, by interest groups, by think tanks, and by universities. Such networks play an important role in developing the national policy agenda, shaping consensus about

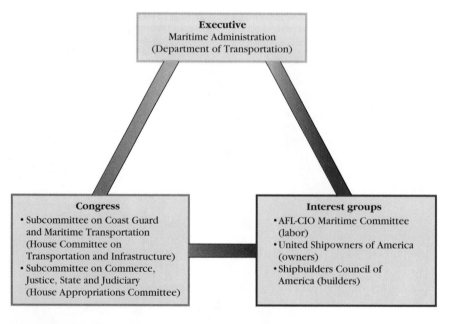

FIGURE 14-3
The iron triangle of merchant shipping policy.

*Prominent public figures and celebrities have helped draw attention to the AIDS epi-
demic and have urged government to fund research. Here Naomi Campbell and
Sharon Stone, the new spokesperson for the American Foundation for AIDS Research
(AMFAR), appear at a fundraising party for the organization.*

preferred policies, and directing political leaders to develop and implement new
proposals.

To take just one example, as government struggled to address the terrifying threat
of the AIDS epidemic, an issue network quickly developed. As knowledge about
AIDS grew, it was widely shared among experts in and out of government. They
worked together in a variety of ways to develop a sense of direction for public policy and then to put pressure on public agencies to implement that agenda. Few
issues have risen to prominence as quickly as AIDS did in the 1980s.

Organizational vitality   Like people, organizations have the capacity to stir the
emotions. Such organizational vitality is most likely in an agency that is new and
fresh. The agency bursts onto the scene, full of enthusiasm, staffed by bright, aggressive people carrying out a popular mission. Many of the New Deal agencies did
this in the 1930s. The Peace Corps did it in the early 1960s, and so did the Army's
Green Berets a few years later. A high level of vitality facilitates the recruitment of
talented people and opens the budget floodgates. The president is happy to be associated with such a popular enterprise, and people are likely to defer to the agency's
judgment.

Unfortunately, organizational vitality is difficult to sustain. The enthusiasm of an
agency's youth rarely lasts. As an agency ages, it makes enemies. Its routines harden,
slowing the decision-making process. The enthusiasts who ran the agency in its early
days go on to other pursuits, and the quality of performance declines. Before long
the agency begins to drop back into the pack. As its vitality decreases, so too does
its influence on policy making.

Leadership   The way an agency is run can make a difference in the way the agency
is perceived and in the attention given to its recommendations. To improve an

agency's effectiveness, leaders can boost internal morale. By providing a sense of excitement and improving the work environment, they can enhance performance. Good leaders can also be persuasive and effective in dealing with the agency's constituencies, especially with the interest groups and the congressional committees most concerned with the agency's programs. For example, in a study of the congressional appropriations process, political scientist Richard Fenno discovered that appropriations subcommittees were much more likely to support an agency's budget request when they had confidence in its leader.[23]

Toward the end of the Reagan administration, many of the members of Congress who dealt regularly with the Department of Housing and Urban Development (HUD) had lost confidence in the leadership of Secretary Samuel R. Pierce because of a pattern of weak management and favoritism in the awarding of grants and contracts. The failures of Pierce's leadership were later revealed in a series of hearings about what came to be known as the "HUD scandals." After his election in 1988, President Bush selected Jack Kemp to be the new HUD secretary. Kemp had served in Congress for eighteen years and was trusted and well regarded by most members. His vigorous early efforts to replace the top leadership at HUD and to correct the lamentable legacy of his predecessor accelerated the restoration of congressional confidence in the department.

PROBLEMS OF ACCOUNTABILITY

Although bureaucrats are not elected, many of them spend their entire careers in government, often in the same agency. Although they make critical decisions about the economy, human welfare, protection of the environment, and war and peace, only the most important, the most misguided, or the most blatantly corrupt of those decisions attract much public attention. Although bureaucrats operate in a political environment, they are often isolated from direct public scrutiny and public review.

That isolation is a significant concern in a democracy, where public policy is supposed to serve the public interest. What can be done to ensure that bureaucratic choices will give due priority to the public interest and that bureaucrats will be held accountable for their actions? How can the checks and balances that are so essential to curb the excesses of authority be imposed on agencies and individuals whose work is so often out of public view? Chapter 13 discussed what efforts presidents undertake to control and direct the work of the executive branch. Several other approaches have been used to accomplish these objectives, including legal controls, legislative controls, and popular participation.

Legal Controls

Bureaucratic decisions are subject to judicial review—that is, they may be challenged in the federal courts. Most legal challenges are based on one of two grounds. The first is that the agency has acted outside its legal authority or jurisdiction. The second is that the agency's decision-making process has violated one or more of the legal rights and protections guaranteed by the Constitution. If a court finds that such a challenge is valid, it can respond in several ways. It can issue a declaratory judgment against the agency, restricting its actions in specified ways. Or it can grant an **injunction**—an order that usually prohibits the agency from taking further action against the aggrieved party until certain conditions, such as a rehearing, are satisfied.

If the plaintiff has sued for damages, the court may also order an agency to pay a sum of money as compensation for those damages.

At any given time, thousands of lawsuits are pending against federal agencies. They serve as an important control technique, but a difficult and inconsistent one. Often such suits take many years to wend their way through the courts, and the high cost of litigation deters the filing of suits by many people who have a genuine grievance. Even those who file suits rarely get satisfaction, because agencies win most of the cases in which they are involved. Legal controls thus provide an imperfect guarantee of bureaucratic accountability.

Legislative Controls

Because administrative oversight is conducted by Congress, the popularly elected branch of the government, it provides the most important guarantee of agency responsiveness to the public interest. Chapter 12 identified some of the ways in which Congress performs its oversight function. The most important of these are its review of personnel policy and presidential appointments and its ultimate control over agency budgets. Congress also exercises oversight through its central role in determining the organizational structure and location of administrative agencies. Congress determines the maximum number of people an agency may employ. It also determines the qualifications that certain executive-branch officials must possess. Statutes require, for example, that the head of the Federal Aviation Administration be a civilian and that one of the members of the Federal Coal Mine Safety Board of Review be a "graduate engineer with experience in the coal mining industry."

Congress determines which positions are subject to Senate confirmation, and it has tended to expand that requirement when it has been in conflict with the executive branch. During the Nixon administration, for example, the Senate confirmation requirement was imposed on appointments of the director and deputy director of OMB and the director of the FBI. In the case of most senior, noncareer appointments in the executive branch, the Senate exercises direct oversight through the confirmation power.

Congress determines the location and level of new agencies and sometimes alters these aspects of existing agencies. When it approved the establishment of the Environmental Protection Agency (EPA) as an independent agency, for example, it did so to keep the EPA from falling under the control of one of the existing cabinet departments. Independent status was the structure preferred by most of the environmentalists who worked for the EPA's creation. Similarly, Congress responded to pressure from veterans' groups by elevating the existing Veterans Administration to cabinet status as the Department of Veterans' Affairs. Organizational decisions of this sort are one of the ways in which Congress imposes its political preferences on the executive branch.

The General Accounting Office (GAO), an arm of Congress, plays a very important role in legislative efforts to control the bureaucracy. The GAO was first created in 1921 to perform financial audits of agency accounts. Over the years its functions have expanded, and now congressional committees often ask it to investigate agency management practices and the effectiveness of substantive programs. GAO reports cover a wide range of subjects and often lead to congressional oversight hearings and to changes in the way agencies do business.[24]

The most important form of legislative control is the power of the purse—the control that Congress exercises over agency budgets.[25] Each year, agencies must appear before congressional appropriations subcommittees to present and defend their budgets. Those subcommittees then make recommendations that find their way into budget and appropriations bills.

Subcommittee decisions rarely follow the agency presentations precisely. Sometimes the subcommittees add funds for certain programs; more often they reduce funding. Frequently the subcommittees or the full Congress shift funds from

Seven astronauts died in a televised instant when the space shuttle Challenger *exploded on January 28, 1986. Millions of eyewitnesses, from schoolchildren to senators, wanted to know what happened, and President Reagan immediately appointed an investigatory commission, including astronaut Sally Ride (below), shown at the State Department hearing on February 26. The commission found that small components called O-rings were not designed to function at the temperatures that prevailed on the day the shuttle was launched. When an executive agency fails so visibly and tragically, a public investigation is almost certain.*

one program to another, replacing agency and presidential preferences with those that have gained political support in the subcommittee or in Congress. One of Jimmy Carter's first initiatives on becoming president, for example, was to cut funding for nineteen dams, reservoirs, and other water development projects in different areas of the country. Because these projects were very important to the representatives from those areas, however, they were able to build coalitions to support them. As a result, the projects were included in the budget that was finally enacted.[26]

Popular Participation

The opportunity of the American people to know about, participate in, and respond to bureaucratic decisions is greater now than it has ever been. Part of the reason for this increase in popular participation is the constantly expanding access to employment in federal agencies. Most federal jobs are now filled through competitive examinations open to all citizens, and equal opportunity and affirmative action programs are designed to ensure the inclusion of female and minority employees in every agency. Moreover, the dispersion of agency staffs into local and regional offices around the country has enhanced geographic representation among federal employees.

Agencies also take steps to encourage public comment on the issues they confront. Often they hold hearings in Washington and elsewhere before making preliminary decisions on new rules or regulations. The Administrative Procedures Act requires that proposed rules be published to permit public comment; so-called **sunshine laws** require that important agency meetings and hearings be open to the public; and the Freedom of Information Act of 1967 permits public access to all but the most sensitive of government documents.[27] (See pages 372–373 for more about this act and sample FOIA letters.)

When agencies take actions that threaten the public interest, they are often called to account by groups representing the public. There is a network of public interest groups—such as Common Cause, environmental groups, and the organizations founded by consumer advocate Ralph Nader—that monitor agency decisions and are quick to criticize those that seem to favor special interests at a high cost or real danger to the public. Other groups with special interests that may be adversely affected by bureaucratic actions also mount public relations campaigns aimed at increasing bureaucratic accountability and getting the bureaucracy to change its ways.

Another, perhaps more important, external source of pressure for accountability is investigative journalism. Print and broadcast reporters uncover and publicize stories that reveal the character of bureaucratic decisions and identify inadequacies or ineptitude in bureaucratic performance. Frequently they provide the leads that result in legislative investigations and legal action or remedial legislation. In 1975, for example, a series of articles in the *New York Times* by investigative reporter Seymour Hersh revealed domestic spying by the CIA, in violation of the agency's charter. Hersh's articles stimulated congressional hearings that resulted in new legislative restrictions on the CIA and the creation of more effective oversight procedures.

The Adequacy of Controls

As the United States government's reliance on bureaucracies increases and as the complexity and power of bureaucracies increase, the need for effective control mechanisms grows more acute. Bureaucracies are crucial to the efficient manage-

POLICING THE FEDERAL POLICE

For much of the twentieth century, members of the federal police forces have loomed large, and largely benevolent, in the minds of Americans. Radio and television programs heralded the exploits of "crime busters," "Feds," and "G-men." As director of the Federal Bureau of Investigation (FBI), J. Edgar Hoover became a national hero—so popular that successive presidents kept him in office for more than 40 years. Congressional appropriations committees rarely questioned or criticized the FBI; frequently, in fact, they appropriated more funds for it than the president had requested.

But after Hoover's death in 1972, revelations of his abuses of power—including disruption of dissident groups and blackmail of their leaders and perhaps even of presidents—tarnished the FBI's reputation and led

to large-scale reforms of its operations. Although these made progress in restoring public confidence in the FBI, in recent years the climate of public and political opinion again seemed to turn against federal law enforcement agencies—not only the FBI, but also the Drug Enforcement Administration (DEA), the U.S. Marshals service, and the Bureau of Alcohol, Tobacco, and Firearms (ATF). Deeply shaken by recurring evidence of misdeeds, deceit, and incompetence, these agencies are now frequently the subject of intense controversy and highly politicized scrutiny. By the mid 1990s, congressional investigations of their activities had become common events.

Some mark the beginning of the turnaround as 1990, when an Idaho resident named Randy Weaver was indicted for allegedly selling illegal guns to an

During a 1993 raid on the Branch Davidian compound in Waco, Texas, the deaths of four federal officers and of some eighty people inside the compound led many to call for better coordination among law enforcement agencies.

ment of the national government, because of their expertise and their ability to simplify and routinize complex tasks. To get those benefits, however, Congress and the president have to delegate considerable authority and discretion to bureaucratic agencies. Delegation creates the problem of ensuring that authority and discretion are used in the public interest.

That is no easy task. Effective checks and balances, ever difficult to create and sustain, are especially elusive in the web of relationships that enmesh the bureaucratic

former for ATF. Weaver was known to be a white supremacist and to have espoused violent antigovernment opinions. When he failed to appear for his date in court in 1992, U.S. marshals surrounded his cabin in the woods of Ruby Ridge. The FBI was then called in to assist. In the 11-day siege that followed, a federal agent and Weaver's wife and son were shot to death before Weaver surrendered. Subsequent investigation determined that the FBI had violated its own procedures in managing the incident and that some FBI officials had tried to cover up the flaws. In 1995, FBI Director Louis Freeh disciplined 12 FBI officials and agents for their handling of the siege at Ruby Ridge.

An even worse incident resulted in 1993 when federal agents sought to enter the Waco, Texas, compound of the Branch Davidians, a religious sect that was thought to have stockpiled a large cache of illegal weapons. The initial ATF effort to enter the compound was badly bungled, and four ATF agents and six Davidians were killed when the Davidians opened fire. The FBI then joined the ATF in what became a 51-day standoff. When federal agents attempted a second assault in April, a fire broke out and 80 Davidians, including 18 children, perished. The federal agencies maintained that they had acted properly and that the fire was set by the Davidians. But a subsequent congressional investigation raised many questions about the handling of the Waco siege.

A similar situation developed in 1996 when a group of antigovernment activists calling themselves the Montana Freemen, who had refused to pay federal taxes and were accused of various financial frauds, holed up on a ranch in Jordan, Montana. More than 100 federal agents, led by the FBI, surrounded the ranch for another lengthy siege. In this episode, however, the FBI was much more cautious about inciting violence, and the Freemen eventually surrendered peacefully.

All of these incidents demonstrate the complexity of federal law enforcement operations targeted against American citizens. Although Americans expect vigorous enforcement of the laws, some also worry about the specter of a federal police force operating without caution or constraint. To some Americans in the 1990s, the federal government seems a rogue force, brutally infringing on the basic freedoms of its people and unnecessarily using tactics that may result in injury or death for overmatched or innocent citizens. After the Ruby Ridge and Waco events, for example, an official of the National Rifle Association, a large interest group composed of gun owners and opponents of gun control legislation, referred to the federal agents involved as "jack-booted storm troopers." Even some of the members of the NRA thought this language too strong. But it reflected a potent strain of contemporary political concern.

How to balance effective federal law enforcement with minimal use of force and close compliance with the Constitution? That is an issue that all federal law enforcement agencies have had to confront in the 1990s. Their responses have been complicated by the overheated political passions that envelop the debate. As these bureaucratic agencies struggle to review and revise their own operating procedures, they are closely scrutinized by politicians and political interests deeply concerned about and acutely anxious to affect their decisions.

agencies of the executive branch. The executive bureaucracy is huge, many of its functions are technically complex, and some of its functions must be conducted in secret. Moreover, the routine and repetitive nature of much government work encourages bureaucrats and other political actors to develop and maintain enduring and mutually beneficial relationships. The desire to sustain these relationships and the shared rewards they produce often inhibits efforts to control bureaucratic activity.

The quest for accountability thus imposes a burden of vigilance on the political system and on the public. The media, special interest groups, and public opinion, however, are inconsistent monitors of bureaucratic activity. The record shows that oversight has been uneven and incomplete, and there is no reason to expect that it will improve significantly in the years ahead. It is hard to strike the proper balance between giving bureaucracies the freedom and encouragement they need to be effective, and at the same time retaining sufficient control to redirect them when they go astray.

SUMMARY

Bureaucracy is a system for carrying on the business of an organization by means of a clear hierarchy of authority and an emphasis on fixed routines. Bureaucracies have jurisdictions established by law, employ specialists trained to perform assigned tasks, and maintain written records of their decisions and activities. The federal bureaucracy—the executive branch—is the largest component of the federal government and includes several types of organizations. The fourteen *departments* are the government's major operating units. *Agencies* have responsibility for a narrower set of functions and may exist either within a department or independently. Bureaus, offices, administrations, and services are subunits of agencies.

Independent regulatory commissions are independent of any departmental affiliation and to some extent are independent of presidential control. Commissions have quasi-legislative and quasi-judicial authority to regulate commerce and trade in an assigned area of jurisdiction. Commission members serve for fixed terms, but the terms are staggered.

The federal government owns a variety of economic enterprises, most of which are operated as *government corporations*. Most government corporations have boards of directors whose members are appointed by the president, usually for long and staggered terms. Some corporations are totally independent; others fall within the jurisdiction of a department.

Before 1883, nonelective positions in the federal bureaucracy were filled by means of *patronage*. People who had supported winning candidates received government jobs, in what was known as the *spoils system*. Calls for reform led to the establishment of the *civil service system*, in which federal employment is based on merit rather than on political considerations. The regular *civil service* now includes most of the career employees of the departments and the major agencies. All civil service positions are graded according to the character of the work to be done, and a pay range is assigned to each grade level. The positions of senior managers and technical specialists are covered by the *Senior Executive Service*, which has its own pay grades. Federal employees are relatively secure in their jobs, although they can be removed when there is a *reduction in force*.

Nearly all the top-level positions in the executive branch are held by political appointees. Most of them can be removed by a president who is unhappy with their performance or loyalty.

The primary task of federal agencies is to interpret and implement the public policies that emerge from the legislative process. They do this in a number of ways, one of which is regulation. *Economic regulation* aims to control prices, market entry, and conditions of service in specific industries. In recent decades there has been a movement toward *deregulation* of some industries. *Social regulation* is concerned with such matters as environmental protection, equal employment opportunity, and product safety. The emphasis on social regulation in recent decades has greatly expanded the scope of federal regulatory activity. Most agencies have the authority to issue rules, or elaborations of laws. The draft of a new rule must be published in the *Federal Register* at least thirty days before it is to go into effect. The agency invites and reviews public comment on the rule and then publishes the rule in its final form. In 1981 the Reagan administration required that all major proposed rules be reviewed and approved by the Office of Management and Budget, but in 1990 the Supreme Court limited the scope of OMB's power in this area.

Executive agencies perform quasi-judicial functions when they hold hearings to resolve conflicting interpretations of a rule. The hearings are often presided over by an *administrative law judge*, whose rulings are binding on both the agency and the complainant.

To ensure that laws and rules are obeyed, agencies make scheduled inspections, conduct audits, and impose reporting requirements. Agencies also oversee compliance by responding to complaints by parties that believe they have been harmed as a result of non-compliance.

Executive agencies also play an important role in the initiation of policy, because agency employees usually are experts in a particular policy area. Their training, experience, and values shape their perceptions of the form policies should take.

Bureaucratic policy making is influenced by the distinctive characteristics of bureaucracy. Hierarchical decision making results in filtering, which eliminates some proposals because they are unnecessary, too costly, or untimely, and in the coordination of the proposals of various subunits. The character and culture of an agency also affect the policies it generates, and the biases of an agency may become institutionalized in its *standard operating procedures*. In recent years, decision making by the executive agencies has become increasingly professionalized. As a result, striking a balance between professional advice and political realities is a constant struggle for executive-branch officials.

The natural characteristics of bureaucratic agencies often produce certain pathologies. Among these unhealthy characteristics are persistence, conservatism, expansionism, capture, and the territorial imperative. *Capture* is the tendency of agencies to develop symbiotic relationships with the special interests they oversee, becoming protectors rather than regulators of those interests. The *territorial imperative* is the common urge of an agency to jealously guard its own territory or turf.

Several factors determine an agency's ability to affect public policy; they include expertise, political support, organizational vitality, and leadership. The more technical and specialized an agency's expertise is, the greater will be the agency's opportunity to dominate policy making in its area of concern. Similarly, the more widespread and intense an agency's external political support is, the greater will be the agency's ability to affect policy making. Agencies try to develop supportive clienteles among the groups that benefit from their programs. The resulting close relationships among agencies, interest groups, and congressional committees are called *iron triangles* or *subgovernments*. However, recent changes in American political life suggest that political power increasingly resides in *issue networks* consisting of specialists in a variety of public and private agencies.

Organizational vitality, another source of influence, is difficult to sustain. A good leader can increase an agency's influence by boosting internal morale and dealing persuasively with the agency's constituencies.

Several approaches have been used to make bureaucratic agencies more accountable to the public. Bureaucratic decisions are subject to judicial review, and courts can issue a declaratory judgment against an agency, grant an *injunction* that prevents the agency from taking certain actions, or order an agency to compensate a plaintiff for damages. Legislative controls on the bureaucracy include congressional review of personnel policy and presidential appointments, control of the structure of administrative agencies, and control over agency budgets. *Sunshine laws* require that important agency meetings and hearings be open to the public. Other sources of pressure for accountability are the activities of public interest groups and investigative journalism.

KEY TERMS

bureaucracy
department
agency
independent regulatory
   commission
government corporation
patronage
spoils system
civil service system

civil service
Senior Executive Service (SES)
reduction in force
economic regulation
deregulation
social regulation
administrative law judge
standard operating procedures
   (SOPs)

capture
territorial imperative
iron triangle
subgovernment
issue network
injunction
sunshine laws

SCHOLARLY STUDIES

Goodsell, Charles. *The Case for Bureaucracy: A Public Administration Polemic.* 3d ed. Chatham, N.J.: Chatham House, 1994. A vigorous defense of the contemporary federal bureaucracy; employs a broad array of empirical evidence to rebut many of the stereotypes that dominate public debate about the role of bureaucrats and public agencies.

Heclo, Hugh. *A Government of Strangers.* Washington, D.C.: Brookings Institution, 1977. An important analysis of the cultures and work environments of senior federal officials. Indicates that government leaders come from such a variety of backgrounds, are selected for such widely differing reasons, and are motivated by so broad an array of incentives that they often have little in common.

Kaufman, Herbert. *The Forest Ranger: A Study in Administrative Behavior.* Baltimore, Md.: Johns Hopkins University Press, 1967. A classic study of bureaucratic culture. Focuses on the development of the United States Forest Service and the highly refined set of values and perceptions that govern the behavior of its employees.

Lynn, Naomi B., and Aaron Wildavsky, eds. *Public Administration: The State of the Discipline.* Chatham, N.J.: Chatham House, 1990. An exploration of the approaches that are currently used to study and explain the actions of public agencies.

Rourke, Francis E. *Bureaucracy, Politics, and Public Policy.* 3d ed. New York: HarperCollins, 1987. A clear and comprehensive exploration of the way politics shapes the organization, operation, and policy products of the federal executive branch.

Seidman, Harold, and Robert Gilmour. *Politics, Position, and Power.* 4th ed. New York: Oxford University Press, 1986. A study of the creation and management of political influence within the federal bureaucracy. Provides a good feel for how the bureaucratic universe appears from the inside.

Shafritz, Jay M., and Albert C. Hyde, eds. *Classics of Public Administration.* 3d ed. Belmont, Calif.: Wadsworth Publishing, 1992. A book of readings that includes most of the seminal articles in the literature of public administration and bureaucratic operation. A good place to identify the principles and theories that have guided the scholarly study of the executive branch.

LEISURE READING

Dickson, Paul. *The Official Rules.* New York: Dell, 1981. A sometimes tongue-in-cheek compilation of the "rules" and proverbs that determine outcomes in the bureaucratic world.

Halberstam, David. *The Best and the Brightest.* New York: Random House, 1993. A reporter's account of the backgrounds, motivations, and mindsets of the leading figures in the development of American policy in Vietnam.

Lowi, Theodore, and Benjamin Ginsberg. *Poliscide.* Lanham, Md.: University Press of America, 1990. An ingenious case study in which the decision to place an atom smasher in Illinois becomes an opportunity for political actors at every level to accomplish political objectives, with grave consequences for the residents of the community in which the project is to be located.

Osborne, David, and Ted Gaebler. *Reinventing Government: How the Entrepreneurial Spirit Is Transforming the Public Sector.* Reading, Mass.: Addison-Wesley, 1992. The original source on the major effort of the 1990s to reform government by making it more responsive to citizens and more entrepreneurial in approach.

PRIMARY SOURCES

The Budget of the United States Government. Washington, D.C.: U.S. Government Printing Office, annual. A detailed account of each year's federal budget proposal, with explanations of programs and contemporary and historical data on government spending.

Statistical Abstract of the United States. Washington, D.C.: Bureau of the Census, annual. A compendium of data on every aspect of American life and government, collected and updated by the Census Bureau and the Department of Commerce.

The United States Government Manual. Washington, D.C.: U.S. Government Printing Office, biennial. A volume describing the functions, authority, and structure of every agency of the federal government, including those that no longer exist.

ORGANIZATIONS

American Society for Public Administration, 1120 G Street, N.W., Washington, DC 20005; phone (202) 393-7878; fax (202) 638-4952; e-mail dcaspa@aol.com Sponsors workshops and conferences, disseminates information about public administration. The society's mission is to promote high ethical standards for public service.

Council for Excellence in Government, 1620 L Street, N.W., Suite 850, Washington, DC 20036; phone (202) 728-0418; fax (202) 728-0422; e-mail mcginnis2@aol.com Works to broaden understanding of public service and management in the government; conducts outreach activities that encourage public and media discussion of public service.

National Academy of Public Administration, 1120 G Street, N.W., Washington, DC 20005; phone (202) 347-3190; fax (202) 393-0993; e-mail napa@tmn.com Conducts studies and offers assistance to federal, state, and local government agencies and public officials on problems of public administration and public policy implementation.

The Judiciary

W ith public concern about teenage pregnancy and the spread of AIDS growing, in 1991 the Falmouth Public Schools in Falmouth, Massachusetts, joined many other school districts around the country in making condoms available free of charge to high school students. But the condom distribution program, in which students were also counseled about the proper use of condoms and about sexually transmitted diseases, was challenged in court by parents who argued that it violated their rights to familial privacy and freedom of religion. Although a New York

state court had struck down a similar program in 1993, the Massachusetts state supreme court upheld the Falmouth program. In January 1996 the United States Supreme Court declined to consider an appeal of the decision.

The Court's refusal to take the case did not mean that its nine justices agreed with the Massachusetts court. Nor did letting the Massachusetts decision stand mean that the New York decision was overruled. Rather, it simply meant that no more than three of the justices, if that, considered the issue worth reviewing at the time. The Court has almost absolute power to decide what issues it wants to decide and when it wants to decide them.

The issue of access to contraceptives has long been politically controversial and subject to litigation. In 1943 a doctor brought a lawsuit challenging the constitutionality of an 1879 Connecticut law that prohibited virtually all individuals, whether married or single, from using contraceptives and barred physicians from giving advice about their use. When the state court upheld the law, the doctor appealed that decision to the United States Supreme Court. But the Court ruled that he failed to meet its tests for bringing such a lawsuit. Because he had not been arrested and had failed to show that he had suffered any personal injury as a result of the statute, the Court said, he lacked standing—the basis for bringing a lawsuit.

Over a decade later, Dr. C. Lee Buxton and a patient were likewise denied standing on the grounds that the law had not been enforced for eighty years, even though the state had begun to close birth control clinics. In this case, *Poe v. Ullman* (1961), Justice Felix Frankfurter argued that the Court should exercise judicial self-restraint by not declaring a largely unenforced law unconstitutional.

Finally, after Dr. Buxton and Estelle Griswold, executive director of the Planned Parenthood League of

Connecticut, had been found guilty of prescribing contraceptives to a married couple, the Court struck down what Justice Potter Stewart called Connecticut's "uncommonly silly law." In announcing the Court's ruling in the case, *Griswold v. Connecticut* (1965), Justice William O. Douglas explained why challengers of the law were now being granted standing. Because Buxton and Griswold had given medical advice on how to prevent conception, he said, they therefore had a professional relationship with the couple. This gave them standing to challenge the constitutionality of Connecticut's law as a violation of a married couple's right to privacy.

No less important for the Court's ruling in Griswold was the fact that in 1962, the year after *Poe v. Ullman*, Justices Frankfurter and Charles Whittaker had resigned from the Court. They had been replaced by President John F. Kennedy's two appointees, Justices Byron White and Arthur Goldberg. With that change in the Court's composition came major changes in the Court's view of individuals' standing to sue and the kinds of rights they could claim in the courts. The Court's recognition of a constitutional right of privacy in *Griswold*, in turn, provided a basis for extending that right to include a woman's right to decide whether to have an abortion in *Roe v. Wade* (1973).

The controversy that began with challenges to the constitutionality of Connecticut's birth control law illustrates the importance of the Supreme Court's power to decide what cases it will review as well as how the Court responds to social forces. Individuals must have standing to bring cases and controversies to the courts, but whether they are granted standing may also depend on the composition of the court. In addition, the controversy illustrates the operation of the American system of judicial federalism, in which each state maintains a system of courts whose standards and rulings may differ from those of other states and of the federal court system.

The shift in the Court's position in the Connecticut birth control cases also indicates how political dynamics affect judicial decision making and how changes in the composition of the bench may significantly alter the Court's role in larger controversies. Although the judiciary can decide only cases and controversies that are properly brought to it, it is nevertheless a political institution. Judges and justices are political actors who exercise great power in the United States, far more than their counterparts in other democracies. Their decisions, based on interpretations of law, sometimes have enormous political consequences. They may affect millions of people and involve billions of dollars. They may settle conflicts between special interest groups, alter the relationship between the president and Congress or between the federal and state governments, and defend the rights of individuals and businesses against the coercive powers of government.

This chapter begins by focusing on the organization and operation of courts and the politics of judicial federalism. It looks at the power of judicial review, the politics of selecting and appointing judges, the judicial process itself, and the Supreme Court. Finally, it examines the politics of judicial decision making and explores the interaction between courts and other political institutions. In all these areas, courts and judges are integral players in the politics of American government.

In most countries there is a single, unitary system of courts, but in the United States judicial power is decentralized and divided between two separate judicial systems. Alongside the federal judiciary, each of the fifty states has its own independent judiciary. Within both the federal and the state systems, judicial power is further divided between trial courts (and other lesser courts such as traffic courts) and one or two levels of appellate courts, which hear appeals from the lower courts. (The organization of the federal judicial system is shown in Figure 15-1; the box on page 556 presents the basic types of law.)

The importance of these dual judicial systems, termed **judicial federalism**, is that federal courts largely consider disputes over national law and state courts consider only disputes arising under state law. If there is a conflict between national and state law, the matter is settled by the federal courts and ultimately by the Supreme Court. This is so because (as discussed in Chapter 2) the Constitution and federal law are supreme over state law. Judicial federalism and the decentralized structure of federal and state courts have a number of important consequences for judicial policy making, as we will see in this chapter.

Federal Courts

Article III of the Constitution vests judicial power "in one Supreme Court, and in such inferior courts as Congress may from time to time ordain and establish." Courts created under Article III are called **constitutional courts**. In addition, under

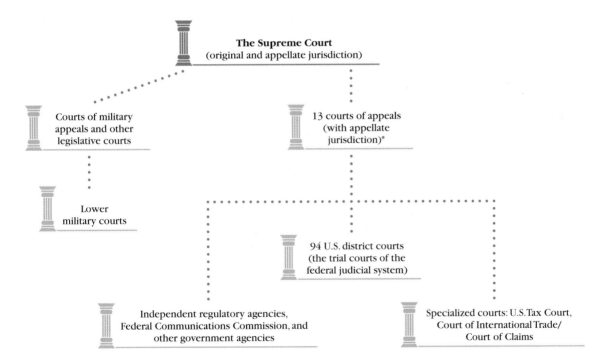

*This includes eleven regional courts of appeals, one Court of Appeals for the District of Columbia Circuit, and one Court of Appeals for the Federal Circuit.

FIGURE 15-1
The organization of the federal judicial system.

TYPES OF LAW

Admiralty and maritime law: Law governing shipping and commerce on the high seas and on the navigable waters of the United States.

Administrative law: Law governing the decision-making procedures and decisions of public agencies and public administrators.

Civil law: Law dealing with the private rights and relations of individuals, though the government may become a party to civil actions when it seeks to prevent violations of law, as under the Sherman Anti-Trust Act.

Common law: Judge-made law, originating in England in the twelfth century and based on the principle of *stare decisis* ("let the decision stand"), or precedent.

Constitutional law: Rulings by the Supreme Court interpreting the United States Constitution.

Criminal law: Law that defines crimes against the public order and specifies punishment for those crimes.

Statutory law: Laws passed by legislatures and judges' interpretations of legislative enactments.

Article I Congress may create **legislative courts** to carry out its own powers. The United States Court of Military Appeals, which applies military law, is one such court; federal bankruptcy courts are another type of legislative court. These courts have more specialized jurisdiction than those created under Article III, and their judges do not hold lifetime appointments.

Congress has established a number of courts under Article III. In 1789 it divided the country into thirteen districts (one in each state) and created a federal district court for each. **District courts** are the trial courts of the federal system. In addition, the Judiciary Act of 1789 created three federal **courts of appeals** to hear appeals from decisions of the district courts or from state courts. But Congress did not provide for any appellate court judges. Instead, these courts were staffed by two Supreme Court justices who twice a year sat with a district court judge to hear cases. The federal courts of appeals were not staffed by full-time appellate judges for another hundred years.

As the country grew, so did the number of district courts, along with the number of appeals of their rulings to the Supreme Court. Eventually the workload of the Supreme Court became too large for the justices to handle. Congress responded in 1891 by creating the circuit courts of appeals, which now hear most of the appeals coming from them or from state courts. Today, aside from legislative courts, the federal judiciary consists of ninety-four district courts, thirteen courts of appeals, and the Supreme Court.

District courts There is at least one federal district court in each state and at least one judge assigned to each court; the number of courts depends on the state's population, and the number of judges on the size of the court's workload. In 1995 there were 649 district judges in all. Every judge has the assistance of one law clerk, one or two secretaries, and additional staff research and clerical support if needed. In criminal cases, district courts may also use *grand juries* (juries consisting of more than twelve jurors) to determine whether to indict individuals, and *petit juries* (twelve-member juries) to try individuals who are indicted.

District judges preside over cases alone; they hear oral arguments at trial, decide cases if a jury is not involved, and impose sentences. They handle the bulk of all litigation in the federal system. Each year, almost 250,000 civil cases and over 45,000 criminal cases are filed in federal district courts.[1] The cases generally involve federal law, but district judges may also decide disputes between citizens of different states and, when authorized by legislation, apply state law.

In most cases a district court is the court of first and last resort in the federal judicial system—the place where a case begins and ends. In fact, a substantial number of federal criminal defendants do not even go to trial because they plead guilty, often as a result of plea bargaining. (As explained in Chapter 4, a plea bargain is a deal between a prosecutor and a defendant in which the defendant agrees to plead guilty to a lesser offense in exchange for a lesser sentence or probation.) Of the criminal cases that do go to trial, less than 15 percent are later appealed. Thus most of what district judges do is never reviewed by a higher court. As one federal judge puts it: "Justice stops in the district. They either get it here or they can't get it at all."[2]

Because district judges preside over trials, they experience the drama of the adversary process to a greater degree than do appellate judges, who rarely hear arguments in cases on appeal. As discussed in Chapter 4, the adversary process is based on the idea that two sides of a dispute should argue their cases before a neutral third party—a judge or a jury—that ensures procedural fairness and, after hearing the evidence from both sides, decides the dispute. Each side argues as hard as it can, and trial judges themselves often feel embattled, rather than like impartial and detached arbitrators.

Appellate courts In contrast with the individual decision making of district judges, appellate court judges decide cases in a collegial manner. Judges on the thirteen federal courts of appeals sit in rotating panels of three and decide most cases solely on the basis of written **briefs** filed by attorneys for both sides in a dispute. These documents discuss the facts of the case and relevant laws and precedents (prior rulings by the Supreme Court or federal circuit courts). Occasionally the entire appellate court sits as a panel, or **en banc**. The dynamics of decision making in federal courts of appeals therefore vary with the rotation of judges and the number of judges sitting *en banc*. Indeed, as the number of judges on appellate courts has increased from three to twenty or more, some judges complain that they function more like a legislative body, dividing into groups and being forced to seek compromises with each other when deciding cases.

Although appellate judges share responsibility for decisions, their mounting caseloads present serious problems. Federal courts of appeals face close to fifty thousand cases a year. The Ninth Circuit alone, which includes the Pacific Coast states, Alaska, Hawaii, and Guam, now issues over four thousand opinions a year. As the number of appeals has risen, Congress has increased the number of judges. But more cases, more judges, and more opinions place greater strain on working relationships and threaten the stability and continuity of the law. Judges have had to delegate more of their work to law clerks, and the number of clerks assigned to an appellate judge has risen from one or two to three or four (at the Supreme Court). Some judges now warn of the bureaucratization of the federal courts and the advent of "bureaucratic justice."[3]

State Courts

State courts are by no means inferior to the federal judiciary, even though their decisions may be appealed to the federal courts and to the Supreme Court if they involve the application of federal law or issues governed by the federal Constitution. State

DOING JURY DUTY

Trial by jury is guaranteed in four different places in the Constitution: in Article III, Section 2, and in the Fifth, Sixth, and Seventh Amendments. The purpose of a jury trial is to protect the accused from government oppression by demanding that members of the community—not a single judge or prosecutor—determine guilt or innocence.

The average citizen can expect to be called for service as a trial juror for a civil or criminal trial every three to five years or so. When calling individuals for jury duty, the courts seek to select at random a fair cross-section of the community. To do this, names are usually randomly drawn from lists of voters and holders of driver's licenses. This method arguably excludes younger, poorer, and minority citizens, who are less likely to register to vote.

Although serving on a jury is an obligation of citizenship, jury duty is often considered a nuisance or a burden. In many ways, it is. Jurors in federal courts receive about $30 a day, which works out to about the minimum wage. Jurors in state courts receive a token daily payment that is even less. In addition, jury service can be very time-consuming.

Many prospective jurors ask to be excused or to have their service postponed. The requests are usually granted to those who would find jury duty particularly burdensome (an elderly person in poor health, for example) or temporarily inconvenient (conflicting with a planned vacation or business trip). In some states, members of certain occupations such as lawyers and police officers are automatically excused; housewives with young children are also automatically excused in some states. Many other states, however, have sharply curtailed automatic excuses. Many states have also moved to streamlined systems that put jurors "on call" and have them report to the courthouse only when they are actually needed.

Relatively few jurors actually participate in a full trial. In the *voir dire*, or selection process, judges and attorneys can challenge, or disqualify, prospective jurors in one of two ways. Peremptory challenges remove a juror, usually a person who appears unsympathetic to one side or the other, without giving a specific reason. Challenges "for cause" remove people who under questioning express a specific bias that could prevent them from being impartial.

Once a jury of twelve has been selected, the trial proceeds. In most cases, trials last only a day or so (many cases are settled after the jury is selected but before the actual trial begins). The jurors listen to the evidence and then begin their deliberations. Generally a decision is reached quickly and unanimously. Reaching a decision in a complex case can take longer, sometimes several days. Often jurors in these cases are sequestered to keep them from outside influences during the deliberations. In some notorious criminal cases, the jurors serve anonymously and are sequestered during the entire trial.

The six jurors and three alternates who were chosen in 1991 to hear the West Palm Beach, Florida, rape trial of William Kennedy Smith. Smith was eventually acquitted of the charges.

courts play a crucial role in the administration of justice. When interpreting state constitutions and bills of rights, they have great freedom to pursue their own directions in policy making rather than simply following the direction of the Supreme Court.

State courts handle by far the greatest volume of litigation. Well over 90 percent of all lawsuits filed each year are in state courts. The business of state courts also tends to diverge from that in federal courts. Apart from criminal cases, the largest portion of state supreme court litigation involves economic issues. State courts face, for instance, a large number of cases involving zoning ordinances, minor business disputes, and government regulation of public utilities, as well as controversies over labor relations and the use of natural resources. The nature of such litigation varies from one state to another, depending on factors such as population size, urbanization, and socio-economic conditions.[4] In the large, populous state of New York, with New York City being the headquarters of major stock exchanges and of many large corporations, a higher percentage of the litigation involves disputes over economic regulations, antitrust laws, and commercial transactions, as well as criminal cases.

The Supreme Court intrudes on state-court policy making only in a very narrow class of litigation: cases in which state courts deal with **federal questions**. A federal question involves a disagreement over the interpretation or application of the Constitution, the Bill of Rights, or other federal laws; such a question rarely emerges from the cases that normally come to the state courts. If a state-court case is decided on **independent state grounds**—such as a state constitution or a state bill of rights—the Court will not overturn the decision, out of respect for the **principle of comity** between federal and state courts. In other words, the Court defers out of courtesy to the decisions of state supreme courts that are based on a state, not the federal, constitution.

Despite the principle of comity, tensions do exist in relations between state and federal courts. These tensions reflect the politics of a changing federal judiciary. In the 1950s and 1960s, for example, the Supreme Court applied the guarantees of the federal Bill of Rights to the states. Many state judges opposed these liberal rulings and attacked the Court for intruding on the autonomy of state courts. By contrast, during the 1970s, 1980s, and 1990s, under more conservative chief justices, the Court tended to take a more limited view of the role of the federal judiciary in protecting and expanding civil liberties and civil rights. As a result, some liberal state-court judges are now going in the opposite direction from the Supreme Court, extending greater protection for civil rights and liberties under their state constitutions. Since 1969, in over seven hundred cases state supreme courts have interpreted their state constitutions and bills of rights to provide greater protection and to afford rights that the United States Supreme Court has refused to recognize under the federal Constitution and Bill of Rights.[5] For example, some courts have recognized a right to education, a right to die, and broader rights to privacy on the basis of their state constitutions.

THE POWER OF JUDICIAL REVIEW

Unlike other political institutions, courts are passive and reactive. They are not, as Justice Benjamin Cardozo once observed, "knights-errant" or "roving commissions." Rather than initiating policy, they must await disputes in the form of a lawsuit—that is, an actual "case or controversy."

Article III of the Constitution, along with congressional legislation, specifies the **jurisdiction** of federal courts, the kinds of cases and controversies that courts may

REQUIREMENTS FOR GAINING STANDING

1. *A personal injury must be claimed.* For example, an individual must have been denied some right under federal or state law.
2. *The dispute must not be hypothetical.* Real adverse interests must be at stake.
3. *A case must be brought before a court authorized to hear such disputes.* Cases must be within a court's jurisdiction.
4. *Other remedies must have been exhausted.* For example, litigants must have exhausted administrative appeals and appeals in other lower courts.
5. *The dispute must not be moot.* Circumstances since filing the lawsuit must not have changed so as to end the dispute or make it hypothetical.
6. *A case must be ripe for judicial resolution.* The dispute must not be hypothetical, and other opportunities for resolving it must have been exhausted.
7. *The dispute must be capable of judicial resolution.* The dispute must not involve a political question that should be decided by other branches of government.

decide. Under Article III the Supreme Court has **original jurisdiction** in all cases involving disputes between two or more states and in cases brought against the United States by ambassadors of foreign countries. Original jurisdiction means that the case originates in the Supreme Court rather than a lower court, but in practice the Court appoints a "special master" to hear the case and to recommend a decision. Out of the more than six thousand cases that come to the Court each year, only two or three involve matters of original jurisdiction. The rest arrive under the Court's **appellate jurisdiction**, as established by congressional legislation. Under its appellate jurisdiction the Court hears appeals from lower federal courts and state courts. Federal legislation also defines the jurisdiction of the lower federal courts; state constitutions and legislation define the jurisdiction of state courts.

Courts have jurisdiction only over disputes involving adverse interests and a real controversy. They will not take "friendly lawsuits" brought by two parties who simply want to have some question settled. The parties must have **standing to sue**; they must show that they are suffering or are in danger of suffering an immediate and substantial personal injury (see the box above). Traditionally individuals could challenge government action only if they could demonstrate a personal and monetary injury. But since the 1960s Congress and the courts have expanded the law of standing in cases like *Griswold v. Connecticut*. As a result, today lawsuits may also involve nonmonetary interests such as aesthetic and environmental well-being. For example, in *United States v. Students Challenging Regulatory Agency Procedures (SCRAP)* (1973), the Court granted standing to a group of law students attacking a proposed surcharge on railroad freight. The students contended that the surcharge would discourage the recycling of bottles and cans and thus contribute to environmental pollution. When granting SCRAP standing to bring its suit, the Court made the following observation: "Aesthetic and environmental well-being, like economic well-being, are important ingredients of the quality of life in our society, and the fact that particular environmental interests are shared by the many rather than the few does not make them less deserving of legal protection through the judicial process."[6]

George E. C. Hayes, Thurgood Marshall, and James M. Nabrit celebrate on the steps of the United States Supreme Court after hearing its decision in Brown v. Board of Education of Topeka, Kansas *(1954). As attorneys for the National Association for the Advancement of Colored People's legal defense fund, they had spearheaded the litigation that led to the decision, which abolished legal segregation in public schools.*

More individuals and interest groups may now gain access to the courts, and they may raise a wider range of disputes. They may bring test cases and controversies in which they have a stake in the outcome but which also represent a conflict over the public interest. In the 1940s and 1950s, the National Association for the Advancement of Colored People brought a series of test cases challenging the constitutionality of racially segregated public schools. These cases led to the Supreme Court's landmark ruling, in *Brown v. Board of Education of Topeka, Kansas* (1954), that struck down the doctrine of "separate but equal" facilities. More recently, environmental groups like the Natural Resources Defense Council and the Sierra Club have brought suits against polluters in order to protect the environment; and the U.S. Chamber of Commerce, business groups, and conservative legal foundations have used litigation to challenge the enforcement of health, safety, and environmental regulations.[7]

The Political Question Doctrine

After a lawsuit has been filed, judges may still refuse to decide a dispute. For example, they will not decide hypothetical disputes or give "advisory opinions" on possible future conflicts. Courts also avoid deciding **political questions**—issues that judges think should be resolved by other branches of government, either because of the separation of powers or because the judiciary is not in a position to provide a remedy. Thus courts generally avoid disputes involving foreign policy and international relations. But this does not make the judiciary less political. Deciding what is a "political question" is itself a political decision and an exercise of judicial review.

The Constitution and legislation stipulate the kinds of cases and controversies that courts may consider. Yet as Chief Justice Charles Evans Hughes once remarked, "We are under the Constitution, but the Constitution is what the judges say it is."[8] Legal doctrines governing access to the courts mean what judges and justices say they mean. Courts change, and judges change their minds. For many decades, for instance, courts applied the political question doctrine to avoid entering the "political thicket" of state elections and representation.[9] But under these conditions urban voters were often denied equal voting rights. The Court finally responded to this injustice in *Baker v. Carr* (1962), holding that such disputes were within its jurisdiction and were **justiciable disputes**—that is, open to judicial resolution and a judicial remedy. After abandoning the political question doctrine in this area, the Court forced state and local governments to provide equal voting rights and established the principle of one person, one vote.

Judicial Review and Political Influence

In the United States the judiciary, particularly the Supreme Court, exercises great political power because its members have the authority to interpret the Constitution and the laws of the nation. This power of *judicial review* (see Chapter 2) gives the courts the power to strike down any law enacted by Congress or by the states and to declare official government actions unconstitutional.

Judicial review has remained controversial ever since Chief Justice John Marshall asserted that power in the landmark case of *Marbury v. Madison* (1803). By striking down acts of Congress or state legislatures, the Court thwarts the democratic process and majority rule as expressed by elected representatives. This is so even when the Court uses its power to promote the democratic process, as it does when it enforces the First Amendment guarantees of freedom of speech and press and when it strikes down barriers to the electoral process.

The political influence of the judiciary has grown dramatically since the nation's founding. No longer is the judiciary, as Alexander Hamilton claimed in *The Federalist, No. 78*, "the least dangerous branch" of the government. Instead, it has become truly a coequal branch. The Supreme Court increasingly asserts its power in striking down congressional legislation, state laws, and municipal ordinances. Likewise, lower courts no longer serve simply as tribunals for private dispute resolution but more often serve as problem solvers and policy makers.

Courts have also increasingly become, as Judge Irving Kaufman points out, "an accelerator of government rather than a brake." In some instances, judges have taken over the management of schools, hospitals, and prisons when ordering changes to make up for past discrimination or substandard facilities.[10] More often, though, Congress has given the courts a role in the implementation of public policies by extending their jurisdiction and giving them the power to hear lawsuits brought under legislation. The National Environmental Protection Act, for example, provides that citizens may file lawsuits in federal courts to challenge the decisions of the Environmental Protection Agency and even to force that agency to promulgate regulations to protect the environment.

Activism Versus Self-Restraint

Do courts exercise too much power? Have they usurped the power of other branches of the government? The power of judicial review has been criticized, at different times, by both liberals and conservatives. In the 1920s and 1930s, liberals attacked the Supreme Court for its **judicial activism** in striking down progressive economic legislation such as minimum-wage laws. (Judicial activism is the use of judicial review to invalidate state and federal laws.) Criticizing the Court for substituting its conservative economic views for the more progressive views of Congress and state legislatures, the liberals urged the Court to exercise **judicial self-restraint** and defer to legislative authority. (Judicial self-restraint is the practice of deferring to the executive and legislative branches, rather than asserting the Court's own view.) By contrast, the Court's activism in defending civil liberties and civil rights in the 1960s and 1970s led conservatives to charge that the Court was usurping the power of other political institutions and thwarting the will of the majority. Presidents Nixon, Reagan, and Bush all called for the appointment of judges who would exercise judicial self-restraint.

But the political role of contemporary courts is only partially explained by judges' exercise of judicial review. Courts respond (more or less slowly) to the problems created by technological advances and political and social changes. The expansion of judicial power is also related to changes in government policies for dealing with illegal activities. For instance, the federal judiciary played a minor role in environmental protection until the 1970s, when Congress passed legislation such as the Clean Air and Clean Water Acts and the National Environmental Protection Act. Then the courts had to resolve conflicts over the implementation of that legislation by federal agencies.

Other social trends have been no less significant in increasing and changing the business of courts. Even before the 1920s and 1930s, railroads and other businesses relied on the judiciary to protect property rights and to strike down progressive economic legislation enacted under the influence of the labor and populist movements beginning in the late nineteenth century. The civil rights movement of the 1950s and 1960s brought lawsuits challenging racial discrimination in schools, in employment, and in public accommodations.

The pace of litigation is also influenced by economic cycles. This is so because increased economic activity gives rise to new issues involving property rights and disputes over government regulations affecting labor-management relations; health, safety, and environmental matters; and other economic issues.

No less important is the fact that American society is exceedingly litigious—so much so that the United States is sometimes called an adversarial democracy. In the mid 1990s, for instance, over 300,000 cases a year were filed in the federal courts, more than twice the number in the preceding decade. Moreover, as noted earlier, the federal judiciary handles but a small percentage of all litigation that occurs in the United States; state courts face over 25 million cases a year. Another measure of the increasing litigiousness of the United States is the rather dramatic increase in the number of lawyers and judges since the end of World War II. In 1990 it was estimated that there was one lawyer for every 298 American citizens.

Even more fundamental to the political role of the judiciary are cultural factors that condition the way democratic politics works in the pluralistic and litigious American society. The competition for power among diverse interest groups in other political arenas inexorably finds its way into the courts. As the astute French commentator Alexis de Tocqueville observed in the 1830s, "Scarcely any political question arises in the United States that is not resolved, sooner or later, into a judicial question."[11] This situation results from a distinguishing feature of democracy in America: the peculiar "legal habit" that accompanies Americans' devotion to civil rights and to the idea of the rule of law.

HOW JUDGES ARE CHOSEN

A hallmark of the federal judiciary is the relative isolation of judges from political pressures such as the direct personal lobbying faced by senators, representatives, and other elected officials. Under the Constitution federal judges are given lifetime appointments, and Congress is barred from decreasing their salaries. Still, judges are appointed largely for political reasons, get involved in political controversies, and make judgments that affect the rules that govern politics.

In contrast with the system for appointing federal judges, the means of selecting state court judges varies from one state to another and among different courts within the states. In states on the Atlantic seaboard, judges have historically been appointed by either the governor or the state legislature. In other states, particularly in the South, they are elected on either a partisan or a nonpartisan basis. In the Midwest and West, as well as in a growing number of states elsewhere, some combination of those methods—a so-called **merit system**—is used. Under a merit system a nonpartisan commission usually provides a list of possible nominees from which the governor or legislature makes appointments to fill vacancies. After one or two years of service, an appointee's name is placed unopposed on a ballot, and voters decide whether he or she should be retained. Under this system, judges may or may not come up for retention elections every ten or fifteen years.

Politics ultimately determines the choice of state court judges. Regardless of the method of selection, the same kinds of individuals tend to be selected. White male lawyers from upper-middle-class Protestant backgrounds who have been politically active have historically predominated. Since the late 1970s, however, an increasing number of women and members of minority groups have been appointed or elected to state judgeships.

Appointment of Federal Judges

Politics also determines who is appointed to the federal bench. Article II of the Constitution gives the president the power to nominate and appoint, with the advice and consent of the Senate, all federal judges. Since federal judgeships provide lifetime tenure, these appointments are a prized form of political patronage. In fact, presidents try to "pack" the federal courts in the hope of influencing the direction of public law and policy long after they have left the Oval Office.

In the 1980s and early 1990s, for instance, Republican presidents Ronald Reagan and George Bush promised to appoint judges who were opposed to abortion. Political scientists studying the decisions of federal judges appointed by recent presidents found that "Reagan appointees were much more resistant to abortion rights than were the appointees of his predecessors, including the appointees of fellow Republican Richard Nixon. Likewise President Carter's appointees were much more supportive of abortion claims than were the appointees of other presidents."[12] Although President Clinton was slow to fill court vacancies in his first year in office, he appointed a near-record number of judges (over 100) in his second year, and by the end of 1995 he had named a total of 182, almost as many as Bush did during his entire four-year term. Of Clinton's appointees, 67 percent were rated by the American Bar Association (ABA) as "well qualified," the ABA's highest ranking. By comparison, 59 percent of Bush's, 55 percent of Reagan's, and 56 percent of Carter's judicial appointees were ranked "well qualified." In addition, 32 percent of Clinton's judges were women and 29 percent were members of racial or ethnic minorities, more nontraditional federal judges than any preceding president ever appointed. Table 15-1 shows the number of judicial appointments made by each of

| TABLE 15-1 | NUMBER OF JUDICIAL APPOINTMENTS FROM ROOSEVELT THROUGH CLINTON |

	ROOSEVELT	TRUMAN	EISENHOWER	KENNEDY	JOHNSON
Supreme Court	9	4	5	2	2
Circuit Court	52	27	45	20	40
District Court	137	102	127	102	122
Special Courts[b]	14	9	10	2	13
Total	212	142	187	126	177
	NIXON	FORD	CARTER	REAGAN	BUSH	CLINTON[a]
Supreme Court	4	1	0	4	2	2
Circuit Court	45	12	56	78	37	28
District Court	182	52	202	290	148	152
Special Courts[b]	7	1	3	10	0	0
Total	238	66	261	382	187	182

[a]Appointments made through 1995.
[b]Includes Customs, Patent Appeals, and Court of International Trade.

the last ten presidents and those made, thus far, by President Clinton; Table 15-2 presents some characteristics of appointees to the federal courts.

Despite their constitutional authority, however, presidents often must compete with the Senate and other political bodies in appointing judges. In addition to the president, the Senate, and judicial candidates themselves, other key actors include the Department of Justice, the Standing Committee on the Federal Judiciary of the American Bar Association, and leading political party officials. The practice of sena-

| TABLE 15-2 | A PROFILE OF PRESIDENTIAL APPOINTEES TO THE LOWER FEDERAL COURTS |

	NUMBER OF APPOINTEES						
	JOHNSON	NIXON	FORD	CARTER	REAGAN	BUSH	CLINTON[a]
Gender							
Male	159	226	63	217	340	149	123
Female	3	1	1	41	28	36	57
Ethnicity or race							
White	152	218	58	202	344	165	128
Black	7	6	3	37	7	12	36
Hispanic	3	2	1	16	15	8	13
Asian		1	2	2	2		2
Native American				1			1
ABA ratings							
Exceptionally/well qualified	89	117	31	145	203	109	120
Qualified	68	110	32	110	165	76	60
Not qualified	4		1	3			
Total number of appointees	162	227	64	258	368	185	180

[a]Appointments made through 1995.
Note: One Johnson appointee did not receive an ABA rating.

Sources: Sheldon Goldman, "Bush's Judicial Legacy: The Final Imprint," Judicature 282 (1993); Alliance for Justice, Judicial Selection Project Annual Report, 1993; and Alliance for Justice Judicial Selection Project Annual Report, 1995 (Washington, D.C.: Alliance for Justice, January 1996).

THE BAER AFFAIR: COURT-BASHING AS A CAMPAIGN STRATEGY

In January 1996 federal District Court Judge Harold Baer, an appointee of President Clinton, was hearing a case in New York City involving a drug bust. A woman leaving the scene in her car had been arrested after police had stopped the car and found in it a large stash of illegal narcotics. Judge Baer ruled the drugs could not be used as evidence against the woman because the police had had no valid grounds for searching the car. Indeed, he said that in the largely minority neighborhood where the incident occurred, running away from the police was a natural and appropriate reaction.

Many politicians were outraged. In March 150 members of Congress, mainly Republicans, sent a letter to Clinton demanding that he "call for the judge's resignation." On March 21 a Clinton spokesman said that Baer's ruling was "wrong-headed" and that the president might ask him to resign if he did not reverse it. Later the White House backtracked from the resignation suggestion, saying Clinton supported the independence of the judiciary and that the controversial ruling "should be resolved in the courts."

In April, Senator Bob Dole of Kansas, soon to be the Republican candidate for president, weighed in on the controversy. Dole said Baer was just one of the "startling numbers" of too-liberal judges Clinton had appointed who "demonstrated an outright hostility to law enforcement." In fact, Dole suggested, Baer might deserve to be impeached.

Later in April, after hearing more testimony, Baer reversed his earlier ruling and allowed the seized drugs to be used as evidence. A short time later he removed himself from the case to try to prevent his reversal from becoming an issue that might invalidate the verdict.

The attacks on Judge Baer and President Clinton's replies were rather standard election-year political fare. Ever since Richard M. Nixon's 1968 presidential campaign, Republican presidential candidates have attacked Democrats for appointing judges who are "soft on criminals." Indeed, Dole continued his attacks throughout the 1996 campaign. By 1996, however, Republican presidents Nixon, Gerald R. Ford, Ronald Reagan, and George Bush had appointed well over

U.S. District Court Judge Harold Baer Jr. was caught in the crossfire of election-year politics.

half the entire federal judiciary; and Democrats threatened to make political issues out of some of those judges' rulings. Moreover, President Clinton had declined to nominate judges who might prove too liberal to win Senate confirmation, particularly after Republicans gained control of the Senate in the 1994 elections.

Yet the controversy over Judge Baer did highlight a serious and long-standing issue. Should judges base their rulings on what will be popular? Surely not, but if the courts stray too far for too long from what public opinion will support, they risk losing the respect that is essential if they are to perform their proper function. Three judges of the U.S. Court of Appeals for the Second Circuit, within which Judge Baer's court sits, denounced the attacks on him for threatening the independence of the judiciary. In an address on April 9, 1996, at the height of the controversy, the Chief Justice of the United States Supreme Court, William H. Rehnquist, remarked that judicial independence was "one of the crown jewels of our system of government." Earlier in the year, however, in his report on the federal judiciary, Rehnquist had observed, "The Constitution places the independent judiciary it creates within a democratic government that is ultimately accountable to the people."

torial courtesy, in which the president consults with senators from the president's party and from a prospective nominee's home state prior to making a formal nomination, developed in part to achieve this accommodation.

The appointment process encourages the Senate and the president to bargain with each other to achieve their political objectives. The president may trade lower-court judgeships for legislation and good relations. That is, the president may agree to nominate a senator's preferred candidate for a district court judgeship in exchange for the senator's vote on crucial legislation and support of the administration's policy goals. Federal judgeships are opportunities for the Senate, no less than for the president, to influence national policy and confer political patronage. As Griffin Bell, a former court of appeals judge and attorney general in the Carter administration, put it, "Becoming a federal judge wasn't very difficult. I managed John F. Kennedy's presidential campaign in Georgia. Two of my oldest friends were the senators from Georgia. And I was campaign manager and special unpaid counsel for the governor."[13]

Indeed, at the lowest level of the federal judicial structure, the district courts, "it's senatorial appointment with the advice and consent of the President," in the words of former attorney general Robert Kennedy.[14] The president has greater discretion at the circuit court level. Since the jurisdiction of these courts spans several states, the president may play senators off against each other by claiming the need for representation of different political parties, geographic regions, religions, races, and so forth within a given circuit.

Appointment of Supreme Court Justices

Unlike other federal judgeships, appointments to the Supreme Court are usually considered a prerogative of the president. As President Herbert Hoover's attorney general, William Mitchell, observed, "with the whole country to choose from, the Senators from one state or another are in no position, even if they were so inclined, to attempt a controlling influence."[15] Although the Senate as a whole has the power to defeat a nominee, in this century only seven have been blocked: four were defeated, two were withdrawn, and no action was taken on one (see Table 15-3).

The rejection of President Reagan's nomination of Robert H. Bork to the Supreme Court in 1987 vividly illustrates the political nature of the appointment process (see the Case Study on pages 570–571). It indicates the range of forces that can affect judicial appointments and the difficulty the president can encounter if he does not take these forces into account. It also demonstrates the need for cooperation in a process that requires agreement between two government institutions.

All presidents try to fill vacancies on the Supreme Court with political associates and individuals who share their ideological views. They make little or no effort to balance the Court by crossing party lines. Of the 108 individuals who have served on the Supreme Court, there have been 13 Federalists, 1 Whig, 8 Democratic-Republicans, 42 Republicans, and 44 Democrats.

In earlier eras presidents sought geographic balance on the Court as well as ideological compatibility. In the early nineteenth century, representation of different geographic regions was considered crucial to establishing the legitimacy of the Court. As the country expanded westward, presidents were inclined to give representation to new states and regions. But in this century appointments have rarely turned on geography. President Nixon, for instance, named two justices from Minnesota, and three of President Reagan's four appointees came from the West.

TABLE 15-3 **SUPREME COURT NOMINATIONS REJECTED, POSTPONED, OR WITHDRAWN BECAUSE OF SENATE OPPOSITION**

Nominee	Year Nominated	Nominated By	Actions[a]
William Paterson[b]	1793	Washington	Withdrawn (for technical reasons)
John Rutledge[c]	1795	Washington	Rejected
Alexander Wolcott	1811	Madison	Rejected
John J. Crittenden	1828	J. Q. Adams	Postponed, 1829
Roger B. Taney[d]	1835	Jackson	Postponed
John C. Spencer	1844	Tyler	Rejected
Reuben H. Walworth	1844	Tyler	Withdrawn
Edward King	1844	Tyler	Postponed
Edward King[e]	1844	Tyler	Withdrawn, 1845
John M. Read	1845	Tyler	No action
George W. Woodward	1845	Polk	Rejected, 1846
Edward A. Bradford	1852	Fillmore	No action
George E. Badger	1853	Fillmore	Postponed
William C. Micou	1853	Fillmore	No action
Jeremiah S. Black	1861	Buchanan	Rejected
Henry Stanbery	1866	Johnson	No action
Ebenezer R. Hoar	1869	Grant	Rejected, 1870
George H. Williams[c]	1873	Grant	Withdrawn, 1874
Caleb Cushing[c]	1874	Grant	Withdrawn
Stanley Matthews[b]	1881	Hayes	No action
William B. Hornblower	1893	Cleveland	Rejected, 1894
Wheeler H. Peckham	1894	Cleveland	Rejected
John J. Parker	1930	Hoover	Rejected
Abe Fortas[f]	1968	Johnson	Withdrawn
Homer Thornberry	1968	Johnson	No action
Clement F. Haynsworth Jr.	1969	Nixon	Rejected
G. Harrold Carswell	1970	Nixon	Rejected
Robert H. Bork	1987	Reagan	Rejected
Douglas H. Ginsburg	1987	Reagan	Withdrawn

[a] A year is given if different from the year of nomination.
[b] Reappointed and confirmed.
[c] Nominated for chief justice.
[d] Taney was reappointed and confirmed as chief justice.
[e] Second appointment.
[f] Associate justice nominated for chief justice.

Source: David M. O'Brien, Storm Center: The Supreme Court in American Politics, *4th ed. (New York: Norton, 1996), 165. Reprinted by permission of W.W. Norton & Company, Inc.*

Most presidents delegate the responsibility for selecting candidates and getting them through the Senate to their attorney general and other close advisers. The assistant attorney general in charge of the Office of Legal Policy in the Department of Justice usually compiles a list of candidates from recommendations by White House staff, members of Congress, governors, and state and local bar associations. The president and a committee of his top advisers narrow the number of candidates to two or three on the basis of a political evaluation and an informal rating by the Standing Committee on the Federal Judiciary of the American Bar Association. (The

ABA committee ranks candidates as "well qualified," "qualified," or "not qualified.") At some point when the president is making the final choice, an exhaustive FBI investigation of the candidate(s) is initiated and a formal evaluation by the ABA is received. Once these reports have been reviewed by the attorney general and White House counsel, a recommendation is sent to the president. If he approves, the nomination is formally submitted to the Senate. The Senate Judiciary Committee then holds a **confirmation hearing** and recommends approval or rejection of the nominee by a vote of the entire Senate.

The role of the ABA in the judicial appointment process has been important but also controversial. Since it began reviewing the records of judicial nominees in 1955, the professional qualifications of the federal judiciary have generally improved. But the ABA has not altered the basic politics of judicial appointments. A former member of the Standing Committee, Leon Jaworski, points out that the ABA typically functions as a "buffer" between the White House and the Senate. Senators may be told, "Well, the American Bar Association has turned [your candidate] down; who can we agree on now?"[16] However, at different times both liberals and conservatives have attacked the ABA's role in the judicial selection process. During the 1960s and 1970s, liberals often criticized the ABA for having too many corporate lawyers on its judicial screening committee and not enough women, minorities, and lawyers with trial-court experience. During the 1980s and 1990s, by contrast, conservative groups and many Justice Department officials in the Reagan and Bush administrations attacked the ABA for being too liberal and for giving low ratings to the administrations' potential judicial nominees. The conservative Washington Legal Foundation even sued to have the ABA's confidential process of evaluating potential nominees opened to the public under the Federal Advisory Committee Act. But in *Public Citizen v. U.S. Department of Justice* (1988) the Supreme Court held that the ABA was not covered by the act and that its participation in the judicial selection process did not violate the president's power to appoint federal judges.[17]

Some observers believe that religion, race, and gender have become more important considerations in judicial selection in recent years. But historically they have been barriers to appointment to the Court. The overwhelming majority (93) of the 108 justices have come from mainstream Protestant backgrounds. Of the remaining 15, 8 were Catholics and 7 were Jews. Justice Thurgood Marshall, who was appointed by President Lyndon Johnson in 1967, was the first African American to serve on the Court. When he retired in 1991, President George Bush named another African American, Judge Clarence Thomas, to fill his seat. In 1981 President Reagan fulfilled a campaign pledge to appoint the first woman to the Supreme Court, nominating Sandra Day O'Connor (see the profile of O'Connor on page 572). In 1986 Antonin Scalia, a Catholic and Reagan's second appointee, became the first Italian American to serve on the Court. Reagan also named another Catholic, Anthony Kennedy, in 1988. President Clinton appointed another female justice, Ruth Bader Ginsburg, in 1993; both she and his second appointee, Stephen G. Breyer, were Jewish.

Considerations such as religion, race, and gender are politically symbolic and largely reflect changes in the electorate. In the future, expectations for more diverse representation—particularly from among Hispanics and Asians—are likely to continue. Still, they are likely to remain less important than personal and ideological compatibility in presidents' attempts to "pack" the Court with justices who share their political views.

THE BATTLE OVER BORK

In 1987 a fierce political battle erupted over President Ronald Reagan's nomination of Judge Robert H. Bork, to the Supreme Court. Instead of becoming the 104th justice, Bork became the 28th Supreme Court nominee to be rejected or forced to withdraw because of opposition in the Senate. This confirmation battle underscored both the Reagan administration's effort to make the Court a symbol and an instrument of the Reagan presidency, and the power of the Senate to defeat a nominee.

In nominating Bork the president chose, over more moderate Republicans and conservative jurists, one of the most outspoken critics of the Court's liberal rulings under chief justices Earl Warren and Warren Burger. The president did so even though Democrats had regained control of the Senate in 1986 and were determined to oppose any nominee who was closely aligned with the right wing of the Republican party. Reagan underestimated the extent of this opposition, which was heightened by the pivotal nature of the appointment. The justice whom Bork was to replace, Lewis Powell, had often cast the crucial fifth vote in cases upholding such liberal-backed policies as legal abortion and affirmative action programs.

The president's nomination of Bork was immediately denounced by Democratic senator Edward Kennedy of Massachusetts and by the chair of the Senate Judiciary Committee, Democratic senator Joseph Biden of Delaware. More than eighty-three organizations followed. Calling Bork "unfit" to serve on the high court, the American Civil Liberties Union abandoned its practice of not opposing nominees. The AFL-CIO also came out in opposition to Bork.

Right-wing organizations were no less active in support of Bork, though they were initially encouraged to downplay their support by White House chief of staff Howard Baker. Over the objections of the Justice Department, the White House adopted a strategy of recasting Bork's conservative record in order to make his opponents appear shrill and partisan. A 70-page White House briefing book was prepared, followed by a 240-page report released by the Justice Department; both attempted to portray Bork as a "mainstream" jurist.

The publicity surrounding the nomination was extraordinary. Numerous reports analyzing Bork's record were distributed to editorial boards around the country by both sides in the struggle. People for the American Way, a liberal group, launched a $2 million media campaign opposing the nomination, and the National Conservative Political Action Committee committed over $1 million to lobbying for Bork's confirmation.

What had far greater impact, however, was Bork's own role in the preconfirmation fray and the Senate confirmation proceedings. Even before the hearings began, Bork took the unusual step of granting newspaper interviews to explain, clarify, and amend his 25-year record as a Yale Law School professor, United States solicitor general in the Nixon administration, and federal judge. These actions broke with tradition and gave the appearance of a public relations campaign.

During his five days and thirty hours of nationally televised testimony before the Judiciary Committee, Bork continued to give the appearance of refashioning himself into a moderate, even "centrist," jurist. By the time he finished, he had contradicted much of what he had stood for in the past. A key consideration thus became, in the words of Senator Patrick Leahy (D-Vermont), one of "confirmation conversion." Noting the "considerable difference between what Judge Bork has written, and what he has testified he will do if confirmed," Arlen Specter, a Republican senator from Pennsylvania, observed, "I think that what many of us are looking for is some assurance of where you are." Even Bork seemed troubled; and at the end of his testimony he told the committee, "It really would be preposterous to say things I said to you and then get on the Court and do the opposite. I would be disgraced in history."

Bork's testimony weighed far more than that of the 110 witnesses assembled for and against him in the following two weeks. To be sure, they contributed to the atmosphere of campaign politics that surrounded the hearings. For the first time a former president,

Judge Robert H. Bork testifying before the Senate Judiciary Committee. Despite his apparent "confirmation conversion" to a more moderate judicial philosophy, his longstanding reputation as a conservative doomed his nomination to the Supreme Court.

Gerald Ford, introduced a nominee to the committee. And former president Jimmy Carter sent a letter expressing his opposition to the nomination. Nor had justices ever before come out as allies of a president or his nominee. Yet retired chief justice Warren Burger testified on behalf of Bork, and justices John Paul Stevens and Byron White publicly endorsed him.

In spite of the publicity and pressure group activities, the hearings were illuminating. They focused on the nature of the Constitution. Is the Constitution defined by the intent of the framers, as Bork's sup-

porters maintained? Or is the Constitution a living document, one that has become more democratic through amendments and interpretations? In the end, this debate turned the tide against Bork in the Senate. Conservative southern Democrats and moderate Republicans joined liberal Democrats to oppose the nomination. The politics in their states, the position of their parties, and the opinion of a majority of the public would not have supported a return to an era in which civil rights and liberties were not protected as they are today.

Discussion Questions

1. What role does and should the Senate play in the appointment of federal judges?
2. Has the appointment of Supreme Court justices become too politicized?
3. What standards should apply in the selection and confirmation of nominees to the federal bench?

SANDRA DAY O'CONNOR: AT THE CENTER OF THE COURT

When Sandra Day O'Connor received a law degree with distinction from Stanford University in 1952, she applied for jobs at a number of law firms. A woman in a field dominated by men, she was turned down everywhere. The firm in which William French Smith (later to become United States attorney general) was a partner offered her a secretarial job. O'Connor eventually went to work as deputy county attorney for San Mateo County in California. She later settled in Phoenix, Arizona, where she practiced law privately.

In 1965 O'Connor became an assistant attorney general in Arizona—the first woman appointed to the position. In 1969 she was appointed to the Arizona State Senate, and the next year she won election on her own. O'Connor served as a state senator for six years. For two of those years she was majority leader—the first woman in the country to hold this position of state legislative leadership. In 1974 she was elected a county judge, and in 1979 she was appointed to the Arizona Court of Appeals.

President Ronald Reagan nominated O'Connor to the Supreme Court of the United States in 1981 to replace the retiring Potter Stewart. She was confirmed by a 99-to-0 vote in the Senate, becoming the first woman justice.

In her first few years on the Court, Justice O'Connor was considered a conservative, usually voting along with Justice William Rehnquist. Within a few years, however, she established a centrist role for herself on many Court decisions. She has often provided the critical fifth vote needed to swing the outcome in one direction or another. In the areas of affirmative action and gender discrimination, Justice O'Connor has been particularly important. It was she who wrote for a bare majority in setting new guidelines for affirmative action in *City of Richmond v. J.A. Croson* (1989) and *Adarand Constructors, Inc. v. Pena* (1995). Her middle-of-the-road interpretation of

Supreme Court justices are asked to speak in all kinds of arenas. Here Sandra Day O'Connor addresses the San Francisco–based Bay Area Council, which conducts research and advocacy on economic issues in that region.

the Fourteenth Amendment allows governments to mandate affirmative action programs as a remedy for their past discriminatory practices but forbids them from adopting such programs simply because of prior discrimination by society in general.

Justice O'Connor's influence on gender discrimination cases has led to the Court's declaration that sexual harassment and sexual stereotyping are forms of gender discrimination and thus are illegal. She has also lent her weight to decisions supporting government attempts to mandate equal opportunity for women in the workplace. Although Justice O'Connor has generally voted in support of restrictions on abortion, she continues to support the basic principle of *Roe v. Wade*.

How successful are presidents in packing the Court? Most succeed to some degree. Others fail, and some completely misjudge their appointees.

Democratic president Franklin Roosevelt succeeded more than most. He made eight new appointments and elevated Justice Harlan Stone to the position of chief justice. Having bitterly attacked the Court for invalidating most of his early New Deal program, in 1937 Roosevelt went so far as to propose expanding the size of the Court from nine to fifteen so that he could appoint justices who supported his economic policies. The Senate defeated this Court-packing plan. Later, however, when vacancies occurred on the Court, Roosevelt succeeded in appointing his

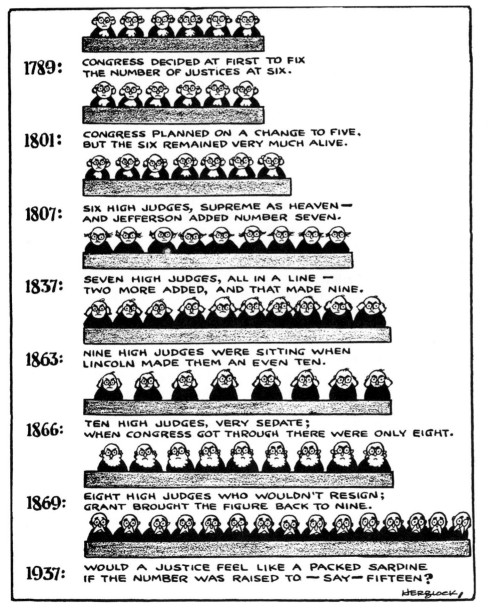

1789: CONGRESS DECIDED AT FIRST TO FIX THE NUMBER OF JUSTICES AT SIX.

1801: CONGRESS PLANNED ON A CHANGE TO FIVE, BUT THE SIX REMAINED VERY MUCH ALIVE.

1807: SIX HIGH JUDGES, SUPREME AS HEAVEN — AND JEFFERSON ADDED NUMBER SEVEN.

1837: SEVEN HIGH JUDGES, ALL IN A LINE — TWO MORE ADDED, AND THAT MADE NINE.

1863: NINE HIGH JUDGES WERE SITTING WHEN LINCOLN MADE THEM AN EVEN TEN.

1866: TEN HIGH JUDGES, VERY SEDATE; WHEN CONGRESS GOT THROUGH THERE WERE ONLY EIGHT.

1869: EIGHT HIGH JUDGES WHO WOULDN'T RESIGN; GRANT BROUGHT THE FIGURE BACK TO NINE.

1937: WOULD A JUSTICE FEEL LIKE A PACKED SARDINE IF THE NUMBER WAS RAISED TO — SAY — FIFTEEN?

HERBLOCK,

A famous cartoon by Herblock that appeared in 1937, when President Franklin D. Roosevelt wanted to expand the Court to secure a majority of justices favorable to his New Deal programs. The Court's size has changed a number of times because of presidential and congressional attempts to alter its direction.

supporters and thereby turning a conservative Court into a more moderately liberal one.

Almost thirty years later, Republican president Richard Nixon achieved some success in remolding the Court in his image. Whereas Roosevelt had attacked the conservative Court in the 1930s, Nixon vehemently opposed the "liberal jurisprudence" of the Court as expressed in its rulings on school desegregation and criminal procedures. However, Nixon's appointments of Chief Justice Warren Burger and justices Harry Blackmun, Lewis Powell, and William Rehnquist failed to turn the Court completely around. Under Chief Justice Burger the Court was increasingly fragmented, with votes often divided 6 to 3 or 5 to 4, and it was pulled in different directions by either its most liberal or its most conservative members.

In his 1980 and 1984 presidential campaigns, Ronald Reagan promised to appoint only justices who were opposed to abortion and to the judicial activism that had characterized the Court under Burger and his predecessor, Earl Warren. No other president since Roosevelt has had as great an impact on the federal judiciary. Before leaving the Oval Office in 1989, Reagan appointed close to half of all lower-court judges and elevated William H. Rehnquist to chief justice, as well as appointing three other justices to the Supreme Court. Although he was hugely successful in appointing lower-court judges, Reagan failed to win over a majority of the Court to his positions on abortion, affirmative action, and other hotly contested issues until Justice Lewis Powell stepped down in 1987. Powell held the pivotal vote; during his last two years on the Court the justices split 5 to 4 in eighty-one cases, with Powell having the deciding vote over 75 percent of the time. A number of these votes came in cases rejecting the Reagan administration's positions on abortion, affirmative action, and some other social policy issues.

With Powell's departure, Reagan had a chance to move the Court in a more conservative direction. His first nominee for Powell's seat, Judge Robert Bork, was defeated after a bitter confirmation battle. His second, Judge Douglas H. Ginsburg, was forced to withdraw after revelations about his personal affairs turned Republican senators against him. However, his third nominee, Judge Anthony M. Kennedy, won easy confirmation. Although Kennedy was not the kind of justice that officials in the Justice Department had hoped would "lock in the Reagan Revolution," there is no doubt that he and Reagan's other appointees brought a new conservatism to the Court. George Bush in turn appointed two more justices, David H. Souter and Clarence Thomas.

In 1993, when Justice Byron White retired, Bill Clinton became the first Democratic president in over twenty-five years to fill a vacancy on the Court. He chose Ruth Bader Ginsburg, a federal appellate court judge who had established a reputation as a moderate jurist and a consensus builder. Clinton's second appointee was Stephen G. Breyer. Both have proven to be moderately left of center and vote most often with justices John Paul Stevens (appointed by President Gerald Ford) and Souter.

Through their appointments, presidents may influence the direction of future Supreme Court policy making, but there is no guarantee that they will succeed. Prior to his elevation to chief justice in 1986, Justice Rehnquist gave a speech at the University of Minnesota in which he indicated some of the reasons why:

> Neither the President nor his appointees can foresee what issues will come before the Court during the tenure of the appointees, and it may be that none had thought very much about these issues. Even though they agree as to the proper resolution of current cases, they may well disagree as to future cases

involving other questions when, as judges, they study briefs and hear arguments. Longevity of the appointees, or untimely deaths such as those of Justice [Frank] Murphy and Justice [Wiley B.] Rutledge [both died in 1949], may also frustrate a President's expectations; so also may the personal antagonisms developed between strong-willed appointees of the same President.[18]

Republican president Dwight D. Eisenhower, for one, was profoundly disappointed by his selection of Chief Justice Earl Warren and Justice William J. Brennan Jr. because of their liberal rulings. And Justice Oliver Wendell Holmes drew the ire of President Theodore Roosevelt by voting against the administration's antitrust policies. As the president put it, he "could carve out of a banana a Judge with more backbone than that!"[19] In 1992 many former Reagan and Bush administration officials and supporters were surprised and disappointed when justices O'Connor, Kennedy, and Souter formed a bare majority with justices Blackmun and Stevens to uphold "the essence" of *Roe v. Wade,* the controversial ruling on a woman's right to have an abortion, in *Planned Parenthood of Southeastern Pennsylvania v. Casey.*

THE SUPREME COURT

The Supreme Court is perhaps the least understood government institution in the United States. Although the public may attend oral arguments and the Court's rulings are handed down in the form of published opinions, a tradition of secrecy surrounds

On August 12, 1994, Stephen Breyer was sworn in as a Supreme Court justice by Associate Justice Antonin Scalia in the East Room of the White House, with Vice President Albert Gore looking on.

THE POLITICS OF APPOINTMENT: CLARENCE THOMAS AND ANITA HILL

In 1991, President George Bush caused an uproar when he nominated Clarence Thomas to replace Thurgood Marshall on the Supreme Court. Thomas was a well-known black conservative judge whom the president had named a year earlier to the Court of Appeals for the District of Columbia Circuit. He had done so in anticipation of the retirement of Marshall, the first black Supreme Court justice and an ardent liberal.

Women's groups, including the National Organization for Women and the National Abortion Rights Action League, immediately opposed Thomas. The civil rights community split, with the Congressional Black Caucus, the NAACP, the Leadership Conference on Civil Rights, and the AFL-CIO ultimately opposing the nomination and the National Urban League and the American Civil Liberties Union staying uncommitted. The American Bar Association rated Judge Thomas "qualified," although two individuals on the fifteen-member committee dissented and one abstained.

During his testimony before the Senate Judiciary Committee, Thomas sought to deflect criticism by emphasizing his "up-by-the-bootstraps" philosophy and personal struggle in overcoming the poverty of his youth. When asked about his prior writings, he gave closely guarded answers. He distanced himself from previous statements advocating a "natural law" approach to constitutional interpretation. And he steadfastly maintained, more than seventy times, that he had never seriously thought about the legitimacy of the controversial ruling in *Roe v. Wade* on a woman's right to choose an abortion. When Senator Howell Heflin (D-Alabama) noted a certain "conflict between what you've said in the past and what you've told us here," Republican senators Orrin Hatch, Alan Simpson, and Arlen Specter sprang aggressively to Thomas's defense. After two weeks of hearings, the judicial committee was deadlocked 7 to 7. Finally it voted 13 to 1 to send Thomas's nomination to the Senate without a recommendation.

Then several new allegations surfaced, including one that Thomas had sexually harassed a female assistant a decade earlier when he chaired the federal Equal Employment Opportunity Commission (EEOC). The committee chair, Senator Joseph Biden, had told several senators of these charges but had not fully investigated them, and then an FBI report was leaked to the press. Finally, law professor Anita Hill—Thomas's assistant at the EEOC—was forced to explain her charges.

Amid rising public anger over the accusations and counter-charges that Hill was part of a conspiracy to derail Thomas's confirmation, the all-white, all-male judiciary committee held hearings that pitted Hill against Thomas on national television. Hill coolly and confidently charged that in the early 1980s Thomas had harassed her by repeatedly pressing for dates, talking explicitly about pornographic movies, and creating a hostile work environment in other ways. Thomas categorically denied the accusations and angrily protested that the confirmation process had become "a circus" and "a high-tech lynching for uppity blacks." "No job is worth it," he said. Thomas's supporters attacked Hill's motives. Senator Specter went so far as to charge her with "flat-out perjury."

The nasty drama of "she said, he said" raised larger issues of racism and sexism, but it failed to resolve the immediate questions about the veracity of either Hill or Thomas. The Senate ultimately voted 52 to 48 to confirm Thomas as the 106th justice.

SOURCE: Adapted from David O'Brien, *Storm Center: The Supreme Court in American Politics*, 4th ed. (New York: Norton, 1996). Reprinted by permission.

the justices' decision making. The Court stands as a temple of law—an arbitrator of political disputes and an expression of the ideal of "a government of laws, and not of men." But it remains a fundamentally political institution. Behind the marble facade, the justices compete for influence.

The Court's annual term (or work year) begins on the first Monday in October and runs until the end of June. For most of this time, the justices are hidden from public view. They hear oral arguments only fourteen weeks a year—on Mondays, Tuesdays, and Wednesdays of every other two-week period from October through April. On Wednesday afternoons and again on most Fridays, they hold private conferences to decide which cases they will review and to make decisions on cases for which they have heard oral arguments. The rest of the time they work alone in their chambers with their law clerks, writing opinions and studying drafts of opinions circulated by other justices.

The Court's Caseload

The public learns about only a few of the Court's rulings each term. Usually only the most controversial decisions are given media coverage. The Court actually reviews and decides by written opinion only about 100 cases each year. Still, that is less than 2 percent of the more than 8,000 cases filed and placed on the Court's **docket** each year. The vast majority of these cases are denied review, leaving the lower-court rulings untouched.

The Court's caseload has grown (see Figure 15-2) and changed throughout its history. In the nineteenth century almost all cases came to the Court as mandatory appeals, which the justices had to decide. But as the caseload grew, Congress eliminated most provisions granting rights of appeal and substituted **petitions for a writ of certiorari** (a petition requesting a court to order a review of the ruling of a lower court), which the Court may simply deny. Congress thus permitted the justices to determine which cases they would review. Figure 15-3 presents the main avenues of appeal to the Supreme Court. The box on page 580 describes the ways in which cases may be appealed to the Court.

The Court now exercises virtually absolute control over its caseload. The power to turn away cases enables it not only to limit the number of cases it reviews but also to pick what issues it wants to decide and when. In this sense the modern Supreme Court functions like a legislative body, setting its own agenda for adjudication and policy making.

When an appeal or certiorari petition arrives at the Court, it immediately goes to the office of the clerk of the Court. There staff determines whether the appeal or petition satisfies requirements for form and length and whether a filing fee of $300 has been paid. Over half the petitions come from indigents, who must file with the brief for their case an *in forma pauperis* ("in the manner of a pauper") petition stating that they are too poor to pay the filing fee. The clerk of the Court then notifies the other party in the case that it must file a brief in response within thirty days. After receiving the briefs, the clerk circulates to the justices a list of cases that are ready for consideration and a set of briefs for each case.

For much of the Court's history, each justice was responsible for reviewing every case; the justices did not delegate to others the responsibility for screening cases. Now, however, the justices have their law clerks do virtually all the screening. The clerks write one- to two-page memos on each case, summarizing the facts and issues and recommending that review be granted or denied. To further cut down the workload, eight members of the Court—all except Justice John Paul Stevens—have

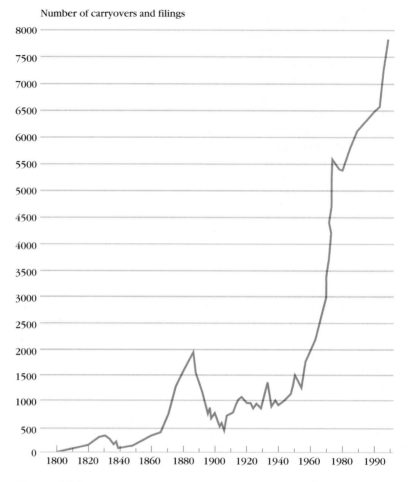

Number of carryovers and filings

FIGURE 15-2
Docket of and filings in the Supreme Court, 1800–1994.

SOURCE: David M. O'Brien, *Storm Center: The Supreme Court in American Politics*, 4th ed. (New York: Norton, 1996), 180. Reprinted by permission of W. W. Norton & Company, Inc.

pooled their clerks in what is called the "cert pool." These clerks divide up all the cases and write memos on each; the memos then circulate to the participating justices for their consideration.

Many observers question the propriety of delegating so much responsibility to law clerks, who are recent law school graduates and will serve for only one year before going on to teach at leading law schools or to join prestigious law firms. The justices counter that most cases are frivolous and that there is no other way to process the heavy caseload.

In the 1990s the Court signaled that it would no longer allow indigents to file petitions in cases that it deemed frivolous, denying several *in forma pauperis* petitions and amending its rules for granting cases. In one case, Michael Sindram was denied the right to file a petition requesting an order directing a state court to expedite his request to expunge a $35 speeding ticket from his record. Sindram was no stranger to the Court. In previous years he had filed forty-two separate petitions and motions on various matters. In denying Sindram's petition, the Court observed that "The goal

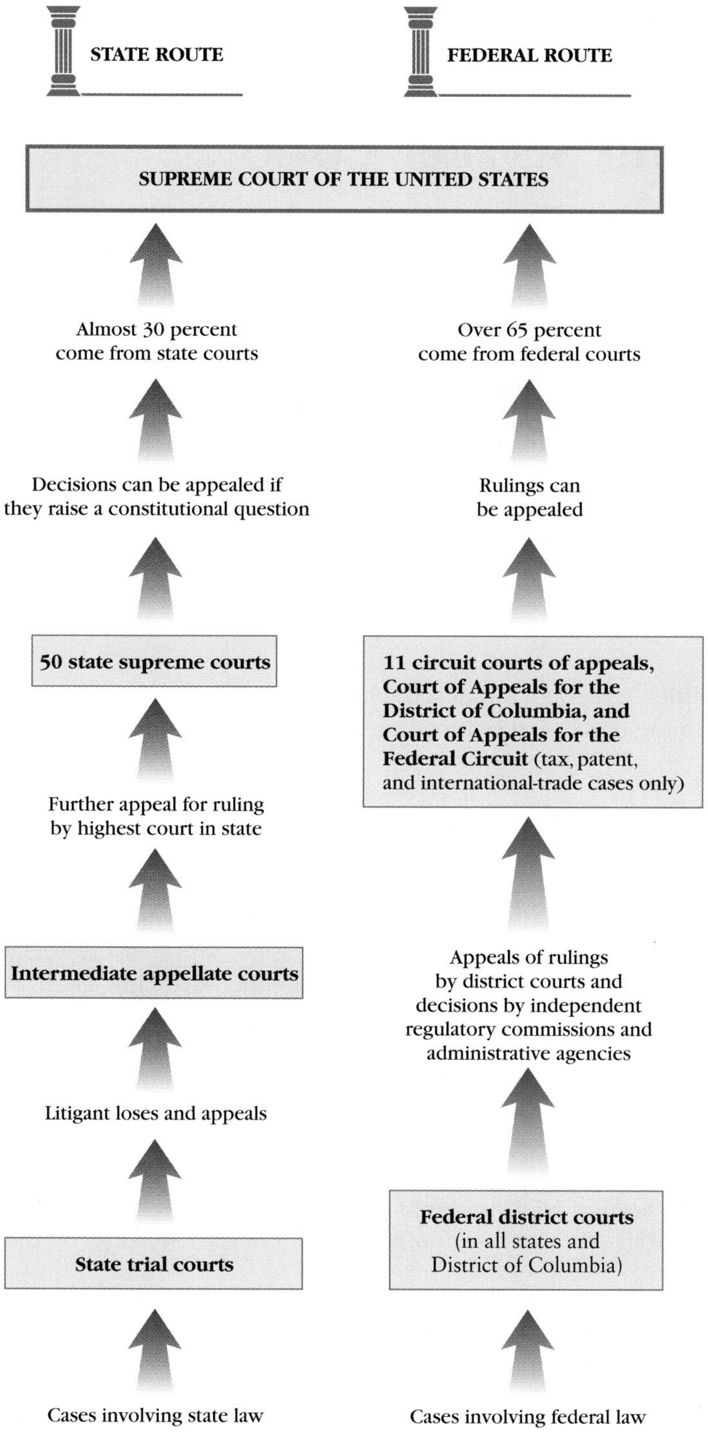

 **STATE ROUTE**    **FEDERAL ROUTE**

SUPREME COURT OF THE UNITED STATES

Almost 30 percent
come from state courts

Over 65 percent
come from federal courts

Decisions can be appealed if
they raise a constitutional question

Rulings can
be appealed

50 state supreme courts

**11 circuit courts of appeals,
Court of Appeals for the
District of Columbia, and
Court of Appeals for the
Federal Circuit** (tax, patent,
and international-trade cases only)

Further appeal for ruling
by highest court in state

Intermediate appellate courts

Appeals of rulings
by district courts and
decisions by independent
regulatory commissions and
administrative agencies

Litigant loses and appeals

State trial courts

Federal district courts
(in all states and
District of Columbia)

Cases involving state law

Cases involving federal law

FIGURE 15-3

Avenues of appeal to the Supreme Court.

SOURCE: David M. O'Brien, *Storm Center: The Supreme Court in American Politics*, 4th ed.
(New York: Norton, 1996), 197. Reprinted by permission of W. W. Norton & Company, Inc.

WAYS OF APPEALING TO THE SUPREME COURT

Mandatory appeal: A formal appeal for review, granted by congressional legislation. The Supreme Court must review and decide all appeals, but only a small fraction of all cases coming to the Court are on appeal.

Writ of certiorari: A petition to the Supreme Court asking it to review the record and decision of a lower court. The Court has discretion to deny or grant petitions for *certiorari.* Over 98 percent of all cases coming to the Supreme Court are on *certiorari.*

Writ of certification: A petition to the Supreme Court from a lower court asking that some question or interpretation of law be clarified, certified, and made more certain.

Writ of habeas corpus: A petition asking a federal court to order officials holding a prisoner to justify the detention or release the person. Cases that assert a violation of constitutional rights and are appealed from state courts to the federal judiciary often come on writs of habeas corpus (Latin for "you have the body").

of fairly dispensing justice . . . is compromised when the Court is forced to devote its limited resources to the processing of repetitious and frivolous requests."[20]

Deciding What to Decide

When the justices meet in conference, they vote on which cases to review. Prior to each conference the chief justice circulates two lists of cases. On the first—the Discuss List—are all the cases he thinks are worth considering, based on a review of the clerks' recommendations. Any justice may add other cases, but the list typically includes only forty to fifty cases. Attached is a second list—the Dead List—containing cases that are considered unworthy of discussion. Over 90 percent of all cases are unanimously denied without discussion, and most of those that make the Discuss List are denied as well. The conference lists are an important technique for saving time and focusing attention on the few cases deemed worthy of consideration.

The chief justice presides over conferences, as he does over oral arguments and all the Court's other public functions. At a conference he usually begins by summarizing each case and indicating why he thinks it should be accepted or denied. Discussion then passes from one justice to another in order of their seniority on the bench.

Although the Court decides all other matters by majority rule, review can be granted on the vote of only four justices—the informal **rule of four**. However, only a small number of the cases granted review are actually accepted on this basis. For well over 70 percent of the cases accepted for review, a majority of the justices agree on the importance of the issues presented. The rule of four was adopted by the Supreme Court when Congress expanded the Court's discretionary power to pick the cases it accepts. The purpose was to assure Congress that important cases would be granted review even if less than a majority of the justices deemed them to present substantial questions of federal law. In addition, because less than a majority of the Court may grant review, the denial of a particular case is not considered a precedent that would be binding on lower courts.

Because of the Court's heavy docket, it does not grant cases in order to decide questions of fact, such as a person's guilt or innocence, or simply to correct mistakes made in lower courts. Instead, it takes cases that involve questions of law on which lower courts have disagreed. The Court thus tends to decide only cases that have national scope and involve significant controversies over public law and policy.

After a conference, the clerk of the Court is told which cases have been accepted or denied. The justices do not explain why they deny review of a case. This policy not only saves them time but also enhances their flexibility: the Court may take up an issue in a later case without feeling bound by an earlier denial. For the few cases that are granted review, the clerk notifies the litigants that they have thirty days to submit briefs on the **merits**—the questions to be decided. The clerk then sets a date for oral argument, usually about four months later.

Oral Argument

Counsel once had unlimited time to present oral arguments; but as the caseload increased, the justices cut back on the time. Each case now gets only one hour—thirty minutes for each side. The Court hears four cases on each oral argument day, which is virtually the only time that the public may see the justices. In a crowded

The United States Supreme Court in 1995. The chief justice always sits in the middle, with associate justices alternating out to his right and left, in descending order of years of service. (Seated) Antonin Scalia (appointed by Reagan in 1986); John Paul Stevens (Ford, 1975); Chief Justice William Rehnquist (associate justice, Nixon, 1972; chief justice, Reagan, 1986); Sandra Day O'Connor (Reagan, 1981); Anthony M. Kennedy (Reagan, 1988). (Standing) Ruth Bader Ginsburg (Clinton, 1993); David H. Souter (Bush, 1990); Clarence Thomas (Bush, 1991); and Stephen G. Breyer (Clinton, 1994).

courtroom, the marshal of the Court announces the sitting of the justices with the traditional introduction:

> Oyez! Oyez! Oyez! All persons having business before the Honorable, the Supreme Court of the United States, are admonished to draw near and give their attention, for the Court is now sitting. God save the United States, and this Honorable Court.

The chief justice proceeds into the courtroom from behind the velvet curtains in back of the bench, and the other justices follow and take their seats in order of seniority. Seating in the courtroom is limited to about 250 spectators, most of whom hear only three to four minutes of oral arguments before they are ushered out. Only by special request may members of the public hear entire arguments in a case. The press may hear all arguments, but no cameras are allowed in the courtroom when the Court is in session.

Oral arguments are the only opportunity attorneys have to communicate directly with the justices, who want crisp, concise, and conversational presentations. They do not want attorneys to read their briefs, and the time limit is strictly enforced. Although Chief Justice Charles Evans Hughes reportedly called time on a lawyer in the middle of the word "if," the Court is more tolerant now. As former chief justice Warren Burger once explained, "We allow a lawyer to finish a sentence that is unfolding when the red light goes on, provided, of course, the sentence is not too long."[21]

Justices differ in their own attitudes toward oral arguments and their preparation for them. Justice William O. Douglas insisted that "oral arguments win or lose a case," but Chief Justice Earl Warren found them "not highly persuasive." Most come prepared with **bench memos** drafted by their law clerks that identify central facts, issues, and possible questions. Chief Justice Rehnquist and justices Ginsburg, O'Connor, Scalia, and Stevens aggressively ask questions; the other justices usually say very little.

Discussing Cases and Voting in Conference

Within a day or two after oral arguments, the justices meet in secret conference to discuss and vote on the cases. The chief justice opens the discussion, which moves to each of the other justices in order of their seniority. For much of the Court's history the justices voted in reverse order of seniority, the junior ones voting first so as not to be swayed by the votes of their senior colleagues. But that practice has been abandoned. Because of the heavier caseload, each justice has only about three minutes to express his or her views and vote on each case. As a result, conferences involve less collective deliberation than was generally true in the past.

The justices' votes at conference are always tentative. Until the day the final decision comes down, justices may use their votes in strategic ways to influence the disposition of a case, offering or threatening to switch sides depending on whether or not their conditions are met. Before and during conference as well, justices bargain and negotiate the treatment of issues and the language of opinions. Justice Harlan F. Stone, for example, once candidly told Justice Frankfurter: "If you wish to write [the opinion] placing the case on the ground which I think tenable and desirable, I shall cheerfully join you. If not, I will add a few observations for myself."[22] On another occasion Justice James McReynolds gently appealed to Justice Stone: "All of us get into a fog now and then, as I know so well from my own experience. Won't you 'Stop, Look, and Listen'?"[23]

After every three-day oral argument session, one of the justices is assigned to write the **opinion** for the Court on each case. This is a crucial aspect of the work of the Court because how an opinion is written—the legal reasoning used to justify the decision—is just as important as the decision itself. The justice selected must be one who voted with the majority during conference, and if the chief justice did so he assigns the opinion, either to himself or to another justice. By tradition, if the chief justice did not vote with the majority, the senior associate justice who was in the majority makes the assignment.

The power of opinion assignment presents significant opportunities for the chief justice to influence the final outcome of cases. In unanimous and landmark cases, chief justices often write opinions themselves. Chief Justice Earl Warren wrote the opinion striking down segregated schools in *Brown v. Board of Education* (1954). Chief Justice Warren Burger likewise delivered the opinion in *United States v. Nixon* (1974), rejecting President Nixon's claim of executive privilege to withhold tape recordings made in the Oval Office during the Watergate crisis.[24]

Chief justices usually try to see that all the justices are assigned about the same number of opinions (thirteen to fifteen per year), so as to distribute the workload evenly and to avoid angering their colleagues. They may make assignments on the basis of a justice's background and particular expertise or in anticipation of public reactions to a ruling. In addition, they sometimes ask the justice who is closest to the dissenters to write the opinion in the hope that other justices will switch their votes and thereby bolster the authority of the Court's decision. Not surprisingly, the power of assigning opinions invites resentment and lobbying by other members of the Court.

Writing and circulating opinions is the justices' most difficult and time-consuming task. Although the justices differ in their styles and approaches to writing opinions, most delegate the preliminary drafting of opinions to their law clerks. Only after a justice is satisfied with an initial draft does it go to other justices for their reactions.

How long does opinion writing take? In the average case, Justice Tom Clark observed, about three weeks of work is required before an opinion is ready to circulate; "then the fur begins to fly."[25] It is not uncommon for a draft opinion to be revised three or four times and to circulate for three or four months before it becomes final. Justices may suggest minor editorial alterations or major substantive changes. Sometimes they will go to war over an opinion; at other times they may feel that a case is not worth fighting over. A few cases are so controversial that the justices reschedule them for oral argument and decision the next year. This was done with *Brown v. Board of Education* (1954) and *Roe v. Wade* (1973).

Opinions announcing the decision of the Court are not statements of the author's particular views of jurisprudence. Rather, they are negotiated documents forged from ideological divisions within the Court. The justice writing the Court's opinion must avoid pride of authorship and attempt to reach a compromise that will secure a majority and an **institutional opinion** for the Court's decision. If a justice fails to achieve this goal, the opinion is reassigned. For this reason, Justice Oliver Wendell Holmes often complained that the task of writing the Court's opinion was especially difficult; as he put it in 1918, "The boys generally cut one of the genitals out of mine, in the form of some expression that they think too free."[26]

What makes writing an opinion for the Court so difficult is that all the other justices are free to write their own individual opinions. They may write **concurring**

JUDICIAL PAPERS: A BREACH OF CONFIDENTIALITY?

In 1993, when the late justice Thurgood Marshall's working papers—including memos and draft opinions circulated by other justices—became available to the public, some of his former colleagues on the Court created a minor controversy by pushing to curtail access to the papers, which they deemed a breach of confidentiality. Following his retirement in 1991, Marshall had donated his papers to the Library of Congress with the stipulation that, upon his death and "at the discretion of the Library," the collection could be opened to "researchers or scholars engaged in serious research." Less than two years later Marshall died, and the Library opened his papers to the public.

At first, without controversy, only a few scholars studied the collection. But within a few months the *Washington Post* ran a three-part series of articles based on Marshall's memos. The articles portrayed the conservative shift of the Rehnquist Court and detailed how close the justices had come to overruling the 1973 *Roe v. Wade* decision, which guaranteed a woman's right to abortion, in *Webster v. Reproductive Health Services* (1989). Chief Justice Rehnquist promptly protested the Library's release of the collection and asked that it be closed. Claiming to "speak for a majority of the active Justices of the Court," he also threatened that "future donors of judicial papers will be inclined to look elsewhere for a repository." Congress held hearings on the matter, but the Library refused to yield and Marshall's papers remain open.

Even more unprecedented was Justice William J. Brennan's making some of his papers available in the 1980s while still sitting on the bench. This angered several other sitting justices, because his collection also contains memos written by them and reveals their tentative thinking about cases, their attempts to influence each other, and the Court's inner workings.

Justices' papers also show that the Court as an institution has become more bureaucratic over recent decades, as seen in the increased number of law clerks, secretaries, and other personnel, as well as in the addition of word-processing technology. The papers of justices Felix Frankfurter, Hugo Black, and William O. Douglas—who served thirty to fifty years ago—include many handwritten or typewritten letters and notes about pending cases and drafts of opinions circulated among the justices. But the collections of justices Brennan and Marshall provide fewer examples of such correspondence. Instead, there are more memos from law clerks and communications from other justices that are often short and to the point, such as "Please join me in your opinion" or "I await the circulation of the dissent."

In 1990, as revealed in a memo from Marshall's papers, Justice Brennan (who retired that year) defended his decision to allow scholars access to his papers. He did change his policies in response to colleagues' criticism and concerns about the Court's confidentiality; now he requires researchers to write in advance about their projects and to obtain his permission to use the papers. Moreover, a researcher's access to them is now limited to six months.

No rules or common practice governs what justices may do with their papers. About 40 percent of them have destroyed their papers, particularly during the nineteenth century, but in this century justices have tended to give their papers to the Library of Congress or to the law school from which they graduated. Usually their papers may not be made available for a period of time after their death, or until all the justices with whom they served have left the bench. In addition, Justice Hugo Black burned his docket books and conference notes before giving his files to the Library of Congress. Others, like Justice Douglas, also purged their collections of papers they deemed too sensitive, and they inserted personal notes for "posterity."

584

opinions—opinions agreeing with the result reached by a majority but disagreeing with its reasons or legal analysis. Justices differ on the propriety of such opinions, which reflect failure or unwillingness to compromise. Some think that they are a sign of "institutional disobedience"; others believe that they are a valuable record of the justices' differing views. In any event, every justice now writes several concurring opinions each term.

Justices who disagree with the majority opinion usually write **dissenting opinions**. In the words of Chief Justice Hughes, dissenting opinions appeal "to the brooding spirit of the law, to the intelligence of a future day, when a later decision may possibly correct the error into which the dissenting judge believes the Court to have been betrayed."[27] Because dissenting opinions undercut the Court's decision, justices may use them as threats when trying to persuade the majority to narrow the scope of its ruling or tone down its language. Some justices write more dissents than others, but as a group they average about ten each term.

Opinion Days

Litigants, lawyers, the media, and the public finally learn the outcome of the justices' votes on opinion days, the days when the Court hands down its final published opinions. The Court once announced opinions only on "Decision Mondays," but now it may do so on any day of the week. By tradition, there is no prior announcement as to when cases will be handed down. Instead of reading their opinions from the bench, as was once done, the justices simply announce them in two to four minutes, merely stating the result in each case. Copies of opinions may be obtained from the offices of the clerk of the Court and the public information officer at the Court. The Where on the Web? box on page 586 suggests ways to access opinions as well as other legal materials in electronic form.

Supreme Court Decision Making as a Political Process

Decision making by the Supreme Court is a political process. The justices often follow their own political agendas when granting and deciding cases. Because the Court decides what cases to review on the basis of the vote of only four justices, the justices may form voting blocs to determine which cases will be granted review. But the justices decide the merits of those few cases by majority vote. In deciding those cases, the process of opinion writing is crucial to the final outcome and affords the justices opportunities to bargain and compromise with each other, as well as to write concurring or dissenting opinions.

The political struggles within the Court come to an end on opinion days, though the justices continue to compete for influence and try to persuade each other to reconsider their views in other cases. Opinion days, however, may also mark the beginning of larger struggles for influence between the Court and rival political forces.

THE POLITICS OF JUDICIAL POLICY MAKING

The Court is an independent arbitrator of political conflicts. Through its decisions it legitimates one set of government policies or another, and in so doing it invites political controversy. But in most areas of public law and policy the fact that the Court

SUPREME COURT DECISIONS AND OTHER LEGAL MATERIALS

Are you especially interested in a decision that's just been handed down by the Supreme Court? Do you need to research the history of the Court's decisions on civil rights or flag burning? Are you interested in copyrighting a story or song you've written? The following information will be invaluable to you in finding what you need in electronic form.

In 1991 the Supreme Court began a project called *Hermes* that makes Court decisions available on the Internet on the day they are announced. Also, a number of university servers, such as Cornell Law School, are part of network sites that make the Court's opinions available to the public. Here are several ways to reach the Cornell server:

Gopher: **law.cornell.edu** or
  http://www.law.cornell.edu (specify the path:
  U.S. Law: Primary Documents and Commentary)
On the World Wide Web: **http://www.law.cornell.edu**
On Telnet: **telnet gopher.law.cornell.edu**   or
  telnet www.law.cornell.edu (specify the path
  above)

This server is one of the most accessible and useful; it contains all Supreme Court decisions from the 1991 term to the present, as well as some earlier landmark rulings. A database on selected state and federal judges, along with federal laws on copyright, patents, and other commercial practices, is also available.

listserv@law.cornell.edu (leave the subject line blank
  and in the message area, type: subscribe liibulletin
  your name, address, phone number)

Syllabi and opinions of the court may be accessed through e-mail on the above list server. On the very day the Court hands down a decision, syllabi of the decisions will be sent to your address. The full opinions may be requested through the methods given above or through e-mail. To receive a decision, you must submit the docket number of the case—for example: 95-0000, where 95 is the year and 0000 is the number of the case. Send an e-mail message to: **liidelivery@law.cornell.edu** and leave the subject blank. In the message area, type **request 95-0000**. To stop the messages from this site, send an e-mail message to **listserv@law.cornell.edu** and type **unsubscribe liibulletin** in the message area. New cases are also available from the base address for Supreme Court materials at **http://www.law.cornell.edu/supct/**

makes decisions is more important than the decisions themselves. Much of the Court's work involves disputes over the interpretation and enforcement of statutes, and it is essential that those disputes be settled in one way or another. Moreover, relatively few of the many controversies over domestic and foreign policy that arise in government actually reach the Court. Yet those few cases are almost always hard cases and politically controversial ones.

The Court decides conflicts over public law and policy by bringing them within the language, structure, and spirit of the Constitution. In this way the Court determines public policy. The struggles that follow are central to American politics. The key actors in that competition are the lower courts, Congress, the president, political interest groups, and ultimately the general public. Their reactions may enhance or thwart the implementation of the Court's rulings and determine the extent of compliance with judicial policy making.

Although the Court depends on lower courts to enforce its rulings, compliance is invariably uneven because the ambiguity of judicial opinions allows lower courts to pursue their own policy goals. Crucial language in an opinion may be treated like *dicta*—language that is not binding in other cases. Or differences between the facts on which the Court ruled and the circumstances of another case may be emphasized so as to reach a result opposite to that reached by the Court. For example, lower courts interpreted *Abington School District v. Schempp* (1963), which struck down a law requiring the reciting of the Lord's Prayer in public schools, to permit voluntary and nondenominational prayer in public schools.[28] Likewise, state courts in Texas refused to extend the Court's ruling in *Norris v. Alabama* (1935) forbidding racial discrimination against blacks in the selection of juries.[29] They continued to allow the exclusion of Mexican Americans from juries until the Court finally ruled, in *Hernandez v. Texas* (1954), that all kinds of racial discrimination in jury selection violate the Fourteenth Amendment's equal protection clause.[30] In sum, open defiance is infrequent but not unprecedented. When it occurs, it reflects the differing policy preferences of state and federal judges.

On major issues of public policy, Congress is likely to prevail or at least to temper the impact of the Court's rulings. Congress may pressure the Court in a number of ways. The Senate may try to influence future judicial appointments, and the House may even try to impeach the justices. More often, Congress uses institutional and jurisdictional changes as weapons against the Court.

Under Article III of the Constitution, Congress has the power to "make exceptions" to the appellate jurisdiction of the federal courts. That authorization has been viewed as a way of denying courts the power to review certain kinds of cases. During the Reagan administration, for instance, there were numerous unsuccessful proposals to deny courts the power to decide cases involving school prayer and abortion. But Congress has succeeded only once in cutting back on the Supreme Court's jurisdiction; this occurred in 1868 with the repeal of the Court's jurisdiction over writs of habeas corpus (see the Constitutional Conflict box on page 588).

Congress has had slightly greater success in reversing the Court by means of a constitutional amendment, which three-fourths of the states must ratify. The process is cumbersome, and thousands of amendments designed to overrule the Court have failed. But four Court decisions (see the box on page 589) have been overturned by constitutional amendments.

More successful has been congressional enactment or rewriting of legislation in response to the Court's rulings. In *Zurcher v. The Stanford Daily* (1978), for example, the Court held that there is no constitutional prohibition against police searching newsrooms without a warrant for "mere evidence" of a crime, such as photographs.[31] Two years later, however, Congress essentially reversed that ruling by passing the Privacy Protection Act of 1980, which prohibits unannounced searches of newsrooms and requires that police obtain a subpoena ordering writers to turn over desired evidence. So, too, Congress overrode more than a dozen rulings of the conservative Rehnquist Court when it enacted the Civil Rights Act of 1991.

But Congress is not always successful in reversing the Court's decisions through legislation. In response to the Court's ruling in *Texas v. Johnson* (1989), which held that a state law prohibiting desecration of the American flag violated the First Amendment's guarantee of freedom of speech, Congress enacted the Flag Protection Act of 1989, which also forbade desecration of the flag.[32] But when that law was challenged, the Court again defended the First Amendment and struck down the act in *United States v. Eichman* (1990).[33]

Although Congress cannot always overturn the Court's rulings, it can often thwart their implementation. For example, Congress delayed implementation of the school

LIMITING THE JURISDICTION OF THE FEDERAL COURTS

Does and should Congress have the power to deny the Supreme Court and lower federal courts the authority to decide cases that raise controversial issues such as abortion or prayer in public schools? The Constitution, in Article III, Section 2, says that "the Supreme Court shall have appellate jurisdiction, both as to law and fact, with such exceptions, and under such regulations, as the Congress shall make." From time to time members of Congress claim that this "exceptions" clause gives Congress the power to curb the federal judiciary's jurisdiction over certain kinds of cases.

During the 1950s, for example, a number of senators proposed legislation forbidding the Court to review cases challenging congressional investigations of "un-American activities." A decade later, in response to the Supreme Court's rulings protecting the rights of the accused, other proposals were made that would have deprived the Court of the power to review certain state criminal cases. In 1979 the Senate passed by a vote of 51 to 40 an amendment eliminating federal court jurisdiction over cases involving school prayer, but the House of Representatives never considered the bill. And in the early 1980s several Republican senators unsuccessfully sought to deny federal courts jurisdiction over abortion controversies.

In fact, Congress has succeeded only once in limiting the Supreme Court's jurisdiction. In 1868 it repealed the Court's jurisdiction over writs of habeas corpus, and the Court upheld that restriction on its power in *Ex parte MacCardle* (1869). Because of the overwhelming failure of congressional attempts to strip the Court of jurisdiction, political scientists and legal scholars disagree about whether Congress may still claim the authority granted it in Article III. Some contend that Congress should continue to try to curb the Court in this way. Others counter that the Court could strike down a repeal of jurisdiction if it deprived the Court of the power to protect constitutional rights.

desegregation decision in *Brown v. Board of Education* (1954) by not authorizing the executive branch to enforce the ruling until the passage of the Civil Rights Act of 1964. Later, by cutting back on appropriations for the Department of Justice and the Department of Health, Education, and Welfare during the Nixon and Ford administrations, Congress registered opposition to busing and further attempts to achieve integrated public schools.

Presidents may undercut the Court's policy making as well. By issuing contradictory directives to federal agencies and assigning low priority to enforcement by the Department of Justice, they may limit the impact of the Court's decisions. Presidents may also make broad moral appeals in opposition to the Court's rulings. For example, President Reagan's opposition to abortion served to legitimate resistance to the Court's decisions in this area.

When it threatens to go too far or too fast in its policy making, the Court is ultimately curbed by public opinion. Except during transitional periods or critical elections, however, the Court has usually been in step with major political and social movements.[34] Moreover, the public tends to perceive the Court as a temple of law rather than of politics—as impartial and removed from the pressures of special or partisan interests. But the public also tends to understand little about the operation

SUPREME COURT DECISIONS OVERTURNED BY CONSTITUTIONAL AMENDMENT

Chisholm v. Georgia (1793), holding that citizens of one state could sue another state in federal court, was reversed by the Eleventh Amendment, guaranteeing sovereign immunity for states from suits by citizens of another state.

Dred Scott v. Sanford (1857), ruling that blacks were not citizens under the Constitution, was technically overturned by the Thirteenth and Fourteenth Amendments, abolishing slavery and making blacks citizens of the United States.

Pollock v. Farmer's Loan and Trust Co. (1895), invalidating a federal income tax, was reversed in 1913 with ratification of the Sixteenth Amendment.

Oregon v. Mitchell (1970), in which a bare majority of the Court held that Congress could not lower the voting age for state and local elections, was reversed in less than a year by the Twenty-Sixth Amendment, extending the franchise to 18-year-olds in all elections.

of the Court, and for this reason only about 30 percent of Americans express "great confidence" in the Court.

Public opinion about the Supreme Court also tends to fluctuate with public reactions to government as a whole. Issues such as school desegregation, school prayer, and abortion focus public attention and mobilize political interest groups in support of or in opposition to the Court. But those issues are also the most likely to sharply

As the first two female Supreme Court justices, Sandra Day O'Connor and Ruth Bader Ginsburg are in frequent demand for speaking engagements. Here O'Connor delivers the commencement address at New York Law School's 100th graduation ceremony, where she also received an honorary doctor of laws degree, and Ginsburg addresses an audience at Harvard University.

589

divide public opinion while fueling political struggles at all levels of government. Thus, in the late 1960s, public confidence in the Court declined when it was widely criticized for handing down rulings guaranteeing the rights of those accused of crimes. But in the early 1970s the Court's standing improved, largely because its rulings helped to resolve a "crisis in confidence" in the presidency that had resulted from the Nixon administration's involvement in the Watergate episode and attempts to cover up other illegal activities. In the 1980s, public confidence in the Court increased further as confidence in government grew owing to the influence of the highly popular President Reagan. By the mid 1990s public opinion polls showed that the Court and the majority of the electorate largely agreed on issues ranging from abortion to matters of criminal justice.

Some Court watchers warn of an "imperial judiciary" and a "government by the judiciary."[35] They point out that judicial review is antidemocratic because it enables the Court to overturn laws enacted by popularly elected legislatures. But the Court's duty is to interpret the Constitution, and compliance with and enforcement of the Court's rulings depend on the cooperation of other political institutions as well as on public acceptance. Major confrontations over public policy are determined as much by what is possible in a pluralistic society with a system of free government as by what the Court says about the meaning of the Constitution.[36] That is the essence of politics in a constitutional democracy.

SUMMARY

The judiciary is a political institution and often must rule on some of the most divisive social issues of the day. Courts provide forums for individuals and interest groups to obtain hearings of their disputes and legal claims. Courts and judges are thus integral players in the politics of American government.

The United States has two separate judicial systems, federal and state; these dual systems are termed *judicial federalism*. If there is a conflict between national and state law, the matter is settled by the federal courts and ultimately by the Supreme Court. Article III of the Constitution vests judicial power in the Supreme Court and any other courts created by Congress. Courts created under Article III are *constitutional courts*. Under Article I Congress may also create specialized courts, such as the United States Court of Military Appeals, which are called *legislative courts*.

In 1789 Congress divided the country into thirteen districts and created a federal *district court* for each. District courts remain the trial courts of the federal system. Congress also created federal *courts of appeals* to hear appeals from decisions of the district

courts and state courts. Aside from legislative courts, today the federal judiciary consists of ninety-four district courts, thirteen courts of appeals, and the Supreme Court. There is at least one federal district court in each state, and each district court has at least one judge. These courts may also use grand juries to determine whether to indict individuals for crimes and petit juries to try those indicted. A substantial number of federal criminal defendants do not go to trial because they plead guilty, often as a result of plea bargaining. Those who do go to trial are tried in an adversary process in which the two sides argue the case and the jury determines which side has done so more convincingly.

Judges on the federal courts of appeals usually sit in rotating panels of three and decide most cases on the basis of written *briefs* submitted by the litigants. Occasionally the entire court sits as a panel, or *en banc*.

The Supreme Court hears cases from state courts only if the cases deal with *federal questions*, or issues involving the interpretation of the Constitution or other federal laws. Under the *principle of comity* the Court does not review cases decided on *independent state grounds* such as a state constitution. The *jurisdiction* of a court determines the kinds of cases and controversies it may decide. The Supreme Court has *original jurisdiction* in cases involving disputes between two or more states and cases brought against the United States by foreign ambassadors; such cases originate in the Supreme Court. However, the majority of the cases that come to the Court arrive under its *appellate jurisdiction*: they are appealed from lower federal courts and state courts.

Courts have jurisdiction only over disputes involving adverse interests and a real controversy. The parties must have *standing to sue*; they must show that they are suffering or are in danger of suffering an immediate and substantial personal injury. Courts avoid deciding *political questions* that the judges think should be resolved by other branches of government. Disputes that are open to judicial resolution are referred to as *justiciable disputes*.

The power of judicial review gives the courts the ability to strike down any law enacted by Congress or by the states and to declare official government actions unconstitutional. Although judicial review is controversial because it enables the Supreme Court to thwart the democratic process, the Court has nevertheless increasingly asserted this power. As a result it has been criticized for its *judicial activism* and urged to exercise *judicial self-restraint*—to defer to Congress and state legislatures.

The method of selecting state court judges varies from one state to another. Some judges are appointed by governors or legislatures; some are elected; and others are appointed under a *merit system* in which a nonpartisan commission provides a list of possible nominees and voters eventually decide whether to retain those who are appointed. Federal judges are appointed by the president with the advice and consent of the Senate. Senators exercise considerable influence on lower-court appointments; and the president often encounters considerable senatorial opposition to his nominations of Supreme Court justices, who are usually political associates and individuals who share his political views.

Candidates for federal judgeships are investigated by the FBI and evaluated by the American Bar Association. The Senate Judiciary Committee then holds a *confirmation hearing* and recommends approval or rejection of nominees by a vote of the entire Senate. The overwhelming majority of the justices appointed to the Supreme Court have been white Protestant men.

Some presidents have been more successful than others in "packing" the Court. Franklin Roosevelt was unable to change the size of the Court, but he succeeded in appointing enough of his supporters to turn a conservative Court into a liberal one. Presidents Nixon, Reagan, and Bush each appointed several conservative justices, thereby shifting the Court away from the "liberal jurisprudence" of earlier decades. The Supreme Court decides less than 2 percent of the cases placed on its *docket* each year. Most cases come to the Supreme Court through *petitions for a writ of certiorari*, which request the Court to review the ruling of a lower court; it may deny such a petition. The grant of review requires the vote of four justices (the *rule of four*), but usually a majority of the justices vote for the grant. The Court takes only cases that involve questions of law on which lower courts have disagreed. Litigants then submit briefs on the *merits*—the questions to be decided.

The Court hears oral arguments in only about 100 cases a year. Each side in a case has thirty minutes to present its arguments. Most justices use *bench memos* to prepare for oral arguments. Within a day or two after oral arguments, the justices meet in secret conference to discuss and vote on the case. One of the justices in the majority is assigned to write an *opinion* for the Court on the case. The justice writing the opinion must attempt to reach a compromise that will serve as an *institutional opinion* stating the reasons for the Court's decision. The other justices are free to write *concurring opinions*, which agree with the decision but for different reasons, or *dissenting opinions*.

The Court decides conflicts by bringing them within the language, structure, and spirit of the Constitution. In this way it determines public policy. The reactions of other institutions of government and the public may enhance or thwart the implementation of the Court's rulings. Congress can temper the impact of a ruling by means of jurisdictional changes, through a constitutional amendment, or by rewriting legislation. The president can undercut the Court by issuing contradictory directives to federal agencies, assigning low priority to enforcement, or publicly disagreeing with its rulings. Ultimately, however, the Court is curbed by public opinion.

judicial federalism
constitutional courts
legislative courts
district courts
courts of appeals
brief
en banc
federal question
independent state grounds
principle of comity

jurisdiction
original jurisdiction
appellate jurisdiction
standing to sue
political question
justiciable dispute
judicial activism
judicial self-restraint
merit system
confirmation hearing

docket
petitions for a writ of certiorari
rule of four
merits
bench memo
opinion
institutional opinion
concurring opinion
dissenting opinion

SCHOLARLY STUDIES

Abraham, Henry. *Justices and Presidents*. 3rd ed. New York: Oxford University Press, 1992. An excellent political history of appointments to the Supreme Court.

Cannon, Mark, and David M. O'Brien, eds. *Views from the Bench: The Judiciary and Constitutional Politics*. Chatham, N.J.: Chatham House, 1985. A collection of writings by justices and judges on the role and function of courts as well as theories of constitutional interpretation.

Gates, John, and Charles Johnson, eds. *The American Courts: A Critical Assessment*. Washington, D.C.: Congressional Quarterly, 1991. A good overview of the social science literature on judicial policy making.

O'Brien, David. *Storm Center: The Supreme Court in American Politics*. 4th ed. New York: Norton, 1996. A detailed institutional history of Supreme Court politics.

Rosenberg, Gerald. *The Hollow Hope: Can Courts Bring About Social Change?* Chicago: University of Chicago Press, 1991. A well-written, provocative study that argues that courts cannot bring about massive social change.

LEISURE READING

Abramson, Jeffrey. *We, the Jury: The Jury System and the Ideal of Democracy*. New York: Basic Books, 1994. An engaging book based on stories of controversial jury trials that raise the larger issue of how effectively the jury system serves the ideal of democratic control over the judiciary.

Craig, Barbara, and David M. O'Brien. *Abortion and American Politics*. Chatham, N.J.: Chatham House, 1993. A balanced examination of how the abortion controversy has played out in interest group politics, public opinion polls, the states, Congress, the presidency, and the courts from *Roe v. Wade* (1973) to *Planned Parenthood of Southeastern Pennsylvania v. Casey* (1992).

Lewis, Anthony. *Gideon's Trumpet*. New York: Random House, 1989. A classic discussion of the watershed ruling on the right to counsel; an excellent introduction to the judicial process.

PRIMARY SOURCE

Congressional Quarterly. *Guide to the United States Supreme Court*. 2d ed. Washington, D.C.: Congressional Quarterly, 1989. A comprehensive reference work on the Supreme Court and its processes and history.

ORGANIZATIONS

Administrative Office of the United States Courts, Thurgood Marshall Federal Judiciary Building, One Columbus Circle, N.E., Washington, DC 20544; (202) 273-3000; Internet http://www.ncsc.dni.us/ Conducts some research and collects data on federal caseloads; is responsible for the administration of the federal courts.

Federal Judicial Center, Thurgood Marshall Federal Judiciary Building, One Columbus Circle, N.E., Washington, DC 20544; (202) 273-4000. Conducts research and training programs for the federal judiciary and publishes a newsletter, *The Third Branch*.

Public Information Office, Supreme Court of the United States, One 1st Street, Washington, DC 20543; (202) 223-2584. Distributes opinions of the Court and occasional speeches by the justices.

Supreme Court Historical Society, 111 2nd Street, N.E., Washington, DC 20002; (202) 543-0400. Collects materials related to the history of the Supreme Court and funds research projects. Publishes newsletters and *The Yearbook of the Supreme Court Historical Society*.

APPENDIXES

A

The Declaration of Independence

B

The Constitution of the United States of America

C

From The Federalist, *Nos. 10 and 51*

D

Presidential Elections

E

Party Control of Congress, 1901–1999

F

United States Supreme Court Justices, 1789–1996

The Declaration of Independence

When in the Course of human events, it becomes necessary for one people to dissolve the political bands which have connected them with another, and to assume among the Powers of the earth, the separate and equal station to which the Laws of Nature and of Nature's God entitle them, a decent respect to the opinions of mankind requires that they should declare the causes which impel them to the separation.

We hold these truths to be self-evident, that all men are created equal, that they are endowed by their Creator with certain unalienable Rights, that among these are Life, Liberty and the pursuit of Happiness. That to secure these rights, Governments are instituted among Men, deriving their just powers from the consent of the governed. That whenever any Form of Government becomes destructive of these ends, it is the Right of the People to alter or to abolish it, and to institute new Government, laying its foundation on such principles and organizing its powers in such form, as to them shall seem most likely to effect their Safety and Happiness. Prudence, indeed, will dictate that Governments long established should not be changed for light and transient causes; and accordingly all experience hath shown, that mankind are more disposed to suffer, while evils are sufferable, than to right themselves by abolishing the forms to which they are accustomed. But when a long train of abuses and usurpations, pursuing invariably the same Object evinces a design to reduce them under absolute Despotism, it is their right, it is their duty, to throw off such Government, and to provide new Guards for their future security.—Such has been the patient sufferance of these Colonies; and such is now the necessity which constrains them to alter their former Systems of Government. The history of the present King of Great Britain is a history of repeated injuries and usurpations, all having in direct object the establishment of an absolute Tyranny over these States. To prove this, let Facts be submitted to a candid world.

He has refused his Assent to Laws, the most wholesome and necessary for the public good.

He has forbidden his Governors to pass Laws of immediate and pressing importance, unless suspended in their operation till his Assent should be obtained; and when so suspended, he has utterly neglected to attend to them.

He has refused to pass other Laws for the accommodation of large districts of people, unless those people would relinquish the right of Representation in the Legislature, a right inestimable to them and formidable to tyrants only.

He has called together legislative bodies at places unusual, uncomfortable, and distant from the depository of their public Records, for the sole purpose of fatiguing them into compliance with his measures.

He has dissolved Representative Houses repeatedly, for opposing with manly firmness his invasions on the rights of the people.

He has refused for a long time, after such dissolutions, to cause others to be elected; whereby the Legislative Powers, incapable of Annihilation, have returned to the People at large for their exercise; the State remaining in the mean time exposed to all the dangers of invasion from without, and convulsions within.

He has endeavoured to prevent the population of these States; for that purpose obstructing the Laws of Naturalization of Foreigners; refusing to pass others to encourage their migration higher, and raising the conditions of new Appropriations of Lands.

He has obstructed the Administration of Justice, by refusing his Assent to Laws for establishing Judiciary powers.

He has made Judges dependent on his Will alone, for the tenure of their offices, and the amount and payment of their salaries.

He has erected a multitude of New Offices, and sent hither swarms of Officers to harass our People, and eat out their substance.

He has kept among us in times of peace, Standing Armies without the Consent of our legislature.

He has affected to render the Military independent of and superior to the Civil power.

He has combined with others to subject us to a jurisdiction foreign to our constitution, and unacknowledged by our laws; giving his Assent to their acts of pretended Legislation.

For quartering large bodies of armed troops among us;

For protecting them, by a mock Trial, from punishment for any Murders which they should commit on the inhabitants of these States;

For cutting off our Trade with all parts of the world;

For imposing taxes on us without our Consent;

For depriving us in many cases, of the benefits of Trial by Jury;

For transporting us beyond Seas to be tried for pretended offences;

For abolishing the free System of English Laws in a neighbouring Province, establishing therein an Arbitrary government, and enlarging its Boundaries so as to render it at once an example and fit instrument for introducing the same absolute rule into these Colonies;

For taking away our Charters, abolishing our most valuable Laws, and altering fundamentally the Forms of our Governments;

For suspending our own Legislature, and declaring themselves invested with Power to legislate for us in all cases whatsoever.

He has abdicated Government here, by declaring us out of his Protection and waging War against us.

He has plundered our seas, ravaged our Coasts, burnt our towns, and destroyed the lives of our people.

He is at this time transporting large Armies of foreign Mercenaries to compleat the works of death, desolation and tyranny, already begun with circumstances of Cruelty & perfidy scarcely paralleled in the most barbarous ages, and totally unworthy the Head of a civilized nation.

He has constrained our fellow Citizens taken Captive on the high Seas to bear Arms against their Country, to become the executioners of their friends and Brethren, or to fall themselves by their Hands.

He has excited domestic insurrections amongst us, and has endeavoured to bring on the inhabitants of our frontiers, the merciless Indian Savages, whose known rule of warfare, is an undistinguished destruction of all ages, sexes and conditions.

In every stage of these Oppressions We have Petitioned for Redress in the most humble terms: Our repeated Petitions have been answered only by repeated injury. A Prince, whose character is thus marked by every act which may define a Tyrant, is unfit to be the ruler of a free People.

Nor have We been wanting in attention to our British brethren. We have warned them from time to time of attempts by their legislature to extend an unwarrantable jurisdiction over us. We have reminded them of the circumstances of our emigration and settlement here. We have appealed to their native justice and magnanimity, and we have conjured them by the ties of our common kindred to disavow these usurpations, which, would inevitably interrupt our connections and correspondence. They too have been deaf to the voice of justice and of consanguinity. We must, therefore, acquiesce in the necessity, which denounces our Separation, and hold them, as we hold the rest of mankind, Enemies in War, in Peace Friends.

We, therefore, the Representatives of the United States of America, in General Congress, Assembled, appealing to the Supreme Judge of the world for the rectitude of our intentions, do, in the Name, and by Authority of the good People of these Colonies, solemnly publish and declare, That these United Colonies are, and of right ought to be Free and Independent States; that they are Absolved from all Allegiance to the British Crown, and that all political connection between them and the State of Great Britain, is and ought to be totally dissolved; and that as Free and Independent States, they have full Power to levy War, conclude Peace, contract Alliances, establish Commerce, and to do all other Acts and Things which Independent States may of right do. And for the support of this Declaration, with a firm reliance on the protection of divine Providence, we mutually pledge to each other our Lives, our Fortunes and our sacred Honor.

The Constitution of the United States of America

We the People of the United States, in Order to form a more perfect Union, establish Justice, insure domestic Tranquility, provide for the common defence, promote the general Welfare, and secure the Blessings of Liberty to ourselves and our Posterity, do ordain and establish this Constitution for the United States of America.

[THREE BRANCHES OF GOVERNMENT]

[*The legislative branch*]

Article I

[*Powers vested*]

SECTION 1   All legislative Powers herein granted shall be vested in a Congress of the United States, which shall consist of a Senate and House of Representatives.

[*House of Representatives*]

SECTION 2   The House of Representatives shall be composed of Members chosen every second Year by the People of the several States, and the Electors in each State shall have the Qualifications requisite for Electors of the most numerous Branch of the State Legislature.

No Person shall be a Representative who shall not have attained to the Age of twenty-five Years, and been seven Years a Citizen of the United States, and who shall not, when elected, be an Inhabitant of that State in which he shall be chosen.

[Representatives and direct Taxes shall be apportioned among the several States which may be included within this Union, according to their respective Numbers, which shall be determined by adding to the whole Number of free Persons, including those bound to Service for a Term of Years, and excluding Indians not taxed, three fifths of all other Persons.][1] The actual Enumeration shall be made within three Years after the first Meeting of the Congress of the United States, and within every subsequent Term of ten Years, in such Manner as they shall by Law direct. The Number of Representatives shall not exceed one for every thirty Thousand, but each State shall have at Least one Representative; and until such enumeration shall be made, the State of New Hampshire shall be entitled to chuse three, Massachusetts eight, Rhode-Island and Providence Plantations one, Connecticut five, New York six, New Jersey four, Pennsylvania eight, Delaware one, Maryland six, Virginia ten, North Carolina five, South Carolina five, and Georgia three.

When vacancies happen in the Representation from any State, the Executive Authority thereof shall issue Writs of Election to fill such Vacancies.

The House of Representatives shall chuse their Speaker and other Officers; and shall have the sole Power of Impeachment.

[*The Senate*]

SECTION 3   The Senate of the United States shall be composed of two Senators from each State, [chosen by the Legislature thereof],[2] for six Years; and each Senator shall have one Vote.

Immediately after they shall be assembled in Consequence of the first Election, they shall be divided as equally as may be into three Classes. The Seats of the Senators of the first Class shall be vacated at the Expiration of the Second Year, of the second Class at the Expiration of the fourth Year, and of the third Class at the Expiration of the sixth Year, so that one-third may be chosen every second Year; [and if Vacancies happen by Resignation, or otherwise, during the Recess of the Legislature of any State, the Executive thereof may make temporary Appointments until the next Meeting of the Legislature, which shall then fill such Vacancies].[3]

No person shall be a Senator who shall not have

[1] Changed by Section 2 of Amendment XIV.

[2] Changed by Amendment XVII.
[3] Changed by Amendment XVII.

attained to the Age of thirty Years, and been nine Years a Citizen of the United States, and who shall not, when elected, be an Inhabitant of that State for which he shall be chosen.

The Vice President of the United States shall be President of the Senate, but shall have no Vote, unless they be equally divided.

The Senate shall chuse their other Officers, and also a President pro tempore, in the absence of the Vice President, or when he shall exercise the Office of President of the United States.

The Senate shall have the sole Power to try all Impeachments. When sitting for that Purpose, they shall be on Oath or Affirmation. When the President of the United States is tried, the Chief Justice shall preside: And no Person shall be convicted without the Concurrence of two-thirds of the Members present.

Judgment in Cases of Impeachment shall not extend further than to removal from Office, and disqualification to hold and enjoy any Office of honor, Trust, or Profit under the United States: but the Party convicted shall nevertheless be liable and subject to Indictment, Trial, Judgment, and Punishment, according to Law.

[*Elections*]

SECTION 4   The Times, Places and Manner of holding Elections for Senators and Representatives, shall be prescribed in each State by the Legislature thereof; but the Congress may at any time by Law make or alter such Regulations, except as to the Places of chusing Senators.

The Congress shall assemble at least once in every Year, and such Meeting shall be on the first Monday in December, [unless they shall by Law appoint a different Day].[4]

[*Powers, duties, procedures of both bodies*]

SECTION 5   Each House shall be the Judge of the Elections, Returns, and Qualifications of its own Members, and a Majority of each shall constitute a Quorum to do Business; but a smaller Number may adjourn from day to day, and may be authorized to compel the Attendance of absent Members, in such Manner, and under such Penalties as each House may provide.

Each House may determine the Rules of its Proceedings, punish its Members for disorderly Behavior, and, with the Concurrence of two thirds, expel a Member.

Each House shall keep a Journal of its Proceedings, and from time to time publish the same, excepting such Parts as may in their Judgment require Secrecy; and the Yeas and Nays of the Members of either House on any question shall, at the Desire of one fifth of those Present, be entered on the Journal.

[4]Changed by Section 2 of Amendment XX.

Neither House, during the Session of Congress, shall, without the Consent of the other, adjourn for more than three days, nor to any other Place than that in which the two Houses shall be sitting.

[*Compensation, privileges, limits on other government service*]

SECTION 6   The Senators and Representatives shall receive a Compensation for their Services, to be ascertained by Law, and paid out of the Treasury of the United States. They shall in all Cases, except Treason, Felony and Breach of the Peace, be privileged from Arrest during their Attendance at the Session of their respective Houses, and in going to and returning from the same; and for any Speech or Debate in either House, they shall not be questioned in any other Place.

No Senator or Representative shall, during the Time for which he was elected, be appointed to any civil Office under the Authority of the United States, which shall have been created, or the Emoluments whereof shall have been encreased during such time; and no Person holding any Office under the United States, shall be a Member of either House during his Continuance in Office.

[*Origin of revenue bills; presidential approval or disapproval of legislation; overriding the veto*]

SECTION 7   All Bills for raising Revenue shall originate in the House of Representatives; but the Senate may propose or concur with Amendments as on other Bills.

Every Bill which shall have passed the House of Representatives and the Senate, shall, before it become a Law, be presented to the President of the United States; if he approve he shall sign it, but if not he shall return it, with his Objections to that House in which it shall have originated, who shall enter the Objections at large on their Journal, and proceed to reconsider it. If after such Reconsideration two thirds of that House shall agree to pass the Bill, it shall be sent, together with the Objections, to the other House, by which it shall likewise be reconsidered, and if approved by two thirds of that House, it shall become a Law. But in all such Cases the Votes of both Houses shall be determined by Yeas and Nays, and the Names of the Persons voting for and against the Bill shall be entered on the Journal of each House respectively. If any Bill shall not be returned by the President within ten Days (Sundays excepted) after it shall have been presented to him, the Same shall be a Law, in like Manner as if he had signed it, unless the Congress by their Adjournment prevent its Return, in which Case it shall not be a Law.

Every Order, Resolution, or Vote to which the Concurrence of the Senate and House of Representatives may be necessary (except on a question of Adjournment) shall be presented to the President of the United States;

and before the Same shall take Effect, shall be approved by him, or being disapproved by him, shall be repassed to two thirds of the Senate and House of Representatives, according to the Rules and Limitations prescribed in the Case of a Bill.

[*Powers granted to Congress*]

SECTION 8   The Congress shall have power

To lay and collect Taxes, Duties, Imposts and Excises, to pay the Debts and provide for the common Defence and general Welfare of the United States; but all Duties, Imposts and Excises shall be uniform throughout the United States;

To borrow money on the credit of the United States;

To regulate Commerce with foreign Nations, and among the several States, and with the Indian Tribes;

To establish an uniform Rule of Naturalization, and uniform Laws on the subject of Bankruptcies throughout the United States;

To coin Money, regulate the Value thereof, and of foreign Coin, and fix the Standard of Weights and Measures;

To provide for the Punishment of counterfeiting the Securities and current Coin of the United States;

To Establish Post Offices and post Roads;

To promote the Progress of Science and useful Arts, by securing for limited Times to Authors and Inventors the exclusive Right to their respective Writings and Discoveries;

To constitute Tribunals inferior to the Supreme Court;

To define and punish Piracies and Felonies committed on the high Seas, and Offences against the Law of Nations;

To declare War, grant Letters of Marque and Reprisal, and make Rules concerning Captures on Land and Water;

To raise and support Armies, but no Appropriation of Money to that Use shall be for a longer Term than two Years;

To provide and maintain a Navy;

To make Rules for the Government and Regulation of the land and naval Forces;

To provide for calling forth the Militia to execute the Laws of the Union, suppress Insurrections and repel Invasions;

To provide for organizing, arming, and disciplining the Militia, and for governing such Part of them as may be employed in the Service of the United States, reserving to the States respectively, the Appointment of the Officers, and the Authority of training the Militia according to the discipline prescribed by Congress;

To exercise exclusive Legislation in all Cases whatsoever, over such District (not exceeding ten Miles square) as may, by Cession of particular States, and the acceptance of Congress, become the Seat of the Government of the United States, and to exercise like Authority over all Places purchased by the Consent of the Legislature of the State in which the Same shall be, for the Erection of Forts, Magazines, Arsenals, dock-Yards, and other needful Buildings;—And

[*Elastic clause*]

To make all Laws which shall be necessary and proper for carrying into Execution the foregoing Powers, and all other Powers vested by this Constitution in the Government of the United States, or in any Department or Officer thereof.

[*Powers denied to Congress*]

SECTION 9   The Migration or Importation of Such Persons as any of the States now existing shall think proper to admit, shall not be prohibited by the Congress prior to the Year one thousand eight hundred and eight, but a tax or duty may be imposed on such Importation, not exceeding ten dollars for each Person.

The privilege of the Writ of Habeas Corpus shall not be suspended, unless when in Cases of Rebellion or Invasion the public Safety may require it.

No Bill of Attainder or ex post facto Law shall be passed.

[No capitation, or other direct, Tax shall be laid, unless in Proportion to the Census or Enumeration herein before directed to be taken.][5]

No Tax or Duty shall be laid on Articles exported from any State.

No preference shall be given by any Regulation of Commerce or Revenue to the Ports of one State over those of another: nor shall Vessels bound to, or from, one State be obliged to enter, clear, or pay Duties in another.

No money shall be drawn from the Treasury, but in Consequence of Appropriations made by Law; and a regular Statement and Account of the Receipts and Expenditures of all public Money shall be published from time to time.

No Title of Nobility shall be granted by the United States: And no Person holding any Office of Profit or Trust under them, shall, without the Consent of the Congress, accept of any present, Emolument, Office, or Title, of any kind whatever, from any King, Prince, or foreign State.

[*Powers denied to states*]

SECTION 10   No State shall enter into any Treaty, Alliance, or Confederation; grant Letters of Marque and Reprisal; coin Money; emit Bills of Credit; make any Thing but gold and silver Coin a Tender in Payment of Debts; pass any Bill of Attainder, ex post facto Law, or Law impairing the Obligation of Contracts, or grant any Title of Nobility.

[5]Changed by Amendment XVI.

No State shall, without the Consent of the Congress, lay any Imposts or Duties on Imports or Exports, except what may be absolutely necessary for executing its inspection Laws: and the net Produce of all Duties and Imposts, laid by any State on Imports or Exports, shall be for the Use of the Treasury of the United States; and all such Laws shall be subject to the Revision and Control of the Congress.

No State shall, without the Consent of Congress, lay any duty of Tonnage, keep Troops, or Ships of War in time of Peace, enter into any Agreement or Compact with another State, or with a foreign Power, or engage in War, unless actually invaded, or in such imminent Danger as will not admit of delay.

[*The executive branch*]

Article II

[*Presidential term, choice by electors, qualifications, payment, succession, oath of office*]
SECTION 1   The executive Power shall be vested in a President of the United States of America. He shall hold his Office during the Term of four Years, and, together with the Vice President, chosen for the same Term, be elected, as follows:

Each State shall appoint, in such Manner as the Legislature thereof may direct, a Number of Electors, equal to the whole Number of Senators and Representatives to which the State may be entitled in the Congress: but no Senator or Representative, or Person holding an Office of Trust or Profit under the United States, shall be appointed an Elector.

[The Electors shall meet in their respective States, and vote by Ballot for two persons, of whom one at least shall not be an Inhabitant of the same State with themselves. And they shall make a List of all the Persons voted for, and of the Number of Votes for each; which List they shall sign and certify, and transmit sealed to the Seat of the Government of the United States, directed to the President of the Senate. The President of the Senate shall, in the Presence of the Senate and House of Representatives, open all the Certificates, and the Votes shall then be counted. The Person having the greatest Number of Votes shall be the President, if such Number be a Majority of the whole Number of Electors appointed; and if there be more than one who have such Majority, and have an equal Number of Votes, then the House of Representatives shall immediately chuse by Ballot one of them for President; and if no Person have a Majority, then from the five highest on the List the said House shall in like Manner chuse the President. But in chusing the President, the Votes shall be taken by States, the Representation from each State having one Vote; A quorum for this Purpose shall consist of a Member or Members from two-thirds of the States, and a Majority of all the States shall be necessary to a Choice. In every Case, after the Choice of the President, the Person having the greatest Number of Votes of the Electors shall be the Vice President. But if there should remain two or more who have equal Votes, the Senate shall chuse from them by Ballot the Vice President.][6]

The Congress may determine the Time of chusing the Electors, and the Day on which they shall give their Votes; which Day shall be the same throughout the United States.

No person except a natural born Citizen, or a Citizen of the United States, at the time of the Adoption of this Constitution, shall be eligible to the Office of President; neither shall any Person be eligible to that Office who shall not have attained to the Age of thirty-five Years, and been fourteen Years a Resident within the United States.

[In case of the removal of the President from Office, or of his Death, Resignation, or Inability to discharge the Powers and Duties of the said Office, the same shall devolve on the Vice President, and the Congress may by Law provide for the Case of Removal, Death, Resignation or Inability, both of the President and Vice President, declaring what Officer shall then act as President, and such Officer shall act accordingly, until the Disability be removed, or a President shall be elected.][7]

The President shall, at stated Times, receive for his Services, a Compensation, which shall neither be encreased nor diminished during the Period for which he shall have been elected, and he shall not receive within that Period any other Emolument from the United States, or any of them.

Before he enter on the Execution of his Office, he shall take the following Oath or Affirmation:—"I do solemnly swear (or affirm) that I will faithfully execute the Office of President of the United States, and will to the best of my Ability, preserve, protect and defend the Constitution of the United States."

[*Powers to command the military and executive departments, to grant pardons, to make treaties, to appoint government officers*]
SECTION 2   The President shall be Commander in Chief of the Army and Navy of the United States, and of the Militia of the several States, when called into the actual Service of the United States; he may require the Opinion, in writing, of the principal Officer in each of the executive Departments, upon any subject relating to the Duties of their respective Offices, and he shall have Power to grant Reprieves and Pardons for Offenses against the United States, except in Cases of Impeachment.

He shall have Power, by and with the Advice and Consent of the Senate, to make Treaties, provided two-

[6]Changed by Amendment XII.
[7]Changed by Amendment XXV.

thirds of the Senators present concur; and he shall nominate, and by and with the Advice and Consent of the Senate, shall appoint Ambassadors, other public Ministers and Consuls, Judges of the Supreme Court, and all other Officers of the United States, whose Appointments are not herein otherwise provided for, and which shall be established by Law; but the Congress may by Law vest the Appointment of such inferior Officers, as they think proper, in the President alone, in the Courts of Law, or in the Heads of Departments.

The President shall have Power to fill up all Vacancies that may happen during the Recess of the Senate, by granting Commissions which shall expire at the End of their next Session.

[*Formal duties*]
SECTION 3 He shall from time to time give to the Congress Information of the State of the Union, and recommend to their Consideration such Measures as he shall judge necessary and expedient; he may, on extraordinary Occasions, convene both Houses, or either of them, and in Case of Disagreement between them, with Respect to the Time of Adjournment, he may adjourn them to such Time as he shall think proper; he shall receive Ambassadors and other public Ministers; he shall take Care that the Laws be faithfully executed, and shall Commission all the Officers of the United States.

[*Conditions for removal*]
SECTION 4 The President, Vice President and all civil Officers of the United States, shall be removed from Office on Impeachment for, and Conviction of, Treason, Bribery, or other high Crimes and Misdemeanors.

[*The judicial branch*]

Article III

[*Courts and judges*]
SECTION 1 The judicial Power of the United States, shall be vested in one supreme Court, and in such inferior Courts as the Congress may from time to time ordain and establish. The Judges, both of the supreme and inferior Courts, shall hold their Offices during good Behaviour, and shall, at stated Times, receive for their Services a Compensation which shall not be diminished during their Continuance in Office.

[*Jurisdictions and jury trials*]
SECTION 2 The judicial Power shall extend to all Cases, in Law and Equity, arising under this Constitution, the Laws of the United States, and Treaties made, or which shall be made, under their Authority;—to all Cases affecting Ambassadors, other public Ministers and Consuls;—to all Cases of admiralty and maritime Jurisdiction;—to Controversies to which the United States shall be a Party;—to Controversies between two

or more States;—[between a State and Citizens of another State;—][8] between Citizens of different States;—between Citizens of the same State claiming Lands under Grants of different States, [and between a State, or the Citizens thereof, and foreign States, Citizens or Subjects].[9]

In all Cases affecting Ambassadors, other public Ministers and Consuls, and those in which a State shall be Party, the supreme Court shall have original Jurisdiction. In all the other Cases before mentioned, the supreme Court shall have appellate Jurisdiction, both as to Law and Fact, with such Exceptions, and under such Regulations as the Congress shall make.

The trial of all Crimes, except in Cases of Impeachment, shall be by Jury; and such Trial shall be held in the State where the said Crimes shall have been committed; but when not committed within any State, the Trial shall be at such Place or Places as the Congress may by Law have directed.

[*Treason and its punishment*]
SECTION 3 Treason against the United States, shall consist only in levying War against them, or, in adhering to their Enemies, giving them Aid and Comfort. No Person shall be convicted of Treason unless on the Testimony of two Witnesses to the same overt Act, or on Confession in open Court.

The Congress shall have power to declare the Punishment of Treason, but no Attainder of Treason shall work Corruption of Blood, or Forfeiture except during the Life of the Person attainted.

[THE REST OF THE FEDERAL SYSTEM]

Article IV

[*Relationships among and with states*]
SECTION 1 Full Faith and Credit shall be given in each State to the public Acts, Records, and judicial Proceedings of every other State. And the Congress may by general Laws prescribe the Manner in which such Acts, Records and Proceedings shall be proved, and the Effect thereof.

[*Privileges and immunities, extradition*]
SECTION 2 The Citizens of each State shall be entitled to all Privileges and Immunities of Citizens in the several States.

A Person charged in any State with Treason, Felony, or other Crime, who shall flee from Justice, and be found in another State, shall on demand of the executive Authority of the State from which he fled, be delivered up, to be removed to the State having Jurisdiction of the Crime.

[8]Changed by Amendment XI.
[9]Changed by Amendment XI.

[No Person held to Service or Labour in one State, under the Laws thereof, escaping into another, shall, in Consequence of any Law or Regulation therein, be discharged from such Service or Labour, but shall be delivered up on Claim of the Party to whom such Service or Labour may be due.][10]

[*New states*]

SECTION 3 New States may be admitted by the Congress into this Union; but no new State shall be formed or erected within the Jurisdiction of any other State; nor any State be formed by the Junction of two or more States, or parts of States, without the Consent of the Legislatures of the States concerned as well as of the Congress.

The Congress shall have Power to dispose of and make all needful Rules and Regulations respecting the Territory or other Property belonging to the United States; and nothing in this Constitution shall be so construed as to Prejudice any Claims of the United States, or of any particular State.

[*Obligations to states*]

SECTION 4 The United States shall guarantee to every State in this Union a Republican Form of Government, and shall protect each of them against Invasion; and on Application of the Legislature, or of the Executive (when the Legislature cannot be convened) against domestic Violence.

[MECHANISM FOR CHANGE]

Article V

[*Amending the Constitution*]

The Congress, whenever two-thirds of both Houses shall deem it necessary, shall propose Amendments to this Constitution, or, on the Application of the Legislatures of two-thirds of the several States, shall call a Convention for proposing Amendments, which, in either Case, shall be valid to all Intents and Purposes, as part of this Constitution, when ratified by the Legislatures of three-fourths of the several States, or by Conventions in three-fourths thereof, as the one or the other Mode of Ratification may be proposed by the Congress; Provided that no Amendment which may be made prior to the Year One thousand eight hundred and eight shall in any Manner affect the first and fourth Clauses in the Ninth Section of the first Article; and that no State, without its Consent, shall be deprived of its equal Suffrage in the Senate.

[10]Changed by Amendment XIII.

[FEDERAL SUPREMACY]

Article VI

All Debts contracted and Engagements entered into, before the Adoption of this Constitution shall be as valid against the United States under this Constitution, as under the Confederation.

This Constitution, and the Laws of the United States which shall be made in Pursuance thereof; and all Treaties made, or which shall be made, under the Authority of the United States, shall be the supreme Law of the Land; and the Judges in every State shall be bound thereby, any Thing in the Constitution or Laws of any State to the Contrary notwithstanding.

The Senators and Representatives before mentioned, and the Members of the several State Legislatures, and all executive and judicial Officers, both of the United States and of the several States, shall be bound by Oath or Affirmation, to support this Constitution; but no religious Test shall ever be required as a Qualification to any Office or public Trust under the United States.

[RATIFICATION]

Article VII

The Ratification of the Conventions of nine States shall be sufficient for the Establishment of this Constitution between the States so ratifying the Same.

Done in Convention by the Unanimous Consent of the States present the Seventeenth Day of September in the year of our Lord one thousand seven hundred and eighty seven and of the Independence of the United States of America the twelfth. In witness whereof We have hereunto subscribed our Names.

[BILL OF RIGHTS AND OTHER AMENDMENTS]

Articles in addition to, and amendment of, the Constitution of the United States of America, proposed by Congress, and ratified by the several States, pursuant to the fifth Article of the original Constitution.

Amendment I [1791]

[*Freedoms of religion, speech, press, assembly*]

Congress shall make no law respecting an establishment of religion, or prohibiting the free exercise thereof; or abridging the freedom of speech, or of the press; or the right of the people peaceably to assemble and to petition the Government for a redress of grievances.

Amendment II [1791]

[*Right to bear arms*]

A well regulated Militia, being necessary to the security of a free State, the right of the people to keep and bear Arms, shall not be infringed.

Amendment III [1791]

[*Quartering of soldiers*]

No Soldier shall, in time of peace be quartered in any house, without the consent of the Owner, nor in time of war, but in a manner to be prescribed by Law.

Amendment IV [1791]

[*Protection against search and seizure*]

The right of the people to be secure in their persons, houses, papers, and effects, against unreasonable searches and seizures, shall not be violated, and no Warrants shall issue, but upon probable cause, supported by Oath or affirmation, and particularly describing the place to be searched, and the persons or things to be seized.

Amendment V [1791]

[*Protection of citizens before the law*]

No person shall be held to answer for a capital, or otherwise infamous crime, unless on a presentment or indictment of a Grand Jury, except in cases arising in the land or naval forces, or in the Militia, when in actual service in time of War or public danger; nor shall any person be subject for the same offence to be twice put in jeopardy of life or limb; nor shall be compelled in any criminal case to be a witness against himself, nor be deprived of life, liberty, or property, without due process of law; nor shall private property be taken for public use, without just compensation.

Amendment VI [1791]

[*Rights of the accused in criminal cases*]

In all criminal prosecutions, the accused shall enjoy the right to a speedy and public trial, by an impartial jury of the State and district wherein the crime shall have been committed, which district shall have been previously ascertained by law, and to be informed of the nature and cause of the accusation; to be confronted with the witnesses against him; to have compulsory process for obtaining witnesses in his favor, and to have the Assistance of Counsel for his defence.

Amendment VII [1791]

[*Rights of complainants in civil cases*]

In suits at common law, where the value in controversy shall exceed twenty dollars, the right of trial by jury shall be preserved, and no fact tried by jury, shall be otherwise reexamined in any Court of the United States, than according to the rules of the common law.

Amendment VIII [1791]

[*Constraints on punishments*]

Excessive bail shall not be required, nor excessive fines imposed, nor cruel and unusual punishments inflicted.

Amendment IX [1791]

[*Rights retained by the people*]

The enumeration in the Constitution, of certain rights, shall not be construed to deny or disparage others retained by the people.

Amendment X [1791]

[*Rights reserved to states*]

The powers not delegated to the United States by the Constitution, nor prohibited by it to the States, are reserved to the States respectively, or to the people.

Amendment XI [1798]

[*Restraints on judicial power*]

The Judicial power of the United States shall not be construed to extend to any suit in law or equity, commenced or prosecuted against one of the United States by Citizens of another State, or by Citizens or Subjects of any Foreign State.

Amendment XII [1804]

[*Mechanism for presidential elections*]

The electors shall meet in their respective states and vote by ballot for President and Vice-President, one of whom, at least, shall not be an inhabitant of the same state with themselves; they shall name in their ballots the person voted for as President, and in distinct ballots the person voted for as Vice-President, and they shall make distinct lists of all persons voted for as President, and of all persons voted for as Vice-President, and of the number of votes for each, which lists they shall sign and certify, and transmit sealed to the seat of the government of the United States, directed to the President of the Senate;—The President of the Senate shall, in presence of the Senate and House of Representatives, open all the certificates and the votes shall then be counted;—The person having the greatest number of votes for President, shall be the President, if such number be a majority of the whole number of Electors appointed; and if no person have such majority, then from the persons having the highest numbers not exceeding three on the list of those voted for as President, the House of

Representatives shall choose immediately, by ballot, the President. But in choosing the President, the votes shall be taken by states, the representation from each state having one vote; a quorum for this purpose shall consist of a member or members from two-thirds of the states, and a majority of all the states shall be necessary to a choice. [And if the House of Representatives shall not choose a President whenever the right of choice shall devolve upon them, before the fourth day of March next following, then the Vice-President shall act as President, as in the case of the death or other constitutional disability of the President.—][11] The person having the greatest number of votes as Vice-President, shall be the Vice-President, if such number be a majority of the whole number of Electors appointed, and if no person have a majority, then from the two highest numbers on the list, the Senate shall choose the Vice-President; a quorum for the purpose shall consist of two-thirds of the whole number of Senators, and a majority of the whole number shall be necessary to a choice. But no person constitutionally ineligible to the office of President shall be eligible to that of Vice-President of the United States.

Amendment XIII [1865]

[*Abolishment of slavery*]

SECTION 1   Neither slavery nor involuntary servitude, except as a punishment for crime whereof the party shall have been duly convicted, shall exist within the United States, or any place subject to their jurisdiction.

SECTION 2   Congress shall have power to enforce this article by appropriate legislation.

Amendment XIV [1868]

[*Citizens' rights and immunities, due process, equal protection*]

SECTION 1   All persons born or naturalized in the United States, and subject to the jurisdiction thereof, are citizens of the United States and of the State wherein they reside. No State shall make or enforce any law which shall abridge the privileges or immunities of citizens of the United States; nor shall any State deprive any person of life, liberty, or property, without due process of law; nor deny to any person within its jurisdiction the equal protection of the laws.

[*Basis of representation*]

SECTION 2   Representatives shall be appointed among the several States according to their respective numbers, counting the whole number of persons in each State, excluding Indians not taxed. But when the right to vote at any election for the choice of electors for President and Vice-President of the United States,

Representatives in Congress, the Executive and Judicial officers of a State, or the members of the Legislature thereof, is denied to any of the male inhabitants of such State, being twenty-one years of age, and citizens of the United States, or in any way abridged, except for participation in rebellion, or other crime, the basis of representation therein shall be reduced in the proportion which the number of such male citizens shall bear to the whole number of male citizens twenty-one years of age in such State.

[*Disqualification of Confederates for office*]

SECTION 3   No person shall be a Senator or Representative in Congress, or elector of President and Vice-President, or hold any office, civil or military, under the United States, or under any State, who, having previously taken an oath, as a member of Congress, or as an officer of the United States, or as a member of any State legislature, or as an executive or judicial officer of any State, to support the Constitution of the United States, shall have engaged in insurrection or rebellion against the same, or given aid or comfort to the enemies thereof. But Congress may by a vote of two-thirds of each House, remove such disability.

[*Public debt arising from insurrection or rebellion*]

SECTION 4   The validity of the public debt of the United States, authorized by law, including debts incurred for payment of pensions and bounties for services in suppressing insurrection or rebellion, shall not be questioned. But neither the United States nor any State shall assume or pay any debt or obligation incurred in aid of insurrection or rebellion against the United States, or any claim for the loss or emancipation of any slave; but all such debts, obligations and claims shall be held illegal and void.

SECTION 5   The Congress shall have power to enforce, by appropriate legislation, the provisions of this article.

Amendment XV [1870]

[*Explicit extension of right to vote*]

SECTION 1   The right of citizens of the United States to vote shall not be denied or abridged by the United States or by any State on account of race, color, or previous condition of servitude.

SECTION 2   The Congress shall have power to enforce this article by appropriate legislation.

Amendment XVI [1913]

[*Creation of income tax*]

The Congress shall have power to lay and collect taxes on incomes, from whatever source derived, without apportionment among the several States, and without regard to any census or enumeration.

[11]Superceded by Section 3 of Amendment XX.

Amendment XVII [1913]

[Election of senators]

The Senate of the United States shall be composed of two Senators from each State, elected by the people thereof, for six years; and each Senator shall have one vote. The electors in each State shall have the qualifications requisite for electors of the most numerous branch of the State legislatures.

When vacancies happen in the representation of any State in the Senate, the executive authority of such State shall issue writs of election to fill such vacancies: *Provided*, That the legislature of any State may empower the executive thereof to make temporary appointments until the people fill the vacancies by election as the legislature may direct.

This amendment shall not be so construed as to affect the election or term of any Senator chosen before it becomes valid as part of the Constitution.

Amendment XVIII [1919]

[Prohibition of alcohol]

[SECTION 1   After one year from the ratification of this article the manufacture, sale, or transportation of intoxicating liquors within, the importation thereof into, or the exportation thereof from the United States and all territory subject to the jurisdiction thereof for beverage purposes is hereby prohibited.

SECTION 2   The Congress and the several States shall have concurrent power to enforce this article by appropriate legislation.

SECTION 3   This article shall be inoperative unless it shall have been ratified as an amendment to the Constitution by the legislatures of the several States, as provided in the Constitution, within seven years from the date of the submission hereof to the States by the Congress.][12]

Amendment XIX [1920]

[Voting rights and gender]

The right of citizens of the United States to vote shall not be denied or abridged by the United States or by any State on account of sex.

Congress shall have the power to enforce this article by appropriate legislation.

Amendment XX [1933]

[Terms of executives, assembly of Congress, presidential succession]

SECTION 1   The terms of the President and Vice President shall end at noon on the 20th day of January,

[12]Repealed by Amendment XXI.

and the terms of Senators and Representatives at noon on the 3d day of January, of the years in which such terms would have ended if this article had not been ratified; and the terms of their successors shall then begin.

SECTION 2   The Congress shall assemble at least once in every year, and such meeting shall begin at noon on the 3d day of January, unless they shall by law appoint a different day.

SECTION 3   If, at the time fixed for the beginning of the term of the President, the President elect shall have died, the Vice President elect shall become President. If a President shall not have been chosen before the time fixed for the beginning of his term, or if the President elect shall have failed to qualify, then the Vice President elect shall act as President until a President shall have qualified; and the Congress may by law provide for the case wherein neither a President elect nor a Vice President elect shall have qualified, declaring who shall then act as President, or the manner in which one who is to act shall be selected, and such person shall act accordingly until a President or Vice President shall have qualified.

SECTION 4   The Congress may by law provide for the case of the death of any of the persons from whom the House of Representatives may choose a President whenever the right of choice shall have devolved upon them, and for the case of the death of any of the persons from whom the Senate may choose a Vice President whenever the right of choice shall have devolved upon them.

SECTION 5   Sections 1 and 2 shall take effect on the 15th day of October following the ratification of this article.

SECTION 6   This article shall be inoperative unless it shall have been ratified as an amendment to the Constitution by the legislatures of three-fourths of the several States within seven years from the date of its submission.

Amendment XXI [1933]

[Repealing of prohibition]

SECTION 1   The eighteenth article of amendment to the Constitution of the United States is hereby repealed.

SECTION 2   The transportation or importation into any State, Territory, or possession of the United States for delivery or use therein of intoxicating liquors, in violation of the laws thereof, is hereby prohibited.

SECTION 3   This article shall be inoperative unless it shall have been ratified as an amendment to the Constitution by conventions in the several States, as provided in the Constitution, within seven years from the date of the submission hereof to the States by the Congress.

Amendment XXII [1951]

[*Limits on presidential term*]

SECTION 1   No person shall be elected to the office of the President more than twice, and no person who has held the office of President, or acted as President, for more than two years of a term to which some other person was elected President shall be elected to the office of the President more than once. But this Article shall not apply to any person holding the office of President when this Article was proposed by the Congress, and shall not prevent any person who may be holding the office of President, or acting as President, during the term within which the Article becomes operative from holding the office of President or acting as President during the remainder of such term.

SECTION 2   This article shall be inoperative unless it shall have been ratified as an amendment to the Constitution by the legislatures of three-fourths of the several States within seven years from the date of its submission to the States by the Congress.

Amendment XXIII [1961]

[*Voting rights of District of Columbia*]

SECTION 1   The District constituting the seat of Government of the United States shall appoint in such manner as the Congress may direct:

A number of electors of President and Vice President equal to the whole number of Senators and Representatives in Congress to which the District would be entitled if it were a State; but in no event more than the least populous State; they shall be in addition to those appointed by the States, but they shall be considered, for the purposes of the election of President and Vice President, to be electors appointed by a State; and they shall meet in the District and perform such duties as provided by the twelfth article of amendment.

SECTION 2   The Congress shall have power to enforce this article by appropriate legislation.

Amendment XXIV [1964]

[*Prohibition of poll tax*]

SECTION 1   The right of citizens of the United States to vote in any primary or other election for President or Vice President, for electors for President or Vice President, or for Senator or Representative in Congress, shall not be denied or abridged by the United States or any State by reason of failure to pay any poll tax or other tax.

SECTION 2   The Congress shall have power to enforce this article by appropriate legislation.

Amendment XXV [1967]

[*Presidential disability and succession*]

SECTION 1   In case of the removal of the President from office or his death or resignation, the Vice President shall become President.

SECTION 2   Whenever there is a vacancy in the office of the Vice President, the President shall nominate a Vice President who shall take the Office upon confirmation by a majority vote of both houses of Congress.

SECTION 3   Whenever the President transmits to the President pro tempore of the Senate and the Speaker of the House of Representatives his written declaration that he is unable to discharge the powers and duties of his office, and until he transmits to them a written declaration to the contrary, such powers and duties shall be discharged by the Vice President as Acting President.

SECTION 4   Whenever the Vice President and a majority of either the principal officers of the executive departments, or of such other body as Congress may by law provide, transmit to the President pro tempore of the Senate and the Speaker of the House of Representatives their written declaration that the President is unable to discharge the powers and duties of his office, the Vice President shall immediately assume the powers and duties of the office as Acting President.

Thereafter, when the President transmits to the President pro tempore of the Senate and the Speaker of the House of Representatives his written declaration that no inability exists, he shall resume the powers and duties of his office unless the Vice President and a majority of either the principal officers of the executive department, or of such other body as Congress may by law provide, transmit within four days to the President pro tempore of the Senate and the Speaker of the House of Representatives their written declaration that the President is unable to discharge the powers and duties of his office. Thereupon Congress shall decide the issue, assembling within 48 hours for that purpose if not in session. If the Congress, within 21 days after receipt of the latter written declaration, or, if Congress is not in session, within 21 days after Congress is required to assemble, determines by two-thirds vote of both houses that the President is unable to discharge the powers and duties of his office, the Vice President shall continue to discharge the same as Acting President; otherwise, the President shall resume the powers and duties of his office.

Amendment XXVI [1971]

[Voting rights and age]

SECTION 1 The right of citizens of the United States, who are eighteen years of age, or older, to vote shall not be denied or abridged by the United States or by any state on account of age.

SECTION 2   The Congress shall have the power to enforce this article by appropriate legislation.

Amendment XXVII [1992]

[Congressional pay]

No law varying the compensation for the services of the Senators and Representatives shall take effect until an election of Representatives shall have intervened.

From *The Federalist,* Nos. 10 and 51

FEDERALIST NO. 10 [1787]

To the People of the State of New York: Among the numerous advantages promised by a well-constructed union, none deserves to be more accurately developed than its tendency to break and control the violence of faction. The friend of popular governments, never finds himself so much alarmed for their character and fate, as when he contemplates their propensity to this dangerous vice. He will not fail, therefore, to set a due value on any plan which, without violating the principles to which he is attached, provides a proper cure for it. The instability, injustice, and confusion introduced into the public councils, have, in truth, been the mortal diseases under which popular governments have everywhere perished; as they continue to be the favourite and fruitful topics from which the adversaries to liberty derive their most specious declamations. The valuable improvements made by the American constitutions on the popular models, both ancient and modern, cannot certainly be too much admired; but it would be an unwarrantable partiality, to contend that they have as effectually obviated the danger on this side, as was wished and expected. Complaints are everywhere heard from our most considerate and virtuous citizens, equally the friends of public and private faith, and of public and personal liberty, that our governments are too unstable; that the public good is disregarded in the conflicts of rival parties; and that measures are too often decided, not according to the rules of justice, and the rights of the minor party, but by the superior force of an interested and overbearing majority. However anxiously we may wish that these complaints had no foundation, the evidence of known facts will not permit us to deny that they are in some degree true. It will be found, indeed, on a candid review of our situation, that some of the distresses under which we labour have been erroneously charged on the operation of our governments; but it will be found, at the same time, that other causes will not alone account for many of our heaviest misfortunes; and, particularly, for that prevailing and increasing distrust of public engagements, and alarm for private rights, which are echoed from one end of the continent to the other. These must be chiefly, if not wholly, effects of the unsteadiness and injustice, with which a factious spirit has tainted our public administrations.

By a faction, I understand a number of citizens, whether amounting to a majority or minority of the whole, who are united and actuated by some common impulse of passion, or of interest, adverse to the rights of other citizens, or to the permanent and aggregate interests of the community.

There are two methods of curing the mischiefs of faction: The one, by removing its causes; the other, by controlling its effects.

There are again two methods of removing the causes of faction: The one, by destroying the liberty which is essential to its existence; the other, by giving to every citizen the same opinions, the same passions, and the same interests.

It could never be more truly said, than of the first remedy, that it was worse than the disease. Liberty is to faction what air is to fire, an ailment without which it instantly expires. But it could not be a less folly to abolish liberty, which is essential to political life, because it nourishes faction, than it would be to wish the annihilation of air, which is essential to animal life, because it imparts to fire its destructive agency.

The second expedient is as impracticable, as the first would be unwise. As long as the reason of man continues fallible, and he is at liberty to exercise it, different opinions will be formed. As long as the connection subsists between his reason and his self-love, his opinions and his passions will have a reciprocal influence on each other; and the former will be objects to which the latter will attach themselves. The diversity in the faculties of men, from which the rights of property originate, is not less an insuperable obstacle to an uniformity of interests. The protection of these faculties is the first object of government. From the protection of different and unequal faculties of acquiring property, the possession of different degrees and kinds of property immediately results;

and from the influence of these on the sentiments and views of the respective proprietors, ensues a division of the society into different interests and parties.

The latent causes of action are thus sown in the nature of man; and we see them everywhere brought into different degrees of activity, according to the different circumstances of civil society. A zeal for different opinions concerning religion, concerning government, and many other points, as well as of speculation as of practice; an attachment to different leaders ambitiously contending for preeminence and power; or to persons of other descriptions whose fortunes have been interesting to the human passions, have, in turn, divided mankind into parties, inflamed them with mutual animosity, and rendered them much more disposed to vex and oppress each other, than to cooperate for their common good. So strong is this propensity of mankind, to fall into mutual animosities, that where no substantial occasion presents itself, the most frivolous and fanciful distinctions have been sufficient to kindle their unfriendly passions and excite their most violent conflicts. But the most common and durable source of factions, has been the various and unequal distribution of property. Those who hold, and those who are without property, have ever formed distinct interests in society. Those who are creditors, and those who are debtors, fall under alike discrimination. A landed interest, a manufacturing interest, a mercantile interest, a moneyed interest, with many lesser interests, grow up of necessity in civilized nations, and divide them into different classes, actuated by different sentiments and views. The regulation of these various and interfering interests forms the principal task of modern legislation, and involves the spirit of the party and faction in the necessary and ordinary operations of the government.

No man is allowed to be a judge in his own cause; because his interest will certainly bias his judgment, and, not improbably, corrupt his integrity. With equal, nay, with greater reason, a body of men are unfit to be both judges and parties at the same time; yet what are many of the most important acts of legislation, but so many judicial determinations, not indeed concerning the right of single persons, but concerning the rights of large bodies of citizens? And what are the different classes of legislators, but advocates and parties to the causes which they determine? Is a law proposed concerning private debts? It is a question to which the creditors are parties on one side, and the debtors on the other. Justice ought to hold the balance between them. Yet the parties are, and must be, themselves the judges; and the most numerous party, or, in other words, the most powerful faction, must be expected to prevail. Shall domestic manufactures be encouraged, and in what degree, by restrictions on foreign manufactures? are questions which would be differently decided by the landed and the manufacturing classes; and probably by

neither with a sole regard to justice and the public good. The apportionment of taxes, on the various descriptions of property, is an act which seems to require the most exact impartiality; yet there is, perhaps, no legislative act, in which greater opportunity and temptation are given to a predominant party to trample on the rules of justice. Every shilling, with which they overburden the inferior number, is a shilling saved to their own pockets.

It is in vain to say, that enlightened statesmen will be able to adjust these clashing interests, and render them all subservient to the public good. Enlightened statesmen will not always be at the helm: nor, in many cases, can such an adjustment be made at all, without taking into view indirect and remote considerations, which will rarely prevail over the immediate interest which one party may find in disregarding the rights of another, or the good of the whole.

The inference to which we are brought is, that the *causes* of faction cannot be removed; and that relief is only to be sought in the means of controlling its *effects*.

If a faction consists of less than a majority, relief is supplied by the republican principle, which enables the majority to defeat its sinister views, by regular vote. It may clog the administration, it may convulse the society; but it will be unable to execute and mask its violence under the forms of the constitution. When a majority is included in a faction, the form of popular government, on the other hand, enables it to sacrifice to its ruling passion or interest, both the public good and the rights of other citizens. To secure the public good, and private rights, against the danger of such a faction, and at the same time to preserve the spirit and the form of popular government, is then the great object to which our inquiries are directed. Let me add, that it is the great desideratum, by which alone this form of government can be rescued from the opprobrium under which it has so long laboured, and be recommended to the esteem and adoption of mankind.

By what means is this object attainable? Evidently by one of two only. Either the existence of the same passion or interest in a majority, at the same time, must be prevented; or the majority, having such coexistent passion or interest, must be rendered, by their number and local situation, unable to concert and carry into effect schemes of oppression. If the impulse and the opportunity be suffered to coincide, we well know that neither moral nor religious motives can be relied on as an adequate control. They are not found to be such on the injustice and violence of individuals, and lose their efficacy in proportion to the number combined together; that is, in proportion as their efficacy becomes needful.

From this view of the subject, it may be concluded, that a pure democracy, by which I mean a society consisting of a small number of citizens, who assemble and administer the government in person, can admit of no cure for the mischiefs of faction. A common passion or interest will, in almost every case, be felt by a majority of the whole; a communication and concert, results from the form of government itself; and there is nothing to check the inducements to sacrifice the weaker party, or an obnoxious individual. Hence, it is, that such democracies have ever been spectacles of turbulence and contention; have ever been found incompatible with personal security, or the rights of property; and have in general been as short in their lives, as they have been violent in their deaths. Theoretic politicians, who have patronized this species of government, have erroneously supposed, that by reducing mankind to a perfect equality in their political rights, they would, at the same time, be perfectly equalized and assimilated in their possessions, their opinions, and their passions.

A republic, by which I mean a government in which the scheme of representation takes place, opens a different prospect, and promises the cure for which we are seeking. Let us examine the points in which it varies from pure democracy, and we shall comprehend both the nature of the cure and the efficacy which it must derive from the union.

The two great points of difference, between a democracy and a republic, are, first, the delegation of the government, in the latter, to a small number of citizens, elected by the rest; secondly, the greatest number of citizens, and greater sphere of country, over which the latter may be extended.

The effect of the first difference is, on the one hand, to refine and enlarge the public views, by passing them through the medium of a chosen body of citizens, whose wisdom may best discern the true interest of their country, and whose patriotism and love of justice, will be least likely to sacrifice it to temporary or partial considerations. Under such a regulation, it may well happen, that the public voice, pronounced by the representatives of the people, will be more consonant to the public good, than if pronounced by the people themselves, convened for the purpose. On the other hand the effect may be inverted. Men of factious tempers, of local prejudices, or of sinister designs, may by intrigue, by corruption, or by other means, first obtain the suffrages, and then betray the interest of the people. The question resulting is, whether small or extensive republics are most favourable to the election of proper guardians of the public weal; and it is clearly decided in favour of the latter by two obvious considerations.

In the first place, it is to be remarked that, however small the republic may be, the representatives must be raised to a certain number, in order to guard against the cabals of a few; and that however large it may be, they must be limited to a certain number, in order to guard against the confusion of a multitude. Hence, the number of representatives in the two cases not being in proportion to that of the constituents, and being proportionally greatest in the small republic, it follows, that if the pro-

portion of fit characters be not less in the large than in the small republic, the former will present a greater option, and consequently a greater probability of a fit choice.

In the next place, as each representative will be chosen by a greater number of citizens in the large than in the small republic, it will be more difficult for unworthy candidates to practise with success the vicious arts, by which elections are too often carried; and the suffrages of the people being more free, will be more likely to centre in men who possess the most attractive merit, and the most diffusive and established characters.

It must be confessed, that in this, as in most other cases, there is a mean, on both sides of which inconveniences will be found to lie. By enlarging too much the number of electors, you render the representatives too little acquainted with all their local circumstances and lesser interests; as by reducing it too much, you render him unduly attached to these, and too little fit to comprehend and pursue great and national objects. The federal constitution forms a happy combination being referred to the national, the local and particular, to the state legislatures.

The other point of difference is, the greater number of citizens, and extent of territory, which may be brought within the compass of republican, than of democratic government; and it is this circumstance principally which renders factious combinations less to be dreaded in the former, than in the latter. The smaller the society, the fewer probably will be the distinct parties and interests composing it; the fewer the distinct parties and interests, the more frequently will a majority be found of the same party; and the smaller the number of individuals composing a majority, and the smaller the compass within which they are placed, the more easily will they concert and execute their plans of oppression. Extend the sphere, and you take in a greater variety of parties and interests; you make it less probable that a majority of the whole will have a common motive to invade the rights of other citizens; or if such a common motive exists, it will be more difficult for all who feel it to discover their own strength, and to act in unison with each other. Besides other impediments, it may be remarked, that where there is a consciousness of unjust or dishonourable purposes, communication is always checked by distrust, in proportion to the number whose concurrence is necessary.

Hence, it clearly appears, that the same advantage, which a republic has over a democracy, in controlling the effects of faction, is enjoyed by a large over a small republic,—is enjoyed by the union over the states composing it. Does this advantage consist in the substitution of representatives, whose enlightened views and virtuous sentiments render them superior to local prejudices, and to schemes of injustice? It will not be denied that the representation of the union will be most likely to possess these requisite endowments. Does it consist in the greater security afforded by a greater variety of parties, against the event of any one party being able to outnumber and oppress the rest? In an equal degree does the increased variety of parties, comprised within the union, increase the security? Does it, in fine, consist in the greater obstacles opposed to the concert and accomplishment of the secret wishes of an unjust and interested majority? Here, again, the extent of the union gives it the most palpable advantage.

The influence of factious leaders may kindle a flame within their particular states, but will be unable to spread a general conflagration through the other states; a religious sect may degenerate into a political faction in a part of the confederacy; but the variety of sects dispersed over the entire face of it, must secure the national councils against any danger from that source: a rage for paper money, for an abolition of debts, for an equal division of property, or for any other improper or wicked project, will be less apt to pervade the whole body of the union than a particular member of it; in the same proportion as such a malady is more likely to taint a particular county or district, than an entire state.

In the extent and proper structure of the union, therefore, we behold a republican remedy for the diseases most incident to republican government. And according to the degree of pleasure and pride we feel in being republicans, ought to be our zeal in cherishing the spirit, and supporting the character of federalists.

JAMES MADISON

FEDERALIST NO. 51 [1788]

To the People of the State of New York: To what expedient then shall we finally resort for maintaining in practice the necessary partition of power among the several departments, as laid down in the constitution? The only answer that can be given is, that as all these exterior provisions are found to be inadequate, the defect must be supplied, by so contriving the interior structure of the government, as that its several constituent parts may, by their mutual relations, be the means of keeping each other in their proper places. Without presuming to undertake a full development of this important idea, I will hazard a few general observations, which may perhaps place it in a clearer light, and enable us to form a more correct judgment of the principles and structure of the government planned by the convention.

In order to lay a due foundation for that separate and distinct exercise of the different powers of government, which to a certain extent, is admitted on all hands to be essential to the preservation of liberty, it is evident that each department should have a will of its own; and consequently should be so constituted, that the members of each should have as little agency as possible in the appointment of the members of the others. Were this principle rigorously adhered to, it would require that all the appointments for the supreme executive, legislative, and judiciary magistracies, should be drawn from the same fountain of authority, the people, through channels, having no communication whatever with one another. Perhaps such a plan of constructing the several departments would be less difficult in practice than it may in contemplation appear. Some difficulties however, and some additional expense, would attend the execution of it. Some deviations therefore from the principle must be admitted. In the constitution of the judiciary department in particular, it might be inexpedient to insist rigorously on the principle; first, because peculiar qualifications being essential in the members, the primary consideration ought to be to select that mode of choice, which best secures these qualifications; secondly, because the permanent tenure by which the appointments are held in that department, must soon destroy all sense of dependence on the authority conferring them.

It is equally evident that the members of each department should be as little dependent as possible on those of the others, for the emoluments annexed to their offices. Were the executive magistrate, or the judges, not independent of the legislature in this particular, their independence in every other would be merely nominal.

But the great security against a gradual concentration of the several powers in the same department, consists in giving to those who administer each department, the necessary constitutional means, and personal motives, to resist encroachments of the others. The provision for defense must in this, as in all other cases, be made commensurate to the danger of attack. Ambition must be made to counteract ambition. The interest of the man must be connected with the constitutional rights of the place. It may be a reflection on human nature, that such devices should be necessary to control the abuses of government: But what is government itself but the greatest of all reflections on human nature? If men were angels, no government would be necessary. If angels were to govern men, neither external nor internal controls on government would be necessary. In framing a government which is to be administered by men over men, the great difficulty lies in this: You must first enable the government to control the governed; and in the next place, oblige it to control itself. A dependence on the people is no doubt the primary control on the government; but experience has taught mankind the necessity of auxiliary precautions.

This policy of supplying by opposite and rival interests, the defect of better motives, might be traced through the whole system of human affairs, private as well as public. We see it particularly displayed in all the subordinate distributions of power; where the constant aim is to divide and arrange the several offices in such a manner as that each may be a check on the other; that the private interest of every individual, may be a sentinel over the public rights. These inventions of prudence cannot be less requisite in the distribution of the supreme powers of the state.

But it is not possible to give to each department an equal power of self defense. In republican government the legislative authority, necessarily, predominates. The remedy for this inconveniency is, to divide the legislature into different branches; and to render them by different modes of election, and different principles of action, as little connected with each other, as the nature of their common functions, and their common dependence on the society, will admit. It may even be necessary to guard against dangerous encroachments by still further precautions. As the weight of the legislative authority requires that it should be thus divided, the weakness of the executive may require, on the other hand, that it should be fortified. An absolute negative, on the legislature, appears at first view to be the natural defense with which the executive magistrate should be armed. But perhaps it would be neither altogether safe, nor alone sufficient. On ordinary occasions, it might not be exerted with the requisite firmness; and on extraordinary occasions, it might be perfidiously abused. May not this defect of an absolute negative be supplied, by some qualified connection between this weaker department, and the weaker branch of the stronger department, by which the latter may be led to support the constitutional rights of the former, without being too much detached from the rights of its own department?

If the principles on which these observations are founded be just, as I persuade myself they are, and they be applied as a criterion, to the several state constitutions, and to the federal constitution, it will be found, that if the latter does not perfectly correspond with them, the former are infinitely less able to bear such a test.

There are moreover two considerations particularly applicable to the federal system of America, which place that system in a very interesting point of view.

First. In a single republic, all the power surrendered by the people, is submitted to the administration of a single government; and usurpations are guarded against by a division of the government into distinct and separate departments. In the compound republic of America, the power surrendered by the people, is first divided between two distinct governments, and then the portion allotted to each, subdivided among distinct and separate departments. Hence a double security arises to the rights of the people. The different governments will control each other; at the same time that each will be controlled by itself.

Second. It is of great importance in a republic, not only to guard the society against the oppression of its rulers; but to guard one part of the society against the injustice of the other part. Different interests necessarily exist in different classes of citizens. If a majority be united by a common interest, the rights of the minority will be insecure. There are but two methods of providing against this evil: The one by creating a will in the community independent of the majority, that is, of the society itself; the other by comprehending in the society so many separate descriptions of citizens, as will render an unjust combination of a majority of the whole, very improbable, if not impracticable. The first method prevails in all governments possessing an hereditary or self appointed authority. This at best is but a precarious security; because a power independent of the society may as well espouse the unjust views of the major, as the rightful interests, of the minor party, and may possibly be turned against both parties. The second method will be exemplified in the federal republic of the United States. While all authority in it will be derived from and dependent on the society, the society itself will be broken into so many parts, interests and classes of citizens, that the rights of individuals or of the minority, will be in little danger from interested combinations of the majority. In a free government, the security for civil rights must be the same as for religious rights. It consists in the one case in the multiplicity of sects. The degree of security in both cases will depend on the number of interests and sects; and this may be presumed to depend on the extent of country and number of people comprehended under the same government. This view of the subject must particularly recommend a proper federal system to all the sincere and considerate friends of republican government: Since it shows that in exact proportion as the territory of the union may be formed into more circumscribed confederacies or states, oppressive combinations of a majority will be facilitated; the best security under the republican form, for the rights of every class of citizens, will be diminished; and consequently, the stability and independence of some member of the government, the only other security, must be proportionally increased. Justice is the end of government. It is the end of civil society. It ever has been, and ever will be pursued, until it be obtained, or until liberty be lost in the pursuit. In a society under the forms of which the stronger faction can readily unite and oppress the weaker, anarchy may as truly be said to reign, as in a state of nature where the weaker individual is not secured against the violence of the stronger: And as in the latter state even the stronger individuals are prompted by the uncertainty of their condition, to submit to a government which may protect the weak as well as themselves: So in the former state, will the more powerful factions or parties be gradually induced by alike motives, to wish for a government which will protect all parties, the weaker as well as the more powerful. It can be little doubted, that if the state of Rhode Island was separated from the confederacy, and left to itself, the insecurity of rights under the popular form of government within such narrow limits, would be displayed by such reiterated oppressions of factious majorities, that some power altogether independent of the people would soon be called for by the voice of the very factions whose misrule had proved the necessity of it. In the extended republic of the United States, and among the great variety of interests, parties and sects which it embraces, a coalition of a majority of the whole society could seldom take place on any other principles than those of justice and the general good; and there being thus less danger to a minor from the will of the major party, there must be less pretext also, to provide for the security of the former, by introducing into the government a will not dependent on the latter; or in other words, a will independent of the society itself. It is no less certain than it is important, notwithstanding the contrary opinions which have been entertained, that the larger the society, provided it lie within a practicable sphere, the more duly capable it will be of self government. And happily for the *republican cause,* the practicable sphere may be carried to a very great extent, by a judicious modification and mixture of the *federal principle.*

JAMES MADISON

Presidential Elections

CANDIDATES	PARTY	ELECTORAL VOTE
1789		
George Washington	Federalist	69
John Adams	Federalist	34
Others		35
1792		
George Washington	Federalist	132
John Adams	Federalist	77
George Clinton		50
Others		5
1796		
John Adams	Federalist	71
Thomas Jefferson	Democratic-Republican	68
Thomas Pinckney	Federalist	59
Aaron Burr	Democratic-Republican	30
Others		48
1800		
Thomas Jefferson[1]	Democratic-Republican	73
Aaron Burr	Democratic-Republican	73
John Adams	Federalist	65
Charles C. Pinckney		64
1804		
Thomas Jefferson	Democratic-Republican	162
Charles C. Pinckney	Federalist	14
1808		
James Madison	Democratic-Republican	122
Charles C. Pinckney	Federalist	47
George Clinton	Independent-Republican	6
1812		
James Madison	Democratic-Republican	122
DeWitt Clinton	Federalist	89
1816		
James Monroe	Democratic-Republican	183
Rufus King	Federalist	34
1820		
James Monroe	Democratic-Republican	231
John Quincy Adams	Independent-Republican	1

CANDIDATES	PARTY	ELECTORAL VOTE
1824		
John Quincy Adams[1]	Democratic-Republican	84
Andrew Jackson	Democratic-Republican	99
Henry Clay	Democratic-Republican	37
William H. Crawford	Democratic-Republican	41
1828		
Andrew Jackson	Democratic	178
John Quincy Adams	National-Republican	83
1832		
Andrew Jackson	Democratic	219
Henry Clay	National-Republican	49
William Wirt	Anti-Masonic	7
John Floyd	National-Republican	11
1836		
Martin Van Buren	Democratic	170
William H. Harrison	Whig	73
Hugh L. White	Whig	26
Daniel Webster	Whig	14
1840		
William H. Harrison[2]	Whig	234
(John Tyler)	Whig	
Martin Van Buren	Democratic	60
1844		
James K. Polk	Democratic	170
Henry Clay	Whig	105
James G. Birney	Liberty	
1848		
Zachary Taylor[2]	Whig	163
(Millard Fillmore)	Whig	
Lewis Cass	Democratic	127
Martin Van Buren	Free Soil	
1852		
Franklin Pierce	Democratic	254
Winfield Scott	Whig	42

CANDIDATES	PARTY	ELECTORAL VOTE
1856		
James Buchanan	Democratic	174
John C. Fremont	Republican	114
Millard Fillmore	American	8
1860		
Abraham Lincoln	Republican	180
Stephen A. Douglas	Democratic	12
John C. Breckinridge	Democratic	72
John Bell	Constitutional Union	39
1864		
Abraham Lincoln[2]	Republican	212
(Andrew Johnson)	Republican	
George B. McClellan	Democratic	21
1868		
Ulysses S. Grant	Republican	214
Horatio Seymour	Democratic	80
1872		
Ulysses S. Grant	Republican	286
Horace Greeley	Democratic	66
1876		
Rutherford B. Hayes	Republican	185
Samuel J. Tilden	Democratic	184
1880		
James A. Garfield[2]	Republican	214
(Chester A. Arthur)	Republican	
Winfield S. Hancock	Democratic	155
James B. Weaver	Greenback-Labor	
1884		
Grover Cleveland	Democratic	219
James G. Blaine	Republican	182
Benjamin F. Butler	Greenback-Labor	
1888		
Benjamin Harrison	Republican	233
Grover Cleveland	Democratic	168
1892		
Grover Cleveland	Democratic	277
Benjamin Harrison	Republican	145
James R. Weaver	People's	22
1896		
William McKinley	Republican	271
William J. Bryan	Democratic, Populist	176
1900		
William McKinley[2]	Republican	292
(Theodore Roosevelt)	Republican	
William J. Bryan	Democratic, Populist	155
1904		
Theodore Roosevelt	Republican	336
Alton B. Parker	Democratic	140
Eugene V. Debs	Socialist	

CANDIDATES	PARTY	ELECTORAL VOTE
1908		
William H. Taft	Republican	321
William J. Bryan	Democratic	162
Eugene V. Debs	Socialist	
1912		
Woodrow Wilson	Democratic	435
Theodore Roosevelt	Progressive	88
William H. Taft	Republican	8
Eugene V. Debs	Socialist	
1916		
Woodrow Wilson	Democratic	277
Charles E. Hughes	Republican	254
1920		
Warren G. Harding[2]	Republican	404
(Calvin Coolidge)	Republican	
James M. Cox	Democratic	127
Eugene V. Debs	Socialist	
1924		
Calvin Coolidge	Republican	382
John W. Davis	Democratic	136
Robert M. LaFollette	Progressive	13
1928		
Herbert C. Hoover	Republican	444
Alfred E. Smith	Democratic	87
1932		
Franklin D. Roosevelt	Democratic	472
Herbert C. Hoover	Republican	59
Norman Thomas	Socialist	
1936		
Franklin D. Roosevelt	Democratic	523
Alfred M. Landon	Republican	8
William Lemke	Union	
1940		
Franklin D. Roosevelt	Democratic	449
Wendell L. Wilkie	Republican	82
1944		
Franklin D. Roosevelt[2]	Democratic	432
(Harry S Truman)	Democratic	
Thomas E. Dewey	Republican	99
1948		
Harry S Truman	Democratic	303
Thomas E. Dewey	Republican	189
J. Strom Thurmond	States' Rights	39
Henry A. Wallace	Progressive	
1952		
Dwight D. Eisenhower	Republican	442
Adlai E. Stevenson	Democratic	89
1956		
Dwight D. Eisenhower	Republican	457
Adlai E. Stevenson	Democratic	73

CANDIDATES	PARTY	ELECTORAL VOTE
1960		
John F. Kennedy[2]	Democratic	303
(Lyndon B. Johnson)	Democratic	
Richard M. Nixon	Republican	219
1964		
Lyndon B. Johnson	Democratic	486
Barry M. Goldwater	Republican	52
1968		
Richard M. Nixon	Republican	301
Hubert H. Humphrey	Democratic	191
George C. Wallace	American Independent	46
1972		
Richard M. Nixon[3]	Republican	520
(Gerald R. Ford)	Republican	
George S. McGovern	Democratic	17
1976		
Jimmy Carter	Democratic	297
Gerald R. Ford	Republican	240

CANDIDATES	PARTY	ELECTORAL VOTE
1980		
Ronald Reagan	Republican	489
Jimmy Carter	Democratic	49
John Anderson	Independent	
1984		
Ronald Reagan	Republican	525
Walter Mondale	Democratic	13
1988		
George Bush	Republican	426
Michael Dukakis	Democratic	111
1992		
Bill Clinton	Democratic	370
George Bush	Republican	168
Ross Perot	Independent	
1996		
Bill Clinton	Democratic	379
Bob Dole	Republican	159
Ross Perot	Reform Party	

[1]Elected by the House of Representatives.

[2]Died while in office.

[3]Resigned from office.

1996 Electoral and Popular Vote Summary

STATE	ELECTORAL VOTE		POPULAR VOTE						TOTAL POPULAR VOTE
	CLINTON	DOLE	CLINTON	PERCENT	DOLE	PERCENT	PEROT	PERCENT	
Ala.	0	9	664,503	43	782,029	51	92,010	06	1,538,542
Alaska	0	3	66,508	33	101,234	51	21,536	11	189,278
Ariz.	8	0	612,412	47	576,126	44	104,712	08	1,293,250
Ark.	6	0	469,164	54	322,349	37	66,997	08	858,510
Calif.	54	0	4,639,935	51	3,412,563	38	667,702	07	8,720,200
Colo.	0	8	670,854	44	691,291	46	99,509	07	1,461,654
Conn.	8	0	712,603	52	481,047	35	137,784	10	1,331,434
D.C.	3	0	140,209	52	98,906	37	28,693	11	267,808
Del.	3	0	152,031	85	16,637	09	3,479	02	172,147
Fla.	25	0	2,533,502	48	2,226,117	42	482,237	09	5,241,856
Ga.	0	13	1,047,214	46	1,078,972	47	146,031	06	2,272,217
Hawaii	4	0	205,012	57	113,943	32	27,358	08	346,313
Idaho	0	4	165,545	34	256,406	52	62,506	13	484,457
Ill.	22	0	2,299,476	54	1,577,930	37	344,311	08	4,221,717
Ind.	0	12	874,668	42	995,082	47	218,739	10	2,088,489
Iowa	7	0	615,732	50	490,949	40	104,462	09	1,211,143

State	Electoral Vote		Popular Vote						Total Popular Vote
	Clinton	Dole	Clinton	Percent	Dole	Percent	Perot	Percent	
Kans.	0	6	384,399	36	578,572	54	92,093	09	1,055,064
Ky.	8	0	635,804	46	622,339	45	118,768	09	1,376,911
La.	9	0	928,983	52	710,240	40	122,981	07	1,762,204
Me.	4	0	311,092	52	185,133	31	85,290	14	581,515
Md.	10	0	924,284	54	651,682	38	113,684	07	1,689,650
Mass.	12	0	1,567,223	62	717,622	28	225,594	09	2,510,439
Mich.	18	0	1,941,126	52	1,440,977	38	326,751	09	3,708,854
Minn.	10	0	1,096,355	51	751,971	35	252,986	12	2,101,312
Miss.	0	7	385,005	44	434,547	49	51,500	06	871,052
Mo.	11	0	1,024,817	48	889,689	41	217,103	10	2,131,609
Mont.	0	3	167,169	41	178,957	44	55,017	14	401,143
Nebr.	0	5	231,906	35	355,665	53	76,103	11	663,674
Nev.	4	0	203,388	44	198,775	43	43,855	09	446,018
N.H.	4	0	245,260	50	196,740	40	48,140	10	490,140
N.J.	15	0	1,599,932	53	1,080,041	36	257,979	09	2,937,952
N.Mex.	5	0	252,215	49	210,791	41	30,978	06	493,984
N.Y.	33	0	3,513,191	59	1,861,198	31	485,547	08	5,859,936
N.C.	0	14	1,099,132	44	1,214,399	49	165,301	07	2,478,832
N.Dak.	0	3	106,405	40	124,597	47	32,594	12	263,596
Ohio	21	0	2,100,690	47	1,823,859	41	470,680	11	4,395,229
Okla.	0	8	488,102	40	582,310	48	130,788	11	1,201,200
Oreg.	7	0	326,099	47	256,105	37	73,265	11	655,469
Pa.	23	0	2,206,241	49	1,793,568	40	430,082	10	4,429,891
R.I.	4	0	220,592	60	98,325	27	39,965	11	358,882
S.C.	0	8	495,878	44	564,856	50	63,324	06	1,124,058
S.Dak.	0	3	139,295	43	150,508	46	31,248	10	321,051
Tenn.	11	0	905,599	48	860,809	46	105,577	06	1,871,985
Tex.	0	32	2,455,735	44	2,731,998	49	377,530	07	5,565,263
Utah	0	5	220,197	33	359,394	54	66,100	10	645,691
Vt.	3	0	138,400	54	80,043	31	30,912	12	249,355
Va.	0	13	1,070,990	45	1,119,974	47	158,707	07	2,349,671
Wash.	11	0	899,645	51	639,743	36	161,642	09	1,701,030
W.Va.	5	0	324,394	51	231,908	37	70,853	11	627,155
Wis.	11	0	1,071,859	49	845,172	39	227,426	10	2,144,457
Wyo.	0	3	77,897	37	105,347	50	25,854	12	209,098
Total:	**379**	**159**	**45,628,667**	**50**	**37,869,435**	**41**	**7,874,283**	**09**	**91,372,385**

Source: Associated Press. Unofficial results as of November 6, 1996.

Party Control of Congress, 1901–1999

		SENATE			HOUSE		
	DEM.	REP.	OTHER	DEM.	REP.	OTHER	PRESIDENT
57th Congress, 1901–1903	31	55	4	151	197	9	McKinley T. Roosevelt
58th Congress, 1903–1905	33	57	—	178	208	—	T. Roosevelt
59th Congress, 1905–1907	33	57	—	136	250	—	T. Roosevelt
60th Congress, 1907–1909	31	61	—	164	222	—	T. Roosevelt
61st Congress, 1909–1911	32	61	—	172	219	—	Taft
62nd Congress, 1911–1913	41	51	—	228	161	1	Taft
63rd Congress, 1913–1915	51	44	1	291	127	17	Wilson
64th Congress, 1915–1917	56	40	—	230	196	9	Wilson
65th Congress, 1917–1919	53	42	—	216	210	6	Wilson
66th Congress, 1919–1921	47	49	—	190	240	3	Wilson
67th Congress, 1921–1923	37	59	—	131	301	1	Harding
68th Congress, 1923–1925	43	51	2	205	225	5	Coolidge
69th Congress, 1925–1927	39	56	1	183	247	4	Coolidge
70th Congress, 1927–1929	46	49	1	195	237	3	Coolidge
71st Congress, 1929–1931	39	56	1	167	267	1	Hoover
72nd Congress, 1931–1933	47	48	1	220	214	1	Hoover
73rd Congress, 1933–1935	60	35	1	319	117	5	F. Roosevelt
74th Congress, 1935–1937	69	25	2	319	103	10	F. Roosevelt
75th Congress, 1937–1939	76	16	4	331	89	13	F. Roosevelt
76th Congress, 1939–1941	69	23	4	261	164	4	F. Roosevelt
77th Congress, 1941–1943	66	28	2	268	162	5	F. Roosevelt
78th Congress, 1943–1945	58	37	1	218	208	4	F. Roosevelt
79th Congress, 1945–1947	56	38	1	242	190	2	Truman
80th Congress, 1947–1949	45	51	—	188	245	1	Truman
81st Congress, 1949–1951	54	42	—	263	171	1	Truman
82nd Congress, 1951–1953	49	47	—	234	199	1	Truman
83rd Congress, 1953–1955	47	48	1	211	221	—	Eisenhower
84th Congress, 1955–1957	48	47	1	232	203	—	Eisenhower
85th Congress, 1957–1959	49	47	—	233	200	—	Eisenhower
86th Congress, 1959–1961	65	35	—	284	153	—	Eisenhower
87th Congress, 1961–1963	65	35	—	263	174	—	Kennedy
88th Congress, 1963–1965	67	33	—	258	177	—	Kennedy Johnson
89th Congress, 1965–1967	68	32	—	295	140	—	Johnson
90th Congress, 1967–1969	64	36	—	247	187	—	Johnson
91st Congress, 1969–1971	57	43	—	243	192	—	Nixon
92nd Congress, 1971–1973	54	44	2	254	180	—	Nixon

	SENATE			HOUSE			
	DEM.	REP.	OTHER	DEM.	REP.	OTHER	PRESIDENT
93rd Congress, 1973–1975	56	42	2	239	192	1	Nixon
							Ford
94th Congress, 1975–1977	60	37	2	291	144	—	Ford
95th Congress, 1977–1979	61	38	1	292	143	—	Carter
96th Congress, 1979–1981	58	41	1	276	157	—	Carter
97th Congress, 1981–1983	46	53	1	243	192	—	Reagan
98th Congress, 1983–1985	45	55	—	267	168	—	Reagan
99th Congress, 1985–1987	47	53	—	252	183	—	Reagan
100th Congress, 1987–1989	54	46	—	257	178	—	Reagan
101st Congress, 1989–1991	55	45	—	262	173	—	Bush
102nd Congress, 1991–1993	56	44	—	276	167	—	Bush
103rd Congress, 1993–1995	57	43	—	258	176	1	Clinton
104th Congress, 1995–1997	47	53	—	204	230	1	Clinton
105th Congress, 1997–1999	45	55	—	207	227	1	Clinton

Numbers indicate initial composition of the Congress. For the 105th Congress, numbers are projections based on unofficial election returns as of November 7, 1996. The outcomes of several House races were subject to change because of recounts or runoffs.

SOURCES: Department of Commerce, Bureau of the Census, *Statistical Abstract of the United States* (Washington, D.C.: U.S. Government Printing Office); and *Members of Congress Since 1789,* 2d ed. (Washington, D.C.: Congressional Quarterly Press, 1981), 176–177; Updated by the authors.

United States Supreme Court Justices, 1789–1996

JUSTICE	PRESIDENT	YEARS OF SERVICE
John Jay	Washington	1789–1795
John Rutledge	Washington	(1789–1791)*
William Cushing	Washington	1789–1810
James Wilson	Washington	1789–1798
John Blair Jr.	Washington	1789–1796
James Iredell	Washington	1790–1799
Thomas Johnson	Washington	1791–1793
William Paterson	Washington	1793–1806
John Rutledge	Washington	(1795)*
Samuel Chase	Washington	1796–1811
Oliver Elsworth	Washington	1796–1800
Bushrod Washington	J. Adams	1798–1829
Alfred Moore	J. Adams	1799–1804
John Marshall	J. Adams	1801–1835
William Johnson	Jefferson	1804–1834
Henry B. Livingston	Jefferson	1806–1823
Thomas Todd	Jefferson	1807–1826
Gabriel Duval	Madison	1811–1835
Joseph Story	Madison	1811–1845
Smith Thompson	Monroe	1823–1843
Robert Trimble	J. Q. Adams	1826–1828
John McLean	Jackson	1829–1861
Henry Baldwin	Jackson	1830–1844
James M. Wayne	Jackson	1835–1867
Roger B. Taney	Jackson	1836–1864
Philip P. Barbour	Jackson	1836–1841
John Catron	Jackson	1837–1865
John McKinley	Van Buren	1837–1852
Peter V. Daniel	Van Buren	1841–1860
Samuel Nelson	Tyler	1845–1872
Levi Woodbury	Polk	1846–1851
Robert C. Grier	Polk	1846–1870
Benjamin R. Curtis	Fillmore	1851–1857
John A. Campbell	Pierce	1853–1861
Nathan Clifford	Buchanan	1858–1881
Noah H. Swayne	Lincoln	1862–1881
Samuel F. Miller	Lincoln	1862–1890
David Davis	Lincoln	1862–1877
Stephen J. Field	Lincoln	1863–1897
Salmon P. Chase	Lincoln	1864–1873
William Strong	Grant	1870–1880
Joseph P. Bradley	Grant	1870–1892

JUSTICE	PRESIDENT	YEARS OF SERVICE
Ward Hunt	Grant	1872–1882
Morrison R. Waite	Grant	1874–1888
John M. Harlan	Hayes	1877–1911
William B. Woods	Hayes	1880–1887
Stanley Matthews	Garfield	1881–1889
Horace Gray	Arthur	1881–1902
Samuel Blatchford	Arthur	1882–1893
Lucius Q. C. Lamar	Cleveland	1888–1893
Melville W. Fuller	Cleveland	1888–1910
David J. Brewer	Harrison	1889–1910
Henry B. Brown	Harrison	1890–1906
George Shiras Jr.	Harrison	1892–1903
Howell E. Jackson	Harrison	1893–1895
Edward D. White	Cleveland	1894–1910
Rufus W. Peckham	Cleveland	1895–1909
Joseph McKenna	McKinley	1898–1925
Oliver W. Holmes Jr.	T. Roosevelt	1902–1932
William R. Day	T. Roosevelt	1903–1922
William H. Moody	T. Roosevelt	1906–1910
Horace H. Lurton	Taft	1909–1914
Charles E. Hughes	Taft	1910–1916
Edward D. White	Taft	1910–1921
Willis Van Devanter	Taft	1910–1937
Joseph R. Lamar	Taft	1910–1916
Mahlon Pitney	Taft	1912–1922
James C. McReynolds	Wilson	1914–1941
Louis D. Brandeis	Wilson	1916–1939
John H. Clarke	Wilson	1916–1922
William H. Taft	Harding	1921–1930
George Sutherland	Harding	1922–1938
Pierce Butler	Harding	1922–1939
Edward T. Sanford	Harding	1923–1930
Harlan F. Stone	Coolidge	1925–1941
Charles E. Hughes	Hoover	1930–1941
Owen J. Roberts	Hoover	1930–1945
Benjamin N. Cardozo	Hoover	1932–1938
Hugo Black	F. Roosevelt	1937–1971
Stanley F. Reed	F. Roosevelt	1938–1957
Felix Frankfurter	F. Roosevelt	1939–1962
William O. Douglas	F. Roosevelt	1939–1975
Frank Murphy	F. Roosevelt	1940–1949
James F. Byrnes	F. Roosevelt	1941–1942

Justice	President	Years of service	Justice	President	Years of service
Harlan F. Stone	F. Roosevelt	1941–1946	Thurgood Marshall	Johnson	1967–1991
Robert H. Jackson	F. Roosevelt	1941–1954	**Warren E. Burger**	Nixon	1969–1986
Wiley B. Rutledge	F. Roosevelt	1943–1949	Harry A. Blackmun	Nixon	1970–1994
Harold H. Burton	Truman	1945–1958	Lewis F. Powell Jr.	Nixon	1972–1988
Fred M. Vinson	Truman	1946–1953	William H. Rehnquist	Nixon	1972–1986
Tom C. Clark	Truman	1949–1967	John Paul Stevens	Ford	1975–
Sherman Minton	Truman	1949–1956	Sandra Day O'Connor	Reagan	1981–
Earl Warren	Eisenhower	1953–1969	**William H. Rehnquist**	Reagan	1986–
John M. Harlan	Eisenhower	1955–1971	Antonin Scalia	Reagan	1986–
William J. Brennan Jr.	Eisenhower	1956–1990	Anthony M. Kennedy	Reagan	1988–
Charles E. Whittaker	Eisenhower	1957–1962	David H. Souter	Bush	1990–
Potter Stewart	Eisenhower	1958–1981	Clarence Thomas	Bush	1991–
Byron R. White	Kennedy	1962–	Ruth Bader Ginsburg	Clinton	1993–
Arthur J. Goldberg	Kennedy	1962–1965	Stephen Breyer	Clinton	1994–
Abe Fortas	Johnson	1965–1969			

Bold type indicates chief justice.

*Rutledge resigned after his confirmation to become chief justice of South Carolina; in 1795 he served during a Court recess.

GLOSSARY

administrative law judge a quasi-independent employee of a federal agency who supervises hearings at which disputes between the agency and a regulated party are resolved. The judge's rulings are binding on both the agency and the complainant, although either side may appeal a ruling in the federal courts.

administrative oversight the review and control by congressional committees of the work conducted by the executive branch of the federal government.

adversary (accusatory) system a system of criminal justice in which a neutral judge presides over the introduction of evidence by a prosecutor and a defense attorney. The defendant is presumed to be innocent until proven guilty and cannot be forced to testify.

affirmative action government and private policies or programs designed to help women and minorities advance in areas in which they have historically been discriminated against or disadvantaged.

agency a unit of the federal government with responsibility for a set of functions that are generally less broad than those of a department. Some agencies are independent; others exist within departments.

agents of political socialization groups and individuals, such as parents, peers, and churches, from whom citizens acquire political information and learn political attitudes and values.

America 2000 a report issued during the presidency of George Bush that established six national educational goals to be attained by the year 2000.

American ethos what Americans believe; the attitudes, values, and traditions of American society. At its core, the American ethos consists of a commitment to a democratic political system and a capitalistic economic system.

***amicus curiae* brief** a written opinion on a judicial case submitted to the court by a party who is not directly involved in the litigation but has an interest in the outcome. Such a brief is also known as a "friend of the court" brief.

Anti-Federalists the group of people who opposed adoption of the Constitution following its drafting in 1787.

appellate jurisdiction the authority of courts to review decisions of lower courts and administrative agencies. Under Article III of the U.S. Constitution, Congress has the power to provide for the appellate jurisdiction of the Supreme Court and courts of appeals.

Articles of Confederation the first constitution of the United States, approved by the Second Continental Congress in 1777 but not ratified by all thirteen former colonies until 1781. It provided for a unicameral legislature, the Continental Congress, which had extremely limited powers.

astroturfing the practice by interest groups of mounting grassroots lobbying campaigns that evoke a highly charged but artificial public response.

attentive public the people in a society who follow political issues and politically relevant events but do not usually participate in political activities other than voting. The attentive public constitutes about 15 to 20 percent of the population.

attitudes broad orientations people have toward areas of public policy. Attitudes consist of a number of interrelated opinions that provide a basis for interpreting events and making judgments on issues.

authoritarian personality a personality type that requires a highly structured environment with precise rules and guidelines in order to function. People with such a personality tend to be most willing to adopt doctrinaire beliefs and to follow strong and inflexible political leaders.

authority lawful power. In a democracy, authority is derived directly or indirectly from the people. It is embodied in the rule of law—the Constitution, statutes, treaties, executive orders, and judicial opinions.

bandwagon effect a shift in support to a front-running candidate. At a presidential nominating convention the front-runner tries to create such an effect by demonstrating the ability to win crucial votes that occur before the nomination and thus removing any doubt about who the nominee will be.

belief system a set of related ideas, such as a religion or a political ideology, that helps people understand and cope with the world around them. People use belief systems as guides for thought and action.

bench memos notes written by law clerks that Supreme Court justices take with them to the bench when hearing oral arguments in a case. They typically summarize the questions presented by the case, the lower court's decision, and the arguments presented by both sides.

bicameral legislature a legislature composed of two houses, such as the U.S. Congress.

bill a proposal, drafted in the form of a law, that a member of Congress would like the other members to consider. A bill may be introduced into either house of Congress by any member of that house.

bill of information a document specifying the charges and evidence against a criminal defendant, which in some states prosecutors may obtain from a judge instead of seeking a grand jury indictment.

Bill of Rights the first ten amendments to the U.S. Constitution, which guarantee specific civil rights and liberties. Introduced in the First Congress, the amendments were ratified by the states in 1791.

Bill of Rights, nationalization of the Supreme Court's application to the states of guarantees in the Bill of Rights, made on the basis of the guarantee of "due process of law" in the Fourteenth Amendment to the Constitution. As a result, the First Amendment, for example, limits the power of both the national government and the states.

block grants grants-in-aid that state and local governments can spend as they wish within specified broad policy areas, such as housing, transportation, or job training.

briefs written legal arguments filed by each side in cases or controversies before a court.

broad reading an approach to interpreting the U.S. Constitution that allows its general principles to be widely applied to different cases in light of changing circumstances.

bundling a means by which political action committees circumvent rules limiting their donations to individual candidates. A PAC solicits donations for a group of candidates but asks that the checks be made out to specific candidates. The checks received for each candidate are then bundled together and sent to that candidate.

bureaucracy an organization of activity based on hierarchies of authority and fixed routines. Bureaucracies have jurisdictions established by law or administrative rules. Their employees are specialists, and they maintain written records of their decisions and activities. Bureaucracies are created to achieve objectivity, precision, efficiency, continuity, consistency, and fairness.

cabinet a body consisting of the heads of the executive departments of the federal government, plus the vice president. Historically, presidents have used the cabinet to counsel them on policy issues, to build support for their programs and positions, and to gain legitimacy for their administrations. In recent decades, however, the cabinet has become less important as an advisory body.

capitalism a system of private ownership and control of the means of economic production and distribution that operates within a free market. It is often contrasted with socialism

and communism, systems in which government controls some or all of the means of production and distribution.

capture the tendency of federal agencies to develop symbiotic relationships with the special interests that they oversee and thus to become protectors rather than regulators of those interests. This has been a special problem with regulatory commissions.

casework the individual problems that constituents bring to the attention of a member of Congress for assistance or solution.

categorical grants grants-in-aid that can be used only for narrowly defined purposes, such as education for homeless children or prevention of drug abuse.

caucus a meeting of partisans. Both major political parties permit the use of caucuses at the precinct level as the first stage in a process by which delegates may be chosen for the parties' national nominating conventions. The Democratic party requires that the number of delegates awarded to each candidate be proportional to the support the candidate receives in the caucus; the Republican party does not impose this requirement.

central clearance process a procedure by which all legislative proposals, positions, and testimony of the executive departments and agencies are cleared beforehand by the Office of Management and Budget to ensure that they are in accord with the president's program.

citizen a member of a political society, with rights and obligations that structure political participation.

civil liberties freedoms that the government must respect, such as the freedom of speech, press, and assembly, that are guaranteed under the U.S. Constitution or legislation or through judicial interpretation of laws.

civil rights rights that the government may not deny or infringe on because of an individual's race, gender, national origin, age, or ethnicity.

civil service the career employees of the federal departments and major agencies whose salaries and fringe benefits are determined by Congress and implemented by the Office of Personnel Management.

civil service system the system for filling most federal government jobs that was established by the 1883 Pendleton Act, whereby jobs must be open to any citizen and merit must be the basis for choosing employees.

Clean Air Act, 1963 the first major federal law attempting to set standards of air quality and to regulate air pollution.

Clean Water Act, 1972 the law by which the federal government took over from the states the establishment of minimum water quality standards.

clear and present danger test a test created by Supreme Court Justice Oliver Wendell Holmes for determining the scope of freedom of speech under the First Amendment to the U.S. Constitution. Under this test, only speech that poses a "clear and present danger" to the country may be punished.

closed-ended question a question on a public opinion

poll that forces respondents to choose from a designated list of answers. Most polls consist of closed-ended questions because they are easier to categorize and analyze than open-ended questions.

cloture the limitation of debate on a measure before the Senate. It takes a vote by three-fifths of the entire Senate (sixty senators) to invoke cloture and thereby end a filibuster.

comity the principle by which federal courts respect and leave undisturbed rulings of state courts that are based solely on independent state grounds.

commercial speech advertising, which for many years was interpreted by the Supreme Court as lacking social redeeming value and thus falling outside the scope of protection for free speech under the First Amendment. But recent rulings of the Court have extended First Amendment protection to many kinds of commercial speech, so long as it is truthful and not deceptive.

concurrent powers powers shared by both the national government and the state governments, such as the power to tax.

concurring opinion a document submitted by one or more justices or judges of a court that agrees with the decision reached in a case but not with all of the reasoning or explanations offered in the institutional opinion. It explains how the same result would have been reached by different reasoning.

confirmation hearings hearings held by a legislative body before approving the appointment of a government official. Under the U.S. Constitution, the president nominates federal judges and other high officials in the executive branch, but they must be confirmed by the Senate.

confront witnesses, right to a criminal defendant's right, guaranteed by the Sixth Amendment to the U.S. Constitution, to call and question witnesses who testify as to the defendant's guilt.

conservatism a political ideology that emphasizes economic rights and liberties for individuals with a minimum of government restraint. Compared with liberals, conservatives favor a more active role for government in national defense and law enforcement and tend to be more satisfied with the status quo.

constituency the residents of the state or district that elects a particular member of Congress.

constitutional courts the U.S. Supreme Court and other federal courts created under Article III of the U.S. Constitution, which gives Congress the power to establish "inferior courts" below the Supreme Court. Federal district courts and courts of appeals are constitutional courts and have general jurisdiction over virtually all matters of federal law.

cooperative federalism a view of federalism held between the mid 1930s and the 1960s that stressed a partnership and sharing of government functions between the states and the national government.

courts of appeals the courts within the federal judicial system that hear appeals of decisions of lower courts, state courts, or administrative agencies. There are thirteen courts of appeals.

crosscutting requirements conditions imposed on almost all grants-in-aid to further various social and economic objectives, such as nondiscrimination or environmental protection.

crossover sanctions conditions imposed on grants-in-aid in one program area that are designed to influence state and local government policy in another area.

dealignment a weakening of the attachment people feel toward political parties. A dealignment of the American electorate has been occurring since the 1960s, with the result that increasing numbers of voters consider themselves independent and vote on the basis of candidates' qualifications rather than party affiliation.

de facto segregation racial segregation due to housing patterns rather than laws or official government policies.

de jure segregation racial segregation due to laws or government policies. The Fourteenth Amendment to the U.S. Constitution has been interpreted by the Supreme Court as forbidding de jure segregation.

democracy a political system in which the people as a whole have the ultimate authority; citizens make public policy themselves or choose people to make it for them. In an ideal democracy, all citizens have the same opportunity to affect policy; this goal is accomplished by having equal representation and by having electoral and governing decisions made on the basis of majority rule.

democratic elitists scholars who believe that as long as people in leadership positions support the principles and practices of democracy, the apathy and intolerance of the masses do not in and of themselves threaten the democratic character of the political system.

Democratic-Republicans (Republicans) the principal opponents of George Washington's administration. Backers of Thomas Jefferson, they favored policies that would benefit their primary support groups, farmers and laborers, and are considered the forerunners of the contemporary Democratic party.

Democrats the faction of the Democratic-Republican party that supported Andrew Jackson. The Democrats consisted primarily of small farmers, new immigrants, and other recently enfranchised voters in the West and the South.

department one of the major operating units of the federal government and of the president's cabinet.

deregulation an effort begun in the late 1960s to reform the federal regulatory process by reducing or eliminating regulations that seemed to stifle competition.

determinate sentencing a system of sentencing criminals in which mandatory sentences are specified for particular offenses, leaving judges and juries little discretion in individual cases.

devolution federalism a possible contemporary trend, beginning with the 1994 Republican congressional victories, in which many federal government responsibilities may be returned to state and local governments.

direction in reference to public opinion, the proportion of the population that holds a particular view.

direct orders legal measures adopted by the national government, and enforced by civil or criminal penalties, that require certain actions by state and local governments.

dissenting opinion a document submitted by one or more justices or judges of a court that disagrees with the majority's reasoning and decision in a case.

district courts the trial courts of the federal judicial system. There are ninety-four federal district courts, at least one in each state.

disturbance theory a theory that explains why political interest groups develop and flourish. It holds that changes within the political environment encourage people to organize to protect or promote their interests and that the organization and activity of these groups spur others to organize and become active.

docket the list of filings or cases that come before a court. The U.S. Supreme Court, for example, has an annual docket of over seven thousand cases.

double jeopardy trying a person in court more than once for the same crime, a practice forbidden by the Fifth Amendment to the U.S. Constitution.

dual federalism a view of federalism held between the time of the Civil War and the mid 1930s that attempted to recognize and maintain separate spheres of authority for the national and state governments.

due process fair and regular or usual procedures. The Fifth and Fourteenth Amendments to the U.S. Constitution provide that no one shall be deprived of life, liberty, or property by the government "without due process of law."

economic regulation government regulation of particular industries to correct what economists call market failures, such as natural monopolies.

Education Consolidation and Improvement Act, 1981 a federal education program consolidating a number of small categorical grants into one major block grant.

elector a person chosen to vote for candidates to office. In presidential elections, the voters of each state select electors to vote for president. Initially these electors were expected to exercise independent judgment in their choice; today they are expected to ratify the choice of the majority or plurality of the state's voters.

Electoral College the body that selects the president and vice president, consisting of the 538 electors chosen in the fifty states and the District of Columbia. A majority of the college's votes is required for election.

Elementary and Secondary Education Act, 1965 one of the most significant federal education programs, which distributes aid to school districts on the basis of the proportion of low-income-family children in those districts.

elites people in leadership positions. Elites tend to be more tolerant than the average citizen of beliefs and behavior that deviate from social and political norms.

en banc as a panel; with all judges participating. Cases in federal courts of appeals are usually heard and decided by three-judge panels, but in especially important cases the entire court will sit en banc.

enrolled bill process a procedure by which the Office of Management and Budget coordinates executive branch recommendations on legislation that has been passed by Congress and is awaiting presidential action.

Environmental Protection Agency the federal agency, created in 1970, that is charged with enforcing the nation's environmental laws.

equal time rule the requirement that broadcasters who allow political candidates to appear or advertise on their station permit other candidates equal opportunities. The rule, from which news reports and public debates are excluded, has actually discouraged broadcasters from providing free time to any candidate.

equality of opportunity a situation in which members of historically disadvantaged or discriminated-against groups, such as women or ethnic minorities, have a chance to obtain an education or employment that is equal to that of other individuals in a society.

equality of result a situation in which groups unequal in terms of such factors as educational background and historical socio-economic advantages enjoy the same benefits or status in income or employment.

establishment clause the part of the First Amendment to the U.S. Constitution that forbids Congress from establishing a national religion or favoring particular religions. As a result of the Supreme Court's interpretation of the amendment, state governments are subject to the same prohibitions.

exacting scrutiny test (strict rationality test) the test generally used by federal courts when reviewing whether laws and regulations involving nonracial discrimination violate the equal protection clause of the Fourteenth Amendment to the U.S. Constitution. Under this test, discrimination on the basis of gender, age, or wealth is unconstitutional unless it furthers some legitimate government interest in a reasonable way. This test is more rigorous than the minimal scrutiny test but less rigorous than the strict scrutiny test.

exclusionary rule the rule that evidence obtained illegally by police cannot be used against a defendant at trial.

executive agreement an agreement between heads of governments on a matter of mutual concern. Presidents often enter into executive agreements to avoid the more rigorous requirements involved in making a treaty. Executive agreements must be reported to Congress, but they do not require Senate ratification.

executive memorandum a formal statement of official policy or procedure, issued by the president to inform his subordinates of what he wishes them to do.

Executive Office of the President a bureaucracy created in 1939 to provide institutional staff support for the president.

executive order a presidential order to subordinates to perform a particular task in a particular way.

executive privilege the power claimed by the president to keep certain communications within the White House confidential from Congress and the courts.

express powers powers that are enumerated in a constitution. Article I, Section 8, of the U.S. Constitution, for example, enumerates seventeen specific powers of Congress, including the power to tax, coin money, regulate commerce, and provide for the national defense.

fairness doctrine a requirement that broadcasters provide time for the discussion of issues of public concern and that conflicting sides of the issue be presented. The doctrine, which encouraged the media to avoid airing controversial issues because of the demand for time to reply, was suspended by the Federal Communications Commission in 1987.

federal questions issues concerning the interpretation and application of federal as opposed to state law.

federalism a system of government in which powers are shared between a central or national government and state or regional governments. The U.S. Constitution establishes a federal system.

Federalists the name given to the people who supported ratification of the U.S. Constitution following its drafting in 1787 and also to the principal supporters of George Washington's administration (many of whom were the same people). The Federalists of the Washington administration, men of property and social standing, favored policies that benefited commercial and manufacturing interests—policies that the administration pursued.

fighting words words that may incite violence or a breach of the peace and public order. Historically, they have not been considered protected speech under the First Amendment to the U.S. Constitution, but in recent years the Supreme Court has overturned all convictions on these grounds.

filibuster a technique for preventing a vote in the Senate, in which senators gain recognition to speak in debate and then do not relinquish the floor. A filibuster can be ended only by a vote of cloture, and even then, loopholes in the Senate rules permit a single senator to prolong debate.

financial controls the most important and effective of Congress's techniques for overseeing the work of the executive branch. Before it appropriates funds to an agency or a program, Congress assesses the manner in which previous appropriations have been used and examines the stated plans for use of the funds currently being requested.

fluidity changeableness; instability. When public opinion is fluid, it shifts quickly from one judgment or set of judgments to another.

formula grants grants-in-aid distributed on the basis of a formula applied to all eligible recipients.

franking privilege the right of members of Congress to mail newsletters and questionnaires free of charge to every mailbox in their states or districts.

free exercise clause the part of the First Amendment to the U.S. Constitution that guarantees individuals the freedom of religious belief. As a result of the Supreme Court's interpretations of the amendment, state governments are barred from coercing individuals' religious beliefs.

freedom of association a right that the First Amendment to the U.S. Constitution has been interpreted as guaranteeing to individuals, including the right to organize and to belong to political parties and religious, economic, and other kinds of social organizations.

free-enterprise system a competitive economic system in which people are encouraged to pursue their own financial interests and the market determines their success or failure. Such a system rewards individual initiative and discourages government involvement.

general revenue sharing a federal program existing between 1972 and 1986 in which grants-in-aid were distributed to state and local governments with few strings attached.

general ticket system a winner-take-all method of selecting presidential and vice presidential electors that is used in all states but two, Maine and Nebraska. Under this system, the entire slate of electors pledged to the candidate who receives the most votes in the state is elected.

gerrymandering the practice of drawing legislative districts in such a way as to give one party an advantage.

going public making an appeal to the people for support for presidential policies. Presidents go public to obtain the backing they need from other public officials, particularly members of Congress.

government the formal institutions within which processes and procedures of decision making about public policy are formulated, implemented, and adjudicated.

government corporation an economic enterprise owned in whole or in part by the federal government; examples are the Tennessee Valley Authority and the Federal Deposit Insurance Corporation.

grand jury a group of twelve to twenty-three persons who meet in private to determine, on the basis of evidence presented by prosecutors, whether to approve an indictment against an individual.

grant of immunity a judicial order giving an individual who testifies in court or before a congressional committee legal protection from subsequent prosecution on the basis of incriminating testimony.

grants-in-aid federal payments to state and local governments.

grantsmanship efforts by state and local governments to maximize the federal aid they receive.

Great Compromise the compromise reached at the Constitutional Convention in 1787 between the Virginia and New Jersey plans. It provided that each state would be equally represented in the Senate and that representation in the House of Representatives would be based on population.

Housing and Community Development Act, 1974 the

legislation that established the Community Development Block Grant program, which provided cities with money for a wide variety of housing and development needs such as public housing, street paving, lighting, and attracting commercial development.

ideological party a political party whose members share a belief system distinct from those of other parties. Ideological parties in the United States, such as the Socialists and the Libertarians, have been minor parties with a limited membership base.

impeachment the power of Congress to remove any civil officer of the United States who has been found guilty of "treason, bribery, or other high crimes and misdemeanors." The impeachment process begins with the introduction of a bill of impeachment in the House of Representatives. If the House approves the bill by majority vote, the impeached person is then tried in the Senate. Conviction requires the votes of two-thirds of the senators present and voting.

implied powers government powers that are inferred from the powers expressly enumerated in a written constitution. The "necessary and proper" clause of Article I, Section 8, of the U.S. Constitution has been interpreted to give Congress broad implied powers.

independent regulatory commission a unit of the federal government whose principal purpose is to regulate commerce and trade in an assigned area of jurisdiction. Commissions are independent of any department and, to some extent, of presidential control. All are run by a group of commissioners rather than a single executive.

independent state grounds a state constitution or state law used as the basis for a decision by a state court instead of federal law or federal courts' interpretation of the U.S. Constitution and Bill of Rights.

indictment the formal statement of charges against a criminal defendant, based on evidence presented by a prosecutor to a grand jury.

in forma pauperis "in the manner of a pauper." When appealing a decision to the U.S. Supreme Court, indigents may file an *in forma pauperis* petition, stating that they are too poor to pay the Court's $300 fee for filing an appeal and asking that it be waived.

inherent powers powers possessed by a national government that are not enumerated in a constitution. In the conduct of foreign affairs, presidents have often claimed that they possess inherent powers.

injunction a prohibitory court order, such as one that prevents a federal agency from taking further action against an aggrieved party until certain conditions—a rehearing, for example—have been met.

inquisitorial system a system of criminal justice used in some countries, such as France, in which the accused person is presumed guilty, interrogated by magistrates, and denied other rights afforded in adversary systems.

institutional opinion an official explanation or justification of a decision by a court with multiple judges or justices.

intensity in reference to public opinion, the depth of feeling on an issue.

intergovernmental lobby the group of state and local government organizations, such as the National League of Cities and the National Governors' Association, that lobby the national government for legislation and decisions favorable to state and local governments.

iron triangle the close, mutually supportive relationship that often develops among executive agencies, special interest groups, and congressional subcommittees.

issue entrepreneurs individual members of Congress who tend to specialize in particular substantive matters and to seek support among their colleagues for policies dealing with those matters. In the House, these are often subcommittee chairs; in the Senate, entrepreneurship is widely dispersed and bears little relation to formal institutional roles.

issue network an interconnected group of specialists in a particular subject area working in bureaucratic agencies at all levels of government, along with experts employed by legislative committee staffs, interest groups, think tanks, and universities. Issue networks play an important role in developing the national policy agenda, shaping consensus about preferred policies, and directing political leaders to develop and implement new policy proposals.

issue party a party created out of dissatisfaction with one or both of the major parties when they ignore an important issue, take an unpopular stand, or nominate an unattractive candidate. An issue party exercises power by threatening the major parties with loss of electoral support until they change their ways. In recent decades issue parties have tended to become vehicles for individuals to promote their presidential candidacy.

Jim Crow laws laws passed in the late nineteenth century that required racial separation in public transportation, restaurants, and other places of accommodation and discriminated against African Americans in various other ways.

joint committees committees composed of members of both houses of Congress. They are permanent study committees with no authority to initiate legislation.

joint conference committees temporary joint committees whose principal function is to resolve the differences between forms of the same bill passed by the House and the Senate, respectively.

judicial activism the use of judicial review to invalidate a law or other official action.

judicial double standard the Supreme Court's tendency since 1937 to uphold virtually all economic regulations under the Fifth and Fourteenth Amendments' guarantees of due process but to give heightened scrutiny to laws and regulations that affect individuals' noneconomic civil rights and liberties.

judicial federalism the dual judicial system in the United States, consisting of a system of federal courts and separate judicial systems in each of the fifty states.

judicial review, power of the power and authority of a court to determine whether acts of a legislature or an executive violate a constitution. The U.S. Supreme Court, for instance, has the power to strike down any congressional or state legislation, as well as any other official government action, that it deems to violate the U.S. Constitution.

judicial self-restraint deference by courts to the decisions of other branches of government.

jurisdiction the authority of a court to decide particular cases. The jurisdiction of federal courts is provided for in Article III of the U.S. Constitution and by Congress in statutes.

justiciable disputes disputes that are within a court's jurisdiction and do not present a political question.

lame duck a label often applied to a president in the last two years of a second term because the president is ineligible to run for reelection and may thus have difficulty building and maintaining political support.

legislation the making of laws, one of the major functions of Congress.

legislative courts courts created by Congress under Article I of the U.S. Constitution and having jurisdiction or authority over particular areas of law. The U.S. Court of Military Appeals, which applies military law, is one such court.

level of confidence the degree of certainty that the results of a public opinion poll (within the range of sampling error) are accurate for the population as a whole. Most national surveys are based on a level of confidence of about 95 percent, meaning that nineteen times out of twenty, the results will be accurate.

libel false statement of fact about a person or defamation of his or her character in print or by visual portrayal on television. Libel falls outside the scope of protection for free speech under the First Amendment to the U.S. Constitution.

liberalism a political ideology that emphasizes political rights and liberties for individuals and equal opportunity for all. Liberals oppose government restraints on the exercise of political freedoms but favor government programs that help the less fortunate.

limited government the idea that government powers are limited and specified or are traceable to enumerated powers in a written constitution.

line-item veto the presidential power, created in 1996, to veto portions of certain kinds of legislation while allowing the rest of the bill to become law.

lobbying the art of persuading public officials to support a particular policy position. The term alludes to legislators' being accosted by interest group representatives in the lobby outside the legislative chamber.

mark-up session a meeting at which all of the members of a congressional subcommittee or committee participate in revising a bill to put it into a form that is acceptable to a majority of them.

mass public the people in a society who do not follow political issues closely, whose mood and opinions change the most rapidly, and who may thus be the easiest to manipulate by others who wish to affect public policy outcomes. The mass public is the largest group (75 to 80 percent) within the general population.

meaningful choice the opportunity for voters to select among at least two candidates whose views are dissimilar and who have sufficient resources to present their views to the public.

merit system a system of appointing judges or other government officials on the basis of ability, competitive examinations, or comparisons with other qualified candidates. Some states have so-called merit systems for the selection of state judges, in which a nonpartisan commission recommends a list of possible nominees from which the governor or legislature makes appointments.

minimal scrutiny test the test used by federal courts when reviewing whether laws and regulations dealing with economic matters violate the equal protection clause of the Fourteenth Amendment to the U.S. Constitution. On this test, laws and regulations will be upheld if they have a rational basis.

***Miranda* warnings** a set of reminders about constitutional rights that police must give before interrogating criminal suspects. Suspects must be told that they have the right to remain silent and to consult an attorney and that an attorney can be provided if they cannot afford to hire one. This requirement was the result of the Supreme Court's ruling in *Miranda v. Arizona* (1966).

multimember district an electoral district in which more than one of the candidates for a particular office is elected. The winners are determined on the basis of the proportion of votes that they or their party receive. Some states and cities in the United States have multimember legislative districts.

National Defense Education Act, 1958 a federal program designed to upgrade the science, math, and foreign-language skills of schoolchildren.

National Service Act, 1993 a federal program providing college loans that can be paid off by working at community service jobs.

nation-centered federalism a view of federalism held in the pre–Civil War era that advocated an active and expanded role for the national government.

negative advertising commercials that seek to discredit a political candidate. First used in 1964, such advertising has come to characterize modern media campaigns.

new federalism the view of federalism associated with presidents Nixon and Reagan, which stressed greater flexibility in the use of grants-in-aid by the recipients and, in the Reagan years, reductions in the total amount of grants.

New Jersey Plan one of the main proposals for the overall structure of government that was presented at the Constitutional Convention in 1787. It was proposed by

William Paterson and called for a unicameral legislature in which all states would be represented equally, a multimember executive with no power to veto legislation, and a supreme court. This plan was favored by smaller states.

newsworthiness the characteristic of stories and events that merit attention by the news media because they capture public interest. Frequently they involve conflict, drama, and surprise in addition to timeliness and importance.

nullification, doctrine of the claim, associated most closely with South Carolina senator John C. Calhoun, that states could declare acts of Congress null and void within their borders.

obscenity material that because of its sexual content is not considered protected speech under the First Amendment to the Constitution. The Supreme Court determines obscenity by three measures: (1) whether local community standards would find a work prurient; (2) whether the work depicts sexual conduct defined as obscene under the law; and (3) whether the work lacks serious literary, artistic, political, or scientific value.

Office of Management and Budget (OMB) the president's principal office for preparing a budget, coordinating legislative and regulatory activities, and improving management in the executive branch.

one person, one vote the principle that all legislative districts within the same state must be approximately equal in population in order to ensure that all citizens have equal representation in government. This principle was enunciated by the Supreme Court in *Westberry v. Sanders* (1964).

open-ended question a question on a public opinion poll that allows respondents to frame their own answers in their own words. Responses to open-ended questions may reflect personal opinions more accurately than answers to closed-ended questions, but they are very difficult to categorize and subsequently to analyze.

opinion (1) a judgment made about current issues, including feelings people have, positions they take, and conclusions they reach. (2) the written explanation or justification of a court's or an individual judge's decision.

opinion makers the people in a society who shape the opinions of others. The opinion makers, who constitute less than 5 percent of the population, are well informed about political issues and are often directly involved in political activities and in positions to affect public debate.

original jurisdiction the authority of a court to have a case originate in it. Article III of the U.S. Constitution specifies the "cases or controversies" over which the Supreme Court has original jurisdiction.

oversight hearings regular in-depth reviews by congressional committees of the activities of executive agencies or the management of specific programs. Such a hearing is usually preceded by an investigation by the committee staff. At the hearing itself, executive branch officials are called to explain their activities and to answer the committee's questions. The product of an oversight hearing may be a report

suggesting changes in administrative procedures, remedial legislation, or reauthorization of the agency or program.

partial preemption the national government's establishment of minimum standards in a policy area and its requiring state and local governments to meet those standards or lose their authority in that area.

partisan a person who identifies with a political party.

party caucus a meeting of all members of a party in a legislative body to set legislative strategy or seek to determine a party position on important policy decisions.

party discipline the ability of party leaders in a legislature to count on the members of their party to support them on votes and to impose sanctions on members who do not. It is normal in legislatures in other countries but rare in the U.S. Congress.

party platform a formal statement of a party's beliefs, opinions, and policy stands, tied together by a set of underlying principles based on the party's ideological orientation.

patronage the distribution of government jobs as a reward for working on a winning candidate's campaign or providing other service to a party or political machine.

personnel control congressional control over presidential appointments and over the number, qualifications, salaries, and employment conditions of all federal employees.

petition for a writ of *certiorari* a legal request that the U.S. Supreme Court hear an appeal of a particular case.

petit jury a trial jury, made up traditionally of twelve persons but in some states now as few as six, that hears evidence and decides whether the defendant is guilty of the charges.

plea bargaining an arrangement whereby a criminal defendant pleads guilty to lesser charges than those originally brought in exchange for a reduced sentence. As a result, both the prosecution and the defense are saved the time and expense of a trial.

pocket veto a presidential veto of a bill that occurs when a congressional session concludes within ten days of the bill's passage and without the president having signed it. Because Congress is not in session, the president does not return the bill, nor is there any possibility of a congressional override.

political action committee (PAC) a nonparty group that solicits contributions from its members and uses the money to influence the outcome of elections.

political correctness the avoidance or prohibition of language and behavior that are offensive to certain segments of the population, such as women or minority groups. Opponents claim that such a prohibition violates individuals' rights protected by the First Amendment to the U.S. Constitution.

political culture the dominant values, beliefs, and attitudes of members of a society about their governance, their history, and their rights and responsibilities as citizens. A political culture conditions the structure of the society's political system, the rules by which it operates, and the bounds of acceptable behavior within it.

political efficacy an individual's sense of his or her own ability to influence political outcomes and to participate in politics in ways that make a difference.

political equality the principle that the vote of each citizen in a democracy counts equally. Two conditions apply: the majority rules, and the candidate with the most votes wins.

political ideology a set of interrelated attitudes that shape judgments about and reactions to political issues. Political ideologies, such as liberalism and conservatism, provide people with a general orientation toward government that helps them form opinions and react to events.

political interest group an organization that attempts to influence the staffing and policies of government.

political party a group organized to win elections in order to influence the policies of government. American political parties are broad-based, decentralized, pragmatic political organizations.

political questions issues presented to courts that judges decide would more appropriately be resolved by other branches of government.

political socialization the ongoing process whereby individuals acquire the information, beliefs, attitudes, and values that help them comprehend the workings of a political system and orient themselves within it.

politics the process by which people pursue their own needs and preferences within a society. Politics frequently involves a struggle to achieve power in order to attain individual and group goals.

popular sovereignty the idea that government is based on the consent of the people and is accountable to the people for its actions.

power the influence that some individuals, groups, or institutions have over others; the ability to get people to do something they might not otherwise do. It may be exercised through the use of persuasive skills, legal authority, force or the threat of force, or the promise of rewards.

preemption the national government's removal of an area of authority from state and local governments.

principle of comity the principle by which the U.S. Supreme Court will not hear an appeal of a state court case if the case was decided on the basis of a state constitution or a state bill of rights.

prior restraint issuing a judicial restraining order to prevent the publication or broadcasting of information that might be harmful to the nation's security. The U.S. Supreme Court has upheld the principle of prior restraint but has been reluctant to approve it in practice.

privacy, right of a constitutional right not enumerated in the Bill of Rights but construed by the U.S. Supreme Court to be in the "penumbras," or shadows, of the First, Third, Fourth, and Fifth Amendments and enforceable against the states under the Fourteenth Amendment.

probable cause reasonable justification; specifically, sufficient evidence for an arrest or a police search, a requirement of the Fourth Amendment to the U.S. Constitution.

procedural due process the application of laws and regulations according to fair and regular procedures. It imposes limits on how government may carry out its activities.

project grants grants-in-aid for which potential recipients must apply to a federal agency; such grants are usually awarded on a competitive basis.

proportional voting the principle by which delegates chosen in the Democratic party's presidential nominating primaries and caucuses are awarded to candidates in proportion to the number of popular votes that they receive.

prospective voting judgments about how to vote that anticipate candidates' future decisions and actions. According to this model of voting behavior, voters compare their own values and positions on issues with those of the candidates and parties in an effort to determine which party and which candidates are likely to benefit them the most.

public opinion the opinions, attitudes, and values of the public as they relate to the issues of the day.

public opinion poll a survey of the beliefs, attitudes, and/or opinions of the general population. Public opinion polls have been conducted regularly since the 1940s to gauge opinion on a wide range of contemporary issues.

public policy government decisions designed to address public problems. Public policy is established by Constitution, law, and precedent; it constitutes the rules by which a society lives.

random selection the process of choosing a representative sample for a public opinion poll. In random selection, every element of the population must have an equal chance of being included in the sample, and the choice of any one element should not preclude the choice of any other.

realignment a shifting of partisan attitudes among the electorate. Realignment occurs over a period of years when the dominant party loses the allegiance of some of its supporters and the other party gains the allegiance of some of these voters as well as a majority of newer ones coming into the electorate. The last realignment in American politics occurred during the 1930s, when the Democrats became the dominant party.

reapportionment the redistribution of seats in the U.S. House of Representatives among the states every ten years on the basis of population changes since the previous census.

rebuttal, right of the requirement that broadcasters give people who are criticized on the air or political candidates whose opponents are endorsed by a station the opportunity to reply free of charge. This right, upheld by the U.S. Supreme Court in 1969, has discouraged broadcasters from airing controversial issues or endorsing candidates.

redistricting redrawing the boundaries of legislative districts to reflect geographic shifts in population.

reduction in force an overall reduction in employment within a federal agency or the federal bureaucracy as a whole, which permits the removal of career employees from their jobs.

regulatory review a procedure by which the Office of Management and Budget oversees regulations that executive agencies wish to issue to implement legislation. In assessing regulations, the OMB examines their necessity, cost-effectiveness, and consistency with administration policy and congressional intent.

representation the processes through which members of Congress seek to determine, articulate, and act on the interests of residents of their state or district.

republic a government whose powers are exercised by elected representatives, who are directly or indirectly accountable to the people governed.

Republicans the party formed in the 1850s by disillusioned Whigs and supporters of other minor parties who opposed the expansion of slavery and new immigration. Composed primarily of laborers, small farmers, and entrepreneurs, it was the forerunner of the contemporary Republican party.

reserved powers powers that have not been delegated to a government body. The Tenth Amendment to the U.S. Constitution provides that powers not delegated to the national government are reserved to state governments or the people of the states.

responsible party government the idea that a party that controls the government must try to implement its platform and the promises made by its candidates.

restrictive covenants contracts in which it is stipulated that property may not be sold or leased to members of certain racial or religious groups. In *Shelley v. Kraemer* (1948), the Supreme Court held that such covenants were unconstitutional under the Fourteenth Amendment.

retrospective voting judgments about how to vote that are based on the past performance of the parties and their elected officials in light of the promises they made and the conditions that resulted from their actions. According to this theory of voting behavior, voters look back and decide whether they (and society) are better or worse off as a result of the performance of the people in power.

reverse discrimination discrimination against whites and/or men, the basis on which affirmative action programs have been challenged under the equal protection clause of the Fourteenth Amendment to the U.S. Constitution.

revolving door politics the practice by which former government officials represent organized interests in the private sector.

rider one or more controversial provisions attached to a piece of legislation. Proposals that might have difficulty surviving on their own are thereby permitted to "ride through" the legislative process on the backs of other bills.

rule of four the informal rule that for a case to be accepted for review by the U.S. Supreme Court, at least four of the justices must vote to take it.

salience importance. The most salient public policy issues are those that arouse the most attention and interest.

sample the portion of the general population that is selected for a public opinion poll. A sample must be representative of the entire population if pollsters are to make generalizations from it.

sampling error the degree to which the opinions of people questioned in a public opinion poll could diverge from the opinions of the population as a whole. Sampling error depends on the size of the sample. For a sample of about one thousand, the error will be in the range of plus or minus 3 percent.

secondary group a group, such as a labor union, church congregation, or bridge club, that individuals choose to join and that may help shape or reinforce their political views and values.

Section 8 a provision of the 1974 Housing and Community Development Act that established a rental subsidy program for needy families and encouraged the construction of subsidized rental housing units.

secular regulation rule a rule used by the U.S. Supreme Court in applying the First Amendment's guarantee of the free exercise of religion. It requires that national and state laws have a secular (nonreligious) purpose and not discriminate on the basis of religion.

seditious libel libel or slander that defames or criticizes the government or its officials. The First Amendment to the U.S. Constitution has been interpreted as forbidding governments from punishing seditious libel.

select committees (special committees) temporary congressional committees created to deal with a specific set of issues. They usually disappear once they have completed their work. Many such committees have explicitly limited functions and authority, and most are not authorized to recommend legislation.

selective benefits, theory of a theory that explains why people join political interest groups. It holds that the primary incentives for joining a group are the benefits that members receive by doing so.

selective perception the tendency of most people to use their reading and television watching to acquire information and opinions that support their existing political views and party preferences.

self-incrimination confessing to a crime or testifying in a court in a way that implicates oneself in a crime. The Fifth Amendment to the U.S. Constitution provides a guarantee against forced self-incrimination.

senatorial courtesy consultation by the president with senators prior to making a formal nomination that requires Senate confirmation. Begun during the Washington administration, this practice gives senators influence over potential presidential nominations, but it also enhances the prospects of nominees who have received prior clearance.

Senior Executive Service (SES) the highest-ranking group of federal civil service employees, created in 1979 to provide agencies with greater flexibility in deploying, compensating, and, if necessary, removing their senior managers and technical specialists. There are now about eight thousand SES members, of whom at least 90 percent must always be career federal employees.

seniority system the former system under which the member of the majority party with the longest consecutive service on each congressional committee was automatically its chair for as long as he or she remained in Congress.

separate but equal doctrine the principle that laws requiring separate facilities for white and black citizens were permissible under the U.S. Constitution's Fourteenth Amendment guarantee of equal protection. The doctrine was upheld by the Supreme Court in *Plessy v. Ferguson* (1896) but abandoned in the mid twentieth century.

separation of powers the division of power and authority within a government among three branches, typically the legislature, the executive, and the judiciary.

Servicemen's Readjustment Act, 1944 a federal program, also known as the G.I. Bill, that provided financial assistance to military veterans for completing their education.

shield laws laws in many states that protect journalists from being forced to reveal their sources. The protection of shield laws is similar to that enjoyed by doctors, lawyers, and clergy but does not extend to information subpoenaed by courts of law.

single-member district an electoral district in which only one of the candidates for a particular office can be elected. Districts for members of Congress are of this type.

slander a false statement of fact about a person or defamation of his or her character by speech, for which individuals may be subject to prosecution.

social regulation government regulation of certain economic functions that are common to many or most industries to ensure that specific objectives are pursued. Typically, the process involves setting standards that are deemed to be in the national interest, applying those standards to all industries, and enforcing them.

social redeeming value the criterion used by the Supreme Court in determining whether speech is protected under the First Amendment. Only the categories of libel and slander, obscenity, fighting words, and commercial speech have been deemed to lack social redeeming value and to receive less protection under the First Amendment.

socio-economic status (SES) an analytic measure of relative social and economic standing.

Speaker of the House the elected leader of the majority party in the House of Representatives, who serves as the presiding officer of the House.

special committees select committees.

special investigations special examinations by Congress of executive branch or presidential activities. Some are conducted by permanent committees and subcommittees with no special appropriations of funds or additions to committee staffs. More commonly, however, investigations differ from routine oversight hearings in the depth of their examinations, the vigor with which they are conducted, and the amount of funds and staff resources committed to them.

speech-plus-conduct the communication of ideas through marching, picketing, and sit-in demonstrations. Under the Supreme Court's interpretation of the First Amendment, such forms of expression are protected speech so long as they are not disruptive or destructive of public or private property.

speedy and public trial a right guaranteed to criminal defendants by the Sixth Amendment to the U.S. Constitution. As a result, secret trials are forbidden, and an arrested person must be tried within a period specified by Congress.

split-ticket voting the practice of voting for candidates of different parties on the same ballot. Split-ticket voting has increased in recent decades with the weakening of partisan allegiances.

spoils system the distribution of federal jobs to supporters of the victorious presidential candidate. It was the primary way of staffing the federal bureaucracy prior to the creation of the civil service system.

stability permanence; persistence. When public opinion is stable, it persists with little or no change.

standard operating procedures (SOPs) predetermined ways of responding to a particular problem or set of circumstances. SOPs simplify bureaucratic decisions and contribute to their consistency, but they also channel bureaucratic activity into rigid patterns and make agencies less adaptable to change.

standing committees permanent congressional committees that have full authority to recommend legislation. A few, like the Rules Committee in the House, are responsible for organizing and regulating the operations of Congress; most have jurisdictions defined along substantive policy lines.

standing to sue the right or legal status to initiate a lawsuit or judicial proceedings. To have standing to sue, parties must show that they are suffering or in danger of suffering an immediate and substantial personal injury.

state-centered federalism a view of federalism held in the pre–Civil War era that opposed increasing national power at the expense of the states.

strict construction the idea that the U.S. Constitution can and should be interpreted in a narrowly literal sense, as it was written and understood by its framers.

strict rationality test the exacting scrutiny test.

strict scrutiny test the test used by federal courts when reviewing whether the equal protection clause of the Fourteenth Amendment to the U.S. Constitution is violated by laws or regulations that limit or deny individuals' "fundamental rights" or that discriminate on the basis of race, national origin, or religion. Under this test, government must have a "compelling interest" that justifies the law or regulation.

subgovernment an alliance that develops among executive agencies, interest groups, and congressional committees in a particular policy area. (Also called an *iron triangle*.)

substantive due process conformity of the subject matter of laws and regulations to a standard of reasonableness. It imposes limits on what government may do.

subversive speech speech that is considered likely to

undermine the government. Until the mid twentieth century, the Supreme Court allowed the national and state governments to punish subversive speech, but more recently the Court has interpreted the First Amendment as protecting it.

suffrage   the right to vote.

sunshine laws   laws requiring that important meetings and hearings of federal agencies be open to the public.

superdelegates   delegates to the Democratic party's national nominating convention who are chosen from among the party's elected and appointed leaders. Unpledged to any candidate, they constituted approximately 18 percent of the convention's delegates in 1996.

supremacy clause   a clause of Article VI of the U.S. Constitution providing that the Constitution and other national laws are "the supreme law of the land." National laws thus supersede state and local laws when there is a conflict between them.

symbolic speech   nonverbal communication through the use of symbols that the U.S. Supreme Court has ruled to be protected speech under the First Amendment, such as the wearing of black armbands as a sign of protest.

Synthetic Fuels Corporation   a program passed during the Carter presidency that provided subsidies for the production of fuel from sources other than oil, such as wind, garbage, and plants. It was abolished during the Reagan presidency.

territorial imperative   the tendency of federal agencies to guard their own area of jurisdiction against other agencies that seem to be trespassing on it.

three-fifths compromise   the decision made at the Constitutional Convention in 1787 to count three-fifths of slaves as persons for the purposes of determining taxation and representation in the U.S. House of Representatives.

Three Mile Island   a nuclear power plant in Pennsylvania that in 1979 experienced the worst nuclear accident in United States history. That event dramatically focused the public's attention on energy issues in general and nuclear dangers in particular.

travel, right to   a right not enumerated in the Bill of Rights but construed by the U.S. Supreme Court to be a basic guarantee of the Fourteenth Amendment. As a result, states are forbidden from infringing on individuals' right to travel from one state to another.

unalienable rights   in the social theory of John Locke, certain natural rights of individuals that are believed to precede the creation of government and that government may not deny. The Declaration of Independence proclaimed that individuals have the unalienable right to "Life, Liberty, and the Pursuit of Happiness."

unanimous consent   a common device used for procedural efficiency in the Senate, in which action is taken without debate when all members consent to it.

unconventional participation   efforts to influence public policy, such as street demonstrations, boycotts, and sit-ins, that fall outside the normal channels of political participation.

universal suffrage   the right of all citizens who have reached maturity to vote. It reflects the democratic principle that if government is to be based on the consent of the governed, all citizens should be able to participate in the selection of their public officials.

values   the most important attitudes and beliefs people have; the ideas, principles, and opinions that are most intensely felt and rank as the most significant for an individual.

Virginia Plan   one of the main proposals for the overall structure of government that was presented at the Constitutional Convention in 1787. It was drafted by James Madison and called for a strong central government, including a bicameral legislature with representation of states based on their wealth and population, a chief executive chosen by the legislature, and a powerful judiciary. This plan was favored by larger states.

void for vagueness   a judicial standard used to strike down laws that are overly broad or so vague that it is uncertain what they apply to or whether they infringe on freedoms such as those protected under the First Amendment to the U.S. Constitution.

Water Quality Act, 1965   the first major federal law attempting to establish standards for water quality.

Whigs   the opponents of Andrew Jackson. The Whigs were a diverse, decentralized group that stayed unified in elections by nominating military heroes as candidates.

whip   the member of each party's leadership structure in the House and the Senate who works closely with rank-and-file members to determine party positions and to seek to form legislative coalitions.

White House Office   the president's principal political aides, who provide staff support for formulating presidential policy, communicating it to the public, and helping the president meet the day-to-day responsibilities of the office.

winner-take-all voting   the principle by which the candidate who receives the most votes in an electoral district or state wins all of the delegates or electors at stake. The Republicans permit this method of voting in their presidential nominating primaries and caucuses; the Democrats do not.

writ of *certiorari*   a formal order issued by the U.S. Supreme Court to a lower federal court or state court requesting the record of the decision in a case that the Supreme Court has accepted for review. Four of the Court's nine justices must agree to grant a writ of certiorari in order for a case to be reviewed.

writ of mandamus   an order issued by a superior court that directs a lower court or other government authority to perform a particular act.

yellow journalism   reporting that emphasizes sensationalism—crime, sex, and other issues that grab readers' attention. The term had its origin in the fight between publishers Joseph Pulitzer and William Randolph Hearst over rights to the comic strip "The Yellow Kid."

REFERENCES

Chapter 1 The American Political Environment

1. Prior to that date, the only appropriation bills enacted into law for the 1996 fiscal year were those that funded the Department of Agriculture, energy and water development, and military construction.
2. Senate Majority Leader Robert Dole tried to break the impasse. Stating that enough was enough, he proposed legislation, which the Senate promptly enacted, that would have allowed federal workers to return to work. The House, however, refused to go along with Dole's plan.
3. For example, the *New York Times* reported on the day of the president's State of the Union address that a survey conducted January 18-20, 1996, found 6 out of 10 people saying that the president really wanted to find a political compromise while only 4 out of 10 felt that way about the Republicans. Richard L. Berke, "Good News for President in Latest Poll," *New York Times*, January 23, 1996, p. B7.
4. The budget enacted in April 1996 provided 9.1 percent less domestic spending than the previous year's, compared with a 14 percent cut between 1982 and 1983.
5. Law Day address by Sen. J. William Fulbright, University of Arkansas, 1974.
6. Herbert McClosky and John Zaller, *The American Ethos: Public Attitudes Toward Capitalism and Democracy* (Cambridge, Mass.: Harvard University Press, 1984).
7. Richard W. Stevenson, "Rich Are Getting Richer, But Not the Very Rich," *New York Times*, March 13, 1996, p. D1, 7.
8. "Serious Christians," *The American Enterprise* (November/December, 1995), p. 19.

Chapter 2 The Constitutional Basis of American Politics

1. See Max Farrand, *The Framing of the Constitution* (1913); and John P. Roche, "The Founding Fathers: A Reform Caucus in Action," *American Political Science Review* (December 1961): 799.
2. For further discussion, see Gordon S. Wood, *The Creation of the American Republic, 1776-1787* (Chapel Hill: University of North Carolina Press, 1969).
3. "Resolution of Federal Convention (May 30, 1787)," in *The Records of the Federal Convention of 1787*, ed. Max Farrand (New Haven, Conn.: Yale University Press, 1913), vol. 1, 30.
4. "James Madison," in *The Federalist Papers*, ed. Clinton Rossiter (New York: New American Library, 1961), no. 39, 240-246.
5. See Forrest McDonald, *Novus Ordo Seclorum: The Intellectual Origins of the Constitution* (Lawrence: University of Kansas Press, 1985).
6. "James Madison," in Farrand, *The Records of the Federal Convention of 1787*, vol. 1, 122-123.
7. "Patrick Henry," in *The Complete Anti-Federalist*, ed. Herbert J. Storing (Chicago: University of Chicago Press, 1981), vol. 5, 211.
8. For studies of the debates in the various state ratification conventions, see *Ratifying the Constitution*, ed. Michael Gillespie and Michael Lienesch (Lawrence: University of Kansas Press, 1989).
9. Quoted and discussed in David O'Brien, "The Framers' Muse on Republicanism, the Supreme Court, and Pragmatic Constitutional Interpretivism," *The Review of Politics* 53 (1991): 251.
10. See Charles A. Beard, *An Economic Interpretation of the Constitution* (New York: Macmillan, 1913).
11. See Bernard Bailyn, *The Ideological Origins of the American Revolution* (Cambridge, Mass.: Harvard University Press, 1967); Forrest McDonald, *We the People: The Economic Origins of the Constitution* (Chicago: University of Chicago Press, 1958); Gordon S. Wood, *The Creation of the American Republic, 1776-1787*; and Gordon S. Wood, *The Radicalism of the American Revolution* (New York: Knopf, 1992).
12. Martin Diamond, "The Declaration and the Constitution: Liberty, Democracy, and the Founders," *The Public Interest* 41 (Fall 1975): 40.
13. "James Wilson," in *The Debates in the Several State Conventions on the Adoption of the Federal Constitution*, ed. Jonathan Elliot, 2nd ed. (Washington, D.C., 1836), vol. 2, 524.
14. Thomas Paine, *Common Sense* (1776), excerpts reprinted in *Free Government in the Making*, ed. Alpheus T. Mason and Gordon E. Baker, 4th ed. (New York: Oxford University Press, 1985).
15. See Peter Onuf, "State Sovereignty and the Making of the Constitution," in *Conceptual Change and the Constitution*, ed. Terence Ball and J. G. A. Pocock (Lawrence: University of Kansas Press, 1988).
16. See John Reid, *The Concept of Liberty in the Age of the American Revolution* (Chicago: University of Chicago Press, 1988).
17. *McCulloch v. Maryland*, 17 U.S. 316 (1819).
18. See Ellis Sandoz, *A Government of Laws: Political Theory, Religion, and the American Founding* (Baton Rouge: Louisiana State University Press, 1990).

19. *Meyers v. United States*, 272 U.S. 52 (1926).

20. This discussion draws on David O'Brien, "Federalism as a Metaphor in the Constitutional Politics of Public Administration," *Public Administration Review* 49 (1989): 411.

21. For two studies of judicial review and the founding, see Robert Clinton, *Marbury v. Madison and Judicial Review* (Lawrence: University of Kansas Press, 1989); and Sylvia Snowiss, *Judicial Review and the Law of the Constitution* (New Haven, Conn.: Yale University Press, 1990).

22. James Madison, speech in the House of Representatives, in *Annals of the First Congress* (Washington, D.C.: Gales and Seaton, 1834), vol. 1, 532.

23. Charles Evans Hughes, *Addresses of Charles Evans Hughes* (New York: Putnam's 1916), 185-186.

24. See Howard Ball, *"We Have a Duty": The Supreme Court and the Watergate Tapes Litigation* (Westport, Conn.: Greenwood, 1990).

25. Felix Frankfurter, "The Zeitgeist and the Judiciary," in *Law and Politics*, ed. A. MacLeish and E. Prichard (New York: Capricorn, 1939), 6.

26. Edward White, "The Supreme Court of the United States," *American Bar Association Journal* 7 (1921), 341.

Chapter 3 Federalism in Theory and Practice

1. Remarks to the National Governors' Association meeting in Washington, D.C., February 2, 1993; published in *Weekly Compilation of Presidential Documents* 29, No. 5 (Washington, D.C.: Office of the Federal Register, National Archives and Records Administration, February 2, 1993): 125-128.

2. *McCulloch v. Maryland*, 17 U.S. 316 (1819).

3. Quoted in Alfred H. Kelly and Winfred A. Harbison, *The American Constitution* (New York: Norton, 1955), 180.

4. The laws known as the Alien and Sedition Acts were four separate acts. The Naturalization Act raised from five to fourteen years the period an alien had to wait to acquire citizenship. The Alien Act empowered the president to order out of the country all aliens judged dangerous to the peace and safety of the nation. The Alien Enemies Act empowered the president in case of war to remove or detain as enemy aliens all male subjects of a hostile power. The Sedition Act provided for fines against or imprisonment of any persons conspiring against the United States government.

5. It should be noted that the Virginia and Kentucky Resolutions were drawn to address specific political issues of the time and that neither Madison nor Jefferson governed as president in a way that was congruent with the resolutions. Further, neither accepted Calhoun's extended nullification theories. For further discussion, see Andrew C. McLaughlin, *A Constitutional History of the United States* (New York: Appleton-Century, 1935).

6. See Edward S. Corwin, *The Twilight of the Supreme Court* (New Haven, Conn.: Yale University Press, 1934), ch. 1.

7. *Texas v. White*, 74 U.S. 700 (1869).

8. *United States v. E. C. Knight Company*, 156 U.S. 1 (1895).

9. *Hammer v. Dagenhart*, 247 U.S. 251 (1918).

10. *Schechter Poultry Corporation v. United States*, 295 U.S. 495 (1935).

11. For elaboration, see David B. Walker, *The Rebirth of Federalism* (Chatham, N.J.: Chatham House Publishers, Inc., 1995), 76-91.

12. *National League of Cities v. Usery*, 426 U.S. 833 (1976).

13. See *Hodel v. Virginia Surface Mining & Reclamation, Inc.*, 452 U.S. 264 (1981); and *EEOC v. Wyoming*, 460 U.S. 226 (1983).

14. *Intergovernmental Perspective* 11, No. 2/3 (Spring-Summer 1985): 23. In response to this "Garcia update," it should be noted that Congress in 1986 amended the Fair Labor Standards Act to allow states and localities to use compensatory time in lieu of overtime pay for their workers. See John J. Harrigan, *Politics and Policy in States and Communities* (New York: HarperCollins, 1991), 58.

15. *Garcia v. San Antonio Metropolitan Transit Authority*, 469 U.S. 528 (1985).

16. Quoted in Rochelle L. Stanfield, "Holding the Bag?" *National Journal*, September 9, 1995, 2206.

17. Timothy J. Conlan, James D. Riggle, and Donna E. Schwartz, "Deregulating Federalism? The Politics of Mandate Reform in the 104 Congress" *Publius: The Journal of Federalism* 25 (Summer 1995): 23-40. U.S. Advisory Commission on Intergovernmental Relations, Intergovernmental Perspective (Fall, 1993).

18. U.S. Congress, House Committee on Ways and Means, *Hearings on the Subject of General Revenue Sharing*, 92nd Cong., 1st sess., June 28, 1971, 1305-1306.

19. Statement of Rev. Fred Kammer, S.J., President, Catholic Charities, USA, Hearing titled "Reforming the Present Welfare System," before the Subcommittee on Department Operations, Nutrition, and Foreign Agriculture, of the Committee on Agriculture, U.S. House of Representatives (104th Cong. 2nd sess.), February 14, 1995, 555-556.

20. For background on this controversy, see Ann Markusen and Jerry Fastrup, "The Regional War for Federal Aid," *The Public Interest* 53 (Fall 1978): 87-99.

21. For an interesting look at these regional debates, see Dick Kirschten, "Formula Friction," *National Journal*, February 2, 1991, 272-273.

22. *National Journal*, June 24, 1995, p. 1842.

23. Quoted in Dick Kirschten, "Formula Friction," *National Journal*, February 2, 1991, 272-273.

24. Quoted in John Rehfuss, *The Job of the Public Manager* (Chicago: Dorsey, 1989), 154.

25. For an excellent discussion of this issue, see Sarah F. Liebschutz, "The National Minimum Drinking-Age Law," *Publius: The Journal of Federalism* 15 (Summer 1985): 39-51.

26. Quoted in *Congressional Quarterly Weekly Reports*, June 30, 1984, 1557.

27. Ibid.

28. President Ronald Reagan, "Remarks on Signing H.R. 4614 into Law," July 17, 1984.

29. Charles Corker, "Water Rights and Federalism: The Western Water Rights Settlement Bill of 1957," *California Law Review* 45 (December 1957), 604.

30. Quoted in Daniel McCool, *Command of the Waters* (Berkeley: University of California Press, 1987), 19.

31. Quoted in ibid., 22.

32. Quoted in Richard D. Lamm and Michael McCarthy, *The Angry West* (Boston: Houghton Mifflin, 1982), 192.

33. *Congressional Quarterly Weekly Reports*, November 4, 1995, 3366.

Chapter 4   Civil Rights and Liberties

1. *Barron v. Baltimore*, 32 U.S. 243 (1833).
2. On the debate over whether the Fourteenth Amendment was intended to apply to the states, see Horace E. Flack, *The Adoption of the Fourteenth Amendment* (Baltimore, Md.: Johns Hopkins University Press, 1908); Charles Fairman, *Reconstruction and Reunion, 1864–88* (New York: Macmillan, 1971); and Raoul Berger, *Government by Judiciary* (Cambridge, Mass.: Harvard University Press, 1977).
3. *Gitlow v. New York*, 268 U.S. 652 (1925).
4. For an excellent history of the nationalization of the Bill of Rights, see Richard C. Cortner, *The Supreme Court and the Second Bill of Rights: The Fourteenth Amendment and the Nationalization of Civil Liberties* (Madison: University of Wisconsin Press, 1981).
5. "Text of 96 Congressmen's Declaration on Integration," *New York Times,* March 12, 1956, A19. (Five congressmen later joined the manifesto as well.)
6. *Joint Anti-Fascist Refugee Committee v. McGrath*, 341 U.S. 123 (1951).
7. *Rochin v. California*, 341 U.S. 165 (1952).
8. *Connolly v. General Construction Co.*, 269 U.S. 385 (1976).
9. See, for example, *Goldberg v. Kelly*, 397 U.S. 254 (1970); *In re Ruffalo*, 390 U.S. 544 (1968); *Goss v. Lopez*, 419 U.S. 565 (1975); and *Memphis Light, Gas & Water Division v. Craft*, 436 U.S. 1 (1978).
10. See *Gray v. Mississippi*, 481 U.S. 648 (1987); and *Rose v. Clark*, 478 U.S. 570 (1986).
11. *Griswold v. Connecticut*, 391 U.S. 145 (1965).
12. *DeShaney v. Winnebago County Department of Social Services*, 489 U.S. 189 (1989).
13. Quoted in *Frank v. Maryland*, 359 U.S. 360, 378 (1959).
14. *California v. Hodari D.*, 499 U.S. 621 (1991).
15. *National Treasury Employees Union v. Von Raab*, 489 U.S. 656 (1989).
16. *Skinner v. Railway Labor Executives' Association*, 489 U.S. 602 (1989).
17. *Vernonia School District 47J v. Acton*, 115 S.Ct. 2386 (1995).
18. *Olmstead v. United States*, 277 U.S. 438 (1928).
19. *Katz v. United States*, 389 U.S. 347 (1967).
20. *Escobedo v. Illinois*, 378 U.S. 478 (1964).
21. *Gideon v. Wainwright*, 372 U.S. 335 (1963).
22. *Miranda v. Arizona*, 384 U.S. 436 (1966).
23. For further discussion of rulings that have cut back or refused to extend the *Miranda* ruling, see David M. O'Brien, *Constitutional Law and Politics*, vol. 2, *Civil Rights and Civil Liberties* 3d ed. (New York: Norton, 1997).
24. Jerome Frank, *Courts on Trial* (Princeton, N.J.: Princeton University Press, 1949), 80 (quoting Macaulay, a legal scholar).
25. *Michigan v. Lucas*, 500 U.S. 145 (1991).
26. *White v. Illinois*, 112 S.Ct. 736 (1992).
27. *Nebraska Press Association v. Stuart*, 427 U.S. 539 (1976); and *Seattle Times Co. v. Rhinehart*, 467 U.S. 20 (1984).
28. *Chandler v. Florida*, 449 U.S. 560 (1981).
29. See, for example, *Georgia v. McCollum*, 505 U.S. 42 (1992).
30. *Williams v. Florida*, 399 U.S. 78 (1970) (criminal cases); and *Colegrove v. Batten*, 413 U.S. 149 (1973) (civil cases).
31. *Burch v. Louisiana*, 441 U.S. 130 (1979) (unanimity required in six-member juries in criminal cases); and *Johnson v. Louisiana*, 406 U.S. 356 (1972) (approval of nonunanimous verdicts).
32. *Rummell v. Estelle*, 445 U.S. 263 (1980).
33. *Solem v. Helm*, 463 U.S. 277 (1983).
34. *Furman v. Georgia*, 408 U.S. 238 (1972).
35. See *Gregg v. Georgia*, 428 U.S. 153 (1976); and cases discussed in O'Brien, supra note 23, 1074–1145.
36. *Griffin v. Illinois*, 360 U.S. 252 (1959).
37. *Ake v. Oklahoma*, 470 U.S. 68 (1985).
38. *Bounds v. Smith*, 430 U.S. 817 (1977).
39. See *Tate v. Short*, 401 U.S. 395 (1971); and *Williams v. Illinois*, 399 U.S. 235 (1970).
40. *Olmstead v. United States*, 277 U.S. 438, 478 (1928) (Brandeis, J. dis. op.).
41. See *National Association for the Advancement of Colored People v. Alabama*, 357 U.S. 449 (1958).
42. *Bowers v. Hardwick*, 478 U.S. 186 (1986).
43. In *BMW of North America v. Gore*, 116 S.Ct. 1589 (1996), however, the court held that a punitive damage award that was 500 times the amount of actual damages violated due process.
44. *Nollan v. California Coastal Commission*, 483 U.S. 825 (1987); also see *Lucas v. South Carolina Coastal Commission*, 505 U.S. 647 (1992).
45. *West Virginia State Board of Education v. Barnette*, 319 U.S. 624 (1943).
46. Edward White, "The Supreme Court of the United States," 7 *American Bar Association Journal* (1921), 341.

Chapter 5   Issues of Freedom and Equality

1. *Texas v. Johnson*, 491 U.S. 397 (1989).
2. Quoted in David M. O'Brien, *Storm Center: The Supreme Court in American Politics*, 4th ed. (New York: Norton, 1996), 124.
3. *United States v. Eichman*, 110 S.Ct. 2404 (1990).
4. *Everson v. Board of Education of Ewing Township*, 330 U.S. 1 (1947).
5. See Walter Berns, *The First Amendment and the Future of American Democracy* (New York: Basic Books, 1976), ch. 1.
6. *Engel v. Vitale*, 370 U.S. 421 (1962); and *Abington School District v. Schempp*, 374 U.S. 203 (1963).
7. *Wallace v. Jaffree*, 472 U.S. 38 (1985).
8. *Lynch v. Donnelly*, 465 U.S. 668 (1984).
9. *County of Allegheny v. American Civil Liberties Union Greater Pittsburgh Chapter*, 492 U.S. 573 (1989).
10. *Lee v. Weisman*, 505 U.S. 577 (1992).
11. *Witters v. Washington Department of Services for the Blind*, 474 U.S. 481 (1986); and *Rosenberger v. The Rector and Visitors of the University of Virginia*, 115 S.Ct. 2510 (1995).
12. *Reynolds v. United States*, 98 U.S. 145 (1879).
13. *Wisconsin v. Yoder*, 406 U.S. 208 (1972).
14. *Employment Division, Department of Human Resources of Oregon v. Smith*, 494 U.S. 872 (1990).
15. *West Virginia State Board of Education v. Barnette*, 319 U.S. 624 (1943).
16. *New York Times Co. v. Sullivan*, 376 U.S. 254 (1964).
17. *Gitlow v. New York*, 268 U.S. 652 (1925).
18. *Schenck v. United States*, 249 U.S. 47 (1919).
19. *Dennis v. United States*, 341 U.S. 494 (1951).

20. *Smith v. California*, 361 U.S. 147 (1959).
21. See, for example, *Yates v. United States*, 356 U.S. 363 (1957) (overturning the convictions of six functionaries of the American Communist party under the Smith Act); and *Scales v. United States*, 367 U.S. 203 (1961) (limiting prosecutions under the Smith Act to only those who are shown to have "a specific intent to bring about violent overthrow" of the government).
22. *Brandenburg v. Ohio*, 395 U.S. 444 (1969).
23. *New York Times Co. v. United States*, 403 U.S. 670 (1971).
24. *R.A.V. v. City of St. Paul, Minnesota*, 505 U.S. 377 (1992).
25. *Wisconsin v. Mitchell*, 113 S.Ct. 2194 (1993).
26. *Chaplinsky v. New Hampshire*, 315 U.S. 568 (1942).
27. *Roth v. United States*, 354 U.S. 476 (1957).
28. *Miller v. California*, 413 U.S. 15 (1973).
29. See *Cohen v. California*, 403 U.S. 15 (1971).
30. *Bethel School District No. 403 v. Fraser*, 478 U.S. 675 (1986).
31. *New York v. Ferber*, 458 U.S. 747 (1982).
32. *California v. LaRue*, 409 U.S. 109 (1972); and *Barnes v. Glen Theatre, Inc.*, 501 U.S. 560 (1991).
33. *Renton v. Playtime Theatres*, 475 U.S. 41 (1986).
34. *Federal Communications Commission v. Pacifica Foundation*, 438 U.S. 726 (1978).
35. *New York Times Co. v. Sullivan*, 376 U.S. 254 (1964).
36. *Hustler Magazine v. Falwell*, 485 U.S. 46 (1988).
37. See *Pacific Gas & Electric v. Public Utilities Commission of California*, 475 U.S. 1 (1986).
38. *Tinker v. Des Moines Independent Community School District*, 393 U.S. 503 (1969).
39. *Stromberg v. California*, 283 U.S. 359 (1931).
40. *Spence v. Washington*, 418 U.S. 405 (1974).
41. *Brown v. Socialist Worker '74 Campaign Committee*, 459 U.S. 87 (1982).
42. *Gibson v. Florida Legislative Investigating Committee*, 371 U.S. 539 (1963).
43. *Elfrandt v. Russell*, 384 U.S. 11 (1966).
44. *Application of Stolar*, 401 U.S. 23 (1971).
45. *United States v. Harris*, 347 U.S. 612 (1954).
46. *Minor v. Happersett*, 88 U.S. 162 (1875).
47. *Baker v. Carr*, 369 U.S. 186 (1962).
48. *Miller v. Johnson*, 115 S.Ct. 2475 (1995).
49. *Plessy v. Ferguson*, 163 U.S. 537 (1896).
50. *Brown v. Board of Education of Topeka*, 347 U.S. 483 (1954).
51. *Brown v. Board of Education of Topeka*, 349 U.S. 294 (1955).
52. *Alexander v. Holmes County Board of Education*, 396 U.S. 19 (1969).
53. *Milliken v. Bradley*, 418 U.S. 717 (1974).
54. *Freeman v. Pitts*, 503 U.S. 467 (1992). Also see *Board of Education of Oklahoma City Public Schools v. Dowell*, 498 U.S. 237 (1991).
55. *United States v. Fordice*, 505 U.S. 717 (1992).
56. *Missouri v. Jenkins*, 115 S.Ct. 2038 (1995).
57. *Rostker v. Goldberg*, 453 U.S. 57 (1981).
58. *Michael M. v. Superior Court*, 450 U.S. 464 (1981).
59. *Craig v. Boren*, 429 U.S. 190 (1976).
60. *Dothard v. Rawlinson*, 433 U.S. 321 (1977).
61. *Geduldig v. Aiello*, 417 U.S. 484 (1974).
62. *Frontiero v. Richardson*, 411 U.S. 677 (1973).
63. *Nashville Gas Co. v. Satty*, 434 U.S. 136 (1977).
64. *Meritor Savings Bank, FBD v. Vinson*, 477 U.S. 57 (1986).
65. *International Union, Automobile Workers, Aerospace, Agricultural Implement Workers of America, UAW v. Johnson Controls, Inc.*, 499 U.S. 187 (1991).
66. *United States v. Virginia*, 116 S.Ct. 2264 (1996).
67. *Gregory v. Ashcroft*, 501 U.S. 452 (1991).
68. *Plessy v. Ferguson*, 163 U.S. 537 (1896).
69. *Regents of the University of California v. Bakke*, 438 U.S. 265 (1978).
70. *City of Richmond v. J.A. Croson*, 488 U.S. 469 (1989).
71. *Metro Broadcasting, Inc. v. Federal Communications Commission*, 497 U.S. 547 (1990).
72. *Adarand Constructors, Inc. v. Pena*, 115 S.Ct. 2097 (1995).
73. Overturning *Wards Cove Packing Co. v. Atonio*, 490 U.S. 642 (1989), which had reversed an earlier ruling and had shifted to employees the burden of proving that an employer's hiring practices had a discriminatory impact.
74. Overturning *Patterson v. McLean Credit Union*, 491 U.S. 164 (1989).
75. Overturning *Equal Employment Opportunity Commission v. Arabian American Oil*, 499 U.S. 244 (1991).
76. Overturning *Price Waterhouse v. Hopkins*, 490 U.S. 228 (1989); and *West Virginia University Hospitals v. Casey*, 499 U.S. 83 (1991).
77. Overturning *Lorance v. AT&T*, 490 U.S. 900 (1989); and *Martin v. Wilks*, 490 U.S. 755 (1989).

Chapter 6   Political Socialization and Participation

1. David Maraniss, *First in His Class* (New York: Simon and Schuster, 1995), 55-56.
2. On research in political socialization, see *Handbook of Political Socialization*, ed. Stanley Allen Renshon (New York: Free Press, 1977).
3. Roberta S. Sigel, "The Case for Educating for Gender Equality," in *Political Socialization, Citizenship Education, and Democracy*, ed. Orit Ichilov (New York: Teachers College Press, 1990), 243-265.
4. M. Kent Jennings and Richard G. Niemi, "Patterns of Political Learning," in *Political Opinion and Behavior*, ed. Edward C. Dreyer and Walter A. Rosenbaum (North Scituate, Mass.: Duxbury, 1976), 80-97; and Martin P. Wattenberg, *The Decline of American Political Parties* (Cambridge, Mass.: Harvard University Press, 1984).
5. Fred I. Greenstein, *Children and Politics* (New Haven, Conn.: Yale University Press, 1965).
6. Jennings and Niemi, "Patterns of Political Learning."
7. See Michael X. Delli Carpini, *Stability and Change in American Politics* (New York: New York University Press, 1986).
8. For a discussion of different explanations of the socialization process, see David O. Sears, "Whither Political Socialization Research? The Question of Persistence," in *Political Socialization, Citizenship Education, and Democracy*, 69-97.
9. R. W. Connell, "Political Socialization in the American Family: The Evidence Re-Examined," *Public Opinion Quarterly* 36 (1972): 330.
10. Bryant Robey, *The American People: A Timely Exploration of a Changing America and the Important New Demographic Trends Around Us* (New York: Dutton, 1985), 55.

R-4

11. M. Kent Jennings, Kenneth P. Langton, and Richard G. Niemi, "Effects of the High School Civics Curriculum," in *The Political Character of Adolescence*, ed. M. Kent Jennings and Richard G. Niemi (Princeton, N.J.: Princeton University Press, 1974), 181-206.

12. M. Kent Jennings, Lee H. Ehman, and Richard G. Niemi, "Social Studies Teachers and Their Pupils," in *The Political Character of Adolescence*, 207-228.

13. Frank P. Scioli and Thomas J. Cook, "Political Socialization Reasearch in the United States: A Review," in *Political Attitudes and Public Opinion*, ed. Dan D. Nimmo and Charles M. Bonjean (New York: McKay, 1972), 154-174.

14. Theodore M. Newcomb, *Persistence and Change: Bennington College and Its Students After Twenty-Five Years* (New York: Wiley, 1967).

15. Renshon, *Handbook of Political Socialization*, 133; and Kenneth B. Clark, *Dark Ghetto* (New York: Harper & Row, 1965), 63-64.

16. Harold W. Stanley and Richard G. Niemi, *Vital Statistics on American Politics* (Washington, D.C.: CQ Press, 1995), 47, 49.

17. Steven H. Chaffee, Clifford I. Nass, and Seung-Mock Yang, "The Bridging Role of Television in Immigrant Political Socialization," *Human Communication Research* 17, No. 2 (Winter 1990): 266-288.

18. See, for example, Douglas Kellner, *Television and the Crisis of Democracy* (Boulder, Colo.: Westview, 1990).

19. Paul C. Light, *Baby Boomers* (New York: Norton, 1988), 125.

20. E. J. Dionne, *Why Americans Hate Politics* (New York: Simon and Schuster, 1991), 17.

21. See Henry E. Brady, Sidney Verba, and Kay Lehman Schlozman, "Beyond SES: A Resource Model of Political Participation," *American Political Science Review* 89, No. 2 (1995): 271-294.

22. See, for example, Stephen Earl Bennett, *Apathy in America, 1960-1984: Causes and Consequences of Citizen Political Indifference* (Dobbs Ferry, N.Y.: Transnational, 1986), 63-70.

23. See Samuel L. Popkin, *The Reasoning Voter: Communication and Persuasion in Presidential Campaigns* (Chicago: University of Chicago Press, 1991).

24. Samuel H. Barnes et al., *Political Participation in Five Western Democracies* (Beverly Hills, Calif.: Sage, 1979), 541-542.

25. Fred I. Greenstein and Nelson Polsby, eds., *Handbook of Political Science* (Reading, Mass.: Addison-Wesley, 1975).

26. Ibid., 27.

27. Calculated from the 1992 National Election Study.

28. Brady, Verba, and Schlozman, "Beyond SES."

29. "Low-Income Voters' Turnout Fell in 1994, Census Reports," *New York Times*, June 11, 1995.

30. Steven J. Rosenstone and John Mark Hansen, *Mobilization, Participation, and Democracy in America* (New York: Macmillan, 1993), 36.

31. See, for example, Verba and Nie, *Participation in America*, 284-285; Rosenstone and Hansen, *Mobilization, Participation, and Democracy*, 244-248; Brady, Verba, and Schlozman, "Beyond SES," 285.

Chapter 7   Public Opinion

1. Johnson believes he contracted the virus that causes AIDS through an unprotected heterosexual affair. Ashe, who has subsequently died from the disease, contracted it from a blood transfusion necessitated by heart surgery.

2. James N. Rosenau, ed., *Public Opinion and Foreign Policy* (New York: Random House, 1961), 34-35.

3. Herbert McClosky, "Consensus and Ideology in American Politics," *American Political Science Review* 58 (June 1964): 363; and Herbert McClosky and Alida Brill, *Dimensions of Tolerance* (New York: Russell Sage, 1983), 239.

4. The discussion that follows on the history and mechanics of polling is drawn primarily from Stephen J. Wayne, *The Road to the White House,* 5th ed. (New York: St. Martin's, 1996), 262-272.

5. Steven J. Rosenstone, *Forecasting Presidential Elections* (New Haven, Conn.: Yale University Press, 1983), 24.

6. Ibid., 27-28.

7. *The Gallup Poll,* November 1992, unnumbered cover.

8. "Poll Watch," *The Pew Research Center for The People & The Press,* January 3, 1996, 5.

9. "Some Pitfalls in Polling," *New York Times,* August 9, 1992, E5.

10. "Politics Quiz," *Washington Post,* January 29, 1996, A6.

11. Joan Biskupic, "Has the Court Lost Its Appeal?" *Washington Post,* October 12, 1995, A23.

12. The Center reported that only 20 percent of those under age 30 followed the news very closely, compared with 23 percent of those between age 30 and 40 and 29 percent of people over age 50. "The Times Mirror News Interest Index: 1989-1995," *The Pew Research Center for The People & The Press,* 7.

13. "How Americans View the Contract with America," *New York Times/CBS News Poll,* February 28, 1995, A21.

14. Angus Campbell, Philip E. Converse, Warren E. Miller, and Donald E. Stokes, *The American Voter* (New York: Wiley, 1960), 249.

15. Norman H. Nie and Kristi Anderson, "Mass Belief Systems Revisited: Political Change and Attitude Structure," *Journal of Politics* 36 (September 1974): 541-591.

16. In 1988, approximately 80 percent of people who identified themselves as conservative supported Bush, and a similar percentage of self-identified liberals supported Dukakis. In 1992, although the candidacy of independent H. Ross Perot reduced these percentages, 68 percent of the liberals voted for Clinton and 64 percent of the conservatives cast their ballots for Bush, according to the large exit poll conducted for the major news networks on election day.

17. One question that pollsters have asked with some frequency in recent years is "Which do you say you favor—a larger government with many services or a smaller government with fewer services?" Here are some of the responses, given in percentages:

	Larger	Smaller
1984	43	49
1988	45	49
1992	38	55
1993	29	60
1994	24	66

"Disillusionment with Washington," *American Enterprise,* January/February 1994, 101; "The Mood on Washington," *American Enterprise,* November/December 1995, 106.

18. Thomas B. Edsall, "Public Grows More Receptive to Anti-Government Message," *Washington Post,* January 31, 1996, A5.

19. Richard Morin and Dan Balz, "Americans Losing Trust in Each Other and Institutions," *Washington Post,* January 28, 1996, A6.

20. Martin B. Abravnel and Ronald J. Busch, "Political Competence, Political Trust, and the Action Orientation of University Students," *Journal of Politics* 37 (February 1975): 57–82; and Joel Aberbach and Jack L. Walker, "Political Trust and Racial Ideology," *American Political Science Review* 64 (December 1970): 1199–1219.

21. James W. Prothro and Charles M. Gregg, "Fundamental Principles of Democracy: Bases of Agreement and Disagreement," *Journal of Politics* 22 (May 1960): 276–294. Also see McClosky, "Consensus and Ideology"; and McClosky and Brill, *Dimensions of Tolerance.*

22. John Muller, "Trends in Political Tolerance," *Public Opinion Quarterly* 52 (Spring 1988): 1–25; and Paul R. Abramson, *Political Attitudes in America* (San Francisco: Freeman, 1983). For a summary of this literature, see Robert Erikson, Norman Luttbeg, and Kent L. Tedin, *American Public Opinion: Its Origins, Content, and Impact,* 4th ed. (New York: Macmillan, 1991), 109–112.

23. McClosky, "Consensus and Ideology"; McClosky and Brill, *Dimensions of Tolerance;* Clyde Z. Nunn, Harry J. Crockett Jr., and J. Allen Williams Jr., *Tolerance for Nonconformity* (San Francisco: Jossey-Bass, 1978); and James L. Gibson and Richard D. Bingham, *Civil Liberties and the Nazis: The Skokie Free-Speech Controversy* (New York: Praeger, 1985).

24. This position is well stated in Stephen Earl Bennett, " 'Know Nothings' Revisited: The Meaning of Political Ignorance Today," *Social Science Quarterly* 69 (June 1988): 476–490.

25. The seminal work on this topic is Theodore Adorno, E. Frankel-Brunswik, D. J. Levinson, and R. N. Sanford, *The Authoritarian Personality* (New York: Harper, 1950). For a more recent discussion, see Fred I. Greenstein, *Personality and Politics* (Chicago: Markham, 1969).

26. Benjamin I. Page and Robert Y. Shapiro, "Effects of Public Opinion on Policy," *American Political Science Review* 77 (March 1983): 175–190; and Gerald C. Wright Jr., Robert S. Erikson, and John P. McIver, "Public Opinion and Policy Liberalism in the American States," *American Journal of Political Science* 31 (November 1987): 980–1001.

27. Erikson, Luttbeg, and Tedin, *American Public Opinion,* 332.

Chapter 8   Political Interest Groups

1. Jimmy Carter, *Why Not The Best?* (New York: Bantam, 1975), 4.

2. For an extended discussion of interest groups and political systems, see Gabriel A. Almond and G. Bingham Powell Jr., *Comparative Politics Today* (New York: HarperCollins, 1992), 61–73.

3. Truman's theory was built on the writings of another student of social and political movements, Arthur F. Bentley, who was the first to study group behavior systematically in his book *The Process of Government* (1908).

4. David B. Truman, *The Governmental Process* (New York: Knopf, 1960).

5. Ibid., 97.

6. Mancur Olson Jr., *The Logic of Collective Action* (New York: Schocken, 1968).

7. Robert H. Salisbury, "An Exchange Theory of Interest Groups," *Midwest Journal of Political Science* 13 (February 1969): 1–32.

8. Jack L. Walker, "The Origins and Maintenance of Interest Groups in America," *American Political Science Review* 77 (June 1983): 390–406.

9. Mark P. Petracca, "The Rediscovery of Interest Group Politics," in *The Politics of Interests,* ed. Mark P. Petracca (Boulder, Colo.: Westview, 1992), 14.

10. Walker, "The Origins," 403.

11. As discussed in Chapter 6, college graduates tend to be more aware of and concerned about the policy issues that affect them and their environment than are people with less education.

12. *The Washington Representatives 1995,* 19th ed. (Washington, D.C.: Columbia Books, 1995), 2.

13. Ibid., 3–4.

14. Ibid.

15. The law also requires those who receive $5,000 from a single client in a six-month period to register. Ruth Marcus and Guy Gugliotta, "Number of Lobbyists Who Register Doubles," *Washington Post,* March 16, 1996, A4.

16. For an excellent discussion of the monitoring function, see Robert H. Salisbury, "The Paradox of Interest Groups in Washington—More Groups, Less Clout," in *The New American Political System,* 2d ed., ed. Anthony King (Washington, D.C.: American Enterprise Institute, 1990), 203–230.

17. Edward O. Laumann and David Knoke, *The Organizational State: Social Choice in National Policy Domains* (Madison: University of Wisconsin Press, 1987), 3.

18. Disagreements within the group, however, may exist over specifics. During the national health-care debate in 1993, the national organization of the AARP supported the managed-care, private-insurer approach of the Clinton administration, whereas its California affiliate backed the single-payer option. David S. Hilzenrath, "AARP's Nonprofit Status Comes Under Scrutiny," *Washington Post,* May 22, 1995, A8.

19. Today, with a larger membership of approximately 2.5 million, the NRA is not as powerful because of the rise of opposition groups and general public concern with crime.

20. *Encyclopedia of Associations 1996,* 30th ed. (New York: Gale Research, 1996), 1489.

21. Ibid., 1671.

22. Hilzenrath, "AARP's Nonprofit Status," A8.

23. Alice A. Love, "The 104th Lobbyists 'In Crowd': A New Pecking Order in Special Interest Washington," *Roll Call,* September 11, 1995.

24. Kevin Sack, "Gaming Lobby Gives Lavishly to Politicians," *New York Times,* December 18, 1995, A1 and B12.

25. The Federal Election Campaign Finance Act permits individuals to donate a maximum of $1,000 per candidate per election, or a total of $2,000, half in the primary and half in the general election. Moreover, the total maximum amount of contributions to candidates that any individual donor can make is $25,000 in any election cycle. On the other hand, PACs can give a maximum of $5,000 per candidate per election, or $10,000 to any one candidate in an election cycle. Nor are they limited in the total amount of contributions they can make. So leadership PACs offer a legal way to circumvent the constrictions of the law.

26. In 1993, Democrats received $24.8 million in PAC contribu-

tions compared with $10.8 million for the Republicans; in 1995, they received $18 million compared with $25.3 million for the Republicans. John E. Yang, "House GOP on a Roll," *Washington Post*, February 12, 1996, A9.

27. John E. Yang, "Parties Got About Equal Pieces of '95 PAC Pie in House, Study Finds," *Washington Post*, April 15, 1996, A4.

28. Charles R. Babcock, "Buying Access to Congress: How a Company Pays to 'Tell Our Story,' " *Washington Post*, June 8, 1992, A17.

29. Frank J. Sorauf, *Money in American Elections* (Glenview, Ill.: Scott, Foresman, 1988), 314.

30. Richard L. Hall and Frank W. Wayman, "Buying Time: Moneyed Interests and the Mobilization of Bias in Congressional Committees," *American Political Science Review* 84 (September 1990): 814.

31. A new business has even been created to help lobbyists perform this task. Since congressional committee rooms have a limited seating capacity and are filled on a first-come, first-served basis, a service now exists to save places in line for busy, highly paid lobbyists. Students are paid by the hour to wait until the committee room opens. Sometimes the lineup for an extremely popular hearing will begin on the previous day and involve camping outside the House and Senate office buildings throughout the night.

32. Richard Viguerie, quoted in Burdett A. Loomis, "A New Era: Groups and the Grass Roots," in *Interest Group Politics*, ed. Allan J. Cigler and Burdett A. Loomis (Washington, D.C.: Congressional Quarterly, 1983), 172.

33. Viguerie usually makes a substantial profit whether or not the drive is successful. Marilyn Werber Serafin, "Senior Schism," *National Journal*, May 6, 1995, 1091.

34. What the ads did not say was that the woman was elderly and suffered third-degree burns from the coffee and that McDonald's had successfully quashed similar negligence suits in the past.

35. David Maraniss and Michael Weisskopf, "Speaker and His Directors Make the Cash Flow Right," *Washington Post*, November 27, 1995, A8.

36. For an excellent discussion of how and why presidents try to mobilize groups' support, see Mark A. Petterson, "The Presidency and Organized Interests: White House Patterns of Interest Group Liaison," *American Political Science Review* 86 (September 1992): 612-625.

37. Gary Lee, "Trade, National Security and the Revolving Door," *Washington Post*, April 13, 1992, A19.

38. *The Washington Representatives 1995*, 974-975.

39. Stephen Engelberg and Martin Tolchin, "Foreigners Find New Ally in U.S. Industry," *New York Times*, November 2, 1993, B8.

40. Charles Trueheart, "Quebec Presses a New Image: Good (Sovereign) Neighbor," *Washington Post*, April 15, 1995, A11.

41. Eric Moses, "Casablanca on the Potomac River?" *National Journal*, November 11, 1995, 2810-2811.

42. One of the changes in rules that the House of Representatives adopted after the Republicans took over in 1995 was to open all committee meetings to the public "except in extraordinary circumstances" and to permit public broadcasting as a matter of right.

43. David Segal, "The Tale of the Bogus Telegrams," *Washington Post*, September 28, 1995, A1 and A8; Juliet Eilperin, "Police Track down Telecom Telegrams," *Roll Call*, August 7, 1995.

44. Consider the case of James H. Lake, a well-known Washington lobbyist who was asked by a senior executive of one of the agricultural companies he represented to help retire the debt of a defeated congressional candidate whose brother just happened to be secretary of agriculture at the time. Lake requested that the five top executives of his firm, including himself, contribute $1,000 each to the defunct but still in debt congressional campaign. Four did; one refused to do so. After checks totaling $4,000 were sent to the campaign, the executive of the agricultural company that had requested the contributions had his company issue a check for $5,000 to Lake's firm for expenses they had incurred on behalf of the company. Lake returned $1,000 to each of the contributors and kept the balance. It is illegal for companies to make campaign contributions and Lake subsequently pleaded guilty to charges that he violated the law. "Prominent GOP Consultant Admits Fraud," *Washington Post*, October 24, 1995, A1 and A6.

45. E. E. Schattschneider, *The Semi-Sovereign People: A Realist's View of Democracy* (Hillsdale, Ill.: Dryden, 1960), 34-35.

46. Ibid., 30-35.

Chapter 9   Political Parties

1. Only two of the original ten proposals failed to gain majority support in the House: a requirement of a three-fifths majority for any income tax increase, and term limits for members of Congress.

2. In *An Economic Theory of Democracy* (New York: HarperCollins, 1957), Anthony Downs provides a logical explanation for the "mainstream" phenomenon.

3. A poll conducted by ABC News/*Washington Post* from October 27 to October 30, 1995, asked the following question: "Would you support or oppose the formation of a third political party that would run candidates for president, Congress, and state offices against Democratic and Republican party candidates?" By a margin of almost two to one, respondents supported the formation of a third party. "Party Systems," *American Enterprise*, January/February 1996, 90. See also surveys conducted by Yankelovich Partners, Inc., for *Time* and CNN as appear in "Third-Party Prospects," *American Enterprise*, May/June 1995, 105. For voting preferences, see "Opinion Outlook," *National Journal*, October 14, 1995, 2558.

4. "Second Thoughts About Third Parties," *American Enterprise*, January/February 1996, 91.

5. However, only 5,000 petition signatures are needed for a single candidate to get on the ballot in Ohio.

6. Jefferson's Republicans were not the forerunners of the modern Republican party, which was organized in 1854 and nominated its first presidential candidate in 1856. Democrats, however, claim Jefferson as their first president and trace their party's origins to the Democratic-Republican party at the end of the eighteenth century.

7. This is the only time a tie occurred. Upon taking office, Jefferson and his supporters proposed a constitutional amendment that required electors to cast separate ballots for president and vice president. The Twelfth Amendment was ratified in 1804.

8. For a more extended discussion of the creation of the American party system, see William Nisbet Chambers,

Political Parties in a New Nation: The American Experience, 1776-1809 (New York: Oxford University Press, 1963). Another helpful interpretation of the beginning of parties in the United States can be found in Wilfred E. Binkley, *American Political Parties: Their National History* (New York: Knopf, 1959).

9. Richard P. McCormick, *The Second American Party System: Party Formation in the Jacksonian Era* (Chapel Hill: University of North Carolina Press, 1966).

10. For an extended discussion of voter turnout during this and subsequent periods, see Walter Dean Burnham, "The Turnout Problem," in *Elections American Style*, ed. A. James Reichley (Washington, D.C.: Brookings Institution, 1987), 112-133.

11. Its presidential candidate in 1992, Earl Dodge, received 935 votes.

12. Voter News Service exit poll.

13. Voter News Service exit poll.

14. For a history of the Republican and Democratic national committees, see Ralph M. Goldman, *The National Party Chairmen and Committees* (Armonk, N.Y.: M. E. Sharpe, 1990).

15. Federal Election Commission, "Record," July 1995, 7; "Parties Raised Nearly $60 million in 'Soft' 1995 Donations," *Washington Post*, March 11, 1996, A17.

16. For an excellent discussion of the strengthening of national party organizations in their campaign activities, see Paul S. Herrnson, *Party Campaigning in the 1980s* (Cambridge, Mass.: Harvard University Press, 1988).

17. See John F. Bibby, Cornelius P. Cotter, James L. Gibson, and Robert J. Huckshorn, "Parties in State Politics," in *Politics in the American States: A Comparative Analysis*, ed. Virginia Gray, Herbert Jacob, and Robert B. Albritton (Glenview, Ill.: Scott, Foresman/Little, Brown, 1990) 108-111.

18. James L. Gibson, Cornelius Cotter, John F. Bibby, and Robert J. Huckshorn, "Assessing Party Organizational Strength," *American Journal of Political Science* 17 (May 1983): 193-222.

19. John F. Bibby, *Politics, Parties, and Elections in America*, 2d ed. (Chicago: Nelson-Hall, 1992), 104.

20. Ibid., 98.

21. For a good study of trends in state parties, see Robert J. Huckshorn and John F. Bibby, "State Parties in an Era of Political Change," in *The Future of American Political Parties*, ed. Joel L. Fleishman (Englewood Cliffs, N.J.: Prentice-Hall, 1982), 70-100.

22. The most comprehensive study of local parties, primarily at the county level, was conducted in 1979-1980 and reported in James L. Gibson, Cornelius P. Cotter, John F. Bibby, and Robert J. Huckshorn, "Whither the Local Parties? A Cross-Sectional and Longitudinal Analysis of the Strength of Party Organizations," *American Journal of Political Science* 29 (February 1985): 139-160.

23. V. O. Key Jr., *American State Politics: An Introduction* (New York: Knopf, 1956), 107-111; and Sarah M. Morehouse, *State Politics, Parties and Policy* (New York: Holt, Rinehart and Winston, 1981), 180-183.

24. Gerald M. Pomper with Susan S. Lederman, *Elections in America* (White Plains, N.Y. : Longman, 1980), 161.

25. Jeff Fishel, *Presidents and Promises* (Washington, D.C.: Congressional Quarterly, 1985), 38.

26. Ibid., 42-43.

27. For a discussion of the concept of responsible party government, see Committee on Political Parties of the American Political Science Association, *Toward a More Responsible Two-Party System* (New York: Holt, Rinehart and Winston, 1950); and Austin Ranney, *The Doctrine of Responsible Party Government* (Urbana: University of Illinois Press, 1962).

28. Parties tend to divide most sharply on the issues that have become salient only in recent election campaigns, not those that have been around for a long time. Jerome M. Clubb and Santa A. Traugott, "Partisan Cleavage and Cohesion in the House of Representatives," *Journal of Interdisciplinary History* 7 (Winter 1977): 374-401.

29. David W. Rohde, "The Reports of My Death Are Greatly Exaggerated: Parties and Party Voting in the House of Representatives," in *Changing Perspectives on Congress*, ed. Glenn R. Parker (Knoxville: University of Tennessee Press, 1990); and Malcolm E. Jewell and David M. Olson, *Political Parties and Elections in American States* (Chicago: Dorsey, 1988), 246-249.

30. "1994 Party Unity Votes," *Congressional Quarterly*, December 31, 1994, 3658.

31. Ibid.

32. Randall L. Calvert and John A. Ferejohn, "Coattail Voting in Recent Presidential Elections," *American Political Science Review* 77 (June 1983): 407-419; and John A. Ferejohn and Randall L. Calvert, "Presidential Coattails in Historical Perspective," *American Journal of Political Science* 28 (February 1984): 164-183.

33. Paul Allen Beck and Frank J. Sorauf, *Party Politics in America*, 7th ed. (New York: HarperCollins, 1992), 423.

34. This subject is discussed for federal judges in Robert A. Carp and Ronald Stidham, *The Federal Courts* (Washington, D.C.: Congressional Quarterly, 1985), 142-148; also see Craig Ducat and Robert L. Dudley, "Federal District Judges and Presidential Power During the Postwar Era," *Journal of*

Politics 51 (February 1989): 98–118. An examination of the influence of party on state judges can be found in Stuart Nagel, "Political Party Affiliation and Judges' Decisions," *American Political Science Review* 55 (December 1961): 843–850; and David W. Adamany, "The Party Variable in Judges' Voting: Conceptual Notes and a Case Study," *American Political Science Review* 63 (March 1969): 57–83.

Chapter 10   Campaigns and Elections

1. For all practical purposes, people are deemed to be responsible for their own actions if they are 18 years of age or older and are mentally competent. In some states, individuals who have been convicted of a felony or dishonorably discharged from the military may not vote.

2. In 1996, however, application of the New York law was successfully challenged by Steve Forbes and Pat Buchanan, who claimed that they had met the statutory requirements and thus should appear on the Republican ballot in districts in which they qualified.

3. For an extended discussion of the early history of campaign finance, see Herbert E. Alexander, *Financing Politics: Money, Elections, and Political Reform* (Washington, D.C.: Congressional Quarterly, 1984), 1–54.

4. Presidential candidates who accept federal funds are limited to a $50,000 personal contribution or loan to their own campaign.

5. Federal Election Commission, *Record* 19, No. 2 (February 1993): 4–5; Federal Election Commission, press release, "PAC Activity in 1994 Elections Remains at 1992 Levels," March 31, 1995, 2–3; and "FEC Releases 18 Month Report on Political Party Finances," Federal Election Commission, August 7, 1996, 1.

6. Angus Campbell, Philip E. Converse, Warren E. Miller, and Donald E. Stokes, *The American Voter* (New York: Wiley, 1960), 101–107.

7. Ibid., 96–101.

8. Raymond E. Wolfinger and Steven J. Rosenstone, *Who Votes?* (New Haven, Conn.: Yale University Press, 1980), 13–26.

9. Ibid., 18–20, 35–36.

10. Paul R. Abramson, John H. Aldrich, and David W. Rohde, *Change and Continuity in the 1988 Elections* (Washington, D.C.: Congressional Quarterly, 1990), 105.

11. James A. Barnes, "Tainted Triumph?" *National Journal*, November 7, 1992, 2539.

12. Rhodes Cook, "Rare Combination of Forces May Make History of '94," *Congressional Quarterly*, April 15, 1995, 1078.

13. Besides, Teixeira notes, "It is a great deal easier to change an election by switching the preferences of existing voters than by adding new voters." Ruy A. Teixeira, "What If We Had an Election and Everybody Came?" *American Enterprise* 3 (July–August 1992): 55.

14. This theory was first postulated in the classic study by Campbell et al., *The American Voter*.

15. William H. Flanagan and Nancy H. Zingale, *Political Behavior of the American Electorate*, 7th ed. (Washington, D.C.: Congressional Quarterly, 1991), 49–54.

16. Campbell et al., *American Voter*, 133–136. Party identification is determined by asking the following question: "Generally speaking, do you usually think of yourself as a Republican, a Democrat, an independent, or what?"

17. The theory of cross-pressures was first advanced by Paul Lazarsfeld, Bernard Berelson, and Hazel Gaudet in *The People's Choice* (New York: Columbia University Press, 1944). See also Bernard Berelson, Paul Lazarsfeld, and William McPhee, *Voting* (Chicago: University of Chicago Press, 1954).

18. Of the Democrats who supported Ronald Reagan in 1984, 56 percent voted for Bill Clinton in 1992, compared with 23 percent for George Bush and 21 percent for H. Ross Perot. "Exit Poll," *USA Today*, November 4, 1992, 6A.

19. Mitofsky International, *New York Times*, November 13, 1994.

20. Flanagan and Zingale, *Political Behavior of the American Electorate*, 124.

21. For an excellent discussion of the retrospective model of voting behavior see Morris Fiorina, *Retrospective Voting in American National Elections* (New Haven, Conn.: Yale University Press, 1981), 65–83.

22. "Primary Turnout: Ups and Downs," *Congressional Quarterly*, July 4, 1992, 71; "1992 Republican Primary Turnout," *Congressional Quarterly*, August 8, 1992, 67; "1996 Republican Primary Results," *Congressional Quarterly*, August 3, 1996, 63; and "1996 Democratic Primary Results," *Congressional Quarterly*, August 17, 1996, 79.

23. John S. Jackson, Barbara Brown, and David Bositis, "Herbert McClosky and Friends Revisited: 1980 Democratic and Republican Party Elites Compared to the Mass Public," *American Politics Quarterly* 10 (1982): 158–180; and Martin Plissner and Warren J. Mitofsky, "The Making of the Delegates, 1968–1988," *Public Opinion* 3 (September–October 1988): 46.

24. The Equal Rights Amendment, which would have prohibited all discrimination on the basis of gender, failed to achieve ratification. In the 1980s, Republican platforms opposed the amendment and Democratic platforms supported it.

25. Quoted in Charles T. Royer, ed., *Campaign for President: The Managers Look at '92* (Hollis, N.H.: Hollis Publishing Co., 1994), 117.

26. Another advantage of having money up front is that the news media interpret it as a sign of strength in the prenomination period prior to caucuses and primaries. The campaign's organization and financial resources are seen as indicators of its electoral potential: well-financed candidates receive more coverage. In 1988, Pat Robertson's organizational and financial strength made him a viable candidate initially despite his status as a political novice and his narrow political base within the Republican party.

27. Quoted in Royer, ed., *Campaign for President*, 14.

28. John Paulik and Mark Thalhimer, "From Wausau to Wichita: Covering the Campaign via Satellite," in Martha FitzSimon, ed., *Covering the Presidential Primaries* (New York: The Freedom Forum Media Studies Center, 1992), 36–37.

29. Dirk Smillie, "Rating an Uncertain Season," in FitzSimon, ed., *Covering the Presidential Primaries*, 20.

30. Thomas E. Patterson, *The Mass Media Election* (New York: Praeger, 1980), 72–74.

31. Ibid., 103.

32. In Maine and Nebraska, one elector is chosen in each state congressional district, and two electors are selected at large; thus in these states a divided electoral vote is possible.

33. The two votes given to every state by virtue of its two senators is what gives those with the smallest populations an advantage.

34. There is a substantial body of literature on the impact of inter- and intraparty competition on the electoral system. See, for example, John F. Bibby, Cornelius P. Cotter, James L. Gibson, and Robert J. Huckshorn, "Parties in State Politics," in *Politics in the American States*, 5th ed., ed. Virginia Gray, Herbert Jacob, and Robert B. Albritton (Glenview, Ill.: Scott, Foresman, 1990); Samuel J. Eldersveld, *Political Parties in American Society* (New York: Basic Books, 1982), 35-36; and James D. King, "Interparty Competition in the American States: An Examination of Index Components," *Western Political Quarterly* 42 (1989): 83-92.

35. Flanagan and Zingale, *Political Behavior of the American Electorate*, 14.

36. To gain an advantage, parties attempt to draw legislative districts so that their partisans constitute a stable but not overwhelming majority in as many districts as possible and their opponents constitute a majority in as few of them as possible.

37. There is a wealth of literature on reapportionment and redistricting. For the political ramifications, see Robert S. Erikson, "The Partisan Impact of State Legislative Reapportionment," *Midwest Journal of Political Science* 15 (1971): 57-71; Timothy G. O'Rourke, *The Impact of Reapportionment* (New Brunswick, N.J.: Transaction, 1980); Amihai Glazer, Bernard Grofman, and Marc Robbins, "Partisan and Incumbency Effects of 1970s Congressional Redistricting," *American Journal of Political Science* 31 (1987): 680-707; and Richard Born, "Partisan Intentions and Election Day Realities in the Congressional Redistricting Process," *American Political Science Association* 79 (1985): 305-319.

38. For a discussion of redistricting in the 1990s, see Beth Donovan, "Political Dance Played Out Through Legal Wrangling," *Congressional Quarterly*, December 21, 1991, 3690-3695.

39. Juan Williams, "Blacked Out in the New Congress," *Washington Post*, November 20, 1994, C1.

40. These conditions require that districts be race-neutral, equal in population, and compact and contiguous; adhere to the state's political subdivisions; and have shared interests. To draw districts that lack these criteria, states have to demonstrate a compelling interest. In other words, the burden of proof is on the state.

41. But they must be careful in using staff that are on the congressional payroll. It is against federal law for United States government employees, such as congressional staffs, to engage in campaign activities in the course of their official duties. To circumvent this rule, candidates may have their staff members take a leave of absence during the campaign.

42. An even smaller proportion of the general public (less than 20 percent) had heard of the Contract prior to the election. Clyde Wilcox, *The Latest American Revolution?* (New York: St. Martin's Press, 1995), 21.

Chapter 11 Politics and the News Media

1. For an extended discussion of how the media reflect and affect society, see Fred S. Siebert, *Four Theories of the Press* (Urbana: University of Illinois Press, 1956).

2. The conviction of Iran-contra defendant Oliver North was overturned by a federal appeals court on the grounds that the testimony of witnesses against North might have been influenced by the congressional hearings in which North was promised immunity from prosecution. The special investigator who prosecuted North could not prove that the witnesses had not been influenced by the hearings, so their testimony could not be used against North in the trial.

3. The country's preoccupation with courtroom drama peaked with the O. J. Simpson murder trial. During the first four months of 1995 the trial received 13.8 hours of evening news coverage compared with only 9.4 hours for President Clinton. "The Invisible Man: TV News Coverage of President Bill Clinton, 1993-1995," *Media Monitor* (May/June 1995): 2.

4. Republican presidential candidate Robert Dole was particularly outspoken in his criticism of the movie industry for its portrayal of and emphasis on sex and violence. The industry, however, saw Dole's criticism as an attempt to muzzle it. If the public didn't like such movies, industry representatives argued, they would not pay to see them.

5. Public television and radio stations in the United States depend primarily on contributions from viewers and listeners and from corporate sponsors. They may receive government grants for specific programs, but their operating costs are not paid by the government.

6. By law the USIA is forbidden to broadcast or even distribute its programs within the United States.

7. According to the 1996 edition of *Editor and Publisher's International Yearbook*, an annual that lists all publications in the United States, there were 1,533 daily newspapers in February 1995. Of these, 25 were published in cities with populations of more than 1 million; 25 served populations between 500,000 and 1 million; and 825 reached populations of less than 25,000.

8. *Times Mirror Company*, "The People and the Press" (November 1989), 13.

9. See, for example, Ben H. Bagdikian, *The Media Monopoly* (Boston: Beacon, 1987); and W. Lance Bennett, *News: The Politics of Illusion* (New York: Longman, 1988).

10. Michael Parenti, *Inventing Reality: The Politics of the Mass Media* (New York: St. Martin's Press, 1986).

11. Austin Ranney, "Broadcasting, Narrowcasting, and Politics," in *The New American Political System*, 2d version, ed. Anthony King (Washington, D.C.: American Enterprise Institute, 1990), 195.

12. "NBC's Believability Burned," *Times Mirror Center for the People and the Press*, March 3, 1993, 1-2.

13. U.S. Bureau of the Census, *Statistical Abstract of the United States 1995* (Washington, D.C., 1995), 571.

14. Ibid., 577.

15. Ranney, "Broadcasting, Narrowcasting, and Politics," 190-191.

16. Ibid., 192.

17. Between 1994 and 1996, 3,500 miles of cable and 312 miles of fiber optic wire were laid on Capitol Hill to congressional offices and to committee and institutional support staffs. Eric Schmitt, "Capitol Hill Takes to Cyberspace, Though in Fits, Starts and Stumbles," *New York Times*, July 10, 1996, A12.

18. "Americans Going Online . . . Explosive Growth, Uncertain Destinations," *Times Mirror Center for the People and the Press*, October 16, 1995, 1.

19. Kara Swisher, "Internet's Reach in Society Grows, Survey Finds," *Washington Post*, October 31, 1995, A1; Peter H. Lewis, "Report of High Internet Use Is Challenged," *New York Times*, December 13, 1995, D5.

20. "Who's on the Internet," *Washington Post*, July 1, 1996, A8.

21. Lewis, "Report of High Internet Use Is Challenged," D5.
22. "Americans Going Online," 8.
23. "Questions of Character," *Media Monitor* (April 1992): 6.
24. "Clinton's the One," *Media Monitor* (November 1992): 2.
25. Ibid.; "The Bad News Campaign," *Media Monitor* (March/April 1996): 2.
26. "Dole's Summer Doldrums: TV News Coverage of the 1996 Presidential Election," *Media Monitor* (July/August 1996): 2.
27. Thomas E. Patterson, *Out of Order* (New York: Alfred A. Knopf, 1993), 106. For an excellent normative discussion of the balance between policy and candidate issues in an election campaign, see Graham P. Ramsden, "Media Coverage of Issues and Candidates: What Balance Is Appropriate in a Democracy?" *Political Science Quarterly*, III (Spring 1996): 65-82.
28. "Clinton's the One," 3-4.
29. "The Bad News Campaign," 2.
30. "Dole's Summer Doldrums," 3.
31. Ibid, 2.
32. Doris Graber, "Presidential Images in the 1968 Campaign" (Paper delivered at the annual meeting of the Midwest Political Science Association, Chicago, April 30–May 2, 1980), 3.
33. Almost 70 percent of Clinton's ads were negative in 1992, compared with 56 percent for Bush. L. Patrick Devlin, "Contrasts in Presidential Campaign Commercials of 1992," *American Behavioral Scientist* 37 (November 1993): 288; Lynda Lee Kaid and Anne Johnston, "Negative Versus Positive Television Advertising in U.S. Presidential Campaigns, 1960-1988," *Journal of Communications* 41 (Summer 1991): 54.
34. Edwin Diamond and Adrian Marin, "Spots," *American Behavioral Scientist* 32 (March/April 1989): 386.
35. Darrell M. West, "Television Advertising in Election Campaigns," *Political Science Quarterly* 108 (Winter 1994-1995): 789-809.
36. S. Robert Lichter, Daniel Amundson, and Richard Noyes, *The Video Campaign: Network Coverage of the 1988 Primaries* (Washington, D.C.: American Enterprise Institute, 1989), 12.
37. "The Bad News Campaign," 2.
38. "The Invisible Man," 1.
39. Ibid.
40. Had that network, CBS, not been the only one of the three major ones to cover the Speaker's speech live several days earlier, it probably would not have done so for the president's news conference. CBS also felt it had to cover the Speaker because one of its correspondents, Connie Chung, had reported a negative comment by Gingrich's mother about her son's opinion of the president's wife.
41. "The Invisible Man," 2.
42. Ibid., 4.
43. Ibid., 2.
44. Timothy E. Cook, *Making News and Making Laws* (Washington, D.C.: Brookings Institution, 1989), 7.
45. O. J. Simpson was acquitted of the murders of his ex-wife, Nicole Brown Simpson, and a friend of hers, Ronald Goldman. Susan Smith was convicted of murdering her two small children by strapping them in seat belts in her car and running the car into a lake. Rodney King was a motorist who was stopped and beaten by Los Angeles police. A private citizen who witnessed the beating recorded it on videotape.
46. "The Invisible Man," 5.
47. "Public Interest and Awareness of the News," *Pew Research Center New Interest Index* (January 1996): 6.
48. Media coverage of the budget battle between Congress and the president, which resulted in two brief partial shutdowns of the government, had an impact on the Republican Congress similar to that which the hostage crisis had had on President Carter. By showing how the shutdowns affected people, the coverage helped turn opinion against Congress.

Chapter 12   Congress

1. Information on the assault weapons ban repeal was drawn from Alan Greenblatt, "Repeal of Assault Weapons Ban Unlikely to Go Beyond House," *Congressional Quarterly Weekly Report*, March 23, 1996, 803; "Victory in the House!" *NRA Grassfire* (newsletter), April 1996; "Clinton Firm on Assault Ban," Associated Press, January 28, 1996; "Assault Weapons Ban, Statement of Senate Majority Leader Bob Dole," March 21, 1996, released by the National Rifle Association Institute for Legislative Action.
2. The members of each Congress and their districts are described in detail in Congressional Quarterly's *Politics in America* series, which is updated after each congressional election.
3. House of Representatives, Commission on Administrative Review, *Administrative Reorganization and Legislative Management*, vol. 2, 95th Cong., 1st sess. (1977), 38.
4. See John R. Johannes, *To Serve the People: Congress and Constituency Service* (Lincoln: University of Nebraska Press, 1984).
5. For an overview of congressional reform, see David W. Brady, Joseph Cooper, and Patricia A. Hurley, "The Decline of Party in the U.S. House of Representatives, 1887-1968," *Legislative Studies Quarterly* 4 (1979): 381-407.
6. The term *whip* derives from a participant in English fox hunts, the "whipper-in," whose task was to keep the hounds from leaving the pack.
7. See Barbara Sinclair, "House Majority Party Leadership in the Late 1980s," in *Congress Reconsidered*, ed. Lawrence C. Dodd and Bruce I. Oppenheimer (Washington, D.C.: Congressional Quarterly, 1989).
8. For a former Speaker's view, see Thomas P. O'Neill Jr. and William Novak, *Man of the House* (New York: Random House, 1987).
9. See Frank H. Mackaman, ed., *Understanding Congressional Leadership* (Washington, D.C.: Congressional Quarterly, 1981).
10. Quoted in Robert L. Peabody, *Leadership in Congress* (Boston: Little, Brown, 1976), 339-340.
11. See Samuel C. Patterson and Gregory A. Caldeira, "Party Voting in the United States Congress," *British Journal of Political Science* 18 (1988): 111-131.
12. See Richard L. Hall, "Participation and Purpose in Committee Decision Making," *American Political Science Review* 81 (1987): 105-127.
13. See Gary C. Jacobson, *The Politics of Congressional Elections*, 2d ed. (Boston: Little, Brown, 1987).
14. See Steven S. Smith and Christopher J. Deering, *Committees in Congress* (Washington, D.C.: Congressional Quarterly, 1984).

15. See Steven S. Smith, *Call to Order: Floor Politics in the House and Senate* (Washington, D.C.: Brookings Institution, 1989).

16. See John W. Kingdon, *Congressmen's Voting Decisions*, 3rd ed. (Ann Arbor: University of Michigan Press, 1989).

17. See Walter J. Oleszek, *Congressional Procedures and Policy Process*, 3rd ed. (Washington, D.C.: Congressional Quarterly, 1989).

18. Richard F. Fenno Jr., *Homestyle: House Members in Their Districts* (Boston: Little, Brown, 1978), 1.

19. House of Representatives, Commission on Administrative Review, *Final Report*, 95th Cong., 1st sess. (1977), 830.

20. See Johannes, *To Serve the People*, 64.

21. See, for example, Morris S. Ogul, *Congress Oversees the Bureaucracy* (Pittsburgh, Penn.: University of Pittsburgh Press, 1976).

22. A dated but rich analysis is Richard F. Fenno Jr., *The Power of the Purse* (Boston: Little, Brown, 1966). A more recent study is D. Roderick Kiewiet and Mathew D. McCubbins, *The Spending Power* (Chicago: University of Chicago Press, 1990).

23. On the actions of congressional appropriations committees, see Aaron Wildavsky, *The New Politics of the Budgetary Process* (Glenview, Ill.: Scott, Foresman, 1988).

24. See Raoul Berger, *Impeachment* (Cambridge, Mass.: Harvard University Press, 1973).

25. Quoted in "Oversight Congress," *Congressional Quarterly Weekly Report*, December 22, 1979, 2880.

26. See Burdett Loomis, *The New American Politician* (New York: Basic Books, 1988).

27. See Burton D. Sheppard, *Rethinking Congressional Reform* (Cambridge, Mass.: Schenkman, 1985).

28. See, for example, David W. Rohde, *Parties and Leaders in the Postreform House* (Chicago: University of Chicago Press, 1991).

Chapter 13   The Presidency

1. For an excellent discussion of the leadership dilemma that contemporary presidents face, see Bert A. Rockman, *The Leadership Question* (New York: Praeger, 1984).

2. See Sidney M. Milkis and Michael Nelson, *The American Presidency: Origins and Development, 1776-1993*, 2d ed. (Washington, D.C.: Congressional Quarterly, 1994), 1-69.

3. Helms also held up other nominees, including Clinton's choice of former senator James Sasser to be ambassador to China. Unhappy that the administration and Senate Democrats refused to consider his proposal to reorganize the State Department, the United States Information Agency, the Agency for International Development, and other foreign policy offices, Helms held ambassadorial nominees hostage until a compromise was reached to consider the Helms plan.

4. In Clinton's case it was Secretary of Defense Les Aspin. In the view of the administration, he was not able to exercise sufficient control over his department. Aspin's forced resignation occurred within the first year of the administration. Secretary of Agriculture Mike Espy was later forced to leave because of his personal use of government transportation, and Energy Secretary Hazel O'Leary got into trouble as a consequence of her extensive travels, her rental of commercial airliners, and her use of a government fund to investigate media coverage of her department.

5. Such agreements have to be reported to Congress, but they do not require Senate ratification. Presidents have used executive agreements to circumvent the treaty-making provision of the Constitution. Treaties require ratification by two-thirds of the Senate; executive agreements do not. In fact, executive agreements may not require any congressional concurrence if no new authorization or appropriations are required.

6. Richard E. Neustadt, *Presidential Power and the Modern Presidents* (New York: Free Press, 1990).

7. In his first year of office George Bush reiterated his pledge not to raise taxes; in his second year he abandoned that pledge. Almost as soon as he took office, Bill Clinton backed away from his campaign promises to cut taxes on the middle class, allow homosexuals to openly serve in the armed forces, and admit Haitian refugees seeking political asylum into the United States. Ronald Reagan, in contrast, stuck to his promises to cut taxes, increase defense spending, and reduce the role of government in the domestic sphere. Bush's and Clinton's vacillation and Reagan's steadfastness helped shape their initial reputations as presidents.

8. George C. Edwards III, *At the Margins* (New Haven, Conn.: Yale University Press, 1989), 124.

9. Samuel Kernell, *Going Public*, 2d ed. (Washington, D.C.: Congressional Quarterly, 1993).

10. For an excellent institutional history of this presidential agency, see Larry Berman, *The Office of Management and Budget and the Presidency, 1921-1979* (Princeton, N.J.: Princeton University Press, 1979).

11. Although President Clinton proposed that the White House Office be reduced by 25 percent, he actually increased its size and cost. The 25 percent reduction was obtained by reducing not the White House Office but the Office of Drug Abuse and several other councils in the Executive Office of the President. Moreover, the budget of the White House Office was increased by more than $3.5 million in 1993 to update its communications technology.

    In addition, the White House Office budget is supplemented by other executive departments that provide services for the president and his staff. These include units of the Defense Department, such as White House Communications (secure communications), the Air Force (air transportation for the president and vice president), the Army (explosives detection and ground transportation), and the Navy (helicopter transportation, Marine guards, food and medical facilities). They also include the General Services Administration (buildings and grounds), National Park Service (visitors and the fine arts collection), National Archives (custody of official documents), Secret Service (protection of the president, the vice president, and their families), and State Department (state visits and receptions).

12. John Sununu, Bush's first chief of staff, had become an embarrassment to the administration because of his personal use of White House cars and airplanes. Moreover, he had become a political liability because he had antagonized many members of Congress and executive-branch officials by his brusque and abrasive manner.

13. John Adams, *The Works of John Adams*, vol. 1, ed. C. F. Adams (Boston: Little, Brown, 1850), 289.

14. Thomas Jefferson, *The Writings of Thomas Jefferson*, vol. 1, ed. P. L. Ford (New York: Putnam, 1896), 98-99.

15. For discussions of presidential illnesses, see Michael P.

Riccards, "The Presidency: In Sickness and Health," *Presidential Studies Quarterly* 7 (Fall 1977): 215-231; Robert E. Gilbert, *The Mortal Presidency: Illness and Anguish in the White House* (New York: Basic Books, 1994); "Special Symposium on Presidential Health," *Political Psychology* 16 (December 1995): 757-860.

16. Tom Mathews, "The Road to War," *Newsweek*, January 28, 1991, 60.

17. James David Barber, *The Presidential Character*, 4th ed. (Englewood Cliffs, N.J.: Prentice-Hall, 1992).

18. Jeffrey Tulis, "On Presidential Character," in *The Presidency in the Constitutional Order*, ed. Joseph M. Bessette and Jeffrey Tulis (Baton Rouge: Louisiana State University Press, 1981), 293-301.

19. John P. Burke and Fred I. Greenstein, *How Presidents Test Reality* (New York: Russell Sage, 1989).

20. Charles O. Jones, "Presidents and Agendas: Who Defines What for Whom?" in *The Managerial Presidency*, ed. James P. Pfiffner (Pacific Grove, Calif.: Brooks/Cole, 1991), 197-213; Jones, *The Presidency in a Separated System* (Washington, D.C.: Brookings Institution, 1994), 147-280.

21. Quoted in Barbara Kellerman, *The Political Presidency* (New York: Oxford University Press, 1984), 25.

22. Edwards, *At the Margins*, 213-234.

23. This theory of the two presidencies was first postulated by Aaron Wildavsky in "The Two Presidencies," *Trans-Action* 4 (December 1966): 7-11. It has subsequently engendered considerable debate. Much of that debate appears in Steven A. Shull, ed., *The Two Presidencies: A Quarter Century Assessment* (Chicago: Nelson-Hall, 1991).

24. Quoted in Bob Woodward, *The Choice* (New York: Simon & Schuster, 1996), 22.

Chapter 14   The Executive Bureaucracy

1. CNN report, "Julie Welch Will Never See Her Future," by correspondent Judy Woodruff, April 27, 1995.

2. See Francis J. Leazes, *Accountability and the Business State: The Structure of Federal Corporations* (New York: Praeger, 1987).

3. See Thomas R. Wolanin, *Presidential Advisory Commissions: Truman to Nixon* (Madison: University of Wisconsin Press, 1975).

4. See Martin Tolchin and Susan Tolchin, *To the Victor: Political Patronage from the Clubhouse to the White House* (New York: Random House, 1971).

5. See G. Calvin Mackenzie, ed., *The In and Outers* (Baltimore, Md.: Johns Hopkins University Press, 1987).

6. Harold Seidman, *Politics, Position, and Power*, 3d ed. (New York: Oxford University Press, 1980), 29.

7. Randall B. Ripley and Grace A. Franklin, *Policy Implementation and Bureaucracy* (Chicago: Dorsey, 1986).

8. Faith Hawkins and John M. Thomas, *Making Regulatory Policy* (Pittsburgh, Penn.: University of Pittsburgh Press, 1989).

9. See Susan J. Tolchin and Martin Tolchin, *Dismantling America: The Rush to Deregulate* (New York: Oxford University Press, 1985).

10. See Susan Rose-Ackerman, *Rethinking the Progressive Agenda: The Reform of the American Regulatory State* (New York: Free Press, 1992).

11. See Jerry L. Mashaw, *Due Process in the Administrative State* (New Haven, Conn.: Yale University Press, 1985).

12. George J. Gordon, *Public Administration in America*, 2d ed. (New York: St. Martin's, 1982), 494. New requirements that most rules must be published twice have accounted for some of the growth in the *Federal Register*.

13. See Philip J. Cooper, *Public Law and Public Administration* (Englewood Cliffs, N.J.: Prentice-Hall, 1988).

14. See John Hanrahan, *Government by Contract* (New York: Norton, 1983).

15. A classic study of such bureaucratic cultures is Herbert Kaufman, *The Forest Ranger: A Study in Administrative Behavior* (Baltimore, Md.: Johns Hopkins University Press, 1967).

16. See Eugene Lewis, *Public Entrepreneurship: Toward a Theory of Bureaucratic Political Power* (Bloomington: Indiana University Press, 1980).

17. Reported in Graham T. Allison, *Essence of Decision: Explaining the Cuban Missile Crisis* (Boston: Little, Brown, 1971), 131-132.

18. Kenneth J. Meier, *Politics and the Bureaucracy: Policymaking in the Fourth Branch of Government*, 2d ed. (Monterey, Calif.: Brooks/Cole, 1987), 65.

19. Francis E. Rourke, *Bureaucracy, Politics, and Public Policy*, 3d ed. (Boston: Little, Brown, 1984), 132-137.

20. See Alfred F. Hurley, *Billy Mitchell: Crusader for Air Power* (New York: Franklin Watts, 1964).

21. See Arthur Belonzi, *The Weary Watchdogs: Governmental Regulators in the Political Process* (Wayne, N.J.: Avery, 1977).

22. Rourke, 91-122.

23. Richard F. Fenno Jr., *The Power of the Purse: Appropriations Politics in Congress* (Boston: Little, Brown, 1966), 288, 337.

24. See Wallace E. Walker, *Changing Organizational Culture: Strategy, Structure, and Professionalization in the U.S. General Accounting Office* (Knoxville: University of Tennessee Press, 1986).

25. The classic and still-valuable study is Fenno, *The Power of the Purse*. Also see Aaron Wildavsky, *The New Politics of the Budgetary Process* (New York: HarperCollins, 1992).

26. See the description of this in Charles O. Jones, *The Trusteeship Presidency: Jimmy Carter and the United States Congress* (Baton Rouge: Louisiana State University Press, 1988), 143-149.

27. For a description of the procedures developed under the Freedom of Information Act, see *How to Use the Freedom of Information Act* (Washington, D.C.: Washington Researchers Publishing, 1986).

Chapter 15   The Judiciary

1. Report of the Director, *Administrative Office of the United States Courts* (Washington, D.C.: Administrative Office of the United States Courts, 1991).

2. Quoted by Rowland Carp and Russell Wheeler, "Sink or Swim: The Socialization of a Federal District Judge," *Journal of Politics* 21 (1972): 359, 361.

3. See Wade McCree Jr., "Bureaucratic Justice: An Early Warning," *University of Pennsylvania Law Review* 129 (1981): 777.

4. See Harry Stumpf and John Culver, *The Politics of State Courts* (New York: Longman, 1992).

5. For further discussion, see Ronald Collins and Peter Galie, "Models of Post-Incorporation Judicial Review," *University of Cincinnati Law Review* 55 (1986): 317.

6. *United States v. Students Challenging Regulatory Agency Procedures*, 412 U.S. 669 (1973).

7. See, for example, Lee Epstein, *Conservatives in Court* (Knoxville: University of Tennessee Press, 1985); Nan Aron, *Liberty and Justice for All: Public Interest Law in the 1980s and Beyond* (Boulder, Colo.: Westview, 1989); and Clement Vose, *Caucasians Only* (Berkeley: University of California Press, 1959).

8. Charles E. Hughes, *Addresses of Charles Evans Hughes* (New York: Putnam, 1916), 185.

9. *Colegrove v. Green*, 328 U.S. 549 (1946).

10. Irving Kaufman, "Chilling Judicial Independence," *Yale Law Journal* 88 (1979): 681, 685. Also see Abraham Chayes, "The Role of the Judge in Public Law Litigation," *Harvard Law Review* 89 (1976): 1281.

11. Alexis de Tocqueville, *Democracy in America*, ed. Philip Bradley (New York: Doubleday, 1945), 151.

12. Steve Alumbaugh and C. K. Rowland, "The Links Between Platform-Based Appointment Criteria and Trial Judges' Abortion Judgments," *Judicature* 74 (1990): 153.

13. Quoted in David M. O'Brien, *Storm Center: The Supreme Court in American Politics*, 4th ed. (New York: Norton, 1996), 73.

14. Ibid., 74; Kennedy oral history interview.

15. Ibid.

16. Ibid., 78.

17. *Public Citizen v. U.S. Department of Justice*, 491 U.S. 440 (1989).

18. William H. Rehnquist, "Presidential Appointments to the Supreme Court" (lecture at the University of Minnesota, 1984), reprinted in *Constitutional Commentary* 2 (1985): 319.

19. Quoted by Henry J. Abraham, *Justices and Presidents*, 3d ed. (New York: Oxford University Press, 1992), 72.

20. *In re Sindram*, 111 S.Ct. 596 (1991).

21. Quoted in O'Brien, *Storm Center*, 290.

22. Quoted by Alpheus T. Mason, *Harlan Fiske Stone: Pillar of the Law* (New York: Viking, 1956), 222.

23. Quoted by Alpheus T. Mason, *The Supreme Court from Taft to Burger*, 3d ed. (Baton Rouge: Louisiana State University Press, 1979), 65.

24. *United States v. Nixon*, 418 U.S. 683 (1974).

25. Tom Clark, "Internal Operation of the United States Supreme Court," *Judicature* 43 (1959): 45, 51.

26. Letter (January 24, 1918), reprinted in *Pollock-Holmes Letters*, vol. 1, ed. Mark DeWolfe Howe (Cambridge, Mass.: Harvard University Press, 1942), 258.

27. Charles E. Hughes, *The Supreme Court of the United States* (New York: Columbia University Press, 1928), 68.

28. *Abington School District v. Schempp*, 374 U.S. 203 (1963).

29. *Norris v. Alabama*, 294 U.S. 587 (1935).

30. *Hernandez v. Texas*, 347 U.S. 475 (1954).

31. *Zurcher v. The Stanford Daily*, 436 U.S. 547 (1978).

32. *Texas v. Johnson*, 491 U.S. 397 (1989).

33. *United States v. Eichman*, 496 U.S. 310 (1990).

34. See Robert Dahl, "Decision-Making in a Democracy: The Supreme Court as a National Policy-Maker," *Journal of Public Law* 6 (1957): 279; and Richard Funston, "The Supreme Court and Critical Elections," *American Political Science Review* 69 (1975): 795.

35. See Donald Horowitz, *The Courts and Social Policy* (Washington, D.C.: Brookings Institution, 1977); and Raoul Berger, *Government by the Judiciary* (Cambridge, Mass.: Harvard University Press, 1977).

36. For further discussion of the Court's role as a policy maker, see Gerald Rosenberg, *The Hollow Hope: Can Courts Bring About Social Change?* (Chicago: University of Chicago Press, 1991).

PHOTO CREDITS

Index to References

INDEX

Throughout this index, the lowercase letters *c, t,* and *f* indicate *captions, tables,* and *figures* respectively.

American Revolution, 11, 16

Americans with Disabilities Act of 1990, 73, 74, 77

Americans United for Separation of Church and State, 26

American Tort Reform Association, 258

Amicus curiae brief, 261-262, 475

Amish, 19, 134*c*

Ancient times, politics in, 4-5

Anderson, George, 536

Anderson, John, 205, 276*t*

Anderson, Marian, 488

Animal sacrifice, and freedom of religion, 133

Anti-Federalists
    on state rights, 41, 64, 66, 97
    view of federalism, 64, 66

Anti-Masons, 276, 282, 283

Appeals
    of court decisions, 117
    to Supreme Court, 579*f*, 580

Appellate courts, 557

Appellate jurisdiction, 560

Appropriations Committees, 451

Arab American Institute, 21

Arafat, Yassir, 505*c*

Argersinger v. Hamlin, 99*t*

Aristotle, 5

Arizona v. Evans, 103

Articles of Confederation, 34-36, 40
    elements of, 34
    weaknesses of, 34-35

Asbestos Hazard Emergency Response Act of 1986, 74

Ashe, Arthur, 196

Aspin, Les, 469*c*

Assault weapons ban, Republican/National Rifle Association relationship, 415-416

Association of State and Interstate Water Pollution Control Officers, 83

Astroturfing, 257-258

Attentive public, and public opinion, 200, 202

Attitudes, and public opinion, 197-198

Authoritarian personality, and tolerance level, 225

Authority
    of government, 12-13
    meaning of, 12

Babbitt, Bruce, 84, 399, 535*c*

Baby boomers, political socialization, 172-173

Bad tendency doctrine, 135

Baer, Harold, Jr., 475, 566

Baker, Howard, 427, 570

Baker v. Carr, 146-147

Bakke, Alan, 157-158

Balanced budget amendment, 1-3, 272

Bandwagon effect, 341

Bankruptcy Act of 1898, 73

Bank of the United States, 43-44

Barbour, Haley, 293*c*

Barr, Bob, 86

Barron v. Baltimore, 98

Barr, William, 468

Belief system
    of presidents, 498-499
    and public opinion, 211

Bell, Griffin, 567

Bench memos, 582

Benham, Philip, 195

Benton v. Maryland, 99*t*

Bernstein, Carl, 385

Bicameral legislature, meaning of, 39, 416

Biden, Joseph, 570, 576

Bill, and lawmaking process, 436, 438

Bill of information, 114

Bill of Rights, 16-17
    amendments of, 41
    and civil rights/liberties, 98-119
    criminal proceedings, guarantees in, 104
    historical roots, 97
    nationalization of, 97, 98-102
    ratification of, 34, 41, 53, 56, 97

Black, Hugo L., 128, 135, 138, 584

Blackmun, Harry, 574

Block grants, 78
    under devolution federalism, 71-72
    types of, 78

Blue books, 85

Blumenthal, Michael, 524

Boehner, John, 416

Boland Amendment, 472

Bork, Robert H., 54, 261, 567, 570-571, 574

Bosnia, 473

Bosses, political, 295

Bowers v. Hardwick, 119

Bradley, Bill, 428

Branch Davidian incident, 407, 408*c*, 546, 547

Brandeis, Louis D., 45, 105*c*, 119

Brandenburg, Charles, 138

Brandenburg v. Ohio, 138

Branzburg v. Hayes, 371

Brennan, William J., Jr., 117, 134, 137, 575, 584

Breyer, Stephen G., 109, 152, 569, 574, 581*c*

Briefs, legal, 557

Broad reading, of Constitution, 57

Brown, Jerry, 338, 340, 399

Brown, Ron, 260

Brown v. Board of Education, 47, 110, 145, 148-151, 261, 561*c*, 583, 588

Bryan, William Jennings, 284*t*, 285, 334

Buchanan, Patrick, 156, 334, 337, 341, 396, 455

Buckley v. Valeo, 318

Buckley, William F., Jr., 178

Budget and Accounting Act of 1921, 480

Bull Moose party, 278, 285

Bundling, and political action committees (PACs), 247

Bundy, Ted, 117*c*

Bureau of Alcohol, Tobacco, and Firearms (ATF), 217, 513-514, 546-547

Bureau of the Budget, 480

Bureaucracy
    cross-cultural view, 526-527
    nature of, 515
    See also Federal bureaucracy

Bureau of Quality Control, 515

Bureaus, federal bureaucracy, 520

Burger, Warren, 102, 570, 571, 574, 583

Burr, Aaron, 44*c*, 490, 492

Bush, George, 126, 160, 290, 304, 311, 367*c*, 391, 494, 495, 507*c*
    election of, 328, 331, 332, 356
    environmental policy under, 232
    managerial style of, 497
    personality type, 497

Bus Regulatory Reform Act, 75

Buxton, Dr. C. Lee, 553

Byrd, Robert, 427

Cabinet, 478-479
    cross-cultural view, 479
    evolution of, 478, 479*f*
    relationship with president, 479

Cable News Network (CNN), 386

Cable Satellite Public Affairs Network (C-SPAN), 386, 387*c*, 407

Cable television, 385-387
    narrowcasting, 386
    news stations, 386-387

Caddell, Pat, 226

Cajuns, 19

Calhoun, John C., 66*c*, 492

Califano, Joseph, 524

California v. Hodari D., 108

Campaign financing, 318-319
    bundling, 247
    increasing costs for, 334-335
    information sources on, 321
    legal restrictions, 318-319, 320-321
    loopholes to law, 247, 320
    and political action committees (PACs), 247, 319
    and soft-money expenditures, 319, 320-321

Campaigns. *See* Election campaign

Canada, federalism of, 63

Cannon, Joseph G., 423

Capitalism
    definition of, 19
    and democracy, 19
    free-enterprise system, 19

Capital punishment. *See* Death penalty

Capture, by federal bureaucracy, 538

Cardozo, Benjamin, 559